SRA ART Connections

Arts Education for the 21st Century

Culture   Personal Expression   Creativity

History   Beauty   Critical Thinking

Art encourages different ways of learning, knowing, and communicating.

i

All the Resources you Need for Great Art Teaching!

Art Connections provides everything teachers need to offer meaningful art education.

Student Edition K–6

Comprehensive student materials in two formats:

Student Edition

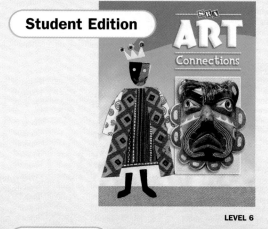

LEVEL 6

Big Book

LEVEL 6

Teacher Edition

Everything classroom and art teachers need to teach art effectively

LEVEL 4

- Complete lesson plans to teach
  - elements and principles of art
  - art history and culture
  - art criticism
  - art production
- Art background
- Cross-curricular connections
- Program resources guide

Technology Components

e-Presentation for students and teachers

LEVEL K

e-Presentation offers the complete Student Edition as a presentation tool for teachers, complete with multimedia experiences, assessments, teacher materials, and a gallery of all artworks in the entire program.

This electronic gallery allows immediate access to all the artwork in the **Art Connections** program.

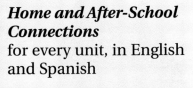

Cross-Curricular Art Connections include practical art projects for the classroom to help meet subject-area guidelines in

- Social Studies
- Mathematics
- Language Arts and Reading
- Science

LEVEL 3

Reading and Writing Test Preparation that reinforces art content

LEVEL 1

Home and After-School Connections for every unit, in English and Spanish

Professional Development Guide for both classroom teachers and art specialists

LEVEL 5

Assessment with tests in English and Spanish for every lesson

Art Around the World CD-ROM includes 150 works of art from the *Art Around the World Collection,* representing a variety of thought-provoking perspectives and activities.

The National Museum of Women in the Arts Collection CD-ROM dynamically explores the 200-print collection to introduce students to key women artists.

ART Connections

Enrich students' lives with exposure to the great masters and cultures of the world.

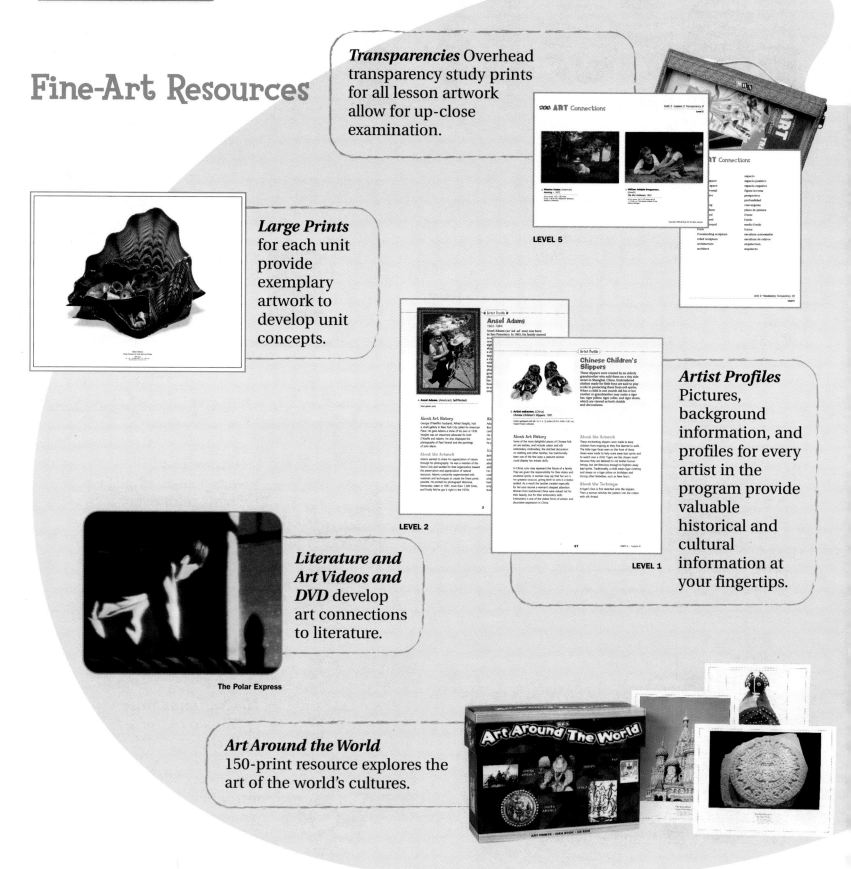

Fine-Art Resources

Transparencies Overhead transparency study prints for all lesson artwork allow for up-close examination.

LEVEL 5

Large Prints for each unit provide exemplary artwork to develop unit concepts.

Artist Profiles Pictures, background information, and profiles for every artist in the program provide valuable historical and cultural information at your fingertips.

LEVEL 2

LEVEL 1

Literature and Art Videos and DVD develop art connections to literature.

The Polar Express

Art Around the World 150-print resource explores the art of the world's cultures.

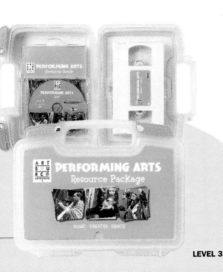

Artsource®
Performing Arts
Resource Package
(Video and DVD)
integrates the
performing arts of
dance, music, and
theatre.

LEVEL 3

Elements and Principles of Art Teaching Resources

Elements of Art
poster reinforces
line, shape, color,
value, form,
space, and
texture.

Principles of Art
poster develops
concepts of
rhythm, balance,
movement,
harmony, variety,
emphasis, and
unity.

*The National Museum of Women
in the Arts Collection* This 200-print
resource provides famous artwork
from famous women artists.

Use the *Color
Wheel* to explore
color concepts.

Theatre Arts Connections
is a complete dramatic
arts program that ties to
Art Connections.

LEVEL 4

Flash Cards
provide a quick review of the
elements and principles of art.

Build a foundation in the elements and principles of art.

36 Lessons at every grade level develop the elements and principles of art in six-lesson units.

◀ **Rembrandt van Rijn.**
Portrait of Rembrandt.

◀ **Frida Kahlo.**
Frida y Diego Rivera.

LEVEL 6

Unit Openers introduce students to unit concepts and master artists.

Unit 5

Space, Proportion, and Distortion

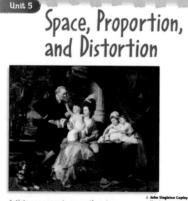

Artists use accurate proportions to realistically depict people and objects.

Copley painted this realistic portrait of the Pepperrell family in 1778. The Pepperrell family lived in New England until about the time of the American Revolution, when they moved to England. At about the same time, Sir William Pepperrell lost most of his wealth. Notice that Copley used correct proportions to make the painting realistic.

▲ **John Singleton Copley.**
(American).
*Sir William Pepperrell
and His Family.* 1778.
Oil on canvas. 90 × 108 inches
(228.6 × 274.32 cm.). North
Carolina Museum of Art, Raleigh,
North Carolina.

154 Unit 5

Artists use space in paintings to give the appearance of depth on a flat surface.
▸ How do you think John Singleton Copley created space in *Sir William Pepperrell and His Family*?
▸ Which objects in the painting look closer to you? Which objects look farther away?

Artists use accurate **proportions** to show people or things realistically.
▸ Do you think the people in Copley's painting look like they have been painted with accurate proportions? Explain.

In This Unit you will learn about different ways that artists show size and placement. Here are the topics you will study:
▸ Foreground, middle ground, and background
▸ Perspective techniques
▸ Point of view
▸ Face proportion
▸ Body proportions
▸ Distortion

Master Artist Profile

John Singleton Copley
(1738–1815)

John Singleton Copley was a popular portrait painter during the eighteenth century. When he was seventeen years old he created a portrait of George Washington. In his attempt to capture details and to make his subjects appear natural, Copley sometimes required fifteen or sixteen sittings for a single portrait. Copley moved to England during the American Revolution and did not return to America.

Unit 5 **155**

LEVEL 4

Unit Wrap-Ups review concepts, explore Art Museums or Art Careers and allow students to experience Artsource® connections to dance, theatre, and music.

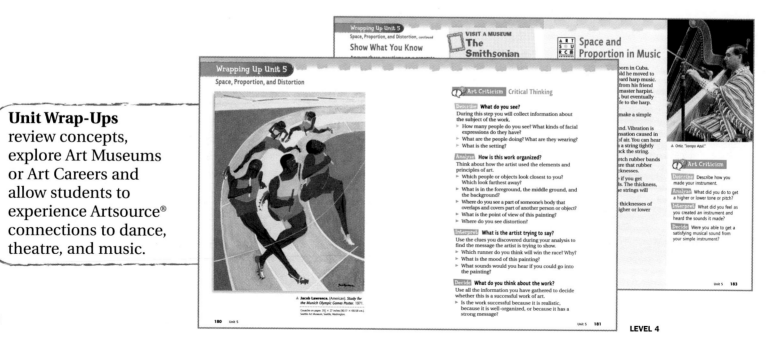

Wrapping Up Unit 5

Space, Proportion, and Distortion

▲ **Jacob Lawrence.** (American). *Study for the Munich Olympic Games Poster.* 1971.
Gouache on paper. 35 × 27 inches (90.17 × 68.58 cm.).
Seattle Art Museum, Seattle, Washington.

180 Unit 5

🎨 Art Criticism | Critical Thinking

Describe **What do you see?**
During this step you will collect information about the subject of the work.
▸ How many people do you see? What kinds of facial expressions do they have?
▸ What are the people doing? What are they wearing?
▸ What is the setting?

Analyze **How is this work organized?**
Think about how the artist used the elements and principles of art.
▸ Which people or objects look closest to you? Which look farthest away?
▸ What is in the foreground, the middle ground, and the background?
▸ Where do you see a part of someone's body that overlaps and covers part of another person or object?
▸ What is the point of view of this painting?
▸ Where do you see distortion?

Interpret **What is the artist trying to say?**
Use the clues you discovered during your analysis to find the message the artist is trying to show.
▸ Which runner do you think will win the race? Why?
▸ What is the mood of this painting?
▸ What sounds would you hear if you could go into the painting?

Decide **What do you think about the work?**
Use all the information you have gathered to decide whether this is a successful work of art.
▸ Is the work successful because it is realistic, because it is well-organized, or because it has a strong message?

Unit 5 **181**

Wrapping Up Unit 5
Space, Proportion, and Distortion, continued
Show What You Know

VISIT A MUSEUM
The **Smithsonian**

Space and Proportion in Music

▲ Ortiz. *"Joropo Azul."*

...born in Cuba. ...old he moved to ...eard harp music. ...from his friend ...master harpist. ...but eventually ...fe to the harp.

...make a simple

...nd. Vibration is ...nsation caused in ...a a string tightly ...ck the string. ...tch rubber bands ...re that rubber ...cknesses.

...if you get ...ls. The thickness, ...e strings will

...thicknesses of ...igher or lower

🎨 Art Criticism

Describe Describe how you made your instrument.
Analyze What did you do to get a higher or lower tone or pitch?
Interpret What did you feel as you created an instrument and heard the sounds it made?
Decide Were you able to get a satisfying musical sound from your simple instrument?

Unit 5 **183**

LEVEL 4

Integrate the four disciplines of art into every lesson for well-rounded exposure to all the dimensions of art.

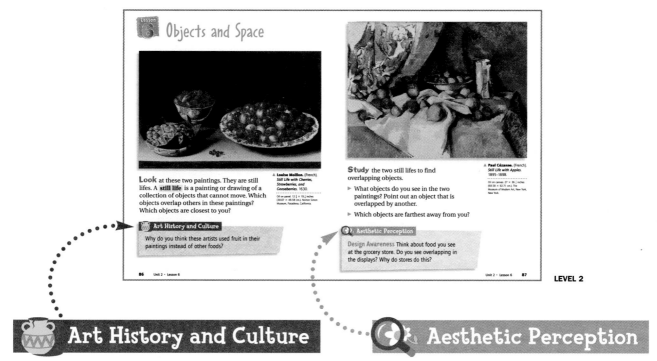

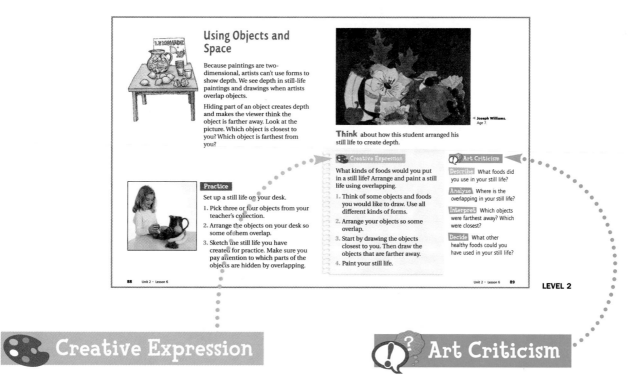

Art History and Culture

Explore the great art, artists, and cultures of the world.

Aesthetic Perception

Develop an understanding and appreciation for art.

Creative Expression

Encounter a broad range of art media in a variety of hands-on art activities that give students an avenue for self-expression and self-esteem.

Art Criticism

Enrich critical-thinking skills as students learn about the elements and principles of art by examining their own and others' artwork.

Add dimension to all subjects with meaningful art connections.

Connect Art to Mathematics, Social Studies, Science, Language Arts and Reading.

History
Develop historical understanding as students explore art history and culture in every lesson.

LEVEL 1

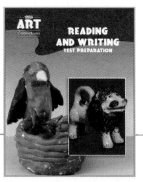

LEVEL 2

Reading and Writing Test Preparation
Use art content, information about artists, art concepts, and art history to practice reading and writing skills in every unit.

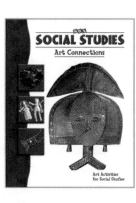
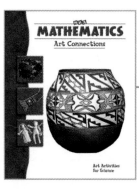

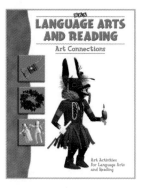

Cross-Curricular Art Connections
These books provide a wealth of exciting art activities designed specifically to support subject-area studies in Science, Mathematics, Social Studies, Language Arts and Reading as they reinforce art concepts.

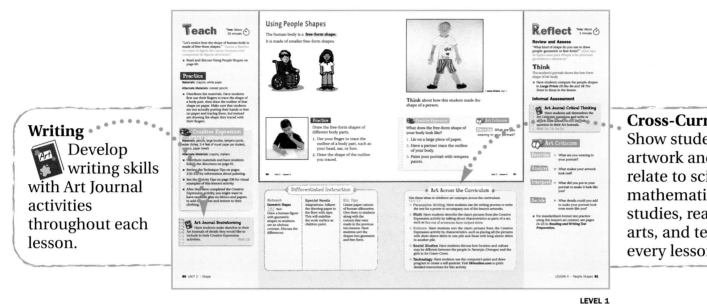

Writing
Develop writing skills with Art Journal activities throughout each lesson.

Cross-Curricular Ideas
Show students how artwork and concepts relate to science, mathematics, social studies, reading/language arts, and technology in every lesson.

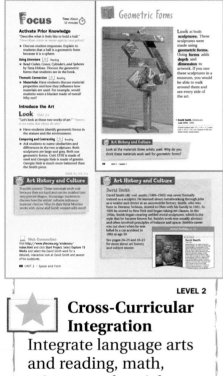

LEVEL 2

Cross-Curricular Integration
Integrate language arts and reading, math, science, and social studies concepts naturally as students work through each art lesson.

LEVEL 4

Vocabulary Development
Key vocabulary terms are highlighted, defined, and reviewed to develop the language of art.

LEVEL 3

Literature Integration
Integrate literature with Illustrator Profiles and Literature and Art video experiences at the beginning of every unit.

Research has shown that incorporating the arts into core curriculum areas in a way that actively involves students in the learning process produces "significant positive effects on student achievement, motivation, and engagement in learning, and notable changes in classroom practices" ("Different Ways of Knowing: 1991-94 National Longitudinal Study Final Report" in Schools, Communities, and the Arts: A Research Compendium).

SRA ART Connections

Integrate all the Performing Arts for a complete Art education.

Expose children to music, dance, and theatre as they explore the visual arts.

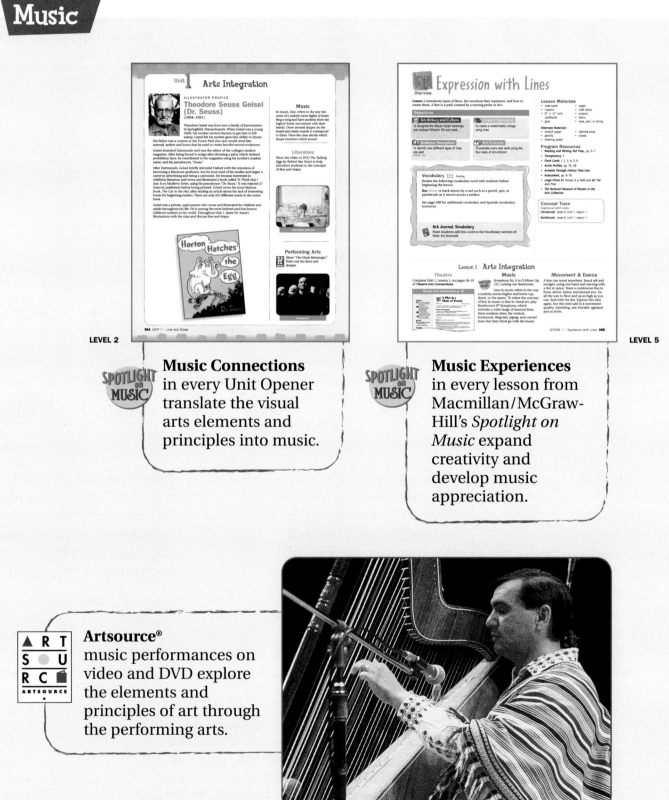

LEVEL 2

LEVEL 5

Music Connections
in every Unit Opener translate the visual arts elements and principles into music.

Music Experiences
in every lesson from Macmillan/McGraw-Hill's *Spotlight on Music* expand creativity and develop music appreciation.

Artsource®
music performances on video and DVD explore the elements and principles of art through the performing arts.

LEVEL 4

A R T
S O U
R C ◼
ARTSOURCE

LEVEL 3

Artsource®
dance performances on
video and DVD explore
the elements and
principles of art through
the performing arts.

A R T
S O U
R C ◼
ARTSOURCE

LEVEL 5

Artsource®
theatre performances on
video and DVD explore
the elements and
principles of art through
the performing arts.

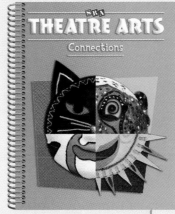

LEVEL 3

**Theatre Arts
Connections** for
grades K–6
lessons explore
the elements
and principles of
theatre arts as
students develop
the elements
and principles of
visual arts.

Case studies have indicated that
students perceive "that the arts
facilitate their personal and social
development." It also appears that to
gain the full benefit of arts education,
students should be exposed to all of the
arts, including fine arts, dance,
theatre, and music ("Arts Education in
Secondary School: Effects and
Effectiveness" in Critical Links, p. 76).

Meet Today's Standards for Art Education.

Art Connections exceeds the national standards for art education.

National Standards for Arts Education

Content Standard #1:

Understanding and applying media, techniques, and processes

The Creative Expression activity in every lesson of *Art Connections* develops understanding and experience with a wide variety of media, techniques, and processes. Practice activities in every lesson focus specifically on techniques.

Content Standard #2:

Using knowledge of structures and functions

Art Connections develops the elements and principles of art in every grade level, K–6. Units and lessons are organized to explore the elements and principles in exemplary art and then to practice techniques and create works of art that employ specific structures and functions of art.

Content Standard #3:

Choosing and evaluating a range of subject matter, symbols, and ideas

Art Connections introduces students to subject matter and symbols at the beginning of every grade level and then uses that knowledge throughout every lesson in the Aesthetic Perception questions and Creative Expression activities as students explore content to develop meaning in artwork.

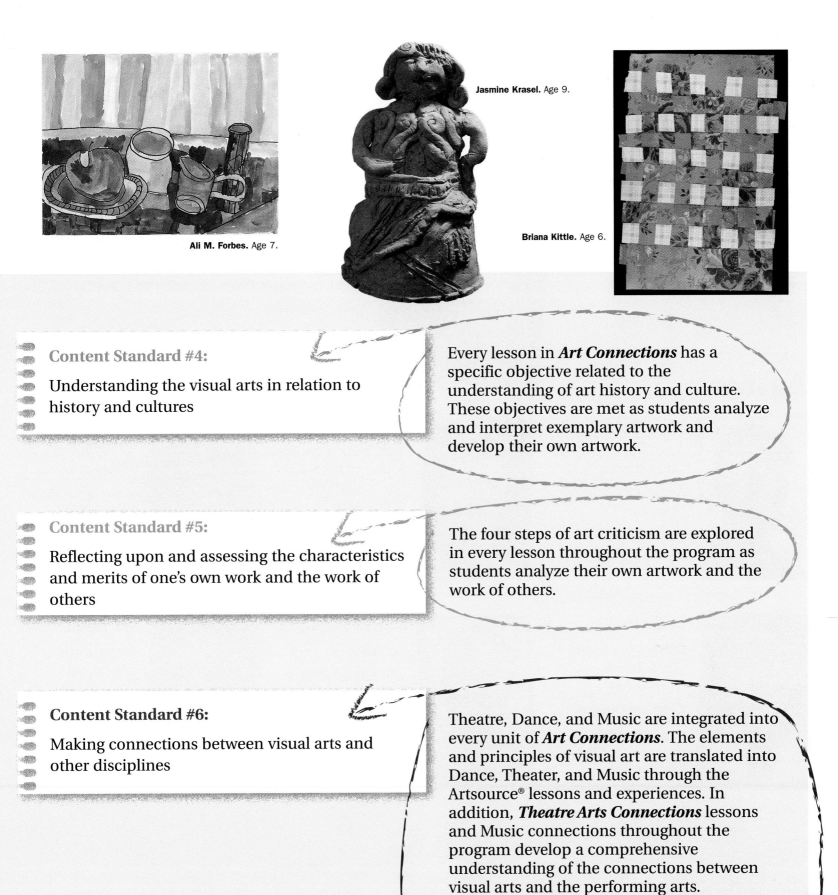

Jasmine Krasel. Age 9.

Ali M. Forbes. Age 7.

Briana Kittle. Age 6.

Content Standard #4:

Understanding the visual arts in relation to history and cultures

Every lesson in *Art Connections* has a specific objective related to the understanding of art history and culture. These objectives are met as students analyze and interpret exemplary artwork and develop their own artwork.

Content Standard #5:

Reflecting upon and assessing the characteristics and merits of one's own work and the work of others

The four steps of art criticism are explored in every lesson throughout the program as students analyze their own artwork and the work of others.

Content Standard #6:

Making connections between visual arts and other disciplines

Theatre, Dance, and Music are integrated into every unit of *Art Connections*. The elements and principles of visual art are translated into Dance, Theater, and Music through the Artsource® lessons and experiences. In addition, *Theatre Arts Connections* lessons and Music connections throughout the program develop a comprehensive understanding of the connections between visual arts and the performing arts.

Cross-curricular connections are built into every lesson through teaching strategies and ideas that integrate language arts and reading, math, science, and social studies concepts. Art Projects for each of the different subject areas are also included in the program.

Let the experts bring the best practices to your classroom.

Rosalind Ragans, Ph.D., Senior Author

Artist, Associate Professor Emerita

Georgia Southern University

Authors

Willis "Bing" Davis

Artist, Art Consultant

Associate Professor Emeritus,

Central State University, Ohio

Tina Farrell

Assisstant Superintendant, Curriculum and Instruction

Clear Creek Independent School District, Texas

Jane Rhoades Hudak, Ph.D.

Professor of Art

Georgia Southern University

Gloria McCoy

Former President, Texas Art Education Association

K–12 Art Director

Spring Branch Independent School District, Texas

Bunyan Morris

Art Teacher

Effingham County School System

Springfield, Georgia

Nan Yoshida

Art Education Consultant

Los Angeles, California

Contributors

Jackie Ellet

Elementary Art Teacher

Duncan Creek Elementary School

Georgia

 Artsource® Music, Dance, and Theatre Lessons

Education Division

The Music Center of Los Angeles County

National Museum of Women in the Arts Collection

National Museum of Women in the Arts

Washington, D.C.

Your Fine-Arts Partner for K–12 Art, Theatre, Dance and Music

McGraw-Hill offers textbook programs to build, support, and extend an enriching fine-arts curriculum from kindergarten through high school.

**Senior Author
Rosalind Ragans**

Start with Art  SRA

SRA/McGraw-Hill presents *Art Connections* for Grades K–6. *Art Connections* builds the foundations of the elements and principles of art across the grade levels as the program integrates art history and culture, aesthetic perception, creative expression in art production, and art criticism into every lesson.

Art Connections also develops strong cross-curricular connections and integrates the arts with literature, *Theatre Arts Connections* lessons, *Artsource*® experiences, and integrated music selections from Macmillan/McGraw-Hill's *Spotlight on Music*.

**Author
Rosalind Ragans
and Gene Mittler**

Integrate with Art Glencoe

Glencoe/McGraw-Hill offers comprehensive middle and high school art programs that encourage students to make art a part of their lifelong learning. All Glencoe art programs interweave the elements and principles of art to help students build perceptual skills, promote creative expression, explore historical and cultural heritage, and evaluate artwork.

- Introduce students to the many themes artists express.
- Explore the media, techniques, and processes of art.
- Understand the historical and cultural contexts of art.

ArtTalk offers high school students opportunities to perceive, create, appreciate, and evaluate art as it develops the elements and principles of art.

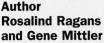

**Author
Rosalind Ragans**

Motivate with Music Macmillan McGraw-Hill

Macmillan/McGraw-Hill's *Spotlight on Music* offers an exiting and comprehensive exposure to music foundations and appreciation.

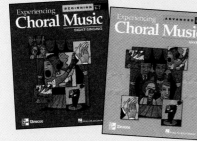

Sing with Style Glencoe

Glencoe/McGraw-Hill introduces *Experiencing Choral Music* for Grades 6–12. This multilevel choral music program includes instruction in the basic skills of vocal production and music literacy, and provides expertly recorded music selections in many different styles and from various periods of history.

Getting Started
The very basics...

Here are some tips for Getting Started with Art Connections.

Before School Begins

1. Explore the components you have (student materials, **Overhead Transparencies**, **Large Prints**, and so on). Consider uses and alternative uses for each of the components.

2. Plan your year.
   - Consider how often you meet with students.
   - Decide how many lessons you can present.
   - Examine your curriculum requirements.
   - Select the lessons that best meet your curriculum requirements.

3. Organize art materials.
   - Identify the *Creative Expression* activities you will have students develop.
   - Determine how you will budget materials to last the entire year.
   - Compile a list of materials and order them.
   - Arrange classroom space to store materials.

4. Arrange classroom space to create and store student artwork.

The First Day of School

1. Give an overview of your expectations, objectives, and what you want students to accomplish.

2. Introduce the artroom to students. Show them where things are kept.

3. Establish and communicate:
   - rules for behavior.
   - rules for handling art materials.
   - rules for cleaning up.

4. Begin the **Art Connections** introductory lessons, including *What Is Art?*, *About Art Criticism*, *About Aesthetic Perception*, and *About Art History and Culture*.

Planning a Lesson

1. Review the lesson in the *Teacher's Edition*, including lesson objectives, in-text questions, *Practice*, and *Creative Expression* activities.

2. Assemble program components, such as **Transparencies, Large Prints,** and the **Big Book**.

3. Make any copies of activities or assessments that will be needed for the lesson.

4. Assemble art materials.

5. Determine how you will assess the lesson.

TEACHER'S EDITION

ART
Connections

Level 1

Authors
Rosalind Ragans, Ph.D., Senior Author

Willis "Bing" Davis   Jane Rhoades Hudak, Ph.D.   Bunyan Morris
Tina Farrell   Gloria McCoy   Nan Yoshida

Contributing Author
Jackie Ellett

Education Division
The Music Center of Los Angeles County

Columbus, OH

The McGraw-Hill Companies

Authors

Senior Author
Dr. Rosalind Ragans, Ph.D.
Associate Professor Emerita
Georgia Southern University

Willis "Bing" Davis
Associate Professor Emeritus
Central State University - Ohio
President & Founder of SHANGO:
The Center for the Study of
African American
Art & Culture

Tina Farrell
Assistant Superintendent,
Curriculum and Instruction
Clear Creek Independent School
District,
League City, Texas

Jane Rhoades Hudak, Ph.D.
Professor of Art
Georgia Southern University

Gloria McCoy
Former President,
Texas Art Education Association
Spring Branch Independent
School District, Texas

Bunyan Morris
Art Teacher
Effingham County School System,
Springfield, Georgia

Nan Yoshida
Art Education Consultant
Retired Art Supervisor,
Los Angeles Unified School
District
Los Angeles, California

Photo Credit **Cover,** Jacob Lawrence, *Builders—Red and Green Ball.* Francine Seders Gallery LTD, Seattle. Photo by Chris Eden. ©Jacob and Gwendolyn Lawrence Foundation.

SRAonline.com

Send all inquiries to:
SRA/McGraw-Hill
8787 Orion Place
Columbus, OH 43240-4027

Printed in the United States of America.

ISBN 0-07-600391-4

3 4 5 6 7 8 9 BCM 10 09 08 07 06

Contributors

Contributing Author
Jackie Ellett, Ed.S
Elementary Art Teacher
Duncan Creek Elementary School
Hoschton, Georgia

Contributing Writer
Lynda Kerr, NBCT
Ed. D. Candidate, Art Teacher
Henry County, Georgia

ARTSOURCE Artsource® Music, Dance, Theatre Lessons
Mark Slavkin, Vice President for Education
The Music Center of Los Angeles County
Michael Solomon, Managing Director
Music Center Education Division
Melinda Williams, Concept Originator and Project Director
Susan Cambigue-Tracey, Project Coordinator and Writer
Madeleine Dahm, Movement and Dance Connection Writer
Keith Wyffels, Staff Assistance
Maureen Erbe, Logo Design

Music Connections
Kathy Mitchell
Music Teacher
Eagan, Minnesota

More about Aesthetics
Richard W. Burrows, Executive Director
Institute for Arts Education
San Diego, California

Art History
Gene A. Mittler, Ph.D.
Professor Emeritus
Texas Tech University

Resources for Students with Disabilities
Mandy Yeager
Ph.D. Candidate
The University of North Texas
Denton, Texas

Brain-Based Learning in the Arts
Jamye Ivey
K-12 Art Supervisor
Dougherty County School System, Georgia

Safe Use of Art Materials
Mary Ann Boykin

Director, The Art School for Children and Young Adults
University of Houston–Clear Lake
Houston, Texas

Integrating the Four Art Forms
Susan Cambigue-Tracey
The Music Center of Los Angeles County

Using Writing to Enhance Your Art Curriculum
Mary Lazzari, EdS
Elementary Art Teacher
Clarke County School District
Athens, Georgia

Museum Education
Marilyn J. S. Goodman
Director of Education
Solomon R. Guggenheim Museum
New York, New York

Displaying Student Artwork
Jackie Ellett
Duncan Creek Elementary School
Hoschton, Georgia

Student Activities

Cassie Appleby
Glen Oaks Elementary School
McKinney, Texas

Maureen Banks
Kester Magnet School
Van Nuys, California

Christina Barnes
Webb Bridge Middle School
Alpharetta, Georgia

Beth Benning
Willis Jepson Middle School
Vacaville, California

Chad Buice
Craig Elementary School
Snellville, Georgia

Beverly Broughton
Gwinn Oaks Elementary School
Snellville, Georgia

Missy Burgess
Jefferson Elementary School
Jefferson, Georgia

Marcy Cincotta-Smith
Benefield Elementary School
Lawrenceville, Georgia

Joanne Cox
Kittredge Magnet School
Atlanta, Georgia

Carolyn Y. Craine
McCracken County Schools
Paducah, Kentucky

Jackie Ellett
Duncan Creek Elementary School
Hoschton, Georgia

Tracie Flynn
Home School
Rushville, Indiana

Phyllis Glenn
Malcom Bridge Elementary
Bogart, Georgia

Dallas Gillespie
Dacula Middle School
Dacula, Georgia

Dr. Donald Gruber
Clinton Junior High School
Clinton, Illinois

Karen Heid
Rock Springs Elementary School
Lawrenceville, Georgia

Alisa Hyde
Southwest Elementary
Savannah, Georgia

Kie Johnson
Oconee Primary School
Watkinsville, Georgia

Sallie Keith, NBCT
West Side Magnet School
LaGrange, Georgia

Letha Kelly
Grayson Elementary School
Grayson, Georgia

Diana Kimura
Amestoy Elementary School
Gardena, California

Desiree LaOrange
Barkley Elementary School
Fort Campbell, Kentucky

Deborah Lackey-Wilson
Roswell North Elementary
Roswell, Georgia

Dawn Laird
Goforth Elementary School
Clear Creek, Texas

Mary Lazzari
Timothy Road Elementary School
Athens, Georgia

Michelle Leonard
Webb Bridge Middle School
Alpharetta, Georgia

Lynn Ludlam
Spring Branch ISD
Houston, Texas

Mark Mitchell
Fort Daniel Elementary School
Dacula, Georgia

Martha Moore
Freeman's Mill Elementary School
Dacula, Georgia

Connie Niedenthal
Rushville Elementary
Rushville, Indiana

Barbara Patisaul
Oconee County Elementary School
Watkinsville, Georgia

Elizabeth Paulos-Krasle
Social Circle Elementary
Social Circle, Georgia

Jane Pinneau
Rocky Branch Elementary School
Watkinsville, Georgia

Marilyn Polin
Cutler Ridge Middle School
Miami, Florida

Michael Ramsey
Graves County Schools
Mayfield, Kentucky

Rosemarie Sells
Social Circle Elementary
Social Circle, Georgia

Jean Neelen-Siegel
Baldwin School
Alhambra, California

Debra Smith
McIntosh County School System
Darien, Georgia

Patricia Spencer
Harmony Elementary School
Buford, Georgia

Melanie Stokes
Smiley Elementary School
Ludowici, Georgia

Rosanne Stutts
Davidson Fine Arts School
Augusta, Georgia

Fran Sullivan
South Jackson Elementary School
Athens, Georgia

Kathy Valentine
Home School
Burkburnett, Texas

Debi West
Rock Springs Elementary School
Lawrenceville, Georgia

Sherry White
Bauerschlag Elementary School
League City, Texas

Patricia Wiesen
Cutler Ridge Middle School
Miami, Florida

Deayna Woodruff
Loveland Middle School
Loveland, Ohio

Gil Young
El Rodeo School
Beverly Hills, California

Larry A. Young
Dacula Elementary School
Dacula, Georgia

Table of Contents

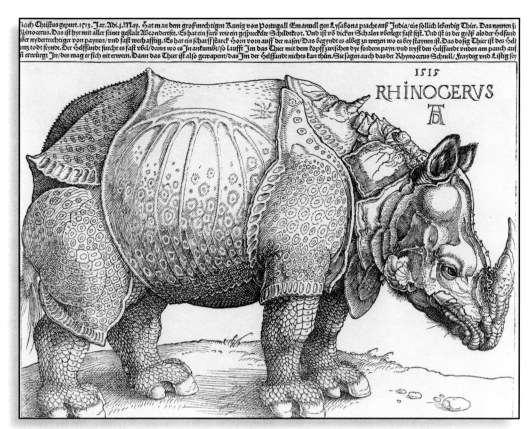

▲ **Albrecht Dürer.** *Rhinoceros.*

Unit 1 Line

●◆ indicates Core Lessons   **5**

Reading Comprehension Skills and Strategies

❶ Vocabulary, Comparing and Contrasting
❷ Vocabulary, Visualizing, Classify and Categorize
❸ Vocabulary, Comparing and Contrasting
❹ Vocabulary, Comparing and Contrasting
❺ Vocabulary, Drawing Conclusions
❻ Vocabulary, Making Inferences

◄ **Loïs Mailou Jones.**
Esquisse for Ode to Kinshasa.

Unit 2 Shape

➦ indicates Core Lessons

Reading Comprehension Skills and Strategies

➊ Vocabulary, Summarizing, Adjectives and Adverbs

➋ Vocabulary, Comparing and Contrasting

➌ Vocabulary, Summarizing

➍ Vocabulary, Summarizing

➎ Vocabulary, Making Connections

➏ Vocabulary, Drawing Conclusions, Adjectives and Adverbs

▲ **Mary Cassatt.** *In the Garden.*

Unit 3 Color

➼ **indicates Core Lessons**

7

Reading Comprehension Skills and Strategies
➊ Vocabulary, Comparing and Contrasting
➋ Vocabulary, Interpreting
➌ Vocabulary, Adjectives and Adverbs
➍ Vocabulary, Comparing and Contrasting
➎ Vocabulary, Main Idea and Details
➏ Vocabulary, Adjectives and Adverbs, Drawing Conclusions

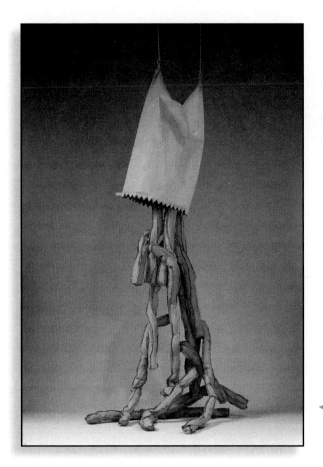

◀ **Claes Oldenburg.**
Shoestring Potatoes
Spilling from a Bag.

Unit 4 Form and Space

8   ➡❖ **indicates Core Lessons**

Reading Comprehension Skills and Strategies

❶ Vocabulary, Comparing and Contrasting   ❸ Vocabulary, Comparing and Contrasting   ❺ Vocabulary, Comparing and Contrasting
❷ Vocabulary, Main Idea and Details   ❹ Vocabulary, Comparing and Contrasting   ❻ Vocabulary, Comparing and Contrasting

◀ **Jesús Moroles.**
Granite Weaving.

Unit 5 Texture, Pattern, and Rhythm

➥ **indicates Core Lessons**

9

Reading Comprehension Skills and Strategies
❶ Vocabulary, Making Inferences
❷ Vocabulary, Summarizing
❸ Vocabulary, Comparing and Contrasting
❹ Vocabulary, Comparing and Contrasting
❺ Vocabulary, Making Connections
❻ Vocabulary, Adjectives and Adverbs

◀ **Leonardo da Vinci.**
Mona Lisa.

Unit 6 Balance, Emphasis, and Unity

10   ➡ indicates Core Lessons

Reading Comprehension Skills and Strategies
➊ Vocabulary, Making Connections
➋ Vocabulary, Making Inferences
➌ Vocabulary, Making Connections
➍ Vocabulary, Summarizing
➎ Vocabulary, Author's (Artist's) Purpose
➏ Vocabulary, Making Connections

Technique Tips

Activity Tips

Overview

The purpose of these pages is to open students' minds to the idea that visual arts include many components and take many forms. The arts satisfy the human needs for display, celebration, personal expression, and communication. We use the visual arts to enhance our innermost feelings and to communicate ideas. Art is made by people. Even people who are not professional artists can enjoy the creative process.

Activating Prior Knowledge

■ Ask students what they think art is. Encourage creative, divergent thinking. In visual art, there are many answers to a question.

Questions to Discuss

■ Have students look at the images on pages 12 and 13 and name the things that are visual art. Then ask the following questions.

▶ Which of these things could you hold in your hands?

▶ Which one could you walk inside?

▶ Which ones would you hang on a wall?

▶ Which ones could you wear?

■ Encourage students to think about things they have at home that fit the categories on these pages. The building they live in is architecture. They have dishes and other containers. Many of them have things hanging on the walls to enhance their visual environments. A few may have sculpture in the home. Many will have seen sculpture in and around public buildings.

What Is Art?

Art is . . .

Painting

▲ **Georgia O'Keeffe.** (American). *Autumn Leaves– Lake George.* 1924.
Oil on canvas. Columbus Museum of Art, Columbus, Ohio.

Drawing

▲ **Leonardo da Vinci.** (Italian). *Self Portrait.* 1514.
Red chalk, Royal Library, Turin, Italy.

Sculpture

▲ **Artist Unknown.** (Italy). *Camillus.* A.D. 41–54.
Bronze. 46⅞ inches high (119.08 cm.). The Metropolitan Museum of Art, New York, New York.

Architecture

▲ **Artist Unknown.** (India). *Taj Mahal.* 1638–1648.
Marble. 240 feet tall (73.15 meters). Agra, India.

Printmaking

▲ **Katsushika Hokusai.** (Japanese). *Kirifuri Waterfall on Mt. Kurokami in Shimotsuke Province.* c. 1833–1834.

Color woodblock print. $15\frac{5}{16} \times 10\frac{3}{8}$ inches (38.9 × 26.3 cm.). Honolulu Academy of Arts, Honolulu, Hawaii.

Pottery

▲ **Harrison Mc Intosh.** (American). *Stoneware Vase #661.* 1966.

Glazed stoneware. $15\frac{1}{4} \times 13$ inches (38.74 × 33.02 cm.). Renwick Gallery, Smithsonian American Art Museum, Washington, D.C.

Weaving

▲ **Artist Unknown.** (Ashanti Peoples, Ghana). *Kente Cloth.*

Museum of International Folk Art, Santa Fe, New Mexico.

Clothing

◄ **Artist Unknown.** (American). *Arapaho Man's Shirt.* c. 1890.

Buckskin and feathers. 37 inches (93.68 cm.) long. Buffalo Bill Historical Center, Cody, Wyoming.

Art is created by people.

What Is Art?   **13**

Using the Credit Line

The credit line is a list of important facts about the work of art that appears below or next to the work. For example, you can help students understand the size of an artwork and how it relates to their own size. Most credit lines contain the following information.

▧ Name of the artist.

▧ Title of the work. This always appears in italics. If the word *detail* follows the title, it means that the image is part of a larger work of art.

▧ Year the work was created. A *c* before the date indicates that the piece was made around the year given.

▧ Medium used by the artist.

▧ Size of the work. The first number is the height, the second is the width, and a third number indicates depth for three-dimensional works.

▧ Location of the work. This tells the museum, gallery, or collection in which the work is housed.

Art Studios, Galleries, and Museums

Works of art are created in *studios.* A studio is an artist's workplace, much like a classroom is a studio for students. Almost everything an artist needs to create an artwork will be found in his or her studio. It is possible for people to visit artist studios, but an invitation from the artist is usually required.

Art galleries are private businesses where art dealers display and sell works of art. Art galleries are typically open to the public and the works of art may be viewed even if the patrons do not intend to buy anything.

A *museum* is a public or private building where valuable and important works of art are cared for and displayed for the public to view. *Curators* are people who supervise the museum and organize exhibitions. *Docents* are special tour directors who help explain the art to visitors.

Overview

These pages introduce students to the three components that define a work of art: the subject, the composition, and the content.

Subject

The subject is the image that the viewer can easily identify in a work of art. The subject may be one person or many people. It may be a thing. It can be an event, such as a party. In recent years, some artists have chosen to create nonobjective art. This is art that has no recognizable subject matter. In this type of art, the elements of art become the subject.

Composition

The composition is the way the principles of art are used to organize the elements of art. Notice the patterns the artist used in *Classic Serape Style Wearing Blanket.*

Content

The content is the message the work communicates to the viewer. The message may be an idea, such as family unity, or an emotion or feeling, such as joy or loneliness. If the work of art is functional, such as *Classic Serape Style Wearing Blanket,* then the function is the meaning. Does the work of art look like it could perform the function it is supposed to?

What Is Art?

Every work of art has three parts.

Subject

This is the object you see in the artwork.

Composition

This is how the artwork is organized.

Content

This is what the artwork means.

▲ **W.H. Brown.** (American). *Bareback Riders.* 1886.
Oil on cardboard mounted on wood. 18½ × 24½ inches (46.99 × 61.60 cm.). National Gallery of Art, Washington, D.C.

What is the subject of this artwork?

▲ **Artist Unknown.** (Native American, Navajo). *Classic Serape Style Wearing Blanket.* 1875.

Plied cotton and Saxony wool. 73½ × 47 inches (186.69 × 119.38 cm.). Utah Museum of Fine Arts, University of Utah, Salt Lake City, Utah.

How is this work organized?

▲ **Jacob Lawrence.** (American). *Children at Play.* 1947.

Tempera on Masonite panel. 20 × 24 inches (50.8 × 60.96 cm.). Georgia Museum of Art, University of Georgia, Athens, Georgia.

What does this artwork mean?

Activating Prior Knowledge

▦ Ask students what is the first thing they look for when they look at a work of art. Students may say they look at color, size, or what it's about. Some may say they look for the feeling or message they get from it. Give students time to explore this question. It will provide a good context for the discussion on these pages.

Questions to Discuss

▦ Read with students the text on pages 14 and 15. Share with them some of the information above. Encourage students to think about their responses during the Activating Prior Knowledge discussion as they look at these images and think about the information you have shared with them.

▶ Read the questions, and discuss the answers. The subject of *Bareback Riders* is two circus riders on a horse. *Classic Serape Style Wearing Blanket* is organized in rows of pattern. *Children at Play,* like all artwork, will mean different things to different people. Possible answers include the joy of friendship and playing together and so on.

Overview

In art, *subject* means something an artist has depicted or represented in an artwork. For example, the subject matter of Claude Monet's painting of trees is called a landscape. Some subject matter, like Monet's landscape, is easy to identify. Others are more difficult because the artwork may be symbolic or nonobjective. Artists create works of art on a variety of subjects: the natural world, literature, religion, the constructed world, history, and so on. These pages deal with several of the most common subject-matter topics—people, objects, everyday life, stories, things outside, colors and shapes, and things that have a deeper meaning.

Talk with students about each subject-matter topic description below. Encourage them to look for examples of different subject matter in the lessons. By helping them to look at each subject in greater detail and by asking thoughtful questions, your students will begin to develop an understanding for differences among subject matter in art.

Nonobjective

Sometimes artwork is nonobjective. It does not have an identifiable subject matter—no familiar subjects are shown. People respond to the way the artwork has been organized and designed. Nonobjective art focuses specifically on the elements and principles of art: line, shape, color, and so on.

▶ **Question:** The artwork does not use a subject we can identify. What are some of the lines, shapes, and colors you see in this picture?

Subject Matter

Artists make art about many subjects. Name the subjects you see on these pages.

Colors and Shapes

▲ **Auguste Herbin.** (French). *Composition on the Word "Vie" 2.* 1950.

Oil on canvas. 57½ × 38¼ inches (146.05 × 97.16 cm.). Museum of Modern Art, New York, New York.

Things Outside

▲ **Claude Monet.** (French). *The Four Trees.* 1891.
Oil on canvas. 32¼ × 32⅜ inches (81.92 × 81.58 cm.). The Metropolitan Museum of Art, New York, New York.

Landscape

This area includes the natural world—plants, animals, or other things outside. The suffix *scape* means "a view of." For example, a *cityscape* is buildings and city life seen in an artwork. A *seascape* is a scene of the sea.

▶ **Question:** What objects do you see in this landscape?

Genre

In art, the term *genre* is used to indicate subjects that have to do with ordinary people engaged in everyday activities.

▶ **Question:** What everyday activities are these people doing?

What Is Art?

Everyday Life

▲ **Carmen Lomas Garza.** (American). *Naranjas (Oranges)*.
Gouache. 20 × 14 inches (50.8 × 35.56 cm.). Collection of Mr. and Mrs. Ira Schneider, Scottsdale, Arizona.

A Story

▲ **Artist Unknown.** (Hmong Peoples, Asia). *Hmong Story Cloth.*
Cotton. 18 × 18 inches (45.72 × 45.72 cm.). Private collection.

A Story

A story is an account of an incident from a real person's life, a historic event, or from a myth, legend, or other piece of symbolic literature.

▶ **Question:** What story do you think is being told in this artwork?

Portrait

This category includes portraits, self-portraits, and group portraits. Portraits are one of the oldest subjects in art history. An artist tries to present both an accurate depiction and other aspects of a person's character in a portrait.

▶ **Question:** What do you think the artist is telling us about these people?

What Is Art?

People

▲ **Isabel Bishop.** (American). *Ice Cream Cones.* 1942.
....
Oil and egg tempera on fiberboard. 33⅞ x 20 inches (86.04 x 50.8 cm.).
Museum of Fine Arts, Boston, Massachusetts.

Objects

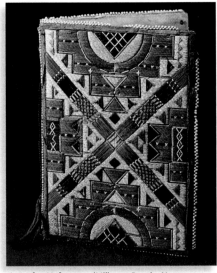

▲ **Artist Unknown.** (Mi'kmaq People, Nova Scotia, Canada). *Letter Holder or Book Cover.*

Birch bark decorated with porcupine quills, glass beads, and silk. $10\frac{1}{4} \times 14\frac{1}{2}$ inches (26.04 × 36.83 cm.). Museum of International Folk Art, Santa Fe, New Mexico.

Things with a Deeper Meaning

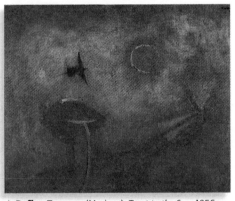

▲ **Rufino Tamayo.** (Mexican). *Toast to the Sun.* 1956.

Oil on canvas. $31\frac{1}{2}$ x 39 inches (80 x 99 cm.). Wichita Art Museum, Wichita, Kansas.

Objects

Sometimes works of art are functional. Pottery, baskets, architecture, teapots, and furniture are just a few examples of artwork that is functional.

▶ **Question:** What do you think this work was used for?

Things with a Deeper Meaning

Sometimes works of art contain symbols—visual signs of something invisible. For example, a dove can be a symbol of peace, or an hourglass may represent the passing of time. Symbols represent a broader idea or sometimes have a secret meaning. Sometimes the title of a work can give you clues to its meaning.

▶ **Question:** What do you think this artwork means?

Overview

Each language has its own system of words and rules of grammar. To learn a new language, you need to learn new words and a new set of rules for putting the words together. The language of visual art also has its own system. The words of the language are the **elements** of art. They are the basic visual symbols in the language of art. Just as there are basic kinds of words such as nouns, verbs, adjectives, and adverbs, there are basic kinds of art elements. These are line, shape, color, value, space, form, and texture. These elements are the visual building blocks that the artist puts together to create a work of art. No matter what materials are used, the artwork will contain all of the visual elements. Sometimes one element will be more important than the others.

Visual images are organized according to rules. In language, these are the rules of grammar. In visual art, the rules for organizing the elements of art are called the **principles** of art. These principles include pattern, rhythm, balance, emphasis, harmony, variety, and unity.

Activating Prior Knowledge

- Ask students what they think of when they hear each of the following words: *line, shape, color.* Encourage them to look around the classroom for examples.

Questions to Discuss

- Have students examine the images on pages 22 and 23. Ask them what they can tell about each photo. What stands out in each image? How does each image help explain the element or principle?

Elements of Art

Art talks with . . .

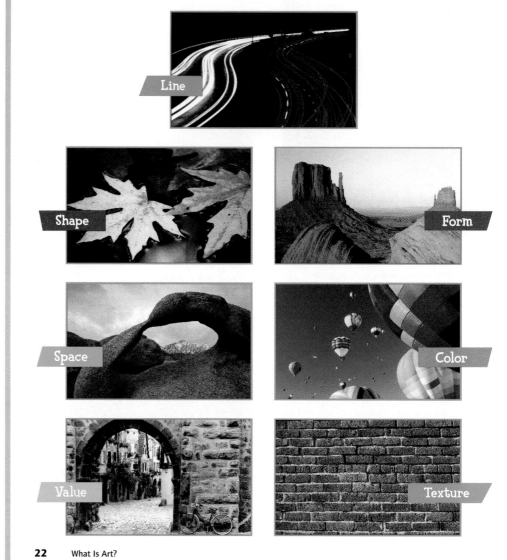

Line

Shape

Form

Space

Color

Value

Texture

Principles of Art

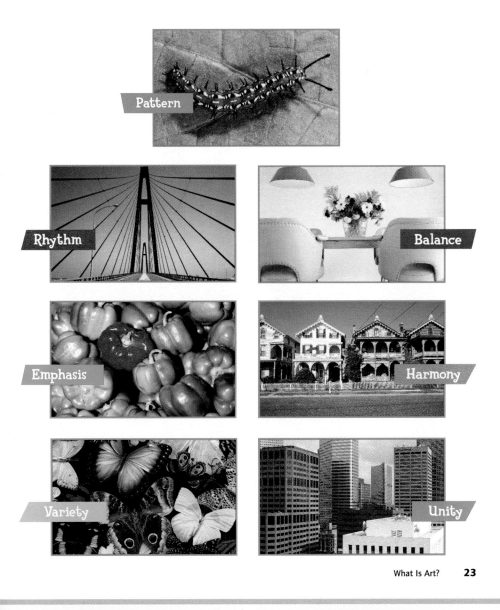

Pattern

Rhythm

Balance

Emphasis

Harmony

Variety

Unity

The Language of Art

The elements and principles of art are the concepts or ideas that artists use to organize their artwork. Artists use a variety of media and materials to make art. *Media* are types of art such as photography, watercolor, and so on. *Materials* are the things used to make the art, such as markers, paint, paper, clay, fabric, wood, metal, or glass.

There are specific techniques and processes that artists use to manipulate the materials. For example, the proper way to hold a brush to create a thin line with watercolor paint is a specific technique unique to watercolor painting. The process of creating a finished watercolor painting consists of many interwoven steps such as thinking about what to paint, sketching several ideas, deciding which elements and principles will enhance the work, choosing the best sketch, deciding which watercolor techniques to use, and finally producing the finished work.

Special techniques and procedures are used with each material. You will need to learn different techniques and follow different procedures for modeling clay than you will for creating paper sculpture. Drawing with crayons requires different techniques and procedures from drawing with oil pastels or chalk. Using the computer to make original art requires that you learn how to use specific computer hardware and software.

Overview

Art History and Culture

Art history is the record of art from the past to the present. By looking at art from the past, we learn what the people who lived before us were like—their feelings and beliefs, clothes, food, houses, and how they viewed the world around them.

Questions to Discuss:

Knowledge
▶ Who created the artwork?

▶ When was the artwork created?

▶ What is the artwork's title?

▶ Have you ever seen an artwork like this? Where?

Comprehension
▶ Is this artwork useful? How is it used?

▶ Compare this artwork with another artwork from a similar time. How are the works of art alike and different?

▶ What interests you most about this artwork?

Application
▶ What types of materials were used to create this artwork?

▶ Demonstrate how the artwork was created.

▶ Explain how this artwork could have a different use today.

Analysis
▶ What are the main lines, shapes, and colors in this artwork?

▶ Compare this painting with another painting in this book. How are they alike? How are they different?

▶ What does this artwork mean?

About Art

▲ **Mary Cassatt.** (American). *Susan Comforting the Baby.* 1881.
Oil on canvas. 25⅝ x 39⅜ inches (65.1 x 100 cm.). Museum of Fine Arts, Houston, Texas.

Art History and Culture

Look at the painting.

▶ How are the people dressed?

▶ What are they doing?

▶ What can you learn about the artist?

Synthesis

▶ How many titles can you create for this artwork? Name them.

▶ Name a person you would like to give this artwork to as a gift. Why?

Evaluation

▶ Do you think this artwork is interesting? Why?

▶ Summarize this artwork's unique qualities.

What to Do

▪ Help students find out more about the life and times of Mary Cassatt. Students may dress up as the artist and tell the artist's story to classmates.

▪ Show students a work by another artist who lived at the same time as Cassatt. Have pairs of students role-play a discussion between the two artists talking about their work.

▪ Have students work in groups to act out this painting. They should act out what happened before, during, and after the moment shown in the painting.

Overview

Aesthetic Perception

Aesthetic perception encourages students to make choices rather than give "right answers." By understanding the process of aesthetic perception, students can see something from a new perspective and ultimately realize that art is all around them.

Journal writing is an integral part of aesthetic perception. It is an ongoing record of what a student does, notices, and thinks. Journals track the evolution of thoughts and experiences over time. Through this recorded journey, the student has the ability to reflect on where one has been and where one is going. Dictating or drawing thoughts and questions intensifies each student's life experiences.

Guidelines for Aesthetic Perception

Students like to know what is important about a work of art and what was important to the artist. They are fascinated with information, questions, and descriptions. There are some guiding principles in the development of aesthetic perception at this level that can profoundly influence teaching practice.

1. All aesthetic perception actively involves the learner.

2. All aesthetic perception involves reflection.

3. The works of art have substance. Their tools and a working vocabulary are vital to empower the learner.

4. Aesthetic perception is a process based upon examination of the artist's choices and the choices in response made by the viewer.

5. All responses are valid. Right and wrong are irrelevant issues when viewing works of art.

6. All works of art relate to each other, and each relates to all other areas of life.

About Art

▲ **Mary Cassatt.** (American). *Susan Comforting the Baby.* 1881.
Oil on canvas. 25⅝ x 39⅜ inches (65.1 x 100 cm.). Museum of Fine Arts, Houston, Texas.

Look

▶ Look at the work of art.
What do you see?

Look Inside

▶ Pretend you are Susan.
Tell a story about this work of art.

Look Outside

▶ What does this work make you feel?

▶ What will you remember about this
work of art?

Questions to Discuss

▶ What is happening in this work of art?

▶ What is this work of art about?

▶ What is your favorite part of this work of
art?

▶ What is most important in this artwork?

▶ What happened just before and just after
in this work of art?

▶ If you were in this work of art, what would
you be doing?

▶ What have you learned about the work of
art?

▶ What does the artist want you to know or
think about in this work of art?

▶ How do you feel about the work of art?

▶ What will you remember about this work
of art?

Things to Do

▪ Draw yourself into the work of art.

▪ Draw what you can't see in the work of art.

▪ Act out or show the story in the work of
art.

▪ Role-play an interview with the artist
about how the work of art was made.

Overview

Art Criticism

Art criticism is an organized system for looking at and talking about art. The purpose of art criticism is to get the viewer involved in a perception process that delays judgment until all aspects of the image have been studied. Learning art criticism also gives each viewer the confidence to discuss a work of art without worrying what other people might think.

Describe What do I see?

During this step, the viewer lists all the obvious things in the artwork. Objectivity is important.

Questions to Discuss

▶ List and describe everything you see in the artwork. Answers may include: In the center of the work is a very young child sitting in a stroller. One hand is clutching her head and the other is reaching toward the viewer. The child is wearing a white dress with a ruffled collar. Susan is leaning close to the child so that her face is touching the baby's face. One arm is around the baby's back. Her hair is pulled into a knot (and so on).

Analyze How is the work organized?

During this step the viewer examines how the elements and principles of art are used in the artwork.

Questions to Discuss

▶ Describe the elements of art you see. Where do you see lines? What shapes can you find? What colors do you see? Answers may include: **Line**—We see lines of brush strokes all over. There are vertical lines on the wall and the shutters. **Shape**—Susan, the child, the stroller, the bird, and the plants are free-form shapes. The shutters are rectangles. **Color**—Most of the colors look dull brown and gray. The faces look very red. There are spots of red in the dull green plants (and so on).

▶ How has the artist used the principles of design? Answers may include: **Emphasis**—The area of emphasis seems to be the two faces (and so on).

▲ **Mary Cassatt.** (American). *Susan Comforting the Baby.* 1881.
Oil on canvas. 25⅝ x 39⅜ inches (65.1 x 100 cm.). Museum of Fine Arts, Houston, Texas.

 **Art Criticism**

Describe

▶ List the people and things you see.

Analyze

▶ What lines, shapes, colors, and textures do you see?

▶ What part stands out?

Interpret

▶ What is happening? What is the artist telling you about Susan and the baby?

Decide

▶ Have you ever seen another artwork like this?

More About Aesthetic Judging

You can use art criticism to make aesthetic judgments about functional objects such as cars or shoes. Follow the first two steps (**Describe** and **Analyze**) as described. During **Interpret,** consider the purpose of the object as its meaning. (Does a pitcher look like it will pour liquid without spilling?) As you **Decide,** consider whether the object works when it is used. (If a chair is not comfortable to sit in, it is not functioning properly and is not successful as a chair.)

 Interpret **What is the artist saying to me?**

During interpretation, viewers will make inferences about the message in the work of art. Each interpretation can be different because each is based upon the feelings and life experiences of the viewer.

Questions to Discuss

▶ What is the artist trying to tell us about these people and their lives? Answers will vary. Some students will think Susan is the mother. Even if she isn't, it is obvious she cares for the child. The child may have awoken from a bad dream, or she may be reaching for a toy that fell.

Decide

This is when the viewer decides whether or not the work is successful. There are two levels of judgment to be made. The first is personal: do you like the work?

The second level is also subjective, but it uses aesthetic theories to help the viewer decide whether the work is successful. More than one theory may be used to judge a work.

▪ Some critics think that the most important thing about a work of art is the realistic presentation of the subject matter. This aesthetic theory is called **imitationalism** or **realism.**

▪ Other critics think that composition is the most important fact in a work of art. This aesthetic theory, called **formalism** or **composition,** emphasizes the design qualities and the arrangement of the elements of art using the principles of art.

▪ Some critics claim that no object should be considered art if it fails to arouse an emotional response in the viewer. **Emotionalism** or **expressionism** is a theory concerned with the content or the meaning of the work of art.

Questions to Discuss

▶ Have you seen another artwork that looks like this? Answers will vary.

▶ Have you seen any works of art in this book that show adults and children relating to each other?

Overview

Creative Expression

The creative process, like the writing process or the scientific method, is an organized approach to creative problem solving that can be used by professional artists and students alike. Throughout *Art Connections,* the Creative Expression activities are presented as problems to be solved. Remind students of the steps in the creative process as they work on the activities.

Get an idea.

■ Inspiration can come from many places. In the *Art Connections* Creative Expression activities, the idea comes from the activity instructions. Professional artists may get ideas from a client who has commissioned a piece of art from nature, from a historical event, from everyday life, or from the available media and materials.

■ Try the following to help students when they have trouble getting an idea.

1. As a class, brainstorm about where to get ideas for artwork: works by other artists, personal experiences, stories students have read, and so on.

2. Encourage students to write ideas in the Ideas section of their Art Journals. Remind students that they can make notes for ideas anytime, not just in art class.

3. Pair students who are having trouble thinking of ideas with students who have many ideas. One student can model getting ideas for the other student.

Plan your work.

■ Once students have an idea, they must decide the best way to execute that idea. Would a two-dimensional or three-dimensional artwork best convey the idea that students are trying to show? Should students use watercolor or pencil?

Make a sketch.

■ Just like professional writers, professional artists do not make a perfect work on the first try. They may make several sketches, evaluate those sketches, and revise them before deciding on a final vision for the artwork.

■ Encourage students to make sketches in the Ideas section of their Art Journals.

▲ **Mary Cassatt.** (American). *Susan Comforting the Baby.* 1881.
Oil on canvas. 25⅝ x 39⅜ inches (65.1 x 100 cm.). Museum of Fine Arts, Houston, Texas.

How can you make art?

1. Get an idea.
2. Plan your work.
3. Make a sketch.
4. Use the media.
5. Share your final work.

Use the media.

- In this stage of the creative process, students make their artwork based on their plans. Encourage students to practice using unfamiliar media, and to try out new techniques on a small practice piece before using those techniques on their artwork.

- Even during this stage of the process, students may get new ideas. Encourage them to be flexible.

Share your final work.

- Art is meant to be shared with and viewed by others. Encourage students to share their artwork with family or friends, display it in the classroom, or display it in the school display area. This is also a good time for students to self-evaluate their work using the four steps of art criticism.

More About Art Journals

- Art Journals are a wonderful way to work through ideas. At the beginning of the school year, help students set up an Art Journal. This can be a spiral notebook or a three-ring binder with pages for writing and sketching. The Art Journal will be divided into sections for Concepts, Ideas, Critical Thinking (Art Criticism), and Vocabulary.

1. Encourage students to use the Concepts section of their journals for summarizing unit and lesson concepts, writing questions they have, and listing other things they want to learn. Younger students may dictate or draw their thoughts.

2. Students can use the Ideas section of their Art Journals for brainstorming, organizing, planning, and sketching. Remind students that they can write ideas in their journals any time; they do not need to wait until a designated time in art class.

3. Students can use the Critical Thinking section of their journals to self-evaluate their work using the four steps of Art Criticism. In *Art Connections* students are asked to self-evaluate after each Creative Expression activity. This can be a valuable tool to help students review art concepts and get ideas for their next work. Younger students may dictate their thoughts.

4. Encourage students to use the Vocabulary section of their Art Journals to record unfamiliar words, summarize or explain definitions, and so on. Developing vocabulary is an important step in being able to think about and communicate about art.

Overview

Elementary teachers are responsible for the safety of their students. Specific guidelines have been established by the Center for Safety in the Arts, and these guidelines should be followed to ensure that both students and teachers use art materials safely. Following are some general tips for using art materials safely. For more detailed information, see "Safe Use of Art Materials" on page T12 of this book.

Safe Art Materials

- Use only water-soluble AP- or CP-designated markers. Never use permanent or scented markers.

- Use only dustless chalk.

- Make sure that crayons have the AP or CP label to ensure that they do not contain lead.

- When using tempera paint, use only liquid tempera, not powdered tempera. Do not use any spray paints or fixatives.

- Use only water-soluble printers' inks.

- Use pencils to carve into soft surfaces for printing blocks. Do not use mat knives or other sharp instruments.

- Do not allow young children to use sharp scissors; blunt points are safe.

- Do not use rubber cement unless it bears the AP or CP label. Do not use solvent-based glues.

Safety

- ▶ Use art materials only on your artwork.
- ▶ Keep art materials out of your mouth, eyes, and ears.
- ▶ Use only safety scissors. Keep your fingers away from the blades.

- ▶ Wash your hands after using the art materials.
- ▶ Wear an art shirt or smock to protect your clothes.
- ▶ Always follow your teacher's directions.

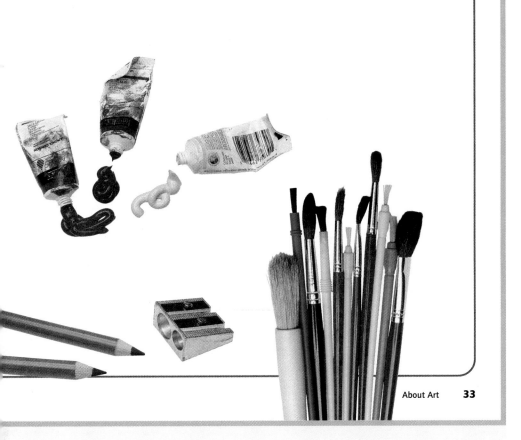

General Safety Precautions for Art

- ■ Read the labels on all materials used in the art room. Look carefully for the AP/CP labels. If these are not present, be suspicious. Imported art materials should be looked upon with extreme caution. Other countries have not developed the rigid safety codes adopted by the United States.

- ■ Do not accept or use old art materials that may have been left in the school or donated by some well-meaning adult. If the materials do not bear the current safety codes, toss them out.

- ■ Never allow food or drink in the room where art activities are being conducted. Dust and even fibers float freely in the air and can readily contaminate food or drink.

- ■ Practice cleanliness. Have children wash their hands thoroughly with soap after using art materials.

- ■ Use absolutely no permanent markers or solvent-based materials in the art room. If a material stains the clothes or hands and does not clean up with simple soap and water, it is not appropriate or safe for young children to use.

- ■ Use plastic containers for washing paintbrushes; glass is dangerous in the hands of young children.

- ■ Paper cutters should not be used by elementary school children. The paper cutter should be kept out of the students' reach, and left in a locked position always with the blade turned to the wall.

- ■ Do not use commercial dyes around children; use vegetable or natural dyes (flowers, teas, onion skins).

- ■ Do not allow children in a room where a kiln is firing; both the heat and the fumes are dangerous.

Unit 1 Planning Guide

	Lesson Title	Suggested Pacing	Creative Expression Activity
Lesson 1	Lines	40 minutes	Create a design with different lines.
Lesson 2	Calm Lines	50 minutes	Create a painting of a quiet place with vertical and horizontal lines.
Lesson 3	Diagonal Lines	50 minutes	Create a torn-paper tree with diagonal lines.
Lesson 4	Curved Lines	50 minutes	Create a monoprint with curved lines.
Lesson 5	Buildings Have Lines	55 minutes	Create a mixed-media collage building.
Lesson 6	Lines Show Movement	45 minutes	Create a computer drawing of self showing movement.
ART SOURCE ARTSOURCE	Lines in Song Writing	35 minutes	Create song lyrics about an endangered animal.

Materials	Program Resources	Fine Art Resources	Literature Resources
oil pastels or crayons, 12" × 18" white paper, watercolors, watercolor brushes, paper towels, water dishes, masking tape	*Reading and Writing Test Preparation,* pp. 6-7 *Flash Cards,* 1-6 *Assessment,* pp. 9-10 *Home and After-School Connections*	*Transparency,* 1 *Artist Profiles,* pp. 32, 63 *Animals Through History Time Line* *Large Prints,* 13 and 14 *The National Museum of Women in the Arts Collection*	*First Day Jitters* by Julie Danneberg
12" × 18" white paper, water containers, liquid tempera paint, watercolor brushes, paper towels, newspaper	*Reading and Writing Test Preparation,* pp. 8-9 *Flash Cards,* 1 and 2 *Assessment,* pp. 11-12	*Transparency,* 2 *Artist Profiles,* pp. 31, 44 *Large Prints,* 13 and 14 *Women in the Arts Collection*	*Amelia's Fantastic Flight* by Rose Bursik
construction paper (brown, black, or grey for the tree and autumn colors for the leaves), glue	*Reading and Writing Test Preparation,* pp. 10-11 *Flash Cards,* 3 and 5 *Assessment,* pp. 13-14	*Transparency,* 3 *Artist Profiles,* pp. 29, 40 *Large Prints,* 13 and 14 *Art Around the World*	*Rosie's Walk* by Pat Hutchins
12" × 18" white paper, tempera paint with media mixer, clear plastic wrap, masking tape, plastic combs, paper towels	*Reading and Writing Test Preparation,* pp. 12-13 *Flash Card,* 4 *Assessment,* pp. 15-16	*Transparency,* 4 *Artist Profiles,* pp. 61, 66 *Large Prints,* 13 and 14 *Art Around the World*	*Homeplace* by Anne Shelby
precut rectangular cardboard or mat board, wooden ice-cream sticks, chenille stems, yarn, scissors, glue	*Reading and Writing Test Preparation,* pp. 14-15 *Assessment,* pp. 17-18	*Transparency,* 5 *Artist Profiles,* pp. 22, 36 *Large Prints,* 13 and 14 *Art Around the World*	*My Town* by Rebecca Treays
computer's paint program	*Reading and Writing Test Preparation,* pp. 16-17 *Flash Cards,* 3-6 *Assessment,* pp. 19-20	*Transparency,* 6 *Artist Profiles,* pp. 3, 35 *Large Prints,* 13 and 14 *Women in the Arts Collection*	*James and the Rain* by Karla Kuskin
"Our Little Blue Planet" including the songs "Dead as a Dodo" and "The Tree Song." Performed by Paul Tracey.			

1 Line

Lesson 1: **Lines** can be described as thick, thin, smooth, rough, solid, or broken.

Lesson 2: **Vertical and horizontal lines** create a feeling of stability. Vertical and horizontal lines are used to paint calm landscapes.

Lesson 3: **Diagonal lines** are slanted. They give a busy, active feeling to artwork.

Lesson 4: **Curved lines** show gentle movement.

Lesson 5: Artists use vertical, horizontal, and diagonal lines to depict **buildings.**

Lesson 6: Artists use lines in their artwork to show **movement.** Diagonal, zigzag, and curved lines can show people and animals moving.

Introduce Unit Concepts

"Artists use different kinds of lines to show different things in their works of art." "Los artistas usan diferentes tipos de líneas para mostrar diferentes cosas en sus obras de arte".

Lines

Have students name humanmade objects and things found in nature that have different line directions. For example:

- **Horizontal lines**—tables, beds, the horizon
- **Vertical lines**—lampposts, chimneys, books on a shelf, tree trunks
- **Diagonal and zigzag lines**—bicycle spokes, sun rays, lightning
- **Curved lines**—tires, flower petals, clouds

Cross-Curricular Projects

- See the *Language Arts and Reading, Mathematics, Science,* and *Social Studies Art Connections* books for activities that further develop line concepts.

National Standards for Arts Education in Visual Arts (NSAE) 6.b

---

Line

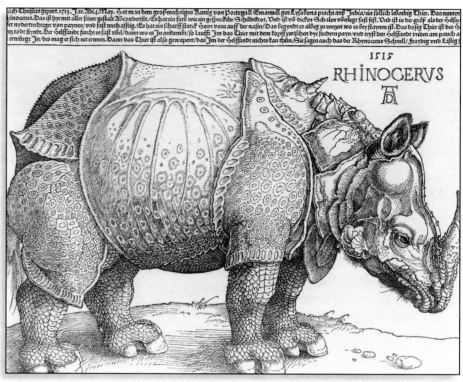

▲ **Albrecht Dürer.** (German).
Rhinoceros. 1515.
Woodcut. 8⅜ × 11⅝ inches (21.27 × 29.53 cm). The Metropolitan Museum of Art, New York, New York.

Artists use lines in their works of art.

This picture of a rhinoceros has many lines.

34 Unit 1

Fine Art Prints

Display **Large Prints 13** *Children at the Ice Cream Stand* and **14** *Night Heron.* Refer to the prints throughout the unit as students learn about lines.

Large Print 13

Large Print 14

Look at the picture.

▶ Where do you see lines that go up and down?

▶ Where do you see lines that are leaning?

▶ Where do you see lines that go from side to side?

In This Unit you will:

▶ learn about different kinds of lines.

▶ find lines in art and the environment.

▶ create art with lines.

Self-Portrait

Albrecht Dürer

(1471–1528)

▶ was a German artist.

▶ made paintings, drawings, and prints.

▶ created art about many subjects.

Unit 1   **35**

Art History and Culture

Albrecht Dürer

In the early 1500s, King Emanuel of Portugal received a rhinoceros as a gift. A man who was visiting Portugal saw the rhinoceros and sent Albrecht Dürer (äl′ brekht do͞or′ ər) (1471–1528) a sketch and description of the animal. Dürer had never actually seen a rhinoceros when he made this piece of art! *Rhinoceros* is a woodcut. Dürer drew the lines of the image on a block of wood, and then he carved away the wood around the image, leaving raised lines. Many prints could be made by inking the woodcut and pressing it onto paper. Dürer was the first artist to use printmaking as a major art form.

See pages 16–21 and 24–25 for more about subject matter and art history.

Artist Profiles, p. 16

· Artist Profile ·

Albrecht Dürer
1471–1528

Albrecht Dürer (al brekt′ dü′ ər) was born in Nuremberg, Germany, in 1471. He was the second son in a family of 18 children. His father was a goldsmith, and it was assumed that he would follow in the family tradition. Because Dürer displayed such skill in drawing, his father apprenticed him to a local painter when he was 15. He married and traveled to Italy when he was 23. In Italy he was introduced to the Renaissance ideal of the artist as an intellectual. He brought this philosophy back to Nuremberg, and set about educating himself in all fields of learning associated with this new approach to art. He studied and wrote about geometry, perspective, proportion, and the nature of art. He also wrote many letters and

Examine the Artwork

"Let's look for lines in Albrecht Dürer's *Rhinoceros.*" "Busquemos líneas en la obra *Rhinoceros* de Albrecht Dürer".

■ Have students look at the artwork and describe what they see.

■ Have students answer the question on page 35. Tell students that lines that go up and down are called vertical lines, lines that are leaning are called diagonal lines, and lines that go from side to side are called horizontal lines.

▶ Vertical lines can be found in the scales on the legs.

▶ Diagonal lines can be found near the face and neck.

▶ Horizontal lines are found on the ground.

■ Additional question:

▶ Does the rhinoceros look like it is moving or does it look calm? The rhinoceros looks calm. If it were moving, the legs would be positioned differently. Instead of having vertical lines, the outlines of the legs would be diagonal.

Unit Pretest

T Display *Transparency 43* as a pretest. Answers: 1. C, 2. A, 3. B

Home Connection

■ See *Home and After-School Connections* for family newsletters and activities for this unit.

National Standards for Arts Education in Visual Arts (NSAE) 2.a; 3.a

ILLUSTRATOR PROFILE
Ashley Bryan
(1923–   )

Ashley Bryan was born and raised in the Bronx, New York. He and his five brothers and sisters enjoyed reading and often borrowed books from the public library. From the time he was in kindergarten, he knew that he was a talented artist. He combined this talent with his love of reading and began making his own books as gifts.

Bryan graduated from Cooper Union Art School and Columbia University. He won a Fulbright Scholarship to study art in Europe. While teaching art classes at Queens College, he began illustrating other authors' books. In 1971 *The Ox of the Wonderful Horns and Other African Folktales,* Bryan's first book as author and illustrator, was published.

In 1973 Bryan joined the faculty of Dartmouth College. He continued to write and illustrate books inspired by African lore. He retired from teaching in 1988 and began writing and illustrating books full-time. He has illustrated or written more than 30 books.

Throughout Unit 1, share Bryan's illustrations with the class and discuss his use of line. Have students identify thick, thin, horizontal, vertical, diagonal, zigzag, and curved lines. Have students discuss the lines used to illustrate people, animals, and buildings.

Music

 Line in music refers to the way a melody moves higher or lower. Sing a song and have students draw lines to show the movement of the melody.

Literature and Art

Use the video or DVD *Mama Don't Allow* by Thatcher Hurd to introduce the concept of line. Point out how the artist used various line qualities and line directions.

Literature and Art

Performing Arts

Play "Our Little Blue Planet" by Paul Tracey. Compare the lines of the song to lines in art.

Artsource

Lesson 1 Lines

Overview

Lesson 1 introduces students to line quality. Lines can be described as thick, thin, smooth, rough, solid, or broken.

Objectives

Art History and Culture
To recognize that some artists create abstract art
NSAE 2.a; 3.a

Creative Expression
To create a design with thick, thin, smooth, rough, solid, and broken lines
NSAE 1.a; 1.c; 1.d

Aesthetic Perception
To identify thick, thin, smooth, rough, solid, or broken lines in artwork and in the environment NSAE 2.a; 6.b

Art Criticism
To evaluate one's own artwork using the four steps of art criticism
NSAE 1.b; 2.b; 3.a; 5.c

Vocabulary ⭐ Reading

Review the following vocabulary words with students before beginning the lesson.

line línea—the mark made by a tool, such as a pencil, pen, or paintbrush, as it moves across a surface

Definitions for the following words appear as art on *Student Edition* page 38 and in the student glossary:

thick gruesa	**rough** áspera	**broken** entre cortada
thin fina	**smooth** suave	**solid** continua

See page 59B for additional Spanish vocabulary resources.

Art Journal: Vocabulary
Have students add these words to the Vocabulary section of their Art Journals.

Lesson Materials
- oil pastels or crayons
- 12" × 18" white paper
- watercolors
- watercolor brushes
- paper towels
- water dishes
- masking tape

Alternate Materials:
- white glue instead of oil pastels or crayons

Program Resources
- *Reading and Writing Test Prep.*, pp. 6–7
- *Transparency 1*
- *Flash Cards 1–6*
- *Artist Profiles*, pp. 32, 63
- *Animals Through History Time Line*
- *Assessment*, pp. 9–10
- *Large Prints 13* Children at the Ice Cream Stand and *14* Night Heron
- *The National Museum of Women in the Arts Collection*

Concept Trace
Lines
Introduced: Level K, Unit 1, Lessons 1, 5, 6

Reinforced: Level 2, Unit 1, Lesson 2

Lesson 1 Arts Integration NSAE 6.a

Theatre
Complete Unit 1, Lesson 1, on pages 18–19 of *Theatre Arts Connections.*

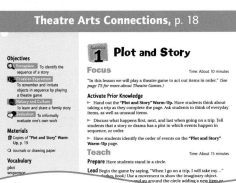

Theatre Arts Connections, p. 18

Music

C-A-G. Billy Taylor.

Line in music refers to the way a melody moves higher and lower (up, down, or the same). To relate the concept of line in music to line in visual art, play Billy Taylor's *C-A-G*, a jazz waltz that creates a melodic line based on the sound of the notes C, A, and G. Have students draw the thick, thin, smooth, rough, solid, or broken lines that they think go with the music.

Movement & Dance
Identify three specific line patterns in the Kandinsky painting: straight lines, *S* curves, and circles. Have students travel through space by creating locomotor (traveling) movements that follow each line path. For example, have students run in the path of a straight line and skip in the path of an *S* curve.

Activate Prior Knowledge

"Do you ever have to stand in a line?"

"¿Alguna vez han tenido que ponerse en una línea?"

- Discuss student responses. Explain that things, including people, can be more organized when they are arranged in a line.

Using Literature ⭐ Reading

- Read *First Day Jitters* by Julie Danneberg. The illustrations by Judy Love contain many different kinds of lines.

Thematic Connection ⭐ Social Studies

- **Cooperation:** Explain that *cooperate* means "to work together." Discuss how people cooperate in a community and how lines cooperate within a work of art.

Introduce the Art

Look
NSAE 2.b; 3.a

"Let's look for lines in the paintings."

"Busquemos líneas en las pinturas".

Comparing and Contrasting ⭐ Reading

- Have students list the similarities and differences in the two works of art. The lines in both paintings are black and the shapes are filled in with color. In *New York City—Bird's Eye View,* the design fills the entire canvas, whereas *Composition 8* has more empty space. The lines and shapes in *Composition 8* are sharper and more precise than the lines and shapes in *New York City—Bird's Eye View.*

🏺 Art History and Culture

Discuss with students that many artists during the early twentieth century created abstract art. Abstract painters did not try to show objects realistically in their art. Sometimes they represented objects in a new way or simplified an object's appearance. Sometimes they made art with no recognizable objects—only the elements of line, shape, and color. This style—first used by Kandinsky—is called *nonobjective.*
NSAE 4.a

💻 Web Connection

Visit **www.ceciliadetorres.com/jt/jt.html** for more information about Torres-García.

Look at the works of art on these pages. The artists used many kinds of lines to create the paintings.

▲ **Joaquín Torres-García.** (Uruguayan). *New York City—Bird's-Eye View.* c. 1920.

Gouache and watercolor on board. $13\frac{1}{2} \times 19\frac{1}{2}$ inches (34.29 × 49.53 cm.). Yale University Art Gallery, New Haven, Connecticut.

🏺 Art History and Culture

At the time these works were painted, many artists were making abstract art. Abstract art does not show objects the way they really look.

🏺 Art History and Culture

Joaquín Torres-García   NSAE 5.a

Joaquín Torres-García (wäh kēn´ tor´ res gär sē´ ä) (1874–1949) was born in Uruguay but moved to Spain when he was 17. As a young man, Torres-García illustrated magazines, created murals, and taught art classes to support himself. Torres-García designed wooden toys and tried to sell them, but he had no luck earning a decent living. He moved with his family to Paris where he was finally recognized as a talented painter. Torres-García helped found Cercle et Carré (Circle and Square), a group of artists who held exhibits and published reviews of abstract art. In the later years of his career, Torres-García's work became less realistic and more abstract.

See pages 16–21 and 24–25 for more about subject matter and art history.

Artist Profiles, p. 63

◆ Artist Profile ◆
Joaquín Torres-Garcia
1874–1949

Joaquín Torres-Garcia (wäh kēn´ tor´ res gär sē´ ä) was born in Uruguay. His family moved to Spain when he was 17 years old. An eager student and deep thinker, he studied many subjects, including art. As a young man, Torres-Garcia illustrated magazines, created murals, and taught art classes to support himself. In 1915 Torres-Garcia designed wooden toys with interchangeable parts to amuse his three children. He moved to New York City, where he hoped to sell the toys. However, they were difficult to manufacture. After trying to sell his toys in Italy, Torres-Garcia and his family settled in Paris. He began to use

Study both works of art to find lines.

▶ Can you find thick, thin, smooth, rough, solid, and broken lines?

▲ **Wassily Kandinsky.** (Russian). *Composition 8.* 1923.

Oil on canvas. 55⅛ × 79⅛ inches (140 × 201 cm.). Solomon R. Guggenheim Museum, New York, New York.

Aesthetic Perception

Seeing Like an Artist Look around. Can you find lines like those in the paintings?

Art History and Culture

Wassily Kandinsky

Wassily Kandinsky (va sēl´ ē kan din´ skē) (1866 –1944) was born in Russia. He studied music at a young age, and he studied law and economics in college. He did not study art until he moved to Germany in 1896. In 1911 Kandinsky helped found Der Blaue Reiter, a group of artists who used art to express spirituality. Kandinsky also taught at the Bauhaus, a school of modern art. In 1933 the Bauhaus was closed by the Nazis and Kandinsky fled to France. Kandinsky is considered one of the most important leaders in modern art because he was the first artist to create non-objective art. He believed color and line in a painting could create feeling just as music did, which is why many of his paintings have musical titles, such as *Composition 8.*

See pages 16–21 and 24–25 for more about subject matter and art history.

Artist Profiles, p. 32

● *Artist Profile* ●
Wassily Kandinsky
1866-1944

Wassily Kandinsky (va sēl´ ē kan din´ skē) first tried painting as a teenager in his native Russia. Even then he felt that each color had a mysterious life of its own. He was still drawn to colors and painting while he studied law and economics in college, but he believed that art was "a luxury forbidden to a Russian." In time, he moved to Germany, studied art, and began his career. Throughout his life Kandinsky moved back and forth between Russia and Germany. In 1933 he settled in France after Nazi storm troopers labeled his painting style "degenerate."

Study

▶ In *New York City—Bird's-Eye View,* thick lines are used to make letters and suggest windows in skyscrapers; thin lines suggest cables of bridges or telephone lines. Most of the thin lines are smooth; the thickest lines, which look like they were made with wide brushstrokes, are rough. Most lines are solid. Broken black lines suggest windows. In *Composition 8,* thick lines make diagonal bars; thin lines make the arcs and many of the other diagonal lines. Most of the diagonal lines are smooth; the "halos" outlining the circles are rough. All of the lines are solid although the grids create the appearance of broken lines.

■ For more examples of abstract/nonobjective art, see *The National Museum of Women in the Arts Collection.*

Art Journal: Concepts

Have students sketch the different types of lines they find in the paintings in the Concepts section of their Art Journals.

Aesthetic Perception

Seeing Like an Artist Discuss with students that lines can be found everywhere around them—in nature as well as in humanmade objects. Have students look around and identify different lines in the environment. Can they find lines like those in the paintings?

Developing Visual Literacy Ask students to tell what they think each painting is about. (Offer the title *New York City—Bird's-Eye View* to help with their interpretation of the Torres-García piece. For the Kandinsky piece, explain that *composition* describes a piece of music.) Students may have trouble with the abstractness of the art. Reassure them that both works of art are open to any interpretation.

Web Connection

Have students visit **www.guggenheimcollection.org** to view other works by Kandinsky. Have students discuss their ideas about his work.

# Teach

"What words can you use to talk about lines?" "¿Qué palabras pueden usar para hablar acerca de líneas?"

- Read and discuss Using Lines on page 38.

Practice

Materials: None

- Read the directions on page 38.

- Have students assemble into small groups and form different lines.

- Ask students to form a thin line by lining up in single file. Then have them change to a thick line by lining up in pairs. Let students experiment to show each kind of line.

Creative Expression

NSAE 1.a; 1.c; 1.d

Materials: oil pastels or crayons, 12" × 18" white paper, watercolors, watercolor brushes, paper towels, water dishes, masking tape

Alternate Materials: white glue instead of oil pastels or crayons

- Distribute materials and have students follow the directions on page 39.

- Make sure students do not brush back and forth when painting over the lines, because this will cause the paint to stick to the lines.

- See the Activity Tips on page 232 for visual examples of this lesson's activity.

- Review the Technique Tips on pages 216–217 and 219 for information about paintbrush care and creating a watercolor resist.

- For an alternate activity, have students create the lines in their designs with white glue instead of oil pastels. Then when the glue dries, have students paint over the picture with watercolor.

Art Journal: Brainstorming

Have students brainstorm ideas for designs that would include many types of lines. Have students make quick sketches in the Ideas section of their Art Journals. Then have students select one to do for the Creative Expression activity.

Using Lines

A **line** is a mark made by an artist's tool as it moves.
Here are different kinds of lines:

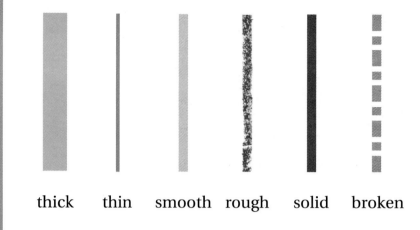

thick   thin   smooth   rough   solid   broken

Practice

Make different lines with your classmates.

1. Line up in single file to make a thin line.

2. Line up in pairs to make a thick line.

3. Can you make other lines?

Differentiated Instruction

Reteach

Make two dots on the board and have a student draw a line between them. Make two more dots and have another student connect them with a line that looks different from the first line.

Special Needs

Adaptations: Provide visual cues of the different types of lines for students as they complete this lesson activity. Learning in other subjects such as math can be reinforced as students are given a certain number of each line to add to their paper.

ELL Tips

Use *Flash Cards 1–6.* Point to a line as you say its name. Have students repeat after you.

Think about how this student used lines.

▲ **Ty Brannen.** Age 7.

(palette icon) **Creative Expression**

How many different ways can you use lines?

1. Think of a design you can make with thick, thin, smooth, rough, solid, and broken lines.
2. Fill your paper with lines.
3. Brush watercolor paint over your lines.

(speech icon) **Art Criticism**

Analyze What kinds of lines did you use? Did you fill your paper?

Unit 1 • Lesson 1   **39**

(decorative banner) **Art Across the Curriculum**

Use these simple ideas to reinforce art concepts across the curriculum.
NSAE 6.b

★ **Expository Writing** Have students use the writing process to write a summary of what they learned in this lesson. The summary should include a list of the different lines.

★ **Math** Distribute index cards with different lines drawn on them. Have students sort the cards by line attributes.

★ **Science** Have students draw different lines and then use their fingertips to measure each line.

★ **Social Studies** Point out how different lines go together in *New York City–Bird's Eye View* to create objects, such as buildings. Discuss characteristics of a city and city life.

★ **Technology** Have students use the computer's paint program to practice making different lines. Visit **SRAonline.com** to print detailed instructions for this activity.

Reflect

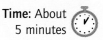
Time: About 5 minutes

Review and Assess
"In what ways can you describe lines?"
"¿De qué maneras pueden describir las líneas?"

Think
The student artist used thick, thin, smooth, rough, solid, and broken lines to create a city scene.

■ Have students identify thick, thin, smooth, rough, solid, and broken lines in *Large Prints 13 Children at the Ice Cream Stand* and *14 Night Heron*.

Informal Assessment

(journal icon) **Art Journal: Critical Thinking**
Have students ask themselves the Art Criticism questions. Then have students write or sketch to answer the Analyze question in their Art Journals.
NSAE 1.b; 2.b; 3.a; 5.c

(speech icon) **Art Criticism**

Describe ▶ What place or thing did you show in your design?

Analyze ▶ What kinds of lines did you use? Did you fill your paper?

Interpret ▶ What is the mood or feeling of your artwork? Give your work a title.

Decide ▶ Did you use six different kinds of lines in your design?

■ For standardized-format test practice using this lesson's art content, see pages 6–7 in *Reading and Writing Test Preparation.*

Focus

Use *Transparency 1* and *Large Print 13 Children at the Ice Cream Stand* to compare ways artists use lines in abstract and narrative art. What types of lines can students identify in each work of art?

Teach

Have students follow your verbal directions to create their abstract line designs.

Reflect

Guide students through evaluation of their works of art using the four steps of art criticism. (See pages 28–29 for more about art criticism.) Then have students share their designs with others in the class, and discuss the variety of designs made from the same set of directions.

Alternate Activity

Materials:
- crayons
- markers
- 12" × 18" white paper

Have students complete an abstract line design based on your verbal directions, such as "Draw a line that changes from thick to thin. Now intersect a solid line with a broken line." Continue until students' papers are filled.

Research
in Art Education

Research has shown that incorporating the arts into core curriculum areas in a way that actively involves students in the learning process produces "significant positive effects on student achievement, motivation, and engagement in learning, and notable changes in classroom practices" ("Different Ways of Knowing: 1991–1994 National Longitudinal Study Final Report" in *Schools, Communities, and the Arts: A Research Compendium*). Because lines can be identified everywhere, it is easy to incorporate this principle of art into other subject areas.

Assessment

Use the following rubric to evaluate the artwork students make in the Creative Expression activity and to assess students' understanding of lines.

Have students complete page 9 or 10 in their *Assessment* books.

	Art History and Culture	Aesthetic Perception	Creative Expression	Art Criticism
3 POINTS	The student can identify that some artists create abstract art.	The student accurately identifies different types of lines in art and in the environment.	The student successfully creates a design using all types of lines introduced in the lesson.	The student thoughtfully and honestly evaluates his or her own work using the four steps of art criticism.
2 POINTS	The student's identification is weak or incomplete.	The student shows emerging awareness of different types of lines, but cannot consistently identify them.	The student creates a design using only a few types of lines introduced in the lesson.	The student attempts to evaluate his or her own work, but shows an incomplete understanding of evaluation criteria.
1 POINT	The student cannot identify that some artists create abstract art.	The student cannot identify different types of lines.	The student's design does not make use of types of lines introduced in the lesson.	The student makes no attempt to evaluate his or her own artwork.

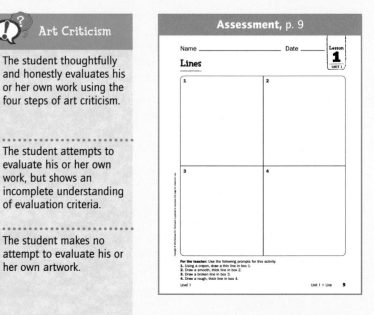

Assessment, p. 9

Name _____ Date _____ Lesson **1** UNIT 1

Lines

For the teacher: Use the following prompts for this activity.
1. Using a crayon, draw a thin line in box 1.
2. Draw a smooth, thick line in box 2.
3. Draw a broken line in box 3.
4. Draw a rough, thick line in box 4.

Level 1   Unit 1 • Line **9**

Lesson 2 Calm Lines

Overview

Lesson 2 introduces vertical and horizontal lines. Artists use vertical and horizontal lines to create a feeling of calm. Calm lines are used to create landscapes.

Objectives

Art History and Culture
To recognize that a landscape is a picture of the outdoors
NSAE 2.a; 3.a

Creative Expression
To paint a calm landscape with vertical and horizontal lines
NSAE 1.a; 1.c; 1.d; 2.c; 3.b

Aesthetic Perception
To locate vertical and horizontal lines in art and the environment
NSAE 2.a; 6.b

Art Criticism
To evaluate one's own artwork using the four steps of art criticism
NSAE 1.b; 2.b; 3.a; 5.c

Vocabulary ⭐ Reading

Review the following vocabulary words with students before beginning the lesson.

horizontal horizontal—from side to side

vertical vertical—up and down

landscape paisaje—a picture of the outdoors

See page 59B for additional Spanish vocabulary resources.

 Art Journal: Vocabulary
Have students add these words to the Vocabulary section of their Art Journals.

Lesson Materials
- 12" × 18" white paper
- water containers
- liquid tempera paint
- watercolor brushes
- paper towels
- newspapers

Alternate Materials
- crayons

Program Resources
- *Reading and Writing Test Prep.,* pp. 8–9
- *Transparency 2*
- *Flash Cards 1* and *2*
- *Artist Profiles,* pp. 31, 44
- *Animals Through History Time Line*
- *Assessment,* pp. 11–12
- *Large Prints 13* Children at the Ice Cream Stand and *14* Night Heron
- *The National Museum of Women in the Arts Collection*

Concept Trace
Calm Lines
Introduced: Level K, Unit 1, Lesson 2

Reinforced: Level 2, Unit 1, Lesson 3

Lesson 2 Arts Integration NSAE 6.a

Theatre
Complete Unit 1, Lesson 2, on pages 20–21 of *Theatre Arts Connections.*

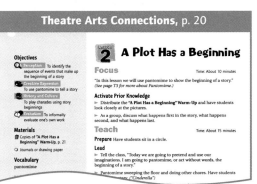
Theatre Arts Connections, p. 20

Music
 Summertime from *Porgy and Bess.* George Gershwin.

Artists use vertical and horizontal lines to make a calm picture. To compare calm lines with calm music, play George Gershwin's *Summertime* from *Porgy and Bess.* Discuss the elements that make the music seem calm. Suggest other songs such as lullabies that have a calm feeling.

Movement & Dance
What action words or phrases can students think of to describe particular line directions? For example, "push and pull" for a horizontal line. Explore each of these in movement.

Focus

Time: About 10 minutes

Activate Prior Knowledge

"What kinds of trees grow where we live? What does the ground look like?" "¿Qué tipos de árboles crecen donde vivimos? ¿Cómo es la tierra?"

■ Discuss your community's natural environment. Ask students if the trees and plants create a peaceful setting.

Using Literature ⭐ Reading

■ Read *Amelia's Fantastic Flight* by Rose Bursik. Have students look for calm lines in the illustrations.

Thematic Connection ⭐ Science

■ **Seasons:** Have students discuss how a landscape might look if it had been painted in spring, summer, autumn, or winter.

Introduce the Art

Look
NSAE 2.a; 2.b; 3.a

"Take a close look at these two paintings."
"Miren de cerca estas dos pinturas".

Visualizing ⭐ Reading

■ Ask students to imagine the setting of *Lilac-colored Landscape*. Why does a landscape have a calm feeling? No action is happening in the picture, so it is probably quiet and still. Vertical and horizontal lines are calm because they represent stability: the trees will remain vertical and the ground will remain horizontal.

Classify and Categorize ⭐ Reading

■ Have students describe *Composition V.* Is it a landscape? The painting is not a landscape, but it still has calm vertical and horizontal lines. The picture looks like a brick wall, which represents stability, just as the trees and ground did in the Kahn piece.

 Art History and Culture

Student answers will vary. Discuss that Kahn's paintings show the calm peaceful feelings he has outdoors.
NSAE 5.a; 5.b

🖥 **Web Connection**

Guide students through an online exhibition of landscape paintings at **www.virtualmuseum.ca/Exhibitions/Landscapes/index.html**. Have students share their ideas about the exhibit.

  Calm Lines

Look at the paintings on these pages. These paintings look calm and quiet.

◄ **Wolf Kahn.** (American). *Lilac-colored Landscape.* 1998.
Oil on canvas. 40 × 42 inches (101.6 × 106.7 cm.). Thomas Segal Gallery, Baltimore, Maryland.

🏺 **Art History and Culture**

These artists made paintings to show their feelings. How do you think they felt about the world around them?

🏺 **Art History and Culture**

Wolf Kahn

Wolf Kahn (wo͞olf kän) (1927–) was born in Germany, but he has lived much of his life in the United States. Kahn uses layers of color and light in his art to show how a scene makes him feel. Kahn is known for his landscape paintings, and most of his works are completed on site in the Vermont countryside.

See pages 16–21 and 24–25 for more about subject matter and art history.

Artist Profiles, p. 31

◆ Artist Profile ◆
Wolf Kahn
b. 1927

Wolf Kahn (wo͞olf kän) was born in Germany to Jewish parents. His mother died when he was five. He lived in Germany with his grandmother for a while. Then he was sent to England in 1939 just before World War II broke out. The next year he traveled to the United States to live with his father. As a young man Kahn studied abstract expressionist painting. Now he has his own approach to art. In the early 1950s, Kahn helped set up an art gallery in New York City. Since then his work has been shown nationwide.

Study both works of art to find different lines.

▶ Which ways do the lines go?

▲ **Piet Mondrian.** (Dutch). *Composition V.* 1914.

Oil on canvas. 21⅝ × 33⅝ inches (54.93 × 85.41 cm.). The Museum of Modern Art, New York, New York.

Aesthetic Perception

Design Awareness Look around. What objects have calm lines?

Study

▶ In *Lilac-colored Landscape,* the ground has horizontal lines and the trees have vertical lines. *Composition V* has horizontal and vertical lines that make rectangles of different sizes.

■ For more examples of landscapes, see *The National Museum of Women in the Arts Collection.*

Art Journal: Concepts

Have students sketch their definition of a landscape in the Concepts section of their Art Journals.

Aesthetic Perception

Design Awareness Discuss objects that have horizontal and vertical lines, such as bookshelves or tables. Mention that a book placed on a horizontal table will not slide off. Discuss how objects are designed with calm lines to make them stable.

Developing Visual Literacy Ask students if they have ever visited a forest or another place like the one in the landscape. Invite students to share their personal experiences and compare them to the artwork. Encourage students to use descriptive adjectives.

NSAE 4.c

Art History and Culture

Piet Mondrian   NSAE 2.a; 3.a; 5.a

Piet Mondrian (pēt môn´ drē än) (1872–1944) could not decide between studying religion or art. He decided to paint, and he became one of the most influential artists of the twentieth century. Mondrian was the leader of the de Stijl, a group that believed art should not show a realistic subject, but instead should express only the universal absolutes of life. Mondrian felt vertical and horizontal lines and primary colors represented these absolutes.

See pages 16–21 and 24–25 for more about subject matter and art history.

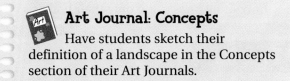

Artist Profiles, p. 44

Artist Profile

Piet Mondrian
1872–1944

Piet Mondrian's given name was Pieter Cornelis Mondriaan, but he liked to be called Piet Mondrian (pēt mōn´ drē än). He was born in the Netherlands to a Calvinist family. At a young age Mondrian could not decide between studying religion or art. He finally decided he wanted to be a painter, but his parents wanted him to be a teacher. He studied to be a teacher and later studied art at the Amsterdam Academy. Mondrian attended evening art classes and worked during the day painting portraits and copying older paintings at museums in Amsterdam. During his life, Mondrian traveled around Europe and lived in many places. He moved to New York City in 1940 to escape the war and

Web Connection

Visit **www.moma.org** for more information about the Piet Mondrian collection at The Museum of Modern Art.

 **each**

"How do artists use vertical and horizontal lines?" "¿Comó usan los artistas las líneas verticales y horizontales?"

- Read and discuss Using Calm Lines on page 42.

- Ask students if they have any ideas about how they could show vertical and horizontal lines using only their bodies.

Practice

Materials: None

- Ask students to stand as vertically as they can. Have them tell how it feels. Ask a few volunteers to lie down horizontally. Have them tell how it feels.

Creative Expression

NSAE 1.a; 1.c; 1.d; 2.c

Materials: 12" × 18" white paper, water containers, liquid tempera paint, watercolor brushes, paper towels, newspapers

Alternate Materials: crayons

- Distribute the materials and have students follow the directions on page 43.

- Review the Technique Tips on page 218 for information about painting with tempera.

- See the Activity Tips on page 232 for visual examples of this lesson's activity.

Art Journal: Brainstorming

Have students brainstorm different scenes that are calm. Have them make sketches in the Ideas section of their Art Journals. Did they use mostly vertical and horizontal lines? Have students select one idea to use for the activity.

NSAE 3.b

Using Calm Lines

Artists use **vertical** and **horizontal** lines to make a picture look calm.

Calm lines are used to make a **landscape,** or picture of the outdoors.

vertical

horizontal

Practice

Use your body to make calm lines.

1. Stand straight like a vertical line. Stand as tall as you can.

2. Lie on the ground like a horizontal line. Be very still.

3. Did you feel calm when you made each kind of line?

Differentiated Instruction

Reteach
Have students find an item in the classroom that is horizontal (such as a desktop), and an item that is vertical (such as a wall). Have them touch the objects to feel the different line directions.

Special Needs
Adaptations: Students with cognitive disabilities may need guided practice in order to make a picture of a calm landscape. Begin by showing them a picture of a landscape and having them trace the lines with their hands. Then have them practice drawing the lines.

ELL Tips
Use *Flash Cards 1* and *2.* Have each student repeat the word *horizontal* as he or she points to a horizontal line and moves his or her finger along the line. Then have each student repeat the word *vertical* as he or she points to a vertical line and moves his or her finger along the line.

△ **Anna Pofer.** Age 7.

Think about how this student used calm lines.

How can you show your favorite quiet outdoor place?

1. Start your landscape with calm lines.

2. You can add other lines to complete your picture.

3. Fill the page.

Interpret What season did you show? How can you tell?

Art Across the Curriculum

Have students use these ideas to reinforce art concepts across the curriculum.
NSAE 6.b

★ **Descriptive Writing** Have students use the writing process to describe a landscape with adjectives for each of the five senses.

★ **Math** Make a simple drawing using calm lines. Have students count the horizontal and vertical lines. Which type of line are there more of?

★ **Science** Find images of nature and have students identify which are horizontal and which are vertical.

★ **Social Studies** Have students brainstorm different things that might be included in landscapes in different states. (For example, a California landscape may include palm trees.)

★ **Technology** Have students use the computer's paint or draw program to create a landscape using vertical and horizontal lines. Visit **SRAonline.com** to print detailed instructions for this activity.

 **Time:** About 5 minutes

Review and Assess

"Which two kinds of lines create a feeling of calm?" "¿Cuáles dos tipos de líneas crean un sentido de calma?"

Think

The artist made a calm painting by using horizontal lines for the sky and the ground, and vertical lines for the tree trunks.

■ Have students identify calm lines in **Large Prints 13** *Children at the Ice Cream Stand* and **14** *Night Heron.*

Informal Assessment

Art Journal: Critical Thinking

Have students ask themselves the Art Criticism questions, and then sketch or write to answer the Interpret question in their Art Journals.
NSAE 1.b; 2.b; 3.a; 5.c

Art Criticism

Describe ▶ What did you include in your landscape?

Analyze ▶ What line directions did you use?

Interpret ▶ What season did you show? How can you tell?

Decide ▶ Did you use vertical and horizontal lines to make your landscape? Is this a place you would like to go for a quiet time?

■ For standardized-format test practice using this lesson's art content, see pages 8–9 in **Reading and Writing Test Preparation.**

Calm Lines

Extra! For the Art Specialist

Time: About 45 minutes

Focus

Using *Transparency 2* and *Large Print 14 Night Heron,* have students look for vertical and horizontal lines. Do those lines create a feeling of calm?

Teach

Have students complete the Alternate Activity. Did students' landscapes include any types of lines other than vertical or horizontal? How did the introduction of those lines affect the mood of the landscape?

Reflect

Guide students through evaluation of their works of art using four steps of art criticism. (See pages 28–29 for more about art criticism.) Then have students describe, analyze, and interpret the work of a classmate.

Alternate Activity

Materials:
- oil pastels
- landscapes completed in the Creative Expression activity

Have students use their completed landscapes from the Creative Expression activity. When the paint is dry, have students use the oil pastels to emphasize the horizontal and vertical lines of their compositions.

Research in Art Education

Research has shown that assessing knowledge through a combination of drawing and writing can lead to higher scores for content knowledge. This applies to native English speakers and limited English speakers alike. This suggests "that drawing may be one way to reveal what students know but cannot put into words" ("The Arts, Language, and Knowing: An Experimental Study of the Potential of the Visual Arts for Assessing Academic Learning by Language Minority Students" in *Critical Links,* p. 141). Drawing with horizontal and vertical lines allows students to show feelings of calm and serenity that they may not have the ability to describe with words.

Assessment

Use the following rubric to evaluate the artwork students make in the Creative Expression activity and to assess students' understanding of calm lines.

Have students complete page 11 or 12 in their *Assessment* books.

	Art History and Culture	Aesthetic Perception	Creative Expression	Art Criticism
3 POINTS	The student recognizes that a landscape is a picture of the outdoors.	The student accurately identifies vertical and horizontal lines in art and in the environment.	The student's landscape clearly illustrates vertical and horizontal lines.	The student thoughtfully and honestly evaluates his or her own work using the four steps of art criticism.
2 POINTS	The student's identification is weak or inconsistent.	The student shows emerging awareness of vertical and horizontal lines, but cannot consistently identify them.	The student's landscape shows some awareness of vertical and horizontal lines.	The student attempts to evaluate his or her own work, but shows an incomplete understanding of evaluation criteria.
1 POINT	The student cannot recognize that a landscape is a picture of the outdoors.	The student cannot identify vertical and horizontal lines.	The student's landscape shows no understanding of vertical and horizontal lines.	The student makes no attempt to evaluate his or her own work.

Assessment, p. 11

Name _____ Date _____

Lesson 2 UNIT 1

Calm Lines

1 | 2

For the teacher: Use the following prompts for this activity.
1. Using a crayon, draw a horizontal line in box 1.
2. Draw a vertical line in box 2.

Level 1

Unit 1 • Line **11**

Lesson 3 Overview
Diagonal Lines

Lesson 3 introduces diagonal lines. Diagonal lines are slanted. They make artwork look busy.

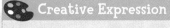
Objectives

Art History and Culture
To identify how artists get ideas for the subjects of their works
NSAE 3.a; 4.c

Creative Expression
To create a torn-paper tree with diagonal branches
NSAE 1.a; 1.c; 1.d

Aesthetic Perception
To locate diagonal and zigzag lines in art and in the environment

Art Criticism
To evaluate one's own artwork using the four steps of art criticism
NSAE 1.b; 2.b; 3.a; 5.c

Vocabulary ⭐ Reading
Review the following vocabulary words with students before beginning the lesson.

diagonal line *línea diagonal*—a slanted line that moves from corner to corner

zigzag *en zigzag*—diagonal lines that connect

See page 59B for additional Spanish vocabulary resources.

Art Journal: Vocabulary
Have students add these words to the Vocabulary section of their Art Journals.

Lesson Materials
- construction paper (brown, black, or gray for the tree and autumn colors for the leaves)
- glue

Alternate Materials:
- other colored paper

Program Resources
- *Reading and Writing Test Prep.,* pp. 10–11
- *Transparency 3*
- *Flash Cards 3* and *5*
- *Artist Profiles,* pp. 29, 40
- *Assessment,* pp. 13–14
- *Large Prints 13* Children at the Ice Cream Stand and *14* Night Heron
- *Art Around the World*

Concept Trace
Diagonal Lines
Introduced: Level K, Unit 1, Lesson 3
Reinforced: Level 2, Unit 1, Lesson 1

Lesson 3 Arts Integration NSAE 6.a

Theatre
Complete Unit 1, Lesson 3, on pages 22–23 of *Theatre Arts Connections.*

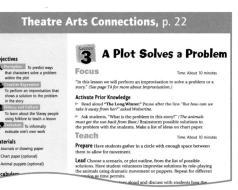

Theatre Arts Connections, p. 22

Objectives
○ To predict ways that characters solve a problem within the plot
○ To perform an improvisation that shows a solution to the problem in the story
○ To learn about the Slavey people using folklore to teach a lesson
○ To informally evaluate one's own work

Materials
○ Journals or drawing paper
○ Chart paper (optional)
○ Animal puppets (optional)

Vocabulary

Lesson 3 A Plot Solves a Problem

Focus *Time: About 10 minutes*
"In this lesson we will perform an improvisation to solve a problem or a story." *(See page T4 for more about Improvisation.)*

Activate Prior Knowledge
► Read aloud **"The Long Winter."** Pause after the line *"But how can we take it away from her?"* asked Wolverine.
► Ask students, "What is the problem in this story?" *(The animals must get the sun back from Bear.)* Brainstorm possible solutions to the problem with the students. Make a list of ideas on chart paper.

Teach *Time: About 10 minutes*
Prepare Have students gather in a circle with enough space between them to allow for movement.
Lead Choose a scenario, or plot outline, from the list of possible solutions. Have student volunteers improvise solutions by role-playing the animals using dramatic movement or puppets. Repeat for different versions as time permits.

Music

Royal March of the Lions, from *Carnival of the Animals.* Camille Saint-Saens.

Diagonal lines give artwork a busy feeling. Diagonal lines can be thick or thin. Play Camille Saint-Saens's *Royal March of the Lions,* which is very regal and grand, featuring a full, swaggering figure in the strings and fast, running scales in the pianos that convincingly mimic lion roars. Have students draw diagonal lines that seem to go with the music.

Movement & Dance
Have students identify letters of the alphabet that have diagonal or zigzag lines, such as K, M, and Z. Have students demonstrate each of these letters by creating them with their bodies. Take 4 counts to create each letter.

Focus

Activate Prior Knowledge

"What kind of tree is most fun to climb?"
"¿Qué tipo de árbol es más divertido de trepar?"

■ Have students compare Sylvia Plimack Mangold's *The Elm Tree (Summer)* with Wolf Kahn's *Lilac-colored Landscape* from page 40. Discuss which tree students think would be better for climbing.

Using Literature ⭐ Reading

■ Read *Rosie's Walk* by Pat Hutchins. Diagonal lines can be found in tree branches and many other places in the illustrations.

Thematic Connection ⭐ Science

■ **Science:** Tree branches can be diagonal lines. A bolt of lightning creates a zigzag line. Discuss other ways diagonal or zigzag lines occur in science.

Introduce the Art

Look

"Let's take a close look at these two works of art." *"Miremos de cerca estas dos obras de arte".*

Comparing and Contrasting ⭐ Reading

■ Have students discuss the similarities and differences between the two works of art. Both have a lot of yellow and green, but *Between the Clock and the Bed* has many more colors. *Between the Clock and the Bed* is nonobjective. *The Elm Tree (Summer)* is realistic, and the subject is a tree.

🏺 Art History and Culture

Discuss with students that artists often get ideas for the subjects of their works from things they see around them. Sylvia Plimack Mangold painted trees she saw in her yard. Jasper Johns got the idea for *Between the Clock and the Bed* from a pattern he saw in another painting.
NSAE 3.a; 4.c

💻 Web Connection

Visit www.jasperjohns.com for more information about Jasper Johns.

Lesson 3 Diagonal Lines

▲ **Jasper Johns.** (American). *Between the Clock and the Bed.* 1981.
Encaustic. $6\frac{1}{8} \times 10\frac{3}{4}$ inches (15.56 × 27.31 cm).
The Museum of Modern Art, New York, New York.

Look at the works of art on these pages. The diagonal lines make your eyes move around the page.

🏺 Art History and Culture

Jasper Johns got the idea for this painting from a pattern he saw in another painting.

🏺 Art History and Culture

Jasper Johns

Jasper Johns (jas´ pər jänz) (1930–) grew up in the South but moved to New York City when he was 24 years old. Much of his artwork has subjects that are everyday images, such as flags or numbers. In 1988, one of Johns's paintings sold for $17 million—more than any other work by a living American artist. Johns often borrows images from other works to incorporate into his art. In 1940, Edvard Munch painted *Self-Portrait Between the Clock and the Bed*. The pattern on the bedspread in Munch's painting is similar to the pattern used in Johns's painting.

See pages 16–21 and 24–25 for more about subject matter and art history.

Artist Profiles, p. 29

Artist Profile

Jasper Johns
b. 1930

Jasper Johns (jas´ pər jänz) was born in Augusta, Georgia. After serving in Japan with the United States Army, he moved to New York City. There he worked in a bookstore and started creating art. When he was 24, he decided to throw away all the art he had ever made. He wanted a fresh start. He was determined to create original art, not copies of the styles of other artists. Since then Johns has been known for his inventiveness.

◀ **Sylvia Plimack
Mangold.**
(American).
*The Elm Tree
(Summer).* 1991.
••••••••••••••••••••
Oil on linen. 80 × 60
inches (203.2 × 152.4 cm.).
Alexander and Bonin,
New York, New York.

Study both works of art.

▶ Where do you see diagonal lines?

🔍 Aesthetic Perception

Seeing Like an Artist Look around. Where do you
see diagonal lines?

🏺 Art History and Culture

Sylvia Plimack Mangold

Sylvia Plimack Mangold (sil´ vē ə pli´ mak man´ gōld´) (1938–) was
born in New York City. She studied art and received a degree from
Yale University. In 1961 she married Robert Mangold, who also is a
well-known artist. Plimack Mangold makes realistic paintings of
things she sees around her, such as rooms or landscapes.

See pages 16–21 and 24–25 for more about subject matter and art
history.

Artist Profiles, p. 40

— Artist Profile —
**Sylvia Plimack
Mangold**
b. 1938
Sylvia Plimack Mangold (sil´ vē ə pli´ mak
man´ gōld) was born in New York City. She
attended several art schools and earned a
degree in fine arts from Yale University. In
1974, she had her first show, and her work
has been much admired ever since.
Mangold taught at the School of Visual Arts
in New York City. She is married to artist
Robert Mangold, and they have two sons.
She lives on a 150-acre farm in
Washingtonville, New York.

Study

▶ *Between the Clock and the Bed* is made
entirely of diagonal lines. The first panel
has prominent yellow lines on a purple
background, the second panel has
prominent blue lines on a yellow
background, and the third panel has
prominent orange lines on a green
background. The bottom of the third panel
has small groups of yellow, blue, and
orange lines. In *The Elm Tree (Summer)*
the tree trunk and the branches start out
as vertical lines, but as the branches grow
higher, they split and become diagonal.

■ For more examples of art from North
America, see *Art Around the World.*

📔 Art Journal: Concepts
Have students sketch an object with
diagonal lines in the Concepts section of
their Art Journals.

🔍 Aesthetic Perception

Seeing Like an Artist Discuss diagonal
lines students see in the classroom. Many
diagonal lines are diagonal because the
object they define is leaning or can be
moved. For example, a book leaning against
a shelf creates a diagonal line. Do students
see any diagonal lines that could be made
horizontal or vertical?

Developing Visual Literacy Have students
discuss how each artwork makes them
feel and why. Do the colors elicit certain
emotions? Does subject matter elicit a
particular emotion? What about the
diagonal lines?
NSAE 2.b; 5.c

💻 Web Connection
Sylvia Plimack Mangold often paints trees. Visit
www.urbanext.uiuc.edu/trees1/ to learn more
about trees.

Teach

Time: About 35 minutes

"How do artists use diagonal and zigzag lines?" *"¿Comó usan los artistas las líneas diagonales y en zigzag?"*

- Read and discuss Using Diagonal Lines on page 46.

Practice

Materials: None

- Have students hold out their arms straight at their sides, and then have them raise their arms to make diagonal branches.

- Students also can experiment with bending their arms at the elbows and wrists to make zigzag lines.

Creative Expression

NSAE 1.a; 1.c; 1.d

Materials: construction paper (brown, black, or gray for the tree and autumn colors for the leaves), glue

Alternate Materials: other colored paper

- Distribute the materials and read the directions on page 47 to students.

- Have students practice holding the paper closely and tearing slowly. Make sure they do not just hold the paper at the top and rip.

- Review the Technique Tips on page 223 for information about tearing paper.

- See the Activity Tips on page 233 for visual examples of this lesson's activity.

Art Journal: Brainstorming

Have students brainstorm ideas for the kind of tree they could create. Have them make sketches in their Art Journals, then choose one to do for the Creative Expression activity.

NSAE 3.b

Using Diagonal Lines

Diagonal lines are slanted. They give artwork a busy feeling.

diagonal

Zigzag lines are made by connecting diagonal lines.

zigzag

Practice

Use your body to make diagonal lines.

1. Pretend you are a tree. Your arms will make the branches.

2. Hold up your arms away from your body. Make them look like diagonal lines.

3. Spread your fingers apart to make thin branches.

46   Unit 1 • Lesson 3

Differentiated Instruction

Reteach

Hang paper on a bulletin board. Draw a diagonal line and a zigzag line. Have students re-create the lines using yarn and pushpins.

Special Needs

Adaptations: Students with disabilities learn best when information is presented in a variety of ways. Bring in a small tree branch for students to examine before they create a tree branch out of torn paper.

ELL Tips

Use *Flash Cards 3* and *5.* Have students trace each line with their fingers as they say the name of the line.

Think about how this student used diagonal lines.

◀ **Peyton Wilker.** Age 6.

Creative Expression

How could you show tree branches that grew in many different directions?

1. Think about how a tree changes as it grows.

2. Tear a sheet of paper to make a tree trunk. Tear thick branches and thin branches. Tear leaves.

3. Glue your tree onto another sheet of paper.

Art Criticism

Decide Do the diagonal lines make your eyes move all around your picture?

Unit 1 • Lesson 3 **47**

Art Across the Curriculum

Use these ideas to reinforce art concepts across the curriculum.
NSAE 6.b

★ **Poetry Writing** Have students use the writing process to write a poem about climbing a tree.

★ **Math** Draw a zigzag line. Have students count by twos the number of diagonal lines.

★ **Science** Demonstrate using a balance scale to weigh small objects. Have students observe that the balance arm will look like a diagonal line unless the objects are of equal weight (and then it will be a horizontal line).

★ **Social Studies** Show students how diagonal and zigzag lines can be useful in constructing a graph or chart.

★ **Technology** Use your computer's paint or draw program to draw diagonal and zigzag lines. Visit **SRAonline.com** to print detailed instructions for this activity.

Reflect

Time: About 5 minutes

Review and Assess

"What kinds of lines give artwork a busy feeling? "¿Qué tipos de líneas hacen una obra de arte tener un sentido ocupado?"

Think

The branches in this student's artwork have diagonal lines.

■ Have students identify diagonal lines in *Large Prints 13* Children at the Ice Cream Stand and *14* Night Heron.

Informal Assessment

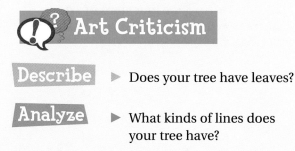

Art Journal: Critical Thinking
Have students ask themselves the Art Criticism questions, and then write or sketch in their Art Journals to answer the Decide question.
NSAE 1.b; 2.b; 3.a; 5.c

Art Criticism

Describe ▶ Does your tree have leaves?

Analyze ▶ What kinds of lines does your tree have?

Interpret ▶ What season did you show? How can you tell?

Decide ▶ Do the diagonal lines in your picture make your eyes move all around?

■ For standardized-format test practice using this lesson's art content, see pages 10–11 in *Reading and Writing Test Preparation.*

Diagonal Lines

Extra! For the Art Specialist

Time: About 45 minutes

Focus

Using **Transparency 3** and **Large Print 14** **Night Heron,** have students look for diagonal and zigzag lines. How do those lines affect the works of art?

Teach

Have students complete the Alternate Activity. When the paintings are dry, assemble them and have students compare the designs. Which design looks the busiest?

Reflect

Guide students through evaluation of their works of art using the four steps of art criticism. (See pages 28–29 for more about art criticism.)

Alternate Activity

Materials:
- sponges embedded with tempera paint
- plastic dish
- thin or corrugated cardboard
- 9″ × 12″ paper

1. Place the paint-filled sponges on plastic dishes to prevent a mess. Several students may share sponges and cardboard.

2. Have students press an edge of the cardboard into the paint, and then press the cardboard onto paper to create a diagonal line.

3. Students should repeat to create a design with diagonal and zigzag lines.

Research in Art Education

Although one examination of nine studies showed only "a positive, moderately sized relationship between reading improvement and an integrated arts-reading form of instruction," it did show a stronger relationship between integrated arts-reading instruction and reading readiness ("Instruction in Visual Art: Can It Help Children to Read?" in *Critical Links*, p. 138). Developing the ability to recognize lines and associate names with them will help students recognize that specific arrangements of lines create letters of the alphabet.

Assessment
Use the following rubric to evaluate the artwork students make in the Creative Expression activity and to assess students' understanding of diagonal lines.

Have students complete page 13 or 14 in their *Assessment* books.

	Art History and Culture	Aesthetic Perception	Creative Expression	Art Criticism
3 POINTS	The student successfully identifies some places where artists get ideas for the subjects of their works.	The student accurately identifies diagonal and zigzag lines in art and in the environment.	The student's torn-paper picture illustrates a clear understanding of diagonal and zigzag lines.	The student thoughtfully and honestly evaluates his or her own work using the four steps of art criticism.
2 POINTS	The student's identification is weak or incomplete.	The student shows emerging awareness of diagonal and zigzag lines, but cannot consistently identify them.	The student's torn-paper picture illustrates some awareness of diagonal and zigzag lines.	The student attempts to evaluate his or her own work, but shows an incomplete understanding of evaluation criteria.
1 POINT	The student cannot identify where artists get ideas for the subjects of their work.	The student cannot identify diagonal and zigzag lines.	The student's torn-paper picture does not illustrate an understanding of diagonal and zigzag lines.	The student makes no attempt to evaluate his or her own artwork.

Assessment, p. 13

Name _____ Date _____

Diagonal Lines

Lesson **3** UNIT 1

For the teacher: Use the following prompt for this activity. Using a crayon, draw a diagonal line from the upper left corner of the box to the bottom right corner of the box.

Level 1   Unit 1 • Line **13**

Lesson 4 Overview · Curved Lines

Lesson 4 introduces curved lines. Artists use curved lines to show gentle movement.

Objectives

Art History and Culture
To understand that some art is to be looked at and some is to be used
NSAE 2.a; 3.a; 5.a

Creative Expression
To create a monoprint with curved lines
NSAE 1.a; 1.c; 1.d

Aesthetic Perception
To identify curved lines in art

Art Criticism
To evaluate one's own artwork using the four steps of art criticism
NSAE 1.b; 2.b; 3.a; 5.c

Vocabulary ⭐ Reading

Review the following vocabulary word with students before beginning the lesson.

curved line línea curva—a line that is always bending

See page 59B for additional Spanish vocabulary resources.

Art Journal: Vocabulary
Have students add this word to the Vocabulary section of their Art Journals.

Lesson Materials
- markers
- sketch paper
- 12" × 18" paper
- tempera paint with media mixer
- clear plastic wrap
- masking tape
- plastic combs
- paper towels

Alternate Materials:
- crayons
- finger paint
- plastic plates

Program Resources
- *Reading and Writing Test Prep.,* pp. 12–13
- *Transparency 4*
- *Flash Card 4*
- *Artist Profiles,* pp. 61, 66
- *Animals Through History Time Line*
- *Assessment,* pp. 15–16
- *Large Prints 13 Children at the Ice Cream Stand* and *14 Night Heron*
- *Art Around the World*

Concept Trace
Curved Lines
Introduced: Level K, Unit 1, Lesson 4

Reinforced: Level 2, Unit 1, Lesson 1

Lesson 4 Arts Integration NSAE 6.a

Theatre
Have students complete pages 24–25 of *Theatre Arts Connections.*

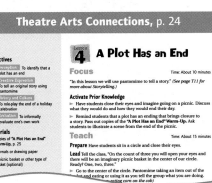

Music
 The Skater's Waltz. Emile Waldteufel.

Curved lines make your eyes move gently, as in Agnes Tait's *Skating in Central Park.* To reinforce the concept of curved lines, play Emile Waldteufel's *The Skater's Waltz.* Have students trace their fingers over the curved lines in the painting as they listen to the music. Play the music again during the Practice activity as students draw the lines a figure skater makes on ice.

Movement & Dance
Have students identify letters of the alphabet that have *C* curves, *S* curves, or circles, such as *B, S,* and *O.* Have students demonstrate each of these letters by creating them with their bodies. Take 4 counts to create each letter.

Time: About 10 minutes ⏱

Activate Prior Knowledge

"Have you ever seen someone ice skate?"

"¿Alguna vez han visto a una persona patinando sobre hielo?"

■ Discuss the kinds of movements a figure skater makes. Explain that a skater's movements are graceful and fluid.

Using Literature ⭐ Reading

■ Read *Homeplace* by Anne Shelby. The illustrations of family life on a farm contain many curved lines that create a comfortable setting.

Thematic Connection

■ **Families:** Discuss the works of art as they relate to students' families. Do their families participate in pastimes together (such as ice skating)? Do they have any family heirlooms (like the bedcover)?

Introduce the Art

Look
NSAE 3.a; 5.a

"Let's take a look at these two works of art."

"Veamos estas dos obras de arte".

Comparing and Contrasting ⭐ Reading

■ Have students discuss the differences between subject matter of each work of art. *Skating in Central Park* is a genre painting: the artist has captured a moment in a scene from everyday life. The scene extends beyond the edges of the painting. *Bridal Bed Cover* is utilitarian: it is something people use. The artist chose to arrange the objects in a particular way within the boundaries of the bedcover to make a decorative design.

🏺 Art History and Culture

Discuss with students that the unknown artist who created *Bridal Bed Cover* wanted to make a useful object that was also decorative. The symbols included in the design represent objects that had meaning in the artist's culture. See the Art History and Culture section on the next page for more information.

NSAE 4.a; 5.a; 5.b

💻 Web Connection

Visit **www.nmaa.si.edu** for information about the Smithsonian American Art Museum, which houses *Skating in Central Park*.

▲ **Agnes Tait.** (American). *Skating in Central Park.* 1934.
Oil on canvas. $33\frac{7}{8} \times 48\frac{1}{8}$ inches (86.04 × 122.24 cm.). Smithsonian American Art Museum, Washington, D.C.

Look at the works of art on these pages. The curved lines make your eyes move gently around the page.

🏺 Art History and Culture

Bridal Bed Cover was made for a newly married couple. Each picture on the bedcover has a special meaning.

🏺 Art History and Culture

Agnes Tait

Agnes Tait (ag′ nəs tāt) (1894–1981) was born in New York City and received art training at the National Academy of Design. During the Depression, Tait worked as an artist through the Works Projects Administration. The WPA provided government jobs so that people could continue to work despite the poor economy. Some artists supported by the WPA produced art on and inside government buildings across the United States.

See pages 16–21 and 24–25 for more about subject matter and art history.

Artist Profiles, p. 61

◆ Artist Profile ◆
Agnes Tait
1894–1981

Agnes Tait (ag′ nəs tāt) was born in New York City in 1894. She studied art there at the National Academy of Design. Until the Great Depression, Tait was able to show her work regularly. However, with a poor economy, people did not buy art. Through the Works Progress Administration (WPA), thousands of people, including artists, were given jobs, and Tait was able to continue painting. In 1943, funding by the WPA ended. Tait moved to Santa Fe, New Mexico, to live in an artists' colony. She was later recognized for her illustrations in children's books.

Study both works of art.

▶ Where do you see curved lines?

Aesthetic Perception

Design Awareness Look around for curved lines. Where do you see them?

Art History and Culture

The artist who created *Bridal Bed Cover* is unknown, but the bedcover was created in Western Japan during the nineteenth century. The family of the bride spent a long time creating and embellishing the bedcover, called a *futonji* in Japan. The futonji was used on the wedding night and then carefully stored away. The futonji is decorated with images that symbolize wishes of happiness and longevity for the newly married couple. At the top is the family crest. The lobsters (whose bent bodies suggest old age) play with a sacred rope used to prevent the entry of evil. The leaves adorning the rope symbolize purity, happiness, and continuity.

See pages 16–21 and 24–25 for more about subject matter and art history.

Artist Profiles, p. 66

◇ Artist Profile ◇

Bridal Bed Cover

This bridal bed cover was made during the nineteenth century by an unknown Japanese artist. It was designed and crafted as a wedding gift to a young Japanese couple. The expensive materials used to create these bedcovers, as well as their beauty and grandeur, made them symbols of the wealth and social status of the bride's family. Because these bedcovers were so delicate and valuable, they were carefully stored or displayed as wall hangings, not used as everyday household items. Thanks to this gentle treatment and protection from bright light, these textiles have retained their original colors for hundreds of years.

Artist unknown. (Western Japan).

Study

▶ In *Skating in Central Park,* curved lines are seen in each hill, the bridge, the outline of the pond, the bodies of people and dogs, and some of the trees. In *Bridal Bed Cover,* curved lines are seen in the bodies of the lobsters, the rope, the leaves, the flowers, and the circle.

■ For more examples of art from Asia, see *Art Around the World.*

Art Journal: Concepts

Have students sketch an object with curved lines in the Concepts section of their Art Journals.

Aesthetic Perception

Design Awareness Discuss with students the curved lines that can be seen all around them. Look for curved lines in nature and in the humanmade environment.

Developing Visual Literacy ⭐ Math
Have students think about the moment in time depicted in *Skating in Central Park.* If they were to revisit the scene an hour later, which curved lines would have changed? Which would have stayed the same? If the scene were represented at a later moment in time, the lines making the bodies of the people and dogs would have changed, but the lines of the hills, the bridge, the pond, and the trees would be the same.

Web Connection
Visit **www.jinjapan.org/kidsweb/** for more information about Japan.

Teach

"How can you use curved lines to show gentle movement?" *"¿Como pueden usar líneas curvas para mostrar un movimiento delicado?"*

■ Read and discuss Using Curved Lines on page 50.

Practice

Materials: markers, sketch paper

Alternate Materials: crayons

■ Distribute the materials and have students follow the directions on page 50.

Creative Expression

NSAE 1.a; 1.c; 1.d
Materials: 12" × 18" paper, tempera paint with media mixer, clear plastic wrap, masking tape, plastic combs, paper towels

Alternate Materials: finger paint, plastic plates

■ Distribute the materials and have students follow the directions on page 51.

■ Review the Technique Tips on page 228 for information about making a monoprint.

■ See the Activity Tips on page 233 for visual examples of this lesson's activity.

■ Tape plastic wrap to the table and spread paint on it for each student. Have students use plastic combs to make curved line designs. Students can also use their fingers to add more curved lines.

■ Instead of using a comb, cut a rectangle out of a plastic plate. Make cuts into one side of the rectangle as if you were making fringe. Then cut off every other fringe piece to make a comb.

■ When each student is finished with his or her design, center a sheet of paper over the plastic wrap and gently rub the back. Peel from the corner to reveal the print.

Art Journal: Brainstorming

Have students plan their ideas for the Creative Expression activity design by making preliminary sketches in their Art Journals.

Using Curved Lines

Curved lines bend. They change direction slowly.

Practice

Draw the lines a figure skater makes on ice.

1. Think about a figure skater moving gracefully across the ice.

2. Pretend your marker is the skater. Pretend your paper is the ice. Move your marker and draw the lines.

Differentiated Instruction

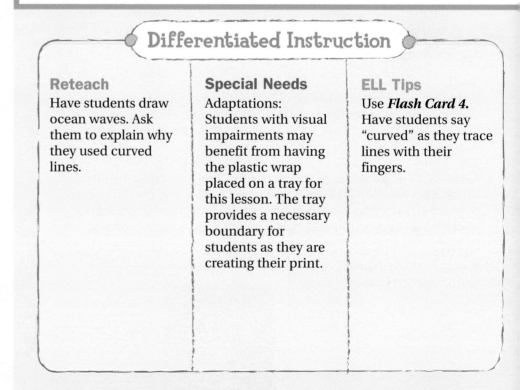

Reteach
Have students draw ocean waves. Ask them to explain why they used curved lines.

Special Needs
Adaptations:
Students with visual impairments may benefit from having the plastic wrap placed on a tray for this lesson. The tray provides a necessary boundary for students as they are creating their print.

ELL Tips
Use *Flash Card 4.* Have students say "curved" as they trace lines with their fingers.

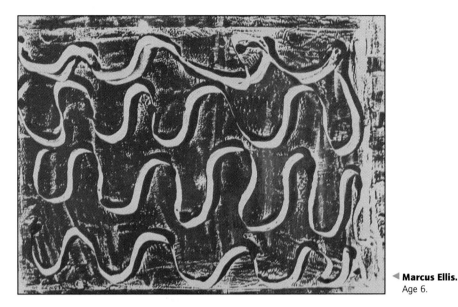

◄ **Marcus Ellis.**
Age 6.

Think about how this student used curved lines.

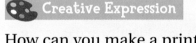
Creative Expression

How can you make a print of curved lines?

1. Tape a square of plastic wrap to the table. Spread paint on it.

2. Pull a comb through the paint to make curved lines. Use gentle movement.

3. Lay paper on top of the paint to make a print.

Art Criticism

Decide If you made the artwork again, what would you change?

Art Across the Curriculum

Use these ideas to reinforce art concepts across the curriculum.
NSAE 6.b

★ **Persuasive Writing** Have students pretend they are trying to sell a bedcover like the one in *Bridal Bed Cover.* Have them write adjectives to describe the bedcover in an appealing way.

★ **Math** Draw three curved lines of different lengths and explain that each line represents a hill. Have students order the lines by how long it would take to walk each one.

★ **Science** Have students brainstorm living things that have curved lines. Then have students think of nonliving things that have curved lines.

★ **Social Studies** Have students choose a leisure activity that could be painted with curved lines (such as ice-skating in *Skating in Central Park*). Then have students imagine what the rules should be for participating in the activity.

★ **Technology** Have students use the computer's paint or draw program to make a picture with curved lines. Visit **SRAonline.com** to print detailed instructions for this activity.

Reflect

Time: About 5 minutes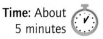

Review and Assess

"How are curved lines different from straight lines?" "¿En qué se diferencian las líneas curvas de las líneas rectas?"

Think

The student made a monoprint of curved lines.

■ Have students identify curved lines in *Large Prints 13* Children at the Ice Cream Stand and *14* Night Heron.

Informal Assessment

Art Journal: Critical Thinking
Have students ask themselves the Art Criticism questions, and then write or sketch to answer the Decide question in their Art Journals.
NSAE 1.b; 2.b; 3.a; 5.c

Art Criticism

Describe ▶ Describe how you made your artwork.

Analyze ▶ Do all the lines in your artwork curve?

Interpret ▶ What feeling does your design suggest? Give your work a title.

Decide ▶ If you did the artwork again, what would you change?

■ For standardized-format test practice using this lesson's art content, see pages 12–13 in *Reading and Writing Test Preparation.*

Curved Lines

For the Art Specialist

Time: About 45 minutes

Focus

Have students look for curved lines in *Transparency 4.* How do the curved lines create comfortable designs?

Teach

Have students complete the Alternate Activity. How did they choose what to include in their pillow design?

Reflect

Guide students through evaluation of their works of art using the four steps of art criticism. (See pages 28–29 for more about art criticism.) Create a class exhibition by drawing large beds on mural paper, and arranging the students' pillow designs on the beds. Have students share their ideas about the exhibition.

Alternate Activity

Materials:
- square sheet of paper (8" × 8" to 12" × 12")
- oil pastels

1. Have students brainstorm things with curved lines that could decorate a bedroom.

2. Have students draw a design for a comfortable pillow using curved lines, shapes with curves, and objects that have curves.

Research in Art Education

"The elementary classroom offers an environment that can foster creativity, independence, self-awareness, self-expression, and an understanding of the visual world. Education through art can provide opportunities for exploring one's creativity, for communicating ideas, and enabling students to express themselves through the use of materials, processes, and tools."Andra Nyman, "Cultural Content, Identity, and Program Development: Approaches to Art Education for Elementary Educators," in *Contemporary Issues in Art Education,* edited by Y. Gaudelius and P. Speirs, 61–69. New Jersey: Prentice Hall, 2002

Assessment

Use the following rubric to evaluate the artwork students make in the Creative Expression activity and to assess students' understanding of curved lines.

Have students complete page 15 or 16 in their *Assessment* books.

	Art History and Culture	Aesthetic Perception	Creative Expression	Art Criticism
3 POINTS	The student can identify and compare the purposes of genre and utilitarian works of art.	The student accurately identifies curved lines in art.	The student's monoprint clearly illustrates curved lines.	The student thoughtfully and honestly evaluates his or her own work using the four steps of art criticism.
2 POINTS	The student's identification and comparison is weak or incomplete.	The student shows emerging awareness of curved lines but cannot consistently identify them.	The student's monoprint shows some understanding of curved lines.	The student attempts to evaluate his or her own work, but shows an incomplete understanding of evaluation criteria.
1 POINT	The student cannot identify and compare the purposes or genre and utilitarian works of art.	The student cannot identify curved lines.	The student's monoprint shows no understanding of curved lines.	The student makes no attempt to evaluate his or her own artwork.

Assessment, p. 15

Name _____ Date _____

Lesson 4 UNIT 1

Curved Lines

For the teacher: Use the following prompt for this activity.
Using a crayon, draw a curved line from one corner of the box to another corner.

Level 1

Unit 1 • Line **15**

Lesson 5 Overview

Buildings Have Lines

Lesson 5 teaches that vertical, horizontal, and diagonal lines are used to depict buildings in art.

Objectives

Art History and Culture

To compare artists' depictions of buildings
NSAE 3.a

Creative Expression

To create a picture of a house using mixed-media collage
NSAE 1.a; 1.c; 1.d

Aesthetic Perception

To locate lines in buildings and identify them by name

Art Criticism

To evaluate one's own artwork using the four steps of art criticism
NSAE 1.b; 2.b; 3.a; 5.c

Vocabulary ⭐ Reading

Review the following vocabulary word with students before beginning the lesson.

building *edificio*—a place where we live, work, meet or play

See page 59B for additional Spanish vocabulary resources.

Art Journal: Vocabulary

Have students add this word to the Vocabulary section of their Art Journals.

Lesson Materials

- white chalk
- black construction paper
- precut rectangular cardboard or mat board
- wooden ice-cream sticks
- chenille stems
- yarn
- scissors and glue

Alternate Materials

- white crayon
- other linear things to add details to houses

Program Resources

- *Reading and Writing Test Prep.,* pp. 14–15
- *Transparency 5*
- *Artist Profiles,* pp. 22, 36
- *Animals Through History Time Line*
- *Assessment,* pp. 17–18
- *Large Prints 13* Children at the Ice Cream Stand and *14* Night Heron
- *Art Around the World*

Concept Trace

Buildings Have Lines

Introduced: Level 1, Unit 1, Lesson 5

Reinforced: Level 2, Unit 1, Lesson 1

Lesson 5 Arts Integration NSAE 6.a

Theatre

Complete Unit 1, Lesson 5, on pages 26–27 of *Theatre Arts Connections.*

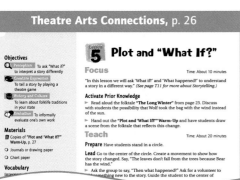

Music

Sesame Street. Joe Raposo, Bruce Hart, and Jon Stone.

Buildings have all kinds of lines. Have students draw the lines they visualize in buildings as they listen to or sing the theme from *Sesame Street.*

Movement & Dance

Divide the class into four groups. Name a type of structure, such as bridge or church. Give all groups 10 counts to create the structure using their combined bodies. Then, ask each group to choose a structure and take one minute to create it, focusing on the details of line, size, and shape. Have each group share their design with the class.

Activate Prior Knowledge

"What buildings did you go into yesterday?"

"¿Qué edificios visitaron ayer?"

- Discuss what happens in each type of building and who uses it. Have students describe common features of buildings (such as a door or roof).

Using Literature ☆ Reading

- The book *My Town* by Rebecca Treays has illustrations of many different buildings by Rachel Wells.

Thematic Connection ☆ Social Studies

- **Jobs/Work:** Discuss buildings that are designed differently for specific jobs (such as a greenhouse or a fire station).

Introduce the Art

Look
NSAE 3.a

"Let's look closely at these works of art."

"Miremos de cerca estas obras de arte".

Drawing Conclusions ☆ Reading

- Ask students what they think each building is used for. The buildings in *Shacks* are probably homes. Smoke is coming from the chimneys, which indicates that the buildings are probably being used as shelters to keep families from the cold. The water towers and tall chimneys suggest that the buildings in *The Monongahela at Morgantown* are probably factories that are used by workers.

🏺 Art History and Culture

Student answers will vary. Discuss with students that although these works of art were made over 70 years ago, students may see buildings like these in their neighborhoods. This is because buildings can last for a long time.

NSAE 4.c

💻 Web Connection

Visit **www.groupofsevenart.com** to view more works of art by Lawren S. Harris.

▲ **Lawren S. Harris.** (Canadian). *Shacks.* 1919.
....
Oil on canvas. $42\frac{1}{2} \times 50\frac{3}{8}$ inches (107.9 × 128 cm.). National Gallery of Canada, Ottawa, Ontario, Canada.

Look at the works of art on these pages. The artists used lines to make buildings.

🏺 Art History and Culture

Do the buildings in these works of art look like buildings you might see in your neighborhood today?

🏺 Art History and Culture

Lawren S. Harris

Lawren S. Harris (lôr´ ən ha´ rəs) (1885–1970) is one of Canada's most important artists. He was born to a wealthy family and studied art in Germany. He began his career illustrating magazine articles even though his wealth did not require him to earn a living. Harris and six other Canadian painters formed the Group of Seven, an artists' organization designed to promote Canadian artists.

See pages 16–21 and 24–25 for more about subject matter and art history.

Artist Profiles, p. 22

Artist Profile

Lawren S. Harris
1885-1970

Lawren Harris (lôr´ ən här´ is) came from a wealthy Canadian family. He was in college when a math professor noticed his pencil drawings. The professor talked Harris's mother into sending him to art school. After studying art in Germany, Harris began his career by illustrating magazine articles. In 1908, on a trip for a magazine, Harris saw his first winter in the Canadian wilderness. He showed that winter beauty in his realistic art. By the time Harris married in 1910 he was already selling his paintings. In 1930 he took a dangerous two-month cruise on a Canadian supply ship into the frozen Arctic. Afterward he painted many scenes from that vast wilderness. After a divorce and remarriage, Harris

▲ **Blanche Lazzell.** (American).
*The Monongahela at
Morgantown.* 1935.
....
Color woodcut. $11\frac{15}{16} \times 13\frac{7}{8}$ inches
(30.3 × 35.2 cm.). Amon Carter Museum,
Fort Worth, Texas.

Study both works of art to find lines.

▶ What lines did each artist use to
make the buildings?

Aesthetic Perception

Design Awareness Look at your school building.
Can you find lines like those you saw in the works
of art?

Art History and Culture

Blanche Lazzell

Blanche Lazzell (blanch lə zel´) (1878–1956) was born in West
Virginia. She attended a number of American universities and the
Art Students League in New York, where Georgia O'Keeffe was also
enrolled at the same time. Lazzell also studied in Paris, but she
returned to the United States when World War I began. She lived in
Provincetown, Massachusetts, where she and several other
woodblock artists formed the Provincetown Printers Group.
Lazzell's prints are considered some of the earliest abstract and
cubist works by a female
American artist.

See pages 16–21 and 24–25
for more about subject
matter and art history.

Artist Profiles, p. 36

Artist Profile

Blanche Lazzell
1878–1956

Blanche Lazzell (blanch lə zel´) was credited
with being one of the first women to
introduce modern art to America. Born in
Maidsville, West Virginia, she earned several
university degrees, which was unusual for a
woman of her time. Lazzell was respected
for her printmaking skills and for her
experimental woodblock techniques, in
which she tried new methods with
watercolor instead of ink. Her bold colors
and angular compositions hint at an
impressionistic influence, while highlighting
her innovative style of printmaking.

Study

▶ Vertical lines form the edges of the
buildings' walls, and horizontal lines form
the tops and bottoms of the buildings'
walls. The windows and doors have
vertical and horizontal lines. Some of the
roofs are diagonal.

Additional Study Question

▶ What do you see in each picture that has
lines that are different from the lines used
in the buildings? What lines do you find
there? The swirling snowdrifts in *Shacks*
are made with curved lines. The hills and
the banks of the river in *The Monongahela
at Morgantown* are made with curved
lines. In both works of art, the natural
objects are made with lines that are
different from the lines that make up the
humanmade objects.

■ For more examples of art from North
America, see *Art Around the World.*

Art Journal: Concepts

Have students sketch their school
building in the Concepts section of their
Art Journals. Then have students list the
lines they used.

Aesthetic Perception

Design Awareness Discuss with students what
your school building looks like. Have
students discuss different parts and identify
the types of lines that make each part.
Compare and contrast your school building
with the buildings shown in the works of art.

Developing Visual Literacy Discuss with
students why they think the artists did not
include people in these works of art. If
people had been included, what would they
be doing? How would the addition of people
change the way the students feel about the
works of art?
NSAE 3.a

Web Connection

Visit **www.cartermuseum.org** to learn more about
the Amon Carter Museum.

 **Teach**

"How do the parts of a building come together?" "¿Cómo se unen las partes de un edificio?"

■ Discuss Using Lines to Make Buildings on page 54.

Practice

Materials: white chalk, black construction paper

Alternate Materials: white crayon

■ Distribute the materials and read the directions on page 54 to students.

■ Have students practice drawing common parts of buildings, such as doors, roofs, and windows.

Creative Expression

NSAE 1.a; 1.c; 1.d; 2.c

Materials: precut rectangular cardboard or mat board, wooden ice-cream sticks, chenille wires, yarn, scissors, glue

Alternate Materials: other linear things to add details to houses

■ Distribute the materials and have students follow the directions on page 55.

■ Review the Technique Tips on page 223 for more information about making a collage.

■ See the Activity Tips on page 234 for visual examples of this lesson's activity.

Art Journal: Brainstorming

Have students brainstorm ideas for kinds of buildings they could design. Have them make sketches in their Art Journals of details they could include in their building, such as doors and windows.

NSAE 3.b

Using Lines to Make Buildings

Artists use vertical, horizontal, and diagonal lines to make pictures of **buildings.**

vertical   horizontal   diagonal

Practice

Draw different parts of buildings.

1. Think of parts that most buildings have.

2. Draw the parts with chalk on black construction paper.

3. Notice the lines you used.

Differentiated Instruction

Reteach

Take students outside to look at the school building. Identify the vertical and horizontal lines.

Special Needs

Adaptations: Some students may need assistance transferring information about lines in buildings to the creation of a building. Help students make the transition by showing them a completed example and having them trace with their fingers the lines they see in the building.

ELL Tips

Bring in pictures of buildings from magazines. Use a black marker to emphasize the vertical and horizontal lines on the buildings as you say the name of each line.

Think about how this student used lines to make a building.

◄ **Tricia Scott.** Age 6.

 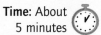
Review and Assess

"What kinds of lines are used most often in buildings?" "¿Qué tipos de líneas se usan más a menudo en los edificios?"

Think

The student used mixed-media materials to make the horizontal, vertical, and diagonal lines of her building.

■ Use *Large Prints 13 Children at the Ice Cream Stand* and *14 Night Heron* to identify lines like those used in buildings.

Informal Assessment

Art Journal: Critical Thinking
Have students ask themselves the Art Criticism questions, and then write or sketch in their Art Journals to answer the Interpret question.
NSAE 1.b; 2.b; 3.a; 5.c

 **Creative Expression**

What could you use to make the lines of a building?

1. Start with a piece of cardboard for the building.

2. Use different objects to add parts to the building. Add windows, doors, and a roof.

3. What else can you add to make the building unique?

 Art Criticism

Interpret Who would use a building like the one you made?

Art Criticism

Describe ▶ What kind of building did you create? What parts does it have?

Analyze ▶ What kinds of lines did you use to make your building?

Interpret ▶ Who would live in a building like the one you made?

Decide ▶ If you could design your building again, what would you do differently?

■ For standardized-format test practice using this lesson's art content, see pages 14–15 in *Reading and Writing Test Preparation.*

Art Across the Curriculum

Use these ideas to reinforce art concepts across the curriculum.
NSAE 6.b

★ **Personal Writing** Have students imagine they are designing their dream houses. Have them list features they would like their houses to have.

★ **Math** Buildings are usually made with an even number of lines. Have students count the number of lines they see in each building.

★ **Science** Have students identify the buildings in *The Monongahela at Morgantown* in order from smallest to largest.

★ **Social Studies** *Shacks* was painted in 1919. Discuss with students the differences between the houses in the painting and the houses that are built today.

★ **Technology** Have students use the line tool in the computer's drawing and painting program to make pictures of buildings. Visit **SRAonline.com** to print detailed instructions for this activity.

Buildings Have Lines

Extra! For the Art Specialist

Time: About 45 minutes

Focus

Use *Transparency 5* and *Large Print 13 Children at the Ice Cream Stand* to compare ways artists use lines to depict buildings in art. Discuss who students think would live or work in each building.

Teach

Have students complete the Alternate Activity. Discuss how students can make each building unique, even though they start with the same lines.

Reflect

Guide students through evaluation of their works of art using the four steps of art criticism. (See pages 28–29 for more about art criticism.) Have students share their buildings with a classmate. The classmates should see if they can make any guesses about the people who live there, based on details in the work of art.

Alternate Activity

Materials:
- 12" × 18" manila paper
- crayons
- markers

1. Have students fold the 12" × 18" manila paper in half, bringing the short sides together. Open the folded paper, and then fold each short side of the paper into the middle, lining it up with the fold.

2. Have students cut the top of the paper to depict the diagonal lines of a roof. Students should design the closed paper to represent the outside of a building. Students should add details such as windows, doors, bricks, and so on.

3. When the outside of the building is completed, students should open the folded papers to design the inside of the building. They should include details to reveal things about the people who live or work inside the building.

Research in Art Education

"The arts help students develop their abilities to appreciate and interpret art of other cultures and to learn about people of the past through exposure to reproductions, to art works in museums and galleries, or through discussions about contemporary artists and art works." Andra Nyman, "Cultural Content, Identity, and Program Development: Approaches to Art Education for Elementary Educators," in *Contemporary Issues in Art Education*, edited by Y. Gaudelius and P. Speirs, 61–69. New Jersey: Prentice Hall, 2002

Assessment

Use the following rubric to evaluate the artwork students make in the Creative Expression activity and to assess students' understanding of the lines used to depict the buildings.

Have students complete page 17 or 18 in their *Assessment* books.

	Art History and Culture	Aesthetic Perception	Creative Expression	Art Criticism
3 POINTS	The student can compare the artists' depictions of buildings.	The student accurately identifies vertical and horizontal lines in buildings and identifies them by name.	The student's mixed-media collage shows a clear understanding of the lines in buildings.	The student thoughtfully and honestly evaluates his or her own work using the four steps of art criticism.
2 POINTS	The student's comparison is weak or incomplete.	The student shows emerging awareness of vertical and horizontal lines in buildings but cannot always identify them.	The student's mixed-media collage shows some understanding of the lines in buildings.	The student attempts to evaluate his or her own work, but shows an incomplete understanding of evaluation criteria.
1 POINT	The student cannot compare the artists' depictions of buildings.	The student cannot identify vertical and horizontal lines in buildings.	The student's collage shows no understanding of the lines in buildings.	The student makes no attempt to evaluate his or her own artwork.

Assessment, p. 17

Name _____ Date _____

Lesson **5** UNIT 1

Buildings Have Lines

For the teacher: Use the following prompt for this activity.
Using a crayon, draw a building shape using two vertical lines, two horizontal lines, and two diagonal lines.

Level 1

Unit 1 • Line   **17**

Lines Show Movement

Lesson 6 teaches that artists show movement by using diagonal, zigzag, and curved lines.

Objectives

Art History and Culture

To identify and compare the cultures of Jacob Lawrence and Harrison Begay
NSAE 1.a; 4.b; 4.c; 5.b

Creative Expression

To paint a picture on the computer using diagonal, zigzag, or curved lines to show movement NSAE 1.a; 1.c; 2.c

Aesthetic Perception

To identify diagonal, zigzag, and curved lines and the movements they represent
NSAE 2.a

Art Criticism

To evaluate one's own artwork using the four steps of art criticism
NSAE 1.b; 2.b; 3.a; 5.c

Vocabulary ⭐ Reading

Review the following vocabulary words with students before beginning the lesson.

curved line _línea curva_—a line that bends

diagonal line _línea diagonal_—a slanted line that moves from corner to corner

zigzag _en zigzag_—diagonal lines that connect

See page 59B for additional Spanish vocabulary resources.

Art Journal: Vocabulary

Have students add these words to the Vocabulary section of their Art Journals.

Lesson Materials
- computer's paint program

Alternate Materials
- watercolors on paper

Program Resources
- _Reading and Writing Test Prep.,_ pp. 16–17
- _Flash Cards 3–6_
- _Transparency 6_
- _Artist Profiles,_ pp. 3, 35
- _Animals Through History Time Line_
- _Assessment,_ pp. 19–20
- _Large Prints 13_ Children at the Ice Cream Stand and _14_ Night Heron
- _The National Museum of Women in the Arts Collection_

Concept Trace
Lines Show Movement
Introduced: Level K, Unit 1, Lesson 3

Reinforced: Level 2, Unit 1, Lesson 4

Lesson 6 Arts Integration NSAE 6.a

Theatre

Complete Unit 1, Lesson 6, on pages 28–33 of _Theatre Arts Connections._

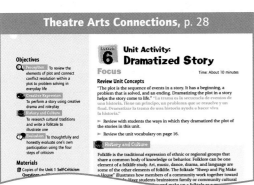

Music

Dance Myself to Sleep. Christopher Cerf and Norman Stiles.

Artists use active lines to show people and animals moving. Have students pantomime to the words and music of _Dance Myself to Sleep._ Have them identify movements of stretching, yawing, turning, tossing, and gently rocking and what types of lines might show those movements.

Movement & Dance

Select three line patterns, such as straight lines, _S_ curves, and zigzags, for students to use pathways to travel on. Have students create locomotor movement for each pathway, then select a sequence and perform each one. After exploring each idea, try arranging them in a different order.

Activate Prior Knowledge

"Have you ever seen photographs of athletes playing sports?" "¿Alguna vez han visto fotografías de atletas jugando deportes?"

- If possible, show students such a photograph. Discuss the action the athletes may have been performing when the photograph was taken, and how the photograph freezes the action at a single moment.

Using Literature Reading

- Read *James and the Rain* by Karla Kuskin. The illustrations by Reg Cartwright have many lines that show the movement of James and the animals as they stroll through the rain.

Thematic Connection ⭐ Social Studies

- **Sports/Games:** The girls in *Children at Play* seem to be enjoying themselves. Have students discuss how to make a sport or game more enjoyable for all participants.

Introduce the Art

Look
NSAE 2.b; 3.a

"The lines in these works of art help us imagine the people moving." "Las líneas en estas obras de arte nos ayudan a imaginarnos a la gente moviéndose".

Making Inferences ⭐ Reading

- Ask students who they think the groups of people are in each work of art. Are they families? If not, what do the people have in common? Answers will vary. Students may say that the girls in *Children at Play* are friends and that they know each other because they live in the same neighborhood. The men in *Night Chant Ceremonial Hunt* are part of the same Navajo tribe. They might be related.

🏺 Art History and Culture

Share with students the Art History and Culture information about Harrison Begay from page 57.

💻 Web Connection

Visit **www.jacoblawrence.org** for more information about Jacob Lawrence.

▲ **Jacob Lawrence.** (American). *Children at Play.* 1947.
• • • • • • • • • • • • • • • •
Tempera on Masonite panel. 20 × 24 inches (50.8 × 60.96 cm.). Georgia Museum of Art, University of Georgia, Athens, Georgia.

Look at the works of art on these pages. The artists used active lines to show people and animals moving.

🏺 Art History and Culture

Harrison Begay was a Native American artist. He painted pictures of traditional Navajo activities.

🏺 Art History and Culture

Jacob Lawrence
NSAE 4.a; 4.b; 4.c; 5.b

Jacob Lawrence (jā´ kəb lär´ ənz) (1917–2000) was born in Atlantic City, New Jersey, but moved to Harlem in 1930. He attended the Harlem Art Workshop after school. Most of Lawrence's work portrays the lives of African Americans. Lawrence also made paintings about his personal experiences, including his service in the Coast Guard during World War II. Lawrence later became an art professor. He retired from teaching in 1983 but continued to paint until his death.

See pages 16–21 and 24–25 for more about subject matter and art history.

Artist Profiles, p. 35

● Artist Profile ●
Jacob Lawrence
1917–2000

Jacob Lawrence (jā´ kəb lär´ ənz) had parents who met on their migration to the North. His father was born in South Carolina, and his mother in Virginia. Lawrence was born in Atlantic City, New Jersey, in 1917. The family finally settled in Harlem in 1929 at the end of the Harlem Renaissance. Because his mother worked all day, she enrolled Lawrence in the Harlem Art Workshop after school to keep him out of trouble. He had many excellent teachers there, including Charles Alston. Lawrence won a scholarship to the American Artists School. He taught at New York's Pratt Institute from 1958 to 1965. From 1970, he taught at the University of Washington in Seattle, where he also served as head of the

Study both works of art.

▶ What things are moving?

▶ What kinds of lines do those things have?

Unit 1 • Lesson 6   **57**

▲ **Harrison Begay.** (Native American, Navajo). *Night Chant Ceremonial Hunt.* 1947.
....
Watercolor on paper. 20 × 30 inches (50.8 × 76.2 cm). The Philbrook Museum of Art, Tulsa, Oklahoma.

Aesthetic Perception

Seeing Like an Artist Look around. Do you see anything with active lines?

Art History and Culture

Harrison Begay

NSAE 4.a; 4.b; 4.c; 5.b

Harrison Begay (ha′rə sən be gā′) (1917–2003) was born in White Cone, Arizona, to a Navajo family. As a boy, Begay attended a government-run boarding school where he learned English. He went on to study architecture and to create murals for the Works Projects Administration. In 1951 he created Tewa Enterprises, which produced Native American artwork. Begay has had a difficult life, often selling his work at very low prices just to make ends meet. Begay's paintings depict the Navajo way of life, including traditional activities, such as the ceremonial hunt depicted in this artwork.

See pages 16–21 and 24–25 for more about subject matter and art history.

Artist Profiles, p. 3

● Artist Profile ●

Harrison Begay
1917–2003

Harrison Begay (hār′ is sən be gā′) was born in White Cone, Arizona. A member of the Navajo tribe, he and his family lived in a hogan and herded sheep and goats for a living. His family found or raised most of what they needed on their own land because the trading post was a long way from their home. Begay studied art under Dorothy Dunn at the Santa Fe Indian School before attending Black Mountain College in North Carolina and Phoenix Junior College in Arizona. He also served three years in the army. Begay began exhibiting his paintings, watercolors, and silkscreens in 1946. He is most famous for his renditions of horses and deer, which were among his favorite subjects. His works are included

Study

▶ In *Children at Play,* the girls are moving. In *Night Chant Ceremonial Hunt,* the men and the animals are moving.

▶ The people and animals are made with curved and diagonal lines.

Additional Study Questions

▶ What in the works of art is not moving? What kinds of lines make those things? In *Children at Play,* the building is not moving. It has vertical and horizontal lines. Some of the girls look like they are still. Their bodies and legs have lines that are more vertical than those of the girls in action. In *Night Chant Ceremonial Hunt,* the plants are not moving. The plants have diagonal lines, and there are horizontal lines where they meet the ground.

■ For more examples of genre art see the *The National Museum of Women in the Arts Collection.*

Art Journal: Concepts

Have students make sketches in their Art Journals of an animal at rest and the same animal running fast. How are the sketches different?

Aesthetic Perception

Seeing Like an Artist Students may see movement through the window, such as branches blowing in a breeze. Students may be moving in the classroom. If there is not much movement going on, create some for the students to observe. Have students notice the lines created by the movement.

Developing Visual Literacy Have students discuss what they think the outcome will be of *Night Chant Ceremonial Hunt.* Will the hunters catch the animals? Do any details in the artwork give them clues about who is faster?
NSAE 5.c

Web Connection

Visit **www.philbrook.org** for more information about the Philbrook.

Teach

Time: About 30 minutes

"What lines are used to show movement?"
"¿Qué líneas se usan para mostrar movimiento?"

- Read and discuss Using Lines to Show Movement on page 58.

Practice

Materials: None

- Divide students into small groups and have them complete the Practice activity on page 58.

Creative Expression

NSAE 1.a; 1.c; 2.c
Materials: computer's paint program

Alternate Materials: watercolors on paper

- Have students follow the directions on page 59.

- See the Activity Tips on page 234 for visual examples of this lesson's activity.

Art Journal: Brainstorming

Have students brainstorm ideas for ways they could show themselves playing. Have students make sketches of their ideas in their Art Journals and then select one to do for the Creative Expression activity.

Using Lines to Show Movement

Diagonal, zigzag, and curved lines are active lines. They are used to show movement.

diagonal   zigzag

curved

Practice

Show movement with your classmates.

1. Think of a game or sport you like to play.

2. Pretend to play the game. Stop when your teacher says, "Freeze!"

3. Look at the lines made by your classmates' arms and legs.

Differentiated Instruction

Reteach
Show students a picture of athletes in motion from a newspaper or magazine. Use a black marker to outline the athletes. Have students identify the lines you drew.

Special Needs
Adaptations: Students with low vision may have trouble seeing the images on the screen. Changing the display properties of your computer can enlarge the size of the images and fonts. In Windows, these settings can be accessed through the control panel display options.

ELL Tips
Use *Flash Cards 1–6.* Point to a line and say its name. Have students repeat after you.

Think about how this student showed movement.

Creative Expression

How can you show the movement you make when you play?

1. Think about the lines that show this movement.
2. Use the brush tool in your computer's paint program to draw yourself at play.
3. Fill the page.

Art Criticism

Describe What are you doing in the picture? Tell about the game you are playing.

Art Across the Curriculum

Use these ideas to reinforce art concepts across the curriculum.
NSAE 6.b

★ **Narrative Writing** Have students imagine that one of the works of art in the lesson is an illustration in a book, and then use the writing process to write a few sentences telling what the story is about.

★ **Math** Have students describe the colors of the girls' dresses in *Children at Play* as part of a set, such as "three out of nine dresses are green."

★ **Science** Have students look at *Night Chant Ceremonial Hunt* and describe how the horses and the deer are similar and how they are different.

★ **Social Studies** Harrison Begay is a Navajo artist. Discuss with students the important contributions of Native Americans.

★ **Technology** Have students use the computer's paint or draw program to create an active picture. Visit **SRAonline.com** to print detailed instructions for this activity.

Reflect
Time: About 5 minutes

Review and Assess

"What lines can show movement in your artwork?" "¿Qué líneas pueden mostrar movimiento en sus obras de arte?"

Think

The student artist used curved lines to show the movement of her arms and diagonal lines to show the movement of her legs.

■ Have students identify movement and the types of lines the artists used in *Large Prints 13 Children at the Ice Cream Stand* and *14 Night Heron*.

Informal Assessment

Art Journal: Critical Thinking
Have students ask themselves the Art Criticism questions, and then write or sketch to answer the Describe question in their Art Journals.
NSAE 1.b; 2.b; 3.a; 5.c

Art Criticism

Describe ▶ What are you doing in the picture? Tell about the game you are playing.

Analyze ▶ What lines did you use to show movement?

Interpret ▶ What does your picture suggest will happen next?

Decide ▶ Did you choose the best lines to show the movement you are making?

■ For standardized-format test practice using this lesson's art content, see pages 16–17 in *Reading and Writing Test Preparation.*

Lines Show Movement

Extra! For the Art Specialist

Time: About 45 minutes

Focus

Use **Transparency 6** and **Large Print 13** *Children at the Ice Cream Stand* to discuss the types of lines artists use to show movement. Who is moving in each picture? Who is not moving? What types of lines do those people have?

Teach

Have students think of an activity they like to do that involves movement, and then pose to represent that activity. Have students notice the way their arms, legs, or bodies are positioned. Then have students complete the Alternate Activity.

Reflect

Guide students through evaluation of their works of art using the four steps of art criticism. (See pages 28–29 for more about art criticism.) Discuss how the lines in the works would be different if the action had been depicted at another moment.

Alternate Activity

Materials:
- colored construction paper
- wallpaper samples
- scissors
- glue
- 12" × 18" white paper

Have students make a collage depicting themselves doing their favorite activity. Students should begin by cutting shapes that represent body parts from construction paper and wallpaper. Students should arrange the shapes on the white paper and glue them to make the collage.

Research in Art Education

One case study showed that students who were "learning disabled and who were 'reluctant' readers" were better able to engage in reading when the creation and analysis of visual art was incorporated into their discussions of stories. This suggests that combining visual art with reading may help certain readers ("Reading Is Seeing: Using Visual Response to Improve the Literary Reading of Reluctant Readers" in *Critical Links*, p. 144). Students' understanding that lines show movement will aid them in their interpretation of illustrations.

Assessment

Use the following rubric to evaluate the artwork students make in the Creative Expression activity and to assess students' understanding of using lines to show movement.

Have students complete page 19 or 20 in their **Assessment** books.

	Art History and Culture	Aesthetic Perception	Creative Expression	Art Criticism
3 POINTS	The student can identify and compare the cultures in the works of art.	The student accurately identifies diagonal, zigzag, and curved lines and the movements they represent.	The student's artwork clearly uses lines to show movement.	The student thoughtfully and honestly evaluates his or her own artwork using the four steps of art criticism.
2 POINTS	The student's identification or comparison is weak or incomplete.	The student shows emerging awareness of diagonal, zigzag, and curved lines and the movements they represent.	The student's artwork shows some awareness of using lines to show movement.	The student attempts to evaluate his or her own work, but shows an incomplete understanding of evaluation criteria.
1 POINT	The student cannot identify or compare the cultures in the works of art.	The student cannot identify diagonal, zigzag, and curved lines and the movements they represent.	The student's artwork does not use lines to show movement.	The student makes no attempt to evaluate his or her own artwork.

Assessment, p. 19

Name _____ Date _____

Lines Show Movement

Lesson **6**
UNIT 1

For the teacher: Use the following prompts for this activity.
Using a crayon or a pencil, draw a diagonal line, a curved line, and a zigzag line. Beside each line, draw a letter of the alphabet that is made with the same kind of line.

Level 1

Unit 1 • Line   **19**

building—a place where we live, work, meet, or play
edificio—un lugar donde vivimos, comemos, trabajamos o jugamos

curved line—a line that is always bending línea curva—una línea que siempre se dobla

diagonal—a slanted line that moves from corner to corner diagonal—una línea oblicua que se mueve de esquina a esquina

horizontal—from side to side horizontal—de lado a lado

line—the mark made by a tool, such as a pencil, pen, or paintbrush, as it moves across a surface línea—la marca trazada por una herramienta, como lápiz, bolígrafo o pincel, a medida que se mueve por una superficie

vertical—up and down vertical—de arriba hacia abajo

zigzag—diagonal lines that connect zigzag—líneas diagonales que se conectan

Definitions for the following words appear as art on *Student Edition* page 38 and in the student glossary:

broken—entre cortada

rough—áspera

smooth—suave

solid—continua

thick—gruesa

thin—fina

Vocabulary Practice

T Display *Transparency 37* to review unit vocabulary words.

Answering Questions ⭐ Vocabulary

Discuss the possibilities of certain relationships among the vocabulary words. Have students answer questions such as "Can a line be thick?" or "Can a horizontal be vertical?" to practice critical thinking skills.

Examples ⭐ Vocabulary

Without identifying the vocabulary word, name or describe an object in the classroom that illustrates the word's meaning. Ask students to identify the vocabulary word you gave an example of.

Visualization Strategies ⭐ Vocabulary

Write the word *line* on the board and draw a circle around it. Have students name other words from the vocabulary list that can describe *line*. Create a word web based on their responses.

Line

Line

▲ **Joseph Norman.** (American).
Spanish Garden #IV. 1994–1995.
Acrylic on paper. 50 × 40 inches (127 × 101.6 cm.).
Private collection.

Art Criticism

Critical Thinking Art criticism is an organized system for looking at and talking about art. You can criticize art without being an expert. The purpose of art criticism is to get the viewer involved in a perception process that delays judgment until all aspects of the artwork have been studied.

■ See page 28–29 for more about art criticism.

Describe

■ What do you see? During this step the student will collect information about the subject of the work.

▶ Have students describe what they see in *Spanish Garden #IV.* On the right side of the painting is a long-neck vase with two rounded handles. A plant with leaves is growing out of the vase. There are more leaves on the left side of the painting. There are black vertical and horizontal lines that are part of a gate.

Analyze

■ How is this work organized? During this step the student thinks about how the artist has used the elements and principles of art.

▶ Where do students see thick lines in the painting? Where do students see thin lines? The thickest black line is behind the vase. The other black vertical and horizontal lines are thick. Thin lines are crisscrossing in the lower right. The curved lines all over the work are thin.

▶ Where do students see vertical lines? Where do students see horizontal lines? There is a red vertical line down the left edge of the painting. Near the upper left, there is a light-colored vertical line and two red horizontal lines. At the bottom left, there is a dark green horizontal line. There are many black vertical lines and horizontal lines on the right side of the painting. There is a row of short vertical lines across the lower center of the

Art History and Culture

Joseph Norman

Joseph Norman (jō´ sef nôr´ mən) (1957–   ) grew up in a poor neighborhood on the south side of Chicago. He enjoyed drawing, and he was encouraged by his family to pursue art as a way to avoid local street gangs. The brother of one of Norman's friends was an illustrator, which made Norman realize he too could someday be a professional artist. Norman was also an excellent football player, which earned him an athletic scholarship to Central State University. He received art degrees and an art education degree from three other universities.

See pages 16–21 and 24–25 for more about subject matter and art history.

Artist Profiles, p. 48

┌ Artist Profile ┐
Joseph Norman
b. 1957

Joseph Norman (jō´ sef nôr´ mən) was born and raised in Chicago, Illinois. He received a degree in art education from the University of Arkansas and a masters degree in Art Education from the University of Illinois. His artistic studies took him to locations such as Germany, Costa Rica and Cuba. Printing, painting, and drawing since the 1980s, Norman is a poetic realist and credits his ability to understand and analyze his work to his studies in art education. He has exhibited widely throughout the country, and his work is in collections at The Museum of Modern Art, The National Gallery of Art, and the National Museum of American Art. Norman resides in Atlanta, Georgia, where he is a professor at the

Art Criticism — Critical Thinking

Describe

▶ What objects do you see in this painting?

Analyze

▶ Where do you see thick lines in this painting?

Interpret

▶ Do the lines make this work look busy or calm?

Decide

▶ Is this a realistic painting?

painting. There is a green vertical line on the upper right edge.

▶ Where do students see diagonal lines? Where do students see curved lines? There are diagonal lines below the blue leaves on the left. At the bottom right there are thin diagonal lines that cross. At the bottom left, the edge of the blue shape is a curved line. The leaf shapes in the painting have curved edges. There are curved lines at the right.

Interpret

■ What is the artist trying to say? Students use the clues they discovered during their analysis to find the message the artist is trying to show.

▶ Ask students whether the lines make the painting look busy or calm. Even though there are many vertical and horizontal lines, the movement of the diagonal and curved lines makes this work look busy.

▶ Ask students if they would like to walk inside this painting. Answers will vary. Some students might say it would be scary because of all the line movement. Others might like to because of the bright colors.

Decide

■ What do you think about the work? Students use all the information they have gathered to decide whether this is a successful work of art.

▶ Ask students if this is a realistic painting. Discuss with students that it is abstract.

 Art Journal: Critical Thinking
Have students write or sketch the answers to the Aesthetic Perception questions in their Art Journals.

Aesthetic Perception

Seeing Like an Artist Joseph Norman's painting is called *Spanish Garden #IV.* Have students think about a real garden they have seen, or bring in a photograph of a garden to display. How does it compare with the work of art?

Describe ▶ Have students list and describe everything in the scene.

Analyze ▶ What lines do students see in the scene?

Interpret ▶ What is the mood of the scene?

Decide ▶ What feeling do students get when they look at the scene?

"Artists use many kinds of lines in their works of art." "Los artistas usan muchos tipos de líneas en sus obras de arte".

T Review unit vocabulary with students using *Transparency 37.*

Art Journal: Writing
Have students answer the questions on page 62. (1. C, 2. B, 3. C)

T For further assessment, have students complete the unit test on *Transparency 43.*

LEARNING ABOUT MUSEUMS

Telfair Museum of Art

► The mansion which houses the Telfair Museum of Art was built in 1818–1819. It was home to the Telfair family until 1875, when it was passed on to the Georgia History Society to be turned into a museum. In 1886 it was opened to the public. The collection of over 4,500 pieces includes fine art, decorative arts, and historic buildings. The Jepson Center for the Arts, an addition to the Telfair Museum of Art, is scheduled open in Spring 2005. It will include interactive galleries, an auditorium, and a sculpture garden.

"Art is a method of opening up areas of feeling rather than merely an illustration of an object."

—Francis Bacon (1909–1992), artist

Line, continued

Show What You Know

Write your answers on a sheet of paper.

❶ Choose the thick line.

A. ————————

B. ▪▪▪▪▪▪▪▪▪▪

C. ▬▬▬▬▬▬▬

❷ Which lines are not calm lines?

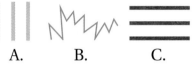

  A.   B.   C.

❸ Which lines show movement?

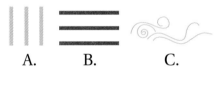

  A.   B.   C.

62 Unit 1

This museum is in Savannah, Georgia. It is the oldest art museum in the South. The museum's collection is located in a mansion that used to be the home of the Telfair family.

Unit Assessment Options

 **Aesthetic Perception**

Practice Have students find examples of thick, thin, smooth, rough, solid, broken, vertical, horizontal, diagonal, zigzag, and curved lines in the classroom.

Creative Expression

Student Portfolio Have students review all of the artwork they have created during this unit and select the pieces they wish to keep in their portfolios.

Art Criticism

Activity Have students select their favorite work of art from the unit. Guide students through study of their selected work using the four steps of art criticism. (See pages 28–29 for more about Art Criticism.)

Lines in Song Writing

▲ Paul Tracey. "Our Little Blue Planet."

A songwriter writes lines for songs. The lines are made up of words. Sometimes the lines rhyme.

What to Do Write two rhyming lines about an endangered animal.

1. Listen to Paul Tracey's song about endangered animals. Talk about what the lines of the song mean.

2. Work in a group. Choose an endangered animal. Write two lines about why the animal is special.

3. Read or sing your lines for others.

 Art Criticism

Describe What did you learn about writing lines for a song?

Unit 1   **63**

 Art History and Culture

Paul Tracey

Paul Tracey draws upon his cultural heritage and broad personal experience to communicate ideas about life through original songs. He became an environmentalist by working on his father's farm in South Africa. His father and the foreman, a Swazi man named Simon Shabalala, taught him about farming, building, and appreciating nature. This inspired his musical show, "Our Little Blue Planet."

Lines in Song Writing   NSAE 6.a

Objective: To create rhyming lines about an endangered animal

Materials: "Our Little Blue Planet" including the songs "Dead as a Dodo" and "Save the Forests, Save the Trees," performed by Paul Tracey. Running time: 5:00

Focus
Time: About 5 minutes

- Read and discuss the information about songwriting on page 63.

 Art History and Culture

- Discuss endangered species with students. Help students create a list of endangered species.

Teach
Time: About 20 minutes

 Aesthetic Perception

- Play the songs for students. Discuss that "Dead as a Dodo" is about endangered species, and that the lines of the song rhyme.

Creative Expression

- Divide students into groups. Have each group select an animal from the list. Provide information about the animals. Have students write two rhyming lines about the animal or why it should be saved. Have students share or sing their lines.

- **Informal Assessment** Identify the rhyming words in each group's lines. Comment positively.

Reflect
Time: About 10 minutes

 Art Criticism

- Have students answer the questions.

Describe ▶ What did you learn about writing lines for a song?

Analyze ▶ How are your lines similar to the lines from Paul Tracey's song? How are they different?

Interpret ▶ What feelings about endangered species do your lines create?

Decide ▶ How well did you describe your animal?

Unit 2 Planning Guide

	Lesson Title	Suggested Pacing	Creative Expression Activity
Lesson 1	Lines Outline Shapes	55 minutes	Create a crayon-resist watercolor ocean.
Lesson 2	Geometric Shapes	55 minutes	Create a geometric shape design.
Lesson 3	Free-Form Shapes	35 and 20 minutes	Create a free-form shape picture.
Lesson 4	People Shapes	65 minutes	Create a life-sized self-portrait with free-form shapes.
Lesson 5	Shapes of People in Action	45 minutes	Create a drawing showing self in action.
Lesson 6	Still-Life Shapes	50 minutes	Create a still life with geometric and free-form shapes.
ARTSOURCE	Shapes in Theatre	35 minutes	Create a tableau using an illustration from a book.

Materials	Program Resources	Fine Art Resources	Literature Resources
12" × 18" white paper, crayons, watercolors, salt, watercolor brushes, paper towels, water dishes, masking tape	*Reading and Writing Test Preparation*, pp. 18–19 *Assessment*, pp. 21–22 *Home and After-School Connections*	*Transparency*, 7 *Artist Profiles*, pp. 8, 53 *Animals Through History Time Line* *Large Prints*, 15 and 16 *Art Around the World*	*Moongame* by Frank Asch
black construction paper (at least 9" × 12"), newsprint or copy paper (cut into 4" × 4½" pieces), crayons (with paper peeled off), scissors, glue, rubbing plates, geometric shape templates	*Reading and Writing Test Preparation*, pp. 20–21 *Flash Cards*, 7 and 9–11 *Assessment*, pp. 23–24	*Transparency*, 8 *Artist Profiles*, pp. 25, 41 *Large Prints*, 15 and 16 *Art Around the World*	*I Read Signs* by Tana Hoban
old magazines, large construction paper, pencils, black glue, dry pastels	*Reading and Writing Test Preparation*, pp. 22–23 *Flash Card*, 8 *Assessment*, pp. 25–26	*Transparency*, 9 *Artist Profiles*, pp. 37, 54 *Large Prints*, 15 and 16 *Women in the Arts Collection*	*The Old Woman Who Loved to Read* by John Winch
pencils, large brushes, tempera paints, water dishes, 3–4 feet of mural paper per student, scissors, paper towels	*Reading and Writing Test Preparation*, pp. 24–25 *Assessment*, pp. 27–28	*Transparency*, 10 *Artist Profiles*, pp. 6, 20 *Large Prints*, 15 and 16 *Art Around the World*	*Miss Malarkey Doesn't Live in Room 10* by Judy Finchler
12" × 8" white paper, markers, crayons	*Reading and Writing Test Preparation*, pp. 26–27 *Assessment*, pp. 29–30	*Transparency*, 11 *Artist Profiles*, pp. 18, 35 *Large Prints*, 15 and 16 *Women in the Arts Collection*	*Mommy Works, Daddy Works* by Marika Pedersen and Mikele Hall
computer's paint program, teacher-provided still-life items	*Reading and Writing Test Preparation*, pp. 28–29 *Assessment*, pp. 31–32	*Transparency*, 12 *Artist Profiles*, pp. 11, 51 *Large Prints*, 15 and 16 *Women in the Arts Collection*	*My House Mi Casa* by Rebecca Emberley
The Story of Babar, the Little Elephant performed by the Children's Theatre Company			

2 Shape

Lesson 1: Lines outline shapes. **Shapes** are created when lines connect.

Lesson 2: Geometric shapes have names. Circles, squares, rectangles, and triangles are geometric shapes.

Lesson 3: Free-form shapes are not geometric. Living things have free-form shapes.

Lesson 4: People have free-form shapes.

Lesson 5: Artists show **people in action** by changing the position of body parts.

Lesson 6: A **still life** shows an arrangement of objects.

1ntroduce Unit Concepts

"Let's talk about the shapes of things you see around you." "Vamos a hablar de las formas de las cosas que ven a su alrededor".

Shapes
Geometric Shapes ⭐ Math

■ Hold up an envelope and a puppet. Explain that the envelope is a geometric shape (a rectangle). Ask students if all rectangles have the same shape. Then ask if all puppets have the same shape. Explain that because not all puppets have the same shape, the shape of a puppet is a free-form shape.

■ Have students name other objects with geometric shapes. Have students name other objects that have free-form shapes.

Cross-Curricular Projects
■ See the *Language Arts and Reading, Mathematics, Science,* and *Social Studies Art Connections* books for activities that further develop line concepts.

National Standards for Arts Education in Visual Arts (NSAE) 6.b

Shape

◀ **Loïs Mailou Jones.** (American). *Esquisse for Ode to Kinshasa.* 1972.
⋯⋯⋯⋯⋯⋯⋯⋯⋯
Acrylic on paper.
11 × 8 inches
(27.9 × 91.4 cm.). The National Museum of Women in the Arts, Washington, D.C.

Artists use shapes in their works of art.

This artwork has many shapes.

64   Unit 2

Fine Art Prints

Display *Large Prints 15 She-Ba* and *16 Dos Niños (Two Children)*. Refer to the prints throughout the unit as students learn about shapes.

Large Print 15

Large Print 16

A **shape** is created by the line all around it.

▶ What shapes can you find in the artwork?

▶ What kinds of lines make each shape?

In This Unit you will:

▶ learn about geometric and free-form shapes.

▶ find shapes in art and the environment.

▶ create art with shapes.

Loïs Mailou Jones

(1905–1998)

▶ was an American artist.

▶ made paintings.

▶ used African themes.

Examine the Artwork

"Let's look for shapes in this artwork."
"Vamos a buscar figuras en esta obra de arte".

■ Have students look at Jones' *Esquisse for Ode to Kinshasa.* Ask them to describe what they see.

■ Have students answer the questions on page 65.

▶ There is a circle around the eye. The large orange shape also has triangles, diamonds, and half-circles on it. There are blue diamonds in the background. The rest of the shapes—the large orange, brown, green, yellow, red, and blue shapes—do not have names because they are free-form shapes.

▶ Most of the shapes are outlined by smooth lines. The free-form and geometric shapes are made of curved, vertical, horizontal, and diagonal lines.

Unit Pretest

T Display **Transparency 44** as a pretest. Answers: 1. A, 2. B, 3. C

Home Connection

■ See **Home and After-School Connections** for family newsletters and activities for this unit.

Art History and Culture

Loïs Mailou Jones

When Loïs Mailou Jones (lō´ əs mā loo´ jōnz) (1905–1998) was in high school, she assisted a designer who made costumes for a dance company. Jones studied design and graduated with honors. She taught at Palmer Memorial Institute and established the art department there. In 1930 Jones became a professor at Howard University, where she taught for 47 years. Jones often used African-inspired themes in her artworks, such as *Esquisse for Ode to Kinshasa,* which pays tribute to the capital city of Zaire.

See pages 16–21 and 24–25 for more about subject matter and art history.

Artist Profiles, p. 30

Artist Profile

Loïs Mailou Jones
1905-1998

Loïs Mailou Jones (lō´ is mī´ lū jōnz) had a long, successful career as an artist and received national and international recognition. As a teacher she affected generations of students. Her early studies at the School of the Museum of Fine Arts in Boston, Massachusetts, emphasized design. She also worked as a textile designer. A 1937–1938 fellowship at the Académie Julian in Paris introduced her to European modernism. Between 1930 and 1977, Jones taught art at Howard University in Washington, D.C. In 1953, she married a Haitian artist and began to travel to Haiti. In the late 1960s and early 1970s, she undertook a massive research project at Howard University called "The Black Visual

National Standards for Arts Education in Visual Arts (NSAE) 3.a; 4.c

Arts Integration

NSAE 6.a

ILLUSTRATOR PROFILE

Rosemary Wells

(1943–   )

Rosemary Wells was born in New York City. Her father was a playwright and her mother was a ballet dancer. She began drawing at the age of two, and her family continually supported and encouraged her. Wells's family didn't have a television, so as a child she spent her free time reading, playing outside, or drawing.

After high school, Wells attended the Boston Museum School. She left school at the age of nineteen and got a job as a book designer at a publishing company. After she showed her boss some illustrations she had drawn to accompany a Gilbert and Sullivan song, Wells's employer published her first book.

Since then, Wells has written and illustrated more than 60 books. Most of her books feature animals rather than children. Many feature recurring characters, such as the bunnies Max and Ruby.

Throughout Unit 2, share Wells's illustrations with the class and discuss her use of shape. Where do students see geometric shapes? Where do students see free-form shapes?

Music

The shapes of instruments contribute greatly to their beauty and tone. Draw students' attention to the shapes of various orchestral instruments. Have students observe how the instruments can be recognized by their shapes.

Literature and Art

Use the video or DVD *The Relatives Came* by Cynthia Rylant to help emphasize the differences between geometric and free-form shapes.

Literature and Art

Performing Arts

Show "The Story of Babar." Discuss how the actors brought the shapes of the illustrations to life.

Artsource

Lines Outline Shapes

Lesson 1 teaches that objects are represented in art by shapes, which are defined by the lines that outline them.

Objectives

🐻 Art History and Culture

To recognize that some artists create artwork with animals as the subject
NSAE 3.a

🔍 Aesthetic Perception

To understand that the shape of an object is formed by the line that surrounds it
NSAE 1.a

🎨 Creative Expression

To create a crayon-resist watercolor ocean
NSAE 1.a; 1.c; 1.d; 2.c; 3.b

❗ Art Criticism

To evaluate one's own artwork using the four steps of art criticism
NSAE 1.b; 2.b; 3.a; 5.c

Vocabulary ⭐ Reading

Review the following vocabulary words with students before beginning the lesson.

shape *forma*—a figure or area that is defined in some way

outline *contorno*—a line that shows or creates the outer edges of a shape

See page 89B for additional Spanish vocabulary resources.

Art Journal: Vocabulary

Have students add these words to the Vocabulary section of their Art Journals.

Lesson Materials

- chenille stems
- 12" × 18" white paper
- crayons
- watercolors
- salt
- watercolor brushes
- water dishes
- paper towels
- masking tape

Alternate Materials:

- yarn
- black paper
- white glue
- oil pastels

Program Resources

- *Reading and Writing Test Prep.,* pp. 18–19
- *Transparency 7*
- *Artist Profiles,* pp. 8, 53
- *Animals Through History Time Line*
- *Assessment,* pp. 21–22
- *Large Prints 15 She-Ba* and *16 Dos Niños (Two Children)*
- *Art Around the World*

Concept Trace

Lines Outline Shapes
Introduced: Level K, Unit 2, Lesson 1

Reinforced: Level 3, Unit 1, Lesson 3

Lesson 1 Arts Integration NSAE 6.a

Theatre

Complete Unit 2, Lesson 1, on pages 36–37 of *Theatre Arts Connections.*

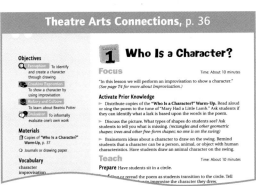

Music

You can create an outline of a melody by tracing the pitches rising and falling in the air with your fingers. Sing *Naughty Kitty Cat.* As you trace the outline notice how you hardly go very high or very low. Repeat with *Goin' to the Zoo.* Did you find any straight lines? Find the jagged outline of *One Little Elephant.*

Movement & Dance

Ask students to imagine a large, empty canvas in front of them, and then place an imaginary paint brush on different parts of the body and paint designs on the canvas using movement. Explore stretching, turning, tilting and jumping to reaching all parts of the canvas.

Activate Prior Knowledge

"When you see an animal, how do you know what animal it is?" "Cuando ven un animal, ¿Cómo saben qué animal es?"

- Discuss students' responses. Explain that we can recognize and identify animals (as well as other living and nonliving things) because of their shapes.

Using Literature ⭐ Reading

- Read *Moongame* by Frank Asch. Discuss how each object in the illustrations has an outline of a different color.

Thematic Connection ⭐ Science

- **Ocean Life:** Discuss the shapes of fish and other animals and plants found in the ocean.

Introduce the Art

Look
NSAE 3.a

"Let's look at the animal in each artwork." "Vamos a ver el animal en cada obra de arte".

Summarizing ⭐ Reading

- Have students describe the subject matter of each artwork. *Muniti Red Snapper* shows a fish on a patterned background. *Rex* depicts a horse. The body of the horse is made of metal and the inside is hollow.

Adjectives and Adverbs ⭐ Language Arts

- List on a chart the adjectives and adverbs students use to describe each work of art.

🏺 Art History and Culture

Discuss with students that some artists often make art with similar subjects and materials. Explain that found objects are objects that were not originally intended to be incorporated into a work of art.
NSAE 3.a

💻 **Web Connection**
Visit www.aboriginalartonline.com to learn more about aboriginal cultures and the art they produce.

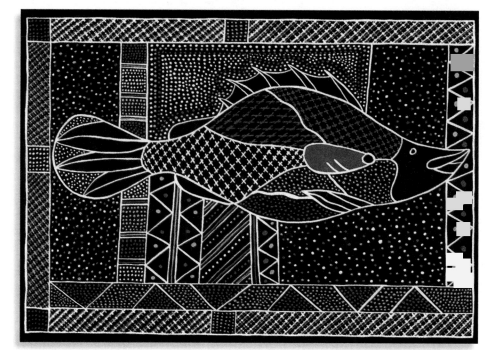

▲ **Francesca Puruntatameri.** (Australian). *Muniti Red Snapper.* c. 1998.
Gouache on paper. 20 × 28 inches (50.8 × 71.12 cm.). Private collection.

Look at the works of art on these pages. The artists used lines to make animal shapes.

🏺 Art History and Culture

Deborah Butterfield only makes art about horses! She often uses found materials in her horse sculptures.

🏺 Art History and Culture

Francesca Puruntatameri

Francesca Puruntatameri (1965–   ) is from the Tiwi Islands, which are located off the northern coast of Australia. On the islands there are three major art centers where artists work. Puruntatameri works at the Munupi Arts and Crafts Association, which was formed in 1990. Many aboriginal artists work in other professions before becoming artists. Puruntatameri worked in a bank, a bakery, and a library before joining the Munupi art center. Aboriginal paintings often depict animals on top of colorful background designs.

See pages 16–21 and 24–25 for more about subject matter and art history.

Artist Profiles, p. 53

Artist Profile
Francesca Puruntatameri
b. 1965

Francesca Puruntatameri is from the Tiwi Islands, which are located off the northern shore of Australia. Before pursuing painting and traditional artistry, and like the majority of Tiwi artists who work in other professions prior to becoming artists, she worked in a bank, bakery, and library. The Tiwi Islands have three main art centers, and Puruntatameri works at the Munupi Arts and Crafts Association, which was formed in 1990. She uses her painting to express a cultural and social link between her heritage and her life today.

Study both works of art to find shapes.

▶ What kinds of lines make the shapes?

▲ **Deborah Butterfield.**
(American). *Rex.* 1991.
....
Found, painted steel. 77 × 110
× 24 inches (195.58 × 279.4
× 60.96 cm.). Lowe Art
Museum, Coral Gables, Florida.

Aesthetic Perception

Seeing Like an Artist Find an object near you.
Trace its outline.

Art History and Culture

Deborah Butterfield NSAE 4.c; 5.b

Deborah Butterfield (deb´ brə bə´ tər fēld) (1949–   ) had trouble
deciding whether to study art or veterinary medicine in college.
Butterfield chose art but still maintained her love for animals,
especially horses. This comes through in her artwork, as Butterfield
sculpts only horses. Throughout history, horses have been depicted
in art for their importance to humans for use in transportation,
work, and sports. (For an example see Harrison Begay's *Night
Chant Ceremonial Hunt* on page 57.) Butterfield does not depict
her horses in that traditional
way. Her horses do not have
riders, and they seem simple
and gentle.

See pages 16–21 and 24–25
for more about subject
matter and art history.

Artist Profiles, p. 8

Artist Profile
Deborah Butterfield
b. 1949

Deborah Butterfield (deb´ə rä but´ tər fēld)
was born in San Diego, California, on the
75th anniversary of the Kentucky Derby. She
thought about becoming a veterinarian, but
decided to study art instead and received
her graduate degree in fine arts from the
University of California at Davis. In 1976 she
moved to Bozeman, Montana. Butterfield
lives on a ranch and trains horses for
competition. Her love of horses translates
into her sculptures; horses have been her
sole subject for many years.

Study

▶ The shape of the fish is outlined by a
smooth, curved white line. Individual
parts of the fish are also outlined in white.
Muniti Red Snapper has triangles,
rectangles, and squares that are outlined
with smooth, straight white lines. In *Rex*
the metal used to make the sculpture
creates the lines that outline the shape of
the horse. Some of the metal pieces are
straight and some are curved. As students
talk about the lines that make the shapes,
ask them to notice the places where the
lines come together.

■ For more examples of art from North
America see *Art Around the World.*

Art Journal: Concepts
Ask students to think of their
favorite animal. Have them draw the
animal's outline in the Concepts section of
their Art Journals. Have students discuss
how they knew what parts of the animal
made the outline.

Aesthetic Perception

Seeing Like an Artist Discuss with students
how every shape has an outline. It may not
be a distinct outline like the white line in
Muniti Red Snapper, but the outline is always
there. Without it the edge of the shape would
not be defined. When a student runs his or
her finger around the edge of an object, he or
she is tracing its outline.

Developing Visual Literacy Do the animals in
Muniti Red Snapper and *Rex* look the way
they would in nature? Have students discuss
the similarities and differences between real
animals and the animals in these artworks.
Also discuss students' ideas for ways the
artists could have made the animals more
realistic.

Web Connection
Visit **www.moma.org/momalearning/artsafari/** to
view an online exhibition of animals in art. Have
students discuss the lines used to outline shapes in
the exhibit's works of art.

each

Time: About 40 minutes

"What happens when you bend a line and connect the ends?" "¿Qué pasa cuando doblan una línea y conectan los extremos?"

- Draw a vertical line and a circle on the board. Discuss how, if you bend the line and connect the ends, you can make a shape. Demonstrate using a chenille stick.

- Read and discuss Using Lines to Outline Shapes on page 68.

Practice

Materials: chenille sticks

Alternate Materials: yarn (lay on a flat surface and form into shapes)

- Distribute the materials and have students follow the directions on page 68.

Creative Expression

NSAE 1.a; 1.c; 1.d; 2.c
Materials: 12" × 18" white paper, crayons, watercolors, salt, watercolor brushes, water dishes, paper towels, masking tape

Alternate Materials: black paper, white glue, oil pastels

- Distribute materials and have students follow the directions on page 69.

- Make sure students press firmly with the crayons. The wax in the crayon will resist the paint, showing the outlines of the shapes.

- After students complete the Creative Expression activity (but while the paint is still wet) sprinkle salt on the picture. It will look like tiny bubbles after the salt has absorbed the paint.

- Review the Technique Tips on page 219 for information about watercolor resist.

- See the Activity Tips on page 235 for visual examples of this lesson's activity.

Art Journal: Brainstorming
Have students brainstorm ideas for fish, plants, and other things they can include in their ocean scenes. Have students make sketches of their ideas in their Art Journals and choose what they will use for the Creative Expression activity.

NSAE 3.b

Using Lines to Outline Shapes

Shapes are made when lines come together. A line around the edge of a shape is its **outline.**

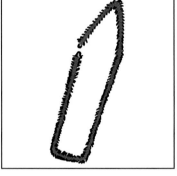

Practice

Practice making outlines.

1. Choose an object in the classroom.

2. Trace the outline of the shape with your finger.

3. Bend a chenille stem to make the outline.

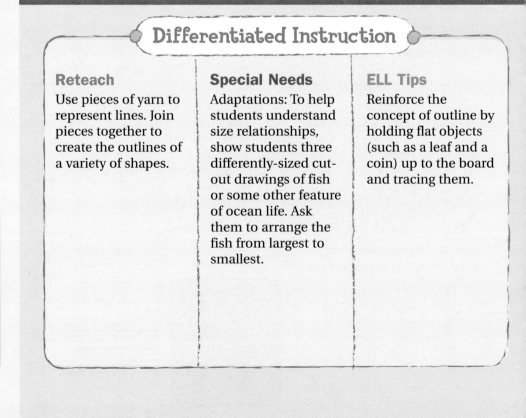

Differentiated Instruction

Reteach
Use pieces of yarn to represent lines. Join pieces together to create the outlines of a variety of shapes.

Special Needs
Adaptations: To help students understand size relationships, show students three differently-sized cut-out drawings of fish or some other feature of ocean life. Ask them to arrange the fish from largest to smallest.

ELL Tips
Reinforce the concept of outline by holding flat objects (such as a leaf and a coin) up to the board and tracing them.

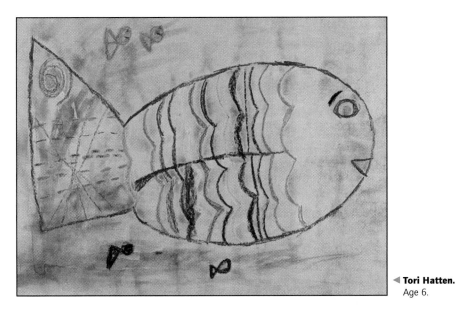

◀ **Tori Hatten.**
Age 6.

Think about how this student used lines to outline shapes.

Creative Expression

What shapes would you put in an ocean scene?

1. Use crayons to draw outlines of fish shapes and plant shapes.

2. Use big shapes, medium-sized shapes, and small shapes.

3. Brush watercolor over your page.

Art Criticism

Interpret Is your ocean a friendly place or a scary place? How can you tell?

Art Across the Curriculum

Use these ideas to reinforce art concepts across the curriculum.
NSAE 6.b

★ **Descriptive Writing** Have students imagine what it might be like if *Rex* were a real horse, then write descriptive words for each of the five senses.

★ **Math** Create a sequence of repeating shapes. Have students predict which shape will come next in the pattern.

★ **Science** Draw the outline of the moon in different phases. Discuss with students that the amount of moon we see changes over time and repeats in a cycle.

★ **Social Studies** Have students identify the United States by its outline. Then have students identify their state by its outline.

★ **Technology** Have students use the computer's paint and draw program to draw the outline of a shape. Then have them fill the shape with a different color using the Fill tool. Visit **SRAonline.com** to print detailed instructions for this activity.

Reflect

Time: About 5 minutes

Review and Assess

"How do you create the shape of an object?"
"¿Cómo crea la figura de un objeto?"

Think

The student used lines to outline the fish shapes.

■ Have students compare the shape outlines in *Large Prints 15 She-Ba* and *16 Dos Niños (Two Children)* to those in the artwork for this lesson.

Informal Assessment

Art Journal: Critical Thinking
Have students ask themselves the Art Criticism questions, and then write or sketch their answers to the Interpret question in their Art Journals.
NSAE 1.b; 2.b; 3.a; 5.c

Art Criticism

Describe ▶ What plants and animals did you include in your ocean scene?

Analyze ▶ How many different shapes did you create?

Interpret ▶ Is your ocean a friendly place or a scary place? How can you tell?

Decide ▶ Did you use lines to outline shapes?

■ For standardized-format test practice using this lesson's art content, see pages 18–19 in *Reading and Writing Test Preparation.*

Lines Outline Shapes

Extra! For the Art Specialist

Time: About 45 minutes

Focus

Use *Transparency 7* to discuss how lines outline shapes. What types of lines make the shape of each animal?

Teach

Have students follow the directions to complete their paintings. How did students know where to paint and draw the outlines of each object?

Reflect

Guide students through evaluation of their paintings using the four steps of art criticism. (See pages 28–29 for more about art criticism.) Encourage students to locate outlines in the classroom.

Alternate Activity

Materials:
- white paper
- tempera paints
- mixing palettes or paper plates
- brushes
- newspaper
- water dishes
- paper towels
- black markers

1. Have students paint fish shapes with a pure paint color. Add white to the paint, letting students mix a tint of the pure paint color. Students can then paint the background around the fish shapes.

2. Black can be added to the tint to produce a shade color for painting fins and other details.

3. When the paintings are dry, students can outline the fish shapes with a marker.

Research in Art Education

"Children respond to art in a holistic manner; their reactions are immediate, subjective, and rarely go beyond the 'like/don't like' stage . . . It takes a sensitive teacher to help educate the vision of the child so that appreciation may occur." Hurwitz, Al, and Stanley Madeja. *The Joyous Vision*. New Jersey: Prentice Hall, 1997.

Assessment

Use the following rubric to evaluate the artwork students make in the Creative Expression activity and to assess students' understanding of the lesson concepts.

Have students complete page 21 or 22 in their *Assessment* books.

	Art History and Culture	Aesthetic Perception	Creative Expression	Art Criticism
3 POINTS	The student can repeat information about both of the artists' use of animals as the subject of the artwork in this lesson.	The student recognizes shapes and understands that they are outlined by lines.	The student's painting shows a clear understanding that lines outline shapes.	The student thoughtfully and honestly evaluates his or her own work using the four steps of art criticism.
2 POINTS	The student can repeat information about one artist's use of an animal as the subject of the artwork in this lesson.	The student recognizes shapes, but does not understand that they are outlined by lines.	The student's painting shows emerging awareness that lines outline shapes.	The student attempts to evaluate his or her own work, but shows an incomplete understanding of evaluation criteria.
1 POINT	The student cannot repeat any information about the artists' use of an animal as the subject of the artwork in this lesson.	The student does not recognize shapes.	The student's painting shows no understanding that lines outline shapes.	The student makes no attempt to evaluate his or her own artwork.

Assessment, p. 21

Name _____ Date _____

Lines Outline Shapes

Lesson **1** UNIT 2

For the teacher: Use the following prompt for this activity.
Using a crayon, draw the outline of the shape of an art tool, such as a paintbrush.

Level 1   Unit 2 • Shape   **21**

Lesson 2 — Geometric Shapes

Overview

Lesson 2 introduces students to geometric shapes, including circles, squares, triangles, and rectangles.

Objectives

Art History and Culture
To recognize that artists use geometric shapes for realistic and nonobjective subjects
NSAE 2.a; 3.a

Creative Expression
To create a geometric shape design
NSAE 1.a; 1.c; 1.d

Aesthetic Perception
To identify geometric shapes by name and locate them in art
NSAE 2.a

Art Criticism
To evaluate one's own artwork using the four steps of art criticism
NSAE 1.b; 2.b; 3.a; 5.c

Vocabulary ⭐ Reading

Review the following vocabulary words with students before beginning the lesson.

geometric shape figura geométrica—a precise mathematical shape, such as a circle, square, rectangle, or triangle.

Definitions for the following words appear as art on **Student Edition** page 72 and in the student glossary:

circle círculo   **square** cuadrado   **rectangle** rectángulo
triangle triángulo

See page 89B for additional Spanish vocabulary resources.

Art Journal: Vocabulary
Have students add these words to the Vocabulary section of their Art Journals.

Lesson Materials
- black construction paper (at least 9″ × 12″)
- newsprint or copy paper (cut into 4″ × 4½″ pieces)
- crayons with paper peeled off
- scissors
- glue or glue sticks
- rubbing plates
- geometric shape templates for students to trace (can be made from posterboard or corrugated cardboard)

Alternate Materials
- found textures

Program Resources
- *Reading and Writing Test Prep.,* pp. 20–21
- *Transparency 8*
- *Flash Cards 7* and *9–11*
- *Artist Profiles,* pp. 25, 41
- *Animals Through History Time Line*
- *Assessment,* pp. 23–24
- *Large Prints 15 She-Ba* and *16 Dos Niños (Two Children)*
- *Art Around the World*

Concept Trace
Geometric Shapes
Introduced: Level K, Unit 2, Lesson 2
Reinforced: Level 2, Unit 1, Lesson 5

Lesson 2 Arts Integration   NSAE 6.a

Theatre
Complete Unit 2, Lesson 2, on pages 38–39 of *Theatre Arts Connections.*

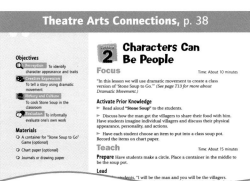

Music
Borrow a poster of orchestral instruments from the library or music teacher. As you name each one, have students find geometric shapes within each.

Movement & Dance
Identify the geometric shapes found inside other geometric shapes in the Auguste Herbin painting. Have students create these shapes in small groups, then repeat, incorporating level changes within each shape. For example, have students make a square on the floor by sitting and then create a circle inside it by standing.

ocus

Time: About 10 minutes

Activate Prior Knowledge

"What shapes can you name?" "¿Qué figuras pueden nombrar?"

■ List students' responses. Explain that geometric shapes are special because although they can differ in size, they are formed the same way every time. Explain that if two students were told to draw a geometric shape (such as a circle), their drawings would be very similar. However if two students are told to draw a non-geometric shape (for instance, the shape of a fish), their drawings would probably be very different.

Using Literature ⭐ Reading

■ Read *I Read Signs* by Tana Hoban. Many geometric shapes can be found in the photographs of signs.

Thematic Connection

■ **Safety:** Discuss with students that safety symbols, such as stop signs, often have distinct shapes to make them easily recognizable.

Introduce the Art

Look
NSAE 1.b; 2.b

"Let's look for geometric shapes in the paintings." "Vamos a observar las figuras geométricas en las pinturas".

Comparing and Contrasting ⭐ Reading

■ Ask students which painting has more easily identifiable geometric shapes and why. It is easier to identify the shapes in *Life No. 1* because it is a nonobjective painting and the shapes are simply geometric shapes, whereas the shapes in *Le Pont Saint-Michel in Paris* represent real objects. Also the shapes in *Life No. 1* are a single color, while the shapes in *Le Pont Saint-Michel in Paris* may have more than one color.

🏺 Art History and Culture

Discuss with students that artists create art about many subjects. Sometimes the subject is something the artist sees in the world and sometimes it is not.
NSAE 2.a; 3.a; 5.a

💻 **Web Connection**
Visit **www.tangram.i-p.com** for online puzzles using geometric shapes.

Geometric Shapes

Look at the paintings on these pages. The artists used geometric shapes in their works of art.

◀ **Auguste Herbin.** (French). *Vie No. 1 (Life No. 1)*. 1950.
....
Oil on canvas. 57 × 38 inches (144.78 × 96.52 cm.). Albright-Knox Art Gallery, Buffalo, New York.

🏺 Art History and Culture

Le Pont Saint-Michel in Paris shows a real place. The artist lived near the river. He made many paintings of it.

🏺 Art History and Culture

Auguste Herbin

Auguste Herbin (ō gōōst âr ban´) (1882–1960) was born in France and studied art in Paris. Herbin traveled around Europe, met many artists, and explored different styles of painting. His artwork became more simple and less detailed until he developed the symbolic style seen in *Life No. 1*. Herbin was France's leading geometrical abstractionist. In abstract painting, the artist seeks to convey meaning using color and shape rather than recognizable objects.

See pages 16–21 and 24–25 for more about subject matter and art history.

Artist Profiles, p. 25

Artist Profile
Auguste Herbin
1882-1960

Auguste Herbin (ō gūst´ âr´ ban) was born in France and studied at the École des Beaux-Arts. Later he went to other countries to paint. In Italy, he noticed how different kinds of light changed the way things look. From then on he tried to ignore little details and paint only the main part of his subject. Herbin was enthusiastic and curious and loved his work. During the last years of his life Herbin created tapestry designs.

▲ **Albert Marquet.** (French).
Le Pont Saint-Michel in Paris.
1908.

Oil on canvas. 25⅝ × 31⅞ inches
(65.09 × 80.96 cm.). The State
Pushkin Museum, Moscow, Russia.

Study both works of art to find
geometric shapes.

▶ What shapes can you name?

🔍 Aesthetic Perception

Design Awareness Look around. Do you see any
geometric shapes?

🏺 Art History and Culture

Albert Marquet   NSAE 5.b

Albert Marquet (äl ber´ mär kā´) (1875–1947) was born in France.
He studied art in Paris, where he met and became good friends
with Henri Matisse. They even exhibited their artworks together.
Marquet lived on the Seine and made many paintings depicting
the river at different times of the day and in different weather
conditions.

See pages 16–21 and 24–25 for more about subject matter and
art history.

Artist Profiles, p. 41

● Artist Profile ●
Albert Marquet
1875–1947

Albert Marquet (äl ber´ mär kā´), the only
son of a railway clerk, was born in Bordeaux,
France. When he was only 16, he went to
Paris to study art at the École des Beaux-
Arts. Marquet experimented with new
styles of painting, and during the early
1900s his works gained popularity. Marquet
traveled more and more as he grew older,
painting scenes from cities across Europe
and northern Africa.

◀**Charles Camoin.** (French).
Portrait of Albert Marquet. 1904.
Oil on canvas. 36½ × 28½ inches (92 × 72.5 cm.).

Study

▶ *Life No. 1* has squares, rectangles, circles,
triangles, and semicircles. *Le Pont Saint-
Michel in Paris* has squares, rectangles,
circles, and triangles.

Additional Study Questions

▶ What kinds of lines make the shapes in
each painting? The shapes in *Life No. 1* are
made with smooth lines. The squares,
rectangles, and triangles are outlined with
perfectly straight lines. The lines used in
Le Pont Saint-Michel in Paris are rougher
and less precise.

▶ In each painting, do any of the shapes
seem more important than others? Why?
Shapes that are larger than others or
appear more frequently seem more
important.

■ For more examples of art from Europe see
Art Around the World.

📓 Art Journal: Concepts

Have students draw the four
geometric shapes taught in this lesson in
the Concepts section of their Art Journals.

🔍 Aesthetic Perception

Design Awareness Discuss with students
geometric shapes they find in their
surroundings. Discuss why those objects
may have been designed with geometric
shapes. A geometric design can give an
object uniformity and compatibility—books
fit neatly on a shelf when they have similar
shapes.

Developing Visual Literacy Have students
imagine that each painting extends beyond
the current borders. What would they see?
Have students make a sketch of what they
could add to "extend" the edge of each
painting. (For instance, add another row of
shapes in *Life No. 1* or more buildings in *Le
Pont Saint-Michel in Paris*.)

💻 Web Connection

Visit **www.pariswater.com/ponts/** to learn about
and see photographs of the bridges crossing the
Seine River.

Teach

Time: About 40 minutes

"What shapes have names?" "¿Qué figuras tienen nombres?"

- Read and discuss Using Geometric Shapes on page 72.

Practice

Materials: None

- Divide the class into four groups. Assign each group one of the four geometric shapes on page 72.

- Record the number of times each group finds their shape. Which group found the most objects with their shape? Discuss why that shape was found so frequently.

Creative Expression

NSAE 1.a; 1.c; 1.d

Materials: black construction paper (at least 9" × 12"), newsprint or copy paper (cut into 4" × 4½" pieces), crayons (with paper peeled off), scissors, glue or glue sticks, rubbing plates, geometric shape templates for students to trace (can be made from posterboard or corrugated cardboard)

Alternate Materials: found textures

- Distribute materials and have students follow the directions on page 73.

- Review the Technique Tips on page 215 for information about texture rubbings. Demonstrate this technique and have students practice it before doing the Creative Expression activity.

- Review the Technique Tips on pages 221–223 for information about making a collage.

- See the Activity Tips on page 235 for visual examples of this lesson's activity.

- When students are finished, you might want to have them glue their designs onto square paper. Then assemble the squares on a large piece of paper to make a class "quilt."

Art Journal: Brainstorming

Have students brainstorm ideas for ways they could arrange geometric shapes to make a design. Have them make sketches of their ideas in their Art Journals and then choose one to make in the Creative Expression activity.

Using Geometric Shapes

Some shapes are **geometric shapes.**

Geometric shapes have names.

circle

square

triangle

rectangle

Practice

Find objects that look like geometric shapes.

1. Form a group with other students.

2. Look around the classroom for objects with the shape your teacher tells you.

3. Count the objects your group finds.

Differentiated Instruction

Reteach

Review geometric shapes using **Flash Cards 7** and **9–11.** Then place a clear transparency over **Transparency 8.** Have students identify geometric shapes. Trace them in red.

Special Needs

Adaptations: Put a small piece of tape underneath the object to be rubbed in order to keep it in place. Also, the use of lightweight typing or computer printing paper will make the object partially visible as the student produces the rubbing.

ELL Tips

Create paper cutouts of each of the geometric shapes. Say the name of a shape and have students pick up the appropriate shape, or hold up the shape and have students identify it by name.

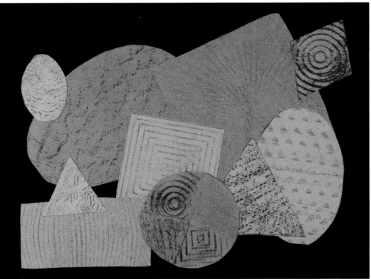

◄ **Lauren Faske.**
Age 6.

Think about how this student used geometric shapes.

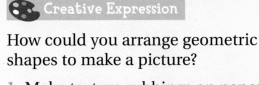 **Creative Expression**

How could you arrange geometric shapes to make a picture?

1. Make texture rubbings on paper.

2. Trace the outlines of geometric shapes on the paper.

3. Cut out the shapes. Arrange them to make a design. Glue the shapes to black paper.

 Art Criticism

Analyze Which colors and shapes look the most important? Why?

 **Reflect**   Time: About 5 minutes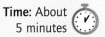

Review and Assess
"What are the names of the geometric shapes you learned about?" "¿Qué nombres tienen las figuras que estudiaron?"

Think
The student arranged a design of circles, ovals, squares, rectangles, and triangles.

■ Have students look for geometric shapes in *Large Prints 15 She-Ba* and *16 Dos Niños (Two Children)*.

Informal Assessment

 **Art Journal: Critical Thinking**
Have students ask themselves the Art Criticism questions, and then write or sketch their answers to the Analyze question in their Art Journals.
NSAE 1.b; 2.b; 3.a; 5.c

 Art Criticism

Describe ► Which geometric shapes did you use in your design?

Analyze ► Which colors and shapes look the most important? Why?

Interpret ► Do the shapes remind you of real or imaginary objects?

Decide ► Did you like using only geometric shapes in your artwork?

■ For standardized-format test practice using this lesson's art content, see pages 20–21 in *Reading and Writing Test Preparation.*

✦ **Art Across the Curriculum** ✦

Use these ideas to reinforce art concepts across the curriculum.
NSAE 6.b

★ **Poetry Writing** Have students use the writing process to write a shape poem about something that has a geometric shape.

★ **Math** Provide students with cutouts of geometric shapes and have them experiment combining shapes to make other geometric shapes. (For example, two equal size triangles can form a square.)

★ **Science** Have students create a simple spreadsheet to record and compare the number of sides each geometric shape has.

★ **Social Studies** Have students use squares and rectangles to make a calendar.

★ **Technology** Have students experiment with Shape tools in the computer's paint and draw program. Visit **SRAonline.com** to print detailed instructions for this activity.

Geometric Shapes

Extra! For the Art Specialist

Time: About 45 minutes

Focus

Place a clear transparency over *Transparency 8.* Trace the geometric shapes as students identify them. In which artwork were the shapes easier to identify?

Teach

Have students follow the directions to complete their collages. Would the creatures be different if students had used free-form shapes instead of geometric shapes?

Reflect

Guide students through evaluation of their works of art using the four steps of art criticism. (See pages 28–29 for more about art criticism.) Encourage students to locate geometric shapes in the classroom.

Alternate Activity

Materials:
- 12" × 18" newsprint
- construction paper
- crayons
- found textures
- scissors
- glue or glue sticks
- markers

1. Have students fold a sheet of newsprint into eight sections. Using different colors of crayons, make a different texture rubbing in each of the sections.

2. Have students draw a geometric shape in each section, then cut out the shapes. Have students arrange and glue the shapes on a sheet of construction paper to make the shape of an imaginary creature.

3. Have students add details to the creatures and backgrounds using crayons and markers.

Research in Art Education

Artistically talented students engage in more self-regulatory behavior in classes with arts integration than in classes without arts integration. ("Using Art Processes to Enhance Academic Self-Regulation" in *Critical Links*, p. 64) These self-regulatory behaviors include paying attention, problem solving, asking questions, taking risks, and being prepared. Because shapes are useful in many subject areas, such as mathematics or physical education, art lessons about shapes can be easily integrated into other subjects.

Assessment

Use the following rubric to evaluate the artwork students make in the Creative Expression activity and to assess students' understanding of the lesson concepts.

Have students complete page 23 or 24 in their *Assessment* books.

	Art History and Culture	Aesthetic Perception	Creative Expression	Art Criticism
3 POINTS	The student recognizes that artists use geometric shapes in artworks with nonobjective subjects, as well as realistic subjects.	The student can identify by name all the geometric shapes taught in the lesson and locate them in art.	The student's shape design clearly illustrates geometric shapes.	The student thoughtfully and honestly evaluates his or her own work using the four steps of art criticism.
2 POINTS	The student shows an incomplete understanding that geometric shapes can be used in artworks with nonobjective, as well as realistic subjects.	The student can identify by name some of the geometric shapes taught in the lesson and locate them in art.	The student's shape design shows some awareness of geometric shapes.	The student attempts to evaluate his or her own work, but shows an incomplete understanding of evaluation criteria.
1 POINT	The student does not recognize that artists use geometric shapes in their artworks.	The student cannot identify by name the geometric shapes taught in the lesson or locate them in art.	The student's shape design shows no understanding of geometric shapes.	The student makes no attempt to evaluate his or her own artwork.

Assessment, p. 23

Name _____ Date _____

Lesson 2 UNIT 2

Geometric Shapes

1	2

For the teacher: Use the following prompts for this activity.
1. Using a crayon, draw a geometric shape in box 1.
2. Draw a different geometric shape in box 2.

Level 1

Unit 2 • Shape **23**

Lesson 3 · Free-Form Shapes
Overview

Lesson 3 introduces students to free-form shapes, which are shapes that are not geometric. Artists use free-form shapes to show living things.

Objectives

Art History and Culture
To recognize some sources from which artists get ideas
NSAE 4.a; 4.c

Aesthetic Perception
To locate free-form shapes in art and the environment
NSAE 2.a

Creative Expression
To create a glue and pastel free-form shape picture
NSAE 1.a; 1.c; 1.d

Art Criticism
To evaluate one's own artwork using the four steps of art criticism
NSAE 1.b; 2.b; 3.a; 5.c

Vocabulary ⭐ Reading

Review the following vocabulary word with students before beginning the lesson.

free-form shape figura abstracta—any shape that is not a geometric shape

See page 89B for additional Spanish vocabulary resources.

Art Journal: Vocabulary
Have students add this word to the Vocabulary section of their Art Journals.

Lesson Materials
- old magazines
- large construction paper
- pencils
- black glue (made by adding black tempera or India ink to white glue)
- assorted dry pastels

Alternate Materials
- books
- watercolors

Program Resources
- *Reading and Writing Test Prep.*, pp. 22–23
- *Transparency 9*
- *Flash Card 8*
- *Artist Profiles*, pp. 37, 54
- *Animals Through History Time Line*
- *Assessment*, pp. 25–26
- *Large Prints 15* She-Ba and *16* Dos Niños (Two Children)
- *The National Museum of Women in the Arts Collection*

Concept Trace
Free-Form Shapes
Introduced: Level K, Unit 2, Lesson 3
Reinforced: Level 2, Unit 1, Lesson 6

Lesson 3 Arts Integration NSAE 6.a

Theatre
Complete Unit 2, Lesson 3, on pages 40–41 of *Theatre Arts Connections.*

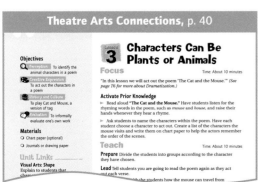

Music

When a melody is fast it might be difficult to describe any specific geometric shapes. Listen to *Symphony no. 4, Movement 4,* by Piotr Ilyich Tchaikovsky. Which instruments seem to be most free-form, the high or the low? Does it ever change?

Movement & Dance
Have students study the painting by Henri Rousseau and select an animal or plant from the painting as an idea to work with. Have students copy the shapes in the painting using their bodies. Then ask students to explore ways to move their shape, by incorporating changes in level, energy, and speed.

Focus

Time: About 10 minutes

Activate Prior Knowledge

"What are some different shapes of leaves you have seen?" "¿Cuáles son algunas figuras y algunos colores de hojas que han visto?"

- Discuss students' responses. Bring leaves of different shapes and sizes to class or draw examples of different leaves on the board. Explain that although they are all leaves, their shapes are not all the same.

Using Literature ⭐ Reading

- Read *The Old Woman Who Loved to Read* by John Winch. The free-form shapes of the woman, animals, and plants can be contrasted with the geometric shapes of the nonliving things such as books and plates.

Thematic Connection ⭐ Science

- **Plants:** Discuss with students how plants change shape and appearance as they grow. Talk about what plants need to grow and to survive.

Introduce the Art

Look
NSAE 3.a

"Let's look at these two paintings." "Vamos a observar estas dos pinturas".

Summarizing ⭐ Reading

- Have students describe the subject matter in each painting. *The Equatorial Jungle* shows jungle animals hiding in the foliage. They are surrounded by trees, flowers, and other plants. *Hong Shancha: Red Camellia* shows a Chinese girl standing behind a large red flower. Two birds are sitting on the flower stem.

🏺 Art History and Culture

Share with students the information from the Art History and Culture sections on pages 74 and 75 about where each artist found inspiration for the subjects of their paintings.

NSAE 4.c; 5.b

💻 Web Connection

Visit the National Gallery of Art's web site for teachers, **www.nga.gov/education/classroom/**, for more information about Rousseau.

Free-Form Shapes

Look at the shapes of the animals and the leaves. The shape of a living thing is a free-form shape.

◀ **Henri Rousseau.** (French). *The Equatorial Jungle.* 1909.
Oil on canvas. 55¼ × 51 inches (140.6 × 129.5 cm). National Gallery of Art, Washington, D.C.

🏺 Art History and Culture

Henri Rousseau never went to the jungle, but he painted many jungle scenes. He got his ideas from reading books and visiting the zoo.

🏺 Art History and Culture

Henri Rousseau

Henri Rousseau (än rē´ rōō sō´) (1844–1910) worked as a toll collector with the Paris Customs Office in order to support his wife and nine children. He never received any art training. In his free time, he taught himself to paint. Rousseau often displayed his work at a show of independent artists. Anyone could enter artwork in the show as long as they paid a fee. Rousseau painted many jungle scenes, although he had never actually been to such an exotic place. The plants are inspired by those Rousseau saw when he visited botanical gardens around Paris. The monkeys are modeled on animals Rousseau saw in a book and at the Paris zoo.

See pages 16–21 and 24–25 for more about subject matter and art history.

Artist Profiles, p. 54

Artist Profile ◆
Henri Rousseau
1844–1910
Henri Rousseau (än rē´ rōō sō´) was born in a small town in France. When he was young he played the clarinet. He also spent some time in the French army. At the age of 25 he moved to Paris, where he spent most of his life. For a long time he worked as a customs clerk. He never went to art school. He learned to paint by practicing in gardens around the city.

◀ **Henri Rousseau.** (French). *Myself* (detail). 1890.

◀ **Hung Liu.** (Chinese American). *Hong Shancha: Red Camellia.* 2002.

Oil on canvas. 60 × 48 inches (152.4 × 121.92 cm.). Bernice Steinbaum Gallery, Miami, Florida.

Study both works of art to find free-form shapes.

▶ What free-form shapes do you see?

🔍 **Aesthetic Perception**

Seeing Like an Artist Look around. What things can you find that have free-form shapes?

🏺 Art History and Culture

Hung Liu

Hung Liu (hung lē ōō´) (1948–) was born in China and lived the first part of her life there. She received two art degrees from two colleges in China. In the 1970s Liu gave art lessons on her own weekly children's television show. In 1984 Liu immigrated to the United States. She became a professor of art at Mills College in California. Her artwork is inspired by historical photographs of Chinese people. Liu often includes plants and animals in her paintings that were symbols traditionally used in Chinese art.

See pages 16–21 and 24–25 for more about subject matter and art history.

Artist Profiles, p. 37

◀ Artist Profile ▶

Hung Liu
b. 1948

Hung Liu (hung lē ōō´) was born in Changchun, China. In the year she was born, her father was taken as a political prisoner. She did not see him again until Father's Day, 50 years later. Although she was a stellar student, political events disrupted her education. She finally graduated from Beijing Teacher's College in 1972, and went on to teach art. Liu began giving lessons in art on her weekly television program, *How to Draw and Paint,* which became extremely popular.

Study

▶ The free-form shapes in *The Equatorial Jungle* are the leaves, the trees, the animals, and the flowers. The free-form shapes in *Hong Shancha: Red Camellia* are the flower, the birds, the leaves, and the girl.

■ For more examples of narrative art see *The National Museum of Women in the Arts Collection.*

📔 **Art Journal: Concepts**
Encourage students to make sketches in the Concepts section of their Art Journals to illustrate the difference between geometric shapes and freeform shapes.

🔍 **Aesthetic Perception**

Seeing Like an Artist Discuss the free-form shapes students find. They should notice that people have free-form shapes. Anything else in the classroom that is living, such as plants or a classroom pet, will also have free-form shapes. Some objects, such as clothing, will have free-form shapes.

Developing Visual Literacy Have students imagine that each artwork is an illustration accompanying a story. What would each story be about? If there were other works of art illustrating the stories, what would they look like? Invite students to share their ideas.

💻 **Web Connection**
Visit Hung Liu's Web site at **www.kelliu.com.**

Teach

Time: About two 20-minute periods

"How are free-form shapes different from geometric shapes?" "¿En qué se diferencian las figuras abstractas de las figuras geométricas?"

- Read and discuss Using Free-Form Shapes on page 76.

Practice

Materials: old magazines

Materials: books

- Have students look through magazines to find free-form shapes. Discuss their findings.

Creative Expression

NSAE 1.a; 1.c; 1.d

Materials: old magazines, large construction paper, pencils, black glue (made by adding black tempera or India ink to white glue), assorted dry pastels

Alternate Materials: watercolors

- Distribute materials and have students follow the directions on page 77.
- Review the Technique Tips on page 216 for information about using pastels.
- See the Activity Tips on page 236 for visual examples of this lesson's activity.
- Allow the glue to dry overnight before students color the shapes.

Art Journal: Brainstorming

Have students make sketches of free-form shapes they found in the magazines in their Art Journals. Have them choose one to do in the Creative Expression activity.

Using Free-Form Shapes

Free-form shapes are not geometric shapes.

  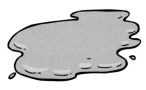

Practice

Look for free-form shapes in magazines.

1. Look for pictures of living things.
2. Can you find other free-form shapes?

Differentiated Instruction

Reteach

Review free-form shapes using **Flash Card 8.** Then have students look through the **Student Edition** or **Large Prints** to find other works of art that use free-form shapes to show living things.

Special Needs

Adaptations: Help students understand the difference between geometric and free-form shapes by asking them to compare the shapes they found in magazines to the ones they identified in lesson 2.

ELL Tips

Create paper cutouts of free-form shapes (using nebulous shapes that will not be recognizable as objects) and mix them with the cutouts of geometric shapes that were used in the last lesson. Have students sort the geometric shapes into one pile and the free-form shapes into another pile.

Think about how this student used a free-form shape.

◄ **Jensen Palmer.** Age 7.

Review and Assess

"What kinds of things have free-form shapes?" "¿Qué tipos de cosas son figuras abstractas?"

Think

The student used the free-form shape of a flower.

■ Have students look for free-form shapes in *Large Prints 15 She-Ba* and *16 Dos Niños (Two Children).*

Informal Assessment

Art Journal: Critical Thinking
Have students ask themselves the Art Criticism questions, and then write or sketch to answer the Analyze question in their Art Journals.
NSAE 1.b; 2.b; 3.a; 5.c

Creative Expression

What free-form shapes did you find?

1. Sketch a free-form shape you found in a magazine.
2. Go over the lines with black glue.
3. When the glue is dry, color your picture with pastels.

Art Criticism

Analyze What kinds of lines did you use to make your shape?

Unit 2 • Lesson 3   **77**

Art Criticism

Describe ► What object did you draw?

Analyze ► What kinds of lines did you use to make your shape?

Interpret ► Does your object look realistic?

Decide ► Did you create a free-form shape?

■ For standardized-format test practice using this lesson's art content, see pages 22–23 in *Reading and Writing Test Preparation.*

Art Across the Curriculum

Use these ideas to reinforce art concepts across the curriculum.
NSAE 6.b

★ **Personal Writing** Have students pretend they have taken a vacation to the location depicted in one of the artworks, and then have them write a postcard to a friend.

★ **Math** Have students write an addition sentence to describe the number of animals in each picture.

★ **Science** Ask students what they think the animals in *The Equatorial Landscape* eat. Discuss ways the animals in the paintings meet their basic need for food.

★ **Social Studies** Help students locate China, Hung Liu's birthplace, on a map or globe.

★ **Technology** Have students use the computer's paint and draw program to create free-form shapes. They can use the Airbrush tool to create shapes with rough lines and the Paintbrush tool to create shapes with smooth lines. Visit **SRAonline.com** to print detailed instructions for this activity.

Free-Form Shapes

Extra! For the Art Specialist

Time: About 45 minutes

Focus

Use **Transparency 9** to have students identify free-form shapes. Where do students see free-form shapes in the classroom?

Teach

Have students follow the directions to complete the Alternate Activity. How many different free-form shapes did students create?

Reflect

Guide students through evaluation of their works of art using the four steps of art criticism. (See pages 28–29 for more about art criticism.)

Alternate Activity

Materials:
- tagboard or posterboard
- 12" × 18" black construction paper
- pencils
- glue
- chalk pastels or oil pastels

1. Have students cut a free-form shape as large as their hand from the tagboard or posterboard.

2. Have students trace the shape several times on a sheet of black construction paper, sometimes overlapping the shapes or letting the shape run off the edge of the paper.

3. Have students outline the shapes with liquid glue. When the glue is dry, have them color the inside of the shapes with pastels.

Research in Art Education

Research continues to try to answer the questions of if and how the arts have an impact on student learning in other subject areas. Some researchers suggest that the relationship between the arts and other subject areas "may not be as unidirectional—from the arts to other disciplines—as other studies have implied. Rather, the relationship may be more dynamic and interactive." ("Learning In and Through the Arts: Curriculum Implications" in *Champions of Change*, p. 43) As students discuss the use of free-form shapes to depict plants and animals, there is an interactive relationship between the arts and students' scientific understanding of living things.

Assessment

Use the following rubric to evaluate the artwork students make in the Creative Expression activity and to assess students' understanding of the lesson concepts.

	Art History and Culture	Aesthetic Perception	Creative Expression	Art Criticism
3 POINTS	The student can identify sources from which artists get their ideas.	The student accurately identifies free-form shapes in art and the environment.	The student's glue picture shows a clear understanding of free-form shapes.	The student thoughtfully and honestly evaluates his or her own work using the four steps of art criticism.
2 POINTS	The student's identification is weak or incomplete.	The student shows some awareness of free-form shapes in the art and the environment.	The student's glue picture shows some awareness of free-form shapes.	The student attempts to evaluate his or her own work, but shows an incomplete understanding of evaluation criteria.
1 POINT	The student cannot identify sources from which artists get their ideas.	The student cannot identify free-form shapes in the art and the environment.	The student's glue picture shows no understanding of free-form shapes.	The student makes no attempt to evaluate his or her own artwork.

Have students complete page 25 or 26 in their **Assessment** books.

Assessment, p. 25

Name _____ Date _____ Lesson **3** UNIT 2

Free-Form Shapes

1	2

For the teacher: Use the following prompt for this activity.
1. Using a crayon, draw a geometric shape in box 1.
2. Draw a free-form shape in box 2.

Level 1   Unit 2 • Shape   **25**

Lesson 4 · Overview · People Shapes

Lesson 4 teaches students that people's bodies are free-form shapes.

Objectives

Art History and Culture

To recognize that artists can use their artwork to express their culture
NSAE 4.a; 4.b; 4.c; 5.a

Creative Expression

To create a painting of one's self using the free-form outline of one's body
NSAE 1.a; 1.c; 1.d

Aesthetic Perception

To recognize that people's bodies are free-form shapes

Art Criticism

To evaluate one's own artwork using the four steps of art criticism
NSAE 1.b; 2.b; 3.a; 5.c

Vocabulary ⭐ Reading

Review the following vocabulary word with students before beginning the lesson.

free-form shape figura abstracta—any shape that is not a geometric shape

See page 89B for additional Spanish vocabulary resources.

Art Journal: Vocabulary

Have students add this word to the Vocabulary section of their Art Journals.

Lesson Materials

- pencils
- tempera paints
- large brushes
- water dishes
- 3–4 feet of mural paper per student
- scissors
- paper towels

Alternate Materials
- crayons
- markers

Program Resources

- *Reading and Writing Test Prep.*, pp. 24–25
- *Transparency 10*
- *Artist Profiles*, pp. 6, 20
- *Animals Through History Time Line*
- *Assessment*, pp. 27–28
- *Large Prints 15* She-Ba and *16* Dos Niños (Two Children)
- *Art Around the World*

Concept Trace

People Shapes
Introduced: Level K, Unit 2, Lesson 5

Reinforced: Level 3, Unit 1, Lesson 6

Lesson 4 Arts Integration NSAE 6.a

Theatre

Complete Unit 2, Lesson 4, on pages 42–43 of *Theatre Arts Connections.*

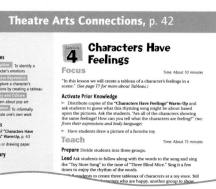

Music

 Listen to *Mi Cuerpo.* There are six phrases to this song. The first two have the same distinctive melodic shape. The next four all have the same contour as each other but contrast the first two. Which start with leaps upward?

Movement & Dance

Have students walk through space, weaving in and around each other to the beat of a drum or other percussive instrument. When the drum stops, call out a specific shape for the students to freeze in. Repeat, this time giving the students 4 counts to make the shape after the drum stops.

Focus

Time: About 10 minutes

Activate Prior Knowledge

"What things do you help your family with around the house?" "¿En qué ayudan a sus familias en sus casas?"

- Discuss students' responses. Have students describe different movements they might make when doing chores, such as leaning over or reaching for something.

Using Literature ⭐ Reading

- Read *Miss Malarkey Doesn't Live in Room 10* by Judy Finchler. The illustrations by Kevin O'Malley show many peoples' shapes and parts.

Thematic Connection ⭐

- **Body:** Discuss the different parts of the human body and their purposes. Talk about how people's features can vary despite having similar parts.

Introduce the Art

Look
NSAE 3.a

"Let's take a close look at these paintings." "Vamos a mirar detalladamente estas pinturas".

Summarizing ⭐ Reading

- Have students describe what they see in each painting. In *Naranjas (Oranges)* the setting is a yard surrounded by a fence. There are a large orange tree, some cacti, a clothesline and clothes basket, and six dogs. Five people are gathering oranges from the ground and in the tree. In *Ice Cream Cones* the setting is a sidewalk. The girls are standing in front of a shop window eating ice cream. There is a fire hydrant on the right.

🏺 Art History and Culture

Share with students information from the Art History and Culture sections for each artist. Discuss that Carmen Lomas Garza portrayed scenes from her culture in her artwork. She painted events she experienced in her life. Isabel Bishop painted scenes of people she observed in Union Square. They did not necessarily share her culture.
NSAE 3.a; 4.a; 4.b; 4.c; 5.a; 5.b

💻 Web Connection

Visit www.carmenlomasgarza.com to learn more about the artist and her work.

People Shapes

Look at the paintings on these pages. The artists used free-form shapes to paint people.

◄ **Carmen Lomas Garza.** (American). *Naranjas (Oranges).*
Gouache. 20 × 14 inches (50.8 × 35.56 cm.). Collection of Mr. and Mrs. Ira Schneider, Scottsdale, Arizona.

🏺 Art History and Culture

Carmen Lomas Garza makes art to show things she did with her family when she was a child.

🏺 Art History and Culture

Carmen Lomas Garza

Carmen Lomas Garza (kär mən lō mäs gär´ sa) (1948–   ), a Hispanic-American artist, was born in Kingsville, Texas, and grew up in a bilingual household. She began painting at age 13. She studied art throughout school and received a graduate degree from San Francisco State University. Garza creates art to celebrate her Hispanic-American culture as well as to show the similarities and differences to other cultures. Many of Garza's paintings are of family activities or of everyday people doing everyday tasks. Many of the scenes reflect her childhood memories.

See pages 16–21 and 24–25 for more about subject matter and art history.

Artist Profiles, p. 20

Artist Profile

Carmen Lomas Garza
b. 1948

Carmen Lomas Garza (kär´ mən lō´ mäs gär´ sä) was born in Kingsville, Texas. She grew up in a Hispanic home where both Spanish and English were spoken. When she and her brother started school, many of their classmates made fun of them for speaking English with an accent. Garza often felt that she did not fit in. This feeling led her to develop stronger ties with her family and community. She decided she wanted to be an artist when she was only 13 years old. She studied art at the Texas Arts and Industry University and earned a master's degree from San Francisco State University.

Study both works of art.

▶ What people shapes do you see?

▶ What other free-form shapes do you see?

◀ **Isabel Bishop.**
(American). *Ice Cream Cones.* 1942.
....
Oil and egg tempera on fiberboard. $33\frac{7}{8} \times 20$ inches (86.04 × 50.8 cm.). Museum of Fine Arts, Boston, Massachusetts.

Aesthetic Perception

Seeing Like an Artist Trace in the air the outline of a classmate. What kind of shape did you make?

Art History and Culture

Isabel Bishop

Isabel Bishop (i´ za bel bi´ shəp) (1902–1988) was born in Cincinnati, Ohio but raised in Detroit, Michigan. She began to take weekend art classes when she was twelve years old. She graduated from high school at the age of fifteen and then moved to New York, New York. She studied illustration at the New York School of Design for Women, and then studied painting at the Art Students League. Bishop rented a studio in Union Square, where she observed strangers as they hurried to work, enjoyed a break, or walked to the store. She sketched as she watched, and later made larger drawings or paintings from her sketches.

See pages 16–21 and 24–25 for more about subject matter and art history.

Artist Profiles, p. 6

Artist Profile
Isabel Bishop
1902-1988
Isabel Bishop (iz´ a bel bish´ ap) was born in Cincinnati, Ohio. A year later, her family moved to a run-down neighborhood in Detroit, Michigan, where her father was employed as the principal of a nearby high school. Her parents didn't think the neighborhood children made good playmates, so Bishop spent much of her time alone. She graduated from high school at age 15 and then studied art. She moved to New York City, where she continued to study art and began exhibiting her work. She loved to paint the people in Union Square.

Bishop married in 1934, moved to the suburbs, and had a son. She commuted

Study

▶ In *Naranjas (Oranges)* there are five people—a woman, two girls, and a boy on the ground and a boy in the tree. The people are standing or crouching. In *Ice Cream Cones* there are two girls. One is leaning against the wall and one is standing.

▶ In *Naranjas (Oranges),* other free-form shapes include the dogs, the tree, and the clothing. The fire hydrant in *Ice Cream Cones* is a free-form shape.

■ For more examples of art from North America see *Art Around the World.*

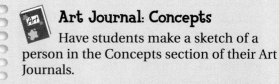

Art Journal: Concepts
Have students make a sketch of a person in the Concepts section of their Art Journals.

Aesthetic Perception

Seeing Like an Artist Discuss with students the shape of a person. Have students try to describe the shape of a person by only talking about the lines they made when they traced the outline (such as curved or horizontal) rather than by naming the parts of a body.

Developing Visual Literacy Have students make inferences about what is happening in each picture. Do these works show families? If not, how do the groups of people know each other? Why are the people in *Naranjas (Oranges)* gathering oranges? What will they do with them? What will the girls in *Ice Cream Cones* do after they eat their ice cream? How do they feel?

Web Connection
Ice Cream Cones is housed at the Museum of Fine Arts in Boston. Visit their web site here: **www.mfa.org**.

 **each**

Time: About 50 minutes

"Let's notice how the shape of human body is made of free-form shapes." *"Vamos a fijarnos en cómo la figura del cuerpo humano está compuesta de figuras abstractas"*.

- Read and discuss Using People Shapes on page 80.

Practice

Materials: crayons, white paper

Alternate Materials: colored pencils

- Distribute the materials. Have students first use their fingers to trace the shape of a body part, then draw the outline of that shape on paper. Make sure that students are not actually putting their hands or feet on paper and tracing them, but instead are drawing the shape they traced with their fingers.

 **Creative Expression**

NSAE 1.a; 1.c; 1.d
Materials: pencils, large brushes, tempera paints, water dishes, 3–4 feet of mural paper per student, scissors, paper towels

Alternate Materials: crayons, markers

- Distribute materials and have students follow the directions on page 81.

- Review the Technique Tips on pages 216–218 for information about painting.

- See the Activity Tips on page 236 for visual examples of this lesson's activity.

- After they have completed the Creative Expression activity, you might want to have students glue on fabrics and papers to add dimension and texture to their clothing.

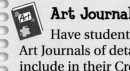 **Art Journal: Brainstorming**

Have students make sketches in their Art Journals of details they would like to include in their Creative Expression activities. NSAE 3.b

Using People Shapes

The human body is a **free-form shape.**

It is made of smaller free-form shapes.

Practice

Draw the free-form shapes of different body parts.

1. Use your finger to trace the outline of a body part, such as your head, ear, or foot.

2. Draw the shape of the outline you traced.

Differentiated Instruction

Reteach

Geometric Shapes

⭐ Math

Draw a human figure with geometric shapes so students see an obvious contrast. Discuss the differences.

Special Needs

Adaptations: Adhere the drawing paper to the floor with tape. This will stabilize the work surface as children paint.

ELL Tips

Create paper cutouts of human silhouettes. Give them to students along with the cutouts that were made in the previous two lessons. Have students sort the shapes into geometric and free-form.

◀ **Jesse Drewa.** Age 7.

Think about how this student made the shape of a person.

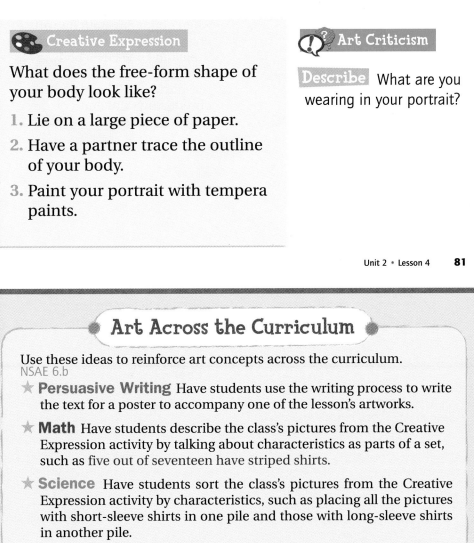

Creative Expression

What does the free-form shape of your body look like?

1. Lie on a large piece of paper.
2. Have a partner trace the outline of your body.
3. Paint your portrait with tempera paints.

Art Criticism

Describe What are you wearing in your portrait?

Art Across the Curriculum

Use these ideas to reinforce art concepts across the curriculum.
NSAE 6.b

★ **Persuasive Writing** Have students use the writing process to write the text for a poster to accompany one of the lesson's artworks.

★ **Math** Have students describe the class's pictures from the Creative Expression activity by talking about characteristics as parts of a set, such as five out of seventeen have striped shirts.

★ **Science** Have students sort the class's pictures from the Creative Expression activity by characteristics, such as placing all the pictures with short-sleeve shirts in one pile and those with long-sleeve shirts in another pile.

★ **Social Studies** Have students discuss how location and culture may be different between the people in *Naranjas (Oranges)* and the girls in *Ice Cream Cones.*

★ **Technology** Have students use the computer's paint and draw program to create a self-portrait. Visit **SRAonline.com** to print detailed instructions for this activity.

Reflect
Time: About 5 minutes

Review and Assess
"What kind of shape do you use to draw people: geometric or free-form?" "¿Qué tipo de figura usan para dibujar a las personas: geométrica o abstracta?"

Think
The student's portrait shows the free-form shape of his body.

■ Have students compare the people shapes in *Large Prints 15 She-Ba* and *16 Dos Niños (Two Children)* to those in the lesson.

Informal Assessment

Art Journal: Critical Thinking
Have students ask themselves the Art Criticism questions and write or sketch their answer to the Describe question in their Art Journals.
NSAE 1.b; 2.b; 3.a; 5.c

Art Criticism

Describe ▶ What are you wearing in your portrait?

Analyze ▶ What makes your artwork look real?

Interpret ▶ What did you put in your portrait to make it look like you?

Decide ▶ What details could you add to make your portrait look even more like you?

■ For standardized-format test practice using this lesson's art content, see pages 24–25 in *Reading and Writing Test Preparation.*

People Shapes

Extra! For the Art Specialist

Time: About 45 minutes

Focus

Use **Transparency 10** to discuss how artists use free-form shapes to depict people in art. Discuss how people would look if artists used geometric shapes to depict them instead.

Teach

Have students complete the Alternate Activity. Create an exhibition of students' self portraits. Can students identify each classmate's portrait?

Reflect

Guide students through evaluation of their works of art using the four steps of art criticism. (See pages 28–29 for more about art criticism.) How many free-form shapes did students combine to make the shape of their bodies?

Alternate Activity

Materials:
- multicultural construction paper
- scissors
- glue or glue sticks
- wrapping paper scraps or fabric
- yarn
- buttons

Have students create a collage self-portrait. Students should first cut from construction paper the shape of their head. Then students may create hair from yarn and eyes from buttons. Students may cut other face and body parts from construction paper, and use the wrapping paper or fabric to cut clothing.

Research in Art Education

Research has shown that the "looking and reasoning skills" learned during visual art training can also be applied to scientific images. ("Investigating the Educational Impact and Potential of the Museum of Modern Art's Visual Thinking Curriculum" in *Critical Links,* p. 142) Students involved in visual arts training showed less circular reasoning and more evidential reasoning when evaluating both fine art images and scientific images. Evaluating one's own body in order to create an accurate self-portrait will build students' observation skills and encourage attention to detail.

Assessment

Use the following rubric to evaluate the artwork students make in the Creative Expression activity and to assess students' understanding of the lesson concepts.

Have students complete page 27 or 28 in their **Assessment** books.

	Art History and Culture	Aesthetic Perception	Creative Expression	Art Criticism
3 POINTS	The student successfully identifies that art can be a reflection of the artist's culture.	The student shows complete understanding that human's bodies are free-form shapes.	The student's painting clearly illustrates that a body is a free-form shape.	The student thoughtfully and honestly evaluates his or her own work using the four steps of art criticism.
2 POINTS	The student's identification is incomplete.	The student shows some awareness that human's bodies are free-form shapes.	The student's painting shows some awareness that a body is a free-form shape.	The student attempts to evaluate his or her own work, but shows an incomplete understanding of evaluation criteria.
1 POINT	The student cannot identify that art can be a reflection of the artist's culture.	The student does not understand that human's bodies are free-form shapes.	The student's painting shows no understanding that a body is a free-form shape.	The student makes no attempt to evaluate his or her own artwork.

Assessment, p. 27

Name _____ Date _____

Lesson 4
UNIT 2

People Shapes

1	2

For the teacher: Use the following prompts for this activity.
1. Using a crayon or a pencil, use free-form shapes to draw a person in box 1.
2. Use geometric shapes to draw a person in box 2.

Level 1   Unit 2 • Shape   **27**

Shapes of People in Action

Lesson 5 teaches that artists can show people in action by changing the position of their body parts.

Objectives

Art History and Culture
To recognize that artists can use different styles of art to depict people
NSAE 2.a; 2.b; 3.a

Creative Expression
To create a drawing with free-form shapes showing movement
NSAE 1.a; 1.c; 1.d; 2.c

Aesthetic Perception
To describe the free-form shapes that indicate movement and motion in the artwork   NSAE 1.b; 2.a; 2.b

Art Criticism
To evaluate one's own artwork using the four steps of art criticism
NSAE 1.b; 2.b; 3.a; 5.c

Vocabulary ⭐ Reading

Review the following vocabulary word with students before beginning the lesson.

position posición—the placement of an object or shape in relation to another

See page 89B for additional Spanish vocabulary resources.

Art Journal: Vocabulary
Have students add this word to the Vocabulary section of their Art Journals.

Lesson Materials
- 12" × 8" white paper
- markers
- crayons

Alternate Materials
- colored pencils

Program Resources
- *Reading and Writing Test Prep.,* pp. 26–27
- *Transparency 11*
- *Artist Profiles,* pp. 18, 35
- *Animals Through History Time Line*
- *Assessment,* pp. 29–30
- *Large Prints 15 She-Ba* and *16 Dos Niños (Two Children)*
- *National Museum of Women in the Arts Collection*

Concept Trace
Shapes of People in Action
Introduced: Level K, Unit 2, Lesson 6

Reinforced: Level 3, Unit 1, Lesson 6

Lesson 5 Arts Integration NSAE 6.a

Theatre
Complete Unit 2, Lesson 5, on pages 44–45 of *Theatre Arts Connections.*

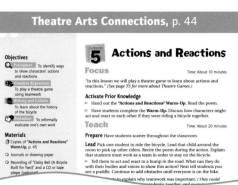

Music
Could you march comfortably to *Waltz of the Flowers* from *The Nutcracker?* It is a style of music that just needs to be danced to. Listen to *Promenade* from *Pictures at an Exhibition* by Modest Mussorgsky. How would you walk through a gallery of beautiful paintings?

Movement & Dance
Have students walk through space, weaving in and around each other to the beat of a drum or other percussive instrument. When the drum stops, call out a specific action for the students to do. Explore each action quickly and in slow motion.

Time: About 10 minutes

Activate Prior Knowledge

"What do you look like when you're sleeping? What do you look like when you're playing?"

"¿Cómo se ven cuando están durmiendo? ¿Cómo se ven cuando están jugando?"

■ Discuss student responses. Discuss how the arms, legs, head, and torso of a person change position depending upon what the person is doing.

Using Literature ⭐ Reading

■ Read *Mommy Works, Daddy Works* by Marika Pedersen and Mikele Hall. The illustrations by Deirdre Betteridge show people doing various jobs.

Thematic Connection ⭐ Social Studies

■ **Social Skills:** People in the lesson's works of art are working or playing in groups. Discuss social skills that make working or playing in a group more enjoyable.

Introduce the Art

Look
NSAE 2.b; 3.a; 4.c; 5.c

"Let's look closely at the busy people in each artwork." "Vamos a mirar detalladamente a las personas que parecen estar muy ocupadas en cada obra de arte".

Making Connections ⭐ Reading

■ Both works of art show groups of people working or playing together. Ask students if either scene reminds them of a time they worked or played with family members or in a group. Student responses will vary.

🏺 Art History and Culture

Discuss with students different styles of art. During the late-twentieth century, artists were using different styles to depict people in works of art. Lawrence used a flat, abstract style to depict people at work and at play in *Builders—Red and Green Ball.* Fish used a very realistic style to depict people playing in *Jump.* NSAE 2.a; 2.b; 3.a

💻 **Web Connection**

Visit www.jacoblawrence.org for more information about Jacob Lawrence.

Look at the shapes of the people in these paintings. Notice the position of each person's arms and legs.

◀ **Jacob Lawrence.** (American). *Builders—Red and Green Ball.* 1979.
Gouache on paper. 30 × 22 inches (76.2 × 55.88 cm). Courtesy of the artist and Francine Seders Gallery LTD., Seattle, Washington.

🏺 Art History and Culture

Jacob Lawrence painted with an abstract style. Janet Fish paints with a realistic style.

🏺 Art History and Culture

Jacob Lawrence

Jacob Lawrence (jā´ kəb lär´ ənz) (1917–2000) was born in Atlantic City, New Jersey, but moved to Harlem in 1930. He attended the Harlem Art Workshop after school. Most of Lawrence's work portrays the lives of African Americans. Lawrence also made paintings about his personal experiences, including serving in the Coast Guard during World War II. Lawrence later became an art professor. He retired from teaching in 1983, but continued to paint until his death.

See pages 16–21 and 24–25 for more about subject matter and art history.

Artist Profiles, p. 35

Artist Profile ♦

Jacob Lawrence
1917–2000

Jacob Lawrence (jā´ kəb lär´ ənz) had parents who met on their migration to the North. His father was born in South Carolina, and his mother in Virginia. Lawrence was born in Atlantic City, New Jersey, in 1917. The family finally settled in Harlem in 1929 at the end of the Harlem Renaissance. Because his mother worked all day, she enrolled Lawrence in the Harlem Art Workshop after school to keep him out of trouble. He had many excellent teachers there, including Charles Alston. Lawrence won a scholarship to the American Artists School. He taught at New York's Pratt Institute from 1958 to 1965. From 1970, he taught at the University of Washington in Seattle, where he also served as head of the

▲ **Janet Fish.** (American).
Jump. 1995.
....
Oil on canvas. 54 × 70 inches
(137.16 × 177.8 cm). D.C. Moore
Gallery, New York, New York.

Study both works of art to find
people in action.

▶ What are the people doing?

▶ How can you tell?

Aesthetic Perception

Seeing Like an Artist Move one hand in the air.
How does the shape of your hand change?

Art History and Culture

Janet Fish

Janet Fish (jan´ ət fish) (1938–   ) was born to a family of artists and
knew from a young age that she also wanted to be an artist. She
was one of the first women to receive a Master of Fine Arts degree
from Yale University. Fish is known for her colorful still lifes that
show the movement of light through glass. Fish's artwork often has
no focal point. Objects fill the entire space of the canvas, and the
painting draws the viewer's eye from one place to another. In *Jump*
the action takes place in the background while the foreground is
filled with inanimate objects.

See pages 16–21 and 24–25
for more about subject
matter and art history.

Artist Profiles, p. 18

Artist Profile
Janet Fish
b. 1938

Janet Fish (jan´ ət fish) earned two degrees
in fine arts from Yale University but
struggled to find work. For a while, she
supported herself by painting bars of soap
for a department store. Since then her large,
lively still lifes have become much admired.
Fish has taught at art schools across the
nation. She now spends half her time in
New York and half in Vermont.

Study

▶ In *Builders—Red and Green Ball* there are
construction workers building at the top
of the painting. At the bottom of the
painting people are playing ball, running,
and pole vaulting. In *Jump*, four children
are jumping into a pool. A woman is
already in the pool and is holding out her
arms to catch a boy. Another boy is in the
pool and is swimming near the edge.

▶ You can tell what each person is doing by
the shape of his or her body. You can also
tell by clues in the picture, such as an
object the person is holding.

■ For more examples of genre art see *The
National Museum of Women in the Arts
Collection.*

Art Journal: Concepts
Ask students what artists do to show
that someone is moving. Have students
show their answers by making sketches in
the Concepts section of their Art Journals.

Aesthetic Perception

Seeing Like an Artist Discuss with students
that depending upon its position the same
hand can have many different shapes.
Students can change the appearance of their
hands in many ways, such as by bending at
the wrists, bending fingers, spreading fingers
apart, and making a fist.

Developing Visual Literacy Have students
compare *Builders—Red and Green Ball* with
Children at Play on page 56. After viewing
two of his works, what ideas do students
have about the work of Jacob Lawrence?
What do they think other works in his
portfolio would look like?

Web Connection
Janet Fish is represented by the D.C. Moore
Gallery in New York City. Visit their Web site
www.artnet.com/dcmoore.html to view more
paintings in Janet Fish's portfolio. Have students
discuss their ideas about Fish's works.

Teach

Time: About 30 minutes

"How can you show a person moving?"
"¿Cómo pueden mostrar a una persona que se mueve?"

- Read and discuss Using Shapes of People in Action on page 84.

- Pantomime a ballerina by holding your hands in the air and twirling around. Have students identify what you are doing. Discuss how they can tell you are a ballerina (because of the position and movement of your arms and legs).

Practice

Materials: None

- Have students follow the directions on page 84.

Creative Expression

NSAE 1.a; 1.c; 1.d; 2.c
Materials: 12″ × 8″ white paper, markers, crayons

Alternate Materials: colored pencils

- Distribute the materials and have students follow the directions on page 85.

- If possible, have a full-length mirror available so students can pose to see how their bodies look. Remind them to take turns and follow safety rules when using the mirror.

- Review the Technique Tips on pages 214–215 for information about using markers and crayons.

- See the Activity Tips on page 237 for visual examples of this lesson's activity.

Art Journal: Brainstorming

Have students brainstorm ideas for games they like to play or activities they like to do by making sketches in their Art Journals. The have students select one and plan how they will show it in the Creative Expression activity.   NSAE 3.b

Using Shapes of People in Action

Changing the **position** of body parts can show how people move.

Practice

Demonstrate movement to your classmates.

1. Decide on a game or sport that you like to play.

2. Pretend to play the game.

3. Have other classmates guess what you are doing. How did they know?

Differentiated Instruction

Reteach
Create silhouettes of athletes playing sports by placing a transparency over a magazine or newspaper picture and tracing the person's outline. Show students the outline and see if they can guess what sport is being played just from the position of the person's body.

Special Needs
Adaptations: To reinforce lesson concepts, students could view works of art that show children at play, such as Pieter Bruegel the Elder's *Children's Games* (1560).

ELL Tips
Find pictures in books or magazines of moving people and still people. Have students identify which pictures have action shapes.

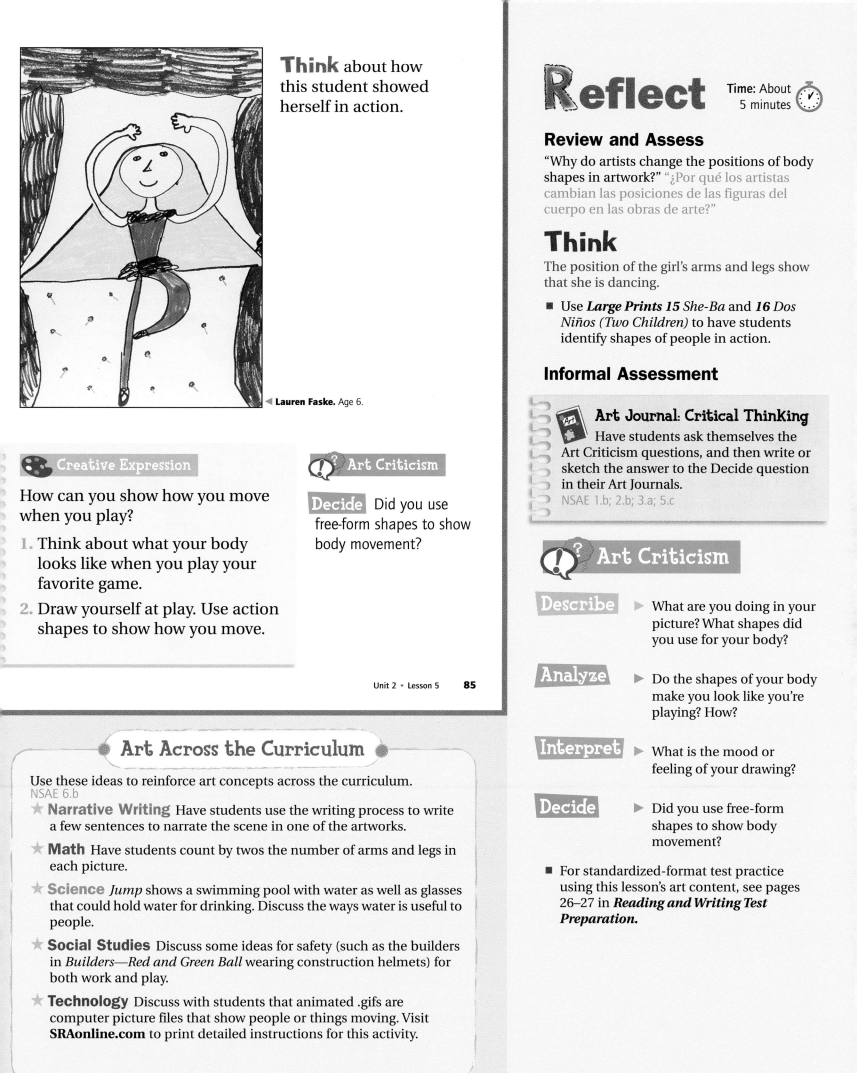

Think about how this student showed herself in action.

◄ **Lauren Faske.** Age 6.

🎨 Creative Expression

How can you show how you move when you play?

1. Think about what your body looks like when you play your favorite game.

2. Draw yourself at play. Use action shapes to show how you move.

💬 Art Criticism

Decide Did you use free-form shapes to show body movement?

Art Across the Curriculum

Use these ideas to reinforce art concepts across the curriculum.
NSAE 6.b

★ **Narrative Writing** Have students use the writing process to write a few sentences to narrate the scene in one of the artworks.

★ **Math** Have students count by twos the number of arms and legs in each picture.

★ **Science** *Jump* shows a swimming pool with water as well as glasses that could hold water for drinking. Discuss the ways water is useful to people.

★ **Social Studies** Discuss some ideas for safety (such as the builders in *Builders—Red and Green Ball* wearing construction helmets) for both work and play.

★ **Technology** Discuss with students that animated .gifs are computer picture files that show people or things moving. Visit **SRAonline.com** to print detailed instructions for this activity.

Reflect   Time: About 5 minutes ⏱

Review and Assess

"Why do artists change the positions of body shapes in artwork?" "¿Por qué los artistas cambian las posiciones de las figuras del cuerpo en las obras de arte?"

Think

The position of the girl's arms and legs show that she is dancing.

■ Use **Large Prints 15** *She-Ba* and **16** *Dos Niños (Two Children)* to have students identify shapes of people in action.

Informal Assessment

Art Journal: Critical Thinking
Have students ask themselves the Art Criticism questions, and then write or sketch the answer to the Decide question in their Art Journals.
NSAE 1.b; 2.b; 3.a; 5.c

💬 Art Criticism

Describe ► What are you doing in your picture? What shapes did you use for your body?

Analyze ► Do the shapes of your body make you look like you're playing? How?

Interpret ► What is the mood or feeling of your drawing?

Decide ► Did you use free-form shapes to show body movement?

■ For standardized-format test practice using this lesson's art content, see pages 26–27 in *Reading and Writing Test Preparation.*

Lesson 5 Wrap-Up

Shapes of People in Action

Extra! For the Art Specialist

Focus

Use **Transparency 11** to discuss how artists vary positions of people's bodies to show what they are doing. What shapes do students' bodies have as they do their favorite activities?

Teach

Have students complete the group murals. How would the people's shapes have changed if students depicted a different activity?

Reflect

Guide students through evaluation of their works of art using the four steps of art criticism. (See pages 28–29 for more about art criticism.) Have groups exhibit their murals for the rest of the class to see.

Alternate Activity

Materials:
- 12" × 18" white paper
- crayons
- markers
- scissors
- glue

1. Assign students to groups of 3 or 4. Have students decide on a group activity or sport they can depict in their mural. Have each student draw a picture of himself or herself participating in the activity.

2. Students should cut out their individual figures and assemble them on another sheet of paper. Students should draw and color a background for the activity before gluing the figures to the paper.

Research in Art Education

It is important that arts education not only be present, but also "rich and continuous" in order to receive the full benefits it can add to "learning and instruction that is critical to healthy development." These benefits include higher levels of cooperation, creativity, and problem-solving skills. ("Learning In and Through the Arts: Curriculum Implications" in *Champions of Change*, p. 36) Group role-playing activities, like those in the Practice section, provide students with an opportunity to practice both observation skills and cooperation skills.

Assessment

Use the following rubric to evaluate the artwork students make in the Creative Expression activity and to assess students' understanding of the lesson concepts.

Have students complete page 29 or 30 in their **Assessment** books.

	Art History and Culture	Aesthetic Perception	Creative Expression	Art Criticism
3 POINTS	The student successfully identifies and compares Lawrence's and Fish's styles of depicting people.	The student successfully identifies the free-form shapes that indicate movement in the artwork.	The student's drawing clearly illustrates the student's understanding of action shapes.	The student thoughtfully and honestly evaluates his or her own work using the four steps of art criticism.
2 POINTS	The student's identification and comparison is weak or incomplete.	The student identifies some of the free-form shapes that indicate movement in the artwork.	The student's drawing shows emerging awareness of action shapes.	The student attempts to evaluate his or her own work, but shows an incomplete understanding of evaluation criteria.
1 POINT	The student cannot identify or compare Lawrence's or Fish's style of depicting people.	The student cannot identify the free-form shapes that indicate movement in the artwork.	The student's drawing shows no understanding of action shapes.	The student makes no attempt to evaluate his or her own artwork.

Assessment, p. 29

Name _____ Date _____

Lesson **5** UNIT 2

Shapes of People in Action

1	2

For the teacher: Use the following prompts for this activity.
1. Using a crayon, draw a person resting in box 1.
2. In box 2, draw a person playing an outdoor game.
3. Tell how your drawing in box 2 shows movement.

Level 1   Unit 2 • Shape   **29**

Lesson 6 Still-Life Shapes

Overview

Lesson 6 introduces students to still lifes.

Objectives

Art History and Culture

To recognize that some artists create still lifes
NSAE 2.a; 3.a

Creative Expression

To create a still life using the computer's paint program
NSAE 1.a; 1.c; 1.d; 2.a; 3.b

Aesthetic Perception

To recognize a still life as an arrangement of objects
NSAE 2.a; 3.a

Art Criticism

To evaluate one's own artwork using the four steps of art criticism
NSAE 1.b; 2.b; 3.a; 5.c

Vocabulary ⭐ Reading

Review the following vocabulary words with students before beginning the lesson.

still life naturaleza muerta—painting or drawing of inanimate (nonmoving) objects

geometric shape figura geométrica—a precise mathematical shape, such as a circle, square, rectangle, triangle

free-form shape figura abstracta—any shape that is not a geometric shape

See page 89B for additional Spanish vocabulary resources.

Art Journal: Vocabulary

Have students add these words to the Vocabulary section of their Art Journals.

Lesson Materials
- computer's paint program
- teacher-provided still-life items

Alternate Materials
- oil pastels
- white paper

Program Resources
- *Reading and Writing Test Prep.,* pp. 28–29
- *Transparency 12*
- *Artist Profiles,* pp. 11, 51
- *Animals Through History Time Line*
- *Assessment,* pp. 31–32
- *Large Prints 15 She-Ba* and *16 Dos Niños (Two Children)*
- *The National Museum of Women in the Arts Collection*

Concept Trace
Still-Life Shapes
Introduced: Level K, Unit 3, Lesson 2

Reinforced: Level 2, Unit 2, Lesson 6

Lesson 6 Arts Integration NSAE 6.a

Theatre

Complete Unit 2, Lesson 6, on pages 46–51 of *Theatre Arts Connections.*

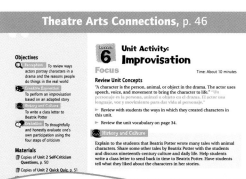

Music

Listen to *Suite #1 for Unaccompanied Cello in G Major BVW 1007 (Movement V 1).* This music has so many shapes of melodies that it is interesting only that one instrument plays the whole piece. Does this music describe anything to you? An action, an experience, or a feeling?

Movement & Dance

A tableaux is a frozen scene that is made of contrasting shapes, levels, and line patterns. Divide students into groups of five and have them create a group tableaux that shows an everyday scene at school, like lunchtime.

Activate Prior Knowledge

"Have you ever helped set the table? Did you arrange the silverware in a certain way?"

"¿Alguna vez han ayudado a poner la mesa? ¿Colocaron los cubiertos en un cierto orden?"

■ Discuss student responses. Discuss the arrangement of other things that may also be included in a place setting, such as plates and cups.

Using Literature ⭐ Reading

■ Read *My House Mi Casa* by Rebecca Emberley. Many of the images of the rooms in the house contain still-life objects.

Thematic Connection ⭐ Science

■ **Food/Nutrition:** Many still lifes include food. Discuss foods that could be included that would provide healthful nutrition.

Introduce the Art

Look
NSAE 2.a; 3.a

"Let's look at the arrangement of objects in each artwork." "Vamos a mirar el orden de los objetos en cada obra de arte".

Drawing Conclusions ⭐ Reading

■ Have students describe what they think a still life is, based on what they see in the two artworks. Students might say that a still life is a painting of objects on a table. They may say that a still life includes a bowl, fruit, and some patterned cloth draped over the table. Explain that many still lifes include those things, but they do not have to.

Adjectives and Adverbs ⭐ Language Arts

■ Have students describe each work of art. List on a chart the adjectives and adverbs students use.

🏺 Art History and Culture

Have students identify variations between the still lifes. Possible answer: Both still lifes show objects on a table, but the objects are different. The objects in *Still Life with Apples and Peaches* are more recognizable than those in *The Red Foulard* because of its abstract style.

💻 **Web Connection**

Visit www.expo-cezanne.com for more information about Cézanne's life and work.

Still-Life Shapes

▲ **Paul Cézanne.** (French). *Still Life with Apples and Peaches.* c. 1905.
Oil on canvas. 32 × 39⅝ inches (81 × 100.5 cm).
National Gallery of Art, Washington, D.C.

Look at the still lifes on these pages. A still life is a picture of things that do not move.

🏺 Art History and Culture

Many artists paint still lifes. How are these still lifes similar? How are they different?

🏺 Art History and Culture

Paul Cézanne NSAE 4.c

Paul Cézanne (pôl sä zan´) (1839–1906) was born in southern France. Cézanne wanted to study painting and had many disagreements about it with his father, who wanted Cézanne to become a banker. Although Cézanne's artwork was not celebrated during his lifetime, he would be considered a great influence for later artists, including Matisse and Picasso. Cézanne is best known for his many still lifes.

See pages 16–21 and 24–25 for more about subject matter and art history.

Artist Profiles, p. 11

• Artist Profile •
Paul Cézanne
1839–1906
Paul Cézanne (paul sä zan´) was born in the south of France in Aix-en-Provence. He is often called the father of modern art. He loved to paint, but people did not like his work much—at least not during his lifetime. He had to beg gallery owners to show his work, and therefore he did not sell many paintings. He inherited money from his parents to pay his bills and buy his paints. He continued painting until a week before he died.

◀ **Pablo Picasso.**
(Spanish). *The Red Foulard.* 1924.
••••••••••••••••••••••
Oil on canvas. 39½ × 32 inches (100.33 × 81.28 cm.). Norton Museum of Art, West Palm Beach, Florida.

Study both works of art to find shapes.

▶ What shapes were used in each painting?

Aesthetic Perception

Design Awareness Look for a still life at home. Is there a plant or a bowl of fruit on a table?

Art History and Culture

Pablo Picasso

Pablo Picasso (pä´ blō pi kä´ sō) (1881–1973) began learning about art at a young age from his father, an art teacher. He exhibited his first paintings when he was 13 years old. He experimented with many styles, and he created the style called Cubism. Picasso was very productive and created more than 20,000 works in his lifetime. When he was 90, the Louvre (a famous museum in Paris) held an exhibition of his work. It was the first time the Grande Galerie of the Louvre had honored the work of a living artist.

See pages 16–21 and 24–25 for more about subject matter and art history.

Artist Profiles, p. 51

◆ Artist Profile ◆
Pablo Picasso
1881–1973
Pablo Picasso (pä´ blō pi kä´ sō) was born in Málaga, Spain. He did poorly in school but his father, an art teacher, taught him to draw and paint. Picasso learned quickly. When he was only 14 he had a painting accepted for an exhibition. Picasso moved to Paris, France when he was 18. At the time he was very poor. Thieves stole what little he had, yet they left his now valuable drawings. In time the outgoing Picasso made many friends. Among them were the American writers Ernest Hemingway and Gertrude Stein and the Russian composer Igor Stravinsky. Picasso painted at night and slept late most mornings. He worked hard his entire life. He completed 200 paintings the year he turned 90.

Study

▶ Students should look for both geometric and free-form shapes. In *Still Life with Apples and Peaches* some pieces of fruit are circles, the design on the pitcher has circles, and parts of the table are rectangles. The free-form shapes are the cloth draped over the table, some of the fruit, the vase, and the bowl. In *The Red Foulard* there are circles and triangles in the design on the cloth and the table has rectangular legs. The other shapes are free-form.

■ For more examples of still lifes see *The National Museum of Women in the Arts Collection.*

Art Journal: Concepts
Have students draw a sketch to show what a still life is in the Concepts section of their Art Journals.

Aesthetic Perception

Design Awareness Discuss with students if they have seen any still-life arrangements in their homes. Who made the arrangement? What was its purpose?

Developing Visual Literacy Have students imagine that the each still life is actually a photograph taken in someone's home. What is the house like? Where is it located? Who lives there? What is happening at the house? Have students use descriptions to represent each of the five senses.

Web Connection
Visit **www.picasso.fr/anglais/** for more information about Pablo Picasso.

 **each**
Time: About 35 minutes

"How would you arrange a still life?" "¿Cómo ordenarían una naturaleza muerta?"

■ Read and discuss Using Still-Life Shapes on page 88.

Practice

Materials: classroom objects

Materials: other items brought from home

■ Read the directions on page 88 and have students complete the activity. Try to have students use both geometric and free-form shapes.

Creative Expression

NSAE 1.a; 1.c; 1.d; 2.a

Materials: computer's paint program, teacher-provided still-life items

Alternate Materials: oil pastels, white paper

■ Distribute the materials and have students follow the directions on page 89.

■ Have students choose three or four objects to use in their still lifes.

■ See the Activity Tips on page 237 for visual examples of this lesson's activity.

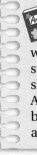 **Art Journal: Brainstorming**
Have students brainstorm ideas for ways they could arrange objects in their still lifes. Have students make a few sketches of different arrangements in their Art Journals, then select the one they like best to use for the Creative Expression activity.
NSAE 3.b

Using Still-Life Shapes

A **still life** has **geometric** and **free-form shapes**.

Practice

Arrange objects that could be used in a still life.

1. Use five objects you find in the classroom.

2. Arrange the objects on a table.

3. What shapes do you see?

Differentiated Instruction

Reteach
Have students describe a still life. Compare their description to the initial sketches they made at the beginning of the lesson in the Concepts section of their Art Journals.

Special Needs
Adaptations: The use of visual prompts in the form of pre-cut geometric shapes will help students name and recognize the shapes found in the still-life arrangement. The use of this instructional strategy prior to the computer activity will enhance student's ability to successfully complete the task.

ELL Tips
Show students some other examples of still-life paintings. Have students repeat after you as you identify them as still lifes.

◀ **Bethany McDaniel.** Age 7.

Think about how this student used geometric and free-form shapes to make a still life.

 Creative Expression

What objects would you place in a still life?

1. Choose your objects. Decide how you would arrange them.

2. Use the shape tools in your computer's paint program to draw objects with geometric shapes. Use the brush tool to draw objects with free-form shapes.

3. Use the fill tool to paint the objects. Use other tools to decorate your picture.

 Art Criticism

Decide If you made another still life, what objects would you include?

Unit 2 • Lesson 6 **89**

Art Across the Curriculum

Use these ideas to reinforce art concepts across the curriculum.
NSAE 6.b

★ **Expository Writing** Have students use the writing process to write instructions about how to create a still-life arrangement.

★ **Math** Have students count and compare the number of objects in each still life.

★ **Science** Have students sort humanmade objects and items from nature in a still-life painting.

★ **Social Studies** The still lifes by Cézanne and Picasso were created in the past. Have students imagine what objects might be included in a still life created in the future.

★ **Technology** Have students make a still life by creating a clip art collage. Visit **SRAonline.com** to print detailed instructions for this activity.

Reflect
Time: About 5 minutes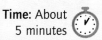

Review and Assess
"What is a still life?" "¿Qué es una naturaleza muerta?"

Think
The objects in the student's still life have geometric and free-form shapes.

■ Have students compare the shapes in *Large Prints 15 She-Ba* and *16 Dos Niños (Two Children)* to those in the still lifes in this lesson.

Informal Assessment

Art Journal: Critical Thinking
Have students ask themselves the Art Criticism questions and write or sketch to answer the Decide question in their Art Journals.
NSAE 1.b; 2.b; 3.a; 5.c

Art Criticism

Describe ▶ What objects did you include in your still life?

Analyze ▶ Are there any geometric shapes in your still life?

Interpret ▶ Does your still life show the kinds of things you like?

Decide ▶ If you made another still life, what objects would you include?

■ For standardized-format test practice using this lesson's art content, see pages 28–29 in *Reading and Writing Test Preparation.*

Still-Life Shapes

Extra! For the Art Specialist

Time: About 45 minutes

Focus

Use *Transparency 12* to discuss how artists use geometric and free-form shapes to create still lifes. Where have students seen a still-life arrangement in the classroom or in their home?

Teach

Have students follow the directions to complete their monoprints. How did students decide what objects to include?

Reflect

Guide students through evaluation of their works of art using the four steps of art criticism. (See pages 28–29 for more about art criticism.)

Alternate Activity

Materials:
- waxed paper
- masking tape
- finger paint or tempera paint with media mixer
- 12" × 18" white paper
- markers or oil pastels

1. On a sheet of waxed paper taped to the table, have students use finger paint or tempera paint with media mixer to paint a still life.

2. Lay white paper over the paint and press to make a monoprint. Peel away from the corner.

3. When the paint is dry, students may use markers or oil pastels to add details to their paintings.

Research in Art Education

"Talk about art, or art criticism, is probably one of the ways we share the contents of our inner lives without embarrassment. Art criticism is very much like teaching: it is the sharing of discoveries about art, or in some cases about life, where art has its ultimate source." Hurwitz, Al, and Stanley Madeja. *The Joyous Vision.* New Jersey: Prentice Hall, 1997.

Assessment

Use the following rubric to evaluate the artwork students make in the Creative Expression activity and to assess students' understanding of the lesson concepts.

Have students complete page 31 or 32 in their *Assessment* books.

	Art History and Culture	Aesthetic Perception	Creative Expression	Art Criticism
3 POINTS	The student successfully recognizes that some artists paint still lifes.	The student successfully recognizes a still life as an arrangement of objects.	The student successfully creates a still life.	The student thoughtfully and honestly evaluates his or her own work using the four steps of art criticism.
2 POINTS	The student shows emerging understanding that artists paint still lifes.	The student shows emerging awareness that a still life is an arrangement of objects.	The student makes a weak attempt at creating a still life.	The student attempts to evaluate his or her own work, but shows an incomplete understanding of evaluation criteria.
1 POINT	The student cannot identify still life as a type of painting.	The student cannot identify a still life as an arrangement of objects.	The student's artwork is not an example of a still life.	The student makes no attempt to evaluate his or her own artwork.

Assessment, p. 31

Name _____ Date _____

Lesson **6** UNIT 2

Still-Life Shapes

For the teacher: Use the following prompt for this activity. Draw a still life. Use at least one geometric shape.

Level 1 — Unit 2 • Shape **31**

free-form shape—any shape that is not a geometric shape
figura abstracta—cualquier figura que no sea geométrica

geometric shape—a precise mathematical shape, such as a circle, square, rectangle, or triangle **figura geométrica**—una figura matemática precisa como un círculo, cuadrado, rectángulo o triángulo

outline—a line that shows or creates the outer edges of a shape **silueta**—una línea que muestra o forma los bordes externos de una figura

position—the placement of an object or shape in relation to another **posición**—la colocación de un objeto o una figura en relación a otra

shape—a figure or area that is defined in some way
figura—una figura o área definida de alguna manera

Definitions for the following words appear as art on **Student Edition** page 72 and in the student glossary:

circle—círculo

rectangle—rectángulo

square—cuadrado

triangle—triángulo

Vocabulary Practice

T Display **Transparency 38** to review unit vocabulary words.

Definitions: Demonstrate Meanings ⭐
Vocabulary
Draw a circle and a square on the board. Ask students which drawing demonstrates the meaning of *circle*. Repeat for other unit vocabulary words.

Words in Context ⭐ Vocabulary
Provide students with clues for each unit vocabulary word. Begin with a general clue that includes a few vocabulary words. For example, *I am a geometric shape.* Then provide a more specific clue, such as *I have three sides.* Have students guess the unit vocabulary word for this clue *(triangle).*

Examples ⭐ Vocabulary
Identify an example of a *free-form shape* in the classroom. Have students name the unit vocabulary word you gave an example of. Repeat for other unit vocabulary words.

Wrapping Up Unit 2

Shape

▲ **Pierre Bonnard.** (French). *The Breakfast Room.*
1930–1931.

Oil on canvas. 62⅞ × 44⅞ inches (159.3 × 113.8 cm.). The Museum of Modern Art, New York, New York.

Art Criticism

Critical Thinking Art criticism is an organized system for looking at and talking about art. You can criticize art without being an expert. The purpose of art criticism is to get the viewer involved in a perception process that delays judgment until all aspects of the artwork have been studied.

- See pages 28–29 for more about art criticism.

Describe

- What do you see? During this step the student will collect information about the subject of the work.

▶ Have students list and describe the objects and people in *The Breakfast Room*. On a blue and white-striped table in the foreground are some cups and saucers, food, pitchers, and a box. Behind the table is a wall with three windows. Through the windows is an outdoor scene. On the left side of the window is a girl holding a cup. The walls on either side of the windows have a diamond pattern on them.

Analyze

- How is this work organized? During this step the student thinks about how the artist has used the elements and principles of art.

▶ Have students list the geometric shapes found in this artwork. The windows and the wood panels around them are rectangles, the cups and saucers have circles, the stripes on the table are rectangles, the box on the table is a square.

▶ Have students list the free-form shapes. The person, the trees, and the food.

Art History and Culture

Pierre Bonnard

Pierre Bonnard (pyâr bô när´) (1867–1947) was born near Paris, France. As he grew up he received a strong education and he was also active in sports. Bonnard attended law school but also took art classes. He began to focus more on his art after failing part of a law test. In the late 1880s Bonnard joined an art group called the Nabis. The group enjoyed making decorative art, such as posters or book illustrations. Bonnard liked to experiment in his art. He often experimented with perception. One way he did this was to paint mirrors and their reflections. Another way was to contrast indoors and outdoors by painting rooms with windows as in *The Breakfast Room*.

See pages 16–21 and 24–25 for more about subject matter and art history.

Artist Profiles, p. 7

◆ Artist Profile ◆

Pierre Bonnard
1867–1947

Pierre Bonnard (pyâr bô när´) was born at Fontenay-aux-Roses, a suburb of Paris, France. Although Bonnard studied law, he spent his free time painting at Académie Julien and the École des Beaux-Arts. Eventually he left law altogether and, after joining with a group of experimental artists, exhibited his paintings throughout France, Europe, and the United States. Despite his fame Bonnard was a quiet, private man.

? Art Criticism | Critical Thinking

Describe

▶ Describe the room and the objects in it.

Analyze

▶ Where do you see geometric shapes?

Interpret

▶ What sounds would you hear if you were in this room?

Decide

▶ Would you like to be in this room? Explain your answer.

Interpret

■ **What is the artist trying to say?** Students use the clues they discovered during their analysis to find the message the artist is trying to show.

▶ **Ask students what sounds they would hear if they were in this room.** Answers will vary. Students may say they would hear people talking, the sounds of food cooking, or dishes rattling.

▶ **Discuss with students what time of day it is in the artwork. Ask what clues the artist used to show this.** The painting is titled *The Breakfast Room* so it is probably morning. The scene through the windows is visible, so it is not night. The food on the table looks like pastries and the settings are like those used for tea or coffee.

Decide

■ **What do you think about the work?** Students use all the information they have gathered to decide whether this is a successful work of art.

▶ **Discuss with students whether they would like to be in this room.** Student responses will vary.

 Art Journal: Critical Thinking
Have students sketch or write the answers to the Aesthetic Perception questions in their Art Journals.

Aesthetic Perception

Seeing Like an Artist Have students look around for a setting where they can see objects on both sides of a window. How is the scene similar to *The Breakfast Room?*

Describe ▶ List and describe the objects you see.

Analyze ▶ What objects have free-form shapes? What objects have geometric shapes?

Interpret ▶ What time of day (or what season) is it? What details would you include to show this?

Decide ▶ What feeling do you have when you look at the scene?

"Artists use geometric and free-form shapes in their works of art." "Los artistas usan figuras geométricas y abstractas en sus obras de arte".

 T Review unit vocabulary with students using *Transparency 38.*

Art Journal: Writing
Have students answer the questions on page 92. Answers: 1. A, 2. C, 3. B

T For further assessment, have students complete the unit test on *Transparency 44.*

 ## CAREERS IN ART
Fashion Design

► Encourage students to think about differences in clothing. Discuss ways the style of a shirt can change (color, length of sleeve, collar, buttons, and so on).

"The object of art is to give life a shape."

—Jean Anouilh
(1910–87), dramatist

Shape, continued

Show What You Know

Write your answers on a sheet of paper.

❶ Choose the free-form shape.

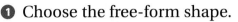
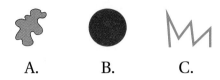

   A.   B.   C.

❷ Choose the geometric shape.

   A.   B.   C.

❸ Choose the shape that shows a person in action.

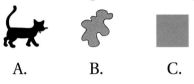

   A.   B.   C.

CAREERS IN ART
Fashion Design

Think about clothing. What different kinds of shirts have you seen? Does your clothing have any patterns on the fabric?

Fashion designers plan what pieces of clothing will look like. They think of ways to change styles or make new styles of the clothes people wear.

Fabric designers create the patterns that appear on fabric.

▲ **Fashion designer**

Unit Assessment Options

Aesthetic Perception

Practice Have students select an artwork from another unit and see how many geometric and free-form shapes they can find.

Creative Expression

Student Portfolio Have students review all the artwork they have created during this unit and select the pieces they wish to keep in their portfolios. Have students view classmates' portfolios and share positive feedback.

Art Criticism

Activity Have students select their favorite work of art from the unit. Guide students through the study of their selected work using the four steps of art criticism. (See pages 28–29 for more about Art Criticism.)

Shape in Theatre

An artist creates shapes and images on paper. When these pictures go with a story, they are called illustrations. Sometimes a theatre director makes a play using the story and illustrations from a book.

What to Do Re-create a scene from an illustration in a book.

1. Choose an illustration that shows characters in action.

2. Work in a group. Use your bodies to show the poses of the characters.

3. Share your scene with the other groups.

▲ The Children's Theatre Company. "The Story of Babar."

 **Art Criticism**

Decide Did your group bring the illustration from the page to the stage?

Art History and Culture

The Children's Theatre Company

The Children's Theatre Company in Minneapolis, Minnesota, is known for its ability to vividly re-create the storybook page on stage. The biggest challenge in bringing a book off the page and onto the stage lies in expanding two-dimensional artwork to three. In this case, it was of primary importance to create an accurate scale of the elephant characters to the human ones. The costumes for Babar and his elephant friends needed to look exactly like the shapes in the book, but have the flexibility to come alive and dance.

Shapes in Theatre NSAE 6.a

Objective: To create a tableau using an illustration from a book

Materials: *The Story of Babar, the Little Elephant* performed by the Children's Theatre Company. Running time: 3:44.

Focus
Time: About 5 minutes

Art History and Culture

- Discuss the information on page 93. Explain to students that a frozen scene that shows the positions of the characters is called a *tableau*.

Teach
Time: About 20 minutes

Aesthetic Perception

- Have students look for illustrations in books that they think will work well in a tableau.

Creative Expression

- Divide students into small groups. Have students create a tableau from their selected illustration.

- **Informal Assessment** Give positive feedback. Talk about using levels and facial expressions in their tableaux.

Reflect
Time: About 10 minutes

Art Criticism

- Have students answer the four art criticism questions.

Describe ▶ What was happening in the scene you re-created?

Analyze ▶ What shapes from the illustrations did you re-create in your tableau?

Interpret ▶ How did it feel to be one of the characters in the story?

Decide ▶ Did your group bring the illustration from the page to the stage?

Unit 3 Planning Guide

	Lesson Title	Suggested Pacing	Creative Expression Activity
Lesson 1	A Rainbow of Colors	55 minutes	Create a drawing and painting of a rainbow world.
Lesson 2	Primary Colors	50 minutes	Create a primary color computer design.
Lesson 3	Red and Yellow Make Orange	55 minutes	Create a red, yellow, and orange shape painting.
Lesson 4	Blue and Yellow Make Green	55 minutes	Create a green outdoor scene.
Lesson 5	Red and Blue Make Violet	55 minutes	Create a violet creature.
Lesson 6	Primary and Secondary Colors	55 minutes	Create a secondary color painting.
ART SOURCE ARTSOURCE	Color in Chinese Dance	35 minutes	Create a colorful rhythm dance.

Materials	Program Resources	Fine Art Resources	Literature Resources
white paper, watercolors, paintbrushes, crayons, water dishes, paper towels, black markers	*Reading and Writing Test Preparation*, pp. 30–31 *Assessment*, pp. 33–34 *Home and After-School Connections*	*Transparency*, 13 *Artist Profiles*, pp. 26, 33 *Animals Through History Time Line* *Large Prints*, 17 and 18 *Women in the Arts Collection*	*The Listening Walk* by Paul Showers
computer's paint program	*Reading and Writing Test Preparation*, pp. 32–33 *Flash Card*, 7 *Assessment*, pp. 35–36	*Transparency*, 14 *Artist Profiles*, pp. 21, 44 *Large Prints*, 17 and 18 *Women in the Arts Collection*	*Ferryboat Ride!* by Anne Rockwell
newspaper, brushes, heavy white paper, paper towels, water dishes, red and yellow liquid tempera paint, palettes	*Reading and Writing Test Preparation*, pp. 34–35 *Assessment*, pp. 37–38	*Transparency*, 15 *Artist Profiles*, pp. 62, 73 *Large Prints*, 17 and 18 *Art Around the World Collection*	*Moo Moo, Brown Cow* by Jakki Wood
blue and yellow oil pastels, white paper, paper towels	*Reading and Writing Test Preparation*, pp. 36–37 *Assessment*, pp. 39–40	*Transparency*, 16 *Artist Profiles*, pp. 17, 49 *Large Prints*, 17 and 18 *Women in the Arts Collection*	*Is Your Mama a Llama?* by Deborah Guarino
9" × 12" white paper, glue dishes, glue brushes, newspaper, diluted white liquid glue, black markers, tissue paper in various shades of red and blue, paper towels	*Reading and Writing Test Preparation*, pp. 38–39 *Assessment*, pp. 41–42	*Transparency*, 17 *Artist Profiles*, pp. 23, 42 *Large Prints*, 17 and 18 *Women in the Arts Collection*	*The Purple Coat* by Amy Hest
mixing trays, water jars, tempera paint (red, blue, and yellow), brushes, 12" × 18" white paper, newspaper	*Reading and Writing Test Preparation*, pp. 40–41 *Flash Cards*, 7 and 8 *Assessment*, pp. 43–44	*Transparency*, 18 *Artist Profiles*, pp. 4, 52 *Large Prints*, 17 and 18 *Women in the Arts Collection*	*This Plane* by Paul Collicutt
Flying Goddess performed by Lily Cai, thin wooden dowels, bamboo, or plastic straw with ribbons or crepe paper in various colors attached with tape or staples			

Unit Overview

3 Color

Lesson 1: Artists use **a rainbow of colors.** The color wheel is like a rainbow bent into a circle.

Lesson 2: **Primary colors** are special because they cannot be made by mixing other colors. Red, yellow, and blue are primary colors.

Lesson 3: **Orange** is a secondary color made by mixing the primary colors **red and yellow.**

Lesson 4: **Green** is a secondary color made by mixing the primary colors **blue and yellow.**

Lesson 5: **Violet** is a secondary color made by mixing the primary colors **red and blue.**

Lesson 6: **Secondary colors** are created by mixing two **primary colors.**

Introduce Unit Concepts

"What colors do you know? Name things found in nature with those colors." "¿Qué colores saben? Nombren cosas que se hallan en la naturaleza con esos colores".

Primary and Secondary Colors

Life Science ⭐ Science

- Have students list things found in nature that are red, yellow, or blue; for example: cherries, sunflowers, and bluebirds.

- Have students list things found in nature that are orange, green, or violet; for example: goldfish, grass, and grapes.

Cross-Curricular Projects

- See the *Language Arts and Reading, Mathematics, Science,* and *Social Studies Art Connections* books for activities that further develop color concepts.

National Standards for Arts Education in Visual Arts (NSAE) 6.b

Color

Artists use many colors in their works of art.

They mix some colors to make other colors.

▲ **Mary Cassatt.** (American). *In the Garden.* 1904.
....
Pastel. 26 × 32 inches (66 × 81.3 cm.). The Detroit Institute of Arts, Detroit, Michigan.

Fine Art Prints

Display *Large Prints 17 Die grossen blauen Pferde* and *18 Dance at Bougival.* Refer to the prints throughout the unit as students learn about color.

Large Print 17

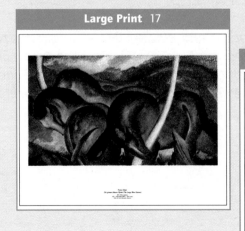

Large Print 18

Look at the artwork.

▶ What colors do you see?

In This Unit you will:

▶ learn about the color wheel, primary colors, and secondary colors.

▶ find colors in art and the environment.

▶ create art with primary and secondary colors.

Mary Cassatt

(1844–1926)

▶ was an American artist.

▶ often painted mothers and their children.

▶ used paint and pastels.

🏺 Art History and Culture

Mary Cassatt

Mary Cassatt (mâr ē kə sat´) (1844–1926) studied art in the United States and Italy before settling in Paris, France, in 1872. She was a member of the French impressionists, artists who believed in the importance of color and light in artwork. Cassatt was the only American artist associated with the French impressionists. She was also the first to promote the impressionists in the United States. Although she had no children of her own, Cassatt often featured mothers and their children in her paintings.

See pages 16–21 and 24–25 for more about subject matter and art history.

Artist Profiles, p. 10

◀ Artist Profile ●

Mary Cassatt
1845–1926

Mary Cassatt (mer´ ē kə sat´) was born into an upper middle-class family in western Pennsylvania in 1884. She was enrolled at the Pennsylvania Academy of the Fine Arts from 1861 to 1865. She later studied in Paris, France, in the studios of Gérôme and Couture. In 1874, she settled permanently in Paris, where she regularly submitted work to the yearly Salon exhibitions. The painter and sculptor Edgar Degas saw her work at the Salon and invited Cassatt to join the Impressionists in 1887. She was the only American ever to exhibit in the group's shows. During her lifetime, Cassatt's work was more popular in Europe than in the United States. In her spare time, she loved to entertain friends and ride her

Examine the Artwork

"Let's look at the colors in Mary Cassatt's painting." "Vamos a ver los colores en la pintura de Mary Cassatt".

■ Have students look at the artwork. Ask them to name the colors they see. Primary colors—red flowers, red lips, yellow spots on dress, yellow flowers, yellow hair, yellow hat, blue sky, blue flowers, blue chair. Secondary colors—green trees, green grass. Other—brown hair, beige skin, black ribbon on hat, pink and white on dress. (Black and white are neutral colors. Brown is created by mixing the complementary colors orange and blue. Pink is a tint created by mixing red with white. Students will not be learning about neutral colors, complementary colors, or tints in this level.)

Unit Pretest

T Display ***Transparency 45*** as a pretest. Answers: 1. A, 2. C, 3. B

Home Connection

■ See ***Home and After-School Connections*** for family newsletters and activities for this unit.

National Standards for Arts Education in Visual Arts (NSAE) 4.a

ILLUSTRATOR PROFILE
Eric Carle
(1929–   )

Eric Carle was born in Syracuse, New York. He attended kindergarten there and loved school. At age six, he and his family moved to Germany. He was no longer enthusiastic about school, but he liked art. At age 17, Carle began studying art at the Akademi der Bilgenden Kunste in Stuttgart, Germany. After graduation he moved back to New York.

Carle worked as a graphic designer and then as an art director for an advertising agency. In 1963 he quit his job and began working as a freelance illustrator. After illustrating several books for other authors, Carle began writing and illustrating his own books. His second original book was *The Very Hungry Caterpillar,* which is his best-known work. It has sold more than 18 million copies, and it has been translated into 30 languages.

Carle has illustrated and written more than 70 books. His illustrations are collages made from painted tissue paper. The pictures often feature animals or scenes from nature.

Throughout Unit 3, share Carle's books with the class and discuss his use of color. What colors can students identify in the illustrations? Where do students see primary colors overlapping to make secondary colors?

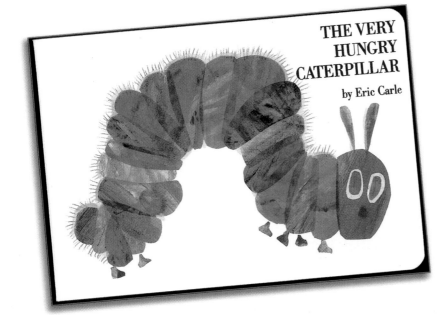

THE VERY HUNGRY CATERPILLAR
by Eric Carle

Music

 Color in music refers to the distinctive tone qualities, or *timbre,* of different instruments and voices. Tone color can be a tool for helping students learn about visual color. Distribute instruments and assign a primary color to each one. Have students play their instruments when you point to the assigned color.

Literature and Art

Have students identify colors as they watch the video or DVD *Ernst* by Elisa Kleven.

Literature and Art

Performing Arts

 Show "Flying Goddess" performed by Lily Cai. Discuss the use of color in Chinese dance.

Artsource®

Lesson 1 Overview

A Rainbow of Colors

Lesson 1 introduces students to the six colors of the color wheel: red, orange, yellow, green, blue, and violet.

Objectives

Art History and Culture
To recognize and compare the subject matter of Kelly's and Hockney's paintings
NSAE 2.a; 3.a

Creative Expression
To create a crayon and watercolor painting with rainbow colors in the correct order
NSAE 1.a; 1.c

Aesthetic Perception
To locate and identify rainbow colors in art and the environment
NSAE 2.a; 6.b

Art Criticism
To evaluate one's own work using the four steps of art criticism
NSAE 1.b; 2.b; 3.a; 5.c

Vocabulary ⭐ Reading

Review the following vocabulary words with students before beginning the lesson.

color wheel *círculo cromático*—design for organizing colors that shows the spectrum bent into a circle

rainbow *arco iris*—red, orange, yellow, green, blue, and violet curved into a semicircle

See page 119B for additional vocabulary and Spanish vocabulary resources.

Art Journal: Vocabulary
Have students add these words to the Vocabulary section of their Art Journals.

Lesson Materials
- white paper
- old magazines
- scissors
- glue
- watercolors
- paintbrushes
- crayons
- water dishes
- paper towels
- black markers

Alternate Materials:
- paint chips in rainbow colors
- markers
- light paper

Program Resources
- *Reading and Writing Test Prep.,* pp. 30–31
- *Flash Card 19*
- *Transparency 13*
- *Artist Profiles,* pp. 26, 33
- *Animals Through History Time Line*
- *Assessment,* pp. 33–34
- *Large Prints 17 Die grossen blauen Pferde* and *18 Dance at Bougival*
- *The National Museum of Women in the Arts Collection*

Concept Trace
A Rainbow of Colors
Introduced: Level K, Unit 3, Lesson 1
Reinforced: Level 2, Unit 3, Lesson 1

Lesson 1 Arts Integration NSAE 6.a

Theatre
Complete Unit 3, Lesson 1, on pages 54–55 of *Theatre Arts Connections.*

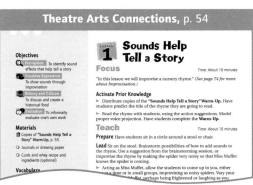

Music
SPOTLIGHT on MUSIC Learning to identify the sound of musical instruments takes experience with both hearing and seeing the instrument. Some pieces are titled with the name of the instrument or instruments that it is written for. Listen to *Trumpet and Drum* from *Jeux d'enfants (Children's Games)* by Georges Bizet. Have students raise their hands when they hear the trumpet.

Movement & Dance
Attach colored ribbon or crepe paper to small garden sticks and divide the students into the following groups: Red, Blue, Green, and Purple. Call out a specific color and have that group travel to the center of the room and explore ways to move with their color for eight counts.

A Rainbow of Colors

Focus

Time: About 10 minutes

Activate Prior Knowledge

"Have you ever seen a rainbow?" "¿Alguna vez han visto un arco iris?"

- Ask what colors are in a rainbow. Discuss how the colors of a rainbow always appear in the same order.

Using Literature ⭐ Reading

- Read *The Listening Walk* by Paul Showers. Discuss how the illustrations by Aliki contain many rainbows and rainbow colors.

Thematic Connection ⭐ Reading

- **Colors:** Discuss colors that do not appear in the rainbow. Have students discuss why they think those colors are not part of the rainbow, and what is special about the colors that are.

Introduce the Art

Look

NSAE 2.b; 3.a

"Let's look at the rainbow colors in these paintings." "Vamos a mirar los colores del arco iris en estas pinturas".

Comparing and Contrasting ⭐ Reading

- Have students discuss the similarities and differences between the subjects of the two works of art. *Spectrum III* is nonobjective, but the subject of *Hollywood Hills House* is a house. Both works have each color of the rainbow and multiple shades of some colors. In *Spectrum III* the colors make your eyes move back and forth across the picture, but the colors in *Hollywood Hills House* make your eyes move all around.

🏺 Art History and Culture

Share with students the information from the Art History and Culture sections on pages 96–97. Discuss the typical subjects of each artist's work. Then ask students to identify how these works of art are typical for the artists.

💻 Web Connection

Spectrum III is housed at the Museum of Modern Art. Visit **www.moma.org** to learn more about the museum.

Look at the works of art on these pages. The artists used the colors of the rainbow.

▲ **Ellsworth Kelly.** (American). *Spectrum III.* 1967.
Oil on canvas. 33¼ × 9⅝ inches (84.46 × 24.45 cm.). The Museum of Modern Art, New York, New York.

🏺 Art History and Culture

Ellsworth Kelly also painted *Spectrum II.* It is identical to *Spectrum III* but more than eight times bigger.

🏺 Art History and Culture

Ellsworth Kelly

Ellsworth Kelly (elz´ wûrth ke´ lē) (1923–) was born in Newburgh, New York, where he grew up with his two brothers. As a high school student, Kelly could not decide whether he wanted to pursue art or theatre as a career. In 1943 he volunteered for the U.S. Army and served during World War II. After the war Kelly trained at the Pratt Institute in Brooklyn, New York, and the School of the Museum of Fine Arts in Boston, Massachusetts. Ellsworth Kelly is known for his experiments with color in works described as hard-edged abstractions.

See pages 16–21 and 24–25 for more about subject matter and art history.

Artist Profiles, p. 33

Artist Profile
Ellsworth Kelly
b. 1923

Ellsworth Kelly (elz´ wûrth ke´ lē) was born in Newburgh, New York. During high school, he studied art and theatre. After graduation, he could not decide which he wanted to pursue as a career, but he eventually chose art. In 1941, he began to study at the Pratt Institute in Brooklyn, New York. In 1943, he volunteered to serve with the army during World War II, and after the war he went back to his art studies. He studied at the School of the Museum of Fine Arts in Boston, Massachusetts. From 1948 to 1954, he lived in France, studying art and architecture. In 1954, he returned to New York.

Study the works of art.

▶ What colors do you see?

▲ **David Hockney.** (British).
Hollywood Hills House. 1982.
....
Oil, charcoal, collage on canvas. Three panels,
60 × 120 inches (152.4 × 304.8 cm.) overall.
Walker Art Center, Minneapolis, Minnesota.

Aesthetic Perception

Design Awareness Find something in the room that matches each color of the rainbow.

Study

▶ *Spectrum III* has yellow, green, blue, violet, red, and orange. Each color appears more than once in different shades, except for violet. *Hollywood Hills House* has the same colors (also in various shades), but also includes black, white, gray, and brown.

■ For more examples of abstract/nonobjective art, see *The National Museum of Women in the Arts Collection.*

Art Journal: Concepts
Have students write the name of each rainbow color in the Concepts section of their Art Journals.

Aesthetic Perception

Design Awareness Discuss with students the items they find for each color. Discuss why each item may have been designed with that color. Do some colors appear more frequently than others? Do any of the colors stand out more than others?

Developing Visual Literacy ☆ Social Studies
Ask students if they have ever been in a house as colorful as the one in *Hollywood Hills House.* Discuss how it would feel to live, work, or play in a house with colors like that.

Art History and Culture

David Hockney NSAE 4.a; 4.c
David Hockney (dā´ vəd häk´ nē) (1937–   ) was born into a working-class family in England. By age 11, he decided to become an artist. Hockney began going to art school at age 16 and went on to study at the Royal College of Art. He was a leader in the pop art movement. Pop artists used popular culture as inspiration for their art. In 1978 Hockney began living permanently in California. Much of his art, including *Hollywood Hills House,* depicts colorful California scenes.

See pages 16–21 and 24–25 for more about subject matter and art history.

Artist Profiles, p. 26

◀ Artist Profile ▶
David Hockney
b. 1937

David Hockney (dā´ vəd häk´ nē) was born in 1937 into a working class family in the northern industrial section of Bradford, England. By the time he was 11, he had decided to become an artist. At 16, he attended the Bradford School of Art, and went on to study at the Royal College of Art. In 1961, he made his first trip to the United States. The brightness and light of California was a sharp contrast from the rain and fog of England. He was impressed by the sense of space in the sprawling city of Los Angeles, and moved permanently to the United States in 1978 to become part of the California art scene.

Web Connection
Visit the Web site of the Walker Art Center at **collections.walkerart.org** for more information on David Hockney.

**each**

Time: About 40 minutes

"Let's find the colors of the color wheel."
"Vamos a buscar los colores del círculo cromático".

■ Read and discuss Using a Rainbow of Colors on page 98.

Practice

Materials: white paper, old magazines, scissors, glue

Alternate Materials: paint chips in rainbow colors

■ Distribute the materials and read the directions on page 98.

■ Have students cut out pictures from magazines for each color in the color wheel.

■ Have students arrange the pictures in the correct color wheel order and glue them to the paper. You might want to first draw the wheel outline on the paper for the students.

Creative Expression

NSAE 1.a; 1.c; 1.d; 2.c
Materials: white paper, crayons, watercolors, paintbrushes, water dishes, paper towels, black markers

Alternate Materials: markers, light paper

■ Distribute materials and have students follow the directions on page 99.

■ Remind students to look at their color wheels for help remembering the order of the colors. Allow students to make the rainbow colors go from side to side or top to bottom.

■ See the Activity Tips on page 238 for visual examples of this lesson's activity.

Art Journal: Brainstorming

Have students brainstorm ideas for things they could include in their rainbow worlds. Then have them make quick sketches of their ideas in the Ideas section of their Art Journals.
NSAE 3.b

Using a Rainbow of Colors

A **color wheel** shows the colors of the **rainbow** in order.

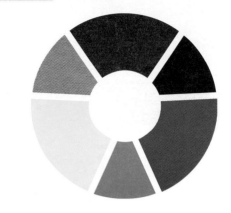

Practice

Make a color wheel.

1. Look in an old magazine.

2. Find and cut out pictures for all colors in the color wheel.

3. Glue the pictures in the order of the color wheel.

Differentiated Instruction

Reteach
Display a picture or photograph of a real rainbow so students can see the order of the colors. Then use *Flash Card 19* to review the color wheel.

Special Needs
Adaptations: Students with a lack of fine motor control may benefit from having their paper stabilized by taping the paper down or having the paper turned as they work.

ELL Tips
Have students point to a color in the artwork, name it, and then point to that color on their color wheels.

Think about how this student used rainbow colors.

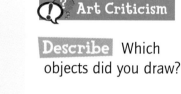

Creative Expression

How would you change the colors of things around you?

1. Think of objects you would like to make colorful. Draw the outlines of the objects with a black marker.

2. Using crayons, color the objects with rainbow colors in order.

3. Paint the background with rainbow colors in order.

Art Criticism

Describe Which objects did you draw?

Art Across the Curriculum

Use these ideas to reinforce art concepts across the curriculum.
NSAE 6.b

★ **Narrative Writing** Have students use the writing process to write a story about what it would be like to live in the rainbow world of their Creative Expression activities.

★ **Math** Ask students if they have ever heard that a pot of gold is at the end of a rainbow. Discuss the monetary value of coins.

★ **Science** Use a prism to demonstrate how light can be separated into the rainbow colors of the spectrum.

★ **Social Studies** Discuss life events in chronological order, noting that they occur in a specific order, just as the colors of the rainbow are always in the same order.

★ **Technology** Discuss the rainbow colors found in the color palette of your computer's paint program. Visit **SRAonline.com** to print detailed instructions for this activity.

Reflect

Time: About 5 minutes

Review and Assess
"What is the order of the rainbow colors?"
"¿Cuál es el orden de los colores del arco iris?"

Think
The student colored the bird and painted the background with rainbow colors.

■ Use *Large Prints 17 Die grossen blauen Pferde* and *18 Dance at Bougival* to have students identify rainbow colors.

Informal Assessment

Art Journal: Critical Thinking
Have students ask themselves the Art Criticism questions, and then write or sketch in their Art Journals to answer the Describe question.
NSAE 1.b; 2.b; 3.a; 5.c

Art Criticism

Describe ▶ Which objects did you draw?

Analyze ▶ What rainbow colors did you use? Did your rainbow colors go in order either across or down in the picture?

Interpret ▶ How does your picture make you feel?

Decide ▶ Does your rainbow world look like a place in which you'd like to live?

■ For standardized-format test practice using this lesson's art content, see pages 30–31 in *Reading and Writing Test Preparation.*

A Rainbow of Colors

Extra! For the Art Specialist

Time: About 45 minutes

Focus

Use *Transparency 13* and have students identify and review the colors of the rainbow. How is the use of color in each work of art similar? How is it different?

Teach

Discuss the correct order of rainbow colors. Have students complete the Alternate Activity.

Reflect

Guide students through evaluation of their work of art using the four steps of art criticism. (See pages 28–29 for more about art criticism.) Then have students describe, analyze, and interpret the work of a classmate.

Alternate Activity

Materials:
- 9″ × 12″ white paper
- watercolors
- watercolor brushes
- water dishes
- paper towels
- pencils
- oil pastels
- scissors
- glue

1. Have students paint horizontal stripes of rainbow colors on a sheet of paper. The stripes should touch each other so the colors will blend along the edges.

2. Have students draw a large animal on another sheet of paper. Using oil pastels, color the animal shape with rainbow colors in vertical stripes.

3. Have students cut out the animal shapes and glue them to the rainbow-colored backgrounds.

Research in Art Education

Competency in the arts can be beneficial when problems need to be solved in other disciplines—for example, "when a theory in science could be understood more fully through the construction of a three-dimensional mobile; or when a mathematical problem could be approached more easily through a closely observed drawing of a shell" ("Learning in and Through the Arts: Curriculum Implications" in *Champions of Change*, p. 42). Understanding the color wheel will be useful for science lessons about properties of light and the color spectrum.

Assessment

Use the following rubric to evaluate the artwork students make in the Creative Expression activity and to assess students' understanding of the lesson concepts.

Have students complete page 33 or 34 in their *Assessment* books.

	Art History and Culture	Aesthetic Perception	Creative Expression	Art Criticism
3 POINTS	The student can identify and compare the subject matter in Kelly's and Hockney's paintings.	The student successfully identifies the rainbow colors in art and the environment.	The student's painting shows a clear understanding of the correct order of the rainbow colors.	The student thoughtfully and honestly evaluates his or her own work using the four steps of art criticism.
2 POINTS	The student's identification or comparison is weak or incomplete.	The student cannot consistently identify the rainbow colors in art and the environment.	The student's painting shows some understanding of the correct order of the rainbow colors.	The student attempts to evaluate his or her own work, but shows an incomplete understanding of evaluation criteria.
1 POINT	The student cannot identify or compare the subject matter in Kelly's and Hockney's paintings.	The student cannot identify the rainbow colors.	The student's painting shows no understanding of the correct order of the rainbow colors.	The student makes no attempt to evaluate his or her own artwork.

Assessment, p. 33

Name _____ Date _____

A Rainbow of Colors

Lesson **1** UNIT 3

For the teacher: Use the following prompt for this activity.
Using crayons, draw the colors of the rainbow in order, starting with red.

Level 1   Unit 3 • Color   **33**

Primary Colors

Lesson 2 introduces students to the primary colors red, yellow, and blue. Primary colors are special because they cannot be made by mixing other colors.

Objectives

Art History and Culture
To recognize that artists sometimes form groups with other artists who have similar beliefs or interests   NSAE 4.a; 4.c

Creative Expression
To use the computer to create a primary color design   NSAE 1.a; 1.c; 2.c; 3.b

Aesthetic Perception
To locate primary colors in art and the environment
NSAE 2.a; 6.b

Art Criticism
To evaluate one's own artwork using the four steps of art criticism
NSAE 1.b; 2.b; 3.a; 5.c

Vocabulary ⭐ Reading

Review the following vocabulary word with students before beginning the lesson.

primary color *color primario*—one of the three basic colors: red, yellow, or blue. Primary colors cannot be made by mixing other colors.

See page 119B for additional vocabulary and Spanish vocabulary resources.

Art Journal: Vocabulary
Have students add this word to the Vocabulary section of their Art Journals.

Lesson Materials
- food coloring (not primary colors)
- bowls
- water
- computer paint program

Alternate Materials:
- colored fruit drinks (not primary colors)
- crayons or markers, white paper

Program Resources
- *Reading and Writing and Test Prep.*, pp. 32–33
- *Flash Card 7*
- *Transparency 14*
- *Artist Profiles*, pp. 21, 44
- *Animals Through History Time Line*
- *Assessment*, pp. 35–36
- *Large Prints 17* Die grossen blauen Pferde and 18 Dance at Bougival
- *The National Museum of Women in the Arts Collection*

Concept Trace
Primary Colors
Introduced: Level K, Unit 3, Lesson 4

Reinforced: Level 2, Unit 3, Lesson 1

Lesson 2 Arts Integration   NSAE 6.a

Theatre

Complete Unit 3, Lesson 2, on pages 56–57 of *Theatre Arts Connections.*

Theatre Arts Connections, p. 56

Music

Musical instruments can be divided into three groups. String instruments make sounds when their strings are vibrated by striking, plucking or bowing. Percussion instruments make sounds when they are shaken or struck. Wind instruments use vibrating air to make their sound. Listen to *The Side Show* by Charles Ives. Have students think about the instruments they hear and classify them.

Movement & Dance

Identify different types of color used to give us signals everyday, such as traffic lights and street signs. Which of these have primary colors? Explore the idea of color signals, using motion. Call out the colors and ask students to respond with motion. Expand the idea by having the class give each color a type of shape rather than an action.

**ocus**

Activate Prior Knowledge

"What can you think of that is always red? Always yellow? Always blue?" *"¿Qué pueden pensar sobre el hecho que siempre es rojo? ¿Siempre es amarillo? ¿Siempre es azul?"*

- Discuss student responses. Some possibilities are stop signs, lemons, and bluebirds.

Using Literature ⭐ Reading

- Read *Ferryboat Ride!* by Anne Rockwell. Have students look for red, yellow, and blue in the illustrations by Maggie Smith.

Thematic Connection ⭐ Social Studies

- **Transportation:** Many types of transportation are mentioned in this lesson, including a fire engine and school bus. Discuss how transportation helps people get things done.

Introduce the Art

Look
NSAE 3.a

"Let's take a look at each work of art." *"Vamos a observar cada obra de arte".*

Interpreting ⭐ Reading

- Ask students what they think is happening in each artwork or what the artwork reminds them of. *Broadway Boogie-Woogie* is nonobjective; it does not have a recognizable subject. The painting looks somewhat like a grid or a map. *Two Fishermen and a Boat* shows men fishing. Another boat is visible in the background.

🏺 Art History and Culture

Share with students the information from the Art History and Culture sections on pages 100–101 about the De Stijl and The Society of Six. Ask students how each artwork in this lesson is representative of its group's style. Discuss with students the possible positive and negative effects of being part of a group. NSAE 4.a; 4.b; 4.c

💻 Web Connection

Broadway Boogie-Woogie is included in the Museum of Modern Art's *Making Choices Guide for Looking,* **www.moma.org/momalearning/makingchoices/.** Have students share their ideas as you guide them through the online exhibition.

  Primary Colors

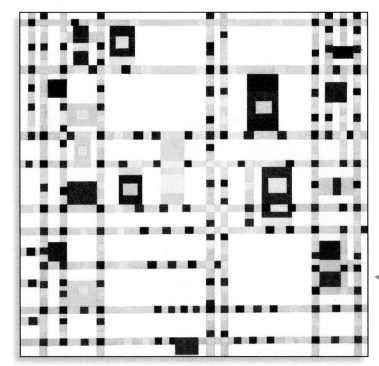

◀ **Piet Mondrian.** (Dutch). *Broadway Boogie-Woogie.* 1942–1943.
....
Oil on canvas. 50 × 50 inches (127 × 127 cm.). The Museum of Modern Art, New York, New York.

Look at the paintings on these pages. They have primary colors.

🏺 Art History and Culture

These artists formed groups with other artists who had similar styles and similar ideas about art.

🏺 Art History and Culture

Piet Mondrian

Piet Mondrian (pēt môn´ drē än) (1872–1944) was born in the Netherlands to a Calvinist family. At a young age, Mondrian could not decide between studying religion or art. He decided to be a painter and became one of the most influential artists of the twentieth century. Mondrian was the leader of the De Stijl, a group of painters and architects who advocated pure abstraction. Neoplasticism was a theory of the De Stijl group. Neoplasticists believe art should not show a realistic subject but instead should express only the universal absolutes of life. Mondrian believed these absolutes were represented by vertical and horizontal lines and primary colors.

See pages 16–21 and 24–25 for more about subject matter and art history.

Artist Profiles, p. 44

Artist Profile
Piet Mondrian
1872–1944
Piet Mondrian's given name was Pieter Cornelis Mondriaan, but he liked to be called Piet Mondrian (pēt môn´ drē än). He was born in the Netherlands to a Calvinist family. At a young age Mondrian could not decide between studying religion or art. He finally decided he wanted to be a painter, but his parents wanted him to be a teacher. He studied to be a teacher and later studied art at the Amsterdam Academy. Mondrian attended evening art classes and worked during the day painting portraits and copying older paintings at museums in Amsterdam. During his life, Mondrian traveled around Europe and lived in many places. He moved to New York City in 1940 to escape the war and

Study the works of art.

▶ What colors do you see?

▲ **Selden Connor Gile.** (American).
Two Fishermen and a Boat. c. 1917.

Oil on panel. 15 × 18 inches (38.1 × 45.72 cm.).
Norton Museum of Art, Palm Beach, Florida.

Aesthetic Perception

Design Awareness What color is a fire engine? A police uniform? A school bus?

Study

▶ *Broadway Boogie-Woogie* has squares and rectangles that are red, yellow, blue, and white. *Two Fishermen and a Boat* is predominantly blue and white, with yellow and red used for accents.

■ For more examples of abstract/ nonobjective art, see ***The National Museum of Women in the Arts Collection.***

Art Journal: Concepts

Have students write the name of each primary color in the Concepts section of their Art Journals.

Aesthetic Perception

Design Awareness Fire engines are red, police uniforms are (usually) blue, and school buses are yellow. Discuss with students that always using the same color makes the objects easily recognizable and makes them stand apart from other objects.

Developing Visual Literacy Discuss the artists' choice to use only primary colors. What was the purpose? What would each artwork be like if the artist had used other colors in addition to red, yellow, and blue?
NSAE 1.b; 2.a; 2.b

Art History and Culture

Selden Connor Gile

Selden Connor Gile (sel´ dən con´ nər gīl) (1877–1947) was born in Maine. He studied business and moved to California after graduation. Gile was a self-taught artist. He joined with five other artists to form a group called The Society of Six. They enjoyed hiking and sketching and painting the scenery while they were outdoors. (This is known as *plein air* painting.)

See pages 16–21 and 24–25 for more about subject matter and art history.

Artist Profiles, p. 21

◆ Artist Profile ◆
Selden Connor Gile
1877-1947
Selden Connor Gile (sel´ dôn con´ nar gil) was born on a farm in Maine and later went to business college. He moved to California, and sold ceramic building materials before teaching himself to paint. Gile loved the outdoors, was an avid hiker, and was known for being an excellent cook and host. Many artists sought his good-natured company, and it was through his warm hospitality and energy that the Society of Six was formed in the 1920s.

Web Connection

Visit **www.thepleinairscene.com** to learn more about plein air painters like Selden Connor Gile.

Teach

Time: About 35 minutes

"Do you think we can create primary colors?"
"¿Creen que podemos crear colores primarios?"

■ Read and discuss Using Primary Colors on page 102.

Practice

Materials: food coloring (not primary colors), bowls, water

Alternate Materials: colored fruit drinks (not primary colors)

■ Distribute the materials and read the directions on page 102.

■ Let students mix food coloring in water to try to make primary colors. Encourage them to suggest other ways colors could be mixed to create red, yellow, or blue.

■ When they see that it doesn't work, explain that *primary* means "first" and that primary colors can't be mixed from other colors.

Creative Expression

NSAE 1.a; 1.c; 2.c
Materials: computer's paint program

Alternate Materials: crayons or markers on white paper

■ Review with students the tools they will be using to create lines and shapes in the paint program. Remind the students that holding the Shift key while using the line tool will make a straight line.

■ Have students follow the directions on page 103.

■ See the Activity Tips on page 238 for visual examples of this lesson's activity.

Art Journal: Brainstorming

Have students brainstorm ideas for ways they could arrange lines and rectangles to represent a city in their primary color design. Have students make quick sketches of their ideas in the Ideas section of their Art Journals. Then have students select an idea to use for the activity.   NSAE 3.b

---

Using Primary Colors

Red, yellow, and blue are **primary colors.**

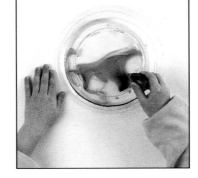

Practice

Try to mix food coloring to make primary colors.

1. Add drops of food coloring to water. Add drops of another color.

2. Try to make red, yellow, or blue.

3. Did it work?

Differentiated Instruction

Reteach
Make transparencies of each rainbow color. Demonstrate that they can be overlapped to make other colors, but no combination will make a primary color.

Special Needs
Adaptations: To help students understand the concept of aerial vantage points, create a small city out of blocks and place it on the floor so that students can look down at it. Activate student's prior knowledge by asking if any have had the experience of seeing the tops of buildings from an airplane.

ELL Tips
Use *Flash Card 7.* Point to each primary color and have students say the name of the color.

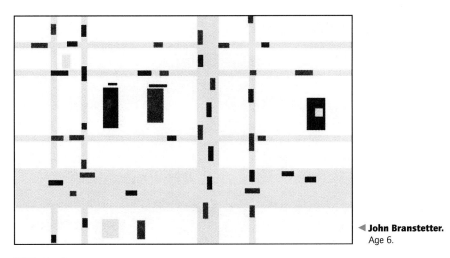

▲ John Branstetter.
Age 6.

Think about how this student used primary colors.

 **Creative Expression**

How could you show what a city looks like from above?

1. Use the computer's paint program. Choose a primary color to draw horizontal and vertical lines that represent streets.

2. Use the other primary colors to draw lines that represent cars and trucks on the streets.

3. Draw primary-colored shapes to represent buildings in the white space.

 **Art Criticism**

Interpret What feeling does your picture create? Give it a title.

Unit 3 • Lesson 2   **103**

Art Across the Curriculum

Use these ideas to reinforce art concepts across the curriculum.
NSAE 6.b

★ **Personal Writing** Have students use the writing process to write a list of their favorite things that are each primary color.

★ **Math** Have students see how many boxes they can count in *Broadway Boogie-Woogie*.

★ **Science** Create a list of items that are red, yellow, and blue. Have students sort the items in the list according to characteristics, such as living or nonliving.

★ **Social Studies** Gile's painting shows two fishermen. Discuss how people can use the sea and other natural resources to meet human needs.

★ **Technology** Have students use the computer's paint program to create a work of art using only primary colors. Visit **SRAonline.com** to print detailed instructions for this activity.

 **Reflect**   Time: About 5 minutes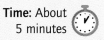

Review and Assess

"What are the primary colors? What is special about them?" "¿Cuáles son los colores primarios? ¿Qué tienen de especial?"

Think

The student artist used primary colors in his computer design.

■ Have students identify primary colors in *Large Prints 17 Die grossen blauen Pferde* and *18 Dance at Bougival.*

Informal Assessment

 **Art Journal: Critical Thinking**
Have students ask themselves the Art Criticism questions, and then write or sketch in their Art Journals to answer the Interpret question.
NSAE 1.b; 2.b; 3.a; 5.c

 Art Criticism

Describe ▶ What colors did you use? What shapes did you use?

Analyze ▶ Which color did you use most? Why?

Interpret ▶ What feeling does your picture create? Give it a title.

Decide ▶ If you added other nonprimary colors, would your picture be more interesting or more confusing?

■ For standardized-format test practice using this lesson's art content, see pages 32–33 in *Reading and Writing Test Preparation.*

LESSON 2 • Primary Colors **103**

Primary Colors

Extra! For the Art Specialist

Time: About 45 minutes

Focus

Use **Transparency 14** to discuss primary colors. What is special about primary colors?

Teach

Have students complete the Alternate Activity. Discuss the creation of any secondary colors. How is the feeling of the painting different from paintings using only primary colors?

Reflect

Guide students through evaluation of their work of art using the four steps of art criticism. (See pages 28–29 for more about art criticism.) Display the works of art as a class exhibition. Have students discuss their ideas about the variety of works created from the same colors.

Alternate Activity

Materials:
- 12″ × 18″ white paper
- liquid tempera paint in primary colors
- paintbrushes
- water containers
- paper towels
- newspaper
- CD of lively music (such as jazz or hip-hop)

1. Play lively music. Have students paint a nonobjective painting, moving their brushes to the music.

2. Discuss the secondary colors that are made as the red, blue, and yellow mix on students' paper.

Research
in Art Education

Some researchers suggest that studying art helps students develop critical thinking and problem-solving skills. Certain aspects of art education may encourage these skills—"art history and art criticism . . . are probably more responsible than studio courses for producing measured improvements in vocabulary, writing, and critical thinking skills" ("Theories and Research That Support Art Instruction for Instrumental Outcomes" in *Schools, Communities, and the Arts: A Research Compendium*). In addition to thinking about the answers, encourage students to write and sketch answers to art criticism questions in their Art Journals.

Assessment
Use the following rubric to evaluate the artwork students make in the Creative Expression activity and to assess students' understanding of the lesson concepts.

Have students complete page 35 or 36 in their **Assessment** books.

	Art History and Culture	Aesthetic Perception	Creative Expression	Art Criticism
3 POINTS	The student can recognize that artists sometimes form groups with other artists who have similar beliefs or interests.	The student accurately identifies primary colors in art and the environment.	The student's shape design incorporates all primary colors.	The student thoughtfully and honestly evaluates his or her own work using the four steps of art criticism.
2 POINTS	The student shows emerging awareness that artists sometimes form groups with other artists.	The student shows emerging awareness of primary colors but cannot consistently identify them.	The student's shape design incorporates some primary colors.	The student attempts to evaluate his or her own work but shows an incomplete understanding of evaluation criteria.
1 POINT	The student does not recognize that artists sometimes form groups with other artists.	The student cannot identify primary colors.	The student's shape design has no primary colors.	The student makes no attempt to evaluate his or her own artwork.

Assessment, p. 35

Name _____ Date _____

Lesson **2** UNIT 3

Primary Colors

For the teacher: Use the following prompt for this activity. Using crayons, draw three different shapes in primary colors.

Level 1

Unit 3 • Color **35**

Red and Yellow Make Orange

Lesson 3 Overview

Lesson 3 teaches that the primary colors red and yellow can be mixed to make the secondary color orange.

Objectives

Art History and Culture

To recognize a few facts about the art and culture of each artist
NSAE 4.a; 4.b; 4.c; 5.a; 5.b

Creative Expression

To create a painting, mixing red and yellow to make orange
NSAE 1.a; 1.c; 1.d

Aesthetic Perception

To identify orange as a secondary color made by mixing the primary colors red and yellow
NSAE 1.a; 2.a

Art Criticism

To evaluate one's own artwork using the four steps of art criticism
NSAE 1.b; 2.b; 3.a; 5.c

Vocabulary ⭐ Reading

Review the following vocabulary words with students before beginning the lesson.

primary color *color primario*—one of the three basic colors: red, yellow, or blue. Primary colors cannot be made by mixing other colors.

secondary color *color secundario*—a color created by mixing two primary colors

See page 119B for additional vocabulary and Spanish vocabulary resources.

Art Journal: Vocabulary

Have students add **secondary color** to the Vocabulary section of their Art Journals.

Lesson Materials

- newspaper
- brushes
- heavy white paper
- paper towels
- water dishes
- red and yellow liquid tempera paint
- palettes

Alternate Materials:
- crayons or markers

Program Resources

- *Reading and Writing Test Prep.,* pp. 34–35
- *Transparency 15*
- *Artist Profiles,* pp. 62, 73
- *Animals Through History Time Line*
- *Assessment,* pp. 37–38
- *Large Prints 17 Die grossen blauen Pferde* and *18 Dance at Bougival*
- *Art Around the World Collection*

Concept Trace
Red and Yellow Make Orange
Introduced: Level 1, Unit 3, Lesson 3
Reinforced: Level 2, Unit 3, Lesson 1

Lesson 3 Arts Integration NSAE 6.a

Theatre

Complete Unit 3, Lesson 3, on pages 58–59 of *Theatre Arts Connections.*

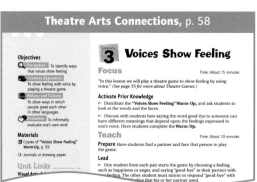

Music

SPOTLIGHT ON MUSIC An instrument everyone has is their voice. Listen to *The Song of the Gingerbread Children Children's Chorus* by Engelbert Humperdink. Can you discern what instruments are blending with the children's voices?

Movement & Dance

Attach colored ribbon or crepe paper to short garden sticks and divide the class into small groups of the same color. Assign action words to each color. Each group moves with their color doing the actions assigned to that color for eight counts. Then combine two groups and have them work together.

Activate Prior Knowledge

"Have you ever mixed two colors of paint to make a new color?" "¿Alguna vez han mezclado dos colores de pintura para crear un nuevo color?"

■ Discuss student responses. Discuss whether they created a muddy color or a color of the rainbow. Explain that when two primary colors (red, yellow, or blue) are mixed, they create a secondary color (orange, green, or violet).

Using Literature ⭐ Reading

■ Read *Moo Moo, Brown Cow* by Jakki Wood, illustrated by Rog Bonner. The illustration of the hen is a great example of red and yellow mixed to make orange.

Thematic Connection ⭐ Math

■ **Numbers/Math:** Equate mixing colors with addition. Tell students they know that $1 + 1 = 2$. Similarly, if they add one primary color to another, they will get a secondary color.

Introduce the Art

Look   NSAE 3.a

"Let's look closely at the colors in these works of art." "Vamos a mirar detalladamente los colores de estas obras de arte".

Adjectives and Adverbs ⭐ Language Arts

■ Have students describe each work of art. List on a chart the adjectives and adverbs students use.

🏺 Art History and Culture

Share information from the Art History and Culture sections with students. Ask students how each work of art reflects information they have learned about each artist. The Shuar people made crowns out of feathers. *Man's Headband of Toucan Feathers* is made of feathers. Tamayo liked to use only a few colors in his paintings. *Toast to the Sun* has mostly orange.
NSAE 4.a; 4.b

💻 **Web Connection**

Visit www.eduweb.com/amazon.html to learn about the Ecuadorian Amazon, where the Shuar people live.

◀ **Artist Unknown.** (Ecuador). *Man's Headband of Toucan Feathers.*
Cotton, feathers, human hair, and thread. Courtesy of the Smithsonian National Museum of the American Indian, New York, New York.

Look at the colors in these works of art. The artists used red, yellow, and orange.

🏺 Art History and Culture

Rufino Tamayo usually liked to use only two or three colors in a painting.

🏺 Art History and Culture

Man's Headband of Toucan Feathers was made by an unknown Shuar artist. The Shuar people are a forest tribe in Ecuador. They use brilliant, tropical bird feathers to create ornaments for tribal ceremonies. In Shuar language, this feathered crown is called a *tawasap*. Older men and political leaders wear tawasaps on special occasions as a symbol of bravery and authority. The crown consists of a woven cotton band, red and yellow toucan feathers, and the black feathers of a bird called *awacha* in Shuar.

See pages 16–21 and 24–25 for more about subject matter and art history.
NSAE 5.a

Artist Profiles, p. 73

Artist Profile

Man's Headband of Toucan Feathers

This headband was made by unidentified Shuar people from Ecuador. Ecuador is part of the Amazon basin. The Amazon covers an area of about six million square miles and extends into nine countries—Peru, Brazil, Ecuador, Colombia, Bolivia, Venezuela, French Guyana, Guyana, and Surinam. Five hundred different tribes live in the Amazon. Each tribe has its own language, beliefs, and customs. Today Amazonian tribes continue to work to preserve their cultures.

Artist unknown. (Ecuador). *Man's Headband of Toucan Feathers.*
Cotton, feathers, human hair, and thread. Courtesy of the Smithsonian

▲ **Rufino Tamayo.** (Mexican).
Toast to the Sun. 1956.
Oil on canvas. 31½ × 39 inches (80 × 99 cm.).
Wichita Art Museum, Wichita, Kansas.

Study the works of art.

▶ Where do you see red?

▶ Where do you see yellow?

▶ Where do you see orange?

🔍 Aesthetic Perception

Design Awareness Look around. Do you see anything orange?

🏺 Art History and Culture

Rufino Tamayo NSAE 5.b

Rufino Tamayo (rōō fēʹ nō tə mīʹ ō) (1899–1991) was born in Mexico. Both of his parents died when he was a boy. Tamayo went to live with his aunt, and he helped run her fruit stand. This had a great influence on him, and Tamayo's future art would often depict fruit or fruit colors. Tamayo's aunt sent him to business school in 1915, but he left after one year to study art. Tamayo worked as a draftsman for the National Museum of Anthropology in Mexico City. There he was exposed to artifacts from earlier Mexican cultures, which also influenced his art. Tamayo often painted with a limited palette. He felt that "with two or three colors at the most you can express more than plenty."

See pages 16–21 and 24–25 for more about subject matter and art history.

Artist Profiles, p. 62

Artist Profile

Rufino Tamayo
1899–1991

Born in Oaxaca, Mexico, in 1899, Rufino Tamayo (rōō fēʹ nō tə mīʹ ō) was orphaned at the age of 12 and sent to live with his aunt in Mexico City. He began taking art lessons at the age of 16 and spent most of his time drawing. This caused his aunt to remove him from school and put him to work as a vendor in her fruit business. She hoped the move would encourage the young Tamayo to concentrate on other things, but he continued to draw—now using the fruit as his subject. This indomitable passion for art was evident throughout Tamayo's career, as he emphasized the universality of painting and the importance of artistic freedom.

Study

▶ The Shuar headband has red feathers. In *Toast to the Sun,* the person's body is red.

▶ The Shuar headband has yellow feathers. In *Toast to the Sun,* yellow is found in the sky and surrounding the sun. Yellow colors are also seen in the glass the person is raising.

▶ Orange can be seen on the Shuar headband where the feathers meet and overlap. The sun and other areas of the sky in *Toast to the Sun* are orange. Orange colors are also seen in the glass the person is raising.

■ For more examples of art from Latin America, see the *Art Around the World Collection.*

📓 Art Journal: Concepts
Have students write the names of the primary colors used to make orange in the Concepts section of their Art Journals.

🔍 Aesthetic Perception

Design Awareness Discuss with students objects that have been designed with the color orange. For example, safety items such as cones or safety patrol vests are usually orange. Orange is a bright color that can be used when someone wants to draw attention to something.
NSAE 2.b

Developing Visual Literacy Have students describe how each artwork makes them feel. What is it about the artwork that makes them feel that way? Would their feelings be different if the works of art had been made with different colors or materials?
NSAE 1.a; 1.b; 2.b; 5.c

💻 Web Connection
Toast to the Sun is housed at the Wichita Art Museum. Visit their Web site **www.wichitaartmuseum.org.**

Teach

Time: About 40 minutes

"Let's practice making the color orange."
"Vamos a practicar cómo hacer el color anaranjado".

- Read and discuss Using Red and Yellow to Make Orange on page 106.

Practice

Materials: red and yellow liquid tempera paint, palettes, brushes

Alternate Materials: red and yellow finger paint, white paper

- Distribute the materials and have students follow the directions on page 106.

- Have students vary the amounts of red and yellow paint to create different shades of orange. The orange paint will be used in the Creative Expression activity.

Creative Expression

NSAE 1.a; 1.c; 1.d

Materials: newspaper, brushes, heavy white paper, paper towels, water dishes, red and yellow liquid tempera paint, palettes

Alternate Materials: red and yellow chalk

- Distribute the materials and have students follow the directions on page 107.

- Review the Technique Tips on pages 216–218 for information about painting with tempera and proper care of the paintbrush.

- See the Activity Tips on page 239 for visual examples of this lesson's activity.

- Students' papers should be filled with color when they are finished.

Art Journal: Brainstorming

Have students brainstorm ideas for shapes they could make in their paintings. Have students make quick sketches of their ideas in the Ideas section of their Art Journals.

NSAE 3.b

Using Red and Yellow to Make Orange

Red and yellow are **primary colors.** They can be mixed to make the **secondary color** orange.

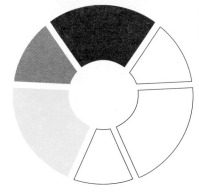

Orange is between red and yellow on the color wheel.

Practice

Mix red and yellow to make orange.

1. Start with yellow paint. Add red. Mix to make orange.

2. Try adding more red. How did the color change?

3. See how many oranges you can make.

Differentiated Instruction

Reteach

Give each student a sheet of primary-colored paper. Ask those students who have one of the colors needed to make orange to stand up. The students who are seated can check to make sure only those with red and yellow are standing.

Special Needs

Adaptations: Reinforce the concept of color mixing by having acetate swatches of red and yellow for each student to manipulate. Have the student look through the yellow swatch and then add the red swatch. Ask them what color they see.

ELL Tips

Have students point to the shapes in their Creative Expression paintings and say the name of each shape's color in their native language and then in English.

◄ **Amy Kuhn.** Age 5.

Think about how this student used red, yellow, and orange.

 **Creative Expression**

How many different oranges can you make using only yellow and red?

1. Think of a shape for yellow and one for red. Paint your shapes.

2. Mix red and yellow paint to make orange. See how many oranges you can make.

3. Fill the rest of the paper with orange.

 **Art Criticism**

Analyze How many different oranges did you create and paint?

Art Across the Curriculum

Use these ideas to reinforce concepts across the curriculum.
NSAE 6.b

★ **Expository Writing** Have students use the writing process to write step-by-step instructions for mixing red and yellow paint to make orange.

★ **Math** Have students write number problems using pictures of yellow and red paint drops equaling orange paint drops.

★ **Science** Red, yellow, and orange are colors that indicate heat. Discuss changes caused by heat.

★ **Social Studies** Pumpkins and autumn leaves can be orange. Discuss holidays and customs that are celebrated in autumn.

★ **Technology** Have students re-create their Creative Expression paintings using the shape tools, the fill tool, and the color palette in the computer's paint program. Visit **SRAonline.com** to print detailed instructions for this activity.

 **Reflect**   Time: About 5 minutes

Review and Assess

"What color do you get if you mix red and yellow?" "¿Qué color obtienen si mezclan el rojo con el amarillo?"

Think

The student's painting has red and yellow shapes and an orange background.

■ Have students look at **Large Prints 17** *Die grossen blauen Pferde* and **18** *Dance at Bougival* and identify where red and yellow mix to make orange.

Informal Assessment

Art Journal: Critical Thinking
Have students ask themselves the Art Criticism questions, and then write or sketch in their Art Journals to answer the Analyze question.
NSAE 1.b; 2.b; 3.a; 5.c

 Art Criticism

Describe ► Name the shapes in your painting. Which are red? Yellow? Orange?

Analyze ► How many different oranges did you create and paint?

Interpret ► What is the mood of your painting? Give your artwork a title.

Decide ► Did you mix red and yellow to make orange? Did you use all three colors in your painting?

■ For standardized-format test practice using this lesson's art content, see pages 34–35 in **Reading and Writing Test Preparation.**

Lesson 3 Wrap-Up

Red and Yellow Make Orange

Extra! For the Art Specialist

Focus

Use **Transparency 15** to discuss how the primary colors red and yellow can mix to create the secondary color orange. What orange objects can students think of?

Teach

Have students complete the Alternate Activity. Did they create different oranges by mixing different ratios of red and yellow?

Reflect

Guide students through evaluation of their work of art using the four steps of art criticism. (See pages 28–29 for more about art criticism.)

Alternate Activity

Materials:

- red and yellow liquid tempera paint
- 9" × 12" white paper
- paintbrushes
- palettes
- water dishes
- paper towels
- newspaper

Have students paint a garden or still life of red, yellow, and orange flowers. Or, have students paint a fruit bowl of oranges, bananas, and apples.

Research in Art Education

Research has shown that "the relevancy of activities [in arts education], respectful climate, and opportunities for learners to take responsibility . . . [provide] a context for learner risk-taking and increased motivation and engagement." Studies also have demonstrated that "these desirable processes and teaching characteristics are inherent to dynamic, multiple-arts teaching environments" ("Promising Signs of Positive Effects: Lessons from the Multi-Arts Studies" in *Critical Links*, p. 99). This lesson provides the opportunity for students to take responsibility by mixing their own shades of orange paint.

Assessment

Use the following rubric to evaluate the artwork students make in the Creative Expression activity and to assess students' understanding of the lesson concepts.

Have students complete page 37 or 38 in their *Assessment* books.

	Art History and Culture	Aesthetic Perception	Creative Expression	Art Criticism
3 POINTS	The student identifies a few facts about the art and culture of each artist.	The student successfully identifies orange as a secondary color made by mixing red and yellow.	The student's shape painting has orange paint that is successfully mixed from red and yellow.	The student thoughtfully and honestly evaluates his or her own work using the four steps of art criticism.
2 POINTS	The student's identification is weak or incomplete.	The student shows emerging awareness that orange is a secondary color made by mixing two primary colors, but cannot consistently identify them.	The student attempts to mix red and yellow to make orange.	The student attempts to evaluate his or her own work but shows an incomplete understanding of evaluation criteria.
1 POINT	The student cannot identify a few facts about the art and culture of each artist.	The student cannot identify orange as a secondary color made by mixing two primary colors.	The student does not mix red and yellow to make orange.	The student makes no attempt to evaluate his or her own artwork.

Assessment, p. 37

Name _____ Date _____

Red and Yellow Make Orange

Lesson **3** UNIT 3

For the teacher: Use the following prompt for this activity.
Using oil pastels, blend yellow on top of red to make orange.

Level 1   Unit 3 • Color **37**

Blue and Yellow Make Green

Lesson 4 teaches that the primary colors blue and yellow can be mixed to make the secondary color green.

Objectives

Art History and Culture
To recognize that many artists paint landscapes showing their surroundings
NSAE 4.b; 4.c; 5.a; 5.b

Creative Expression
To draw a picture using yellow and blue oil pastels to make green
NSAE 1.a; 1.c; 1.d; 2.c

Aesthetic Perception
To identify the secondary color green as a mixture of the primary colors blue and yellow
NSAE 1.a; 2.a

Art Criticism
To evaluate one's own artwork using the four steps of art criticism
NSAE 1.b; 2.b; 3.a; 5.c

Vocabulary ⭐ Reading

Review the following vocabulary words with students before beginning the lesson.

primary color color primario—one of the three basic colors: red, yellow, or blue. Primary colors cannot be made by mixing other colors.

secondary color color secundario—a color created by mixing two primary colors

See page 119B for additional vocabulary and Spanish vocabulary resources.

Art Journal: Vocabulary

Have students review these words in the Vocabulary section of their Art Journals.

Lesson Materials
- blue and yellow oil pastels
- white paper

Alternate Materials:
- crayons

Program Resources
- *Reading and Writing Test Prep.,* pp. 36–37
- *Transparency 16*
- *Artist Profiles,* pp. 17, 49
- *Animals Through History Time Line*
- *Assessment,* pp. 39–40
- *Large Prints 17 Die grossen blauen Pferde* and *18 Dance at Bougival*
- *The National Museum of Women in the Arts Collection*

Concept Trace
Blue and Yellow Make Green
Introduced: Level 1, Unit 3, Lesson 4
Reinforced: Level 2, Unit 3, Lesson 1

Lesson 4 Arts Integration NSAE 6.a

Theatre
Complete Unit 3, Lesson 4, on pages 60–61 of *Theatre Arts Connections.*

Theatre Arts Connections, p. 60

Music
A string quartet blends the sounds of string instruments with each other. There are two violins, one viola and a cello in *String Quartet Op. 33 No. 3 Movement 4* by Franz Joseph Haydn. Listen to the sounds of the blend and the occasional instrument playing on its own.

Movement & Dance
Attach colored ribbon or crepe paper to short garden sticks and have students form a large circle. Have all students with one color travel to the center and move for eight counts. Once all colors have taken their turn, combine two colors by having two groups go to the center at the same time.

Focus

Time: About 10 minutes

Activate Prior Knowledge

"What color do you see most often outdoors?" "¿Qué color ven más a menudo cuando están afuera?"

- Discuss landscapes filled with green grass, trees, and leaves.

Using Literature ⭐ Reading

- Read *Is Your Mama a Llama?* by Deborah Guarino. The outdoor scenes in the illustrations by Steven Kellogg show blue and yellow mixed to make green.

Thematic Connection ⭐ Science

- **Environment:** Discuss the environment with students. Talk about what can be done to protect it and keep it green.

Introduce the Art

Look
NSAE 2.a

"Let's look at these paintings." "Vamos a observar estas pinturas".

Comparing and Contrasting ⭐ Reading

- Have students discuss the variations between the works of art. Both works of art have a lot of yellow and green. *Touchwood Hills* shows an aerial view of many trees and the ground. In *Papaw Tree—'Iao Valley*, the ground is not visible and only a single tree is shown with some mountains in the background.

🏺 Art History and Culture

Remind students that a landscape is a picture of the outdoors. Share the information from the Art History and Culture sections on pages 108–109 and discuss that the artists often painted landscapes showing their surroundings. NSAE 4.b; 4.c; 5.a; 5.b

💻 Web Connection

The Pavilion Gallery Museum, **www.partnersinthepark .org/gallery.html**, is home to the largest permanent collection of Eyre's paintings.

Blue and Yellow Make Green

▲ **Ivan Eyre.** (Canadian). *Touchwood Hills.* 1972–1973.
Acrylic on canvas. 58 × 65 inches (147.3 × 167.6 cm.). National Gallery of Canada, Ottawa, Ontario.

Look at the works of art on these pages. The artists used blue, yellow, and green.

🏺 Art History and Culture

Many artists paint landscapes showing their surroundings.

🏺 Art History and Culture

Ivan Eyre

Ivan Eyre (ī′ vən ēr) (1935–) was born in Saskatchewan, Canada. He studied art at a number of universities and then became a professor of painting and drawing. In 1974 Eyre was chosen to be a member of the Royal Canadian Academy, which recognizes outstanding Canadian artists. Eyre has exhibited his work often and has sold his work to many collectors. He is known for his landscapes depicting Canadian hills and forests.

See pages 16–21 and 24–25 for more about subject matter and art history.

Artist Profiles, p. 17

Artist Profile

Ivan Eyre
b. 1935

Ivan Eyre (ī′ vən ēr) was born in rural Saskatchewan, a province in Canada. His family was extremely poor. They moved from place to place throughout Canada as his father looked for work. When Eyre was in fifth grade, he won a prize for painting. His teachers encouraged him to continue making art. He went to after-school art classes while he was in high school. After he graduated, he went to art school in Winnipeg. In 1967, the Canada Council paid for him to travel around Europe. He returned from his travels to teach in Winnipeg, Manitoba. He has also taught art at the University of North Dakota and the University of Manitoba.

Georgia O'Keeffe. (American). *Papaw Tree—'Iao Valley.* 1939.

Oil on canvas. 19 × 16 inches (48.3 × 40.6 cm.). Honolulu Academy of Arts, Honolulu, Hawaii.

Study both works of art.

▶ How many greens do you see?

Aesthetic Perception

Seeing Like an Artist Collect some green leaves. Arrange them from lightest to darkest green.

Art History and Culture

Georgia O'Keeffe

Georgia O'Keeffe (jor´ jə ō´ kēf´) (1887–1986) knew as a child that she wanted to be an artist when she grew up. She knew she wanted to create art that was different from other art she had seen. O'Keeffe created larger-than-life paintings of natural things such as flowers, bones, or shells. She never painted people. O'Keeffe often painted scenes of the Southwest, especially New Mexico, where she lived for many years. A Georgia O'Keeffe museum opened in Santa Fe, New Mexico, in 1997. It was the first museum in the United States devoted exclusively to the artwork of a female artist.

See pages 16–21 and 24–25 for more about subject matter and art history.

Artist Profiles, p. 49

• Artist Profile •

Georgia O'Keeffe
1887–1986

Georgia O'Keeffe (jōr´ jə ō kēf´) was born in Sun Prairie, Wisconsin. At the age of ten she began taking private art lessons, but the thing she liked most was experimenting with art at home. By 13, she had decided to become an artist. She trained under experts and won many prizes for her art. For years she challenged the art world with her unique vision. She eventually became famous for her spectacular, larger-than-life paintings of natural objects, including flowers, animal skulls, and shells. She loved nature, especially the desert of New Mexico, where she spent the last half of her life. O'Keeffe was married to the famous American photographer Alfred Stieglitz and appears in many of his photographs.

Study

▶ Each artwork has many shades of green, ranging from light to dark. Some greens look more yellow than others.

■ For more examples of landscapes, see *The National Museum of Women in the Arts Collection.*

Art Journal: Concepts

Have students write the names of the primary colors used to make green in the Concepts section of their Art Journals.

Aesthetic Perception

Seeing Like an Artist Bring in leaves or have students collect green leaves. Have students notice the different greens and arrange them in order from lightest to darkest.

Developing Visual Literacy Have students discuss whether they have ever been in a setting like either of those pictured in the works of art. Have students compare the landscapes to their personal experiences. If students have not seen a landscape like one pictured, discuss where it might exist.
NSAE 2.b

Web Connection
Visit the Georgia O'Keeffe Museum Web site at **www.okeeffemuseum.org.** Have students view works from O'Keeffe's portfolio and share their ideas about her art.

Teach

Time: About 40 minutes

"Let's practice mixing blue and yellow to make green." *"Vamos a practicar cómo mezclar el azul y el amarillo para hacer verde".*

- Read and discuss Using Blue and Yellow to Make Green on page 110.

Practice

Materials: blue and yellow oil pastels, white paper

Alternate Materials: blue and yellow tempera paint, brushes

- Distribute the materials and have students follow the directions on page 110.

- Review the Technique Tips on page 216 for information about using oil pastels.

- Students should see that it is better to make green with the stronger color (blue) on the bottom. Demonstrate how to make variations of green by using different amounts of blue and yellow.

Creative Expression

NSAE 1.a; 1.c; 1.d; 2.c
Materials: blue and yellow oil pastels, white paper

Alternate Materials: crayons

- Distribute the materials and have students follow the directions on page 111.

- See the Activity Tips on page 239 for visual examples of techniques.

Art Journal: Brainstorming

Have students brainstorm ideas for outdoor green scenes, such as a jungle, forest, or backyard. Have students make quick sketches of their ideas in the Ideas section of their Art Journals. Then have students select an idea to use for the activity.

NSAE 3.b

Using Blue and Yellow to Make Green

Blue and yellow are **primary colors.** They can be mixed to make the **secondary color** green.

Green is between yellow and blue on the color wheel.

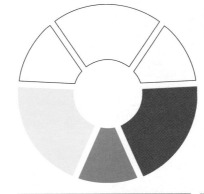

Practice

Mix blue and yellow to make green.

1. Use a blue oil pastel to make a shape on paper.

2. Cover the shape with yellow pastel. Blend the colors.

3. Make another shape with yellow pastel. Then cover it with blue pastel. Blend the colors.

4. Which green is stronger?

110 Unit 3 • Lesson 4

Differentiated Instruction

Reteach

Give each student a primary-colored sheet of paper. Ask those students who have one of the colors needed to make green to stand up. The students who are seated can check to make sure only those with blue and yellow are standing.

Special Needs

Adaptations: Have a labeled color wheel available to reinforce color naming and relationships among primary and secondary colors. Also, a green value scale will demonstrate to students the range of green values that exist.

ELL Tips

Have students point to the colors in their Creative Expression paintings and say the name of each color in their native language and then in English.

◄ **Dustin Durrence.**
Age 7.

Think about how this student made a green scene.

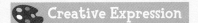 **Creative Expression**

What colors do you see most outdoors? Draw a green scene.

1. Imagine a summer day outside. Choose the green things to put in your scene.

2. Make green things by mixing blue and yellow.

3. Use blue and yellow to fill the background.

 **Art Criticism**

Describe What objects did you draw?

Art Across the Curriculum

Use these ideas to reinforce art concepts across the curriculum.
NSAE 6.b

★ **Poetry Writing** Have students use the writing process to write a short poem about a green outdoor scene.

★ **Math** Have students measure the length of the different leaves used for the Seeing Like an Artist activity.

★ **Science** Have students observe an outdoor scene and describe the plants and animals.

★ **Social Studies** Have students discuss the physical characteristics (such as landforms or weather) of each location in the works of art.

★ **Technology** Have students use the computer's paint or draw program to create a make-believe land filled with yellows, blues, and greens. Visit **SRAonline.com** to print detailed instructions for this activity.

 **Reflect** Time: About 5 minutes

Review and Assess

"What color do you get if you mix blue and yellow?" "¿Qué colores obtienen si mezclan el azul con el amarillo?"

Think

The student made a green frog and green leaves by blending yellow and blue pastels.

■ Have students look at **Large Prints 17** *Die grossen blauen Pferde* and **18** *Dance at Bougival* and identify where blue and yellow mix to make green.

Informal Assessment

Art Journal: Critical Thinking
Have students ask themselves the Art Criticism questions, and then write or sketch in their Art Journals to answer the Describe question.
NSAE 1.b; 2.b; 3.a; 5.c

 Art Criticism

Describe ► What objects did you draw?

Analyze ► How many different greens did you make?

Interpret ► What is the mood of your artwork? Give your work a title.

Decide ► Did you mix blue and yellow to make green? Did you use all three colors in your artwork?

■ For standardized-format test practice using this lesson's art content, see pages 36–37 in **Reading and Writing Test Preparation.**

Blue and Yellow Make Green

Extra! For the Art Specialist

Time: About 45 minutes

Focus

Use *Transparency 16* to discuss how the primary colors yellow and blue mix to create the secondary color green. What green objects can students think of?

Teach

Have students complete the Alternate Activity. Do students' collages have more than one shade of green?

Reflect

Guide students through evaluation of their works of art using the four steps of art criticism. (See pages 28–29 for more about art criticism.)

Alternate Activity

Materials:
- tissue paper (light blue, yellow, and green)
- diluted white glue
- glue dishes
- glue brushes
- 9" × 12" white posterboard
- scissors

1. Have students tear 1" to 2" pieces of light blue and yellow tissue paper. Using diluted white glue, have students paint glue on a small section of posterboard. Then have students place a piece of torn tissue paper on the glue, and paint over it with another layer of glue. As students overlap and glue the light blue and yellow pieces of tissue paper, they will see the colors mix to make green.

2. After the posterboard is covered with blue and yellow tissue paper, have students cut out shapes from green tissue paper to glue on top of the background.

Research in Art Education

Research has indicated that one important outcome of integrating the arts into other curriculum areas is an increased level of classroom discussions and more time spent on problem solving. The level of teacher dedication and experience seems to influence these outcomes ("Different Ways of Knowing: 1991–94 National Longitudinal Study Final Report" in *Schools, Communities, and the Arts: A Research Compendium*). Discussion of colors and color mixing can be integrated easily into math and science classes.

Assessment

Use the following rubric to evaluate the artwork students make in the Creative Expression activity and to assess students' understanding of the lesson concepts.

Have students complete page 39 or 40 in their *Assessment* books.

	Art History and Culture	Aesthetic Perception	Creative Expression	Art Criticism
3 POINTS	The student recognizes that many artists paint landscapes showing their surroundings.	The student successfully identifies green as a secondary color made from mixing blue and yellow.	The student's drawing has green that is successfully mixed from blue and yellow.	The student thoughtfully and honestly evaluates his or her own work using the four steps of art criticism.
2 POINTS	The student shows emerging awareness that many artists paint landscapes showing their surroundings.	The student shows emerging awareness that green is a secondary color made from mixing two primary colors but cannot consistently identify them.	The student attempts to mix blue and yellow to make green.	The student attempts to evaluate his or her own work but shows an incomplete understanding of evaluation criteria.
1 POINT	The student does not recognize that many artists paint landscapes showing their surroundings.	The student cannot identify green as a secondary color made from mixing two primary colors.	The student does not mix blue and yellow to make green.	The student makes no attempt to evaluate his or her own artwork.

Assessment, p. 39

Name _____ Date _____

Lesson **4** UNIT 3

Blue and Yellow Make Green

For the teacher: Use the following prompt for this activity. Using oil pastels, blend yellow on top of blue to make green.

Level 1   Unit 3 • Color   **39**

Red and Blue Make Violet

Lesson 5 teaches that the primary colors red and blue can be mixed to make the secondary color violet.

Objectives

Art History and Culture
To identify a few facts about the fauve style of art
NSAE 4.a; 4.b

Creative Expression
To use red and blue tissue paper to create a creature that looks violet
NSAE 1.a; 1.c; 1.d; 2.c; 3.b

Aesthetic Perception
To identify the secondary color violet as a mixture of the primary colors red and blue
NSAE 1.a; 2.a

Art Criticism
To evaluate one's own artwork using the four steps of art criticism
NSAE 1.b; 2.b; 3.a; 5.c

Vocabulary ⭐ Reading

Review the following vocabulary words with students before beginning the lesson.

primary color color primario—one of the three basic colors: red, yellow, or blue. Primary colors cannot be made by mixing other colors.

secondary color color secundario—a color created by mixing two primary colors

See page 119B for additional vocabulary and Spanish vocabulary resources.

Art Journal: Vocabulary
Have students review these words in the Vocabulary section of their Art Journals.

Lesson Materials
- 9" × 12" white paper
- glue dishes
- glue brushes
- newspaper
- diluted white liquid glue
- black markers
- tissue paper in various shades of red and blue
- paper towels

Alternate Materials:
- crayons or oil pastels on light-colored or white paper

Program Resources
- *Reading and Writing Test Prep.,* pp. 38–39
- *Transparency 17*
- *Artist Profiles,* pp. 23, 42
- *Animals Through History Time Line*
- *Assessment,* pp. 41–42
- *Large Prints 17 Die grossen blauen Pferde* and *18 Dance at Bougival*
- *The National Museum of Women in the Arts Collection*

Concept Trace
Red and Blue Make Violet
Introduced: Level 1, Unit 3, Lesson 5

Reinforced: Level 2, Unit 3, Lesson 1

Lesson 5 Arts Integration   NSAE 6.a

Theatre

Complete Unit 3, Lesson 5, on pages 62–63 of *Theatre Arts Connections.*

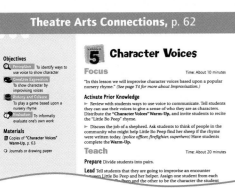

Theatre Arts Connections, p. 62

Objectives
- Perception To identify ways to use voice to show character
- Creative Expression To show character by improvising voices
- History and Culture To play a game based upon a nursery rhyme
- Evaluation To informally evaluate one's own work

Materials
- Copies of "Character Voices" Warm-Up, p. 63
- Journals or drawing paper

Lesson 5 Character Voices

Focus   Time: About 10 minutes

"In this lesson we will improvise character voices based upon a popular nursery rhyme." *(See page T4 for more about Improvisation.)*

Activate Prior Knowledge
▶ Review with students ways to use voice to communicate. Tell students they can use their voices to give a sense of who they are as characters. Distribute the "Character Voices" Warm-Up, and invite students to recite the "Little Bo Peep" rhyme.
▶ Discuss the job of a shepherd. Ask students to think of people in the community who might help Little Bo Peep find her sheep if the rhyme were written today. *(police officer, firefighter, superhero)* Have students complete the Warm-Up.

Teach   Time: About 20 minutes

Prepare Divide students into pairs.

Lead Tell students that they are going to improvise an encounter between Little Bo Peep and her helper. Assign one student from each pair to be Bo Peep and the other to be the character the student

Music

Listen to *Concerto for Two Trumpets RV 537* by Antonio Vivaldi. Trumpets are featured in this composition with full orchestra. Have students raise their hands when they hear the sounds of the brass instruments in the blend. Have students listen again for the times they hear only the orchestra.

Movement & Dance

Attach colored ribbon or crepe paper to short garden sticks and have students form a large circle. Have all students with one color travel to the center, move for eight counts and then freeze in a shape. Another color group enters and moves for eight counts and then also freezes in a shape. Repeat until all groups and colors are in the center.

Focus

Time: About 10 minutes

Activate Prior Knowledge

"Have you ever seen a violet flower?"
"¿Alguna vez han visto una flor violeta?"

- Discuss violets and other purple flowers. Remind students that the color violet is also called *purple*.

Using Literature ⭐ Reading

- Read *The Purple Coat* by Amy Hest. The purple fabric in the illustrations by Amy Schwartz contains flecks of red and blue.

Thematic Connection ⭐ Math

- **Time:** Matisse's painting shows the reflection of the afternoon sunlight on the buildings. Discuss different times of day and the appearance of the sun.

Introduce the Art

Look
NSAE 2.a; 2.b; 3.a

"Let's take a close look at these two works of art." "Vamos a mirar detalladamente estas dos obras de arte".

Main Idea and Details ⭐ Reading

- Have students discuss what they see in each painting. In *A Glimpse of Notre Dame in the Late Afternoon*, students may identify buildings, a river, a bridge, a road, and people walking along the road. *Dido* is nonobjective. It does not have a recognizable subject. Have students discuss what the painting reminds them of.

🏺 Art History and Culture

Share with students the information about Henri Matisse from the Art History and Culture section on page 113. Discuss that Matisse painted in the fauve style of art. Use the **Animals Through History Time Line** to show students when this movement occurred—during the first decade of the 20th century.   NSAE 4.a; 4.b

💻 Web Connection

The Minneapolis Institute of Arts has a Web site at **www.artsmia.org/hartigan/** with activities and information about one of Hartigan's paintings.

Red and Blue Make Violet

▲ **Grace Hartigan.**
(American). *Dido.* 1960.

Oil on canvas. 82 × 91 inches
(208.28 × 231.14 cm.). McNay
Art Museum, San Antonio, Texas.

Look at the works of art on these pages. The artists used red, blue, and violet.

🏺 Art History and Culture

Henri Matisse was the leader of a group of artists called the Fauves. *Fauves* means "wild beasts" in French.

🏺 Art History and Culture

Grace Hartigan   NSAE 4.c

Grace Hartigan (grās härt´ ə gən) (1922–) was born in New Jersey. When Hartigan was five she developed pneumonia and was bedridden for a year. During that time she taught herself to read and draw. After graduating from high school, Hartigan took drawing classes at night school. During World War II she worked as a draftsperson for an airplane factory. Another draftsperson showed her a book of paintings by Henri Matisse, whose work became an influence on and an inspiration to Hartigan. She moved to New York City and became a successful painter. Hartigan is known to be extremely focused on her work and will not leave a painting until it is finished.

See pages 16–21 and 24–25 for more about subject matter and art history.

Artist Profiles, p. 23

▸ Artist Profile ◂

Grace Hartigan
b. 1922

Grace Hartigan (grās härt´ ti gən) began her career in the 1950s as one of the most promising young abstract expressionist painters in New York. A member of the second generation of artists to work in the new style, Hartigan distinguished herself early on. Her art was chosen for important gallery and museum exhibitions, and she was hailed as a rising art star in national magazines such as *Life* and *Fortune*. For the first years of her career, she was known as George Hartigan, after the female novelists George Sand and George Eliot. Hartigan identified passionately with the liberated lifestyles of these women.

Study the paintings.

► Where do you see red?

► Where do you see blue?

► Where do you see violet?

◄ **Henri Matisse.** (French).
A Glimpse of Notre Dame in the Late Afternoon. 1902.
....
Oil on paper mounted on canvas.
28½ × 21½ inches (72.39 × 54.61 cm.).
Albright-Knox Art Gallery, Buffalo,
New York.

Aesthetic Perception

Design Awareness Look around your classroom.
What do you see that is violet?

Art History and Culture

Henri Matisse

Henri Matisse (än´ rē ma tēs´) (1869–1954) was born in France. He studied for a career in law, but in 1890 became ill with appendicitis and was bedridden. While he was recovering from his illness, he began to paint to relieve his boredom. After he recovered, Matisse gave up law and decided to study art. Matisse was the leader of an art movement called fauvism. The name *fauve* means "wild beast" in French and was given to these artists because of their wild use of bright colors.

See pages 16–21 and 24–25 for more about subject matter and art history.

Artist Profiles, p. 42

◄ Artist Profile ►
Henri Matisse
1869-1954
Henri Matisse (än´ rē ma tēs´) was the son of a middle-class couple in the north of France. He was not interested in art while he was in school. After high school his father sent him to law school in Paris. When he was 21 an appendicitis attack changed his life. Because he had to spend a long time in the hospital, his mother brought him a paint box to help him pass the time. Matisse eventually convinced his father to let him drop out of law school and study art. Matisse married and started a family soon after. His paintings were not selling, so he worked for a decorator and his wife opened a hat shop. During the last years of his life he suffered from arthritis. Unable to hold a brush in his hands, he devoted his efforts to

Study

► *Dido* has a large field of red at the top of the painting and red splotches in the middle. In *A Glimpse of Notre Dame in the Late Afternoon,* red accents are found on the edges of the buildings and structures.

► In *Dido,* fields of blue are located on the left of the painting. In *A Glimpse of Notre Dame in the Late Afternoon,* the sky, water, bridge, street, and trees are blue.

► In *Dido,* a large area of violet is in the bottom right, and violet is also in other places where red and blue meet. In *A Glimpse of Notre Dame in the Late Afternoon,* violet is seen on the cathedral, on the walls, and in other places where red and blue mix.

■ For more examples of abstract/ nonobjective art, see ***The National Museum of Women in the Arts Collection.***

Art Journal: Concepts

Have students write the names of the primary colors used to make violet in the Concepts section of their Art Journals.

Aesthetic Perception

Design Awareness The classroom might not have much in it that is violet. Throughout history violet-colored dye was expensive, so violet traditionally has been the color of royalty and authority. Violet is also considered a "polarizing" color—people either love it or hate it.

Developing Visual Literacy Ask students if they have ever seen a building colored by the reflection of the sun like the cathedral in *A Glimpse of Notre Dame in the Late Afternoon.* Invite students to share any personal experiences that contribute to their understanding of the artwork.   NSAE 3.a

Web Connection

Visit **www.musee-matisse-nice.org** for information about the Matisse Museum in Nice, France.

Teach

Time: About 40 minutes

"Let's practice mixing red and blue to make violet." "*Vamos a practicar cómo mezclar el rojo con el azul para hacer violeta*".

- Read and discuss Using Red and Blue to Make Violet on page 114.

Practice

Materials: tissue paper in various shades of red and blue

Alternate Materials: red and blue liquid tempera paint, palettes, brushes

- Distribute the materials and have students follow the directions on page 114. If possible, have students try pink and light blue or darker reds and darker blues to see how many different violet colors can be created.

Creative Expression

NSAE 1.a; 1.c; 1.d; 2.c

Materials: 9" × 12" white paper, glue dishes, glue brushes, newspaper, diluted white liquid glue, black markers, tissue paper in various shades of red and blue, paper towels

Alternate Materials: crayons or oil pastels on light-colored or white paper

- Distribute the materials and have students follow the directions on page 115.

- See the Activity Tips on page 240 for visual examples of this lesson's activity.

- Make sure the red tissue paper is a cool red, not red-orange. If red-orange is mixed with blue, it will make a brown color.

- Have students tear the tissue paper into approximately 1-inch pieces, then glue them on top of one another on the white paper to make violet. Control the amount of glue used so colors do not bleed. Encourage students to add details to their creatures with a black marker.

Art Journal: Brainstorming

Have students brainstorm ideas for a violet creature they could create. Have students make quick sketches of their ideas in the Ideas section of their Art Journals. Then have students select an idea to use for the activity.   NSAE 3.b

---

Using Red and Blue to Make Violet

Red and blue are **primary colors.** They can be mixed to make the **secondary color** violet.

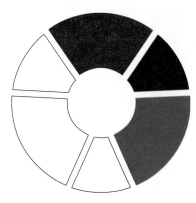

Violet is between blue and red on the color wheel.

Practice

Mix red and blue to create violet.

1. Place red tissue paper on top of blue.

2. Hold the tissue paper up to the light to see the colors mix.

3. Try pink and light blue or dark red and dark blue. See how many different violet colors you can create.

Differentiated Instruction

Reteach

Give each student a sheet of primary-colored paper. Ask those students who have one of the colors needed to make violet to stand. The students who are seated can check to make sure only those with red and blue are standing.

Special Needs

Adaptations: Students who have difficulty controlling their tearing may benefit from having the tissue paper precut in 1-inch pieces.

ELL Tips

Have students point to the colors in their Creative Expression creatures and say the name of each color in their native language and then in English.

◄ **Payton Myers.**
Age 7.

Think about how this student used blue and red to make violet.

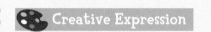 **Creative Expression**

What would a violet creature look like?

1. Overlap torn pieces of red and blue tissue paper.

2. Glue the tissue paper to a sheet of white paper to make the shape of your creature.

3. Add details to your creature with black marker.

 **Art Criticism**

Interpret Is your creature scary or nice? How can you tell?

Art Across the Curriculum

Use these ideas to reinforce art concepts across the curriculum.
NSAE 6.b

★ **Descriptive Writing** Have students imagine they are in a garden surrounded by violet-colored flowers and violet-colored fruits. Have students use the writing process to write descriptive words about the place.

★ **Math** Have students imagine the precise time in *A Glimpse of Notre Dame in the Late Afternoon* and describe the time on a clock.

★ **Science** Violet is also the name of a flower. Discuss with students the things flowers need to survive.

★ **Social Studies** The violet is the state flower of four states. Discuss state symbols.

★ **Technology** Have students use the computer's paint or draw program to re-create the creatures from their Creative Expression activities. Visit **SRAonline.com** to print detailed instructions for the activity.

 **Reflect** **Time:** About 5 minutes

Review and Assess
"What color do you get if you mix blue and red?" "¿Qué color obtienen si mezclan el azul con el rojo?"

Think

The student artist overlapped blue and red tissue paper to make his violet creature.

■ Have students look at *Large Prints 17 Die grossen blauen Pferde* and *18 Dance at Bougival* and identify where red and blue mix to make violet.

Informal Assessment

Art Journal: Critical Thinking
Have students ask themselves the Art Criticism questions, and then write or sketch in their Art Journals to answer the Interpret question.
NSAE 1.b; 2.b; 3.a; 5.c

 **Art Criticism**

Describe ▶ What kind of creature did you invent?

Analyze ▶ How many different violet colors did you make?

Interpret ▶ Is your creature scary or nice? How can you tell?

Decide ▶ Did you mix red and blue to make violet?

■ For standardized-format test practice using this lesson's art content, see pages 38–39 in *Reading and Writing Test Preparation.*

Red and Blue Make Violet

Extra! For the Art Specialist

Time: About 45 minutes

Focus

Use *Transparency 17* to discuss how the primary colors red and blue can mix to create the secondary color violet. What violet objects can students think of?

Teach

Have students complete the Alternate Activity. How else could students have mixed the red and blue paint to make violet?

Reflect

Guide students through evaluation of their works of art using the four steps of art criticism. (See pages 28–29 for more about art criticism.)

Alternate Activity

Materials:
- 12" × 18" manila paper
- tempera paint (red and blue)
- pencils
- newspaper

1. Have students fold a sheet of manila paper in half by bringing the short ends together and creasing the fold. Have students open their papers. Place two small blobs of red paint on the crease of the paper, with a blue blob in between them. The paint blobs should be almost touching. This is the "caterpillar."

2. Have students carefully close the paper into a "cocoon." Have students lay a pencil partly on the table and partly on the fold. Have students push the pencil toward one corner of the paper, then replace it at the fold and push it toward the other corner. Students may need to repeat pushing the paint to the corners of the paper.

3. When students open their papers, they should have a red, blue, and violet butterfly print.

Research in Art Education

Arts involvement increases a student's self-image. Students involved in the arts are "far more likely than their low-arts counterparts to think of themselves as competent in academics" ("Learning in and Through the Arts: Curriculum Implications" in *Champions of Change*, p. 40).

Assessment

Use the following rubric to evaluate the artwork students make in the Creative Expression activity and to assess students' understanding of the lesson concepts.

Have students complete page 41 or 42 in their *Assessment* books.

	Art History and Culture	Aesthetic Perception	Creative Expression	Art Criticism
3 POINTS	The student can identify a few facts about the fauve style of art.	The student successfully identifies violet as a secondary color made from mixing red and blue.	The student successfully combines red and blue to create a violet creature.	The student thoughtfully and honestly evaluates his or her own work using the four steps of art criticism.
2 POINTS	The student's identification is weak or incomplete.	The student shows emerging awareness that violet is a secondary color made from mixing two primary colors but cannot consistently identify them.	The student attempts to mix red and blue to create violet.	The student attempts to evaluate his or her own work but shows an incomplete understanding of evaluation criteria.
1 POINT	The student cannot identify any facts about the fauve style of art.	The student cannot identify violet as a secondary color made from mixing two primary colors.	The student's creature is not violet.	The student makes no attempt to evaluate his or her own artwork.

Assessment, p. 41

Name _____ Date _____

Red and Blue Make Violet

Lesson **5** UNIT 3

For the teacher: Use the following prompt for this activity. Using tempera paints, blend red on top of blue to make violet.

Level 1   Unit 3 • Color   **41**

Lesson 6 Overview
Primary and Secondary Colors

Lesson 6 reviews the primary and secondary colors that were taught in this unit.

Objectives

Art History and Culture

To recognize that some artists paint scenes of everday life
NSAE 4.a; 4.b; 4.c; 5.a; 5.b

Creative Expression

To create a painting with primary colors mixed to make secondary colors
NSAE 1.a; 1.c; 1.d; 2.c; 3.b

Aesthetic Perception

To distinguish between primary and secondary colors in artwork and in the environment NSAE 1.a; 2.a

Art Criticism

To evaluate one's own artwork using the four steps of art criticism
NSAE 1.b; 2.b; 3.a; 5.c

Vocabulary ⭐ Reading

Review the following vocabulary words with students before beginning the lesson.

primary color *color primario*—one of the three basic colors: red, yellow, or blue. Primary colors cannot be made by mixing other colors.

secondary color *color secundario*—a color created by mixing two primary colors

See page 119B for additional vocabulary and Spanish vocabulary resources.

Art Journal: Vocabulary

Have students review these words in the Vocabulary section of their Art Journals.

Lesson Materials

- construction paper in primary and secondary colors (cut into small pieces for students to use as flash cards)
- mixing trays
- water jars
- tempera paint (red, blue, and yellow)
- brushes (3 per student if possible)
- 12" × 18" white paper
- newspaper

Alternate Materials:

- primary- and secondary-colored crayons
- watercolors, crayons, or markers

Program Resources

- *Reading and Writing Test Prep.*, pp. 40–41
- *Flash Cards 7* and *8*
- *Transparency 18*
- *Artist Profiles*, pp. 4, 52
- *Animals Through History Time Line*
- *Assessment*, pp. 43–44
- *Large Prints 17* Die grossen blauen Pferde and *18* Dance at Bougival
- *The National Museum of Women in the Arts Collection*

Concept Trace

Primary and Secondary Colors
Introduced: Level K, Unit 3, Lesson 4

Reinforced: Level 2, Unit 3, Lesson 1

Lesson 6 Arts Integration NSAE 6.a

Theatre

Complete Unit 3, Lesson 6, on pages 64–69 of *Theatre Arts Connections.*

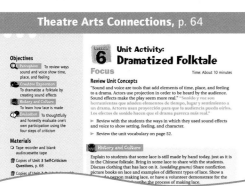

Music

Listen to *Symphony No 9 in D Minor Op 125 ("Choral"), Fourth Movement* by Ludwig van Beethoven. Beethoven was the first composer to add the voice to the blend of the orchestra in the symphonic form. He used a text that was well known at the time, "Ode to Joy," and put it to his melody.

Movement & Dance

Divide students into three groups. Have each group identify an aspect of nature that reminds them of a color. For example, fire is orange. Have students form a large circle, and have each group travel to the center and explore the movement of their selected aspect of nature.

Focus

Activate Prior Knowledge

"What colors would you use to paint a scene from your life?" "¿Qué colores usarían para pintar una escena de sus vidas?"

- Discuss the colors students see in their everyday lives. Encourage them to describe the colors of natural and human-made things.

Using Literature ⭐ Reading

- Read *This Plane* by Paul Collicutt. The illustrations contain primary and secondary colors, and in some places it is possible to see which colors were mixed to make others.

Thematic Connection ⭐ Social Studies

- **America:** Both works of art show summer scenes from America's past. Discuss the way the people were portrayed and whether similar scenes could be found in America today.

Introduce the Art

Look
NSAE 3.a

"Let's look closely at these works of art." "Vamos a mirar detalladamente estas obras de arte".

Adjectives and Adverbs ⭐ Language Arts

- Have students describe what they see in each painting. List on a chart the adjectives and adverbs students use.

Drawing Conclusions ⭐ Reading

- Ask students if they think these works of art show families. Discuss student responses. If students think these works do not show families, ask what the people in each group have in common.

🏺 Art History and Culture

Discuss with students that these works of art are genre paintings. Discuss how these works of art can be a source of information about the past. NSAE 4.a; 4.b; 4.c; 5.a; 5.b

 Web Connection

Visit **www.mostateparks.com/benton.htm** to learn more about Benton's former home and studio.

Primary and Secondary Colors

◀ **Thomas Hart Benton.**
(American). *July Hay.* 1943.
Oil and egg tempera on composition board. 38 × 26¾ inches (96.52 × 67.95 cm). Metropolitan Museum of Art, New York, New York.

Look at the colors in these works of art. The artists used primary and secondary colors.

🏺 Art History and Culture

These artists painted *genre* paintings. A genre painting shows scenes of everyday life.

🏺 Art History and Culture

Thomas Hart Benton

Thomas Hart Benton (to´ məs härt ben´ tən) (1889–1975) was born into a political family. He had the same name as his great-uncle, who was Missouri's first senator. Benton's father was a congressman. Benton studied at the Art Institute of Chicago and later in Paris. After returning to the United States, he taught art and made many paintings and murals. Benton was the leader of the Regionalist art movement, which portrayed scenes of common rural American life during the 1930s. President Truman, also from Missouri, was a great admirer of Benton's work. In 1960 Truman even helped him paint a mural.

See pages 16–21 and 24–25 for more about subject matter and art history.

Artist Profiles, p. 4

◀ Artist Profile ▶

Thomas Hart Benton
1889-1975

Thomas Hart Benton (tom´ əs hart bent´ ən) was a regional American painter known for his energetic, colorful murals. He was the son of a United States congressional representative and named after his great uncle, a famous pre-American Civil War senator. From his family, Benton developed a strong identity as an American. He studied art in Paris and at the Art Institute of Chicago. Benton believed that American artists should develop their own styles and not just copy French painting styles. Although Benton began his art career as a cartoonist, he was known for his murals depicting scenes from the rural past of the

▲ **Maurice Prendergast.**
(Canadian/American).
Summer, New England. 1912.
Oil on canvas. 19¼ × 27½ inches (48.9 × 69.9 cm.).
Smithsonian American Art Museum,
Washington, D.C.

Study the colors in the paintings.

▶ What primary colors do you see?

▶ What secondary colors do you see?

Aesthetic Perception

Seeing Like an Artist Name things in your room with primary colors. Name things with secondary colors.

Art History and Culture

Maurice Prendergast

Maurice Prendergast (mär ēs´ pren´ dər gast) (1859–1924) lived in Newfoundland until his family moved to Boston, Massachusetts, in 1868. After graduating from high school, Prendergast took drawing classes at night and found a job making posters that advertised performances. He often collaborated on works of art with his younger brother Charles. The brothers went to Europe, and Maurice studied in Paris for a few years. When he returned to the United States, he began exhibiting his artwork. He became renowned for his scenes of people in leisure activities at parks or on beaches.

See pages 16–21 and 24–25 for more about subject matter and art history.

Artist Profiles, p. 52

• Artist Profile •
Maurice Prendergast
1859–1924
Born in St. John's, Newfoundland, Maurice Prendergast (mär ēs´ pren´ dar gast) was raised in Boston and began his artistic career painting naturalistic landscapes. He followed the avant-garde art movement of the Ashcan School from Philadelphia to New York, where he experimented with color theory and the depiction of the individual amidst an impersonal city. In his fifties and sixties, Prendergast wanted to create a style all his own, using a modernist freedom of color and form. This desire led him to create the large, expressive seaside paintings for which he is most famous.

▲ **Maurice Prendergast.** (Canadian/American). *Summer, New England.* 1912.
Oil on canvas. 19¼ × 27½ inches (48.9 × 69.9 cm.)

Study

▶ *July Hay* has the primary colors red (flowers), yellow (hay, some tree leaves, men's hats, centers of flowers), and blue (men's pants, sky). *Summer, New England* has the primary colors red (parasol, women's hats, clothing), yellow (clothing, tree leaves), and blue (water, sky, clothing).

▶ *July Hay* has the secondary colors orange (shadows in the hay) and green (leaves, trees). *Summer, New England* has the secondary colors orange (clothing, parasol, buggy), green (leaves, grass, clothing), and violet (clothing, trees).

■ For more examples of genre art, see **The National Museum of Women in the Arts Collection.**

Art Journal: Concepts

Have students list the primary and secondary colors in the Concepts section of their Art Journals.

Aesthetic Perception

Seeing Like an Artist Discuss the primary and secondary colors the students find in the classroom. Have them notice objects in the room as well as people's clothing and even eye color. Have them notice the colors of natural things (such as any plants or food) as well as humanmade things. Discuss which color students see the most.

Developing Visual Literacy Discuss how each color makes students feel. Lead students to discover which are warm colors (red, orange, yellow) and which are cool (green, blue, violet).
NSAE 2.b

Web Connection

Summer, New England was part of the Smithsonian's Treasures to Go exhibit, which can be viewed online at **nmaa-ryder.si.edu/treasures/**. Have students view the exhibition and share their ideas in small groups.

Teach

Time: About 40 minutes

"Let's play a color game to review primary and secondary colors." *"Vamos a jugar a un juego de colores para repasar los colores primarios y secundarios".*

- Read and discuss Using Primary and Secondary Colors on page 118.

Practice

Materials: construction paper in primary and secondary colors (cut into small pieces for students to use as flash cards)

Alternate Materials: primary- and secondary-colored crayons

- Distribute the materials and read the directions on page 118.

- Have students work in small groups. They can take turns holding up color flash cards while other students take turns naming the colors. If it is a secondary color, have another student tell which primary colors are mixed to make it.

Creative Expression

NSAE 1.a; 1.c; 1.d; 2.c

Materials: mixing trays, water jars, tempera paint (red, blue, and yellow), brushes (3 per student if possible), 12" × 18" white paper, newspaper

Alternate Materials: watercolors, crayons, or markers

- Distribute the materials and have students follow the directions on page 119.

- See the Activity Tips on page 240 for visual examples of this lesson's activity.

- Demonstrate how to fold the paper in half and designate six boxes. Have students put each primary color in a box and the other primary color needed to make a secondary color in the box opposite it.

- Have students fold their papers and gently press to mix the colors well. Then tell students to use their craft sticks to draw their summer scene in the wet paint.

Art Journal: Brainstorming

Have students brainstorm ideas for things they can paint in the Creative Expression activity. Have students make quick sketches of their ideas in the Ideas section of their Art Journal. Then have students select an idea to use for the activity.

NSAE 3.b

Using Primary and Secondary Colors

The three **primary colors** can be used to create three **secondary colors.**

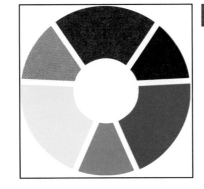

Practice

Review primary and secondary colors.

1. Form a group with some classmates.

2. Use the color flash cards. Take turns naming the colors.

3. Tell which primary colors make each secondary color.

Differentiated Instruction

Reteach
Hold up three containers of primary-colored food coloring. Ask students which colors will result when you mix the colors two at a time in a jar of water.

Special Needs
Adaptations: Give each student a sticky note with the name of a primary or secondary color on it. Have each student find something in the room that is the color listed on the note, and label it with the note.

ELL Tips
Use *Flash Cards 7 and 8.* Point to each color and have students name them. To activate prior knowledge, have students also name each shape.

◀ **Oliver Sandoval.**
Age 6.

Think about how this student used primary and secondary colors.

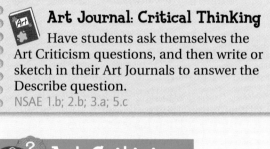

Creative Expression

What kinds of things do you see during summer in your neighborhood?

1. Fold your paper in half. On one half, paint squares of each primary color. On the other half, paint squares of the primary color needed to make each secondary color.

2. Fold your paper and press to mix the paint.

3. Use craft sticks to draw your scene in the wet paint.

Describe What does your painting show?

Art Across the Curriculum

Use these ideas to reinforce art concepts across the curriculum.
NSAE 6.b

★ **Persuasive Writing** Have students write a few sentences about which fine artwork they like better and why.

★ **Math** Have students discuss the probability of certain color combinations making new colors (such as "red and blue make green").

★ **Science** Both works of art in this lesson have summer settings. Discuss temperatures that might occur on a summer day.

★ **Social Studies** The men in *July Hay* are using tools to help them do their work. Discuss how technology has changed the way people work.

★ **Technology** Have students re-create their Creative Expression paintings using the computer's paint program. Visit **SRAonline.com** to print detailed instructions for this activity.

Reflect   Time: About 5 minutes

Review and Assess

"Which colors are primary colors? Which colors are secondary colors?" "¿Qué colores son colores primarios? ¿Cuáles son colores secundarios?"

Think

The student made secondary colors by folding his paper to mix primary colors.

■ Have students identify primary and secondary colors in *Large Prints 17 Die grossen blauen Pferde* and *18 Dance at Bougival.*

Informal Assessment

Art Journal: Critical Thinking
Have students ask themselves the Art Criticism questions, and then write or sketch in their Art Journals to answer the Describe question.
NSAE 1.b; 2.b; 3.a; 5.c

Art Criticism

Describe ▶ What does your painting show?

Analyze ▶ What colors did you create by mixing primary colors?

Interpret ▶ What mood does your painting have? Give it a title.

Decide ▶ Did you mix primary colors to make secondary colors?

■ For standardized-format test practice using this lesson's art content, see pages 40–41 in *Reading and Writing Test Preparation.*

Primary and Secondary Colors

Extra! For the Art Specialist

Time: About 45 minutes

Focus

Use *Transparency 18* to discuss primary and secondary colors. What colors do students see most frequently in the works of art?

Teach

Discuss mixing primary colors to create secondary colors. Have students refer to a color wheel as they complete the Alternate Activity.

Reflect

Guide students through evaluation of their works of art using the four steps of art criticism. (See pages 28–29 for more about art criticism.) Then have students describe, analyze, and interpret the work of a classmate.

Alternate Activity

Materials:
- still-life objects in primary and secondary colors
- black markers
- white paper
- liquid tempera paint in red, blue, and yellow
- paintbrushes
- paper plates
- water dishes
- paper towels

1. Set up a still-life arrangement for students to paint. Have students use the black markers to draw the outlines of objects on their papers. Encourage students to include at least three objects and to draw them touching at least three sides of the paper.

2. Have students use the primary-colored paint to paint primary-colored objects. Have students mix the primary-colored paint to paint secondary-colored objects. Have students fill their paper so no white space remains.

Research
in Art Education

Successful integration of the arts includes lesson plans based on state standards, activities with well-defined objectives and planned assessment (using rubrics or scoring guides) that match these objectives, and content and art lessons that are of equal importance ("Chicago Arts Partnership in Education" in *Champions of Change*, p. 54).

Assessment
Use the following rubric to evaluate the artwork students make in the Creative Expression activity and to assess students' understanding of the lesson concepts.

Have students complete page 43 or 44 in their *Assessment* books.

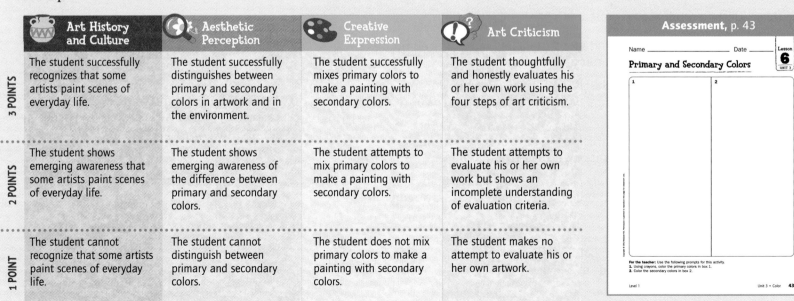

	Art History and Culture	Aesthetic Perception	Creative Expression	Art Criticism
3 POINTS	The student successfully recognizes that some artists paint scenes of everyday life.	The student successfully distinguishes between primary and secondary colors in artwork and in the environment.	The student successfully mixes primary colors to make a painting with secondary colors.	The student thoughtfully and honestly evaluates his or her own work using the four steps of art criticism.
2 POINTS	The student shows emerging awareness that some artists paint scenes of everyday life.	The student shows emerging awareness of the difference between primary and secondary colors.	The student attempts to mix primary colors to make a painting with secondary colors.	The student attempts to evaluate his or her own work but shows an incomplete understanding of evaluation criteria.
1 POINT	The student cannot recognize that some artists paint scenes of everyday life.	The student cannot distinguish between primary and secondary colors.	The student does not mix primary colors to make a painting with secondary colors.	The student makes no attempt to evaluate his or her own artwork.

Assessment, p. 43

Name _____ Date _____

Primary and Secondary Colors

For the teacher: Use the following prompts for this activity.
1. Using crayons, color the primary colors in box 1.
2. Color the secondary colors in box 2.

Level 1 · Unit 3 · Color **43**

color wheel—design for organizing colors that shows the spectrum bent into a circle **círculo cromático**—diseño para organizar los colores que muestra el espectro en un círculo

primary color—one of the three basic colors: red, yellow, or blue. Primary colors cannot be made by mixing other colors **color primario**—uno de los tres colores básicos: rojo, amarillo o azul. Los colores primarios no se pueden crear al mezclar otros colores

rainbow—red, orange, yellow, green, blue, and violet curved into a semicircle **arco iris**—los colores rojo, anaranjado, amarillo, verde, azul y violeta colocados en un semicírculo

secondary color—a color created by mixing two primary colors **color secundario**—un color creado al mezclar dos colores primarios

Vocabulary Practice

 Display *Transparency 39* to review unit vocabulary words.

Visualization Strategies ⭐ Vocabulary

Point to objects in the classroom that are red, orange, yellow, green, blue, or violet. Ask students which vocabulary word describes the color of each object.

Categorizing/Classifying ⭐ Vocabulary

Write the four vocabulary words on the board. Name one of the six colors covered in the unit and have students explain which three unit vocabulary words are associated with that color. For instance, *red* is a *primary color,* and it is part of the *color wheel* and the *rainbow.*

Definitions: Brief Definitions ⭐ Vocabulary

Read the definition of a vocabulary word and have students identify the word.

Color

Critical Thinking Art criticism is an organized system for looking at and talking about art. You can criticize art without being an expert. The purpose of art criticism is to get the viewer involved in a perception process that delays judgment until all aspects of the artwork have been studied.

- See pages 28–29 for more about art criticism.

Describe

- What do you see? During this step the student will collect information about the subject of the artwork.

▶ Have students describe what they see in the painting. There are curved, diagonal, and straight lines in bright colors. There are also free-form shapes.

▶ Share the information from the caption with students. Ask if this is a large or small painting. It is four feet tall. That is as tall as most children in the room, which makes it a large painting.

Analyze

- How is this work organized? During this step the student thinks about how the artist has used the elements and principles of art.

▶ Have students name colors of the color wheel found in this painting. All six of the colors from the color wheel are shown: red, orange, yellow, green, blue, and violet.

▶ Have students identify where they see primary and secondary colors. Red: free-form shape with red dots in upper left, red shapes and lines across the center. Orange: two large free-form shapes on the left. Yellow: vertical lines at upper left, lines throughout center and bottom. Green: large free-form shape on right, lines throughout center and bottom. Blue: large vertical line on right, small lines and shapes throughout. Violet: a few lines in the center, a large shape at the bottom left.

▲ **Hans Hofmann.** (German/American).
Au Printemps, Springtime. 1955.
Oil on canvas. 48 × 36 inches (121.92 × 91.44 cm). Frances Lehman Loeb Art Center, Vassar College, Poughkeepsie, New York.

Art History and Culture

Hans Hofmann

Hans Hofmann (hänz hof´ man) (1880–1966) was born in Germany. He left home at age 16 and began working for an architectural and engineering office. Hofmann used his money to enroll in art school. A department-store owner saw Hofmann's artwork and was so impressed that he financed Hofmann's trip to study in Paris from 1904 to 1914. When Hofmann returned to Germany, he opened an art school. In the 1930s Hofmann moved to the United States and opened an art school in New York. In 1958 he retired from teaching to paint full-time. He achieved international recognition late in life. Hofmann was an abstract expressionist. Abstract expressionists convey strong emotions through line, shape, and color.

See pages 16–21 and 24–25 for more about subject matter and art history.

Artist Profiles, p. 27

• Artist Profile •
Hans Hofmann
1880-1966

Hans Hofmann (hänz hof´ man), a German painter, studied art in his homeland and in Paris before opening his own school of modern art in Munich, Germany. As World War II threatened, some of his students who had already moved to New York City arranged a teaching position for him at the Art Students League. Hofmann immigrated to the United States and settled in New York City in 1932. In 1933, he started the Hans Hofmann School of Fine Art. It became one of the most respected art schools in the United States. For 25 years, Hofmann taught art but did little painting of his own. In 1958, he left his school to paint full time. He eventually achieved international recognition.

Art Criticism Critical Thinking

Describe

▶ Describe what you see in the painting.

Analyze

▶ What colors from the color wheel do you see in this painting?

Interpret

▶ Is this a calm or busy picture? Why?

Decide

▶ Would you like to have this painting in your classroom? Why or why not?

Interpret

- What is the artist trying to say? Students use the clues they discovered during their analysis to find the message the artist is trying to show.

▶ Ask students whether they feel this is a calm or busy picture. Most students will probably say this is a busy picture because there are so many little diagonal lines.

▶ Ask students why they think the artist named this painting *Springtime*. Answers may vary. Some students may say they think it is because the bright colors look like flowers.

Decide

- What do you think about the work? Students use all the information they have gathered to decide whether this is a successful work of art.

▶ Ask students if they would like to have this painting in the classroom. Have them explain their answers. Answers will vary.

 Art Journal: Writing
Have students write or sketch the answers to the Aesthetic Perception questions in their Art Journals.

Aesthetic Perception

Critical Thinking Have students ever been to the circus, or seen one on television? Display a picture of a colorful circus scene, or have students recall their experiences. How do the colors of the circus compare with *Springtime?*

Describe ▶ Have students list everything they see in the scene.

Analyze ▶ Where do students see primary and secondary colors?

Interpret ▶ What feeling do the colors create?

Decide ▶ If the circus was not decorated with primary and secondary colors, how would the feeling change?

"Artists use primary and secondary colors in their art." "Los artistas usan colores primarios y secundarios en sus obras de arte".

T Review unit vocabulary with students using *Transparency 39.*

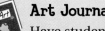 **Art Journal: Writing**
Have students answer the questions on page 122 in their Art Journals or on a separate sheet of paper. Answers: 1. A, 2. C, 3. D

T For further assessment, have students complete the unit test on *Transparency 45.*

LEARNING ABOUT MUSEUMS

The Frances Lehman Loeb Art Center

▶ The Frances Lehman Loeb Art Center was founded in 1864 as the Vassar College Art Gallery. In 1993 a 36,400 square foot facility designed by Cesar Pelli opened and was named in honor of the new building's primary donor. Approximately 400 of the finest works from the permanent collection are exhibited in the Main Gallery in a free-flowing, chronological arrangement. The twentieth-century collection has been built primarily by gifts from Vassar graduates.

"The business of the artist is to tell his audience the secrets of their own hearts."

—Robin George Collingwood (1889–1943), philosopher/historian/ archaeologist

Color, continued

Show What You Know

Write your answers on a sheet of paper.

1 Which is not a primary color?

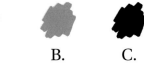

A.   B.   C.

2 Which is not a secondary color?

A.   B.   C.

3 Which color combination is not correct?

A.   B.   C.

LET'S VISIT A MUSEUM

Frances Lehman Loeb Art Center

This museum is located at Vassar College in Poughkeepsie, New York. The collection has over 15,000 pieces. It has art from ancient times to the present.

Unit Assessment Options

Aesthetic Perception

Practice Have students record a list of primary-colored and secondary-colored items they find in the classroom.

Creative Expression

Student Portfolio Have students review all the artwork they have created during this unit and select the pieces they wish to keep in their portfolios. Have students share their portfolios with classmates, and discuss each other's use of color.

Art Criticism

Activity Have students select their favorite artwork from this unit. Guide students through study of their selected work using the four steps of art criticism. (See pages 28–29 for more about art criticism.)

Color in Chinese Dance

Lily Cai performs traditional Chinese ribbon dancing. She moves through space to create patterns with the red ribbons.

What to Do Create a colorful ribbon dance.

1. Choose a color for your ribbon stick. Practice using the ribbon stick. Use full body movements.

2. Choose different movements to create a dance.

3. Perform your ribbon dance with others.

▲ Lily Cai. "Flying Goddess."

Art Criticism

Interpret What feeling did your ribbon dance have?

Art History and Culture

Chinese Dance

Chinese civilization is over 5,000 years old. Chinese classical dance reflects the philosophy and aesthetics of each dynasty of emperors. *The Flying Goddess* ribbon dance is from the T'ang Dynasty. Beauty in this dynasty was represented by dance, music, costumes, and art that were full and round. The flying and floating of colorful ribbons represents the spirit of a goddess.

Color in Chinese Dance NSAE 6.a

Objective: To create a colorful rhythm dance

Materials: *Flying Goddess* performed by Lily Cai (running time: 3:43), thin wooden dowels, bamboo, or plastic straws with ribbons or crepe paper in various colors attached with tape or staples.

Focus
Time: About 5 minutes

- Discuss the information on page 123.

Art History and Culture

- Share the Art History and Culture information with students. Have students discuss different ribbon movements that could be made using arm and hand movement.

Teach
Time: About 20 minutes

Aesthetic Perception

- Have students choose a color for their ribbon stick. Arrange for a space big enough for students to move freely with their ribbon sticks.

Creative Expression

- Direct students to explore making circular patterns and figure eights in many different directions using their ribbon sticks. Encourage them to use high energy.

- **Informal Assessment** Comment positively on students' interpretations.

Reflect
Time: About 10 minutes

Art Criticism

- Have students answer the four art criticism questions orally.

Describe ▶ Describe the movement you created with your ribbon.

Analyze ▶ What ribbon colors did you see as you performed with the group?

Interpret ▶ What feeling did your ribbon dance have?

Decide ▶ Did you create a colorful ribbon dance?

Unit 4 Planning Guide

	Lesson Title	Suggested Pacing	Creative Expression Activity
Lesson 1	**Shapes and Forms**	60 minutes	Create a shapes and forms mobile.
Lesson 2	**Forms Take Up Space**	55 minutes	Create a posterboard sculpture that has space through it.
Lesson 3	**Free-Form Forms**	55 minutes	Create a clay free-form form.
Lesson 4	**3-D Me!**	65 minutes	Create a self-portrait statue.
Lesson 5	**Buildings and Spaces**	65 minutes	Create a three-dimensional house.
Lesson 6	**Space in Pictures**	55 minutes	Create a still-life painting.
ARTSOURCE	**Form and Space in Theatre**	35 minutes	Use body movements to represent an event in nature.

Materials	Program Resources	Fine Art Resources	Literature Resources
9" × 9" cardboard or posterboard squares, string, pencils, colored construction paper, scissors, glue, paper hole punch	*Reading and Writing Test Preparation,* pp. 42–43 *Assessment,* pp. 45–46 *Home and After-School Connections*	*Transparency,* 19 *Artist Profiles,* pp. 9, 59 *Large Prints,* 19 and 20 *Art Around the World*	*America: My Land, Your Land, Our Land* by W. Nikola-Lisa
9" × 12" posterboard, crayons, markers, scissors, colored construction paper (optional)	*Reading and Writing Test Preparation,* pp. 44–45 *Assessment,* pp. 47–48	*Transparency,* 20 *Artist Profiles,* pp. 38, 60 *Large Prints,* 19 and 20 *Women in the Arts Collection*	*Wheels Around* by Shelley Rotner
clay, slip, slip bows, clay tools (pencils, paper clips, craft sticks), clay mats (muslin), paintbrushes, water containers, glaze (optional)	*Reading and Writing Test Preparation,* pp. 46–47 *Assessment,* pp. 49–50	*Transparency,* 21 *Artist Profiles,* pp. 24, 81 *Large Prints,* 19 and 20 *Art Around the World*	*Sweet Dreams: How Animals Sleep* by Kimiko Kajikawa
clay, slip, slip bowls, clay tools (pencils, paper clips, craft sticks), clay mats (muslin), paintbrushes, water containers	*Reading and Writing Test Preparation,* pp. 48–49 *Assessment,* pp. 51–52	*Transparency,* 22 *Artist Profiles,* pp. 78–79 *Large Prints,* 20 *Women in the Arts Collection*	*Communities* by Gail Saunders-Smith
recycled materials (cardboard boxes, cardboard tubes, empty milk cartons, empty plastic bottles), masking tape, glue, acrylic paint, paintbrushes, water dishes, paper towels	*Reading and Writing Test Preparation,* pp. 50–51 *Assessment,* pp. 53–54	*Transparency,* 23 *Artist Profiles,* pp. 68, 82 *Large Prints,* 19 *Women in the Arts Collection*	*The Little House* by Virginia Lee Burton
12" × 18" watercolor paper, pencils, watercolor paints, still-life objects, brushes, water containers, paper towels	*Reading and Writing Test Preparation,* pp. 52–53 *Assessment,* pp. 55–56	*Transparency,* 24 *Artist Profiles,* pp. 47, 64 *Animals Through History Time Line* *Large Prints,* 19 and 20 *Women in the Arts Collection*	*Career Day* by Anne Rockwell
In the Heart of the Beast Puppet and Mask Theatre. "On the Day You Were Born." Running Time: 7:08			

Unit Overview

4 Form and Space

Lesson 1: Shapes are two-dimensional. **Forms** are three-dimensional.

Lesson 2: Forms take up space, are surrounded by space, and can have space inside them.

Lesson 3: Free-form forms are not geometric forms.

Lesson 4: People are free-form forms. Sculptors create statues that are three-dimensional portraits of humans.

Lesson 5: Buildings are three-dimensional forms that students see every day. The spaces inside buildings allow them to be used.

Lesson 6: Two-dimensional pictures also show **space** around objects.

Introduce Unit Concepts

"Let's talk about space and form." "Vamos a hablar del espacio y la forma".

Space
- Have students brainstorm different uses of the word *space*, such as *outer space* or *parking space*. Discuss that space is an empty area, and things can move through space or take up space.

Form
- Have students name natural and humanmade forms they see in the classroom. Discuss that a form can be viewed from all sides.

Cross-Curricular Projects
- See the *Language Arts and Reading, Mathematics, Science,* and *Social Studies Art Connections* books for activities that further develop the concepts of form and space.

National Standards for Arts Education in Visual Arts (NSAE) 6.b

---

Form and Space

Artists create forms that take up space.

This artwork has forms that hang from the ceiling to the floor.

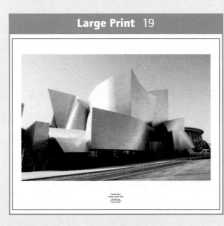

◄ **Claes Oldenburg.** (American). *Shoestring Potatoes Spilling from a Bag.* 1966.

Canvas, kapok, glue, acrylic. 108 × 46 × 42 inches (274.32 × 116.84 × 106.68 cm.). Walker Art Center, Minneapolis, Minnesota.

Fine Art Prints

Display **Large Prints 19** *Disney Concert Hall* and **20** *Ray and Elsie.* Refer to the prints throughout the unit as students learn about space and form.

Large Print 19

Large Print 20

A **form** has height, width, and depth. **Space** is all around it.

Look at the artwork.
▶ What forms do you see?
▶ Where do you see space?

In This Unit you will:
▶ learn about form and space.
▶ find form and space in art and the environment.
▶ create art with form and space.

Claes Oldenburg

(1929 –)

▶ is an American artist.
▶ creates sculptures of everyday objects.
▶ sculpts objects much larger than they really are.

Unit 4 **125**

Art History and Culture

Claes Oldenburg

Claes Oldenburg (kläs ōl´ dən bərg) (1929–) was born in Stockholm, Sweden, but his family moved to the United States when he was a young child. In 1953, he became an American citizen. Oldenburg studied at Yale University and the Art Institute of Chicago. He moved to New York in 1956 and quickly became a well-known artist. Oldenburg is famous for his large-scale sculptures of familiar objects and his monumental outdoor works of art.

See pages 16–21 and 24–25 for more about subject matter and art history.

Artist Profiles, p. 50

● Artist Profile ●

Claes Oldenburg
b. 1929

Born in Sweden, Claes Oldenburg (kläs ōl´ dən bərg) became a United States citizen in 1953. He studied writing at Yale and art at the Art Institute of Chicago. When he moved to New York City in 1956, he felt an urge to sculpt the city, so he created *The Store*. This was a painted sculpture of clothing and food displayed as if they were in a New York shop window. In 1961 Oldenburg opened a real store in New York City and stocked it with plaster food for sale. The next year he created *happenings*—mixtures of sound, movement, people, and giant cloth objects stuffed with rags or paper. This led to his first popular art form—soft sculpture. Recently Oldenburg created metal sculptures of everyday objects, greatly

Examine the Artwork

"Let's take a look at this sculpture and imagine that you are standing next to it."
"Vamos a observar esta escultura e imagínese que están parados al lado de ésta".

■ Tell students that the height of the sculpture is nine feet. It is twice as tall as most people in the class. Have students guess how high their heads would reach on the sculpture if they stood next to it. Have students imagine they could walk all around the sculpture and even through the space between some of the potatoes. Imagine standing underneath the sculpture and looking into the bag. What would they see? Empty space.

■ Have students answer the questions about space and form on page 125.

▶ The bag and the shoestring potatoes are forms.

▶ Space is all around and between the bag and the potatoes. There is space inside the bag.

Unit Pretest

T Display **Transparency 46** as a pretest. Answers: 1. B, 2. B, 3. A

Home Connection

■ See *Home and After-School Connections* for family newsletters and activities for this unit.

National Standards for Arts Education in Visual Arts (NSAE) 3.a

ILLUSTRATOR PROFILE

Barbara Cooney

(1917–2000)

Barbara Cooney and her twin brother were born in Brooklyn, New York. Their mother was an artist, and as a child Cooney always had access to her mother's art supplies. Cooney's favorite hobby was drawing pictures, but she did not consider being a professional artist until after graduating from Smith College with a degree in art history. Cooney decided that she would like to illustrate books as a career, so she began taking classes at the Art Students League in New York City.

Cooney assembled a portfolio and began looking for illustrating jobs, but her job search was soon put on hold. When World War II began, Cooney joined the Women's Army Corp. She then got married in 1944 and had two children. Cooney focused on raising her family until her divorce in 1947 caused her to search for a means of support. She found jobs illustrating other authors' books and eventually began writing and illustrating her own.

During her career Cooney illustrated over 100 books. She often illustrated adaptations of classic tales. Her book *Chanticleer and the Fox* was an adaptation of *The Nun's Priest's Tale* by Geoffrey Chaucer. Cooney is known for her attention to detail, which is attributable to the great amount of research she does for each project. Cooney has traveled the world, including visits to England, Finland, France, Haiti, Ireland, Mexico, Spain, St. Lucia, and Switzerland, in order to study places before illustrating them.

Throughout Unit 4, share Cooney's illustrations with the class and discuss her use of form and space. What kinds of building forms and people forms do students see in the illustrations? Where is there space in and around objects?

Music

Form in music refers to the way a composition is organized. ABA form is one in which the first and last sections are the same and the middle section is contrasting. Students can identify the ABA form in *Eine Kleine Nacht Musik* by Mozart.

Literature and Art

Show the video or DVD *Paper Crane* by Molly Bang to introduce the concepts of form and space. Discuss with students the form of the paper crane and the space around it.

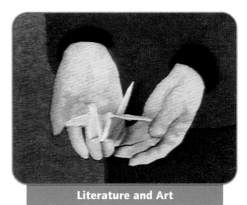

Literature and Art

Performing Arts

Show "On the Day You Were Born." Discuss how the forms of the actors move through space.

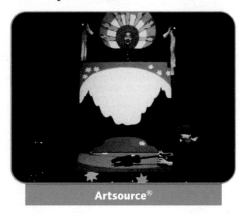

Artsource®

Shapes and Forms

Lesson 1 introduces the difference between two-dimensional shapes and three-dimensional forms.

Objectives

Art History and Culture

To identify and compare how Alexander Calder and Frank Stella used art forms in new ways NSAE 4.a; 4.b; 4.c

Creative Expression

To create a mobile using shapes and forms NSAE 1.a; 1.c; 1.d

Aesthetic Perception

To distinguish between a two-dimensional shape and a three-dimensional form NSAE 2.a

Art Criticism

To evaluate one's own artwork using the four steps of art criticism NSAE 1.b; 2.b; 3.a; 5.c

Vocabulary ⭐ Reading

Review the following vocabulary words with students before beginning the lesson.

height altura o alto—how tall something is

width ancho—how wide something is

depth profundidad—the distance from front to back

See page 149B for additional vocabulary and Spanish vocabulary resources.

Art Journal: Vocabulary

Have students add these words to the Vocabulary section of their Art Journals.

Lesson Materials
- colored construction paper
- 9" × 9" cardboard or posterboard squares
- string
- pencils
- scissors
- tape
- glue
- paper hole punch

Alternate Materials:
- paper

Program Resources
- *Reading and Writing Test Prep.,* pp. 42–43
- *Transparency 19*
- *Artist Profiles,* pp. 9, 59
- *Animals Through History Time Line*
- *Assessment,* pp. 45–46
- *Large Prints 19* Disney Concert Hall and *20* Ray and Elsie
- *Art Around the World*

Concept Trace
Shapes and Forms
Introduced: Level K, Unit 4, Lesson 2

Reinforced: Level 2, Unit 2, Lesson 1

Lesson 1 Arts Integration NSAE 6.a

Theatre
Complete Unit 4, Lesson 1, on pages 72–73 of *Theatre Arts Connections.*

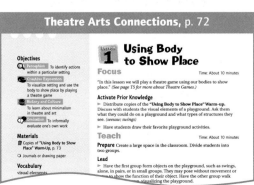

Music
Listen to *Tininkling*. This music is a dance from the Philippines to portray a crane. The dancer always has one knee in the air in a very angular pose. How do the pulses in the music suggest geometric shapes and forms?

Movement & Dance
Group students in pairs. One student in each pair creates a shape and freezes. Have the other students look at their partner's shape. What direction are they facing? What level are they on? Where is their focus? Is the energy going up or down in their shape? Have students repeat, reversing roles.

Shapes and Forms

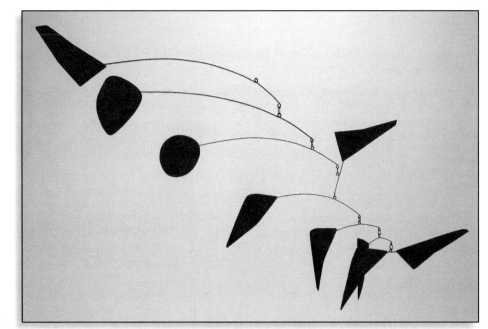

Look at these works of art. The artists combined shapes and forms.

▲ **Alexander Calder.** (American).
Red Rudder in the Air. 1975.
....
Painted sheet metal and steel wire.
31 × 68 inches (78.74 × 172.72 cm.).
Grand Rapids Art Museum, Grand Rapids,
Michigan.

🏺 Art History and Culture

Alexander Calder created a new art form. He invented the mobile in the 1930s.

Focus

Time: About 10 minutes

Activate Prior Knowledge

"What is the difference between a person and a photo of the person?" "¿Cuál es la diferencia entre una persona y la foto de la persona?"

■ If possible, take an instant photo of a student and have students compare the photo to the student. Discuss that you can't see the sides or back of the student. The real person is three-dimensional and can be viewed from all angles.

Using Literature ⭐ Reading

■ Read *America: My Land, Your Land, Our Land* by W. Nikola-Lisa. The book has illustrations by 14 artists. Some images show shapes and others show forms.

Thematic Connection ⭐ Reading

■ **Shapes:** Review with students the free-form and geometric shapes they learned about in Unit 2.

Introduce the Art

Look   NSAE 2.b

"Let's take a close look at these works of art." "Vamos a mirar detalladamente estas obras de arte".

Comparing and Contrasting ⭐ Reading

■ Ask students why the shapes in these works are different from shapes painted on canvas. The shapes in both works can be viewed in three dimensions. Students could look up and down as well as front to back. *Red Rudder in the Air* is a mobile. The shapes can "dance" around in the air if a breeze is blowing.

🏺 Art History and Culture

Discuss with students that these artists thought of new ways to use forms. Alexander Calder invented the *mobile*, which is a sculpture that has moving parts. Frank Stella combined painting and sculpture by painting on three-dimensional forms instead of flat canvases.

💻 Web Connection

Visit **www.calder.org** to learn more about Alexander Calder and his mobiles.

🏺 Art History and Culture

Alexander Calder   NSAE 4.a; 4.b; 4.c

Alexander Calder (a lig zan´ dər kôl´ dər) (1898–1976) was born into a family of artists. His father and grandfather were sculptors, and his mother was a painter. However, Calder was interested in gadgets and technology, so he studied engineering. He eventually combined his mechanical training with his creativity to invent mobiles. Mobiles are hanging sculptures that move in the wind. Calder never named a mobile until it was hung in place. Then he named it for what it looked like to him.

See pages 16–21 and 24–25 for more about subject matter and art history.

Artist Profiles, p. 9

Artist Profile
Alexander Calder
1871-1945
Alexander Calder (a leg zan´ dər ´kôl´ dər) had a mother who painted, and both his father and grandfather were sculptors. Calder liked to make gadgets. He trained to be an engineer. Later he attended art school and worked as a commercial artist. In 1926, he moved to Paris, France, and began to experiment with making tiny circuses out of wood, cork, and wire. In 1931, he used his training as an engineer to create motor-driven sculptures. A year later he invented *mobiles*—sculptures that move in the wind.

Calder traveled to Europe, South America, and Asia with his wife and two daughters. He created works of art wherever he went. His work became very popular. It has

▲ **Frank Stella.** (American).
Loomings 3X. 1986.
....
Ink and oil paint on etched magnesium and aluminum.
$142\frac{1}{8} \times 162\frac{1}{2} \times 44$ inches (361 × 412.75 × 111.76 cm.).
Walker Art Center, Minneapolis, Minnesota.

Study the works of art.

► Where do you see shapes?

► Where do you see forms?

🔍 Aesthetic Perception

Seeing Like an Artist Look at a form. What does it look like from different sides?

🏺 Art History and Culture

Frank Stella

Frank Stella (frangk ste´lə) (1936–) was born in Malden, Massachusetts. He studied art at Phillips Academy and Princeton University. In 1959, Stella exhibited his work at the Museum of Modern Art in a show called Sixteen Americans. He was 23 years old, making him the youngest artist included in that show. In the 1970s, Stella began to combine painting and sculpture by painting on three-dimensional forms made from wood or metal (such as *Loomings 3X*).

See pages 16–21 and 24–25 for more about subject matter and art history.

Artist Profiles, p. 59

◆ Artist Profile ◆
Frank Stella
b. 1936

Frank Stella (frangk ste´ lə) was born in Malden, Massachusetts, in 1936. He studied painting at Phillips Academy and majored in history at Princeton University. He supported himself after college by painting houses. He moved to New York City, where he had his first successful show called *Sixteen Americans*. At the age of 23, he was the youngest artist in the show. At first people were annoyed and shocked by his style. However, his talent was noticed by a few important gallery owners and critics who felt his work was exciting and new. Later in his life he became an architect.

Study

► *Red Rudder in the Air* has red shapes: triangles, a circle, and other shapes. They are connected to and hang from wires. The shapes and wires are surrounded by empty space. *Loomings 3X* was made from flat sheets of metal that were cut into shapes.

► The shapes of *Red Rudder in the Air* are flat, but the mobile as a whole is a form because its pieces extend through three dimensions of space. Some of the metal shapes of *Loomings 3X* were bent or curved to make forms. After a flat shape is bent so that it takes up three dimensions of space, it becomes a form. The sculpture as a whole is a form because it protrudes from the wall.

■ For more examples of art from North America, see *Art Around the World Collection.*

📓 Art Journal: Concepts

Have students sketch a square and a box in the Concepts section of their Art Journals and note the difference.

🔍 Aesthetic Perception

Seeing Like an Artist Have students locate free-form forms (such as a plant or a person) as well as geometric forms (such as a box or ball). Discuss that geometric forms look similar from many angles, and free-form forms can look different from several angles.

Developing Visual Literacy Because students can see only the two-dimensional photographs, they will have to imagine what the three-dimensional works of art would be like. Have students discuss what they think it would be like to see the works in person. Would they like looking at the three-dimensional works more than the photographs? Why?
NSAE 1.b; 2.b; 5.c

💻 Web Connection

Visit **collections.walkerart.org** to search for other works by Frank Stella.

Teach

Time: About 45 minutes

"Let's see how forms can be created from shapes." *"Vamos a ver cómo se pueden crear las formas a partir de las figuras".*

- Read and discuss Using Shapes and Forms on page 128.

Practice

Materials: construction paper, scissors, tape

Alternate Materials: scrap paper

- Distribute the materials and have students follow the directions on page 128.

- Show that paper can be measured in two ways: height and width. Have students fold, curl, and bend two-dimensional paper in different ways to create three-dimensional forms. Ask students if they can measure their forms in three ways: height, width, and depth.

Creative Expression

NSAE 1.a; 1.c; 1.d

Materials: 9″ × 9″ cardboard or posterboard squares, string, pencils, colored construction paper, scissors, glue, paper hole punch

Alternate Materials: paper glued to paper instead of cardboard

- Distribute materials and have students follow the directions on page 129.

- Review the Technique Tips on page 224 for information about making paper forms.

- See the Activity Tips on page 241 for visual examples of this lesson's activity.

- When students are finished, punch a hole in the top of the mobile and pull a string through for hanging.

Art Journal: Brainstorming

Have students brainstorm ideas for shapes they would like to include in their mobile. Have them make quick sketches of their ideas in the Ideas section of their Art Journals.
NSAE 3.b

Using Shapes and Forms

Shapes have **height** and **width.**
Forms have height, width, and **depth.**

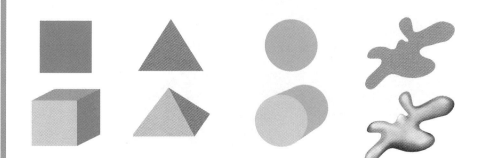

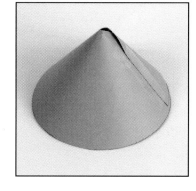

Practice

Make paper shapes into forms.

1. Start with a paper shape.
2. Fold, curl, or bend the paper shape to make a form.
3. Can you measure the depth of your paper form?

Differentiated Instruction

Reteach
Cut out a circle from construction paper and display it next to a ball (or use a construction-paper square and a box). Have students describe the similarities and differences.

Special Needs
Adaptations: Some students may find it difficult to differentiate between a shape and a form. Have manipulatives available of shapes and their corresponding forms.

ELL Tips
Point to a classroom object and ask if it is a form. Ask students whether they can walk around the object and see it from behind and from the sides.

Think about how this student used shapes and forms.

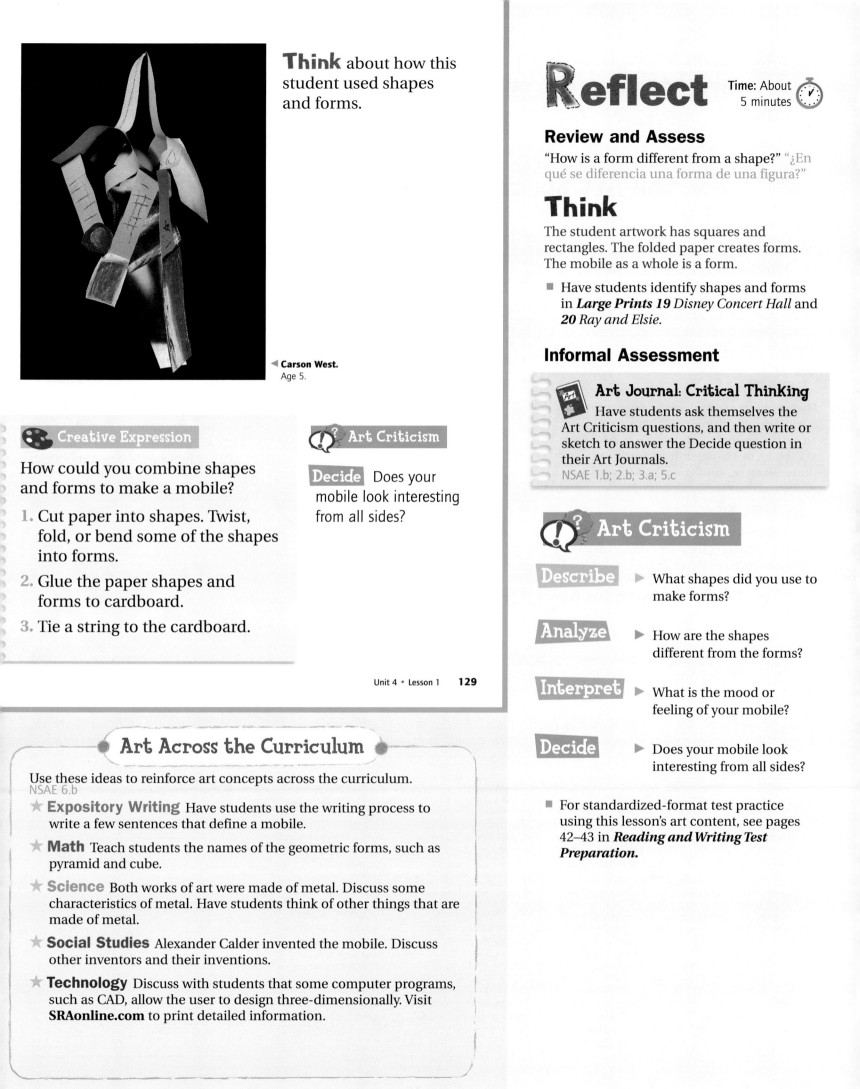

◄ **Carson West.**
Age 5.

Creative Expression

How could you combine shapes and forms to make a mobile?

1. Cut paper into shapes. Twist, fold, or bend some of the shapes into forms.

2. Glue the paper shapes and forms to cardboard.

3. Tie a string to the cardboard.

Art Criticism

Decide Does your mobile look interesting from all sides?

Art Across the Curriculum

Use these ideas to reinforce art concepts across the curriculum.
NSAE 6.b

★ **Expository Writing** Have students use the writing process to write a few sentences that define a mobile.

★ **Math** Teach students the names of the geometric forms, such as pyramid and cube.

★ **Science** Both works of art were made of metal. Discuss some characteristics of metal. Have students think of other things that are made of metal.

★ **Social Studies** Alexander Calder invented the mobile. Discuss other inventors and their inventions.

★ **Technology** Discuss with students that some computer programs, such as CAD, allow the user to design three-dimensionally. Visit **SRAonline.com** to print detailed information.

Reflect

Time: About 5 minutes

Review and Assess

"How is a form different from a shape?" "¿En qué se diferencia una forma de una figura?"

Think

The student artwork has squares and rectangles. The folded paper creates forms. The mobile as a whole is a form.

■ Have students identify shapes and forms in *Large Prints 19 Disney Concert Hall* and *20 Ray and Elsie.*

Informal Assessment

Art Journal: Critical Thinking
Have students ask themselves the Art Criticism questions, and then write or sketch to answer the Decide question in their Art Journals.
NSAE 1.b; 2.b; 3.a; 5.c

Art Criticism

Describe ► What shapes did you use to make forms?

Analyze ► How are the shapes different from the forms?

Interpret ► What is the mood or feeling of your mobile?

Decide ► Does your mobile look interesting from all sides?

■ For standardized-format test practice using this lesson's art content, see pages 42–43 in *Reading and Writing Test Preparation.*

Shapes and Forms

Extra! For the Art Specialist

Time: About 45 minutes

Focus

Use *Transparency 19* to discuss the difference between shapes and forms. Have students point out shapes and forms in the works of art. If students could view each artwork from another angle, how would it look different?

Teach

Have students complete the Shape-into-Form Animal Alternate Activity. Do students' animals stand on their legs? How is their form animal different from a two-dimensional animal drawn on paper?

Reflect

Guide students through evaluation of their works of art using the four steps of art criticism. (See pages 28–29 for more about art criticism.) Encourage students to locate other examples of shapes and forms in the classroom.

Alternate Activity

Materials:
- 9" × 12" oak tag (or one side of a manila folder)
- scissors
- pencils
- markers or crayons
- construction paper
- yarn scraps
- glue or glue sticks

1. Have students select an animal they would like to make. Four-legged animals with short necks and thick bodies will work well for this activity. Have students fold the oak tag in half. Explain that the fold of the paper will be the spine of the animal.

2. Have students draw a silhouette of the animal, starting at the head, from the folded edge of the paper. Have students cut out their animal shapes, leaving the folded edges intact.

3. Have students decorate the animals.

Research in Art Education

A link exists between "arts education and creative thinking, academic self-concept, and school climate" ("Learning In and Through the Arts: The Question of Transfer" in *Critical Links*, p. 66). Students in schools with quality arts programs tend to use more creativity, take more risks, and view themselves as academically competent. Encourage students to think creatively and to take risks as they make their paper mobiles.

Assessment

Use the following rubric to evaluate the artwork students make in the Creative Expression activity and to assess students' understanding of shapes and forms.

Have students complete page 45 or 46 in their *Assessment* books.

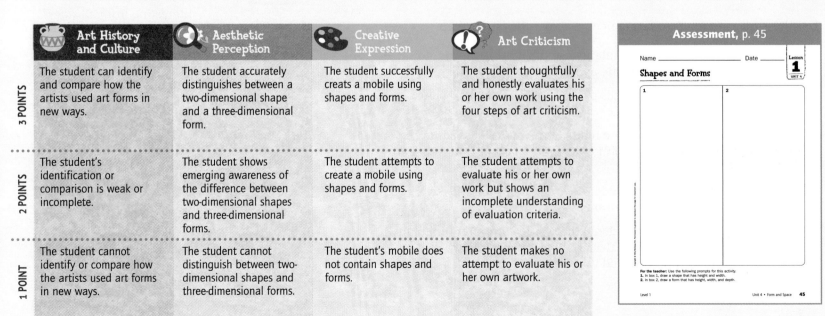

	Art History and Culture	Aesthetic Perception	Creative Expression	Art Criticism
3 POINTS	The student can identify and compare how the artists used art forms in new ways.	The student accurately distinguishes between a two-dimensional shape and a three-dimensional form.	The student successfully creates a mobile using shapes and forms.	The student thoughtfully and honestly evaluates his or her own work using the four steps of art criticism.
2 POINTS	The student's identification or comparison is weak or incomplete.	The student shows emerging awareness of the difference between two-dimensional shapes and three-dimensional forms.	The student attempts to create a mobile using shapes and forms.	The student attempts to evaluate his or her own work but shows an incomplete understanding of evaluation criteria.
1 POINT	The student cannot identify or compare how the artists used art forms in new ways.	The student cannot distinguish between two-dimensional shapes and three-dimensional forms.	The student's mobile does not contain shapes and forms.	The student makes no attempt to evaluate his or her own artwork.

Assessment, p. 45

Name _____ Date _____

Lesson **1** UNIT 4

Shapes and Forms

1	2

For the teacher: Use the following prompts for this activity.
1. In box 1, draw a shape that has height and width.
2. In box 2, draw a form that has height, width, and depth.

Level 1   Unit 4 • Form and Space **45**

Forms Take Up Space

Lesson 2 teaches students that forms are surrounded by space. Forms also can have space inside them.

Objectives

Art History and Culture

To recognize that sculptors are artists who create three-dimensional works of art
NSAE 1.a

Aesthetic Perception

To recognize that space surrounds a form
NSAE 3.a

Creative Expression

To create a posterboard sculpture
NSAE 1.a; 1.c; 1.d

Art Criticism

To evaluate one's own artwork using the four steps of art criticism
NSAE 1.b; 2.b; 3.a; 5.c

Vocabulary ★ Reading

Review the following vocabulary words with students before beginning the lesson.

form forma—any object that can be measured in three ways: height, width, and depth

space espacio—the element of art that refers to the area between, around, above, below, and within objects

See page 149B for additional vocabulary and Spanish vocabulary resources.

Art Journal: Vocabulary

Have students add these words to the Vocabulary section of their Art Journals.

Lesson Materials

- 9" × 12" posterboard
- crayons
- markers
- scissors
- colored construction paper (optional)

Alternate Materials:
- construction paper

Program Resources

- *Reading and Writing Test Prep.*, pp. 44-45
- *Transparency 20*
- *Artist Profiles*, pp. 38, 60
- *Animals Through History Time Line*
- *Assessment*, pp. 47-48
- *Large Prints 19* Disney Concert Hall and *20* Ray and Elsie
- *The National Museum of Women in the Arts Collection*

Concept Trace

Forms Take Up Space
Introduced: Level K, Unit 4, Lesson 3
Reinforced: Level 2, Unit 2, Lesson 1

Lesson 2 Arts Integration NSAE 6.a

Theatre

Complete Unit 4, Lesson 2, on pages 74–75 of *Theatre Arts Connections.*

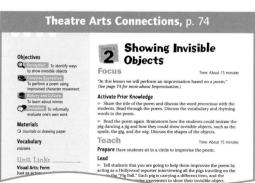

Music

Listen to *Variations on Simple Gifts* from *Appalachian Spring* by Aaron Copland. He created the ballet for the dancer Martha Graham in 1944. *Simple Gifts* is a Shaker hymn, and Copland repeated the melody by varying it in some way.

Movement & Dance

Have a small group of students create a group sculpture. Encourage them to include contrasting levels and line. Ask a second group to explore moving around and through the human sculpture. What happens to the sculpture when movement is added?

Focus

Activate Prior Knowledge

"What is in this bag?" "¿Qué hay en la bolsa?"

- Show students an empty bag. Discuss that it is empty, but air is inside it. Air is also all around it. Then put an object inside the bag. Explain that the object takes up space that used to be filled with air.

Using Literature ⭐ Reading

- Read *Wheels Around* by Shelley Rotner. The photographs of vehicles show space through forms (such as between the spokes of a bicycle wheel) and space in forms (such as inside a car).

Thematic Connection ⭐ Science

- **Space:** Discuss space exploration. Talk about the planets and their relationship to each other in space.

Introduce the Art

Look
NSAE 3.a

"Let's take a look at these sculptures." "Vamos a mirar estas esculturas".

Main Idea and Details ⭐ Reading

- Have students describe each sculpture. *Yellow Top* has horizontal pieces that are yellow, green, blue, red, brown, and orange. They are separated by white vertical pieces. *Figure* is a dark metal color. It looks like a body with a head and eyes at the top.

🏺 Art History and Culture

Explain that the GI Bill (formally known as the Servicemen's Readjustment Act of 1944) provided federal funds for education of World War II veterans. Veterans could attend any college and study any subject, and the government helped to pay for tuition, books, supplies, and living expenses. Discuss with students ways that artists are involved in their communities, such as through military service.

 Web Connection

Visit www.tatintsian.com/sugarman.html for more information about George Sugarman and to view other works.

Lesson 2 # Forms Take up Space

Look at these sculptures. They have forms. They also have open spaces for air to go through.

◄ **George Sugarman.** (American). *Yellow Top.* 1959.
....
Acrylic on laminated wood. 89 × 46 × 34 inches (226.06 × 116.84 × 86.36 cm.). Walker Art Center, Minneapolis, Minnesota.

🏺 Art History and Culture

George Sugarman served in the U.S. Navy. This allowed him to study art through the G.I. Bill program.

🏺 Art History and Culture

George Sugarman NSAE 1.a

George Sugarman (jorj shu´ gər mən) (1912–1999) was born in New York City. He began to paint in 1950. The following year he went to Paris, France, on the G.I. Bill program and studied sculpture. An artist who creates sculptures, or three-dimensional works of art, is called a sculptor. He was one of the first sculptors to consider the negative space around a sculpture as part of the sculpture itself. By 1969, he was one of the United States' most celebrated sculptors.

See pages 16–21 and 24–25 for more about subject matter and art history.

Artist Profiles, p. 60

Artist Profile
George Sugarman
1912-1999

George Sugarman (jorj shu´ gər mən) was born in New York City in 1912, however, he did not begin to paint until 1950. The following year he went to Paris, France, on the G.I. Bill to study sculpture with the Russian-born sculptor Ossip Zadkine. He was inspired to develop his own unique style of wood sculpture. He returned to New York City and had his first exhibition in 1960. By 1969 he was one of the most celebrated sculptors in the United States. He had many one-man shows and won many awards and grants for his artwork.

Study the works of art.

▶ Where do you see space in and around the sculptures?

◀ **Jacques Lipchitz.** (Lithuanian/American). *Figure*. 1929-1930.
Bronze (cast 137). 7 feet $\frac{1}{4}$ inch × $38\frac{5}{8}$ inches (2.14 meters × 98.11 cm.). Museum of Modern Art, New York, New York.

Aesthetic Perception

Seeing Like an Artist Your hand is a form. Open and close your fingers. How does the space change?

Art History and Culture

Jacques Lipchitz

Jacques Lipchitz (zhäk lēp shēts) (1891–1973) was born in Lithuania. He moved to Paris, France, when he was 18 years old to study art. While in Paris he became friends with many other artists, including Pablo Picasso. After World War II began, Lipchitz moved to the United States, where he became a citizen in 1958. Throughout his life Lipchitz held many exhibitions and received many commissions. He is considered the most important cubist sculptor of the twentieth century.

See pages 16–21 and 24–25 for more about subject matter and art history.

Artist Profiles, p. 38

● Artist Profile ●
Jacques Lipchitz
1891-1973
Jacques Lipchitz (zhäk lēp shēts) was born in Lithuania and later moved to France. During World War II Lipchitz, who was Jewish, fled Europe to escape the Nazis. He left Paris and came to the United States. In 1952 a fire destroyed everything in his New York art studio, and he had to start all over. In 1957 he became a citizen of the United States.

Study

▶ The forms of *Yellow Top* are different-colored pieces that have space between them because they are separated by the white pieces. The forms of *Figure* have spaces that go all the way through them. *Figure* also has indentations that have space inside. Both sculptures have space all around them.

■ For more examples of abstract/nonobjective art, see **The National Museum of Women in the Arts Collection.**

Art Journal: Concepts

Have students think of an everyday object that has space around it and through it, and sketch it in the Concepts section of their Art Journals.

Aesthetic Perception

Seeing Like an Artist Discuss with students that when they hold their fingers tightly together, no space is between them. As they spread their fingers wider and wider, they create more space between their fingers. Their hands do not actually get larger, but as their fingers spread apart, their hand takes up more space.

Developing Visual Literacy Discuss with students how each sculpture makes them feel. Do they like one more than the other? Discuss the properties of each sculpture that influence their feelings. Discuss different materials artists can use to make a form, such as papier-mâché, clay, or glass.
NSAE 1.b; 2.b; 5.c

Web Connection

Visit *The Estate of Jacques Lipchitz* at **www.marlboroughgallery.com/artists.html** for more information.

Teach

Time: About 40 minutes

"Let's notice how a form can have space around it and through it." *"Vamos a fijarnos en cómo una forma puede tener espacio a su alrededor y a través de ella".*

- Read and discuss Using Forms and Space on page 132.

Practice

Materials: None

- Have students follow the directions on page 132.

- Students should think of different ways to join hands to create a form. For instance, students might attach by wrapping just one finger around the next student's finger. Have them try standing close together or stretching their arms out to stand far apart. Ask each group to describe the space in and around the forms of their bodies.

Creative Expression

NSAE 1.a; 1.c; 1.d

Materials: 9" × 12" posterboard, crayons, markers, scissors, colored construction paper (optional)

Alternate Materials: construction paper

- Distribute materials and have students follow the directions on page 133.

- Review the Technique Tips on page 221 for information about properly using scissors.

- See the Activity Tips on page 241 for visual examples of this lesson's activity.

- Students may also choose to tear strips of construction paper and insert them into the slits.

Art Journal: Brainstorming

Have students brainstorm ideas for shapes and colors they would like to use in their Creative Expression sculptures. Have students make quick sketches of their ideas in the Ideas section of their Art Journals.

Using Forms and Space

A **form** takes up **space** and has space all around it. A form also can have space inside it or through it.

Practice

Make a human sculpture.

1. Form a group with your classmates.
2. Join hands to make an interesting form.
3. Notice the space around your bodies.

Differentiated Instruction

Reteach

Stand with your arms straight down at your sides. Bend your arms and put your hands on your hips. Discuss with students how the space around your body changed.

Special Needs

Adaptations: For students with low vision, ensure that there is high contrast between the color of the posterboard and the color of the markers.

ELL Tips

Hold up a hoop or another form with space through it. Have students identify *form* or *space* as you touch the object or move your hand through the space.

◄ **Alexandra Andrews.** Age 6.

◄ **Zachary Locotti.** Age 6.

Think about how these students made designs that take up space.

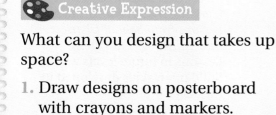 **Creative Expression**

What can you design that takes up space?

1. Draw designs on posterboard with crayons and markers.

2. Fold your posterboard in half. Cut slits into it.

3. Bend the posterboard to make some sections stand out.

Art Criticism

Describe Describe your sculpture. What materials did you use to make it?

Art Across the Curriculum

Use these ideas to reinforce art concepts across the curriculum.
NSAE 6.b

★ **Descriptive Writing** Have students write a few adjectives to describe each artwork.

★ **Math** Have students count the colored pieces and the white pieces in *Yellow Top* and compare the numbers.

★ **Science** Discuss that removing pieces from the forms of everyday objects can change how they work as well as how they look.

★ **Social Studies** Jacques Lipchitz was born in Lithuania but moved to France and then the United States. Locate these countries on a map or globe.

★ **Technology** Discuss that a computer takes up space and has space inside it. Demonstrate that inserting a disk into a disk drive takes up some of the space inside the computer. Visit **SRAonline.com** to print detailed instructions for this activity.

 **Reflect** Time: About 5 minutes

Review and Assess

"What is the relationship between forms and space?" "¿Cuál es la relación entre las formas y el espacio?"

Think

The students bent the panels of the posterboard to create sculptures that have height, width, and depth. These forms take up space. The sculptures also have space through them and around them.

■ Have students identify space and forms in *Large Prints 19* Disney Concert Hall and *20 Ray and Elsie.*

Informal Assessment

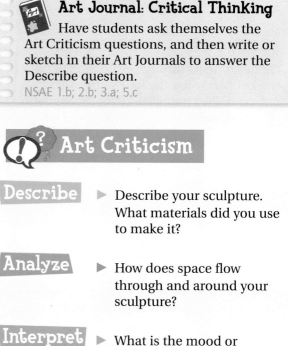 **Art Journal: Critical Thinking**
Have students ask themselves the Art Criticism questions, and then write or sketch in their Art Journals to answer the Describe question.
NSAE 1.b; 2.b; 3.a; 5.c

Art Criticism

Describe ► Describe your sculpture. What materials did you use to make it?

Analyze ► How does space flow through and around your sculpture?

Interpret ► What is the mood or feeling of your sculpture? Give it a title.

Decide ► How could you change your sculpture to change the space around it?

■ For standardized-format test practice using this lesson's art content, see pages 44–45 in *Reading and Writing Test Preparation.*

Forms Take Up Space

For the Art Specialist

Time: About 45 minutes

Focus

Ask students if their bodies are shapes or forms. Have a student stand and strike a pose. Ask students to point out space around the student's position.

Teach

Have students complete the Alternate Activity. Where do they see space around the forms of their circus scene? How would the space change if the forms were arranged differently?

Reflect

Guide students through evaluation of their works of art using the four steps of art criticism. (See pages 28–29 for more about art criticism.)

Alternate Activity

Materials:
- shallow boxes or shoe box lids, one per every 3 or 4 students
- oil-based clay
- construction paper scraps
- scissors
- glue or glue sticks

1. Divide students into groups of 3 or 4. Have students brainstorm information about a circus. How many rings does a circus usually have? What kinds of performers and animals are there?

2. Tell students they are going to construct a scene from a circus. Each person in the group will have an assigned part of the scene, such as a person, animal, or prop.

3. Have students create their circus forms using the clay and construction paper, and arrange them in the shallow box. Have students design and arrange their forms to be interesting from more than one angle.

Research in Art Education

It has been shown that "elementary [art] programs establish a foundation in the arts for all students, not just for those in specialized programs or those who choose an arts course of study in high school." Providing consistent, quality instruction in the arts in elementary school also ensures that students have the time to foster skills in the arts. Many of these skills take time to develop (*Gaining the Arts Advantage: Lessons from School Districts that Value Arts Education*). Lessons in future levels will build upon skills developed in this level.

Assessment

Use the following rubric to evaluate the artwork students make in the Creative Expression activity and to assess students' understanding of forms and space.

Have students complete page 47 or 48 in their *Assessment* books.

	Art History and Culture	Aesthetic Perception	Creative Expression	Art Criticism
3 POINTS	The student successfully identifies a sculptor as an artist who creates three-dimensional works of art.	The student consistently recognizes that space surrounds a form.	The student's posterboard sculpture clearly illustrates form.	The student thoughtfully and honestly evaluates his or her own work using the four steps of art criticism.
2 POINTS	The student's identification is weak or incomplete.	The student shows emerging awareness that space surrounds a form.	The student's posterboard sculpture shows some awareness of form.	The student attempts to evaluate his or her own work, but shows an incomplete understanding of evaluation criteria.
1 POINT	The student cannot identify a sculptor as an artist who creates three-dimensional works of art.	The student does not recognize that space surrounds a form.	The student's posterboard sculpture shows no understanding of form.	The student makes no attempt to evaluate his or her own artwork.

Assessment, p. 47

Name _____ Date _____

Lesson **2** UNIT 4

Forms Take Up Space

For the teacher: Use the following prompt for this activity.
Using a crayon, draw a form that takes up space and has spaces in it or through it.

Level 1   Unit 4 • Form and Space   **47**

Free-Form Forms

Lesson 3 introduces students to free-form forms.

Objectives

Art History and Culture
To recognize that artists create realistic free-form forms as well as abstract ones
NSAE 2.a; 3.a

Creative Expression
To create a free-form form with clay
NSAE 1.a; 1.c; 1.d; 2.c; 3.b

Aesthetic Perception
To distinguish between free-form forms and geometric forms
NSAE 2.a

Art Criticism
To evaluate one's own artwork using the four steps of art criticism
NSAE 1.b; 2.b; 3.a; 5.c

Vocabulary ⭐ Reading

Review the following vocabulary words with students before beginning the lesson.

geometric form *forma geométrica*—a three-dimensional figure that has precise measurement and can be described in mathematical terms, such as a sphere, a cube, a pyramid or cone, and a rectangular solid

free-form form *forma abstracta*—an uneven and irregular form; any form that is not geometric

See page 149B for additional vocabulary and Spanish vocabulary resources.

Art Journal: Vocabulary
Have students add these words to the Vocabulary section of their Art Journals.

Lesson Materials
- sketch paper
- colored pencils
- clay
- slip
- slip bowls
- clay mats (muslin)
- clay tools (pencils, paper clips, craft sticks)
- paintbrushes
- water containers
- glaze (optional)

Alternate Materials:
- crayons or markers
- modeling clay
- self-hardening clay, or flour and cornstarch dough

Program Resources
- *Reading and Writing Test Prep.*, pp. 46–47
- *Transparency 21*
- *Artist Profiles*, pp. 24, 81
- *Animals Through History Time Line*
- *Assessment*, pp. 49–50
- *Large Prints 19* Disney Concert Hall and *20* Ray and Elsie
- *Art Around the World*

Concept Trace
Free-Form Forms
Introduced: Level K, Unit 4, Lesson 2
Reinforced: Level 2, Unit 2, Lesson 2

Lesson 3 Arts Integration NSAE 6.a

Theatre
Complete Unit 4, Lesson 3, on pages 76–77 of *Theatre Arts Connections.*

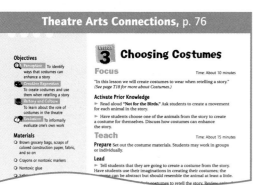

Theatre Arts Connections, p. 76

Music
The form of Western music generally has both large and small patterns. The melodies of Native Americans, however, are less predictable. They are more like free-form forms. Listen to the irregular melodies of *Tekaniontonʼneha.*

Movement & Dance
Have students make a large circle and count off in groups of five. Going clockwise around the circle ask the first number 1 to enter the circle and make a shape. Number 2 then enters and creates a shape that adds onto one's shape and changes level. Number 3 enters and faces a different direction, numbers 4 and 5 enter and find a way to connect to one or more of the shapes. Repeat with all groups.

Focus

Time: About 10 minutes

Activate Prior Knowledge

"What kind of shape is a free-form shape?"

"¿Qué tipo de figura es una figura abstracta?"

- Remind students that in Unit 2 they learned that a free-form shape is any shape that is not a geometric shape. In two-dimensional works of art (such as paintings), living things have free-form shapes. Explain that free-form forms are like free-form shapes, but they have three dimensions.

Using Literature ⭐ Reading

- Read *Sweet Dreams: How Animals Sleep* by Kimiko Kajikawa. Discuss the free-form forms of the animals in the photographs.

Thematic Connection ⭐ Science

- **Living Things:** Discuss that living things are free-form forms. Observe and describe the free-form parts of animals and plants.

Introduce the Art

Look
NSAE 2.a; 3.a

"Let's take a close look at these works of art."

"Vamos a mirar detalladamente estas obras de arte".

Comparing and Contrasting ⭐ Reading

- Have students discuss the similarities and differences between the subjects of the works of art. Similarities: Both works of art are vertical; both have spaces through them; both look different from different sides. Differences: *Standing Youth* is made from bronze and has a realistic, recognizable subject; and *Figure: Churinga* is made from wood and is abstract.

🏺 Art History and Culture

Have students look carefully at *Standing Youth*. What details in the artwork give clues about the history and culture of this person? Discuss with students that works of art can serve as records of history and culture. In their works of art, artists sometimes incorporate images they see in the world around them. Art can be a reflection of the time and place it was created.
NSAE 4.a; 4.b; 4.c

💻 Web Connection

Visit **china.candidemedia.com/html/mfachina .html** for other examples of Chinese art.

Lesson 3

Free-Form Forms

Look at these sculptures. They have free-form forms.

◄ **Artist Unknown.** (China). *Standing Youth*. Late fifth to early fourth century B.C.

Cast bronze with applied jade. Height 11$\frac{13}{16}$ inches (30 cm.). Museum of Fine Arts, Boston, Massachusetts.

🏺 Art History and Culture

Standing Youth was made a very long time ago. It gives clues about the people who lived when it was made.

🏺 Art History and Culture

Standing Youth was created during China's Eastern Zhou period. During this era, representations of humans were more accurate than they had been in the past. Clues in this artwork (such as the man's appearance) led archaeologists to believe that the sculpture depicts a nomad from China's northern border region. This sculpture is similar to other bronze sculptures that were placed in tombs to provide entertainment for the deceased in the afterlife.

See pages 16–21 and 24–25 for more about subject matter and art history.

Artist Profiles, p. 81

⟨ Artist Profile ⟩

Standing Youth

This statue was created in China during the Eastern Zhou dynasty. This time period, spanning the late fifth to the early fourth centuries B.C., is known today as the *Warring States* period. No information as to the identity of the artist has been found.

Study the sculptures.

▶ What would they look like from each side?

◀ **Barbara Hepworth.** (British). *Figure: Churinga.* 1952.

Spanish Mahogany. $52\frac{1}{2} \times 16 \times 15\frac{1}{2}$ inches (133.35 × 40.64 × 39.37 cm.). Walker Art Center, Minneapolis, Minnesota.

Aesthetic Perception

Design Awareness Which of your toys have geometric forms? Which have free-form forms?

Art History and Culture

Barbara Hepworth

Barbara Hepworth (bärb´ ə rə hep´ wûrth) (1903–1975) was one of the most important British sculptors. She was prominent in the development of abstract sculpture. Hepworth was renowned during her lifetime. Her sculptures were exhibited frequently, and she received many awards. She was awarded the title of Dame in the Order of the British Empire. Her former studio in Tate St. Ives is now a museum.

See pages 16–21 and 24–25 for more about subject matter and art history.

Artist Profiles, p. 24

◆ Artist Profile ◆

Barbara Hepworth
1903-1975

Barbara Hepworth (bärb´ ə rə hep´ wûrth) was an English sculptor known for her abstract works in wood, stone, and metal. As a child in Yorkshire, she took car trips through the countryside with her father. She was impressed by the contrast between the beauty of rural areas and the grime of industrial towns. The land became a theme she returned to again and again in her art. After studying art and sculpture in England, Hepworth moved to Rome and then returned to England. She married twice, once to a sculptor and once to a painter. She had a son and a set of triplets. Her relationship with her children also became an important theme of her work. In 1965, she was honored by being named a dame.

Study

▶ If *Standing Youth* was viewed from the side or back, the viewer would see the side or back of the person. The left side of *Standing Youth* is different from the right side because the poles are held at different lengths. One side of *Figure: Churinga* has an indentation, while the other side is smoother.

■ For more examples of art from Asia, see ***Art Around the World Collection.***

Art Journal: Concepts

Have students make a sketch in the Concepts section of their Art Journals to show the difference between a geometric form and a free-form form.

Aesthetic Perception

Design Awareness Have students name some toys with geometric forms (balls, building blocks) and some with free-form forms (action figures, stuffed animals). Discuss the characteristics of toys with each type of form.

Developing Visual Literacy Discuss with students that *Standing Youth* is realistic while *Figure: Churinga* is abstract. Why do students think each artist chose to make a realistic or abstract work? Do students connect more to either work? Which work would students prefer to have in their home?
NSAE 2a; 2.b; 3.a; 5.a; 5.c

Web Connection

Visit **www.sculpture.uk.com/barbara_hepworth_ other_works.htm** to view other sculptures in Hepworth's portfolio. Have students share their ideas about Barbara Hepworth's work in small groups.

each

Time: About 40 minutes

"What is the difference between a geometric form and a free-form form?" "¿Cuál es la diferencia entre una forma geométrica y una forma abstracta?"

- Read and discuss Using Free-Form Forms on page 136.

Practice

Materials: sketch paper, colored pencils

Alternate Materials: crayons or markers

- Distribute the materials and have students follow the directions on page 136.

- Students can choose a free-form form in the classroom to sketch or they can think of one that is familiar to them, such as a favorite animal. Have students sketch the form from at least two different sides.

Creative Expression

NSAE 1.a; 1.c; 1.d; 2.c

Materials: clay, slip, slip bowls, clay mats (muslin), clay tools (pencils, paper clips, craft sticks), paintbrushes, water containers, glaze (optional)

Alternate Materials: modeling clay, self-hardening clay, or flour and cornstarch dough

- Distribute materials and have students follow the directions on page 137.

- Review the Technique Tips on pages 230–231 for information about working with clay.

- See the Activity Tips on page 242 for visual examples of this lesson's activity.

- Demonstrate the use of slip.

- You might allow students to glaze the sculptures when the clay is dry.

Art Journal: Brainstorming

Have students brainstorm ideas for free-form forms they could sculpt. Have students make quick sketches of their ideas in the Ideas section of their Art Journals.

NSAE 3.b

Using Free-Form Forms

Some forms are **geometric forms.**

Other forms are **free-form forms.**

Practice

Sketch a free-form form.

1. Think about what a free-form form looks like from different sides.
2. Sketch the form from different sides.

136 Unit 4 • Lesson 3

Differentiated Instruction

Reteach
Compare premade geometric and free-form forms. Discuss that measuring geometric forms is easy, but measuring free-form forms can be more complicated.

Special Needs
Adaptations: incorporate technology into this lesson for students who need additional ways of understanding the concepts. Many museums have Web sites that allow you to view sculptures from different angles. Preview some and have them available for students to explore.

ELL Tips
Assemble a number of classroom objects with free-form forms or geometric forms. Have students identify the type of form as you point to each.

◄ **Aaron Ragans.**
Age 6.

Think about how this student made
a free-form form.

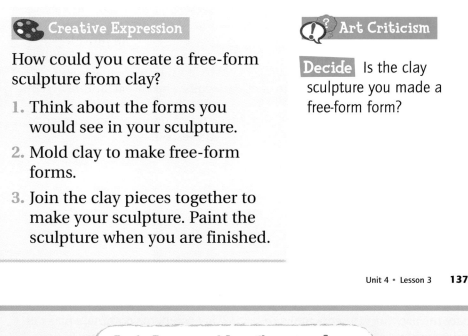

Creative Expression

How could you create a free-form
sculpture from clay?

1. Think about the forms you
   would see in your sculpture.

2. Mold clay to make free-form
   forms.

3. Join the clay pieces together to
   make your sculpture. Paint the
   sculpture when you are finished.

Art Criticism

Decide Is the clay
sculpture you made a
free-form form?

Art Across the Curriculum

Use these ideas to reinforce art concepts across the curriculum.
NSAE 6.b

★ **Narrative Writing** Have students use the writing process to write
a short story about the subject of *Standing Youth*.

★ **Math** Have students make a sketch of what each sculpture would
look like if it were made from geometric forms instead of free-form
forms.

★ **Science** Have students observe that the fronts of their hands are
different from the backs, and make sketches to record their
observations. Have students compare their sketches.

★ **Social Studies** Archaeologists believe that statues like *Standing
Youth* were placed in tombs. Discuss how traditions and customs
vary between cultures.

★ **Technology** Computer monitors and other pieces of technology
equipment are often geometric forms rather than free-form forms.
Discuss with students why they have been designed that way. Visit
SRAonline.com to print detailed instructions for this activity.

Reflect

Time: About
5 minutes

Review and Assess

"Is a shoe a geometric or a free-form form?"
"¿Un zapato es una forma geométrica o
abstracta?"

Think

The student made the free-form form of an
animal.

■ Have students identify free-form forms in
Large Prints 19 Disney Concert Hall and
20 Ray and Elsie.

Informal Assessment

Art Journal: Critical Thinking
Have students ask themselves the
Art Criticism questions and then write or
sketch in their Art Journals to answer the
Decide question.
NSAE 1.b; 2.b; 3.a; 5.c

Art Criticism

Describe ▶ What did you sculpt?

Analyze ▶ Does your statue look
different from each side?

Interpret ▶ Does your statue look like
anything you know? Give it
a title.

Decide ▶ Is the clay sculpture you
made a free-form form?

■ For standardized-format test practice
using this lesson's art content, see pages
46–47 in *Reading and Writing Test
Preparation.*

Free-Form Forms

Extra! For the Art Specialist

Time: About 45 minutes

Focus

Use *Transparency 21* to discuss free-form forms. How are they different from geometric forms?

Teach

Have students complete the Alternate Activity. Could students measure their free-form sculptures in three dimensions?

Reflect

Guide students through evaluation of their works of art using the four steps of art criticism. (See pages 28–29 for more about art criticism.) Then have students describe, analyze, and interpret the work of a classmate.

Alternate Activity

Materials:
- 4" × 6" pieces of tagboard or oak tag (5 or 6 pieces per student)
- scissors
- markers or crayons

1. Distribute 5 or 6 pieces of tagboard to each student. Demonstrate cutting the pieces of tagboard into free-form shapes and cutting two or three 1" slots into the edges of the shapes. Show students how to join free-form shapes together by pushing slots of different pieces of tagboard into each other.

2. Students will cut out different free-form shapes from their pieces of tagboard. Students can use markers or crayons to decorate their tagboard pieces. Have students join their free-form shapes together to create a free-form sculpture.

Research in Art Education

Students are challenged by the comprehensive nature of big art projects, and "in doing so, [they] master an enormous number of artistic skills, direct a myriad of aesthetic and expressive qualities toward given ends, and symbolize human behaviors and emotions in a great variety of ways" (*Gaining the Arts Advantage: Lessons from School Districts that Value Arts Education*). Art projects also can provide students with the opportunity to learn time management skills. The clay sculpture activity will give students a challenge and an opportunity to practice these skills.

Assessment

Use the following rubric to evaluate the artwork students make in the Creative Expression activity and to assess students' understanding of free-form forms.

Have students complete page 49 or 50 in their *Assessment* books.

	Art History and Culture	Aesthetic Perception	Creative Expression	Art Criticism
3 POINTS	The student can identify and compare realistic and abstract free-form works of art.	The student accurately identifies geometric and free-form forms.	The student successfully creates a free-form form with clay.	The student thoughtfully and honestly evaluates his or her own work using the four steps of art criticism.
2 POINTS	The student's identification or comparison is weak or incomplete.	The student shows emerging awareness of geometric and free-form forms.	The student attempts to create a free-form form with clay.	The student attempts to evaluate his or her own work, but shows an incomplete understanding of evaluation criteria.
1 POINT	The student cannot identify or compare realistic and abstract free-form works of art.	The student cannot identify geometric and free-form forms.	The student does not create a free-form form with clay.	The student makes no attempt to evaluate his or her own artwork.

Assessment p. 49

Name _____ Date _____

Free-Form Forms

Lesson **3** UNIT 4

1	2

For the teacher: Use the following prompts for this activity.
1. In box 1, draw a geometric form.
2. In box 2, draw a free-form form.

Level 1   Unit 4 • Form and Space **49**

3-D Me!

Lesson 4 teaches students that the human body is a free-form form. Sculptors create three-dimensional portraits of people.

Objectives

Art History and Culture

To recognize that sculptors create three-dimensional portraits of people
NSAE 5.a

Creative Expression

To create a three-dimensional self-portrait sculpture   NSAE 1.a; 1.c; 1.d; 2.c; 3.b

Aesthetic Perception

To recognize that the human form is a free-form form
NSAE 6.b

Art Criticism

To evaluate one's own artwork using the four steps of art criticism
NSAE 1.b; 2.b; 3.a; 5.c

Vocabulary  Reading

Review the following vocabulary words with students.

height altura o alto—how tall something is

width ancho—how wide something is

depth profundidad—the distance from front to back

form forma—any object that can be measured in three ways: height, width, and depth

See page 149B for additional vocabulary and Spanish vocabulary resources.

Art Journal: Vocabulary

Have students add these words to the Vocabulary section of their Art Journals.

Lesson Materials

- clay
- slip
- slip bowls
- clay tools (pencils, paper clips, craft sticks)
- clay mats (muslin)
- paintbrushes
- water containers

Alternate Materials:
- modeling clay, self-hardening clay, or flour and cornstarch dough

Program Resources

- *Reading and Writing Test Prep.,* pp. 48–49
- *Transparency 22*
- *Artist Profiles,* pp. 78–79
- *Animals Through History Time Line*
- *Assessment,* pp. 51–52
- *Large Prints 20* Ray and Elsie
- *National Museum of Women in the Arts Collection*

Concept Trace

3-D Me!

Introduced: Level K, Unit 4, Lesson 2

Reinforced: Level 2, Unit 2, Lesson 3

Lesson 4 Arts Integration NSAE 6.a

Theatre

Complete Unit 4, Lesson 4, on pages 78–79 of *Theatre Arts Connections.*

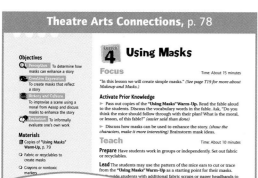

Theatre Arts Connections, p. 78

Music

Listen to the use of dynamics in *Bydlo* from *Pictures at an Exhibition* by Modest Mussorgsky. The music depicts a lumbering cart coming towards us and passing by. What else in the music suggests it is approaching us?

Movement & Dance

Have four students form a circle. Ask number 1 to enter the circle and make a shape. Number 2 then enters and adds on to the shape made by the first, changing the level. The third student enters and creates a shape that faces a different direction. Number 4 enters and finds a way to connect to one of the shapes. Have the rest of the students walk around the sculpture, viewing it from all sides.

Focus

Time: About 10 minutes

Activate Prior Knowledge

"Have you ever seen a sculpture of a person?"

"¿Alguna vez han visto una escultura de una persona?"

- Discuss statues that students have seen. Discuss reasons an artist might choose to make a sculpture of a person.

Using Literature [★] Reading

- Read *Communities* by Gail Saunders-Smith. The photographs show the free-form forms of people doing different jobs.

Thematic Connection [★] Reading

- **About Me:** Discuss with students what makes each of them special and unique. How could this be shown in a statue?

Introduce the Art

Look
NSAE 2.a; 3.a

"Let's take a close look at these two works of art." "Vamos a mirar detalladamente estas dos obras de arte".

Comparing and Contrasting [★] Reading

- Have students list the similarities and differences between the two works of art. Similarities: Both are forms; both show men. Differences: The man in *Ritual Figure* is standing, and the man in *Seated Arhat* is kneeling or seated with one leg bent. The man in *Ritual Figure* is holding a cane and wearing a hat, and the man in *Seated Arhat* is not. *Ritual Figure* is more colorful than *Seated Arhat,* and the two statues are made of different materials.

Art History and Culture

Discuss with students that the sculptures were made thousands of years apart and on different continents. Artists have been making three-dimensional portraits throughout history and all over the world. Each of these sculptures represents a person with ideal qualities in the artist's culture. The Egyptian sculpture represents someone with power, strength, and masculinity. The Chinese sculpture represents someone with spirituality, freedom, and empowerment.
NSAE 4.a; 4.b; 4.c; 5.a

Web Connection
Visit **www.metmuseum.org/collections/index.asp** to view more Egyptian art.

3-D Me!

◀ **Artist Unknown.** (Egypt). *Ritual Figure.* c. 1962–1928 B.C.
Gessoed and painted wood. Height 22⅞ inches (58.10 cm.). Metropolitan Museum of Art, New York, New York.

Look at the works of art on these pages. They are sculptures of people.

Art History and Culture

Each of these sculptures represents someone with ideal qualities from the artist's culture.

Art History and Culture

This statue was discovered during an excavation of the pyramids at Lisht, Egypt, in 1914. Figures like this probably were used in elaborate funeral ceremonies and then buried. The statue has features of royal and divine figures: The crown is the crown of Lower Egypt, but the kilt symbolizes divinity. Men in Egyptian art depict power, strength, and masculinity.

See pages 16–21 and 24–25 for more about subject matter and art history.

Artist Profiles, p. 78

▷ Artist Profile ◁

Ritual Figure
This figure was created during the twelfth dynasty of the Middle Kingdom of ancient Egyptian history. The statue might have been carved by one artist and then painted by another, or it might have been designed and constructed by a larger group of artisans. Little is known about the individuals and groups who created portrait sculptures such as this one, but it is presumed that they enjoyed some degree of recognition as respected members of their communities.

Artist Unknown. (Egypt). *Ritual Figure*

Study the sculptures.

▶ What forms do you see?

◀ **Artist Unknown.** (China). *Seated Arhat.* c. 1300–1450.

Cast iron, traces of pigment. Height 30¹¹⁄₁₆ inches (77.95 cm.). Kimbell Museum of Art, Fort Worth, Texas.

Art History and Culture

An *arhat* (or *lohan* in Chinese) is a Buddhist saint. Arhats are believed to have achieved an elevated level of spirituality, which gives them freedom and empowerment. Portraits of arhats often appeared in Chinese, Indian, and Tibetan art.

See pages 16–21 and 24–25 for more about subject matter and art history.

Artist Profiles, p. 79

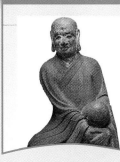

Artist Profile

Seated Arhat

This statue was made by an unknown Chinese artist during the late Yuan dynasty or early Ming dynasty. Portraits of arhats were a popular art form during these time periods. Because many sculptors engaged in the creation of these graceful statues, it has proven difficult for art historians to identify the specific artist who created this piece. Inscribed on the back of this statue are the names of the donors who commissioned the work, as well as the name of the temple that was to receive it as a gift.

Study

▶ Each human is a form. Each form is made up of smaller forms, such as the head or the arms. The hat and the staff in *Ritual Figure* are also forms.

■ For more examples of portraits, see *The National Museum of Women in the Arts Collection.*

Art Journal: Concepts

Have students make a sketch of a human form in the Concepts section of their Art Journals.

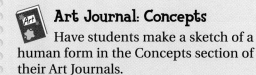

Aesthetic Perception

Seeing Like an Artist Have students look at their bodies and notice that they are made up of smaller forms. Each part also can be made up of smaller forms. For example, a hand is one of the smaller forms that make up an arm. A finger is one of the smaller forms that make up the hand.

Developing Visual Literacy Discuss with students what they think the artists' purposes were for creating each statue. Do the works of art have any clues to show how the artists felt about each person?

NSAE 3.a; 4.c; 5.a; 5.b

Web Connection

Visit **www.kimbellart.org** to view other works in the Kimbell Art Museum's Asian art collection.

Teach

Time: About 50 minutes

"What does the form of a person look like?"
"¿Comó es la forma de una persona?"

- Read and discuss Using People Forms on page 140.

Practice

Materials: sketch paper, crayons

Alternate Materials: markers or colored pencils

- Distribute the materials and have students follow the directions on page 140.

- Discuss the sizes of the smaller forms that make up the human body: a large torso, two long forms for legs, two smaller forms for arms, a neck, and a head. Have students sketch the outlines of the different sizes of forms they would need to make their 3-D self portrait.

Creative Expression

NSAE 1.a; 1.c; 1.d; 2.c

Materials: clay, slip, slip bowls, clay tools (pencils, paper clips, craft sticks), clay mats (muslin), paintbrushes, water containers

Alternate Materials: modeling clay, self-hardening clay, or flour and cornstarch dough

- Distribute materials and have students follow the directions on page 141.

- Review the Activity Tips on page 242 for visual examples of techniques.

- Discuss the process of joining pieces of clay: score, slip, squeeze, and smooth.

- Suggest they make both arms or both legs at the same time so they are approximately the same size and length. Attach the legs so the figure is sitting. Students will not be able to create a standing figure because it is difficult to make the legs so that they will support the body.

- Encourage students to add details so the statues look like them.

Art Journal: Brainstorming

Have students brainstorm ideas for how they would like their self-portrait sculptures to look. Have students make quick sketches of their ideas in the Ideas section of their Art Journals.

NSAE 3.b

140 UNIT 4 • Form and Space

Using People Forms

A person has **height, width,** and **depth.**
A person is a form.

Practice

What sizes are the forms of your body?

1. Think about the forms you would show in a sculpture of yourself.

2. Which forms are big? Which forms are small?

3. Sketch the outline of each form.

140   Unit 4 • Lesson 4

Differentiated Instruction

Reteach
Compare the sculptures with photos of humans. Discuss the different body parts that make up the human form.

Special Needs
Adaptations: Students with developmental disabilities may have difficulty recognizing and applying information about their body forms. Have mirrors available and provide students with the opportunity to recognize the shape and size of each body part.

ELL Tips
Bring pictures of famous statues of people (such as the Statue of Liberty) to class. Ask students if they could walk around the statue and look at the sides and the back. Review the concept that forms, including humans, are three-dimensional.

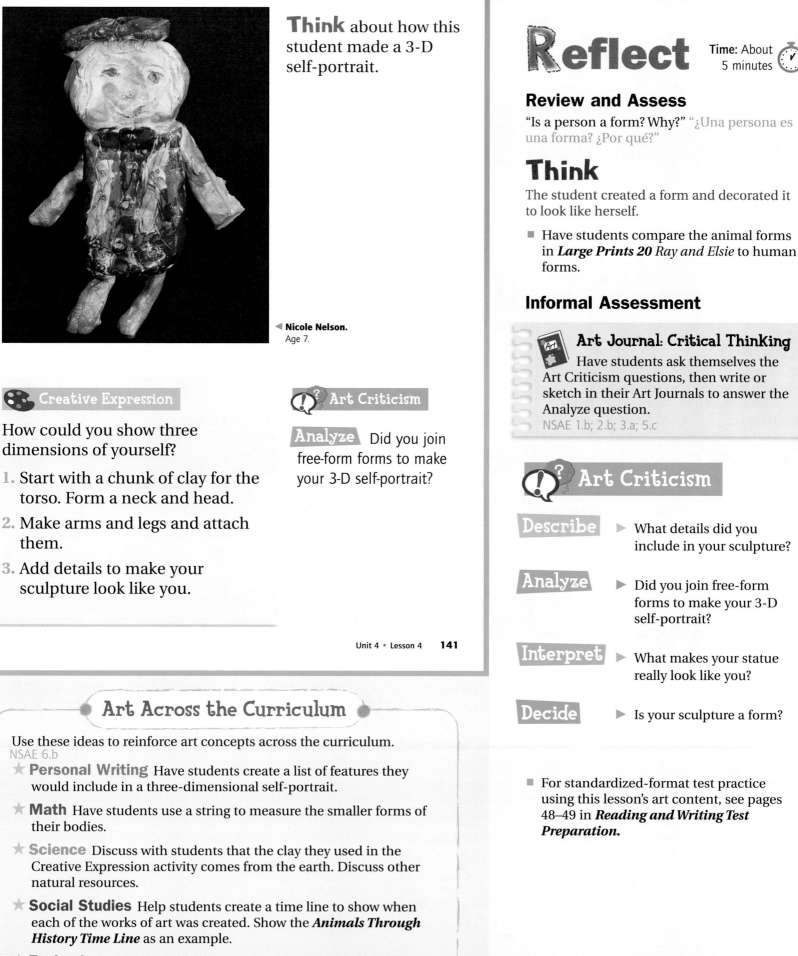

Think about how this student made a 3-D self-portrait.

◀ **Nicole Nelson.**
Age 7.

Creative Expression

How could you show three dimensions of yourself?

1. Start with a chunk of clay for the torso. Form a neck and head.

2. Make arms and legs and attach them.

3. Add details to make your sculpture look like you.

Art Criticism

Analyze Did you join free-form forms to make your 3-D self-portrait?

Art Across the Curriculum

Use these ideas to reinforce art concepts across the curriculum.
NSAE 6.b

★ **Personal Writing** Have students create a list of features they would include in a three-dimensional self-portrait.

★ **Math** Have students use a string to measure the smaller forms of their bodies.

★ **Science** Discuss with students that the clay they used in the Creative Expression activity comes from the earth. Discuss other natural resources.

★ **Social Studies** Help students create a time line to show when each of the works of art was created. Show the ***Animals Through History Time Line*** as an example.

★ **Technology** Students can use a digital camera to photograph a pose they would like to depict in their three-dimensional self-portraits. Visit **SRAonline.com** to print detailed instructions for this activity.

Reflect

Time: About 5 minutes

Review and Assess

"Is a person a form? Why?" "¿Una persona es una forma? ¿Por qué?"

Think

The student created a form and decorated it to look like herself.

■ Have students compare the animal forms in ***Large Prints 20*** *Ray and Elsie* to human forms.

Informal Assessment

Art Journal: Critical Thinking

Have students ask themselves the Art Criticism questions, then write or sketch in their Art Journals to answer the Analyze question.
NSAE 1.b; 2.b; 3.a; 5.c

Art Criticism

Describe ▸ What details did you include in your sculpture?

Analyze ▸ Did you join free-form forms to make your 3-D self-portrait?

Interpret ▸ What makes your statue really look like you?

Decide ▸ Is your sculpture a form?

■ For standardized-format test practice using this lesson's art content, see pages 48–49 in ***Reading and Writing Test Preparation.***

3-D Me!

Extra! For the Art Specialist

Time: About 45 minutes

Focus

Discuss with students famous statues (such as the Lincoln Memorial) or statues they have seen in their community. Use *Transparency 22* to discuss the smaller forms that join together to create the form of a person.

Teach

Have students complete the Alternate Activity. What features will students include in their three-dimensional self-portraits?

Reflect

Guide students through evaluation of their works of art using the four steps of art criticism. (See pages 28–29 for more about art criticism.)

Alternate Activity

Materials:
- low-fire clay (one 3" diameter ball of clay per student)
- 12" × 14" pieces of of burlap
- clay tools (such as pencils, plastic forks, paper clips)

1. Give each student a ball of clay and a piece of burlap. Have students use the heels of their hands to press the clay into a $\frac{1}{2}$" thick slab.

2. Have students use clay tools to lightly incise a drawing of themselves into the clay. It should touch at least three edges of the clay slab. Arms and legs should be thicker than students' thumbs.

3. After the teacher has checked the drawings for correct thickness, students retrace the outlines to cut out the figure. Then students incise facial features and clothing details.

4. Fire clay figures. After firing, they can be painted with watercolors if desired.

Research in Art Education

Learning in the arts may help students develop a positive self-concept. Many studies have shown that the arts seem to "promote learning, interpersonal communication, and the establishment of positive identity." A positive self-concept is important because it has been shown to "aid the development of necessary values and skills" ("The Effects of Arts and Music Education on Students' Self-Concept" in *Schools, Communities, and the Arts: A Research Compendium*). Creating a self-portrait sculpture is a way for students to express their identity.

Assessment

Use the following rubric to evaluate the artwork students make in the Creative Expression activity and to assess students' understanding of three-dimensional portraits.

Have students complete page 51 or 52 in their *Assessment* books.

	Art History and Culture	Aesthetic Perception	Creative Expression	Art Criticism
3 POINTS	The student accurately recognizes that sculptors create three-dimensional portraits of people.	The student accurately identifies the human form as a free-form form.	The student successfully creates a three-dimensional self-portrait sculpture.	The student thoughtfully and honestly evaluates his or her own work using the four steps of art criticism.
2 POINTS	The student shows emerging awareness that sculptors create three-dimensional portraits of people.	The student shows emerging awareness that the human form is a free-form form.	The student attempts to create a three-dimensional self-portrait sculpture.	The student attempts to evaluate his or her own work, but shows an incomplete understanding of evaluation criteria.
1 POINT	The student does not recognize that sculptors create three-dimensional portraits of people.	The student cannot identify the human form as a free-form form.	The student does not create a three-dimensional self-portrait sculpture.	The student makes no attempt to evaluate his or her own artwork.

Assessment, p. 51

Name _____ Date _____

Lesson 4 UNIT 4

3-D Me!

For the teacher: Use the following prompt for this activity. Draw a picture that shows a 3-D statue of a classmate.

Level 1   Unit 4 • Form and Space   **51**

Lesson 5 Overview

Buildings and Spaces

Lesson 5 teaches that buildings are forms. The spaces within and around a building allow it to be used.

Objectives

Art History and Culture
To compare the purposes of buildings
NSAE 5.a

Creative Expression
To create a building form
NSAE 1.a; 1.c; 1.d

Aesthetic Perception
To recognize and distinguish between forms and spaces in buildings
NSAE 3.a

Art Criticism
To evaluate one's own artwork using the four steps of art criticism
NSAE 1.b; 2.b; 3.a; 5.c

Vocabulary ⭐ Reading

Review the following vocabulary word with students before beginning the lesson.

form *forma*—any object that can be measured in three ways: height, width, and depth

See page 149B for additional vocabulary and Spanish vocabulary resources.

Art Journal: Vocabulary
Have students add this word to the Vocabulary section of their Art Journals.

Lesson Materials
- recycled materials: cardboard boxes, cardboard tubes, empty milk cartons, empty plastic bottles
- masking tape
- glue
- acrylic paint
- paintbrushes
- water dishes
- paper towels

Alternate Materials:
- construction paper

Program Resources
- *Reading and Writing Test Prep.,* pp. 50–51
- *Transparency 23*
- *Artist Profiles,* pp. 68, 82
- *Animals Through History Time Line*
- *Assessment,* pp. 53–54
- *Large Prints 19* Disney Concert Hall
- *The National Museum of Women in the Arts Collection*

Concept Trace
Buildings and Spaces
Introduced: Level K, Unit 4, Lesson 4
Reinforced: Level 2, Unit 6, Lesson 6

Lesson 5 Arts Integration NSAE 6.a

Theatre

Complete Unit 4, Lesson 5, on pages 80–81 of *Theatre Arts Connections.*

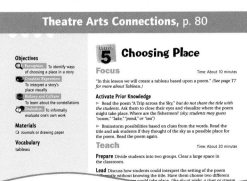

Theatre Arts Connections, p. 80

Music

SPOTLIGHT ON MUSIC Listen to *Promenade* from *Pictures at an Exhibition.* Modest Mussorgsky wrote the piece after viewing paintings at an exhibition. Can you imagine what it would be like to stroll through the building and spaces of this exhibition?

Movement & Dance

Study three types of homes that people in different parts of the world have designed and live in, such as an igloo, a grass hut, and a brick house. Identify the shape, size, and specific features of each dwelling. In small groups create each home using eight counts and holding each for four counts.

Focus

Time: About 10 minutes

Activate Prior Knowledge

"What different rooms does your home have?" "¿Qué cuartos diferentes tienen sus casas?"

- Discuss how buildings have rooms, designated by walls and doorways, that are designed for special purposes.

Using Literature ⭐ Reading

- Read *The Little House* by Virginia Lee Burton. The illustrations include many different buildings.

Thematic Connection ⭐ Social Studies

- **Buildings:** Discuss how buildings help humans meet their need for shelter. What would students' lives be like if no buildings existed?

Introduce the Art

Look
NSAE 3.a

"Let's take a look at these two buildings."
"Vamos a observar estos dos edificios".

Comparing and Contrasting ⭐ Reading

- Have students list the similarities and differences between the buildings. Each building has unique features (such as the turrets on *Corn Palace* and the canopy on *The Dwell House*). *Corn Palace* is decorated with colorful pictures, and *The Dwell House* is plainer. Both buildings have walls and entryways. Both buildings have predominantly vertical and horizontal lines.

🏺 Art History and Culture

Discuss with students the purposes of the buildings. *Corn Palace* was built to show the richness of the farmers' harvests. It is a multipurpose building. It serves as a community center, and different events are held there. *The Dwell House* was designed as an entry in a contest of homes designed from prefabricated materials.
NSAE 5.a

💻 **Web Connection**

Visit www.cornpalace.org/cornpalace.html for more information about Corn Palace.

Buildings and Spaces

▲ **Artist Unknown.** (United States). *Corn Palace.* c. 1892.
Mitchell, South Dakota.

Look at the buildings on these pages. The buildings have different forms and open spaces.

🏺 Art History and Culture

The *Corn Palace* is decorated with corn and other grains. It was built so farmers could show the richness of the harvest.

🏺 Art History and Culture

Corn Palace is located in Mitchell, South Dakota. The original *Corn Palace* was built in 1892 for farmers to display the fruitfulness of the South Dakota harvest. The building is constructed of concrete (not corn), but every year artists decorate the outer walls with locally grown corn, grasses, and other grains. Murals on the walls pay tribute to life in South Dakota. A different artist and mural theme are chosen every year.

See pages 16–21 and 24–25 for more about subject matter and art history.

Artist Profiles, p. 68

▸ Artist Profile

Corn Palace

A variety of architects, contractors, and artists have worked on the Corn Palace in South Dakota. The current building was designed by architects Rapp and Rapp of Chicago. This architectural firm also designed Radio City Music Hall in New York City and many other famous theatrical buildings in the United States. The exterior designs, changed every year, are created by different people. Five of the interior panels were designed by artist Oscar Howe.

▲ **Artist unknown.** (United States). *Corn Palace.* c. 1892.

▲ **Central Office of Architecture.**
(Los Angeles, California).
The Dwell House. 2003.

Study the buildings.

▶ What forms do you see?

▶ What open spaces do you see?

▶ Are there spaces you cannot see?

Aesthetic Perception

Design Awareness Think about your school building. What forms and spaces does it have?

Art History and Culture

In 2003, *Dwell Magazine* held a competition called The Dwell Home Invitational. The contest challenged architects to design a home using prefabricated materials costing $175,000. *The Dwell Home* was the model submitted by the Central Office of Architecture in Los Angeles, California. It did not win the competition, but is still important because it combines economical mass production with unique architectural design.

See pages 16–21 and 24–25 for more about subject matter and art history.

Artist Profiles, p. 82

Artist Profile

The Dwell House

The Dwell House model was designed by a California design group called the Central Office of Architecture. The COA began in 1987 as the dream of three architects: Ron Golan, Eric A. Kahn, and Russell N. Thomsen. These three men wanted to start an architectural firm that was dedicated to creative, quality design work. The COA has prided itself in its ability to find practical, innovative solutions to problems that arise when planning or building a new structure. The San Francisco Museum of Modern Art is home to a permanent exhibit of some of the COA's unique works.

▲ **Central Office of Architecture.** (Los Angeles, California.)

Study

▶ The forms of *Corn Palace* are the walls, roof, minarets, turrets, cupolas, awnings, and flagpoles. The forms of *The Dwell House* are the walls, roof, pipes, and beams.

▶ The spaces of *Corn Palace* are the spaces all around the building and underneath the awning. *The Dwell House* has spaces under the roof, between the beams, within the doorways, and all around it.

▶ Even though it cannot be seen, we know that there are spaces inside the buildings. There must be spaces inside the buildings in order for them to be used.

■ For more examples of utilitarian art, see *The National Museum of Women in the Arts Collection.*

Art Journal: Concepts
Have students make a sketch showing a building and spaces in the Concepts section of their Art Journals.

Aesthetic Perception

Design Awareness Discuss with students the different forms that make up the school building. Discuss the spaces outside and inside the school. Why was the school designed with those forms and spaces?
NSAE 2.b

Developing Visual Literacy Have students discuss how they feel about each building in the photographs. Would they like to live or work in such a building? What properties of each building make them feel that way?

Web Connection
Visit the Central Office of Architecture's Web site at **www.coalabs.com**.

Teach

Time: About 40 minutes

"What are some of the different spaces we use?" "¿Cuáles son algunos de los diferentes espacios que usamos?"

- Read and discuss Using Buildings and Spaces on page 144.

Practice

Materials: None

- Have students name the places they live in, learn in, store things in, play in, watch movies in, and so on. Encourage them to describe the differences and similarities among these places.

Creative Expression

NSAE 1.a; 1.c; 1.d

Materials: recycled materials (cardboard boxes, cardboard tubes, empty milk cartons, empty plastic bottles), masking tape, glue, acrylic paint, paintbrushes, water dishes, paper towels

Alternate Materials: construction paper

- Distribute materials and have students follow the directions on page 145.

- See the Activity Tips on page 243 for visual examples of this lesson's activity.

Art Journal: Brainstorming

Have students brainstorm ideas for ways they could put forms together to design a home. Have students make quick sketches of their ideas in the Ideas section of their Art Journals.   NSAE 3.b

Using Buildings and Spaces

Buildings are forms. The forms have open spaces for people to move through.

Practice

How are different buildings and spaces used?

1. Think about places to live, learn, shop, play, or work.

2. Describe different buildings and their spaces.

3. How are the places the same? How are they different?

Differentiated Instruction

Reteach
Bring in photographs of famous buildings, such as the White House. Have students discuss the purpose of the building and its forms and spaces.

Special Needs
Adaptations: As an extension, ask students to create a picture or sculpture of the imaginary creature for which the house was created.

ELL Tips
Review with students the forms and spaces of the buildings they made in the Creative Expression activity.

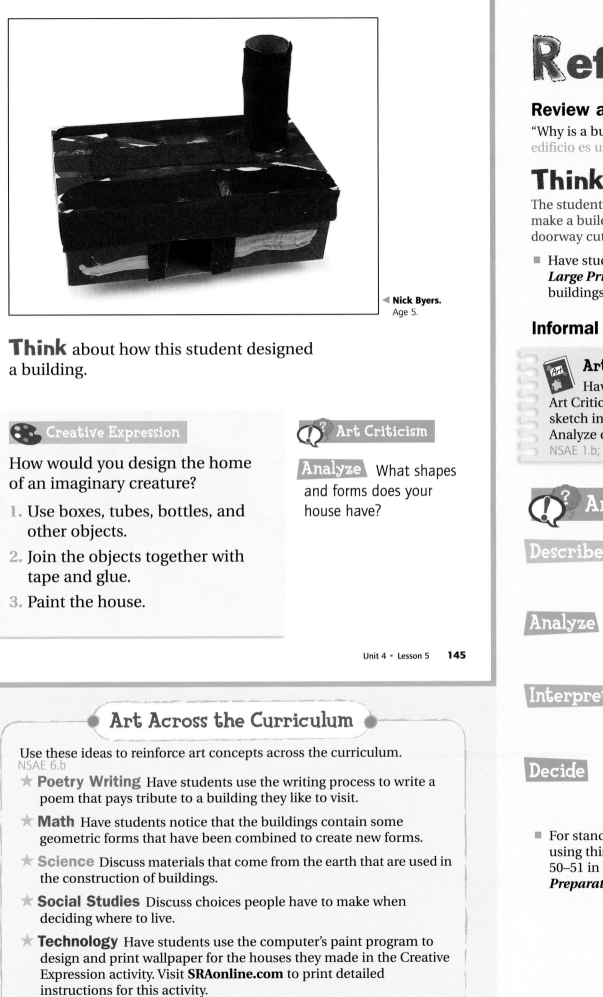

Nick Byers.
Age 5.

Think about how this student designed a building.

Creative Expression

How would you design the home of an imaginary creature?

1. Use boxes, tubes, bottles, and other objects.
2. Join the objects together with tape and glue.
3. Paint the house.

Art Criticism

Analyze What shapes and forms does your house have?

Art Across the Curriculum

Use these ideas to reinforce art concepts across the curriculum.
NSAE 6.b

★ **Poetry Writing** Have students use the writing process to write a poem that pays tribute to a building they like to visit.

★ **Math** Have students notice that the buildings contain some geometric forms that have been combined to create new forms.

★ **Science** Discuss materials that come from the earth that are used in the construction of buildings.

★ **Social Studies** Discuss choices people have to make when deciding where to live.

★ **Technology** Have students use the computer's paint program to design and print wallpaper for the houses they made in the Creative Expression activity. Visit **SRAonline.com** to print detailed instructions for this activity.

Reflect
Time: About 5 minutes

Review and Assess
"Why is a building a form?" "¿Por qué un edificio es una forma?"

Think

The student combined a box and a tube to make a building. The building has an open doorway cut into the side.

- Have students compare the buildings in *Large Print 19 Disney Concert Hall* to the buildings in the lesson.

Informal Assessment

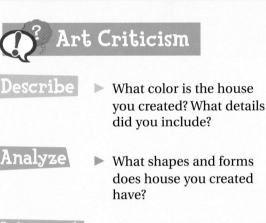

Art Journal: Critical Thinking
Have students ask themselves the Art Criticism questions, and then write or sketch in their Art Journals to answer the Analyze question.
NSAE 1.b; 2.b; 3.a; 5.c

Art Criticism

Describe
▶ What color is the house you created? What details did you include?

Analyze
▶ What shapes and forms does house you created have?

Interpret
▶ Who would live in the house you made? How can you tell?

Decide
▶ Is the house you created a form?

- For standardized-format test practice using this lesson's art content, see pages 50–51 in *Reading and Writing Test Preparation.*

Buildings and Spaces

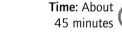 **For the Art Specialist**

Time: About 45 minutes

Focus

Have students identify the forms and spaces of the buildings in *Transparency 23*. What do they think the interiors of the buildings would look like?

Teach

Have students complete the Alternate Activity. When students are finished, have them examine the communities made by the other groups. In which one would they most like to live?

Reflect

Guide students through evaluation of their works of art using the four steps of art criticism. (See pages 28–29 for more about art criticism.)

Alternate Activity

Materials:
- 3′ × 4′ piece of colored roll paper per 3 or 4 students
- markers or crayons
- construction paper scraps
- scissors
- glue or glue sticks

1. Divide students into groups of 3 or 4. Tell them each group will create a community that will incorporate the houses they made in the Creative Expression activity.

2. Give each group a 3′ × 4′ piece of colored roll paper to use as the background for their community. After students decide where to place their buildings, have them draw in streets, parks, and so on.

3. Have students use construction paper scraps to create traffic signals, trees, lakes, and so on.

Research in Art Education

Collaboration is an important benefit of the arts. In the visual arts, students may engage in "enterprises such as painting murals and scenery, producing books, and organizing exhibitions" ("Learning In and Through the Arts: Curriculum Implications" in *Champions of Change,* p. 40). They also often have the opportunity to learn to critique the work of others appropriately. In this lesson, students may collaborate by combining the houses they made in the Creative Expression activity to make a neighborhood.

Assessment

Use the following rubric to evaluate the artwork students make in the Creative Expression activity and to assess students' understanding of buildings and spaces.

Have students complete page 53 or 54 in their *Assessment* books.

	Art History and Culture	Aesthetic Perception	Creative Expression	Art Criticism
3 POINTS	The student successfully compares the purposes of the buildings.	The student accurately recognizes and distinguishes between forms and spaces in buildings.	The student successfully creates a building form.	The student thoughtfully and honestly evaluates his or her own work using the four steps of art criticism.
2 POINTS	The student's comparison is weak or incomplete.	The student shows emerging awareness of forms and spaces in buildings.	The student attempts to create a building form.	The student attempts to evaluate his or her own work, but shows an incomplete understanding of evaluation criteria.
1 POINT	The student cannot compare the purposes of the buildings.	The student cannot recognize forms and spaces in buildings.	The student does not create a building form.	The student makes no attempt to evaluate own artwork.

Assessment, p. 53

Name _____ Date _____

Buildings and Spaces

Lesson **5** UNIT 4

For the teacher: Use the following prompt for this activity.
Using a crayon, draw your school. Show that there is space inside it.

Level 1

Unit 4 • Form and Space **53**

Space in Pictures

Lesson 6 teaches students that two-dimensional works of art show space between objects.

Objectives

Art History and Culture
To compare still lifes painted at different times by artists from different cultures
NSAE 3.a; 4.a; 4.b; 4.c

Creative Expression
To create a still life that shows space between objects
NSAE 1.a; 1.c; 1.d; 2.c

Aesthetic Perception
To recognize the representation of three-dimensional space in two-dimensional works of art   NSAE 2.a; 3.a

Art Criticism
To evaluate one's own artwork using the four steps of art criticism
NSAE 1.b; 2.b; 3.a; 5.c

Vocabulary ⭐ Reading

Review the following vocabulary word with students before beginning the lesson.

space espacio—the element of art that refers to the area between, around, above, below, and within objects

See page 149B for additional vocabulary and Spanish vocabulary resources.

Art Journal: Vocabulary
Have students add this word to the Vocabulary section of their Art Journals.

Lesson Materials
- 12" × 18" watercolor paper
- pencils
- watercolor paints
- still-life objects
- brushes
- water containers
- paper towels

Alternate Materials:
- crayons or markers on light-colored paper

Program Resources
- *Reading and Writing Test Prep.,* pp. 52–53
- *Transparency 24*
- *Artist Profiles,* pp. 47, 64
- *Animals Through History Time Line*
- *Assessment,* pp. 55–56
- *Large Prints 19* Disney Concert Hall and *20* Ray and Elsie
- *National Museum of Women in the Arts Collection*

Concept Trace
Space in Pictures
Introduced: Level K, Unit 4, Lesson 1
Reinforced: Level 2, Unit 2, Lesson 6

Lesson 6 Arts Integration   NSAE 6.a

Theatre
Complete Unit 4, Lesson 6, on pages 82–87 of *Theatre Arts Connections.*

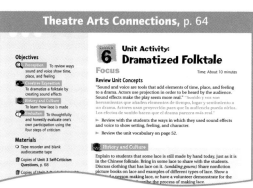

Theatre Arts Connections, p. 64

Music
Negative space in music is silence, the lack of sound. Within a piece it is called *rest.* When orchestration changes some instruments rest while new ones enter. Listen to new entrances in *C A G.*

Movement & Dance
Have students walk through the room, moving around each other. Ask students to keep walking but move to the center of the room, so there is space around the group. Now ask them to move to the edges of the room, so there is space in the middle of the room. How does the way we use space affect our energy and speed? Did the group walk faster when everyone was in the center?

Focus

Time: About 10 minutes

Activate Prior Knowledge

"Are my hands touching? How do you know?"

"¿Mis manos se están tocando? ¿Cómo lo saben?"

■ Hold your hands up next to each other about four inches apart so they are not touching. Discuss with students that they know your hands are not touching because they can see the space between them. Then hold one hand about two inches behind the other. Your hands should slightly overlap. Ask students which hand is in front and how they know. Discuss that they can tell one hand is behind because not all of it can be seen.

Using Literature ⭐ Reading

■ Read *Career Day* by Anne Rockwell. Discuss with students which objects in the illustrations by Lizzy Rockwell are close together and which have a lot of space around them.

Thematic Connection ⭐ Reading

■ **Homes:** Both works of art show things you find in a home. Discuss the purpose of various objects people have in their homes. Discuss reasons people have for choosing what they buy.

Introduce the Art

Look

NSAE 3.a

"Let's take a close look at these two works of art." "Vamos a mirar detalladamente estas dos obras de arte".

Comparing and Contrasting ⭐ Reading

■ Have students describe the similarities and differences between the two works of art. Both works are still lifes, but *Still Life* has useful household objects, including a bowl and vases, and *Still Life with Porcelain Dog* has decorative objects, including a porcelain dog and flowers.

🏺 Art History and Culture

Use the *Animals Through History Time Line* to show students when these still lifes were painted. Discuss with students how they think still lifes may vary depending on the time and place they are painted.

NSAE 4.d; 4.b; 4.c

💻 Web Connection

Search the collection at **www.nmwa.org** to view examples of still lifes from previous centuries.

Space in Pictures

▲ **Patricia Walker.**
(American). *Still Life.*
1995.
....
Oil on canvas. 22 × 22 inches
(55.88 × 55.88 cm.).
Collection of the artist.

Look at the paintings. The artists showed objects and the space around them.

🏺 Art History and Culture

These paintings are still lifes. Artists have been painting still lifes for over 400 years.

146 Unit 4 • Lesson 6

🏺 Art History and Culture

Patricia Walker

Patricia Walker (pə tri´ shə wô´ kər) (1949–) received art degrees from the Rhode Island School of Design and Cornell University. She has a studio in Savannah, Georgia. This still life is one of a series of 20 created as Walker studied the same objects. She constantly searches for interesting objects at antique shops and garage sales so she can study the negative space each form creates.

See pages 16–21 and 24–25 for more about subject matter and art history.

Artist Profiles, p. 64

♦ Artist Profile ♦
Patricia Walker
b. 1949

Patricia Walker (pə tri´ shə wô´ kar) was born in Natrona Heights, Pennsylvania, which is located near the Allegheny River. She received her degree in painting from the Rhode Island School of Design in 1985. In 1987, she completed her master of fine arts degree in painting at Cornell University. Since the fall of 1987, she has enjoyed teaching fine arts at Georgia Southern University.

◀ **Gabriele Munter.**
(German).
*Still Life with
Porcelain Dog.* 1911.
Oil on canvas. $25\frac{3}{4} \times 21\frac{1}{4}$
inches (65.41 × 53.98 cm.).
San Diego Museum of Art,
San Diego, California.

Study the works of art on these pages.

▶ Where do you see space in the pictures?

Aesthetic Perception

Seeing Like an Artist Place two objects on your
desk. How can you change the space around them?

Art History and Culture

Gabriele Munter

Gabriele Munter (gä brā´ lä mün´ tər) (1877–1962) was born in
Germany. She had an interest in art but was not allowed to attend
the art academies because she was a woman. Munter instead had
lessons from private tutors. She traveled frequently (including a
tour of the United States from 1898 to 1900) and made sketches of
what she saw. In 1902, she enrolled in an evening drawing class
taught by Wassily Kandinsky. They developed a close relationship,
and he was her mentor for many years. Munter painted still lifes,
landscapes, and portraits.

See pages 16–21 and 24–25
for more about subject
matter and art history.

Artist Profiles, p. 47

◆ Artist Profile ◆
Gabriele Münter
1877-1962
Gabriele Münter (gä brä´ lä mün´ tər) was
one of the founders of modern German
expressionism. She studied in Düsseldorf,
Germany before traveling to the United
States for two years. She resumed her
studies in Munich, Germany, where she
met many artists who were developing new
styles of painting. She traveled throughout
Europe, spending two years near Paris,
France, where she learned about
innovations in French art. In 1911, she
joined with other radical artists in Munich
to form the Blue Rider group. She painted
in secret when German expressionist art was
outlawed. After World War II she continued
to paint and promoted the history of the
Blue Rider group.

Study

▶ In *Still Life* there is space above the objects
and all around them. The vases have
openings at the top, so space is inside
them. There is not much space between
the vase that is second from the right and
the bowl. In *Still Life with Porcelain Dog*
there is space around the objects. It looks
like there is not much space behind the
porcelain dog.

■ For more examples of still lifes, see *The
National Museum of Women in the Arts
Collection.*

Art Journal: Concepts

Have students make a sketch in the
Concepts section of their Art Journals of
two objects with a lot of space between
them. Then have students sketch the same
objects with only a little space between
them.

Aesthetic Perception

Seeing Like an Artist Have students
experiment by moving objects around on
their desks. They should notice that as they
move the objects, they see different areas of
the background. Students should experiment
with placing objects beside each other as
well as overlapping them.

Developing Visual Literacy Ask students if
any of the objects in the works of art remind
them of things in their own homes. If
students created their own still-life
arrangements at home, how would they be
similar or different?

Web Connection

Still Life with Porcelain Dog is housed at the San
Diego Museum of Art, **www.sandiegomuseum.org.**

Teach

Time: About 40 minutes

"What does space in pictures look like?"
"¿Cómo es el espacio en las pinturas?"

■ Read and discuss Using Space in Pictures on page 148.

Practice

Materials: sketch paper, pencils

Alternate Materials: crayons or markers

■ Create a still-life arrangement for students to observe and sketch. Distribute the materials and have students follow the directions on page 148.

■ Students should notice that the space around and between objects is more visible when the objects are viewed from above rather than from eye level.

■ Point out that when the objects are viewed from eye level some of them overlap. The object that is closer is in front.

Creative Expression

NSAE 1.a; 1.c; 1.d; 2.c

Materials: 12″ × 18″ watercolor paper, pencils, watercolor paints, still-life objects, brushes, water containers, paper towels

Alternate Materials: crayons or markers, light-colored paper

■ Distribute the materials and have students follow the directions on page 149.

■ Review the Activity Tips on page 243 for visual examples of techniques.

■ Students should fill their papers with color. Remind them to always rinse their brushes before using another color. They should blot the brush on a paper towel.

Art Journal: Brainstorming

Have students brainstorm ideas for ways they could arrange objects in their still lifes. Have students make quick sketches of their ideas in the Ideas section of their Art Journals.

Using Space in Pictures

Space is the emptiness around and between objects.

Practice

Look at the space around objects.

1. Look at an arrangement of objects. Look down at it from above.

2. Sketch the space around the objects.

3. Look at the objects from the front. How does the space look now?

Differentiated Instruction

Reteach

Tape cutouts of objects to the board with different amounts of space between them, overlapping some objects. Have students describe the space.

Special Needs

Adaptations: Students may have difficulty seeing the negative space between objects. Help students by providing a backdrop for the still life that contrasts sharply with the objects.

ELL Tips

Review with students vocabulary used to describe the location of objects, such as *near, far, in front of,* and *behind.* Arrange objects to demonstrate.

▲ **Ali M. Forbes.** Age 7.

Think about how this student showed space around the objects.

 Creative Expression

How could you show space around objects?

1. Look at a still-life arrangement.
2. Draw the outlines of the objects. Show the space.
3. Paint your still life.

Art Criticism

Describe What objects are in your still life?

**eflect** Time: About 5 minutes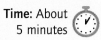

Review and Assess
"How do you know which object in a painting is closer?" "¿Cómo saben qué objeto está más cerca en una pintura?"

Think
The student showed space around the objects by making some of the objects overlap.

- Use **Large Prints 19** *Disney Concert Hall* and **20** *Ray and Elsie* to have students identify space.

Informal Assessment

Art Journal: Critical Thinking
Have students ask themselves the Art Criticism questions, and then write or sketch in their Art Journals to answer the Describe question.
NSAE 1.b; 2.b; 3.a; 5.c

Art Criticism

Describe ▸ What objects are in your still life?

Analyze ▸ Do any objects overlap? How did you show which objects are farther away?

Interpret ▸ Is the setting of your picture a neat or messy place? How did you show this?

Decide ▸ Did you show space in your picture?

- For standardized-format test practice using this lesson's art content, see pages 52–53 in *Reading and Writing Test Preparation.*

Art Across the Curriculum

Use these ideas to reinforce art concepts across the curriculum.
NSAE 6.b

★ **Persuasive Writing** Have students imagine that one of the still lifes is the picture accompanying an advertisement. Have them use the writing process to write the text for the advertisement.

★ **Math** Discuss with students ways of measuring the space between objects.

★ **Science** Have students identify objects in the still lifes as living or nonliving.

★ **Social Studies** Students described the location of objects in the still lifes in relation to each other. Have students also describe the location they are in relative to other geographical locations.

★ **Technology** Have students create a clip-art collage, overlapping images to show depth. Visit **SRAonline.com** to print detailed instructions for this activity.

Space in Pictures

Extra! For the Art Specialist

Time: About 45 minutes

Focus

Use *Transparency 24* to have students identify space. Where is there space around the objects? Which objects are close together and which are farther apart? Have students use classroom objects to recreate the positions of objects in each work of art.

Teach

Have students complete the Alternate Activity. Then assemble the still-life collages to make a class exhibition. Have students share their ideas about the works in the exhibit.

Reflect

Guide students through evaluation of their works of art using the four steps of art criticism. (See pages 28–29 for more about art criticism.) Then have students look for space in another two-dimensional work of art.

Alternate Activity

Materials:
- still life arrangement of objects with simple shapes
- 9″ × 12″ light-colored construction paper
- 6″ × 9″ construction paper pieces
- construction paper scraps
- pencils
- scissors
- glue or glue sticks
- oil pastels or crayons

1. Have students first examine the still-life arrangement and notice the forms and the space around them.

2. Have students draw the still-life objects on 6″ × 9″ construction paper with pencil and cut them out. Then have students arrange and glue the objects on a sheet of 9″ × 12″ light-colored construction paper. Students may have to overlap some objects to accurately represent the still-life arrangement.

3. When the glue is dry, have students use oil pastels or crayons to draw a table and background for their still life. Students may also add details to the objects.

Research in Art Education

It has been theorized that the reasons students who are involved in the arts tend to excel might be because "the arts serve to broaden access to meaning by offering ways of thinking and representation consistent with the spectrum of intelligences scattered unevenly across our population" ("Involvement in the Arts and Human Development: General Involvement and Intensive Involvement in Music and Theater Arts" in *Champions of Change*, p. 4).

Assessment

Use the following rubric to evaluate the artwork students make in the Creative Expression activity and to assess students' understanding of space in pictures.

Have students complete page 55 or 56 in their *Assessment* books.

	Art History and Culture	Aesthetic Perception	Creative Expression	Art Criticism
3 POINTS	The student can compare the still lifes created at different times by artists of different cultures.	The student accurately identifies the representation of three-dimensional space in a two-dimensional picture.	The student's still life clearly shows space between objects.	The student thoughtfully and honestly evaluates his or her own work using the four steps of art criticism.
2 POINTS	The student's comparison is weak or incomplete.	The student shows emerging awareness of the representation of three-dimensional space in a two-dimensional picture.	The student attempts to show space between objects in the still life.	The student attempts to evaluate his or her own work, but shows an incomplete understanding of evaluation criteria.
1 POINT	The student cannot compare the still lifes created at different times by artists of different cultures.	The student cannot identify the representation of three-dimensional space in a two-dimensional artwork.	The student's still life shows no space between objects.	The student makes no attempt to evaluate his or her own artwork.

Assessment, p. 55

Name _____ Date _____

Lesson
6
UNIT 4

Space in Pictures

For the teacher: Use the following prompts for this activity.
1. Using a blue crayon, draw two shapes.
2. Color the space in between the shapes with a red crayon.

Level 1   Unit 4 • Form and Space **55**

Unit 4 Vocabulary Review

height—how tall something is *altura*—o alto; lo alto que es algo

width—how wide something is *ancho*—lo ancho que es algo

depth—the distance from front to back *profundidad*—la distancia desde el frente hasta atrás

form—any object that can be measured in three ways: height, width, and depth *forma*—cualquier objeto que se pueda medir de tres maneras: pro su altura, ancho y profundidad

space—the element of art that refers to the area between, around, above, below, and within objects *espacio*—el elemento artístico que se refiere al área entre, alrededor, arriba, debajo y dentro de los objetos

geometric form—a three-dimensional figure that has precise measurement and can be described in mathematical terms, such as a sphere, a cube, a pyramid or cone, and a rectangular solid *forma geométrica*—una figura tridimensional que tiene una medida precisa y que se puede describir en términos matemáticos, como una esfera, un cubo, una pirámide o un cono, y un cuerpo sólido rectangular

free-form form—an uneven and irregular form; any form that is not geometric *forma abstracta*—una forma irregular; cualquier forma que no sea geométrica

Vocabulary Practice

T Display *Transparency 40* to review unit vocabulary words.

Categorizing/Classifying ⭐ Vocabulary
Choose an object in the classroom. Have students identify it as a *geometric form* or a *free-form form* and explain their answer.

Definitions: Brief Definitions ⭐
Vocabulary
Give a brief definition of *height*. Have students identify the unit vocabulary word you defined. Repeat for other unit vocabulary words.

Examples ⭐ Vocabulary
Display *Large Print 20 Ray and Elsie*. Have each student select a unit vocabulary word and find an example of that word in the artwork.

Form and Space

▲ **Artist Unknown.** (Romania, Hamangia Culture). *The Thinker.* 5500–4700 B.C.
Clay. Height 4½ inches (11.43 cm.). National History Museum, Bucharest, Romania.

Art Criticism   NSAE 2.b; 3.a

Critical Thinking Art criticism is an organized system for looking at and talking about art. You can criticize art without being an expert. The purpose of art criticism is to get the viewer involved in a perception process that delays judgment until all aspects of the artwork have been studied.

■ See pages 28–29 for more about art criticism.

Describe

■ What do you see? During this step the student will collect information about the subject of the work.

► Ask students what the person is doing. The person is seated on a low stool. The person's hands are holding his head. The legs are bent and the elbows rest upon his knees.

■ Ask students what the sculpture is made of. How big is it? How old is it? Direct students to the caption where they can find this information. Use the *Animals Through History Time Line* to show when the work was created.

Analyze

■ How is this work organized? During this step the student thinks about how the artist has used the elements and principles of art.

► Ask students where they see empty spaces between parts of the form. There are empty spaces between the man's arms and his body, between his legs, and under his legs.

► Ask students where they see free-form and geometric forms in this sculpture. The man is a free-form form. His eyes are indented triangular forms and his nose is a protruding triangular form. The stool looks geometric.

► Ask students why a sculpture of a person is a 3-D form. A sculpture of a person is a 3-D form because a person has height, width, and depth.

Art History and Culture

The Thinker was created by an artist in the Hamangia culture, which existed during the Neolithic period from approximately 5000 B.C. to 3000 B.C. The statue was discovered during the excavation of a cemetery in the Hamangia city of Cernavoda, Romania. The Hamangia culture is believed to have been stable, because there is continuity among artifacts dating over a long period of time. The culture disappeared sometime in the fifth millennium B.C., when it assimilated with other cultures in the region.

See pages 16–21 and 24–25 for more about subject matter and art history.

Artist Profiles, p. 83

Artist Profile

The Thinker

Created by an unknown artist over six thousand years ago, *The Thinker* was found in an excavated gravesite of the Neolithic Hamangia peoples of Cernavoda, located in what is today the nation of Romania.

◄ **Artist unknown.** (Hamangia Culture, Romania). *The Thinker.* 5500–4700 B.C.

Art Criticism   Critical Thinking

Describe

▶ What is the person doing?

Analyze

▶ Where do you see empty spaces between parts of the form?

Interpret

▶ How do you think the person is feeling?

Decide

▶ How do you think it would feel to touch something as old as this work?

Interpret

■ What is the artist trying to say? Students use the clues they discovered during their analysis to find the message the artist is trying to show.

▶ Ask students how they think the person is feeling. Answers will vary. Some students may say the person is thinking. They may also say the person is sad, tired, or lonely.

▶ Ask students what they would say to a 6,000-year-old person if this sculpture could talk. Answers will vary. Some students will want to ask the person what he is thinking about. They might ask what he is feeling. Or, they might ask what things were like back when this sculpture was made.

Decide

■ What do you think about the work? Students use all the information they have gathered to decide whether this is a successful work of art.

▶ Ask students how they think it would feel to touch something as old as this work. Answers will vary.

Art Journal: Writing

Have students write or sketch the answers to the Aesthetic Perception questions in their Art Journals.

Aesthetic Perception

Critical Thinking Have students think about another sculpture of a person, or bring in a photograph of a sculpture to display. How does the statue compare with *The Thinker?* Discuss the following questions with students.

Describe ▶ What does the sculpture look like?

Analyze ▶ What forms were combined to make the sculpture? Does it have any spaces?

Interpret ▶ What is the person like? How can you tell?

Decide ▶ Did the artist create a three-dimensional portrait?

"Artists use form and space in their works of art." "Los artistas usan la forma y el espacio en sus obras de arte".

T Review unit vocabulary with students using *Transparency 40.*

 Art Journal: Writing
Have students answer the questions on page 152. Answers: 1. B, 2. A, 3. B

T For further assessment, have students complete the unit test on *Transparency 46.*

CAREERS IN ART
Architecture

► Encourage students to think about buildings they use every day. What do they look like? What forms and spaces do they have?

"Art doesn't transform. It just plain forms."

—Roy Lichtenstein
(1923–1997), painter

Show What You Know

Write your answers on a sheet of paper.

1 Choose the form.

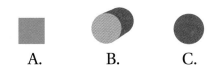

   A.   B.   C.

2 Choose the free-form form.

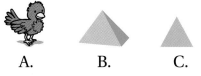

   A.   B.   C.

3 Choose the form that has space through it.

   A.   B.   C.

Unit Assessment Options

🔍 **Aesthetic Perception**

Practice Have students select their favorite form in the classroom or school and discuss the space around it.

🎨 **Creative Expression**

Student Portfolio Have students review the works of art they have created during this unit and select the pieces they wish to keep in their portfolios. Have students view classmates' portfolios and give positive feedback about each other's use of form and space.

💬 **Art Criticism**

Activity Have students select their favorite work of art from the unit. Guide students through study of their selected work using the four steps of art criticism. (See pages 28–29 for more about art criticism.)

CAREERS IN ART
Architecture

Think about your neighborhood. What do the buildings look like? Are there parks?

Architects design buildings. They decide how a building will be used and what it will look like.

Landscape architects design places with plants. They think about how the shapes and colors of different plants will look together.

▲ Architect

Form and Space in Theatre

On the Day You Were Born is a play. It tells about events in nature that happened on the day a child was born. The artists and actors explore space and different forms. They use puppets, paintings, poems, and music.

What to Do Use body movements to represent an event in nature.

1. Work with a partner or a group. Choose an event that happens in nature. You could choose rain falling or a tree growing.

2. Make up movements that represent the event. Use your bodies to make forms. Move through space in different ways.

3. Share your movements with others.

▲ In the Heart of the Beast Puppet and Mask Theatre. "On the Day You Were Born."

 **Art Criticism**

Interpret How did it feel to move through space like your natural event?

Art History and Culture

In the Heart of the Beast Puppet and Mask Theatre

In the Heart of the Beast Puppet and Mask Theatre of Minneapolis, Minnesota, use the ancient tradition of puppet and mask theatre. They produce original works, built by hand with recycled materials. They combine sculpture and painting with poetry, puppets, music, and dance. The idea for the production of *On the Day You Were Born* began when Debra Frasier asked the theatre if they could create something to celebrate the publication of her book. The theatre wanted to do a play about the natural wonders of the world, so they collaborated.

 # Form and Space in Theatre

Objective: To use body movements to represent an event in nature

Materials: In the Heart of the Beast Puppet and Mask Theatre. "On the Day You Were Born." Running time: 7:08

Focus
Time: About 5 minutes

■ Discuss the information on page 153.

Art History and Culture

■ Ask students if they have ever seen a puppet show. Share the information about In the Heart of the Beast Puppet and Mask Theatre.

Teach
Time: About 20 minutes

Aesthetic Perception

■ Help students brainstorm natural events. Discuss the different steps of each event. For instance, rain falls, then collects in puddles.

Creative Expression

■ Have students design movement that represents their chosen nature event, then share with the class.

■ **Informal Assessment** Comment positively on students' use of form and space.

Reflect
Time: About 10 minutes

Art Criticism

■ Have students answer the four art criticism questions.

Describe ▶ What makes your natural event special?

Analyze ▶ How did the forms of your body represent your idea?

Interpret ▶ How did it feel to move through space like your natural event?

Decide ▶ Was your representation successful?

	Lesson Title	Suggested Pacing	Creative Expression Activity
Lesson 1	Real Texture	55 minutes	Create a collage with textured materials.
Lesson 2	Visual Texture	45 minutes	Create a self-portrait showing visual texture.
Lesson 3	Raised Texture	45 minutes	Create a plaque with carved texture.
Lesson 4	Pattern	60 minutes	Create a stamped pattern.
Lesson 5	Changing Pattern	60 minutes	Create a weaving on a wallpaper loom.
Lesson 6	Rhythm	45 minutes	Create a drawing of a parade showing rhythm.
ART SOURCE ARTSOURCE	Texture, Pattern, and Rhythm in Dance	35 minutes	Create a mechanical doll dance with a partner.

Materials	Program Resources	Fine Art Resources	Literature Resources
textured materials, found materials, scissors, glue, white paper, oil pastels or dustless colored chalk	*Reading and Writing Test Preparation,* pp. 54–55 *Assessment,* pp. 57–58 *Home and After-School Connections*	*Transparency,* 25 *Artist Profiles,* pp. 72, 77 *Large Prints,* 21 and 22 *The National Museum of Women in the Arts Collection*	*Snowballs* by Lois Ehlert
crayons, watercolor paints, 12" × 18" white paper, paper towels, paintbrushes, water containers	*Reading and Writing Test Preparation,* pp. 56–57 *Assessment,* pp. 59–60	*Transparency,* 26 *Artist Profiles,* pp. 13, 28 *Large Prints,* 21 and 22 *The National Museum of Women in the Arts Collection*	*Here Is the African Savanna* by Madeleine Dunphy
clay, clay mats (muslin), found objects, carving tools (plastic utensils, paper clips, pencils, craft sticks)	*Reading and Writing Test Preparation,* pp. 58–59 *Assessment,* pp. 61–62	*Transparency,* 27 *Artist Profiles,* pp. 76, 84 *Large Prints,* 21 and 22 *Art Around the World*	*Fossils Tell of Long Ago* by Aliki
clay, clay tools, clay mats (muslin), paper plates, liquid tempera paints, white paper, brushes, water containers, paper towels, newspaper	*Reading and Writing Test Preparation,* pp. 60–61 *Assessment,* pp. 63–64	*Transparency,* 28 *Artist Profiles,* pp. 43, 69 *Large Prints,* 21 and 22 *The National Museum of Women in the Arts Collection*	*The Chick and the Duckling* by Mirra Ginsburg
2" × 18" strips of wallpaper, rulers, scissors, pencils, 12" × 18" pieces of wallpaper	*Reading and Writing Test Preparation,* pp. 62–63 *Assessment,* pp. 65–66	*Transparency,* 29 *Artist Profiles,* pp. 5, 71 *Large Prints,* 21 and 22 *Art Around the World*	*Night Shift Daddy* by Eileen Spinelli
oil pastels, colored paper	*Reading and Writing Test Preparation,* pp. 64–65 *Flash Card,* 10 *Assessment,* pp. 67–68	*Transparency,* 30 *Artist Profiles,* pp. 19, 55 *Large Prints,* 21 and 22 *The National Museum of Women in the Arts Collection*	*One Afternoon* by Yumi Heo
The Nutcracker, "Waltz of the Flowers" excerpt and "The Story of the Nutcracker" performed by the Joffrey Ballet of Chicago. Running time: 5:12			

Unit Overview

5 Texture, Pattern, and Rhythm

Lesson 1: Real texture is texture you can feel. Artists create real texture by making works of art with real objects that can be touched.

Lesson 2: Visual texture is texture you can see but not feel. Artists create visual texture by showing the way an object's real texture looks.

Lesson 3: Carving is cutting away from the surface of an object with a sharp tool. Carving creates raised areas that have real texture.

Lesson 4: Pattern is created by the repetition of a shape, line, or color in a work of art.

Lesson 5: A **motif** is the shape or object that is repeated within a pattern. A changing pattern has more than one motif.

Lesson 6: Repeating a motif creates **rhythm,** which is a feeling of movement in an artwork.

Introduce Unit Concepts

"Let's talk about texture, pattern, and rhythm." "Vamos a hablar de la textura, el patrón y el ritmo".

Texture
▪ Have students feel their hair, the bottoms of their shoes, and their desktops, and describe how each feels.

Pattern and Rhythm
▪ Play some music and have students clap to the rhythm. Then draw simple shapes and lines to represent the pattern of claps and pauses; for example, □ – □ – □ –.

Cross-Curricular Projects
▪ See the **Language Arts and Reading, Mathematics, Science,** and **Social Studies Art Connections** books for activities that further develop texture, pattern, and rhythm concepts.

National Standards for Arts Education in Visual Arts (NSAE) 6.a; 6.b

---

Texture, Pattern, and Rhythm

Artists show texture, pattern, and rhythm in their works of art.

Texture is how something feels if you touch it. Repeating a shape makes a pattern. Rhythm is a feeling of movement because something repeats.

◀ **Jesús Moroles.** (American). *Granite Weaving.* 1988.
....
Georgia gray granite. 98 × 74½ × 11 inches (248.9 × 189.2 × 27.9 cm.). Smithsonian American Art Museum, Washington, D.C.

Fine Art Prints

Display **Large Prints 21** *Farm Scene* and **22** *Petit Chat (Small Cat)*. Refer to the prints throughout the unit as students learn about texture, pattern, and rhythm.

Large Print 21

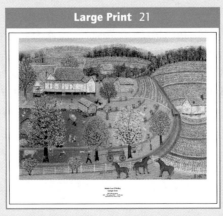

Large Print 22

Look for **texture, pattern,** and **rhythm** in the sculpture.

▶ What would the work feel like if you could touch it?

▶ What things are repeated?

▶ How do your eyes move around the picture?

In This Unit you will:

▶ learn about texture, pattern, and rhythm.

▶ find texture, pattern, and rhythm in art and the environment.

▶ create art that has texture, pattern, and rhythm.

Jesús Moroles

(1950–   )

▶ is an American artist.

▶ creates large sculptures.

▶ sculpts only granite.

Examine the Artwork

"Let's look closely at this sculpture." *"Vamos a mirar detalladamente esta escultura".*

▪ Have students describe what they see in the picture.

▪ Have students answer the questions on page 155.

▶ The sculpture looks like it would be bumpy and rough. The tops of the protruding slabs look smooth.

▶ The protruding horizontal slabs are repeated vertically.

▶ The viewer's eye moves from the top to the bottom, following the repeated slabs.

Unit Pretest

T Display **Transparency 47** as a pretest. Answers: 1. C, 2. B, 3. A

Home Connection

▪ See **Home and After-School Connections** for family newsletters and activities for this unit.

Art History and Culture

Jesús Moroles

Born in Texas to Mexican immigrant parents, Jesús Moroles (hā sōōs´ mo rōo´ lēez) (1950–) creates monumental sculptures from granite. Often more than twenty feet tall, his massive creations can be found in numerous museums as well as in outdoor environments such as the White House sculpture garden. The granite he uses comes from varied locations and he works on it in his Texas studio.

See pages 16–21 and 24–25 for more about subject matter and art history.

Artist Profiles, p. 46

• Artist Profile •

Jesús Moroles
b. 1950

Born in Texas to Mexican immigrant parents, Jesús Moroles (hā sōōs´ mo rō´ léz) creates monumental sculptures from granite, or "living stone." He has been working with granite since 1980 and now has his own successful studio headquarters—Moroles, Inc.—in Rockport, Texas. Moroles's sculptures have been exhibited all over the world, and he has had great success from the very beginning of his career. Often more than 20 feet tall, his massive creations can be found in numerous museums, as well as in outdoor environments such as the CBS Plaza in New York City, the White House sculpture gardens, the Edwin A. Ulrich Museum in Kansas, and the Albuquerque Museum in

National Standards for Arts Education in Visual Arts (NSAE) 2.b

ILLUSTRATOR PROFILE
Tasha Tudor
(1915–   )

Tasha Tudor was born in Boston, Massachusetts. She learned a lot about art from her mother, who was a portrait artist. At the age of nine, Tudor went to live with some family friends in Connecticut. She enjoyed living in the countryside and decided to live on a farm when she grew up. When Tudor left Connecticut to visit her family in Boston, she often drew pictures to remind her of the countryside she loved and missed.

Tudor married Thomas Leighton McCready Jr. and began living the farm lifestyle she had dreamed of as a child. They raised animals and kept a garden. Tudor wove cloth and sewed her own dresses. She cooked over a wood-burning stove. Everything was done without electricity or running water.

Tudor's husband encouraged her to attempt a career as an illustrator. They showed a publisher a book Tudor had made as a Christmas present for their niece. The publisher liked it, and it was published in 1938 as *Pumpkin Moonshine*. Since then, Tudor has illustrated almost 100 books, including books she has written as well as classics such as *The Secret Garden* by Frances Hodgson Burnett and *A Child's Garden of Verses* by Robert Louis Stevenson. Tudor's illustrations reflect her passion for her rural lifestyle. She also loves Corgi dogs and has included many in her books.

Throughout Unit 5, share Tudor's illustrations with the class and discuss her use of texture, pattern, and rhythm. If students could touch the animals or plants in the illustrations, what would they feel like? What motifs are repeated throughout the illustrations?

Music

 Texture refers to the way melody and harmony, or *rhythm patterns,* are combined to create layers of sound. Guide students in finding repeated patterns in music.

Literature and Art

Use the video or DVD *Monster Mama* by Liz Rosenberg to introduce students to the concepts of texture, pattern, and rhythm.

Literature and Art

Performing Arts

Show *The Nutcracker.* Discuss the textures of the dancers' costumes, and the pattern and rhythm of the music and dancing.

Artsource®

Lesson 1 · Real Texture

Overview

Lesson 1 introduces students to real texture. Artists create real texture by using objects with texture that can be touched in their works of art.

Objectives

Art History and Culture
To identify some characteristics of Native American art
NSAE 4.a; 4.b; 4.c

Creative Expression
To create a collage using textured materials
NSAE 1.a; 1.c; 1.d

Aesthetic Perception
To identify and describe real textures in the environment
NSAE 6.b

Art Criticism
To evaluate one's own artwork using the four steps of art criticism
NSAE 1.b; 2.b; 3.a; 5.c

Vocabulary ⭐ Reading

Review the following vocabulary words with students before beginning the lesson.

real texture textura real—texture you can feel

collage collage—objects glued onto paper

See page 179B for additional vocabulary and Spanish vocabulary resources.

Art Journal: Vocabulary
Have students add these words to the Vocabulary section of their Art Journals.

Lesson Materials

- textured materials (such as fabric scraps, waxed paper, corrugated cardboard, sandpaper, wire, string, rope, newspapers, leaves, tree bark, cotton balls, sticks, foil)
- found materials (such as buttons, ribbons, broken jewelry)
- scissors
- glue
- white paper
- oil pastels or dustless, colored chalk

Alternate Materials:
- textured objects found in the classroom
- scrap paper, scissors, paper, glue

Program Resources
- *Reading and Writing Test Prep.*, pp. 54–55
- *Transparency 25*
- *Artist Profiles*, pp. 72, 77
- *Animals Through History Time Line*
- *Assessment*, pp. 57–58
- *Large Prints 21* Farm Scene and *22* Petit Chat (Small Cat)
- *The National Museum of Women in the Arts Collection*

Concept Trace
Real Texture
Introduced: Level K, Unit 5, Lesson 1
Reinforced: Level 2, Unit 5, Lesson 5

Lesson 1 Arts Integration NSAE 6.a

Theatre
Complete Unit 5, Lesson 1, on pages 90–91 of *Theatre Arts Connections.*

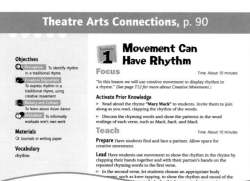

Music
In music, texture is described as thick or thin. One melody line is thin, and each added part adds thickness. Sing *Twinkle, Twinkle, Little Star* with only voice. Repeat, and add piano accompaniment. Repeat again and add drum. Do students prefer a thick or thin texture on this song?

Movement & Dance
Dancers use contrasting movement qualities and force/energy to express different feelings and ideas. Use words such as boil, melt, quiver, jab, or spring as a stimulus for exploring different movement qualities.

Focus

Time: About 10 minutes

Activate Prior Knowledge

"What words can you think of to tell what something feels like when you touch it?"

"¿Qué palabras se les ocurre para decir cómo se siente algo al tocarlo?"

- Make a list of students' answers. Explain that the way something feels when you touch it is its texture. Discuss adjectives that can be used to describe texture, including *fuzzy, prickly, smooth,* and *rough.*

Using Literature ⭐ Reading

- Read *Snowballs* by Lois Ehlert. The illustrations are collages that include materials with real texture.

Thematic Connection ⭐ Social Studies

- **Native Americans:** Discuss with students the communities that existed in the western hemisphere before it was settled by Europeans.

Introduce the Art

Look

NSAE 2.a; 3.a; 5.a

"Let's take a close look at these two works of art." "Vamos a mirar detalladamente estas dos obras de arte".

Making Inferences ⭐ Reading

- Have students make guesses about what each artwork was used for and what it is made of. Student answers will vary. The first artwork is a turban, or hat. It is made of fur and decorated with beads and ribbon. The second artwork is a cover that could hold pages. It was made of bark decorated with porcupine quills, glass beads, and silk.

Art History and Culture

Discuss with students that Native Americans made their art with materials that were recycled from plants and animals that were used for food. They did not want to waste anything that was taken from the earth. Another characteristic of Native American art is that it was often functional as well as decorative. NSAE 4.a; 4.b; 4.c

💻 **Web Connection**

Visit **www.potawatomi.org** for more information about the Potawatomi Nation.

156 UNIT 5 • Texture, Pattern, and Rhythm

Lesson 1 — Real Texture

▲ **Artist Unknown.** (United States). *Potawatomi Turban.* c. 1880.

Otter pelt, silk ribbon, glass beads. 6¼ inches high (15.88 cm.). Chandler-Pohrt Collection, Detroit Institute of the Arts, Detroit, Michigan.

Look at the works of art on these pages. They are real objects.

Art History and Culture

Native Americans made art with materials that came from plants and animals.

Art History and Culture

Potawatomi Tribe

The Potawatomi are a Native American people. They were once part of a larger tribe that split into smaller groups. The Potawatomi kept the council fire that had been used by their former tribe. *Potawatomi* means "people of the place of fire" or "fire keepers." Potawatomi people were fishers, hunters, and farmers. The skins of the animals they killed for food were used to make clothing. This turban was made from otter pelt. Men of the Potawatomi tribe wore fur turbans instead of the feather headdresses that were popular in other tribes.

See pages 16–21 and 24–25 for more about subject matter and art history.

Artist Profiles, p. 77

Artist Profile

Potawatomi Turban

The Potawatomi people were farmers, fishers, hunters, and trappers. They traveled by horse and navigated the rivers in birch bark canoes. Originally from the Great Lakes area, the Potawatomi had a tribal alliance with the Ojibwe and Ottawa peoples known as the Council of Three Fires. During the Indian Removal Act of the 1830s, American troops forced the relocation of the Three Fires peoples to territories in the central plains states. Some Potawatomi fled to Canada to escape the removal. Populations of Ojibwe, Ottawa, and Potawatomi still live in Kansas, Oklahoma, and the Great Lakes regions of the United States and Canada.

◀ **Artist unknown.** (United States).

Study the objects.

▶ What would they feel like if you touched them?

◀ **Artist Unknown.** (Mi'kmaq People, Nova Scotia, Canada). *Letter Holder or Book Cover.* 1900–1925.

Birch bark decorated with porcupine quills, glass beads, and silk. 14½ × 10¼ inches (36.83 × 26.04 cm.). Museum of International Folk Art, Santa Fe, New Mexico.

Aesthetic Perception

Design Awareness Touch some objects in the room. Describe their textures.

Unit 5 • Lesson 1 **157**

Study

▶ The fur would be rough but silky. The beads and quills would be bumpy. The leather would be smooth.

■ For more examples of utilitarian art, see *The National Museum of Women in the Arts Collection.*

Art Journal: Concepts
Provide students with bits of paper or fabric of various textures. Have students select one and glue or tape it in the Concepts section of their Art Journals. Next to the material have students write an adjective that describes its texture.

Aesthetic Perception

Design Awareness Have students touch objects in the classroom and then describe the texture of each. Discuss whether the texture of an object affects its usefulness. Discuss which textures they find most often.

Developing Visual Literacy Discuss with students what it would be like to wear the turban or use the letter holder. Have students compare the works of art to similar objects they use in their everyday lives.

Art History and Culture

Mi'Kmaq People

The Mi'kmaq (or Micmac) are a Native American people. *Mi'kmaq* translates to "my friends." Mi'kmaq people were mainly fishers and hunters. They did not want to waste anything, so they tried to use as much of an animal or plant as they could. The Mi'kmaq are well-known for making art with porcupine quills. To decorate birch bark with quills (such as the letter holder shown), holes are poked through the bark with an awl, and then the quills are threaded through. Geometric patterns are popular for quill decorations.

See pages 16–21 and 24–25 for more about subject matter and art history.

Artist Profiles, p. 72

Artist Profile

Letter Holder or Book Cover

This letter holder or book cover was made by an artist of the Mi'kmaq people, a Native American group located in the far northeastern coastal areas of North America. The unidentified Mi'kmaq artist who made this piece lived on the peninsula that is now called Nova Scotia. The Mi'kmaq were hunters and fishers, usually living in areas where fish were most plentiful. They were resourceful people, finding uses for every part of the animals they killed.

◀ **Artist unknown (Mimac).** (Mi'kmaq People, Nova Scotia, Canada). *Letter Holder or Book Cover.*

Birch bark decorated with porcupine quills, glass beads, and silk.

Web Connection
Visit **museum.gov.ns.ca/arch/infos/mikmaq1.htm** for more information about the Mi'kmaq culture.

LESSON 1 • Real Texture **157**

Teach

Time: About 40 minutes

"What has texture?" "¿Qué tiene textura?"

■ Read and discuss Using Real Texture on page 158.

Practice

Materials: textured materials (such as fabric, wax paper, corrugated cardboard, sandpaper)

Alternate Materials: textured objects found in the classroom

■ Give each student a piece of fabric or other material. Have students feel the material and think about how they could describe its texture. Name a texture and have all students holding that texture raise their hands. For example, "Raise your hand if you are holding something rough."

Creative Expression

NSAE 1.a; 1.c; 1.d

Materials: textured materials (such as fabric scraps, wire, string, rope, cardboard, newspapers, leaves, tree bark, sandpaper, sticks, cotton balls, foil), found materials (such as buttons, ribbons, broken jewelry), scissors, glue, white paper, oil pastels or dustless colored chalk

Alternate Materials: scrap paper, scissors, paper, glue

■ Distribute the materials and have students follow the directions on page 159.

■ Discuss that by using found materials in their collages, students are recycling things that would otherwise have become trash.

■ Review the Technique Tips on pages 221–223 for information about making a collage.

■ See the Activity Tips on page 244 for visual examples of this lesson's activity.

Art Journal: Brainstorming

Ask students to visualize their finished collages. Which materials would look best together? How should they be arranged? Have students make sketches of their ideas in their Art Journals.

Using Real Texture

Texture you can feel is called **real texture.**

Practice

Sort things by how they feel.

1. Your teacher will give each student an object.

2. Touch the object you received. What texture does it have?

3. Raise your hand when your teacher calls the name of your object's texture.

158 Unit 5 • Lesson 1

Differentiated Instruction

Reteach

Compare real things and photos of them. Let students feel the real textures and see that photos can show the textures of the objects, but those textures can't be felt.

Special Needs

Adaptations: Increase students' skills of word recognition by writing down the textures they describe on a class chart. The actual objects whose texture matches each word can also be added to the chart.

ELL Tips

Students might have difficulty thinking of adjectives to describe texture. You might want to phrase questions as an either/or choice so the vocabulary needed to answer the question is contained in the question itself.

Think about how this student used real texture in a collage.

▲ **Titi Lola Abisoye.** Age 6.

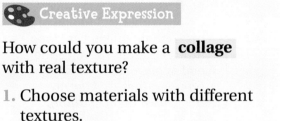 **Creative Expression**

How could you make a **collage** with real texture?

1. Choose materials with different textures.

2. Cut or tear them into geometric and free-form shapes.

3. Arrange the materials. Glue them to the paper.

Art Criticism

Analyze What shapes and textures did you include in your collage?

Art Across the Curriculum

Use these ideas to reinforce art concepts across the curriculum.
NSAE 6.b

★ **Descriptive Writing** Have students use the writing process to write sentences about their favorite animals, using adjectives to describe their textures.

★ **Math** Have students identify the geometric shapes used in the works of art.

★ **Science** Discuss that recycling materials (like using found materials in the Creative Expression activity) is beneficial for the environment.

★ **Social Studies** The Mi'kmaq people live in Nova Scotia, and the Potawatomi people live in Wisconsin. Help students locate these places on a map or globe.

★ **Technology** Have students identify parts of a computer by name and describe their textures. Visit **SRAonline.com** to print detailed instructions for this activity.

 **Reflect**

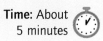

Time: About 5 minutes

Review and Assess
"What is real texture?" "¿Qué es la textura real?"

Think
The student used real texture by making a collage with textured materials.

■ Discuss with students how the artists could have added real texture to *Large Prints 21* Farm Scene and *22* Petit Chat *(Small Cat)*.

Informal Assessment

Art Journal: Critical Thinking
Have students ask themselves the Art Criticism questions, and then write or sketch to answer the Analyze question in their Art Journals.
NSAE 1.b; 2.b; 3.a; 5.c

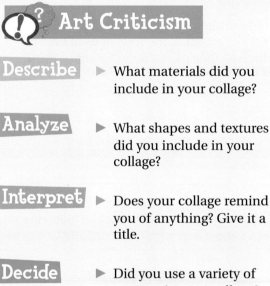 **Art Criticism**

Describe ▶ What materials did you include in your collage?

Analyze ▶ What shapes and textures did you include in your collage?

Interpret ▶ Does your collage remind you of anything? Give it a title.

Decide ▶ Did you use a variety of textures in your collage?

■ For standardized-format test practice using this lesson's art content, see pages 54–55 in *Reading and Writing Test Preparation.*

Real Texture

Extra! For the Art Specialist

Time: About 45 minutes

Focus

Using *Transparency 25,* have students name different textures they see in the works of art. See if students can point out different textures in the classroom and describe how the textures would feel to the touch.

Teach

Have students follow the directions to complete the nature collage. How would the textures of their collages change if they were made with found objects instead of natural materials?

Close

Guide students through evaluation of their works of art using the four steps of art criticism. (See pages 28–29 for more about art criticism.)

Alternate Activity

Materials:

- natural materials gathered on a short nature hike
- lunch-size paper bags to hold items during hike
- 12" × 18" white paper or light-colored construction paper
- white glue in shallow containers
- newspaper to protect tables

1. Take students on a short nature hike around the school grounds. Have them collect items with interesting textures that they could use in a collage.

2. Take students back to the classroom. Have them arrange objects on their papers.

3. Students can pick up items one at a time, touch them to the glue in the tray, and then place the items in the collage.

Research in Art Education

One study showed that when students study art forms from minority cultures (in the case of this particular study, Native American music), the instruction seems to be "effective in diminishing students' stereotypical attitudes and perceptions toward a minority culture." The arts can help teachers become "catalysts for cultural understanding and respect" ("North American Indian Music Instruction: Influences Upon Attitudes, Cultural Perceptions, and Achievement" in *Schools, Communities, and the Arts: A Research Compendium*).

Assessment

Use the following rubric to evaluate the artwork students make in the Creative Expression activity and to assess students' understanding of real texture.

Have students complete page 57 or 58 in their *Assessment* books.

	Art History and Culture	Aesthetic Perception	Creative Expression	Art Criticism
3 POINTS	The student successfully identifies some characteristics of Native American art.	The student accurately identifies and describes textures in the environment.	The student's collage uses materials that clearly have real texture.	The student thoughtfully and honestly evaluates his or her own work using the four steps of art criticism.
2 POINTS	The student's identification is weak or incomplete.	The student shows emerging awareness of textures but cannot consistently describe them.	The student's collage displays some real texture.	The student attempts to evaluate his or her own work but shows an incomplete understanding of evaluation criteria.
1 POINT	The student cannot identify any characteristics of Native American art.	The student cannot identify or describe textures.	The student's collage does not display real texture.	The student makes no attempt to evaluate his or her own artwork.

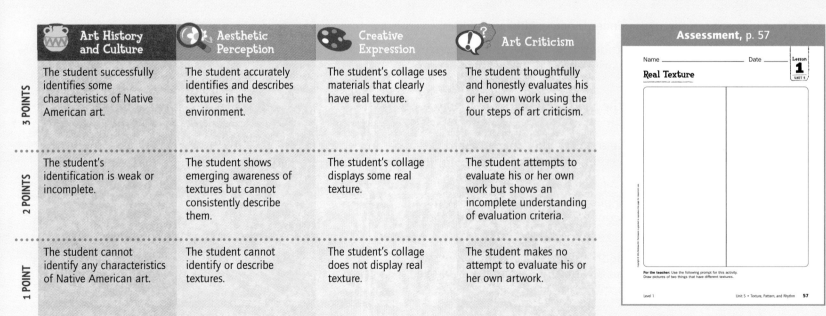

Assessment, p. 57

Name _____ Date _____ **Lesson 1** UNIT 5

Real Texture

For the teacher: Use the following prompt for this activity. Draw pictures of two things that have different textures.

Level 1   Unit 5 • Texture, Pattern, and Rhythm   **57**

Lesson 2 Visual Texture

Overview

Lesson 2 introduces visual texture, which is texture that can be seen but not felt. Artists create visual texture by showing the way an object's real texture looks.

Objectives

Art History and Culture

To describe a portrait as a painting of a specific person
NSAE 1.a; 2.a; 3.a; 5.a

Creative Expression

To create a self-portrait that shows visual textures   NSAE 1.a; 1.c; 1.d; 2.c; 3.b

Aesthetic Perception

To describe visual textures in art

NSAE 1.b; 2.b

Art Criticism

To evaluate one's own artwork using the four steps of art criticism
NSAE 1.b; 2.b; 3.a; 5.c

Vocabulary ⭐ Reading

Review the following vocabulary word with students before beginning the lesson.

visual texture *textura visual*—the way something looks like it might feel if you could touch it

See page 179B for additional vocabulary and Spanish vocabulary resources.

Art Journal: Vocabulary

Have students add this word to the Vocabulary section of their Art Journals.

Lesson Materials
- old magazines
- crayons
- watercolor paints
- 12" × 18" white paper
- paper towels
- paintbrushes
- water containers

Alternate Materials:
- teacher-provided photographs that show texture
- markers

Program Resources
- *Reading and Writing Test Prep.,* pp. 56–57
- *Transparency 26*
- *Artist Profiles,* pp. 13, 28
- *Animals Through History Time Line*
- *Assessment,* pp. 59–60
- *Large Prints 21* Farm Scene and *22* Petit Chat (Small Cat)
- *The National Museum of Women in the Arts Collection*

Concept Trace
Visual Texture
Introduced: Level K, Unit 5, Lesson 2
Reinforced: Level 2, Unit 5, Lesson 6

Lesson 2 Arts Integration NSAE 6.a

Theatre

Complete Unit 5, Lesson 2, on pages 92–93 of *Theatre Arts Connections.*

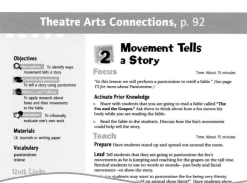

Music

Listen to *The Moldau* by Bedrich Smetana. The Moldau is a river in Czechoslovakia. The piece starts with a small flow of melody from two flutes depicting two streams coming out of the mountains. Listen to the texture change as more instruments are added.

Movement & Dance

Divide the class into small groups in different areas of the room. Give each group two energy qualities such as dash, sizzle, bump, or buzz. Each group travels to the center of the room showing their first quality, freezes, and then exits showing their second quality. Ask the rest of the class to guess the words the group might have been given.

Focus

Activate Prior Knowledge

"What is the texture of this person's hair?" "¿Cuál es la textura del cabello de esta persona?"

▨ Show students a magazine picture of a person with hair that has visual texture, such as a rough-looking beard. Discuss that if they touch the picture, they will only feel the page it is printed on, but they can imagine how the real hair would feel.

Using Literature ★ Reading

▨ Read *Here Is the African Savanna* by Madeleine Dunphy. Discuss with students that they can look at the illustrations by Tom Leonard and imagine what textures can be found in Africa.

Thematic Connection

▨ **Reading:** Just as visual texture helps students imagine texture they cannot touch, reading helps them imagine places and people they have never seen.

Introduce the Art

Look
NSAE 3.a

"Let's take a close look at the two works of art." "Vamos a mirar detalladamente las dos obras de arte".

Summarizing ★ Reading

▨ Have students describe what they see in each artwork. *Mrs. Ezekiel Goldthwait* has a woman sitting in a chair at a wooden table. She is wearing a white bonnet and a brown dress with lace around the sleeves and neck. A bowl of apples and peaches is sitting on the table, and she is touching two pieces of fruit. *The Lookout—"All's Well"* shows a man at the bottom left. His hand is raised and his mouth is open as if he is calling out. Some ropes and poles are in the background. A bell is in the center of the painting.

🏺 Art History and Culture

Discuss with students that a portrait is a work of art that shows a specific person. Before photographs were common, a portrait could be painted to record what a person looked like. Artists can also include details to show something about the person's personality. NSAE 4.c; 5.a

💻 Web Connection

The National Portrait Gallery at **www.npg.si.edu** contains portraits by John Singleton Copley.

Lesson 2 Visual Texture

Look at the paintings on these pages. The artists showed the textures of the people and objects.

◀ **John Singleton Copley.** (American). *Mrs. Ezekiel Goldthwait.* 1771.
....
Oil on canvas. $50\frac{3}{8} \times 40\frac{1}{4}$ inches (127.95 × 102.24 cm.). Museum of Fine Arts, Boston, Massachusetts.

🏺 Art History and Culture

Before photography was common, artists painted portraits of people.

🏺 Art History and Culture

John Singleton Copley

John Singleton Copley (jän sing´ gəl tən kä´ plē) (1738–1815) was born in Boston, Massachusetts. He was influenced by his stepfather, who was an engraver. Copley painted many portraits, which were popular in America at the time. The setting was important in Copley's portraits, and he often included objects used by the subject in his paintings. He painted portraits of many politicians and wealthy New England residents. Copley exhibited one of his paintings in London, and it was successfully received. He then moved there in 1775. The subjects of his paintings later changed from portraits to historical scenes.

See pages 16–21 and 24–25 for more about subject matter and art history.

Artist Profiles, p. 13

◆ Artist Profile ◆

John Singleton Copley
1738-1815

John Singleton Copley (jän sing´ gəl tən kä´ plē) was born in Boston one year after his parents arrived from Ireland. His father died, and his mother supported the family by running a tobacco shop. When Copley was 11, his mother married Peter Pelham, who was a printmaker, a painter, and a teacher. Pelham quickly saw young Copley's talent and gave him his first art lessons. Copley also learned from studying prints of paintings by Michelangelo, Raphael, and Rubens. In 1774, he was encouraged to go to Europe to study. He left his family in Boston and toured Europe. His father-in-law was one of the importers of the famous

◀ **Winslow Homer.** (American).
The Lookout—"All's Well". 1896.
Oil on canvas. 40 × 30¼ inches (101.6 × 76.84 cm.).
Museum of Fine Arts, Boston, Massachusetts.

Study the paintings to find texture.

▶ What looks smooth?

▶ What looks rough?

 Aesthetic Perception

Seeing Like an Artist Look in a mirror. What textures would you show in a self-portrait?

Art History and Culture

Winslow Homer   NSAE 5.b

Winslow Homer (winz´ lō hō´ mər) (1836–1910) was born in Boston, Massachusetts. In 1855, he began working as an apprentice to a lithographer. Homer moved to New York City in 1859 and worked as a freelance illustrator. During the Civil War, Homer traveled to Virginia and made sketches and paintings of the war front. During the 1870s, Homer primarily painted scenes of rural American life. In the early 1880s, he traveled to England and stayed in a fishing village. After that visit he mainly painted scenes of the New England coast and fishermen. Homer created seascapes and narrative works of art.

See pages 16–21 and 24–25 for more about subject matter and art history.

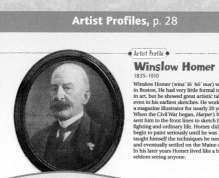

Artist Profiles, p. 28

◆ Artist Profile ◆
Winslow Homer
1835-1910

Winslow Homer (winz´ lō hō´ mər) was born in Boston. He had very little formal training in art, but he showed great artistic talent even in his earliest sketches. He worked as a magazine illustrator for nearly 20 years. When the Civil War began, *Harper's Weekly* sent him to the front lines to sketch both the fighting and ordinary life. Homer did not begin to paint seriously until he was 26. He taught himself the techniques he needed, and eventually settled on the Maine coast. In his later years Homer lived like a hermit, seldom seeing anyone.

Study

▶ In *Mrs. Ezekiel Goldthwait,* the woman's dress, her skin, the table, and the apples look smooth. In *The Lookout—"All's Well"* the bell and the shiny parts of the man's face look smooth.

▶ In *Mrs. Ezekiel Goldthwait,* the edge of the chair and the lace on the woman's dress look rough. The peaches look fuzzy. The rope and the man's beard in *The Lookout—"All's Well"* look rough.

■ For more examples of portraits, see ***The National Museum of Women in the Arts Collection.***

 Art Journal: Concepts

Have students make sketches in the Concepts section of their Art Journals to show the lines they could use to draw something smooth and the lines they could use to draw something rough. What lines could they use to show other textures?

Aesthetic Perception

Seeing Like an Artist Discuss with students the textures they have on their bodies and clothing. If students were to make a self-portrait, what kinds of lines would they use to show these textures?

Developing Visual Literacy Discuss with students why they think the person in *Mrs. Ezekiel Goldthwait* is in the center, but the person in *The Lookout—"All's Well"* is cut off at the corner and the bell is in the center.
NSAE 2.a; 2.b; 3.a

🖥 **Web Connection**

Visit **www.mfa.org/home.htm** to search for more information about the Winslow Homer collection at the Museum of Fine Arts in Boston.

Teach

Time: About 30 minutes

"How do artists show the textures of things?"
"¿Cómo muestran los artistas las texturas de las cosas?"

- Read and discuss Using Visual Texture on page 162.

Practice

Materials: old magazines

Alternate Materials: teacher-provided photographs that show texture

- Distribute the materials and have students follow the directions on page 162.

- Encourage students to look for visual texture in pictures of people, animals, and objects.

Creative Expression

NSAE 1.a; 1.c; 1.d; 2.c
Materials: crayons, watercolor paints, 12" x 18" white paper, paper towels, paintbrushes, water containers

Alternate Materials: markers

- Distribute the materials and have students follow the directions on page 163.

- Review the Technique Tips on pages 214 and 219–220 for information about using crayons and watercolors.

- See the Activity Tips on page 244 for visual examples of this lesson's activity.

Art Journal: Brainstorming

Have students brainstorm ideas for details they will include in their self-portraits. Have them make sketches in their Art Journals to determine what lines they should use to show textures most effectively.
NSAE 3.b

Using Visual Texture

Texture you can see but not feel is called **visual texture.**

Practice

Look for texture in pictures.

1. Look through a magazine.
2. Find pictures that show texture.
3. How many textures can you find in the same picture?

Differentiated Instruction

Reteach
Show students a bell or a peach and have them feel and describe its real texture. Then have students discuss how Copley or Homer showed that object's visual texture in the painting.

Special Needs
Adaptations: Students may need guided practice in creating visual texture. Have several objects available for students to observe and record visual textures. Check for student understanding before proceeding to the activity.

ELL Tips
Show a photograph of clothing from a catalog and have students identify it as visual texture. Then have them touch a real item of clothing and identify it as real texture.

▲ **Brittany Warren.** Age 6.

Think about how this student showed texture in her self-portrait.

 **Creative Expression**

How could you show the textures of you?

1. Draw your self-portrait with crayon.
2. Use lines that show the textures of your body and clothing.
3. Paint over your drawing with watercolors.

 Art Criticism

Interpret What mood do you have in your self-portrait? How did you show this?

Art Across the Curriculum

Use these ideas to reinforce art concepts across the curriculum.

NSAE 6.b

★ **Personal Writing** Have students pretend they know one of the people in this lesson's works of art and use the writing process to write a letter to him or her.

★ **Math** Have students count the number of colors they can name in each artwork. Which painting is more colorful?

★ **Science** A ship's lookout could have used the bell to alert others of danger. Discuss the parts of a bell and how it works.

★ **Social Studies** John Singleton Copley painted portraits of important people. Show students portraits of historical figures and discuss their significance.

★ **Technology** Have students use the computer's photo-editing program to add visual texture to a photograph. Visit **SRAonline.com** to print detailed instructions for this activity.

 **Reflect**   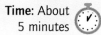 Time: About 5 minutes

Review and Assess

"What is visual texture?" '¿Qué es la textura visual?"

Think

The student showed the texture of her hair, skin, and clothing.

■ Have students describe the visual texture in *Large Prints 21* Farm Scene and *22* Petit Chat (Small Cat).

Informal Assessment

Art Journal: Critical Thinking
Have students ask themselves the Art Criticism questions, and then write or sketch to answer the Interpret question in their Art Journals.
NSAE 1.b; 2.b; 3.a; 5.c

 **Art Criticism**

Describe ▶ What colors did you use in your self-portrait?

Analyze ▶ What different textures did you use? What lines create these textures?

Interpret ▶ What mood do you have in your self-portrait? How did you show this?

Decide ▶ Do the textures you drew look real? What would you do differently next time?

■ For standardized-format test practice using this lesson's art content, see pages 56–57 in *Reading and Writing Test Preparation.*

Visual Texture

Extra! For the Art Specialist

Time: About 45 minutes

Focus

Using *Transparency 26,* have students discuss the different textures in each work of art. Which objects in the classroom have textures like those depicted in the works of art?

Teach

Have students follow the directions to complete the Alternate Activity. How is visual texture different from real texture?

Reflect

Guide students through evaluation of their works of art using the four steps of art criticism. (See pages 28–29 for more about art criticism.)

Alternate Activity

Materials:
- 12" × 18" newsprint
- found textures
- peeled, broken crayons
- 9" × 12" construction paper
- scissors
- glue or glue sticks
- markers

1. Have students fold the newsprint into eight sections.

2. Using various textures found in the classroom, have students use the crayons to fill each section of the paper with different texture rubbings. Have students cut the textures apart on the fold lines.

3. Students will create a texture creature by cutting different textures into shapes to represent body parts. Have students glue the shapes to a sheet of construction paper to make the creature. Details may be added with markers.

Research in Art Education

One study showed that students, on average, gained eight percentile points on a standardized language arts test after one year of learning in an arts-integrated classroom and gained 16 percentile points after two years. After three years, students "outscored non-program students on the writing and drawing assessments of social studies content learning" ("Different Ways of Knowing: 1991–94 National Longitudinal Study Final Report" in *Schools, Communities, and the Arts: A Research Compendium*). By incorporating relevant portraits and historical paintings into social studies lessons, students can visually connect to the content.

Assessment

Use the following rubric to evaluate the artwork students make in the Creative Expression activity and to assess students' understanding of visual texture.

Have students complete page 59 or 60 in their *Assessment* books.

	Art History and Culture	Aesthetic Perception	Creative Expression	Art Criticism
3 POINTS	The student successfully describes a portrait as a painting of a specific person.	The student accurately describes visual textures in art.	The student's self-portrait clearly illustrates visual textures.	The student thoughtfully and honestly evaluates his or her own work using the four steps of art criticism.
2 POINTS	The student's identification is weak or incomplete.	The student shows emerging awareness of visual textures in art but cannot consistently identify them.	The student's self-portrait shows some awareness of visual textures.	The student attempts to evaluate his or her own work but shows an incomplete understanding of evaluation criteria.
1 POINT	The student cannot describe a portrait.	The student cannot identify visual textures in art.	The student's self-portrait shows no understanding of visual textures.	The student makes no attempt to evaluate his or her own artwork.

Assessment, p. 59

Name _____ Date _____

Visual Texture

Lesson
2
UNIT 5

1	2

For the teacher: Use the following prompts for this activity.
1. In box 1, use a crayon to draw lines that visually represent a smooth texture.
2. In box 2, draw lines that represent a rough texture.

Level 1   Unit 5 • Texture, Pattern, and Rhythm   **59**

Lesson 3 Raised Texture

Overview

Lesson 3 introduces carving, which is cutting away from the surface of an object with a sharp tool. Carving creates raised areas that have real texture.

Objectives

Art History and Culture

To compare carvings from different materials and time periods
NSAE 4.a; 4.b; 4.c

Creative Expression

To carve real texture into a clay plaque
NSAE 1.a; 1.c; 1.d; 2.c; 3.b

Aesthetic Perception

To locate objects in the environment that have real texture created by raised areas
NSAE 6.b

Art Criticism

To evaluate one's own artwork using the four steps of art criticism
NSAE 1.b; 2.b; 3.a; 5.c

Vocabulary ⭐ Reading

Review the following vocabulary words with students before beginning the lesson.

carving *tallar o esculpir*—cutting away of a hard material to create a three-dimensional work of art

real texture *textura real*—texture you can feel

See page 179B for additional vocabulary and Spanish vocabulary resources.

 Art Journal: Vocabulary
Have students add these words to the Vocabulary section of their Art Journals.

Lesson Materials

- clay
- carving tools (plastic utensils, paper clips, pencils, craft sticks)
- clay mat (muslin)
- found objects

Alternate Materials:
- plasticine molding clay

Program Resources

- *Reading and Writing Test Prep.,* pp. 58–59
- *Transparency 27*
- *Artist Profiles,* pp. 76, 84
- *Animals Through History Time Line*
- *Assessment,* pp. 61–62
- *Large Prints 21 Farm Scene* and *22 Petit Chat (Small Cat)*
- *Art Around the World*

Concept Trace
Raised Texture
Introduced: Level K, Unit 5, Lesson 5
Reinforced: Level 2, Unit 5, Lesson 5

Lesson 3 Arts Integration   NSAE 6.a

Theatre

Complete Unit 5, Lesson 3, on pages 94–95 of *Theatre Arts Connections.*

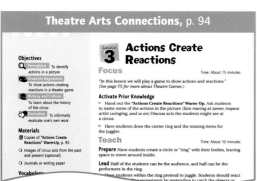

Theatre Arts Connections, p. 94

Music

When students sing a round, the melody overlaps. *Frere Jacque* and *Row, Row, Row Your Boat* can be sung to illustrate this. Divide the class into two sections. One section begins singing. Four beats later, the other section begins singing at the beginning of the song.

Movement & Dance

Call out various words such as flap, pop, slither, or ooze for the students to interpret in movement. Ask students to try each idea in one small part of their body to begin with, like the hand, adding in larger body parts as they go. Ask students to explore moving with a great deal of force and then with just a little.

Activate Prior Knowledge

"Have you ever made a footprint in snow or wet sand?" "¿Alguna vez han hecho una huella de un pie en la nieve o en arena mojada?"

- Discuss how the sand or snow was pressed down, creating a raised area around the footprint. Other examples of the contrast between raised and lowered areas are drawing in dirt with a stick or mowing the grass.

Using Literature   ★ Reading

- Read *Fossils Tell of Long Ago* by Aliki. Point out to students that the fossils create raised texture in the ground or in rock.

Thematic Connection   ★ Science

- **Fossils:** Ask students if they can figure out how a fossil is similar to a work of art. Explain that both objects can provide clues about the past.

Introduce the Art

Look   NSAE 2.a; 3.a

"Let's take a close look at the two works of art." "Vamos a mirar detalladamente las dos obras de arte".

Comparing and Contrasting   ★ Reading

- Have students discuss the similarities and differences between the plaque and the tortilla molds. The plaque and the tortilla molds are similar in size and shape. In both works of art the design is raised and the areas around it have been carved away. Both works of art also have geometric and free-form shapes. The plaque and the tortilla molds were carved from different materials.

🏺 Art History and Culture

Use the *Animals Through History Time Line* to show students when each work of art was made. Compare the materials used, and discuss the durability of each material.
NSAE 4.a; 4.b

💻 Web Connection
Visit **www.brooklynmuseum.org** to learn more about the Brooklyn Museum of Art.

164 UNIT 5 • Texture, Pattern, and Rhythm

Raised Texture

◀ **Artist Unknown.** (Panama). *Plaque.* 700–1100 A.D.
••••••••••••••••••••••••
Gold. 9 × 8½ inches (22.9 × 21.6 cm.). The Brooklyn Museum, New York, New York.

Look at the works of art on these pages. They have raised areas that would feel bumpy if you could touch them.

🏺 Art History and Culture

The *Plaque* looks shiny but it is actually very old! It is made of gold, which lasts for a very long time.

164   Unit 5 • Lesson 3

🏺 Art History and Culture

Archaeologists found this plaque in Panama at a grave site excavated on the banks of the Ciri Grande. The plaque was located near the skull of a person believed to be an important local chief. The figure on the plaque was once thought to be a crocodile god, but scholars have recently reinterpreted it to be a mythical warrior or cult hero. The unknown Panamanian artist who crafted this plaque used almost pure gold. The artist hammered the gold into a thin sheet and then, working over a resilient surface such as leather, tooled the designs on the metal.

See pages 16–21 and 24–25 for more about subject matter and art history.

Artist Profiles, p. 76

⌐ Artist Profile ¬

Plaque

This plaque was made of hammered gold and was found in a burial site near the skull of an important local chief. The plaque was made in Coclé, a province of central Panama on that nation's southern coast, sometime between 700 and 1100 A.D. The individual artist is unknown, but this plaque is typical of Coclé work during this period.

▲ **Artist unknown.** (Panama). *Plaque.* 700–1100 A.D.

▲ **Artist Unknown.** (Vizarron, Queretaro, Mexico). *Tortilla Molds.* 1930s.

Carved wood. Approx. 10 × 2 inches (25.4 × 5.08 cm.). San Antonio Museum of Art, San Antonio, Texas.

Study the objects.

▶ Where do you see raised areas?

Aesthetic Perception

Design Awareness What things in your school or home have texture because of raised areas?

Art History and Culture

Tortillas are a staple of Mexican food. A tortilla is a piece of thin bread made from *masa harina* (corn flour) dough that has been flattened into a circle and then cooked on a skillet or griddle. Tortillas are eaten topped with food, such as meat and beans, or they are dipped in sauces. Tortillas were traditionally pressed by hand and were undecorated. These tortilla molds were used to press designs into tortillas for a special occasion, such as a religious event or a family celebration. These special molds were made only in Vizarrón, Querétaro, Mexico.

See pages 16–21 and 24–25 for more about subject matter and art history.

Artist Profiles, p. 84

Artist Profile

Tortilla Molds

These tortilla molds were made by an unknown artist from Vizarrón, a town in the central Mexican state of Querétaro. Although the identity of the particular artist who carved the three molds shown here is not known, the location of their origin narrows the list of possible artists to those living within Vizarrón during the 1930s.

◄ **Artist unknown.** (Mexico). *Tortilla Molds.* c. 1930.

Study

▶ In both works of art, most of the shapes in the designs (such as the animals and the plants) are raised areas. The shapes were created by carving away or pressing down the areas around the shapes. A few of the shapes (such as the pattern around the outside of the plaque) were created by pressing or carving the shapes into the artwork.

■ For more examples of art from Latin America, see *Art Around the World.*

Art Journal: Concepts

Have students sketch an object with raised texture in the Concepts section of their Art Journals. Have students color the areas of the object that are not raised.

Aesthetic Perception

Design Awareness Discuss objects that have real texture created by indentations or raised areas, for instance, the buttons on a telephone, the keys on a computer keyboard, the texture on the bottoms of athletic shoes, or the texture on a coin.

Developing Visual Literacy The *Tortilla Molds* were used to make decorated tortillas for special occasions. Discuss with students whether they make any foods or decorations with their families, especially for holidays. Ask students how their personal experiences affect their understanding of the artwork.

Web Connection

Visit **www.samuseum.org** to learn more about the San Antonio Museum of Art.

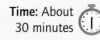

Teach

Time: About 30 minutes

"How can you add real texture to clay?"
"¿Cómo puedes agregar textura real a la arcilla?"

- Read and discuss Using Carved Texture on page 166.

Practice

Materials: clay, carving tools (plastic utensils, paper clips, pencils, craft sticks), found objects

Alternate Materials: modeling compound

- Distribute the materials and have students follow the directions on page 166.

- Let students take turns experimenting with various carving tools to carve texture into clay. Then let students discover what happens when they press various found objects into clay. Discuss each procedure and its results.

Creative Expression

NSAE 1.a; 1.c; 1.d; 2.c

Materials: clay, clay mat (muslin), found objects, carving tools (plastic utensils, paper clips, pencils, craft sticks)

Alternate Materials: plasticine modeling clay

- Distribute the materials and have students follow the directions on page 167.

- Review the Technique Tips on page 230 for information about working with clay.

- See the Activity Tips on page 245 for visual examples of this lesson's activity.

Art Journal: Brainstorming

Have students brainstorm ideas in their Art Journals for designs they could carve into clay to make real texture. Have students notice the lines they used.
NSAE 3.b

Using Raised Texture

Artists create raised areas in their works of art by **carving** and pressing. Works of art with raised areas have real texture.

Practice

Carve and press texture into clay.

1. Experiment with different carving tools.
2. Try pressing something into the clay.
3. Talk about the results.

166 Unit 5 • Lesson 3

Differentiated Instruction

Reteach
Provide objects with raised texture. Have students feel and describe the raised and recessed areas.

Special Needs
Adaptations: Have raised sculptures or objects available for students to feel prior to beginning this project. Reinforce lesson objectives by providing natural textured objects for students to use.

ELL Tips
Compare a bar of soap with a relief carving to a smooth bar of soap. Have students feel the texture of each and identify the raised and carved areas of the bar of soap that has been carved.

Think about how this student carved real texture.

◄ **Amy Marie Kuhn.** Age 5.

How could you carve real texture into clay?

1. Flatten a ball of clay into a square or circle.
2. Carve and press different lines and shapes into the clay to make a design.
3. Carve your initials on the back of the clay.

Describe What image or design did you carve into your plaque?

Art Across the Curriculum

Use these ideas to reinforce art concepts across the curriculum.
NSAE 6.b

★ **Narrative Writing** Have students pretend that one of the works of art is an illustration and use the writing process to write a short story to accompany it.

★ **Math** Have students feel the raised texture on coins as they identify their value.

★ **Science** Discuss raised texture on the bodies of reptiles (such as crocodiles or turtles).

★ **Social Studies** Discuss with students that braille is a technology that has changed communication. Explain how the raised dots allow visually impaired people to read with their fingers.

★ **Technology** Have students use a Web search engine to find images of fossils with raised texture. Visit **SRAonline.com** to print detailed instructions for this activity.

 **Reflect** Time: About 5 minutes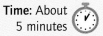

Review and Assess
"How does carving add real texture?" "¿Cómo se agrega textura real al esculpir?"

Think
The student carved a cat design into her plaque.

■ Use *Large Prints 21 Farm Scene* and *22 Petit Chat (Small Cat)* to have students identify objects that might have raised texture.

Informal Assessment

Art Journal: Critical Thinking
Have students ask themselves the Art Criticism questions, then write or sketch in their Art Journals to answer the Describe question.
NSAE 1.b; 2.b; 3.a; 5.c

Art Criticism

Describe ► What image or design did you carve into your plaque?

Analyze ► What kinds of lines did you carve?

Interpret ► Does your plaque stand for anything special?

Decide ► Can you feel the difference between the raised areas and the carved ridges that create textures?

■ For standardized-format test practice using this lesson's art content, see pages 58–59 in *Reading and Writing Test Preparation.*

Raised Texture

Extra! For the Art Specialist

Time: About 45 minutes

Focus

Use *Transparency 27.* Ask students if any parts of the artwork seem to stand out from the background. What kinds of texture did the artists use in the works of art?

Teach

Have students complete the Styrofoam carving. What other materials can students think of that they could carve texture into?

Reflect

Guide students through evaluation of their works of art using the four steps of art criticism. (See pages 28–39 for more about art criticism.)

Alternate Activity

Materials:
- pieces of Styrofoam (meat trays or plates)
- pencils with erasers
- texture tools (plastic forks, paper clips, craft sticks)
- markers

1. Have students choose an animal to illustrate on their texture plaque. Have students use a pencil to incise their animal on the Styrofoam. Students may use pencils and other texture tools to add details to their animals.

2. Have students draw one or two objects in the background to show where their animal lives and what it eats.

3. Students can use the eraser end of the pencil to press on the unincised areas to make the animals stand out in low relief. The plaques may be colored with markers.

Research in Art Education

Case studies have indicated that students perceive "that the arts facilitate their personal and social development." It also appeared that to gain the full benefit of arts education, students should be exposed to all of the arts, including fine arts, dance, theatre, and music ("Arts Education in Secondary School: Effects and Effectiveness" in *Critical Links,* p. 76). See the Arts Integration feature on page 163B for ideas.

Assessment

Use the following rubric to evaluate the artwork students make in the Creative Expression activity and to assess students' understanding of raised texture.

Have students complete page 61 or 62 in their *Assessment* books.

	Art History and Culture	Aesthetic Perception	Creative Expression	Art Criticism
3 POINTS	The student can compare carvings from different materials and time periods.	The student accurately locates raised texture in the environment.	The student's clay plaque clearly has carved texture.	The student thoughtfully and honestly evaluates his or her own work using the four steps of art criticism.
2 POINTS	The student's comparison is weak or incomplete.	The student shows emerging awareness of raised texture but cannot consistently identify it.	The student's clay plaque has some carved texture.	The student attempts to evaluate his or her own work but shows an incomplete understanding of evaluation criteria.
1 POINT	The student cannot compare carvings from different materials and time periods.	The student cannot identify raised texture.	The student's clay plaque does not have carved texture.	The student makes no attempt to evaluate his or her own artwork.

Assessment, p. 61

Name _____ Date _____ Lesson **3** UNIT 5

Raised Texture

For the teacher: Use the following prompt for this activity.
Using a crayon, draw a picture of an object that has raised texture.

Level 1   Unit 5 • Texture, Pattern, and Rhythm   **61**

Lesson 4 Pattern

Overview

Lesson 4 introduces pattern, which is created by the repetition of shapes, lines, or colors in a work of art.

Objectives

Art History and Culture
To recognize that utilitarian objects can be decorative as well as useful
NSAE 5.a

Creative Expression
To make a clay stamp and use it to stamp a pattern   NSAE 1.a; 1.c; 1.d; 2.c; 3.b

Aesthetic Perception
To identify patterns in art
NSAE 2.a; 3.a

Art Criticism
To evaluate one's own artwork using the four steps of art criticism
NSAE 1.b; 2.b; 3.a; 5.c

Vocabulary ⭐ Reading

Review the following vocabulary word with students before beginning the lesson.

pattern patrón—the use of shapes, colors, or lines repeated in a planned way

See page 179B for additional Spanish vocabulary resources.

 Art Journal: Vocabulary
Have students add this word to the Vocabulary section of their Art Journals.

Lesson Materials
- construction paper cut into geometric shapes
- clay
- clay tools
- clay mats (muslin)
- paper plates
- liquid tempera paints
- white paper
- brushes
- water containers
- paper towels
- newspaper

Alternate Materials:
- wrapped candies
- precut vegetables or fruit (such as green peppers, potatoes, apples, pears) instead of clay stamps

Program Resources
- *Reading and Writing Test Prep.,* pp. 60–61
- *Transparency 28*
- *Artist Profiles,* pp. 43, 69
- *Animals Through History Time Line*
- *Assessment,* pp. 63–64
- *Large Prints 21 Farm Scene* and *22 Petit Chat (Small Cat)*
- *The National Museum of Women in the Arts Collection*

Concept Trace
Pattern
Introduced: Level K, Unit 6, Lesson 1
Reinforced: Level 2, Unit 4, Lesson 1

Lesson 4 Arts Integration NSAE 6.a

Theatre
Complete Unit 5, Lesson 4, on pages 96–97 of *Theatre Arts Connections.*

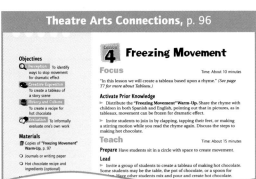
Theatre Arts Connections, p. 96

Music
Listen to *Russian Sailor's Dance* from *The Red Poppy* by Reinhold Gliere. The main melody pattern repeats many times with variations that keep the listener's interest. Discuss how the instrumentation changes without changing the melody.

Movement & Dance
Ask students to think of specific actions that have a repetitive pattern, such as scrubbing or weaving. Explore each of these ideas in movement, and then ask students to select three and organize then in a sequence. Use eight counts for each idea. Have students explore these ideas with a partner.

Focus

Time: About 10 minutes

Activate Prior Knowledge

"What does the American flag look like?"

"¿Cómo se ve la bandera de Estados Unidos?"

- Show students the flag or a picture of the flag. Discuss the design of repeated stars and stripes.

Using Literature ⭐ Reading

- Read *The Chick and the Duckling* by Mirra Ginsburg. The illustrations by Jose Aruego contain patterns of repeated shapes and colors.

Thematic Connection ⭐ Science

- **Insects:** Discuss with students patterns that can be found in nature. Patterns appear on many insects, such as spots on a ladybug or stripes on a bee.

Introduce the Art

Look
NSAE 3.a

"Let's take a close look at the two works of art." "Vamos a mirar detalladamente las dos obras de arte".

Comparing and Contrasting ⭐ Reading

- Have students list the similarities and differences in the two works of art. The vase and the quilt are utilitarian (they can be used). Both have shapes that are repeated to make a pattern, and the patterns have alternating colors. Both have areas of solid color (the brown area on the neck of the vase and the blue stripe around the outside of the quilt). The vase is a form that has space inside, and the quilt is flat.

🏺 Art History and Culture

Both works of art are utilitarian, meaning they are objects that people could use in their homes. *Stoneware Vase #661* could be used to hold flowers. *Four Patch in Triangles Quilt* could be used as a bed cover.
NSAE 5.a; 6.b

💻 Web Connection

Stoneware Vase #661 is part of the collection of American crafts at the Renwick Gallery. Learn more about the gallery at **nmaa-ryder.si.edu/collections/renwick/main.html**.

Pattern

Look at these works of art. Notice the colors and shapes the artists used to decorate the vase and the quilt.

◀ **Harrison Mc Intosh.** (American). *Stoneware Vase #661.* 1966.
Glazed stoneware. 15¼ × 13 inches (38.74 × 33.02 cm.). Renwick Gallery, Smithsonian American Art Museum, Washington, D.C.

🏺 Art History and Culture

How do you think these works of art could be used in everyday life?

🏺 Art History and Culture

Harrison Mc Intosh

Harrison Mc Intosh (ha´ rə sən mak´ ən täsh) (1914–   ) was born in Vallejo, California. He studied art in college and became a professional ceramicist in the 1950s. He has had many individual shows and participated in many exhibitions. His work appears in museums in North America, Japan, and Europe. In addition to selling the individual pottery and ceramic pieces that he makes in his studio, Mc Intosh has designed pieces for tableware companies.

See pages 16–21 and 24–25 for more about subject matter and art history.

Artist Profiles, p. 43

Artist Profile
Harrison Mc Intosh
b. 1914

Harrison Mc Intosh (ha´ rə sən mak´ ən täsh) was born in Vallejo, California, and studied ceramics at the University of Southern California and the Claremont Graduate University. His career has been predominantly based in California, where he has worked as a professional studio potter in Claremont since the mid-1950s. He also creates ceramic and glassware designs with his wife Marguerite for large factories such as the Japanese company Mikasa.

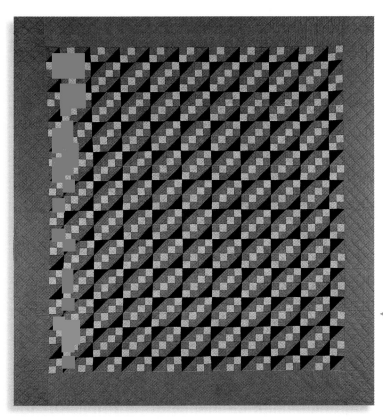

◀ **Barbara Zook Peachey.** (American). *Four Patch in Triangles Quilt.* 1910–1920.

Cotton. $85\frac{1}{2} \times 78\frac{3}{4}$ inches (217.17 × 200 cm.). American Folk Art Museum, New York, New York.

Study the works of art.

▶ What shapes and colors are repeated?

🔍 Aesthetic Perception

Design Awareness Look at your clothing. Find a pattern.

🏺 Art History and Culture

Barbara Zook Peachey   NSAE 4.a; 4.b; 4.c; 5.a; 5.b

Mrs. Peachey was part of an Amish community in Mifflin County, Pennsylvania. The Amish are a Christian group that originated in Europe and moved to North America in the eighteenth century to escape persecution. The Amish wear simple clothing and shun modern conveniences like cars and electricity. Amish women first learned quilt making from their American neighbors in the mid-nineteenth century. The American quilt tradition uses patterns of repeated blocks. Amish women often give quilts as gifts to mark special occasions like births or weddings.

See pages 16–21 and 24–25 for more about subject matter and art history.

Artist Profiles, p. 69

▷ Artist Profile ◁

Four Patch in Triangles Quilt

Barbara Zook Peachey belonged to a community of people who practiced the conservative Christian Amish religion and way of life. The Amish emigrated from Europe to North America during the eighteenth century and settled mainly in the Great Lakes states. The Amish believe in a simple life of devotion to God, separate from and as unaffected as possible by the modern world around them. The Amish are known for their strong work ethic and the excellent quality of the goods they produce.

Barbara Zook Peachey. (American.)

Study

▶ A tear shape is repeated on *Stoneware Vase #661*. Blue and brown tears alternate both horizontally and vertically. *Four Patch in Triangles Quilt* has a four-patch pattern. It is called *four-patch* because four small squares combine to make one patch. The top-left square and bottom-right square of the patch are made of four smaller blue and pink squares. The top-right square of the patch has a red triangle at the top and a black triangle at the bottom. The bottom-left square of the patch has a black triangle at the top and a red triangle at the bottom. It has 11 rows, with 10 patches repeated in each row. Students might have difficulty seeing the patch and will probably just identify that pink and blue squares alternate with red and black triangles.

■ For more examples of utilitarian art, see *The National Museum of Women in the Arts Collection.*

📓 Art Journal: Concepts

Have students make a sketch in the Concepts section of their Art Journals to show a pattern.

🔍 Aesthetic Perception

Design Awareness Have students look for patterns in their clothing. Even if no printed patterns or designs are visible on what they are wearing, almost everyone will be able to find a pattern somewhere: ribs at the cuffs of socks, eyelets for shoelaces, or buttons on a coat are patterns.

Developing Visual Literacy Ask students if they have ever seen in someone's home a decorated vase or quilt like those in the lesson. Have students explain how personal examples help expand their understanding of the works of art. NSAE 4.c; 5.c

💻 Web Connection

Learn more about the American Folk Art Museum at **www.folkartmuseum.org.**

Time: About 45 minutes

"How can you create a pattern?" "¿Cómo puedes crear un patrón?"

- Read and discuss Using Pattern on page 170.

Practice

Materials: construction paper cut into geometric shapes

Alternate Materials: wrapped candies

- Distribute the materials and have students follow the directions on page 170.

- Students can make patterns by repeating the same shape or by repeating a sequence of shapes. The shapes do not have to be arranged in a straight line. They can be arranged in a wave, a circle, and so on. After students make their patterns, have them rearrange their patterns or use different shapes to make another pattern.

Creative Expression

NSAE 1.a; 1.c; 1.d; 2.c
Materials: clay, clay tools, clay mats (muslin), paper plates, liquid tempera paints, white paper, brushes, water containers, paper towels, newspaper

Alternate Materials: precut vegetables or fruit (such as green peppers, potatoes, apples, pears) instead of clay stamps

- Distribute the materials and have students follow the directions on page 171.

- Review the Technique Tips on page 226 for information about printmaking.

- See the Activity Tips on page 245 for visual examples of this lesson's activity.

Art Journal: Brainstorming

Have students brainstorm ideas for designs they could use on their stamps. Have students sketch their ideas in the Ideas section of their Art Journals and then choose one to do for the Creative Expression activity.
NSAE 3.b

Using Pattern

Repeating a line, a shape, or a color creates a **pattern.**

Practice

Make a pattern.

1. Use the paper shapes your teacher gives you.

2. Repeat them to make a design that has a pattern.

3. What other patterns could you make?

Differentiated Instruction

Reteach
On the board, draw a sequence of four identical stars above a sequence of a square, a circle, a triangle, and a rectangle. Ask students to identify which sequence is a pattern.

Special Needs
Adaptations: Have actual stamps available for students to feel and discuss before beginning this activity. Some students may have more success cutting shapes out of foam core and gluing them onto a base for stamp printing.

ELL
On the board, write a pattern of a letter or number repeated five times, for instance, A A A A A. To emphasize the repetition, have students say the name of the letter or number as you point to each one in the pattern.

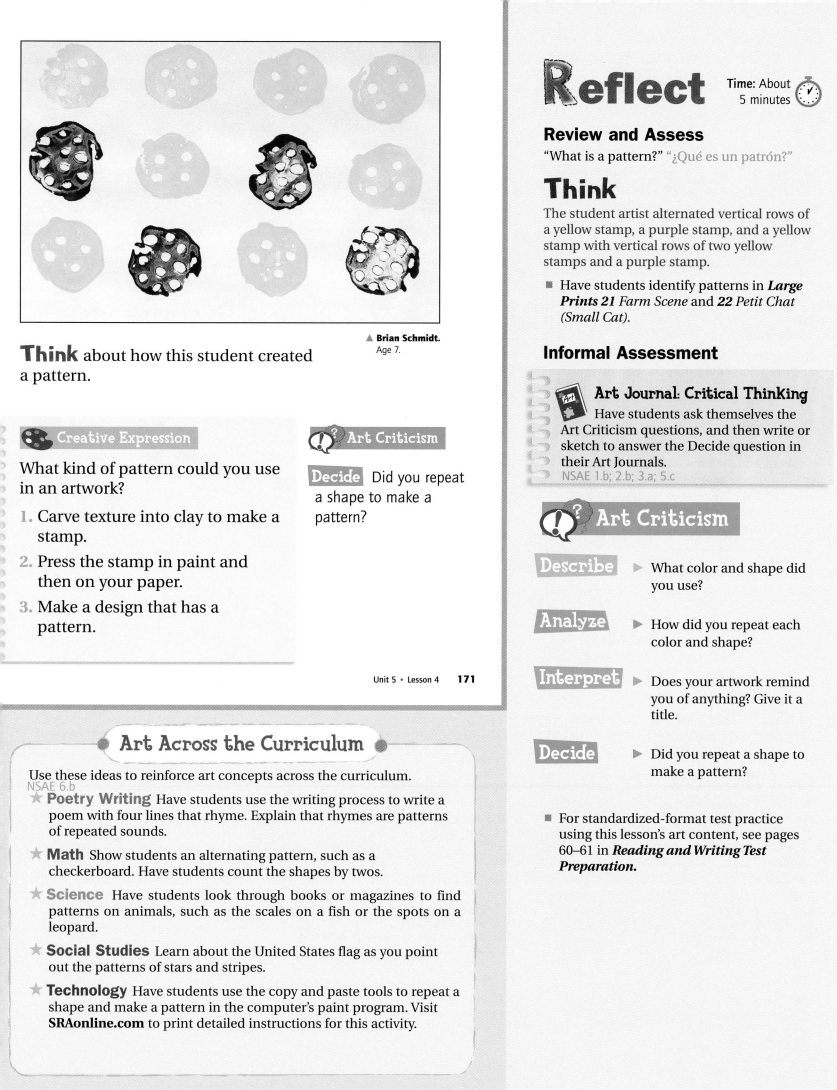

Think about how this student created a pattern.

▲ **Brian Schmidt.**
Age 7.

Creative Expression

What kind of pattern could you use in an artwork?

1. Carve texture into clay to make a stamp.

2. Press the stamp in paint and then on your paper.

3. Make a design that has a pattern.

Art Criticism

Decide Did you repeat a shape to make a pattern?

Unit 5 • Lesson 4 **171**

Art Across the Curriculum

Use these ideas to reinforce art concepts across the curriculum.
NSAE 6.b

★ **Poetry Writing** Have students use the writing process to write a poem with four lines that rhyme. Explain that rhymes are patterns of repeated sounds.

★ **Math** Show students an alternating pattern, such as a checkerboard. Have students count the shapes by twos.

★ **Science** Have students look through books or magazines to find patterns on animals, such as the scales on a fish or the spots on a leopard.

★ **Social Studies** Learn about the United States flag as you point out the patterns of stars and stripes.

★ **Technology** Have students use the copy and paste tools to repeat a shape and make a pattern in the computer's paint program. Visit **SRAonline.com** to print detailed instructions for this activity.

Reflect

Time: About 5 minutes

Review and Assess

"What is a pattern?" "¿Qué es un patrón?"

Think

The student artist alternated vertical rows of a yellow stamp, a purple stamp, and a yellow stamp with vertical rows of two yellow stamps and a purple stamp.

■ Have students identify patterns in *Large Prints 21 Farm Scene* and *22 Petit Chat (Small Cat)*.

Informal Assessment

Art Journal: Critical Thinking

Have students ask themselves the Art Criticism questions, and then write or sketch to answer the Decide question in their Art Journals.
NSAE 1.b; 2.b; 3.a; 5.c

Art Criticism

Describe ▶ What color and shape did you use?

Analyze ▶ How did you repeat each color and shape?

Interpret ▶ Does your artwork remind you of anything? Give it a title.

Decide ▶ Did you repeat a shape to make a pattern?

■ For standardized-format test practice using this lesson's art content, see pages 60–61 in *Reading and Writing Test Preparation.*

Lesson 4 Wrap-Up
Pattern

For the Art Specialist

Time: About 45 minutes

Focus
Use *Transparency 28* to discuss pattern. What kinds of lines, shapes, and colors make the patterns?

Teach
Have students complete the Alternate Activity. What could they do with their patterned paper?

Reflect
Guide students through evaluation of their works of art using the four steps of art criticism. (See pages 28–29 for more about art criticism.) Encourage students to look for examples of pattern in the classroom or on their clothing.

Alternate Activity

Materials:
- 12″ × 18″ manila paper
- crayons or markers

Have students fold a sheet of paper in half three times to create eight sections. Have students use crayons or markers to create a different pattern in each section.

Research in Art Education
Several possible reasons can be cited for the academic achievement associated with student involvement in arts organizations. Arts organizations tend to place high expectations for achievement on participating students; they give students a chance to perform school-related tasks (such as reading, calculating, and planning), and these organizations value and encourage risk-taking ("Living the Arts Through Language and Learning" in *Critical Links,* p. 78).

Assessment
Use the following rubric to evaluate the artwork students make in the Creative Expression activity and to assess students' understanding of pattern.

Have students complete page 63 or 64 in their *Assessment* books.

	Art History and Culture	Aesthetic Perception	Creative Expression	Art Criticism
3 POINTS	The student recognizes that utilitarian objects can be decorative as well as useful.	The student accurately identifies patterns in art.	The student's stamp design clearly shows a pattern.	The student thoughtfully and honestly evaluates his or her own work using the four steps of art criticism.
2 POINTS	The student shows emerging understanding that utilitarian objects can be decorative as well as useful.	The student shows emerging awareness of patterns in art but cannot consistently identify them.	The student attempted to make a stamp design that shows a pattern.	The student attempts to evaluate his or her own work but shows an incomplete understanding of evaluation criteria.
1 POINT	The student shows no understanding that utilitarian objects can be decorative as well as useful.	The student cannot identify patterns in art.	The student's stamp design does not show a pattern.	The student makes no attempt to evaluate his or her own artwork.

Assessment, p. 63

Name _____ Date _____

Lesson 4 UNIT 5

Pattern

For the teacher: Use the following prompt for this activity. Using a crayon, draw a pattern.

Level 1 Unit 5 • Texture, Pattern, and Rhythm **63**

Lesson 5 Overview — Changing Pattern

Lesson 5 introduces motifs, which are the shapes or objects that are repeated within a pattern. A changing pattern has more than one motif.

Objectives

Art History and Culture
To identify and compare art traditions of different cultures
NSAE 4.a; 4.b; 4.c

Creative Expression
To create a weaving with a changing pattern
NSAE 1.a; 1.c; 1.d

Aesthetic Perception
To identify motifs in changing patterns
NSAE 3.a

Art Criticism
To evaluate one's own work using the four steps of art criticism
NSAE 1.b; 2.b; 3.a; 5.c

Vocabulary ⭐ Reading

Review the following vocabulary words with students before beginning the lesson.

motif motivo—a shape or object that is repeated

pattern patrón—the use of shapes, colors, or lines repeated in a planned way

weaving tejer—creating fabric by crisscrossing

See page 179B for additional Spanish vocabulary resources.

Art Journal: Vocabulary
Have students add these words to the Vocabulary section of their Art Journals.

Lesson Materials
- construction paper cut into geometric shapes
- 2" × 18" strips of wallpaper
- rulers
- scissors
- pencils
- 12" × 18" pieces of wallpaper

Alternate Materials:
- construction paper
- markers

Program Resources
- *Reading and Writing Test Prep.*, pp. 62–63
- *Transparency 29*
- *Artist Profiles*, pp. 5, 71
- *Animals Through History Time Line*
- *Assessment*, pp. 65–66
- *Large Prints 21* Farm Scene and *22* Petit Chat (Small Cat)
- *Art Around the World*

Concept Trace
Changing Pattern
Introduced: Level K, Unit 6, Lesson 1
Reinforced: Level 2, Unit 4, Lesson 1

Lesson 5 Arts Integration NSAE 6.a

Theatre
Complete Unit 5, Lesson 5, on pages 98–99 of *Theatre Arts Connections*.

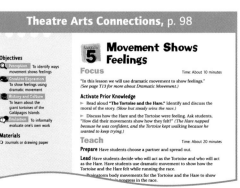

Music
Sing or listen to *Over the Rainbow* by E. Y. Harburg and Harold Arlen. Both the melodic and rhythmic patterns change from the A section to the B section. The held notes on the word *somewhere* are easily identified. The contrasting quick notes in the B section give a feeling of movement.

Movement & Dance
Students explore a variety of simple movement patterns (such as marching, slow motion steps, or jumping), moving to a basic percussive beat or pulse. This can be done traveling across the room in a line or standing in a circle. Build a simple sequence by combining two ideas.

Focus

Time: About 10 minutes

Activate Prior Knowledge

"What is the order of the days of the week?"
"¿Cual es el orden de los días de la semana?"

- Discuss with students that the seven days of the week repeat in the same order, week after week.

Using Literature ⭐ Reading

- Read *Night Shift Daddy* by Eileen Spinelli. Have students look for changing patterns in the illustrations by Melissa Iwai.

Thematic Connection ⭐ Math

- **Numbers/Math:** Discuss changing patterns in math, such as alternating odd and even numbers.

Introduce the Art

Look

"Let's take a close look at the two works of art." "Vamos a mirar detalladamente las dos obras de arte".

Making Connections ⭐ Reading

- Have students make connections to the elements taught in previous units by describing the lines, shapes, colors, and forms of each work of art. *Kente Cloth* has horizontal and vertical lines. These lines come together to make geometric shapes (rectangles). *Kente Cloth* has the primary colors red, yellow, and blue and the secondary color green. *Dance by Numbers* has horizontal, vertical, diagonal, and curved lines. The lines come together to make geometric shapes (circles, triangles, and a square) and free-form shapes (flowers and the bag). *Dance by Numbers* has the primary colors red, blue, and yellow and the secondary colors green and orange. *Dance by Numbers* is a form. The strap creates an opening for space to go through.

🏺 Art History and Culture

Share with students the information about kente cloths from the Art History and Culture section on this page.
NSAE 4.a; 4.b; 4.c

💻 **Web Connection**

Visit **www.virtualexplorers.org/ghana/kente.htm** to learn more about kente cloth and the people of Ghana.

Lesson 5 # Changing Pattern

◀ **Artist Unknown.**
(Ashanti Peoples, Ghana).
Kente Cloth.
Museum of International Folk Art, Santa Fe, New Mexico.

Look at the works of art on these pages. They have patterns.

🏺 Art History and Culture

The Ashanti people are well known for their tradition of weaving kente cloths. There are many kente patterns. Each one has its own name.

🏺 Art History and Culture

The unknown artist who created this kente cloth was one of the Ashanti people, who live principally in central Ghana on the African continent. They are noted artisans, especially for their cotton weaving, and their traditional kente cloth is known around the world. The tradition of weaving and wearing kente cloth dates back to the twelfth century and continues today. The word *kente* means "basket" and refers to the woven pattern on the cloth, which resembles the woven design of a basket. There are many kente designs, and most have stripes and geometric shapes. The kente cloth is worn for special occasions.

See pages 16–21 and 24–25 for more about subject matter and art history.

Artist Profiles, p. 71

◀ Artist Profile ▷

Kente Cloth

Kente cloths are made by the western African Ashanti people of Ghana and the Ewe peoples of Ghana and Togo. The weavers who make kente cloth are traditionally male. The art of weaving kente is passed down from generation to generation.

▲ **Artist unknown.** (Ashanti Peoples, Ghana).

Study the patterns in each work of art.

▶ What lines, shapes, or colors are repeated?

▶ Do they change within each pattern?

◀ **Martha Berry.** (American). *Dance by Numbers Bandolier Bag.* 2000.
Wool, cotton cloth, cotton binding, Czech glass seed beads, yarn, and brass trade beads. 36 × 16 × ½ inches (91.44 × 40.64 × 1.27 cm). Private Collection.

Aesthetic Perception

Design Awareness What things in your home or school have changing patterns?

Art History and Culture

Martha Berry

Martha Berry (märˊ thə bârˊ rē) (1948–   ) was born in Oklahoma to parents of Cherokee heritage. She researches beadwork done by Native Americans and creates art based on their styles. Berry often makes bandolier bags, which were popularized during the nineteenth and twentieth centuries by Native American tribes that lived in the Great Lakes area of the United States. Bandolier bags were used during formal occasions or special ceremonies. They were made exclusively by women to be worn by men. They were worn over the shoulder and used to hold personal items like a purse is used today.

See pages 16–21 and 24–25 for more about subject matter and art history.

Artist Profiles, p. 5

Artist Profile

Martha Berry
b. 1948

Cherokee beadwork artist Martha Berry (märˊ thə bârˊ rē) was born and raised in Oklahoma by parents of Cherokee, English, and Scotch-Irish descent. At the age of five, her mother and grandmother taught her how to sew, and by the time she was nine she was making her own clothes. When Berry was 20, she worked as a seamstress for a touring ice show. She did not explore her Cherokee heritage until she was in her forties. In only six years Berry became an award-winning beadwork artist. She has displayed her work in many exhibitions and museums.

Study

▶ In *Kente Cloth* the stripes are repeated. In *Dance by Numbers* the flowers and *X*s repeat.

▶ Sometimes the stripes in *Kente Cloth* are horizontal, and sometimes they are vertical. The stripes are different colors. In *Dance by Numbers*, the colors of the *X*s alternate.

■ For more examples of art from Africa, see the *Art Around the World Collection.*

Art Journal: Concepts
Have students sketch an example of a changing pattern in the Concepts section of their Art Journals.

Aesthetic Perception

Design Awareness Changing patterns are often used for decoration. Students may have seen a changing pattern on bulletin board borders, wrapping paper, wallpaper, book covers, furniture, bedding, or clothing.

Developing Visual Literacy Discuss students' personal examples that further their understanding of the lesson's works of art. *Kente Cloth* and *Dance by Numbers* were items of importance that were worn on special occasions. Do students have any similar items that they wear on special occasions?

Web Connection
Visit **www.berrybeadwork.com** for more information about bandolier bags by Martha Berry.

Teach

Time: About 45 minutes

"Let's create a changing pattern." *"Vamos a crear un patrón cambiante".*

■ Read and discuss Using Changing Pattern on page 174.

Practice

Materials: construction paper cut into geometric shapes

Alternate Materials: patterns drawn on construction paper with markers

■ Distribute the materials and have students follow the directions on page 174.

■ Students should repeat one motif to create a regular pattern, then say the name of the motif as they point to each shape (for instance, "square, square, square, square"). Then students should create a changing pattern and name the motif as they point to each shape (for instance, "square, circle, square, circle"). Students should notice the difference between a regular pattern and a changing pattern.

Creative Expression

NSAE 1.a; 1.c; 1.d

Materials: 2" × 18" strips of wallpaper, rulers, scissors, pencils, 12" × 18" pieces of wallpaper

Alternate Materials: construction paper

■ Distribute the materials and have students follow the directions on page 175.

■ Review the Technique Tips on page 225 for information about weaving.

■ See the Activity Tips on page 246 for visual examples of this lesson's activity.

Art Journal: Brainstorming

Have students make sketches in their Art Journals to plan the weavings they will make in the Creative Expression activity.

Using Changing Patterns

A **motif** is the line, shape, or color that is repeated in a pattern. If you use more than one motif, you have a changing pattern.

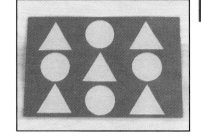

Practice

Use the paper shapes to make patterns.

1. Repeat one motif to make a regular pattern.

2. Say the name of the motif as you point to each shape.

3. Choose two motifs. Make a changing pattern. Say the name of the motif as you point to each one.

Differentiated Instruction

Reteach
On the board, draw a sequence of four identical stars above a sequence of alternating identical stars and moons. Have students identify the changing pattern.

Special Needs
Adaptations: Students who have difficulty understanding the process of weaving may benefit from rhythmically repeating the steps aloud: "Over, under, over, under."

ELL Tips
On the board, write a pattern of letters or numbers repeated, for instance, A B A B A B. To emphasize the changing pattern, have students say the name of the letter or number as you point to each one.

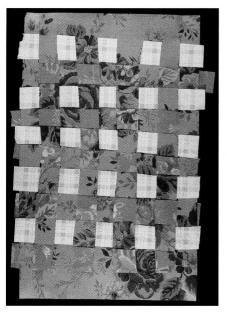

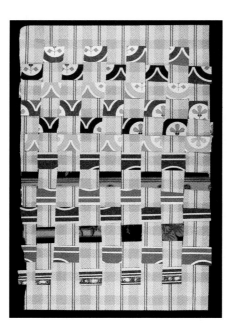

▲ Brianna Kittle. Age 6.

▲ Daniel Tomlinson. Age 6.

Think about how these students created changing patterns.

Creative Expression

How can you **weave** a pattern?

1. Make a paper loom. Your teacher will show you how.

2. Cut strips of paper.

3. Weave the strips over and under the loom.

Art Criticism

Describe What colors did you use for your weaving?

Reflect   Time: About 5 minutes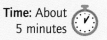

Review and Assess

"What is a motif?" "¿Qué es un motivo?"

Think

The students created changing patterns by weaving wallpaper.

■ Have students look for changing patterns in *Large Prints 21 Farm Scene* and *22 Petit Chat (Small Cat).*

Informal Assessment

Art Journal: Critical Thinking
Have students ask themselves the Art Criticism questions, and then write or sketch the answer to the Describe question in their Art Journals.
NSAE 1.b; 2.b; 3.a; 5.c

Art Criticism

Describe ▶ What colors did you use for your weaving?

Analyze ▶ What are the motifs in your pattern?

Interpret ▶ Is your pattern interesting?

Decide ▶ If you made a weaving again, what would you do differently?

■ For standardized-format test practice using this lesson's art content, see pages 62–63 in *Reading and Writing Test Preparation.*

● **Art Across the Curriculum** ●

Use these ideas to reinforce art concepts across the curriculum.
NSAE 6.b

★ **Expository Writing** Have students use the writing process to write an explanation of how they made their weavings.

★ **Math** Provide students with a list of the whole numbers 1–10. Have students identify each number as odd or even and notice the changing pattern.

★ **Science** Explain that the cycle of day and night is a changing pattern. Have students identify other changing patterns found in nature.

★ **Social Studies** Have students use a calendar to explain the changing pattern of days of the week.

★ **Technology** Have students use the computer's word processing program to key a changing pattern of letters and spaces. Visit **SRAonline.com** to print detailed instructions for this activity.

Changing Pattern

Extra! For the Art Specialist

Time: About 45 minutes

Focus

Have students choose a line, shape, or color in one of the works of art in *Transparency 29,* and point out where it is repeated. What else is repeated in the work of art?

Teach

Have students complete the Alternate Activity. How did they decide what motifs to repeat in their patterns? Do students' bead necklaces remind them of a real necklace they have seen?

Reflect

Guide students through evaluation of their works of art using the four steps of art criticism. (See pages 28–29 for more about art criticism.) Have students look for examples of changing patterns in nature or in the classroom.

Alternate Activity

Materials:
- 9" × 12" construction paper
- 6" × 9" construction paper
- scissors
- glue or glue sticks
- pencils

1. Tell students they are going to design a bead necklace by cutting out different shapes and sizes of beads from paper. Have students select a sheet of 9" × 12" construction paper to use for the background. Students will draw a circle, oval, or teardrop shape on their paper as the shape of the necklace.

2. Show students how to fold a sheet of 6" × 9" construction paper in half two times and cut out a bead shape to make four identical beads. Students can cut out as many beads as needed in groups of four.

3. Have students glue their beads to the necklace shape to create a repeated pattern.

Research in Art Education

It has been proven that "at the level of neuro-function, learning experiences unequivocally impact future learning experiences." Although more research is still needed on exactly how the reorganization of neural pathways and receptors impacts a student's transfer of skills from the arts to reading and math, it is reasonable to assume that experiences with the arts may "enhance performance in related skills" ("The Arts and the Transfer of Learning" in *Critical Links,* p. 152).

Assessment

Use the following rubric to evaluate the artwork students make in the Creative Expression activity and to assess students' understanding of changing patterns.

Have students complete page 65 or 66 in their *Assessment* books.

	Art History and Culture	Aesthetic Perception	Creative Expression	Art Criticism
3 POINTS	The student can identify and compare art traditions of different cultures.	The student accurately identifies motifs in changing patterns.	The student's weaving clearly illustrates changing patterns.	The student thoughtfully and honestly evaluates his or her own work using the four steps of art criticism.
2 POINTS	The student's identification or comparison is weak or incomplete.	The student shows emerging awareness of motifs but cannot consistently identify them in changing patterns.	The student's weaving shows some awareness of changing patterns.	The student attempts to evaluate his or her own work but shows an incomplete understanding of evaluation criteria.
1 POINT	The student cannot identify or compare art traditions of different cultures.	The student cannot identify motifs in changing patterns.	The student's weaving shows no understanding of changing patterns.	The student makes no attempt to evaluate his or her own artwork.

Assessment, p. 65

Name _____ Date _____ Lesson 5 UNIT 5

Changing Pattern

1.

2.

For the teacher: Use the following prompts for this activity.
1. In box 1, use a crayon to draw a changing pattern using two different motifs.
2. In box 2, draw a changing pattern using three different motifs.

Level 1 Unit 5 · Texture, Pattern, and Rhythm **65**

Lesson 6 · Rhythm Overview

Lesson 6 introduces rhythm, which is a feeling of movement in a work of art. Artists create rhythm by repeating objects or elements. The viewer's eyes follow the repeated motifs through the artwork.

Objectives

Art History and Culture

To identify and compare the culture of each artist
NSAE 4.a; 4.b; 4.c

Creative Expression

To create an artwork with rhythm
NSAE 1.a; 1.c; 1.d; 2.c

Aesthetic Perception

To identify repeated motifs in art and describe the rhythm they create
NSAE 3.a

Art Criticism

To evaluate one's own artwork using the four steps of art criticism
NSAE 1.b; 2.b; 3.a; 5.c

Vocabulary ⭐ Reading

Review the following vocabulary words with students before beginning the lesson.

motif motivo—a shape or object that is repeated

rhythm ritmo—the repetition of motifs to create a feeling of movement

See page 179B for additional Spanish vocabulary resources.

Art Journal: Vocabulary

Have students add these words to the Vocabulary section of their Art Journals.

Lesson Materials

- oil pastels
- colored paper

Alternate Materials:

- markers

Program Resources

- *Reading and Writing Test Prep.,* pp. 64–65
- *Transparency 30*
- *Flash Card 10*
- *Artist Profiles,* pp. 19, 55
- *Animals Through History Time Line*
- *Assessment,* pp. 67–68
- *Large Prints 21 Farm Scene* and *22 Petit Chat (Small Cat)*
- *The National Museum of Women in the Arts Collection*

Concept Trace
Rhythm
Introduced: Level K, Unit 6, Lesson 2
Reinforced: Level 2, Unit 4, Lesson 3

Lesson 6 Arts Integration NSAE 6.a

Theatre

Complete Unit 5, Lesson 6, on pages 100–105 of *Theatre Arts Connections.*

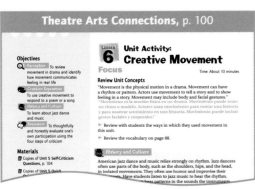

Music

Listen to *In the Hall of the Mountain King* from *Peer Gynt Suite No. 1, Op 46* by Edvard Grieg. Clap the main rhythm pattern. Notice how there is a feeling of anticipation in the second half. What kind of mood is created by the repeated rhythm pattern in combination with the dynamics and tempo?

Movement & Dance

Students sit in a circle with the teacher in the middle. The teacher claps out a simple rhythm that the students repeat by clapping it back (call and response). Once this idea has been explored, add in body percussion.

Focus

Time: About 10 minutes

Activate Prior Knowledge

"Have you ever seen a parade?" *"¿Alguna vez han visto un desfile?"*

■ Discuss students' responses. Ask students to name things that are included in a parade. Discuss reasons a community might have a parade.

Using Literature ⭐ Reading

■ Read *One Afternoon* by Yumi Heo. The repeated motifs in the illustrations of city life create rhythm.

Thematic Connection ⭐ Social Studies

■ **Neighborhoods/Communities:** Discuss motifs that are repeated throughout neighborhoods. Buildings, people, traffic, and landscapes create rhythm.

Introduce the Art
Look

"Let's take a close look at the two works of art." *"Vamos a mirar detalladamente las dos obras de arte".*

Adjectives and Adverbs ⭐ Language Arts

■ Ask students to describe the subject matter of each artwork. List on a chart the adjectives and adverbs students use.

🏺 Art History and Culture

Explain to students that both paintings are *narrative*, meaning they represent a story. *Coyote Koshare* depicts characters from legends in Harry Fonseca's culture. Antonio Ruiz was Mexican, and the children in *School Children on Parade* carry Mexican flags. Ruiz's painting may depict an event he saw in his culture. NSAE 3.a; 4.c; 5.a; 5.b

💻 Web Connection

Examples of kachina dolls can be found at the Adobe Gallery's Web site, **www.adobegallery.com.**

176 UNIT 5 • Texture, Pattern, and Rhythm

▲ **Harry Fonseca.** (American). *Coyote Koshare.* 1993.
Mixed media on canvas. 24 × 30 inches (60.96 × 76.2 cm.). Courtesy of Harry Fonseca.

Look at the works of art on these pages. The artists repeated motifs.

🏺 Art History and Culture

These works of art are *narrative* paintings. Narrative paintings tell a story.

🏺 Art History and Culture

Harry Fonseca NSAE 4.a; 4.b; 4.c

Harry Fonseca (har´ ē fōn´ sā´ kə) (1946–) depicts traditional Native American stories reset in modern life. Though they may wear jeans and tennis shoes, the coyotes that appear in many of Fonseca's works are consistent with traditional legends. The black and white stripes on Fonseca's coyotes in *Coyote Koshare* mimic the Native American koshare kachina doll. Kachina dolls portray kachina dancers, who impersonate spirits during ceremonial dances. The koshare kachinas are sacred clowns. Their actions are amusing yet inappropriate.

See pages 16–21 and 24–25 for more about subject matter and art history.

Artist Profiles, p. 19

● Artist Profile ●
Harry Fonseca
b. 1946

Harry Fonseca (har´ ē fōn´ sā´ kə) was born in California to parents of Maidu, Hawaiian, and Portuguese heritage. The Maidu tribe is a gatherer tribe of central California, and Harry grew up appreciating the culture's use of rich color and design. He also grew up with few books and little exposure to art, but he studied art in college in Sacramento. Fonseca's parents did not understand why he chose to pursue painting and thought it impractical, but he continued to successfully explore his own independent style and method despite the skepticism of others.

Study the works of art.

▶ What motifs are repeated?

▲ **Antonio Ruiz.** (Mexican).
School Children on Parade.
1936.
Oil on canvas. $9\frac{1}{2} \times 13\frac{1}{4}$ inches (24.13 × 33.66 cm.). The Metropolitan Museum of Art, New York, New York.

Aesthetic Perception

Seeing Like an Artist Have you seen any repeated motifs in nature?

Art History and Culture

Antonio Ruiz

Antonio Ruiz (an tōn´ yō rōō ēs´) (1897–1964) was born in Mexico City, Mexico. After studying art in Mexico, he moved to Hollywood, California, where he designed movie sets. He later returned to Mexico and worked with children's theatre. Ruiz painted slowly and completed only a few paintings a year. Because he spent so much time on his paintings he felt a strong attachment to them and rarely sold them. Ruiz's artwork is narrative—his paintings tell a story.

See pages 16–21 and 24–25 for more about subject matter and art history.

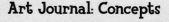

Artist Profiles, p. 55

Artist Profile
Antonio Ruiz
1897–1964
Antonio Ruiz (an tōn´ yō rōō ēs´) was born in Mexico City. He grew up in an educated family that also appreciated the arts. His grandfather was a painter, his mother a concert pianist, and his father a physician. As a child, Ruiz loved to play with construction sets. After studying art in Mexico, he moved to California, where he designed movie sets. After two years he returned to Mexico to paint and to direct children's theatre. In time, he became the director of Mexico's School of Painting and Sculpture. Ruiz also taught scenery design at the University of Mexico.

Study

▶ The motifs repeated in *Coyote Koshare* are the clouds, the stripes of the rainbow, the coyotes, the stripes on the coyotes, the coyotes' eyes, the shoes, the watermelon shapes, and the seeds in the watermelons. The motifs repeated in *School Children on Parade* are the children, the stripes on the flags, the dogs, the people in the crowd, the wooden slats of the planters, and the arches of the building.

■ For more examples of narrative art, see *The National Museum of Women in the Arts Collection.*

Art Journal: Concepts

Have students make a sketch of a repeated motif in the Concepts section of their Art Journals. Have students describe how the viewer's eyes follow the motif through their sketch.

Aesthetic Perception

Seeing Like an Artist Have students think of examples of repeated motifs in nature, such as legs on a spider, petals on a flower, or leaves on a tree. Ask students to describe how their eyes move to follow the motif. For instance, the students' eyes would follow the petals of a daisy from one to the next in a circle around the flower. If possible, bring photos to show examples of rhythm in nature.

Developing Visual Literacy Ask students what they think the mood of each artwork is. Discuss details included by the artists that might reveal the mood, such as the dreamlike background of *Coyote Koshare* or the somber looks on the children's faces in *School Children on Parade.*
NSAE 2.b; 3.a

Web Connection
Visit the Web site of The Metropolitan Museum of Art, **www.metmuseum.org.**

each

Time: About 30 minutes

"How do artists make your eyes move around a picture?" *"¿Qué hacen los artistas para que tu vista se mueva alrededor de una pintura?"*

- Read and discuss Using Rhythm on page 178.

Practice

Materials: None

- Have students follow the directions on page 178.
- Make sure students are repeating the same steps. Emphasize that rhythm is created by repetition.

Creative Expression

NSAE 1.a; 1.c; 1.d; 2.c
Materials: oil pastels, colored paper

Alternate Materials: markers

- Distribute the materials and have students follow the directions on page 179.
- Review the Technique Tips on page 216 for information about using oil pastels.
- See the Activity Tips on page 246 for visual examples of this lesson's activity.

 Art Journal: Brainstorming
Have students brainstorm ideas for things they would like to show in a parade. Then have them select the motifs they will repeat in the Creative Expression activity.

Using Rhythm

Rhythm is a feeling of movement. Artists create rhythm by repeating motifs. Your eyes move along the artwork. They follow the things that are repeated.

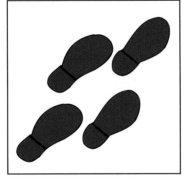

Practice

Create rhythm by walking.

1. Plan a way you could walk in a parade. You could march with a steady beat. Or, you could take a step and then rest.

2. Perform your walk for your classmates. Repeating your steps creates rhythm.

178 Unit 5 • Lesson 6

Differentiated Instruction

Reteach
Use *Flash Card 10.* Discuss with students how their eyes follow the repeated motifs across the card.

Special Needs
Adaptations: Activate students' prior knowledge of motif by reviewing some of the work produced from previous lessons.

ELL Tips
Review directional words, such as *right* and *left,* with students to help them describe the direction of each work's visual movement.

▲ **Steven Reese.** Age 6.
▲ **Taylor Wallace.** Age 7.

Think about how these students created rhythm.

How could you create rhythm in a picture of a parade?

1. Choose a parade theme. Think about what to include. Make yourself an important part of the parade.

2. Draw your parade. Repeat a motif to create rhythm.

Analyze How do your eyes move through your picture?

Art Across the Curriculum

Use these ideas to reinforce art concepts across the curriculum.
NSAE 6.b

★ **Persuasive Writing** Have students write the sentences they would use to make a commercial advertising the parade in the Creative Expression activities.

★ **Math** Have students practice counting by choosing one of the motifs in *Coyote Koshare* or *School Children on Parade* and counting the number of times it appears.

★ **Science** Have students look for rhythm in photographs of plants or animals in their science books.

★ **Social Studies** Have students look for examples of rhythm in paintings or photographs of historical events.

★ **Technology** Have students create a motif using the computer's paint program, and then copy and paste the motif to create a design with rhythm. Visit **SRAonline.com** to print detailed instructions for this activity.

Time: About 5 minutes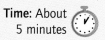

Review and Assess

"What is rhythm?" "¿Qué es el ritmo?"

Think

The students created rhythm by repeating the flags and people. The clothing has repeated stripes.

■ Have students identify how artists created rhythm in **Large Prints 21** *Farm Scene* and **22** *Petit Chat (Small Cat)*.

Informal Assessment

Art Journal: Critical Thinking
Have students ask themselves the Art Criticism questions and then write or sketch in their Art Journals to answer the Analyze question.
NSAE 1.b; 2.b; 3.a; 5.c

Describe ▶ What did you include in your parade?

Analyze ▶ How do your eyes move through your picture?

Interpret ▶ What kind of parade did you show? What details did you include to show this?

Decide ▶ If you made your drawing again, how could you add more rhythm?

■ For standardized-format test practice using this lesson's art content, see pages 64–65 in **Reading and Writing Test Preparation.**

Lesson 6 Wrap-Up

Rhythm

Focus

Using *Transparency 30,* discuss with students how their eyes move around the picture. What motifs did each artist repeat to create this movement?

Teach

Have students brainstorm ideas for ways to create rhythm in the Alternate Activity in their Art Journals. Then have students complete the Alternate Activity.

Reflect

Guide students through evaluation of their works of art using the four steps of art criticism. (See pages 28–29 for more about art criticism.)

Alternate Activity

Materials:
- tempera paint
- brushes
- water containers
- 12″ × 18″ white or manila paper
- pencils
- waxed paper
- masking tape

1. Tell students to choose an event or scene that would have a repeated motif, such as flags blowing in the wind or dolphins jumping out of the water. Tape waxed paper to the table, and have students paint their scene on the waxed paper. Make sure students repeat their motif to create rhythm.

2. Carefully place the paper over the painting and rub the back. Slowly peel back the paper and lay the monoprint flat to dry.

Research in Art Education

Research has shown that "learning happens best when kids have fun, and the arts are fun for kids." It is important to remember that although the arts can act "as catalysts for learning other subject areas across the curriculum," they are also valuable in their own right ("Arts Literacy for Business" in *The Vision for Arts Education in the Twenty-first Century*).

Assessment

Use the following rubric to evaluate the artwork students make in the Creative Expression activity and to assess students' understanding of rhythm.

Have students complete page 67 or 68 in their *Assessment* books.

	Art History and Culture	Aesthetic Perception	Creative Expression	Art Criticism
3 POINTS	The student can identify and compare the culture of each artist.	The student accurately identifies the repeated motifs in each artwork and the rhythm they create.	The student's artwork clearly shows rhythm.	The student thoughtfully and honestly evaluates his or her own work using the four steps of art criticism.
2 POINTS	The student's identification or comparison is weak or incomplete.	The student shows emerging awareness of repeated motifs and rhythm but cannot consistently identify them.	The student's artwork shows some awareness of rhythm.	The student attempts to evaluate his or her own work but shows an incomplete understanding of evaluation criteria.
1 POINT	The student cannot identify or compare the culture of each artist.	The student cannot identify repeated motifs or rhythm.	The student's artwork shows no understanding of rhythm.	The student makes no attempt to evaluate his or her own artwork.

Assessment, p. 67

Name _____ Date _____

Lesson **6** UNIT 5

Rhythm

For the teacher: Use the following prompt for this activity.
Using crayons, draw a picture of your neighborhood. Repeat a motif to create rhythm in your picture.

Level 1   Unit 5 • Texture, Pattern, and Rhythm   **67**

carving—cutting away of a hard material to create a three-dimensional work of art **tallar** o **esculpir**—cortar un material duro para crear una obra de arte tridimensional

collage—objects glued onto paper **collage**—objetos pegados a papel

motif—a shape or object that is repeated **motivo**—una figura u objeto que se repite

pattern—the use of shapes, colors, or lines repeated in a planned way **patrón**—el uso de figuras, colores o líneas que se repiten de una manera planificada

real texture—texture you can feel **textura real**—textura que puedes palpar

rhythm—the repetition of motifs to create a feeling of movement **ritmo**—la repetición de motivos para crear una sensación de movimiento

visual texture—the way something looks like it might feel if you could touch it **textura visual**—la manera en que algo pareciera sentirse si se tocara

weaving—creating fabric by crisscrossing **tejer**—crear una tela entretejiendo

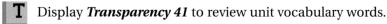

Vocabulary Practice

T Display *Transparency 41* to review unit vocabulary words.

Examples ⭐ Vocabulary

Show students a collage and ask them to name the vocabulary word that identifies your example. Repeat the process for other unit vocabulary words.

Definitions: Brief Definitions ⭐
Vocabulary

Read the definition of each unit vocabulary word, and have students identify the term you are defining.

Categorizing/Classifying ⭐ Vocabulary

Read each vocabulary word, and have students identify whether it is associated with texture or rhythm.

Wrapping Up Unit 5

Texture, Pattern, and Rhythm

Art Criticism

Critical Thinking Art criticism is an organized system for looking at and talking about art. You can criticize art without being an expert. The purpose of art criticism is to get the viewer involved in a perception process that delays judgment until all aspects of the artwork have been studied.

■ See pages 28–29 for more about art criticism.

Describe

■ During this step students will collect information about the subject of the work.

▶ Ask students to describe the people in *Hmong Story Cloth.* Possible answers: There are six women with top-knot hairdos, seven men, and one baby being carried on one woman's back. They all wear black long-sleeved shirts and long pants. The sleeves have blue decorations at the wrists. The women wear red skirts with green and yellow aprons. Their shoes are white. Six of the men wear small black hats with red round shapes on top and red sashes. Their shoes are blue. One woman carries a tea kettle in her hand. Two other women carry baskets on their backs. Two men carry backpacks. The four people in the center of the picture are swimming in a river. They seem to have tubes around their waists to keep them afloat. The tubes are different colors. One man is wearing a black uniform with a black military style hat and a brown belt that may have a holster on it.

▲ **Artist Unknown.** (Hmong Peoples, Asia). *Hmong Story Cloth.* c. 1988.

Cotton. 18 × 18 inches (45.72 × 45.72 cm.). Private Collection.

180 Unit 5

Art History and Culture

The Hmong have endured a history of persecution and forced relocation. They lived in China for thousands of years, but their villages were invaded and the Hmong were forced to flee to Laos. During the Vietnam War, the Hmong were allies of the United States. When the United States withdrew from Vietnam and Laos after the war, the Hmong were in danger, so they swam across the Mekong River to Thailand. From there, many Hmong refugees went to the United States in search of freedom. Until the late 1950s, the Hmong people did not have a written language, so they used art (such as story cloths) to record and preserve their history and culture.

See pages 16–21 and 24–25 for more about subject matter and art history.

Artist Profiles, p. 70

Artist Profile

Hmong Story Cloth

This story cloth was made by an unknown artist of the Hmong people of eastern Asia. Ancestors of the Hmong lived along the banks of the Yellow River in China more than 4,000 years ago. Since that time the Hmong have had a difficult history of persecution, forced relocation, and migration into and out of refugee camps. The Hmong people spent many years working to establish themselves in Laos, Thailand, Vietnam, and Cambodia. Always a minority group wherever they went, they farmed the land and served in the armies of their host countries. In 1976, Hmong families began moving to the United States in search of safe places to live and work.

⟨?⟩ Art Criticism Critical Thinking

Describe

▶ Describe the people you see in this picture.

Analyze

▶ Where do you see rough and smooth textures?

Interpret

▶ What is happening in this picture? Tell the story of these people.

Decide

▶ Does this picture tell an interesting story?

🔍 Aesthetic Perception

Critical Thinking Have students look for illustrations in a storybook or textbook that describe people's history or culture. How do the illustrations compare with *Hmong Story Cloth?*

Describe
▶ List and describe everything you see in the illustrations.

Analyze
▶ Where do you see texture, pattern, and rhythm in the illustrations?

Interpret
▶ What story is the artist trying to tell?

Decide
▶ Do you think the artwork shows what the artist was trying to say?

Analyze

▪ Students think about how the artist has used the elements and principles of art.

▶ Discuss with students how this artwork has texture. Possible answers: The raised embroidery threads of the river and trees look rough. The background fabric and the blue border appear to be smooth.

▶ Discuss with students how this work has pattern. The repeated triangles on the women's skirts and the lines in the river are regular patterns.

▶ Discuss with students how this work has rhythm. Possible answers: The people walking are a repeated motif that draws the viewer's eye from right to left. The swimmers are a repeated motif that draws the viewer's eye from right to left.

Interpret

▪ Students use the clues they discovered during their analysis to find the message the artist is trying to show.

▶ Discuss with students what they think is happening in the artwork. Answers will vary. Some students may realize that the people are walking a long way and swimming in a river to escape from some place.

▶ Discuss with students where they think the action is taking place. Answers will vary. Some will recognize that the trees and river represent the jungle, the building represents the refugee camp, and the man at the bottom seems to be a soldier receiving the travelers.

Decide

▪ Students use the information they have gathered to decide whether this is a successful work of art.

▶ Discuss with students whether they feel this picture tells an interesting story. Answers will vary. Most will probably agree that the story is interesting and that this work of art has a strong message.

📔 Art Journal: Writing
Have students write or sketch answers to the Aesthetic Perception questions in their Art Journals.

"Artists use visual texture to show what something would feel like if you could touch it. They repeat objects to create pattern and rhythm in their work." "Los artistas usan textura visual para mostrar cómo se sentiría algo si se tocara. Ellos repiten objetos para crear patrón y ritmo en sus obras".

 T Review unit vocabulary with students using *Transparency 41.*

 Art Journal: Writing
Have students answer the questions on page 182 in their Art Journals or on a separate sheet of paper. Answers: 1. A, 2. B, 3. B

T For further assessment, have students complete the unit test on *Transparency 47.*

LEARNING ABOUT MUSEUMS

Kimbell Art Museum

► The Kimbell Art Museum opened in 1972 with funds provided by the Kimbell Art Foundation. The founders, Kay and Velma Fuller Kimbell, bequeathed their entire personal fortune to the foundation in order to establish and maintain a first-rate public art museum in Fort Worth, Texas.

"Art does not reproduce the visible; rather, it makes visible."

--Paul Klee
(1879-1940), artist

Show What You Know

Write your answers on a sheet of paper.

1 Which of these has smooth texture?

A.   B.   C.

2 Which of these does not have raised texture?

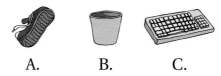

A.   B.   C.

3 Which of these is a changing pattern?

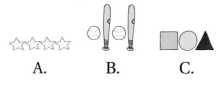

A.   B.   C.

Unit Assessment Options

🔍 Aesthetic Perception

Practice Have students look for texture, pattern, and rhythm in the classroom.

🎨 Creative Expression

Student Portfolio Have students review all the artwork they have created during this unit and select the pieces they wish to keep in their portfolios. Have students share their portfolios with classmates and discuss each other's use of texture, pattern, and rhythm.

❗ Art Criticism

Activity Select another artwork from this unit. Discuss it with students using the four steps of art criticism. (See pages 28–29 for more about Art Criticism.)

 **LET'S VISIT A MUSEUM**

Kimbell Art Museum

This museum is in Fort Worth, Texas. Many paintings and sculptures are exhibited there. The museum also has art workshops for children.

Texture, Pattern, and Rhythm in Dance

The Nutcracker is a traditional holiday ballet. Colorful, textured dolls and flowers come to life and dance. The music has rhythm.

What to Do Create a mechanical doll dance with a partner.

1. One person is the doll. The other person "winds up" the doll with an imaginary key. Then the person turns on the doll's switch.

2. The doll dances in a mechanical way. The other person turns off the doll's switch. The doll freezes.

3. Switch roles. Perform for the class.

▲ The Joffrey Ballet of Chicago. *The Nutcracker*, "Waltz of the Flowers" excerpt and "The Story of the Nutcracker."

 Art Criticism

 **Analyze** What kind of rhythm made the doll seem mechanical?

Unit 5   **183**

 **Art History and Culture**

The Joffrey Ballet of Chicago

Ballet began in the French court of King Louis XIV. It is a classic, academic dance form that is based on five positions of the feet and uses French terminology. The Joffrey Ballet of Chicago conveys a specifically American energy and style. Its purpose is to revive major historical ballets and present new choreography that draws from American life. "The Nutcracker" was first performed in 1892 in St. Petersburg, Russia. The Joffrey Ballet production of "The Nutcracker" was conceived by Gerald Arpino.

Texture, Pattern, and Rhythm in Dance

NSAE 6.a

Objective: To create a mechanical doll dance with a partner.

Materials: *The Nutcracker,* "Waltz of the Flowers" excerpt and "The Story of the Nutcracker" performed by The Joffrey Ballet of Chicago. Running time: 5:12.

Focus

Time: About 5 minutes

■ Discuss the information on page 183.

 **Art History and Culture**

■ Share with students the Art History and Culture information about ballet.

Teach

Time: About 20 minutes

 Aesthetic Perception

■ Have students ever seen a wind-up toy? What kind of movements did it have? Have students discuss the difference between mechanical and natural movements.

Creative Expression

■ Have students follow the directions on page 183 to create their dance.

■ **Informal Assessment** Comment positively on students' performances and teamwork.

Reflect

Time: About 5 minutes

Art Criticism

■ Have students answer the four art criticism question.

Describe What did each partner do to make the mechanical doll dance believable?

Analyze What kind of rhythm made the doll seem mechanical?

Interpret What did it feel like to be the doll? What did it feel like to control the doll?

Decide Were you and your partner successful in performing the mechanical doll dance?

	Lesson Title	Suggested Pacing	Creative Expression Activity
Lesson 1	**Balance**	55 minutes	Create a transfer-print design that has balance.
Lesson 2	**Balance in Masks**	70 minutes	Create a mixed-media face form that has balance.
Lesson 3	**Emphasis in Paintings**	60 minutes	Create a landscape with emphasis.
Lesson 4	**Emphasis in Forms**	70 minutes	Create a cut-paper slipper that has emphasis.
Lesson 5	**Unity with Words and Symbols**	60 minutes	Create a letter creature with unity.
Lesson 6	**Unity in Sculpture**	70 minutes	Create a unified sculpture.
▲RT S▪U RC▪ ARTSOURCE	**Balance, Emphasis, and Unity in Stories**	35 minutes	Create a story with a group.

Materials	Program Resources	Fine Art Resources	Literature Resources
12" × 18" white paper, oil pastels, craft sticks or spoons	*Reading and Writing Test Preparation*, pp. 66–67 *Flash Cards*, 12 and 20 *Assessment*, pp. 69–70 *Home and After-School Connections*	*Transparency*, 31 *Artist Profiles*, pp. 65, 74 *Large Prints*, 23 and 24 *Women in the Arts Collection*	*This is Baseball* by Margaret Blackstone
small brown paper lunch sacks, newspaper, paper towel tubes, glue, masking tape, mixed media materials, 18" × 18" fabric squares	*Reading and Writing Test Preparation*, pp. 68–69 *Assessment*, pp. 71–72	*Transparency*, 32 *Artist Profiles*, pp. 57, 75 *Large Prints*, 23 and 24 *Women in the Arts Collection*	*Feelings* by Aliki
12" × 18" construction paper (light or dark blue), tempera paint, medium brushes, water containers, paper towels, newspaper, magazines, scissors, glue	*Reading and Writing Test Preparation*, pp. 70–71 *Flash Card*, 15 *Assessment*, pp. 73–74	*Transparency*, 33 *Artist Profiles*, pp. 12, 39 *Large Prints*, 23 and 24 *Art Around the World*	*To Market, To Market* by Anne Miranda
9" × 12" construction paper, 3" × 9" construction paper, scissors, glue, paper towels, newspaper, buttons (optional)	*Reading and Writing Test Preparation*, pp. 72–73 *Flash Card*, 15 *Assessment*, pp. 75–76	*Transparency*, 34 *Artist Profiles*, pp. 67, 80 *Large Prints*, 23 and 24 *Art Around the World*	*Snow is Falling* by Franklin M. Branley
9" × 12" white paper, pencils, colored pencils	*Reading and Writing Test Preparation*, pp. 74–75 *Flash Card*, 18 *Assessment*, pp. 77–78	*Transparency*, 35 *Artist Profiles*, pp. 15, 34 *Large Prints*, 23 and 24 *Art Around the World*	*Take Me Out to the Ballgame* by Jack Norworth
wood scraps in a variety of shapes, glue, cardboard or mat board, tempera paint, brushes, water containers, magazines, scissors	*Reading and Writing Test Preparation*, pp. 76–77 *Assessment*, pp. 79–80	*Transparency*, 36 *Artist Profiles*, pp. 48, 58 *Large Prints*, 23 and 24 *Women in the Arts Collection*	*The Josefina Story Quilt* by Eleanor Coerr
Let Them Eat Books excerpt, *The Two Skyscrapers Who Decided to Have a Child* by Carl Sandburg. Running time: 7:00			

6 Balance, Emphasis, and Unity

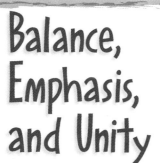

Lesson 1: A shape has **balance** when both halves match.

Lesson 2: **Masks have balance** because they cover faces which have balance.

Lesson 3: Artists can create **emphasis in a painting** by including an unusual or unexpected shape.

Lesson 4: Artists create **emphasis in a form** by making one part different from the rest.

Lesson 5: Artists can create **unity** by making words and symbols fit together with images.

Lesson 6: Artists can create **unity in a sculpture** by repeating colors and forms.

Introduce Unit Concepts

"Let's find balance, emphasis, and unity in the classroom." "Vamos a encontrar equilibrio, énfasis y unidad en la clase".

Balance
- Look for balanced designs in the classroom, such as the arrangement of desks.

Emphasis
- Discuss ways to emphasize a word on the board, such as by circling it or writing it larger than other words.

Unity
- Discuss that the classroom has unity—the students belong together because they are all first graders.

Cross-Curricular Projects
- See the **Language Arts and Reading, Mathematics, Science,** and **Social Studies Art Connections** books for activities that further develop the concepts of balance, emphasis, and unity.

National Standards for Arts Education in Visual Arts (NSAE) 6.b

184 UNIT 6 • Balance, Emphasis, and Unity

Balance, Emphasis, and Unity

This artwork is one of the most famous paintings in the world.

It has balance, emphasis, and unity.

◀ **Leonardo da Vinci.**
(Italian). *Mona Lisa.*
1503.
Oil on wood. 30$\frac{1}{4}$ × 20$\frac{7}{8}$ inches (77 × 53 cm.). Louvre, Paris, France.

184 Unit 6

Fine Art Prints

Display **Large Prints 23** *Lala and Tudi's Birthday Party* and **24** *Nanfang Yendi, Lord of the Southern Quadrant.* Refer to the prints throughout the unit as students learn about balance, emphasis, and unity.

Large Print 23

Large Print 24

A shape has **balance** when both halves match.

▶ Which part of the artwork has balance?

Artists use **emphasis** to show the most important parts of their artwork.

▶ What area of *Mona Lisa* attracts your attention first?

An artwork has **unity** when everything looks like it belongs together.

▶ What colors create unity in the artwork?

In This Unit you will:

▶ learn about balance, emphasis, and unity.

▶ find balance, emphasis, and unity in art and the environment.

▶ create art that has balance, emphasis, and unity.

Self-Portrait

Leonardo da Vinci

(1452–1519)

▶ was an Italian artist and scientist.

▶ filled more than 100 notebooks with drawings and ideas.

▶ drew plans for things we use today, such as helicopters.

Unit 6 **185**

Art History and Culture

Leonardo da Vinci

Leonardo da Vinci (lē ə när´ dō də vin´ chē) (1452–1519) was a scholar, scientist, artist, philosopher, and inventor. He filled many notebooks with his ideas, drawings, poems, and scientific thoughts. He wrote backwards in a right-to-left script, so his notebooks could only be read in a mirror. Da Vinci had ideas for many modern inventions, such as the parachute, the helicopter, and the submarine. Science was always present in da Vinci's art. In his paintings, da Vinci strove to capture the exact appearance of people and objects in nature. In his drawings, he analyzed how things function.

See pages 16–21 and 24–25 for more about subject matter and art history.

Artist Profiles, p. 14

● Artist Profile ●
Leonardo da Vinci
1452–1519
Leonardo (lē ə när´ dō də vin´ chē) was born in 1452, in the small Tuscan town of Vinci. He was the son of a wealthy Florentine notary and a peasant woman. Even when he was a child, people noticed that he had remarkable abilities. He had gracious manners, a fine sense of humor, great strength, and a curiosity that drove him to explore everything. In the mid-1460s, the family settled in Florence, Italy, where Leonardo was given the best available education. He was apprenticed to Verrocchio as a studio boy in 1466. By 1478, he was recognized as an independent master painter.

Examine the Artwork

"Let's look for balance, emphasis, and unity in *Mona Lisa.*" "Vamos a buscar equilibrio, énfasis y unidad en *Mona Lisa*".

■ Have students look at Leonardo da Vinci's *Mona Lisa* and describe what they see.

■ Have students answer the questions on page 185.

▶ The woman's head is balanced. Her hair is parted in the middle. If an imaginary line were drawn from the part in her hair down the middle of her face, everything on both sides of the line would match. Her hair, eyes, nose, and mouth are balanced across the imaginary line.

▶ The woman attracts the viewer's attention first because she takes up the majority of the space in the artwork. The woman's dark eyes are emphasized by the light, pale skin on her face.

▶ Most of the colors in the painting are subtle, darkened browns. This creates unity in the work.

Unit Pretest

T Display *Transparency 48* as a pretest. Answers: 1. A, 2. B, 3. A

Home Connection

■ See *Home and After-School Connections* for family newsletters and activities for this unit.

National Standards for Arts Education in Visual Arts (NSAE) 3.a

NSAE 6.a

ILLUSTRATOR PROFILE
Jose Aruego
(1932–   )

Jose Aruego was born in Manila, Phillipines. As a child, he loved animals. Despite living in a small house, Aruego's family always kept many animals, including horses, dogs, cats, pigs, chickens, roosters, ducks, pigeons, and frogs.

Perhaps because of the influence of the many lawyers he knew, including his father, sister, and friends, Aruego received his law degree from the University of the Philippines in 1955. However he soon decided to give up law and moved to New York City to study art. He received a certificate in Graphic Arts from Parsons School of Design.

Aruego held various design and advertising jobs before he began working on children's books in 1968. Since then he has written and illustrated more than fifty books, and illustrated numerous books that other authors have written. Aruego expresses his childhood love for animals by featuring many in his illustrations.

Throughout Unit 6, share Aruego's illustrations with the class and discuss balance, emphasis, and unity in his works of art. Are the illustrations balanced? What shapes in the illustrations have balance? What parts of the illustrations did Aruego emphasize? How did he create this emphasis? How did Aruego create unity?

Music

Discuss ways musicians can create emphasis, such as with cymbal crashes or sudden pauses. Have students try to find examples of emphasis in music they sing, hear, and create.

Literature and Art

Show the video or DVD *The Little Band*. Discuss examples of balance, emphasis, and unity with students.

Literature and Art

Performing Arts

 Show "Let Them Eat Books." Discuss how the actors create balance, emphasis, and unity in their performance.

Artsource®

Balance of Shape

Lesson 1 introduces the element of balance. Balance occurs when both halves of a shape match. Individual shapes can have balance as well as an entire artwork.

Objectives

Art History and Culture

To compare clothing traditions from different cultures
NSAE 4.a; 4.b; 4.c; 5.a

Creative Expression

To create a transfer print design that has balance
NSAE 1.a; 1.c; 1.d

Aesthetic Perception

To identify examples of balance in art and the environment
NSAE 2.a

Art Criticism

To evaluate own artwork using the four steps of art criticism
NSAE 1.b; 2.b; 3.a; 5.c

Vocabulary ⭐ Reading

Review the following vocabulary words with students before beginning the lesson.

balance equilibrio—the principle of design that deals with the visual weight in a work of art

mola mola—an artwork in reverse appliqué when layers are cut away after stitching.

See page 209B for additional vocabulary and Spanish vocabulary resources.

Art Journal: Vocabulary

Have students add these words to the Vocabulary section of their Art Journals.

Lesson Materials

- 12" × 18" white paper
- oil pastels
- craft sticks or spoons

Alternate Materials:
- fabric crayons

Program Resources

- *Reading and Writing Test Prep.,* pp. 66–67
- *Transparency 31*
- *Flash Cards 12* and *20*
- *Artist Profiles,* pp. 65, 74
- *Animals Through History Time Line*
- *Assessment,* pp. 69–70
- *Large Prints 23* Lala and Tudi's Birthday Party and *24* Nanfang Yendi, Lord of the Southern Quadrant
- *The National Museum of Women in the Arts Collection*

Concept Trace

Balance of Shape
Introduced: Level K, Unit 6, Lesson 3

Reinforced: Level 2, Unit 5, Lesson 1

Lesson 1 Arts Integration NSAE 6.a

Theatre

Complete Unit 6, Lesson 1, on pages 108–109 of *Theatre Arts Connections.*

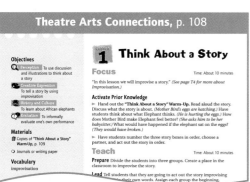

Music

Balance in music can describe how evenly different parts are performed at the same time to make the desired blend. Listen to *Akinla* from *African Suite* by Fela Sowande. Discuss whether all parts are equal in dynamics at all times.

Movement & Dance

Have students explore balance through body shape. Have a student stand tall with arms stretched out to the side. Ask the class to imagine a dotted line dividing the right and left sides of the student's body. Is his or her body balanced? Now ask the student to bend the left arm and lift the left leg. Is the student's body still balanced?

Focus

Time: About 10 minutes

Activate Prior Knowledge

"Do you know anyone who makes things by hand?" "¿Conocen a alguien que hace cosas a mano?"

■ Discuss the various things that craft artists do, such as knitting or wood-working. Help students understand that most people treasure handmade objects because of the time and skill needed to make them.

Using Literature ⭐ Reading

■ Read *This is Baseball* by Margaret Blackstone. Discuss the balance in the illustrations by John O'Brien.

Thematic Connection

■ **Sports/Games:** Discuss balance as it relates to sports or games. For instance, there are a balanced number of people on the court for each basketball team.

Introduce the Art

NSAE 2.a; 3.a

Look

"Let's take a close look at the two shirt designs." "Vamos a mirar detalladamente los dos diseños de camisa".

Making Connections ⭐ Reading

■ Ask students to make connections to other unit concepts (such as line, shape, and color) as they describe each work of art. *Mola* has every kind of line discussed in Unit 1. Some of the lines form the outlines of shapes. Most of the shapes are freeform but a few circles can be found. *Mola* includes primary and secondary colors, as well as white and black. *Arapaho Man's Shirt* has fewer lines than *Mola*. Most of the lines are solid, but there is a broken line down the turtle's back. The person, birds, and turtle are free-form shapes. The squares on the turtle's back are geometric shapes. *Arapaho Man's Shirt* has primary colors as well as white and black.

Art History and Culture

Share with students the Art History and Culture information about the Kuna *Mola* and the *Arapaho Man's Shirt*. Ask students if they are aware of clothing traditions of other cultures. Is the clothing balanced?
NSAE 4.a; 4.b; 4.c; 5.a

🖥 Web Connection

Visit www.panart.com/mola_gallery.htm to view more Mola designs.

Balance

▲ **Artist Unknown.** (Kuna Peoples, Panama). *Mola*.
. . . .
Layered and cut fabric with stitchery. Private Collection.

Look at the shirts on these pages. Draw an imaginary line down the middle of each shirt with your finger. The left side of each shirt matches the right side.

🏺 Art History and Culture

The word *mola* means "blouse" in the Kuna language.

🏺 Art History and Culture

The Kuna people live in small villages on the islands of the San Blas Archipelago off of the eastern coast of Panama. Most families earn a living by farming or fishing. The Kuna women make molas, which are colorfully designed, appliqué blouses. The word *mola* means "blouse" or "cloth" in the Kuna language. Mola blouses have panels on the front and back that are decorated with birds, animals, flowers, and leaves, with geometric patterns in the background. Kuna girls are taught to make the molas by their mothers and grandmothers.

See pages 16–21 and 24–25 for more about subject matter and art history.

Artist Profiles, p. 74

▷ Artist Profile ◁

Mola

The Kuna live on the islands of the San Blas Archipelago off the eastern coast of Panama. In the sixteenth century, they were an important culture and lived in central Panama. Now there are fewer than 40,000 remaining Kuna live in small villages. Most families earn a living by farming or fishing, but some people commute to Panama City to make money.

▲ **Artist unknown (Kuna).** (Panama). *Mola*.
Layered and cut fabric with stitchery. Private collection.

Study the shirts to see how they are balanced.

▶ What is the same on both sides of the imaginary line?

▶ What is balanced across the middle?

◀ **Artist Unknown.** (United States). *Arapaho Man's Shirt.* c. 1890.
Buckskin and feathers. 40 × 24½ inches (101.6 × 62.2 cm.). Buffalo Bill Historical Center, Cody, Wyoming.

 Aesthetic Perception

Design Awareness What furniture can you think of that has a balanced design?

Art History and Culture

The women of Native American Plains tribes (such as Arapaho) usually made clothing for their family members. The *Arapaho Man's Shirt* was made by an unidentified Arapaho Native American artist in about the year 1890. This shirt was worn during a ritual performance called the *Ghost Dance.* The symbols on the shirt represent the spirit world, from which the Arapaho sought blessings.

See pages 16–21 and 24–25 for more about subject matter and art history.

Artist Profiles, p. 65

> *Artist Profile*
>
> **Arapaho Man's Shirt**
>
> An unidentified Arapaho Indian artist made this shirt around 1890. The women of Native American Plains tribes usually made clothing for members of their families. Their designs were mostly abstract and geometric, and the patterns in these designs were often balanced.
>
> ◀ **Artist unknown.** (United States).

Study

▶ The animals are the same on both sides of the *Mola.* On the *Arapaho Man's Shirt,* the stars, birds, fringe, and sleeves are the same on both sides.

▶ In *Mola,* there are two plant-like designs that are balanced across the middle. On the *Arapaho Man's Shirt,* the person and the turtle are balanced across the middle.

■ For more examples of utilitarian art see *The National Museum of Women in the Arts Collection.*

Art Journal: Concepts
Have students sketch their own example of balance in the Concepts section of their Art Journals.

Aesthetic Perception

Design Awareness Examples of furniture with balance include chairs, sofas, tables, and beds. Furniture is designed with balance because it is made to be used by people's bodies, which have balance. A balanced design also makes furniture more functional. If the legs of a table were not balanced, it would be difficult to keep things from sliding off the table.

Developing Visual Literacy Have students imagine who would wear the *Mola* or *Arapaho Man's Shirt.* Have students sketch to show the other items of clothing, such as pants or a skirt, that they think would be worn with each shirt.

Web Connection
For more information about the Arapaho tribe, visit the Culture section of their official Web site, **www.cheyenne-arapaho.org**

each

Time: About 40 minutes

"How do you know if something has balance?" *"¿Cómo saben si algo tiene equilibrio?"*

■ Read and discuss Using Balance on page 188.

Practice

Materials: None

■ Have students follow the directions on page 188.

■ Students should notice that clothing has balance because it is made to fit our bodies, which have balance.

Creative Expression

NSAE 1.a; 1.c; 1.d

Materials: 12" × 18" white paper, oil pastels, craft sticks

Alternate Materials: fabric crayons

■ Distribute the materials and have students follow the directions on page 189.

■ Review the Technique Tips on page 229 for information about making a transfer print.

■ See the Activity Tips on page 247 for visual examples of this lesson's activity.

■ Teachers might wish to draw a shirt pattern (rectangular body and two long sleeves like *Arapaho Man's Shirt*) on the paper before students begin the activity.

■ As students complete step 3 of the activity, they can unfold the paper and check to see what has or has not been transferred. After students complete step 3, they can go back over the transferred design with oil pastels so the colors on both halves of the paper are equally bright.

■ As an alternate activity, students can use fabric crayons on paper and have an adult transfer the finished design onto a real t-shirt by ironing.

Art Journal: Brainstorming

In their Art Journals, have students brainstorm ideas for symbols that are representative of themselves. Then have students choose the symbols they would like to use and plan how they will arrange them in the Creative Expression activity.

Using Balance

When you draw an imaginary line down the middle of a shape and both sides match, the shape has **balance.** The imaginary line is the line of balance.

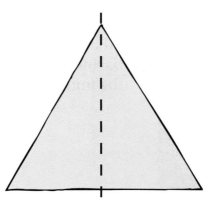

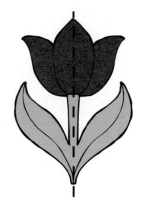

Practice

Look for balance in your classmates' clothing.

1. Look at shirts, pants, jackets, and skirts.
2. Is the shape of the clothing balanced? Is the design on the clothing balanced?
3. Why does clothing usually have balance?

Differentiated Instruction

Reteach
Review balance with students using *Flash Cards 12* and *20.* Have students look for examples of balanced shapes in the classroom.

Special Needs
Adaptations: If students have difficulty creating symbols, ask them to look at the shirt they are wearing (or think of a favorite shirt) and re-create the patterns found there.

ELL Tips
Provide students with pictures of people, animals, or objects that have balance. Have students fold the pictures in half vertically and analyze how the halves match.

◀ **G. P. Lane.**
Age 7.

Think about how this student designed a balanced shirt.

 **Creative Expression**

How could you design a balanced shirt?

1. Think about symbols you would like to wear on a shirt.

2. Fold your paper in half and open it. Draw half of your shirt design on one half of the paper. Press hard with the oil pastels.

3. Refold your paper. Rub the back. Open the paper.

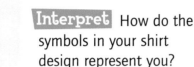 **Art Criticism**

Interpret How do the symbols in your shirt design represent you?

Art Across the Curriculum

Use these ideas to reinforce art concepts across the curriculum.
NSAE 6.b

★ **Narrative Writing** Discuss with students how they use balance in the writing process by making sure their stories have a beginning, a middle, and an end.

★ **Math** Using pictorial models, discuss how both sides of an addition or subtraction sentence are balanced.

★ **Science** Demonstrate how students can use a balance to compare the weights of objects.

★ **Social Studies** Discuss people exchanging money for goods or services as an example of balance.

★ **Technology** Use the computer's paint program to paint half of a design. Copy and paste the half, flip it horizontally, and line it up next to the other half to create a balanced design. Visit **SRAonline.com** to print detailed instructions for this activity.

 **Reflect** 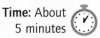 Time: About 5 minutes

Review and Assess
"How can you create balance in a work of art?" "¿Cómo pueden crear equilibrio en una obra de arte?"

Think
The student's shirt has symbols that are repeated on each side.

■ Have students identify balance in *Large Prints 23 Lala and Tudi's Birthday Party* and *24 Nanfang Yendi, Lord of the Southern Quadrant*.

Informal Assessment

Art Journal: Critical Thinking
Have students ask themselves the four Art Criticism questions, and then write or sketch to answer the Interpret question in their Art Journals.
NSAE 1.b; 2.b; 3.a; 5.c

Art Criticism

Describe ▶ What did you include in your design?

Analyze ▶ How does your design have balance?

Interpret ▶ How do the symbols in your shirt design represent you?

Decide ▶ If you could add anything to your design, what would it be?

■ For standardized-format test practice using this lesson's art content, see pages 66–67 in *Reading and Writing Test Preparation*.

Balance of Shape

Extra! For the Art Specialist

Time: About 45 minutes

Focus

Using **Transparency 31,** discuss balance in the works of art. Have students point out matching lines, shapes, colors, and textures on each side.

Teach

Have students complete the Alternate Activity. How did students create balance in their designs?

Reflect

Guide students through evaluation of their works of art using the four steps of art criticism. (See pages 28–29 for more about art criticism.) Encourage students to locate and describe other examples of balance in the classroom.

Alternate Activity

Materials:
- 9" × 12" construction paper
- 6" × 9" construction paper
- scissors
- glue or glue sticks

1. Have students fold a 9" × 12" sheet of construction paper in half by bringing the long sides together and creasing. The paper may be cut into a symmetrical shape when folded, such as a kite or butterfly. Open the papers and explain that the crease is the line of balance.

2. Have students fold a sheet of 6" × 9" construction paper in half and cut out a geometric or freeform shape so there are two identical shapes. Have students glue each of the shapes in the same place on each side of the line of balance.

3. Have students cut out a variety of shapes from folder papers and glue them on each side of the line of balance, overlapping at least two shapes.

Research in Art Education

Students involved in the arts showed higher reading proficiency, higher standardized test scores, and had a lower dropout rate than non-arts-involved students. These results hold true across grade levels and across socio-economic status levels ("Involvement in the Arts and Human Development" in *Champions of Change,* p. 6). However, a similar study conducted in the UK showed that although students perceived that the arts aid personal and social development, there was not a correlation between arts education and increased test scores ("Arts Education in Secondary Schools" in *Critical Links,* p. 76).

Assessment

Use the following rubric to evaluate the artwork students make in the Creative Expression activity and to assess students' understanding of balance of shape.

Have students complete page 69 or 70 in their *Assessment* books.

	Art History and Culture	Aesthetic Perception	Creative Expression	Art Criticism
3 POINTS	The student can compare clothing traditions from different cultures.	The student accurately identifies balance in art and the environment.	The student's transfer print design clearly shows balance.	The student thoughtfully and honestly evaluates his or her own work using the four steps of art criticism.
2 POINTS	The student's comparison is weak or incomplete.	The student shows emerging awareness of balance but cannot consistently identify it.	The student's transfer print design shows some awareness of balance.	The student attempts to evaluate his or her own work but shows an incomplete understanding of evaluation criteria.
1 POINT	The student cannot compare clothing traditions from different cultures.	The student cannot identify balance.	The student's transfer print design does not show balance.	The student makes no attempt to evaluate his or her own work.

Assessment, p. 69

Name _____ Date _____

Lesson 1 UNIT 6

Balance

For the teacher: Use the following prompt for this activity.
Using a pencil, draw a shape that has balance. Draw a line through the shape to show the line of balance.

Level 1   Unit 6 • Balance, Emphasis, and Unity   **69**

Balance in Masks

Lesson 2 teaches students that masks are forms that have balance. Masks have balance because human faces have balance.

Objectives

Art History and Culture
To identify a few facts about the use of masks
NSAE 4.a; 4.b; 4.c; 5.a

Creative Expression
To create a mixed-media face form that has balance   NSAE 1.a; 1.c; 1.d; 2.c; 3.b

Aesthetic Perception
To recognize that the human head is a form that has balance
NSAE 6.b

Art Criticism
To evaluate one's own artwork using the four steps of art criticism
NSAE 1.b; 2.b; 3.a; 5.c

Vocabulary ⭐ Reading

Review the following vocabulary words with students before beginning the lesson.

balance equilibrio—the principle of design that deals with the visual weight in a work of art

mask máscara—three-dimensional art form of a sculpted face, often made to be worn over the face

See page 209B for additional vocabulary and Spanish Vocabulary resources.

 Art Journal: Vocabulary
Have students add these words to the Vocabulary section of their Art Journals.

Lesson Materials
- small brown paper lunch sacks
- newspaper
- paper towel tube
- glue
- masking tape
- mixed media materials (such as yarn, puff balls, foam shapes, buttons)
- 18" × 18" fabric squares

Alternate Materials:
- paper plates stapled together and stuffed

Program Resources
- *Reading and Writing Test Prep.,* pp. 68–69
- *Transparency 32*
- *Artist Profiles,* pp. 57, 75
- *Animals Through History Time Line*
- *Assessment,* pp. 71–72
- *Large Prints 23* Lala and Tudi's Birthday Party and *24* Nanfang Yendi, Lord of the Southern Quadrant
- *The National Museum of Women in the Arts Collection*

Concept Trace
Balance in Masks
Introduced: Level K, Unit 6, Lesson 4
Reinforced: Level 2, Unit 5, Lesson 2

Lesson 2 Arts Integration NSAE 6.a

Theatre
Complete Unit 6, Lesson 2, on pages 110–111 of *Theatre Arts Connections.*

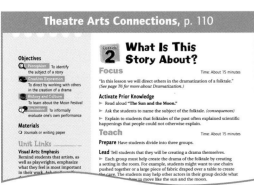

Music
 Faces have balance. Listen to *Contredanse* by Jean-Phillipe Rameau. What form is this piece in? Are the beginning and ending sections exactly the same? How does the orchestration change in the middle section?

Movement & Dance
Have students sit on the floor across from a partner. Ask students to imagine there is a mirror between them and that one student will be the other's reflection. Without touching, have one student slowly move his or her hands in circular patterns in front of them. The partner must mirror the movement exactly. Ask students to explore a wide range of line patterns and shapes with their hands, arms, legs, and torsos.

Focus

Time: About 45 minutes ⏱

Activate Prior Knowledge

"Why do people wear masks?" "¿Por qué la gente usa máscaras?"

- Help students brainstorm reasons to wear masks. Possible answers include: doctors and dentists wear masks to protect themselves and patients; firefighters and scuba divers wear masks to help them breathe; actors and dancers wear masks to pretend they are someone else.

Using Literature ⭐ Reading

- Read *Feelings* by Aliki. Discuss how feelings can be shown through facial expressions.

Thematic Connection

- **Body:** As you discuss how faces and the human body have balance, discuss things students can do to take care of their bodies.

Introduce the Art

Look
NSAE 2.b; 3.a

"Let's take a close look at these masks."
"Vamos a mirar detalladamente estas máscaras."

Making Inferences ⭐ Reading

- Have students discuss the mood or feeling of each mask and speculate about its purpose. *Ngady amwaash (Mweel) Mask* has a sleepy feeling because the eye openings are very small. It could be used to portray a sleepy character when acting out a story. *Mask of the Moon* has a silly feeling because it has a large grin and exaggerated facial expression. It could be used to make people laugh.

🏺 Art History and Culture

Share information from the Art History and Culture sections on these pages about each mask. Discuss how the masks were used in each culture.
NSAE 4.a; 4.b; 4.c; 5.a

💻 Web Connection

For more pieces from the African art collection at the Virginia Museum of Fine Arts, visit **www.vmfa.state.va.us/collections/collect_african.html**.

Lesson 2 Balance in Masks

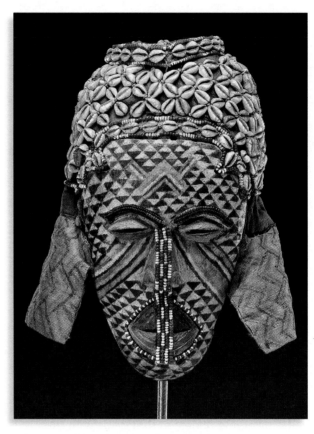

Look at the masks on these pages. Masks are forms that are worn to cover faces.

◀ **Artist Unknown.** (Kuba Peoples, Democratic Republic of the Congo). *Ngady amwaash (Mweel) Mask.* c. 19th–20th century.

Wood, paint, glass beads, cowrie shells, string, raffia, cloth. $12\frac{1}{2} \times 8 \times 9\frac{1}{2}$ inches (31.7 × 20.3 × 24.1 cm.). Virginia Museum of Fine Arts, Richmond, Virginia.

🏺 Art History and Culture

These masks represent characters from legends. They were worn for ritual dances.

🏺 Art History and Culture

The *Ngady amwaash (Mweel) Mask* was made by an unidentified artist of the Kuba peoples of the Democratic Republic of the Congo, formerly known as Zaire, located in central Africa. Kuba peoples are known for their skills in metalwork, woodcarving, and sculpture. The *Ngady amwaash (Mweel) Mask* is one of the ten types of Kuba masks that have been identified by art historians and anthropologists. It is believed that this mask was first introduced in celebration of the role of women in Kuba culture. It represents a female character, but it would have been worn by a male dancer in a ceremonial dance.

See pages 16–21 and 24–25 for more about subject matter and art history.

Artist Profiles, p. 75

▷ Artist Profile

Ngady Amwaash (Mweel) Mask

This mask was made by an unidentified artist of the Kuba peoples of the Democratic Republic of the Congo, formerly known as Zaire, located in central Africa. The Kuba is a large confederation of approximately nineteen different ethnic groups living in central Africa. The ancient Kuba kingdoms were wealthy and rich in cultural traditions, myths, and legends. The Kuba people are known for their skills in metalwork, woodcarving, and sculpture. Traditionally, men and women in Kuba culture practice different art forms.

◀ **Artist Unknown (Kuba).** (Democratic Republic of the Congo). *Ngady Amwaash (Mweel) Mask*

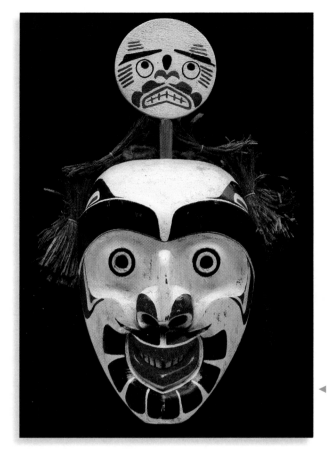

Study the masks to find balance.

▶ What is repeated on each half of the masks?

▶ What is balanced across the middle?

◀ **Joe Seaweed.** (Kwakiutl Peoples, Canada). *Mask of the Moon.* c. 1946.
....
Cedar bark, mink pelts, plywood. 18⅞ × 4⅞ inches (47.94 × 12.38 cm.). Seattle Art Museum, Seattle, Washington.

Aesthetic Perception

Seeing Like an Artist What forms found in nature have balance?

Art History and Culture

Joe Seaweed

Joe Seaweed (jō sē´ wēd) (1910–1983) is an artist of the Kwakiutl nation, a clan of people living on the coast of southeast Alaska, British Columbia, and Washington. He learned to carve from his father, Willie Seaweed, one of the most well known Kwakiutl carvers. Father and son carved a variety of objects used in Kwakiutl society, including totem poles and masks. *Mask of the Moon* would have been worn for a comical performance. The wearer would represent the full moon, and would argue with the crescent moon.

See pages 16–21 and 24–25 for more about subject matter and art history.

Artist Profiles, p. 57

◆ Artist Profile ◆
Joe Seaweed
1910–1983
Joe Seaweed (jō sē´ wēd) was a Native artist of the Kwakwaka'wakw nation of the coast of southeast Alaska, British Columbia, and Washington State. Originally, *Seaweed* was spelled *Siwide* (sē´ wē dē), and meant "recipient of the paddles." The Siwides put the canoe paddles away as fishers returned with their catch. Willie Seaweed, Joe's father, was one of the most inventive Northwest coast native artists of his time. Joe Seaweed created work almost identical to his father's, and the two worked together in the village of Blunden Harbour, British Columbia. His work is part of many private collections, and is often placed alongside his father's.

Study

▶ On *Ngady amwaash (Mweel) Mask* the shell pattern, the ear flaps, the eyebrows, the eyes, and the face pattern are repeated on each half. On *Mask of the Moon* the hair, the ear flaps, the eyebrows, the eyes, the moustache, and the design around the eyes and mouth are repeated on each half.

▶ On *Ngady amwaash (Mweel) Mask* the nose, the mouth, and the blue and white beaded strip that covers the nose and mouth are balanced across the middle. On *Mask of the Moon* the circle at the top, the nose, and the mouth are balanced across the middle.

■ For more examples of art from Africa, see ***The National Museum of Women in the Arts Collection.***

Art Journal: Concepts
Have students think of a balanced mask they have seen and sketch it in the Concepts section of their Art Journals.

Aesthetic Perception

Seeing Like an Artist Discuss with students other balanced forms found in nature. Ideas include turtles, starfish, and butterflies. Discuss that animals almost always have balance. Discuss that plants can have balance as well, but they do not always.

Developing Visual Literacy These masks were worn for ritual dances. How do students think the rest of each dancer's costume would look? How do students think each dancer would dance?

Web Connection
Visit the Seattle Art Museum's Web site at **www.seattleartmuseum.org.**

Teach

"Why do masks usually have balance?" "¿Por qué las máscaras tienen equilibrio, por lo general?"

- Read and discuss Using Balance in Masks on page 192.

Practice

Materials: hand mirrors

Alternate Materials: have students look for balance in each others' faces

- Have students follow the directions on page 192.

- Students should notice that eyes and ears are repeated on each half while the nose and mouth are balanced across the middle.

- Discuss with students that faces are not always perfectly balanced. For instance, students may have missing teeth.

Creative Expression

NSAE 1.a; 1.c; 1.d; 2.c; 3.b
Materials: small brown paper lunch sacks, newspaper, paper towel tubes, glue, masking tape, mixed media materials (such as yarn, puff balls, foam shapes, buttons), 18" × 18" fabric squares

Alternate Materials: paper plates stapled together and stuffed

- Distribute the materials and have students follow the directions on page 193.

- Review the Activity Tips on page 247 for visual examples of techniques.

- Students should stuff the paper lunch sacks with newspaper until they are half full. Place a paper towel tube approximately 3 inches inside the bag and attach with masking tape. Cut a small opening in the center of the fabric square. Slide the fabric over the paper towel tube handle and glue so the fabric covers the masking tape. Use glue to attach buttons, yarn, and other mixed media material to create a face.

Art Journal: Brainstorming

In their Art Journals, have students sketch ideas for ways they could arrange mixed media materials to create a face.

Using Balance in Masks

Artists design **masks** with balance because human faces have balance.

Practice

Look for balance on your face.

1. Look at your face in a mirror.
2. What is repeated on each half?
3. What is balanced across the middle?

Differentiated Instruction

Reteach
Show students large pictures of faces from magazines. Draw a dashed line down the center of each face to show the line of balance. Discuss with students what makes each face balanced.

Special Needs
Adaptations: Help students connect the activity with the art exemplars by asking them to design their mask for a special purpose or celebration.

ELL Tips
Review with students the names of the parts of the face and head. Point to a part of your face and have students identify it.

Think about how this student created a face with balance.

◀ **Anika Chaturvedi.**
Age 6.

 **Creative Expression**

How could you create a face with balance?

1. Stuff a small paper bag with newspaper to make a head.

2. Use tape to attach a paper towel tube to the head. Cover the tube with fabric to make a body.

3. Attach buttons, yarn, and other objects to the head to make a face with balance.

 **Art Criticism**

Decide Does the face you created have balance?

Art Across the Curriculum

Use these ideas to reinforce art concepts across the curriculum.
NSAE 6.b

★ **Expository Writing** Have students use the writing process to write in their own words a list of the steps they did in the Creative Expression activity.

★ **Math** Discuss fractions and equal parts of a whole as you talk about each half of a balanced face.

★ **Science** Discuss how animals' bodies can be balanced. Can students think of any animals whose bodies do not have balance?

★ **Social Studies** Use portraits or photographs of historical figures to discuss balance in faces.

★ **Technology** By using a digital camera or by scanning, open photos of each student's face in the computer's paint program. Allow students to draw the line of balance through the middle of their faces. Visit **SRAonline.com** to print detailed instructions for the activity.

Reflect

Time: About 5 minutes

Review and Assess

"Why do masks and faces have balance?"
"¿Por qué las máscaras y las caras tienen equilibrio?"

Think

The student created a face with balance by making each half of the face match.

■ Have students look for faces with balance in *Large Prints 23* Lala and Tudi's Birthday Party and *24* Nanfang Yendi, Lord of the Southern Quadrant.

Informal Assessment

Art Journal: Critical Thinking
Have students ask themselves the four Art Criticism questions, and then write or sketch to answer the Decide question in their Art Journals.
NSAE 1.b; 2.b; 3.a; 5.c

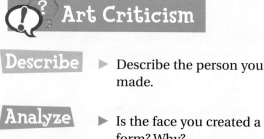 **Art Criticism**

Describe ▶ Describe the person you made.

Analyze ▶ Is the face you created a form? Why?

Interpret ▶ What kind of mood does the person have? How did you show this?

Decide ▶ Does the face you created have balance?

■ For standardized-format test practice using this lesson's art content, see pages 68–69 in *Reading and Writing Test Preparation.*

Balance in Masks

Extra! For the Art Specialist

Time: About 45 minutes

Focus

Using *Transparency 32,* discuss balance in masks. Have students then look at each other's faces to find balance.

Teach

Have students complete the Alternate Activity. For what occasion would students wear their masks?

Reflect

Guide students through evaluation of their works of art using the four steps of art criticism. (See pages 28–29 for more about art criticism.) Have students also look for balance in *Large Print 24.*

Alternate Activity

Materials:
- 9" × 12" white or light colored construction paper
- tempera paint
- brushes
- water containers

1. Have students fold a sheet of paper in half, bringing the long sides together and creasing. While the paper is folded, students should cut a curved line along the open edge of the papers to create the sides of the mask shape.

2. Have students open the papers and paint the features of a mask on one side of the paper only. When they are finished painting, have students refold the paper and rub the back to transfer the design to the other half.

Research in Art Education

In one large study, students involved in arts organizations were compared to a control group. The arts-involved students were shown to be four times more likely to win school-wide attention for academic achievement, four times more likely to participate in a math or science fair, three times more likely to be elected to class office, and four times more likely to engage in community service ("Living the Arts Through Language and Learning" in *Critical Links,* p. 78).

Assessment

Use the following rubric to evaluate the artwork students make in the Creative Expression activity and to assess students' understanding of balance in masks.

Have students complete page 71 or 72 in their *Assessment* books.

	Art History and Culture	Aesthetic Perception	Creative Expression	Art Criticism
3 POINTS	The student can identify a few facts about the use of masks.	The student accurately identifies that the human head is a form that has balance.	The student's mixed media face clearly has balance.	The student thoughtfully and honestly evaluates his or her own work using the four steps of art criticism.
2 POINTS	The student's identification is weak or incomplete.	The student shows emerging awareness that the human head is a form that has balance.	The student's mixed media face shows some attempt to create balance.	The student attempts to evaluate his or her own work but shows an incomplete understanding of evaluation criteria.
1 POINT	The student cannot identify any facts about the use of masks.	The student cannot identify that the human head is a form that has balance.	The student's mixed media face does not show balance.	The student makes no attempt to evaluate his or her own work.

Assessment, p. 71

Name _____ Date _____

Lesson **2** UNIT 6

Balance in Masks

For the teacher: Use the following prompt for this activity. Using a crayon, draw a face that has balance.

Level 1   Unit 6 • Balance, Emphasis, and Unity **71**

Emphasis in Paintings

Lesson 3 introduces the concept of emphasis. Artists create emphasis to attract the viewer's attention to an important part of a work of art. Artists can create emphasis in a painting by including an unusual or unexpected shape.

Objectives

Art History and Culture

To recognize that René Magritte and Marc Chagall were surrealist painters
NSAE 4.a; 4.b; 4.c

Creative Expression

To create a landscape with emphasis
NSAE 1.a; 1.c; 1.d; 2.c; 3.b

Aesthetic Perception

To identify qualities that create emphasis in a painting
NSAE 2.b

Art Criticism

To evaluate one's own artwork using the four steps of art criticism
NSAE 1.b; 2.b; 3.a; 5.c

Vocabulary ⭐ Reading

Review the following vocabulary words with students before beginning the lesson.

emphasis énfasis—the principle of design that makes one part of an artwork stand out more than the other parts

landscape paisaje—a picture of the outdoors

See page 209B for additional Spanish vocabulary resources.

Art Journal: Vocabulary

Have students add these words to the Vocabulary section of their Art Journals.

Lesson Materials

- crayons
- 12" × 18" construction paper (light or dark blue)
- tempera paint
- medium brushes
- water containers
- paper towels
- newspaper
- magazines
- scissors
- glue

Alternate Materials:

- colored candies
- white paper
- crayons

Program Resources

- *Reading and Writing Test Prep.,* pp. 70–71
- *Transparency 33*
- *Flash Card 15*
- *Artist Profiles,* pp. 12, 39
- *Animals Through History Time Line*
- *Assessment,* pp. 73–74
- *Large Prints 23* Lala and Tudi's Birthday Party and *24* Nanfang Yendi, Lord of the Southern Quadrant
- *Art Around the World*

Concept Trace

Emphasis in Paintings
Introduced: Level 1, Unit 6, Lesson 3
Reinforced: Level 2, Unit 5, Lesson 3

Lesson 3 Arts Integration NSAE 6.a

Theatre

Complete Unit 6, Lesson 3, on pages 112–113 of *Theatre Arts Connections.*

Music

The most famous example of emphasis by dynamics, or "accent," is in *The Surprise Symphony No. 94* by Franz Joseph Haydn. When Haydn was frustrated that his audiences were getting sleepy during his after dinner entertainment he added the famous accents to wake them up.

Movement & Dance

Certain ideas may be emphasized in a dance, such as a particular character, shape, locomotor movement, quality, or feeling. The idea can be emphasized by repeating it several times or by changing its size, its placement on stage, or its relationship to other objects in the space. Ask students to think of other ways one might emphasize a particular movement idea.

Focus

Time: About 10 minutes

Activate Prior Knowledge

"Have you ever been the tallest or shortest person in a crowd, or the one with the brightest clothes?" "¿Alguna vez han sido la persona más alta o más baja en una muchedumbre, o la persona vestida con colores más vivos?"

■ Discuss how something that is different gets our attention.

Using Literature ☆ Reading

■ Read *To Market, To Market* by Anne Miranda. Discuss what stands out in the illustrations by Janet Stevens.

Thematic Connection

■ **Safety:** Discuss techniques communities use to emphasize safety, such as using flashing lights or sirens.

Introduce the Art

Look

"Let's take a close look at these paintings."
"Vamos a mirar detalladamente estas pinturas".

Making Connections ☆ Reading

■ Ask students to make connections to line and shape unit concepts as they describe each work of art. *Time Transfixed* has vertical, horizontal, diagonal, and curved lines. Most of the shapes are geometric shapes. *Birthday* contains curved, vertical, horizontal, and diagonal lines. The people are free-form shapes. *Birthday* also has circles, squares, and rectangles.

🏺 Art History and Culture

Ask students if they have ever had a dream where things seemed mixed-up. Discuss that Magritte and Chagall were part of an early-twentieth century art movement called surrealism. The paintings of surrealist artists had dreamlike qualities. Real objects were often depicted in an unusual way. NSAE 4.a; 4.b; 4.c

💻 **Web Connection**
Learn more about René Magritte at **www.magritte.com**.

Emphasis in Paintings

Look at the works of art on these pages. The artists included something unusual in the paintings.

◀ **Rene Magritte.** (Belgian). *Time Transfixed.* 1938.
....
Oil on canvas. $27\frac{1}{2} \times 38\frac{1}{2}$ inches (69.85 × 97.79 cm.). The Art Institute of Chicago, Chicago, Illinois.

🏺 Art History and Culture

These artists were famous for painting pictures that look like dreams. This style was popular at the time.

🏺 Art History and Culture

René Magritte

René Magritte (rə nē´ mə grēt´) (1898–1967) was born in Belgium. He studied art in Brussels and then worked briefly at a wallpaper factory. Magritte was part of the Surrealist movement that developed in the 1920s. Unlike other Surrealist artists, Magritte did not abandon realism, but instead took realistic objects and placed them into a dreamlike environment.

See pages 16–21 and 24–25 for more about subject matter and art history.

Artist Profiles, p. 39

◆ Artist Profile ◆
René Magritte
1898-1967
René Magritte (rə nē´ mə grēt´) was born in Belgium at the end of the nineteenth century. After studying art in Brussels, he worked briefly in a wallpaper factory. The influence of his time at this factory is sometimes evident in his patterned paintings. Magritte had a mischievous attitude, and displayed an avant-garde, poetic energy. He directed this energy into numerous creations and was honored with retrospective exhibitions in both Europe and the United States.

Study the works of art.

▶ What stands out in each painting?

▲ **Marc Chagall.** (Russian).
Birthday. 1945.
Oil on cardboard. $31\frac{3}{4} \times 39\frac{1}{4}$ inches (80.65 × 99.67 cm.). Museum of Modern Art, New York, New York.

Aesthetic Perception

Seeing Like an Artist Look around your classroom. Has your teacher made anything stand out?

Study

▶ In *Time Transfixed* the train stands out. It is unusual for a train to be in a fireplace. In *Birthday* the people stand out. The man is floating in the air and his head is twisted in an unusual way. He has no arms.

▪ For more examples of art from Europe, see *Art Around the World.*

Art Journal: Concepts

In the Concepts section of their Art Journals, have students make a sketch of their family. Have students emphasize themselves in their family portrait.

Aesthetic Perception

Seeing Like an Artist Ask students if there is anything in the classroom that stands out because it has purposely been emphasized. Discuss how the object was emphasized, and why the teacher might have wanted to emphasize it. For instance, important instructions on the board may have been written in a different color or circled.

Developing Visual Literacy Have students imagine that each artwork is an illustration accompanying a story in a book. What would the story be about? How would the illustrations immediately before and after these illustrations look?

Art History and Culture

Marc Chagall

Marc Chagall (märk sha gäl´) (1887–1985) was born in Russia. He studied art in St. Petersburg and then in Paris. He worked as the director of the Art Academy in his hometown and then as the art director of a theatre, where he painted murals in the lobby and created sets for shows. Chagall's Surrealist paintings looked like fantasy and often showed people and animals flying through the air.

See pages 16–21 and 24–25 for more about subject matter and art history.

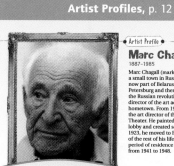

Artist Profiles, p. 12

◆ Artist Profile ◆
Marc Chagall
1887–1985

Marc Chagall (mark sha gäl´) was born in a small town in Russia, Vitebsk, which is now part of Belarus. He studied art in Saint Petersburg and then in Paris, France. After the Russian revolution he served as the director of the art academy in his hometown. From 1919 to 1922, Chagall was the art director of the Moscow Jewish State Theater. He painted murals in the theater lobby and created sets for the shows. In 1923, he moved to France. He spent most of the rest of his life there, except for a brief period of residence in the United States from 1941 to 1948.

Web Connection

Birthday is housed at the Museum of Modern Art. Visit their Web site at **www.moma.org**.

# Teach

Time: About 45 minutes

"How do artists create emphasis?" "¿Cómo crean énfasis los artistas?"

- Read and discuss Using Emphasis in Paintings on page 196.

Practice

Materials: crayons

Alternate Materials: different colored candies

- Have students follow the directions on page 196.

- Students should notice that their eyes are drawn to the crayon or candy that is a different color from the rest.

Creative Expression

NSAE 1.a; 1.c; 1.d; 2.c; 3.b

Materials: 12" × 18" construction paper (light or dark blue), tempera paint, medium brushes, water containers, paper towels, newspaper, magazines, scissors, glue

Alternate Materials: white paper, crayons

- Distribute the materials and have students follow the directions on page 197.

- Review the Activity Tips on page 248 for visual examples of techniques.

- Have students look through magazines for a picture of an object that would appear outside. Students should carefully cut out the shape of the object and glue the image towards the middle or bottom of their paper. Then have students lightly sketch in the rest of their landscape around the object. Students should use tempera to complete their landscapes.

- Display students' works in the classroom. Have students share their ideas about emphasis in the exhibition.

Art Journal: Brainstorming
Have students review their notes about landscapes in their Art Journals from Unit 1, Lesson 2, and use them as they plan this lesson's Creative Expression activity.

Using Emphasis in Paintings

When an object stands out, it has **emphasis.** Artists create emphasis by making an object look different from what the viewer might expect.

Practice

How can you arrange crayons to create emphasis?

1. Look through your crayon box. Find four colors that are similar.

2. Find one crayon that is different. Arrange the crayons.

3. Ask a classmate, "Which crayon do you notice first?"

Differentiated Instruction

Reteach
Using *Flash Card 15,* discuss with students which object has emphasis and why.

Special Needs
Adaptations: Help students make connections between this activity and the works of art by Magritte and Chagall by having them illustrate an image from their dreams for this lesson.

ELL Tips
Students may be hesitant to answer interpretive questions about their artwork. You may wish to phrase questions as an either/or choice so the vocabulary needed to answer the question is contained in the question itself.

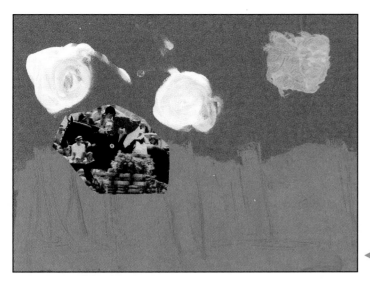
◀ **Caroline Mitchell.**
Age 5.

Think about how this student created emphasis in the landscape.

Creative Expression

How could you create a landscape with emphasis?

1. Look through a magazine. Find a picture of an object you would find outside.

2. Carefully cut out the object.

3. Glue the object to a sheet of paper. Draw and paint a landscape around the object.

Art Criticism

Analyze How did you create emphasis in your landscape?

Art Across the Curriculum

Use these ideas to reinforce art concepts across the curriculum.
NSAE 6.b

★ **Poetry Writing** Have students use the writing process to write a poem that has a feeling of a fantasy or dream, like the paintings.

★ **Math** Create simple drawings of sets of objects, using emphasis to make one object stand out. Have students describe the different objects as parts of a set.

★ **Science** Have students study nature and discover what stands out, as if an artist had created emphasis in the world.

★ **Social Studies** Discuss with students how celebrating a holiday can create emphasis on a special day.

★ **Technology** Have students re-create their Creative Expression activities by inserting a scanned photograph in the computer's paint program and then painting the rest of the landscape around it. Visit **SRAonline.com** to print detailed instructions for this activity.

Reflect

Time: About 5 minutes

Review and Assess
"How can you create emphasis in a work of art?" "¿Cómo pueden crear énfasis en una obra de arte?"

Think
The student created emphasis by including a magazine picture in her landscape.

■ Have students identify areas of emphasis in **Large Prints 23** *Lala and Tudi's Birthday Party* and **24** *Nanfang Yendi, Lord of the Southern Quadrant.*

Informal Assessment

Art Journal: Critical Thinking
Have students ask themselves the four Art Criticism questions, and then write or sketch to answer the Analyze question in their Art Journals.
NSAE 1.b; 2.b; 3.a; 5.c

Art Criticism

Describe ▶ What objects did you include in your landscape?

Analyze ▶ How did you create emphasis in your landscape?

Interpret ▶ Does your landscape remind you of a dream? Why or why not?

Decide ▶ If you could add anything to your design, what would it be?

■ For standardized-format test practice using this lesson's art content, see pages 70–71 in **Reading and Writing Test Preparation.**

Emphasis in Paintings

Extra! For the Art Specialist

Time: About 45 minutes

Focus

Use *Transparency 33.* Ask students what is the first thing they notice about each work of art. What did the artist do to make them notice it? How is that part different from the rest of the work?

Teach

Have students complete the Alternate Activity. Discuss techniques for creating emphasis other than those the students used in the activity.

Reflect

Guide students through evaluation of their works of art using the four steps of art criticism. (See pages 28–29 for more about art criticism.) Encourage students to look for areas of emphasis in the classroom.

Alternate Activity

Materials:
- 9" × 12" white paper
- crayons
- watercolors
- brushes
- water containers

1. Tell students they will be designing a clown's face using geometric and free-form shapes. Have students choose a feature of the clown's face they want to emphasize. Discuss techniques they could use for creating the emphasis, such as making the shape larger or darker than the others.

2. Have students draw clown faces with crayons, pressing hard to leave wax on the paper. Then have students paint the faces with a watercolor wash.

Research in Art Education

Research has shown that incorporating the arts in education can lead to positive school change. Pilot projects demonstrate that "the arts do contribute to the general school curriculum, to learning for all students, to school and professional culture, to educational and instructional practices, and to the schools' neighborhoods and communities" ("The Arts and Education Reform: Lessons from a Four-Year Evaluation of the A+ Schools Program, 1995-1999" in *Critical Links*, p. 84).

Assessment

Use the following rubric to evaluate the artwork students make in the Creative Expression activity and to assess students' understanding of emphasis in paintings.

Have students complete page 73 or 74 in their *Assessment* books.

	Art History and Culture	Aesthetic Perception	Creative Expression	Art Criticism
3 POINTS	The student can identify that the artists from the lesson painted in the Surrealist style.	The student accurately identifies qualities that create emphasis in paintings.	The student's landscape clearly shows emphasis.	The student thoughtfully and honestly evaluates his or her own work using the four steps of art criticism.
2 POINTS	The student's identification is weak or incomplete.	The student shows emerging awareness of qualities that create emphasis in paintings.	The student's landscape shows some awareness of emphasis.	The student attempts to evaluate his or her own work but shows an incomplete understanding of evaluation criteria.
1 POINT	The student cannot identify that the artists from the lesson painted in the Surrealist style.	The student cannot identify qualities that create emphasis in paintings.	The student's landscape does not show emphasis.	The student makes no attempt to evaluate his or her own work.

Assessment, p. 73

Name _____ Date _____

Lesson
3
UNIT 6

Emphasis in Paintings

For the teacher: Use the following prompt for this activity.
Using crayons, draw three shapes. Emphasize one of them.

Level 1   Unit 6 • Balance, Emphasis, and Unity   **73**

Emphasis in Forms

Lesson 4 continues teaching about emphasis. Artists can create emphasis in a form by decorating one part differently from the rest of the artwork.

Objectives

Art History and Culture

To compare footwear traditions from different cultures
NSAE 4.a; 4.b; 4.c; 5.a

Creative Expression

To create a cut paper slipper that has emphasis   NSAE 1.a; 1.c; 1.d; 2.c; 3.b

Aesthetic Perception

To identify examples of emphasis in forms
NSAE 2.a; 2.b

Art Criticism

To evaluate one's own artwork using the four steps of art criticism
NSAE 1.b; 2.b; 3.a; 5.c

Vocabulary [★] Reading

Review the following vocabulary word with students before beginning the lesson.

emphasis énfasis—the principle of design that makes one part of the artwork stand out more than the other parts

See page 209B for additional Spanish vocabulary resources.

Art Journal: Vocabulary

Have students add this word to the vocabulary section of their Art Journals.

Lesson Materials

- 9" × 12" construction paper in various colors
- 3" × 9" construction paper in various colors

- scissors
- glue
- paper towels
- newspaper
- buttons (optional)

Alternate Materials:
- tag board

Program Resources

- *Reading and Writing Test Prep.,* pp. 72–73
- *Transparency 34*
- *Flash Card 15*
- *Artist Profiles,* pp. 67, 80
- *Animals Through History Time Line*
- *Assessment,* pp. 75–76
- *Large Prints 23* Lala and Tudi's Birthday Party and *24* Nanfang Yendi, Lord of the Southern Quadrant
- *Art Around the World*

Concept Trace
Emphasis in Forms
Introduced: Level 1, Unit 6, Lesson 3

Reinforced: Level 2, Unit 5, Lesson 4

Lesson 4 Arts Integration NSAE 6.a

Theatre

Complete Unit 6, Lesson 4, on pages 114–115 of *Theatre Arts Connections.*

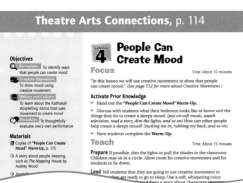

Theatre Arts Connections, p. 114

Music

SPOTLIGHT on MUSIC You can recognize an animal in music by the composer's melodies, dynamics, and rhythm. If you have knowledge of the animal, and perhaps his voice and body shape, you can enjoy guessing the animals represented in each section of *The Carnival of the Animals.* Contrast the music of *The Elephant* and the *Ballet of the Unhatched Chicks.*

Movement & Dance

Discuss with students that there are many different styles of dance. What styles of dance are they familiar with? Where have they seen them? How can they identify the particular style? Tap dancers and ballet dancers both wear shoes, but their dancing is very different. What helps us identify tap and ballet as different styles of dance?

Focus

Activate Prior Knowledge

"Have you ever seen a room that was decorated for a special occasion?" "¿Alguna vez han visto un salón decorado para una ocasión especial?"

- Discuss with students decorations they may have seen or used, such as holiday decorations or balloons and streamers at a birthday party. Discuss how decorations can draw attention to the fact that something is different or special.

Using Literature ⭐ Reading

- Read *Snow is Falling* by Franklin M. Branley. Discuss how the children in the illustrations by Holly Keller create emphasis by decorating certain areas of the snowman.

Thematic Connection ⭐ Social Studies

- **Cultural Diversity** Discuss that clothing traditions differ across cultures.

Introduce the Art

Look
NSAE 3.a

"Let's take a close look at these two pairs of shoes." "Vamos a mirar detalladamente estos dos pares de zapatos".

Summarizing ⭐ Reading

- Ask students to describe each pair of shoes. *Chinese Children's Slippers* are black with colorful decorations. The front part of the shoe has a face with ears, large eyes, eyelashes, a nose, a mouth, and colorful string whiskers around the mouth. The rest of the shoe has colorful line decorations. *Sioux Moccasins* are made of brown leather. There is fringe around the ankle. The tongue of the shoe flops over the top and has geometric designs. There are red tassels at the end of the tongue. The top of the shoe has a beaded geometric design.

 Art History and Culture

Share and discuss with students the information from the Art History and Culture sections on these pages. Have students compare the footwear traditions from the two cultures.
NSAE 4.a; 4.b; 4.c; 5.a

💻 **Web Connection**

For more information about Chinese art and customs, visit **www.chinavista.com/experience/index.html**.

198 UNIT 6 • Balance, Emphasis, and Unity

Emphasis in Forms

Look at the shoes on these pages. The artists decorated them.

▲ **Artist Unknown.** (China). *Chinese Children's Slippers.* 1991.
Cotton appliquéd with silk. 4 × 2 × 1½ inches.
(10.16 × 5.08 × 3.81 cm.). Private collection.

 **Art History and Culture**

The tiger faces on the front of the slippers in *Chinese Children's Slippers* were put there to watch over a child's steps as the child learned to walk.

198 Unit 6 • Lesson 4

 **Art History and Culture**

Some of the most delightful pieces of folk art found in China are textiles, including embroideries of cotton and silk. These slippers were made of cotton, and the design was embroidered with silk thread. Embroidery, the stitched decoration on clothing and other textiles, has traditionally been a way for a woman to express her beauty and display her artistic skills. The faces on the front of the shoes were made to scare away bad spirits and to watch over a child's steps as the child learned to walk.

See pages 16–21 and 24–25 for more about subject matter and art history.

Artist Profiles, p. 67

⟨ Artist Profile ⟩

Chinese Children's Slippers

These slippers were created by an elderly grandmother who sold them on a tiny side street in Shanghai, China. Embroidered clothes made for little boys are said to play a role in protecting them from evil spirits. When a child is one month old his or her mother or grandmother may make a tiger hat, tiger pillow, tiger collar, and tiger shoes, which are viewed as both shields and decorations.

▲ **Artist unknown.** (China).
Chinese Children's Slippers. 1991.
Cotton appliquéd with silk. 4 × 2 × 1½ inches. (10.16 × 5.08 × 3.81 cm.).

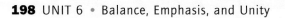

Study the shoes. Imagine that someone is wearing them.

▶ If you saw that person walking, what part of the shoes would you notice first?

▲ **Artist Unknown.** (United States). *Sioux Moccasins.* c. 1900.
....
Cowhides, rawhide, porcupine quills, glass beads, metallic beads, cotton fabric, tin cones, and dyed horsehair. 10¾ inches (27.3 cm.). Detroit Institute of Arts, Detroit, Michigan.

Aesthetic Perception

Design Awareness Have you ever seen a police car? What part of it did you notice first?

Art History and Culture

The *Sioux Moccasins* were made by an artist of the Sioux tribe native to the plains region of North America. Moccasins are soft leather shoes that traditionally have been worn by many different Native American peoples. These beautifully beaded and fringed moccasins were probably worn during ceremonial dances. The geometric designs on the moccasins probably had symbolic meanings.

See pages 16–21 and 24–25 for more about subject matter and art history.

Artist Profiles, p. 80

> Artist Profile
>
>
>
> **Sioux Moccasins**
> These moccasins were made around the turn of the twentieth century by an artist who belonged to the Sioux tribe. The part of North America that is today the states of Minnesota, North Dakota, South Dakota, and Nebraska was once the land of Plains Indians tribes, such as the Sioux, Absarokee, Kickapoo, Sauk, Fox, Hidatsa, and many others. The Plains peoples hunted buffalo and other animals, often following migrating herds over long distances. In the mid-nineteenth century, the Sioux way of life was threatened, and the people were in danger of starvation as settlers and those heading west for the California Gold Rush killed off most of the buffalo on Sioux lands.

Study

▶ Answers will vary. Students will probably say they would first notice the faces on the front of *Chinese Children's Slippers*. The long whiskers would draw the viewer's attention because they would shake at the very front of the shoes. The eyes would probably draw attention next, because of the large pupils. Students will probably say the first part of *Sioux Moccasins* they would notice are the tassels hanging from the tongues across the front of the shoes. The tassels are made of a different material than the rest of the shoe.

■ For more examples of art from Asia see *Art Around the World.*

Art Journal: Concepts
Have students sketch a shirt in the Concepts section of their Art Journals. Have students show how they could decorate one part of the shirt differently to create emphasis.

Aesthetic Perception

Design Awareness Discuss with students that police cars and other emergency vehicles are designed with flashing lights and sirens to draw attention to them.

Developing Visual Literacy Discuss how students feel about each pair of shoes. Would students like to wear them? Is there anything each artist could have changed about the shoes to make them more or less appealing to students?

Web Connection
The Grand River Museum's Web site, **www.grandrivermuseum.org,** has more examples of beaded art by Native Americans.

Time: About 55 minutes

"How can you emphasize one part of a form?" "¿Cómo pueden enfatizar una parte de una forma?"

- Read and discuss Using Emphasis in Forms on page 200.

Practice

Materials: None

- Have students follow the directions on page 200.

- If students feel no area of their shoes have emphasis, discuss what could be done to create emphasis (for instance, adding colorful shoelaces).

Creative Expression

NSAE 1.a; 1.c; 1.d; 2.c

Materials: 9" × 12" construction paper in various colors, 3" × 9" construction paper in various colors, scissors, glue, paper towels, newspaper, buttons (optional)

Alternate Materials: tagboard

- Distribute the materials and have students follow the directions on page 201.

- Review the Technique Tips on pages 221–222 for information about using scissors and glue.

- See the Activity Tips on page 248 for visual examples of this lesson's activity.

Art Journal: Brainstorming

In their Art Journals, have students brainstorm ideas for a real or imaginary animal they could show on their slippers. Have students plan how they will create them in the Creative Expression activity.

NSAE 3.b

Using Emphasis in Forms

Artists can decorate forms to make one part stand out. Artists create **emphasis** by using textures, colors, or shapes that are different from other areas.

Practice

Which part of your shoe is emphasized?

1. Look at your shoes.

2. What part do you like best? Why?

3. How is that part of your shoe different?

Differentiated Instruction

Reteach
Display three objects: two that are very similar and one that is different. Discuss with students why the different object stands out.

Special Needs
Adaptations: Encourage students to apply prior knowledge of texture by using this element in the design of their shoe.

ELL Tips
Students may have difficulty following oral directions without some kind of visual support. Consider modeling the steps of the Creative Expression activity with the whole class.

◀ **Christopher Dickhute.** Age 7.
Tyler Ferguson. Age 7.
Chase Rantamaki. Age 6.
Adam Sanders. Age 6.

Think about how these students created emphasis on the slippers.

Creative Expression

How could you emphasize the front of a slipper?

1. Trace your foot on a sheet of construction paper. Cut out the foot shape.

2. Glue a strip of paper to make the top of the slipper.

3. Decorate the top of the slipper. Make it look like an animal.

Art Criticism

Describe What shapes and colors are on your slipper?

Art Across the Curriculum

Use these ideas to reinforce art concepts across the curriculum.
NSAE 6.b

★ **Descriptive Writing** Have students use the writing process to write a description of the animal on their slipper.

★ **Math** Discuss the value of money as students identify areas of emphasis on coins and bills.

★ **Science** Discuss with students ways animals or plants have natural emphasis, such as colorful feathers or flowers.

★ **Social Studies** Have students create emphasis to make their state stand out on a map of the United States.

★ **Technology** Have students use the computer's paint program to create a geometric shape design. Then have students decorate one of the shapes differently than the rest to create emphasis. Visit **SRAonline.com** to print detailed instructions for this activity.

 **Reflect** Time: About 5 minutes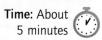

Review and Assess

"How can you make one part of a form stand out?" "¿Cómo pueden destacar una parte de una forma?"

Think

The students created emphasis on the slippers by decorating the fronts of them with animal faces.

■ Discuss with students whether there are any examples of emphasis through decoration in *Large Prints 23* Lala and Tudi's Birthday Party and *24* Nanfang Yendi, Lord of the Southern Quadrant.

Informal Assessment

Art Journal: Critical Thinking
Have students ask themselves the four Art Criticism questions, and then write or sketch to answer the Describe question in their Art Journals.
NSAE 1.b; 2.b; 3.a; 5.c

Art Criticism

Describe ▶ What shapes and colors are on your slipper?

Analyze ▶ How does your slipper have emphasis?

Interpret ▶ Is the animal on your slipper friendly or scary?

Decide ▶ Are you happy with how your artwork turned out?

■ For standardized-format test practice using this lesson's art content, see pages 72–73 in *Reading and Writing Test Preparation.*

Emphasis in Forms

Extra! For the Art Specialist

Time: About 45 minutes

Focus

Use *Transparency 34* to discuss how artists create emphasis in forms by decorating part of the form differently. Have students look for examples of emphasis through decoration on their own shoes or clothing.

Teach

Have students complete the Alternate Activity. What are some other ways they could have created emphasis on the animal?

Reflect

Guide students through evaluation of their works of art using the four steps of art criticism. (See pages 28–29 for more about art criticism.)

Alternate Activity

Materials:
- yarn
- buttons
- blunt tapestry needles
- burlap or squares of old sheets
- markers

1. Discuss students' favorite animals. Do the animals have any natural areas of emphasis? Have students choose an animal they would like to show. Have students draw the outline of that animal on the fabric with marker.

2. Have students stitch over the outline. See the Technique Tips on page 231 for information about stitchery. Have students emphasize the eyes of the animal by sewing buttons for eyes.

Research in Art Education

An overview of research concerning the arts in education shows that high-arts involvement leads to outcomes "central to the goals society typically articulates for public education—productive social membership, critical and higher-order thinking, and commitment to the skills for lifelong learning" ("Promising Signs of Positive Effects: Lessons from the Multi-Arts Studies" in *Critical Links*, p. 99).

Assessment

Use the following rubric to evaluate the artwork students make in the Creative Expression activity and to assess students' understanding of emphasis in forms.

Have students complete page 75 or 76 in their *Assessment* books.

	Art History and Culture	Aesthetic Perception	Creative Expression	Art Criticism
3 POINTS	The student can compare footwear traditions from different cultures.	The student accurately identifies emphasis in forms.	The student's cut paper slipper clearly shows emphasis.	The student thoughtfully and honestly evaluates his or her own work using the four steps of art criticism.
2 POINTS	The student's comparison is weak or incomplete.	The student shows emerging awareness of emphasis in forms.	The student's cut paper slipper shows some awareness of emphasis.	The student attempts to evaluate his or her own work but shows an incomplete understanding of evaluation criteria.
1 POINT	The student cannot compare footwear traditions from different cultures.	The student cannot identify emphasis in forms.	The student's cut paper slipper does not show emphasis.	The student makes no attempt to evaluate his or her own work.

Assessment, p. 75

Name _____ Date _____

Lesson 4 UNIT 6

Emphasis in Forms

For the teacher: Use the following prompt for this activity. Using markers, draw a hat. Emphasize one part of the hat.

Level 1   Unit 6 • Balance, Emphasis, and Unity   **75**

Unity with Words and Symbols

Lesson 5 introduces unity, which is the quality of wholeness or oneness in an artwork. Artists can create unity by making words and symbols fit together with the images.

Objectives

Art History and Culture

To identify simple ideas expressed by the artists through symbols
NSAE 3.a

Creative Expression

To create a letter creature with unity
NSAE 1.a; 1.c; 1.d; 2.c; 3.b

Aesthetic Perception

To identify examples of art unified with words or symbols
NSAE 2.b

Art Criticism

To evaluate one's own artwork using the four steps of art criticism
NSAE 1.b; 2.b; 3.a; 5.c

Vocabulary ⭐ Reading

Review the following vocabulary word with students before beginning the lesson.

unity *unidad*—a feeling of belonging together created by using related elements of art

See page 209B for additional Spanish vocabulary resources.

Art Journal: Vocabulary

Have students add this word to the Vocabulary section of their Art Journals.

Lesson Materials
- old magazines
- 9" × 12" white paper
- pencils
- colored pencils

Alternate Materials:
- posters
- crayons

Program Resources
- *Reading and Writing Test Prep.,* pp. 74–75
- *Transparency 35*
- *Flash Card 18*
- *Artist Profiles,* pp. 15, 34
- *Animals Through History Time Line*
- *Assessment,* pp. 77–78
- *Large Prints 23* Lala and Tudi's Birthday Party and *24* Nanfang Yendi, Lord of the Southern Quadrant
- *Art Around the World*

Concept Trace
Unity with Words and Symbols
Introduced: Level K, Unit 6, Lesson 5
Reinforced: Level 2, Unit 6, Lesson 5

Lesson 5 Arts Integration NSAE 6.a

Theatre

Complete Unit 6, Lesson 5, on pages 116–117 of *Theatre Arts Connections.*

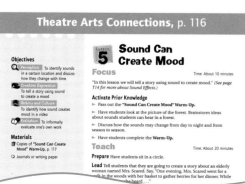

Theatre Arts Connections, p. 116

Music

Listen to *Tuileries* from *Pictures at an Exhibition.* The instrumental sounds stay high and light throughout the piece. There is a contrasting middle section, the "B section," where the melody smoothes out. Why does the total piece have a feeling of unity even with the contrasting rhythms and phrasing of the section in the middle?

Movement & Dance

Have students stand in a circle. While being led by a leader, have them move for eight counts with a specific action or movement such as marching or stretching. Then have students move using their own movement idea for eight counts. Is it more powerful when the group moves in unison or when each person does his or her own movement?

Focus

Time: About 10 minutes

Activate Prior Knowledge

"What does the package of your favorite cereal look like?" "¿Cómo es el paquete de tu cereal favorito?"

- If possible, show students a box of cereal or other product with an interesting logo that unifies words and art. Discuss how packaging often combines words with pictures. The lines, shapes, and colors of the words and pictures come together to capture a shopper's attention.

Using Literature ★ Reading

- Read *Take Me Out to the Ballgame* by Jack Norworth. Have students look for unity with words and pictures in the illustrations by Alex Gillman.

Thematic Connection ★ Social Studies

- **Neighborhoods/Communities** Discuss that neighborhoods or communities can have unity. How is there unity in the classroom?

Introduce the Art

Look

"Let's take a close look at the two works of art." "Vamos a mirar detalladamente estas dos obras de arte".

Artists's Purpose

- Ask students to describe what they see in each work of art. Why do students think each artist made an artwork that included words or symbols rather than only using pictures? *Visa* has shapes and block letters. Each shape or letter is a solid color. *Symbols* has symbols arranged in rows. Students' answers will vary about why they think the artists may have used words or symbols in addition to pictures.

🏺 Art History and Culture

Students' interpretations of the pictographs may vary. Possible answers include music notes, a check mark, and an apple. Discuss other pictographs students may see in their environment, such as the dollar sign and symbols for handicap parking or no smoking.
NSAE 2.b; 3.a

💻 Web Connection

Have students visit **www.ibiblio.org/wm/** and share their ideas about the work of Stuart Davis.

▲ **Stuart Davis.**
(American). *Visa.* 1951.
....
Oil on canvas. 40 × 52 inches
(101.6 × 132.08 cm.). Museum of
Modern Art, New York, New York.

Look at the works of art on these pages. The artists used pictures and words or symbols to make a design.

🏺 Art History and Culture

Ida Kohlmeyer used pictographs, or symbols that represent words, in her artwork. How many pictographs do you recognize?

🏺 Art History and Culture

Stuart Davis

Stuart Davis (stoo´ ərt dā´ vəs) (1894–1964) grew up knowing all the illustrators who worked for the *Philadelphia Press,* where his father was an editor. Davis left high school to attend art school and supported himself by doing illustrations for *Harper's Weekly.* He translated the sights and sounds of American life into calligraphic shapes and words and abstract symbols to represent common objects of the American lifestyle.

See pages 16–21 and 24–25 for more about subject matter and art history.

Artist Profiles, p. 15

Artist Profile
Stuart Davis
1894–1964

Stuart Davis (stoo´ art dā´ vas) was born in Philadelphia. He left high school when he was only 16 years old and went to New York City to study art. His long career began when he showed some paintings in the Armory Show in New York City in 1913. This large and important show introduced modern art to many Americans. Afterward Davis's career took off. By the 1920s, he was studying cubism. Through the 1940s, many of his paintings showed his love of jazz music. He even gave some of his paintings musical titles.

Study the works of art.

▶ What lines, shapes, or colors make each artwork look like everything belongs together?

▲ **Ida Kohlmeyer.**
(American).
Symbols. 1981.

Oil, graphite, and pastel on
canvas. 69⅛ × 69 inches
(176.53 × 175.26 cm.).
National Museum of
Women in the Arts,
Washington, D.C.

🏺 **Art History and Culture**

Ida Kohlmeyer

Ida Kohlmeyer (ī´ də kōl´ mī ûr) (1911–1997) began her artistic career in her late thirties, after taking art classes at a neighborhood art school. At the age of 45, she graduated with her Master of Fine Arts degree in painting from Tulane University. Kohlmeyer's painting style was influenced by Abstract Expressionism, which is a style that uses shapes, lines, brushstrokes, and colors to convey ideas or emotions.

See pages 16–21 and 24–25 for more about subject matter and art history.

Artist Profiles, p. 34

◆ Artist Profile ◆
Ida Kohlmeyer
1911–1997
Ida Kohlmeyer (ĭ´ də kōl´ mī ûr) grew up
Ida Rittenberg in New Orleans, Louisiana.
She began her artistic career in her late
thirties, after taking art classes in a
neighborhood art school. Her talent was
quickly recognized, and she was encouraged
to continue with formal art training. At 45,
she graduated with a master of fine arts
degree in painting from Tulane University.
Kohlmeyer's early work was primarily
figurative, but under the influence of Hans
Hofmann at his school in Provincetown,
Massachusetts, and Mark Rothko, a visiting
artist-in-residence at Tulane University,
she moved toward abstraction. A dedicated,
prolific artist, Kohlmeyer has paintings
and sculptures in many important

Study

▶ In *Visa,* the words, symbols, and shapes are all bright, solid colors without outlines. They were painted in a similar style that looks like a collage of cut paper. The pictographs in *Symbols* were all drawn in similar colors with similar line styles. They also have unity because they are grouped in rows.

■ For more examples of art from North America, see *Art Around the World.*

📓 **Art Journal: Concepts**
Have students sketch their own explanation of unity in the Concepts section of their Art Journals.

🔍 **Aesthetic Perception**

Seeing Like an Artist Discuss examples students may find around them of unity between words and art. Ideas include advertisements in magazines or on billboards, book or album covers, and food packaging. Discuss with students that graphic designers are artists whose job is to design these combinations of words and art with unity in order to grab consumers' attention.

Developing Visual Literacy Discuss with students how graphic designers' or artists' use of art elements in combining words with art can contribute to students' responses. Have students look at the cover of their ***Student Editions.*** Do they like the style of the words? Does it make students interested in the book? What if the letters of the title were instead thin, small, and plain?

💻 **Web Connection**
Symbols is part of the collection of the National Museum of Women in the Arts. Visit their Web site, **www.nmwa.org.**

Teach

Time: About 45 minutes

"How can an artist connect words with pictures?" "¿Cómo puede un artista conectar las palabras con los dibujos?"

- Read and discuss Using Unity with Words on page 204.

Practice

Materials: old magazines

Alternate Materials: posters

- Have students follow the directions on page 204.

- Discuss the lines, shapes, and colors that are used to create unity between words and pictures.

Creative Expression

NSAE 1.a; 1.c; 1.d; 2.c

Materials: 9" × 12" white paper, pencils, colored pencils

Alternate Materials: crayons

- Distribute the materials and have students follow the directions on page 205.

- Review the Technique Tips on page 214 for information about using pencils and crayons.

- See the Activity Tips on page 249 for visual examples of this lesson's activity.

Art Journal: Brainstorming

In their Art Journals, have students brainstorm ideas for how they can turn their favorite letter into a creature. What kind of creature will it be? Where does the creature live? What does it eat? Have students sketch ideas and then choose what they will show in the Creative Expression activity.

NSAE 3.b

Using Unity with Words

A work of art has **unity** when everything looks like it belongs together. Lines, shapes, and colors can connect pictures with words or symbols to create unity.

Practice

Find words or symbols combined with pictures in magazines.

1. Look through magazines.

2. Find pages where words or symbols are combined with pictures.

3. How do the pages have unity?

Differentiated Instruction

Reteach
Use *Flash Card 18* to review and discuss the concept of unity.

Special Needs
Adaptations: Reinforce skills of letter recognition by having students illustrate an animal that begins with the letter they chose.

ELL Tips
Review the letters of the alphabet and have students practice them before beginning the Creative Expression activity.

Think about how this student combined pictures with a symbol.

◀ **Joseph Lazzari.**
Age 6.

🎨 Creative Expression

How could you make an imaginary creature from a letter of the alphabet?

1. Think of your favorite letter. You could choose one of your initials.

2. Draw the letter. Imagine how the shape of the letter could become an animal, person, or creature.

3. Add more lines and shapes to complete the creature.

💬 Art Criticism

Analyze How do the lines, shapes, and colors create unity in your picture?

Reflect

 **Time:** About 5 minutes

Review and Assess

"How can artists create unity between words and pictures?" "¿Cómo pueden los artistas crear unidad entre las palabras y los dibujos?"

Think

The student created unity by using similar colors, shapes, and line styles.

■ Have students identify unity in *Large Prints 23* Lala and Tudi's Birthday Party and *24* Nanfang Yendi, Lord of the Southern Quadrant.

Informal Assessment

Art Journal: Critical Thinking
Have students ask themselves the four Art Criticism questions, and then write or sketch to answer the Analyze question in their Art Journals.
NSAE 1.b; 2.b; 3.a; 5.c

💬 Art Criticism

Describe ▶ What kind of creature did you draw?

Analyze ▶ How do the lines, shapes, and colors create unity in your picture?

Interpret ▶ How does the letter you chose represent you?

Decide ▶ If you could change anything about your picture, what would it be?

■ For standardized-format test practice using this lesson's art content, see pages 74–75 in *Reading and Writing Test Preparation.*

🎨 Art Across the Curriculum

Use these ideas to reinforce art concepts across the curriculum.
NSAE 6.b

★ **Persuasive Writing** After completing the Practice activity, have students use the writing process to write an advertisement similar to those students found in the magazines.

★ **Math** Discuss symbols that are used in mathematics, such as the plus or minus signs.

★ **Science** Discuss machines that have unity among parts, such as cars.

★ **Social Studies** Discuss the concept of unity within families or communities.

★ **Technology** Have students use the computer's paint program to create an artwork showing a family or group the student belongs to. Have students include words in their artwork to explain who the group is. Have students unify the artwork with similar lines, colors, and shapes. Visit **SRAonline.com** to print detailed instructions for this activity.

Lesson 5 Wrap-Up

Unity with Words and Symbols

Extra! For the Art Specialist

Time: About 45 minutes

Focus

Use **Transparency 35** to discuss unity. Discuss that the works of art are different from most works the students have seen because they include words or symbols. Discuss how the artists combined the words or symbols with pictures.

Teach

Have students complete the Alternate Activity to create unity between letters and pictures. What are other ways students could unify words or symbols and pictures?

Reflect

Guide students through evaluation of their works of art using the four steps of art criticism. (See pages 28–29 for more about art criticism.) Encourage students to locate in their environment other examples of words combined with pictures.

Alternate Activity

Materials:
- 9" × 12" white paper
- pencils and erasers
- crayons or colored markers

1. Assign each student a letter of the alphabet. Then have them think of an animal whose name begins with that letter, or the teacher can brainstorm animals and create a reference list. Explain to students they will be making a drawing of the animal in the shape of the letter the animal's name begins with. Have students try to fill the page.

2. Assemble the students' works of art and display them in the order of the alphabet. Have students identify examples of unity in the exhibition of artwork by their peers.

Research in Art Education

Research has shown that "the correlation in the United States between choosing to study the arts and achieving well academically is not a function of SES [socio-economic status]." Although there may still be questions about the relationship between the arts and academic achievement, it is important that we provide opportunities for students of all SES levels to learn about the arts ("Involvement in the Arts and Human Development: Extending an Analysis of General Associations and Introducing the Special Cases of Intensive Involvement in Music and Theatre Arts" in *Critical Links*, p. 70).

Assessment

Use the following rubric to evaluate the artwork students make in the Creative Expression activity and to assess students' understanding of unity with words and symbols.

	Art History and Culture	Aesthetic Perception	Creative Expression	Art Criticism
3 POINTS	The student can identify ideas expressed by artists through words and symbols.	The student accurately identifies examples of art unified with words or symbols.	The student's letter creature clearly shows unity.	The student thoughtfully and honestly evaluates his or her own work using the four steps of art criticism.
2 POINTS	The student's identification is weak or incomplete.	The student shows emerging awareness of art unified with words or symbols.	The student's letter creature shows some awareness of unity.	The student attempts to evaluate his or her own work but shows an incomplete understanding of evaluation criteria.
1 POINT	The student cannot identify ideas expressed by artists through words and symbols.	The student cannot identify art unified with words or symbols.	The student's letter creature does not show unity.	The student makes no attempt to evaluate his or her own work.

Have students complete page 77 or 78 in their **Assessment** books.

Assessment, p. 77

Name _____ Date _____

Lesson 5 UNIT 6

Unity with Words and Symbols

For the teacher: Use the following prompts for this activity.
1. Using a crayon, draw the letters of your first name with some space between the letters.
2. Draw a shape around each letter.
3. Color the shapes to make the letters look like they belong together.

Level 1   Unit 6 • Balance, Emphasis, and Unity   **77**

Unity in Sculpture

Lesson 6 Overview

Lesson 6 continues teaching about unity. Artists can create unity in a sculpture by repeating colors and forms.

Objectives

Art History and Culture

To recognize that some artists create art about personal experiences
NSAE 4.c; 5.b

Aesthetic Perception

To identify examples of unity in forms
NSAE 2.a; 2.b; 3.a

Creative Expression

To create a unified sculpture
NSAE 1.a; 1.c; 1.d; 2.c; 3.b

Art Criticism

To evaluate one's own artwork using the four steps of art criticism
NSAE 1.b; 2.b; 3.a; 5.c

Vocabulary ⭐ Reading

Review the following vocabulary words with students before beginning the lesson.

unity *unidad*—a feeling of belonging together created by using related elements of art

sculpture *escultura*—a three-dimensional work of art

See page 209B for additional Spanish vocabulary resources

Art Journal: Vocabulary

Have students add these words to the Vocabulary section of their Art Journals.

Lesson Materials

- wood scraps in a variety of shapes
- glue (wood glue, white glue, or hot glue)
- cardboard or mat board (6" × 6" or larger)
- tempera paint
- brushes
- water containers
- magazines
- scissors

Alternate Materials:
- precut corrugated cardboard in a variety of shapes

Program Resources

- *Reading and Writing Test Prep.,* pp. 76–77
- *Transparency 36*
- *Artist Profiles,* pp. 48, 58
- *Animals Through History Time Line*
- *Assessment,* pp. 79–80
- *Large Prints 23 Lala and Tudi's Birthday Party* and *24 Nanfang Yendi, Lord of the Southern Quadrant*
- *The National Museum of Women in the Arts Collection*

Concept Trace
Unity in Sculpture
Introduced: Level K, Unit 6, Lesson 6
Reinforced: Level 2, Unit 6, Lesson 5

Lesson 6 Arts Integration NSAE 6.a

Theatre

Complete Unit 6, Lesson 6, on pages 118–123 of *Theatre Arts Connections.*

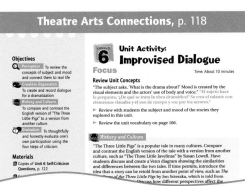

Music

Listen to *Canon in D Major* by Pachebel. The three high voices are playing the same melodic material but entering at different times. The bass line, called "continuo" in Pachebel's time, has a very simple job to create unity. What does it do?

Movement & Dance

Working with partners, have students create three sculptures together: one unified shape, two individual shapes, and then one unified shape. Putting both unified and individual movements together can be very powerful. Why is that?

Focus

Activate Prior Knowledge

"Do you have a souvenir that helps you remember a special place or person?"

"¿Tienen algún recuerdo que les haga acordar de un sitio o una persona especial?"

- Discuss ways in which people are remembered, including statues, collages of favorite things, and sculptures of things that bring back memories.

Using Literature ★ Reading

- Read *The Josefina Story Quilt* by Eleanor Coerr. Discuss how Faith made a quilt patch to help herself remember Josefina. Discuss unity within a quilt.

Thematic Connection ★ Social Studies

- **Time** Sometimes artists create art to remind them of special events. Have students make a time line that shows special events in their lives.

Introduce the Art

Look
NSAE 2.a; 2.b; 3.a

"Let's take a close look at the two works of art." "Vamos a mirar detalladamente las dos obras de arte".

Making Connections ★ Reading

- Ask students to make connections to other unit concepts (such as line, shape, color, and texture) as they describe each work of art. *Monument* has shapes made from mostly diagonal lines. It has triangles and rectangles, and some free-form shapes. It has the primary colors red, yellow, and blue, as well as shades of pink, brown, and black. *Monument* appears to have a rough texture. *Study for Time-Life Frieze* has mostly vertical and horizontal lines. It has rectangular shapes and free-form forms. It is the secondary color green, and appears to have a smooth texture.

🏺 Art History and Culture

Share with students that *Monument* was created after the artist's parents died, and it contains materials and forms that remind the artist of her parents. Discuss other ways artists can remember loved ones or personal experiences in their works of art.
NSAE 4.c; 5.b

💻 Web Connection

Visit Gilda Snowden's personal Web site, **hometown.aol.com/gsnow19543/** to view more of her work.

---

6 Unity in Sculpture

◀ **Gilda Snowden.** (American). *Monument.* 1988.
• • • • • • • • • • • • • •
Encaustic on wood. 76 × 81 × 8 inches (193 × 205.7 × 20.3 cm). Detroit Institute of Arts, Detroit, Michigan.

Look at the works of art on these pages. Each artist put smaller forms together to make a sculpture.

🏺 Art History and Culture

Gilda Snowden created *Monument* as a tribute to her parents. The artwork has symbols that remind her of her family.

🏺 Art History and Culture

Gilda Snowden

Gilda Snowden (gil´ də snō´ dən) (1954–   ) is a contemporary artist from Detroit who creates art from found objects. She decided at a very young age to become an artist when she grew up. She attended art school at Wayne State University in Detroit. During her early career as an artist, Snowden made art that celebrated her life and the people around her. In 1987, both of Snowden's parents died. This changed the purpose of her artwork, and she began to make art reflecting her memories.

See page 16–21 and 24–25 for more about subject matter and art history.

Artist Profiles, p. 58

★ Artist Profile ★
Gilda Snowden
b. 1954

Gilda Snowden (gil´ də snō´ dən) was born in Detroit, Michigan. She decided at a young age to become an artist and attended art school at Wayne State University in Detroit. Early in her career she made genre artwork that celebrated her life and the people around her. In 1987, both of Snowden's parents died. This tragedy changed the direction of her artwork. Her art gained depth and purpose. Snowden still lives in Detroit. She is an associate professor at the Center for Creative Studies College of Art and Design.

Study the sculptures.
► What forms are alike in each sculpture?
► What colors did the artists repeat?

▲ **Henry Moore.** (British).
Study for Time-Life Frieze.
1952.
....
Bronze. $14\frac{7}{8} \times 38\frac{3}{4} \times 1\frac{11}{16}$ inches
($37.78 \times 98.43 \times 4.29$ cm.).
Walker Art Center, Minneapolis,
Minnesota.

🔍 **Aesthetic Perception**

Design Awareness What forms are repeated throughout your classroom?

Study

► The forms of each work of art have similar shapes and sizes.

► Both works of art have the same colors repeated throughout.

■ For more examples of abstract/ nonobjective art, see *The National Museum of Women in the Arts Collection.*

📔 **Art Journal: Concepts**
Have students brainstorm other forms (besides sculpture) that have unity and make sketches in the Concepts section of their Art Journals to show how those forms have unity.

🔍 **Aesthetic Perception**

Design Awareness Have students identify repeated forms that create unity in the classroom. Examples include desks, windows, boards, or bookshelves.

Developing Visual Literacy *Monument* is about Gilda Snowden's memories. What do students think *Study for Time-Life Frieze* is about? Invite students to share their ideas and interpretations about the artwork.

🏺 **Art History and Culture**

Henry Moore

Henry Moore (hen´ rēe mor) (1898–1986) was born in Castleford, England. At 18, he left home to join the army during World War I. He began studying art after the war. By 23, he was a serious sculptor. In the 1930s, many sculptors were producing realistic works, but Moore started creating abstract sculpture. He often used holes in his sculptures, and he focused on making the simplest form of the subject he carved.

See pages 16–21 and 24–25 for more about subject matter and art history.

Artist Profiles, p. 45

● Artist Profile ●
Henry Moore
1898–1986
Henry Moore (hen´ rē mor) was born in Castleford, England. When he was ten, he told his father he wanted to become a sculptor. At 18, he left home to join the army during World War I. He began studying art after the war. By age 23, he was a serious sculptor.

💻 **Web Connection**
The Web site of the Henry Moore foundation, **www.henry-moore-fdn.co.uk,** provides more information about the artist and his work.

Teach

Time: About 55 minutes

"How do artists create unity in sculpture?"
"¿Cómo los artistas crean unidad en una escultura?"

- Read and discuss Using Unity in Sculpture on page 208.

Practice

Materials: None

- Have students follow the directions on page 208.

- Discuss with students that individual pieces of furniture have unity so that they are aesthetically pleasing. If each leg of a chair had different forms and colors then the pieces of the chair would not look like they belonged together. Also discuss that a room can have unity created by matching pieces of furniture.

Creative Expression

NSAE 1.a; 1.c; 1.d; 2.c
Materials: wood scraps in a variety of shapes, glue (wood glue, white glue, or hot glue), cardboard or mat board (6" × 6" or larger), tempera paint, brushes, water containers, magazines, scissors

Alternate Materials: precut corrugated cardboard in a variety of shapes

- Distribute the materials and have students follow the directions on page 209.

- See the Activity Tips on page 249 for visual examples of this lesson's techniques.

- After students paint their sculptures, have them look for letters, words, or pictures in the color that was used on the sculpture, and glue the magazine's pictures to the sculpture.

Art Journal: Brainstorming

Before beginning the Creative Expression activity, have students brainstorm ideas for how they can arrange their wood scraps in their Art Journals.
NSAE 3.b

Using Unity in Sculpture

Colors and forms that are alike create **unity** in **sculpture.**

Practice

Think of pieces of furniture that have unity.

1. List pieces of furniture in your home.
2. Think about colors and forms that are repeated in each piece of furniture.
3. Why does furniture have unity?

Differentiated Instruction

Reteach
Have students study an appliance, such as a radio or clock, and discuss similarities in shapes, sizes, and colors used throughout the appliance.

Special Needs
Adaptations: The works of artist Louise Nevelson (see *The National Museum of Women in the Arts Collection*) are excellent examples of unity in sculpture and should provide additional direction for any students who might have difficulty understanding project objectives.

ELL Tips
Define *unity* for students and use the word in a few sentences.

◄ **Deonte Walton.**
Age 6.

Think about how this student created unity in the sculpture.

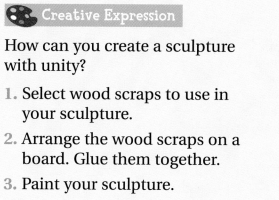

Creative Expression

How can you create a sculpture with unity?

1. Select wood scraps to use in your sculpture.

2. Arrange the wood scraps on a board. Glue them together.

3. Paint your sculpture.

Art Criticism

Describe What colors and forms did you use in your sculpture?

Art Across the Curriculum

Use these ideas to reinforce art concepts across the curriculum.
NSAE 6.b

★ **Personal Writing** *Monument* contains symbols that remind the artist of her family. Have students use the writing process to make a list of symbols that remind them of their families.

★ **Math** Discuss measuring the dimensions and weight of the sculptures students make in the Creative Expression activity.

★ **Science** Have students look for unity in people forms or animal forms.

★ **Social Studies** Have students identify national and state monuments and discuss how the forms have unity.

★ **Technology** Have students look for unity in the forms of technology equipment, such as a computer keyboard. Visit **SRAonline.com** to print detailed instructions for this activity.

Reflect

Time: About 5 minutes

Review and Assess

"How can you create unity in a sculpture?"
"¿Cómo pueden crear unidad en una escultura?"

Think

The student created unity by repeating forms and colors in his sculpture.

■ Have students look for repeated colors and forms that create unity in *Large Prints 23 Lala and Tudi's Birthday Party* and *24 Nanfang Yendi, Lord of the Southern Quadrant.*

Informal Assessment

Art Journal: Critical Thinking
Have students ask themselves the four Art Criticism questions, and then write or sketch to answer the Describe question in their Art Journals.
NSAE 1.b; 2.b; 3.a; 5.c

Art Criticism

Describe ▶ What colors and forms did you use in your sculpture?

Analyze ▶ How did you create unity in your sculpture?

Interpret ▶ Does your work remind you of anything? Give it a title.

Decide ▶ What would you change if you did this project again?

■ For standardized-format test practice using this lesson's art content, see pages 76–77 in *Reading and Writing Test Preparation.*

Unity in Sculpture

Extra! For the Art Specialist

Time: About 45 minutes

Focus

Use *Transparency 36* to discuss ways artists create unity in sculptures. What forms and colors are repeated?

Teach

Have students complete the relief sculptures in the Alternate Activity.

Reflect

Guide students through evaluation of their works of art using the four steps of art criticism. (See pages 28–29 for more about art criticism.) Have students look for other examples of forms with unity in their environment.

Alternate Activity

Materials:
- 7" × 7" poster-board in a variety of colors
- 6" × 9" construction paper in a variety of colors
- scissors
- glue or glue sticks
- oil pastels or markers

1. Have students cut out free-form shapes from construction paper. Have students decorate the shapes with lines, patterns, or textures using the pastels or markers.

2. Students should bend, twist, or fold the shapes so that they will stand out from the posterboard when they are fastened. Have students fasten the shape to the posterboard by putting dots of glue on each end of the shape. Touch the glued ends of the paper to the posterboard so the shape stands out from it.

3. Have students add more shapes to create their relief sculptures. Some shapes can be attached on top of other shapes.

Research in Art Education

Students with rich in-school art programs tend to have a more positive atmosphere—children at these schools are "more likely than children in low-arts schools to have a good rapport with their teachers." This holds true across socio-economic lines ("Learning in and Through the Arts: Curriculum Implications" in *Champions of Change*, p. 41).

Assessment

Use the following rubric to evaluate the artwork students make in the Creative Expression activity and to assess students' understanding of unity in sculpture.

Have students complete page 79 or 80 in their *Assessment* books.

	Art History and Culture	Aesthetic Perception	Creative Expression	Art Criticism
3 POINTS	The student recognizes that some artists create art about personal experiences.	The student accurately identifies examples of unity in forms.	The student's sculpture clearly shows unity.	The student thoughtfully and honestly evaluates his or her own work using the four steps of art criticism.
2 POINTS	The student shows emerging awareness that some artists create art about personal experiences.	The student shows emerging awareness of unity in forms.	The student's sculpture shows some awareness of unity.	The student attempts to evaluate his or her own work but shows an incomplete understanding of evaluation criteria.
1 POINT	The student cannot recognize that some artists create art about personal experiences.	The student cannot identify unity in forms.	The student's sculpture does not show unity.	The student makes no attempt to evaluate his or her own work.

Assessment, p. 79

Name _____ Date _____

Lesson **6** UNIT 6

Unity in Sculpture

For the teacher: Use the following prompt for this activity.
Using crayons, draw a design with shapes and lines. Use color and shape to create unity in your picture.

Level 1   Unit 6 • Balance, Emphasis, and Unity   **79**

balance—the principle of design that deals with the visual weight in a work of art equilibrio—el principio de diseño que trata del peso visual en una obra de arte

emphasis—the principle of design that makes one part of the artwork stand out more than the other parts énfasis—el principio de diseño que hace destacar más una parte de la obra de arte que las otras

landscape—a picture of the outdoors paisaje—una pintura de una escena al aire libre

mask—three-dimensional art form of a sculpted face, often made to be worn over the face máscara—una forma artística tridimensional de una cara esculpida, a menudo hecha para llevarla sobre el rostro

mola—an artwork in reverse appliqué when layers are cut away after stitching mola—una obra de arte al revés que se aplica cuando se recortan capas después de ser cosidas

sculpture—a three-dimensional work of art escultura—una obra de arte tridimensional

unity—a feeling of belonging together created by using related elements of art unidad—una sensación de pertenecer que se crea al usar elementos relacionados de arte

Vocabulary Practice

T Display *Transparency 42* to review unit vocabulary words.

Definitions: Demonstrate Meanings ⭐
Vocabulary

Draw a sketch on the board to demonstrate the meaning of one of the unit vocabulary words. Have students identify the vocabulary word you drew an example of. Repeat for other words.

Dictionary Entries ⭐ Vocabulary

Read aloud the definition of one of the unit vocabulary words. Have students identify the word you are defining.

Examples ⭐ Vocabulary

Display *Large Print 23.* Have students find examples of the unit vocabulary words *balance, emphasis,* and *unity* in the artwork.

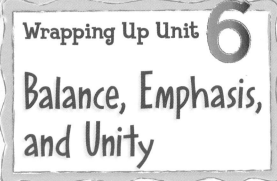

Wrapping Up Unit 6
Balance, Emphasis, and Unity

▲ **Miriam Schapiro.** (Canadian/American).
Offering. 2002.
Acrylic and fabric on canvas. 60 × 58 inches (152.4 × 147.32 cm.).
Private collection.

Art Criticism

Critical Thinking Art criticism is an organized system for looking at and talking about art. You can criticize art without being an expert. The purpose of art criticism is to get the viewer involved in a perception process that delays judgment until all aspects of the artwork have been studied.

■ See page 28–29 for more about art criticism.

Describe

■ During this step, students will collect information about the subject of the work.

▶ Have students describe what they see in the painting. The background is black. There is a large, gold-colored, seven-branched candleholder. On the left and right sides of the candleholder there are brightly-colored free-form shapes. There are eight hands coming out of the candleholder. Three of the hands have thumbs pointing toward the left edge of the painting and three hands have thumbs pointing toward the right edge of the painting. The two hands coming out of the center have their thumbs together.

Analyze

■ During this step, students will think about how the artist has used the elements and principles of art.

▶ Ask students which part of the painting has balance? The candleholder is balanced. The hands holding flowers and the freeform shapes are repeated on both halves of the candleholder.

▶ Ask students to identify the shapes and colors that create emphasis. The candleholder is large and has thick lines. That creates emphasis because it is different from the small free-form shapes with thin lines. The smooth gold color of the candleholder also makes it stand out

Art History and Culture

Miriam Schapiro

Miriam Schapiro (mir´ ē əm shə pir´ ō) (1923–   ) was born in Canada but grew up in New York. Her parents encouraged her interest in art and sent her to art classes at the Museum of Modern Art. Schapiro often includes feminist themes in her art. She also made "femmages." Schapiro invented this word to describe art made with techniques that women traditionally use, such as sewing, embroidery, piecework, and appliqué. Femmages are collages reflecting female emotions and creativity.

See pages 16–21 and 24–25 for more about subject matter and art history.

Artist Profiles, p. 56

◆ Artist Profile ◆

Miriam Schapiro
b. 1923

Miriam Schapiro (mir´ ē əm shə pir´ ō) is an American artist who was born in Toronto, Canada. She grew up in the Flatbush section of Brooklyn, New York. Her parents encouraged her pursuit of a career in art and sent her to art classes at the Museum of Modern Art. She met her husband, artist Paul Brach, while attending college. They married in 1946 and have a son who is a writer. Schapiro organizes her home life so that art is woven into it. She can move from baking in the kitchen to painting in her studio and back to the kitchen without feeling interrupted. Her husband says that she has learned to live a "seamless life."

Art Criticism Critical Thinking

Describe

▶ What do you see in this painting?

Analyze

▶ What part of this painting has balance?

Interpret

▶ What is the mood of this painting?

Decide

▶ Do you think this painting has a story to share with others?

from the busy bright colors of the free-form shapes, the hands, and the flowers.

▶ Ask students what gives this work unity. The work has unity because of the repeated hands, flowers, and free-form shapes. The colors of the free-form shapes and flowers are similar.

Interpret

▪ During this step, students will use clues they discovered during their analysis to find the message the artist is trying to show.

▶ Ask students what the mood of the painting is. Answers will vary. Some may say the flowers give the painting a festive mood. Others may say the bright colors make it look joyful or hopeful.

▶ Ask students why they think there are hands coming out of the candleholder instead of candles. Answers will vary. Students may see the flowers as a sign of peace. Others may say the hands are offering the flowers as a gift. Some may think flowers can brighten a day just like the light from a flame.

Decide

▪ During this step, students will use all the information they have gathered to decide whether this is a successful work of art.

▶ Ask students if they think the painting has a strong message to share with others. Answers will vary. Some may say it has a strong message that is worth sharing because it is about peace.

 Art Journal: Critical Thinking
Have students write the answers to the Aesthetic Perception questions in their Art Journals.

Aesthetic Perception

Critical Thinking Have students ever seen an interesting decoration like the candleholder in *Offering*? How was it similar to this work of art? How was it different?

Describe ▶ Describe the decoration.

Analyze ▶ Is the decoration balanced? What part of it has emphasis?

Interpret ▶ What feeling did the decoration bring to the room?

Decide ▶ If you could change anything about the decoration, what would it be?

"Artists create works of art that have balance, emphasis, and unity." *"Los artistas crean obras de arte que tienen equilibrio, énfasis y unidad".*

T Review unit vocabulary with students using *Transparency 42.*

 Art Journal: Writing
Have students answer the questions on page 212. Answers: 1. A, 2. B, 3. C

T For further assessment, have students complete the unit test on *Transparency 48.*

CAREERS IN ART
Education

► Encourage students to talk about the people and places who helped them learn about art. Share with students your own experiences teaching art.

"Whether in music or architecture, literature, painting, or sculpture, art opens our eyes and ears and feelings to something beyond ourselves, something we cannot experience without the artist's vision and genius of his craft."

—Barbara Tuchman (1912–1989), historian

Show What You Know

Write your answers on a sheet of paper.

1 Which of these shapes has balance?

A.   B.   C.

2 Which of these does not show emphasis?

A.   B.   C.

3 Colors and forms that are alike can create _____ in sculpture.

A. emphasis

B. movement

C. unity

CAREERS IN ART
Education

Think about places where you have learned about art. Who was there to help you learn?

Art teachers work in schools. They teach students how to appreciate and understand art. Art teachers also help students create their own art.

Art museums have **educators.** They help visitors learn about the museum's collection. They plan tours and arrange exhibits.

▲ Art teacher

Unit Assessment Options

Aesthetic Perception

Practice Have students identify examples of balance, emphasis, and unity in nature and in the humanmade environment.

Creative Expression

Student Portfolio Have students review all the artwork they have created during this unit and select the pieces they wish to keep in their portfolios. Have students share their portfolios with classmates and offer positive feedback about each other's work.

Art Criticism

Activity Have students select their favorite work of art from this unit. Guide students through study of their selected work using the four steps of art criticism. (See pages 28–29 for more about art criticism.)

Balance, Emphasis, and Unity in Stories

Let Them Eat Books is a show for children. The actors perform stories from all over the world.

What to Do Build a story with a group.

1. Sit in a circle. One person holds the story stick.

2. The person with the story stick starts the story. After two sentences, that person passes the story stick to the next person.

3. Go around the circle. The last person has to end the story.

▲ We Tell Stories. "Let Them Eat Books."

 **Art Criticism**

Describe Describe the beginning, middle, and end of the story.

Art History and Culture

We Tell Stories

The seeds which began the storytelling troupe, We Tell Stories, were sown in 1974 when founder Carl Weintraub decided to perform some stories for his three-year-old's preschool. Seven years later, he had formed a company which was creating shows for the Los Angeles County Museum of Art, inaugurating new exhibits by crafting participatory drama experiences for children. We Tell Stories is a multi-ethnic troupe which reflects a range of races and cultures. The performers use only a trunk filled with colorful and sometimes wacky costumes and props. The experience has an extemporaneous style and is designed so that children participate as listeners and as performers on stage. At the show's conclusion, the audience is encouraged to seek out books by the authors whose work has been represented.

Balance, Emphasis, and Unity in Stories
NSAE 6.a

Objective: To create a story with a group

Materials: *Let Them Eat Books* excerpt, *The Two Skyscrapers Who Decided to Have a Child* by Carl Sandburg. Running time: 7:00

Focus

Time: About 5 minutes

■ Discuss the information on page 213.

 **Art History and Culture**

■ Discuss elements of a good story, such as a beginning, a middle, and an end.

Teach

Time: About 20 minutes

Aesthetic Perception

■ Show *The Two Skyscrapers Who Decided to Have a Child*. Discuss balance, emphasis, and unity in the story.

Creative Expression

■ Explain how the story stick process will work. Have students create their story.

■ **Informal Assessment** Give students positive feedback and suggestions.

Reflect

Time: About 10 minutes

 **Art Criticism**

■ Have students answer the four Art Criticism questions.

Describe ► Describe the beginning, middle, and end of the story.

Analyze ► Did the story have a clear plot?

Interpret ► What feelings did you have during the story?

Decide ► Do you think you succeeded in building a story with a group?

Drawing

It is important to allow the students to experiment with the drawing media. Use gentle guidance to show them how to properly hold the drawing media. Prior to use, demonstrate the techniques as they are illustrated here. Proper handling and use will increase success and establish good habits for the future. It will also make the media last longer.

Pencil

- Primary pencils with medium-soft lead should be used.

- When making thin lines, the students should hold the pencil as in writing.

- For thick lines, hold the pencil on its side near the point between the thumb and fingertips.

Crayon

- Thin lines and small dots can be created with the sharpened end of the crayon.

- Thick lines and large dots can be made with the flat end. Large areas can be colored in with the side of an unwrapped crayon.

- Students may become concerned over broken crayons. Reassure them that these pieces are still useful for drawing and coloring areas.

Technique Tips

Drawing

Pencil

Thin lines

Thick lines

Crayon

Thin lines

Thick lines

Large spaces

Small dots

Large dots

Technique Tips

Crayon Rubbing

Rub away from your holding hand.

....

Marker

Use the tip.

Use the side of the tip.

Put on the cap.

Crayon Rubbing

- When rubbing textures, have the student hold the uncovered crayon so that he or she is rubbing with the side of the crayon, not the tip.

- With one hand, hold the paper and the edges of the material being rubbed. Then rub away from the holding hand for every stroke. If the student rubs back and forth, the paper will wrinkle up and a smooth rubbing will not be made.

- Rubbings can be made with an uncovered wax crayon, an uncovered oil pastel, or the side of a pencil point.

- It is better to use dark colors to make the rubbing so that the texture impression shows up. Red, green, blue, and violet are good colors to use.

- Some materials that make good rubbings are burlap, lace, weeds, shoe bottoms, and commercial rubbing plates.

Marker

- To avoid damage, students should not press hard on the marker tip. Tell them to handle the marker gently for better control.

- For thin lines and dots, a conical-tipped marker can be used.

- The side of the tip can be used to make wider lines and to color areas.

- Remind students to replace the cap to prevent drying.

Oil Pastels

- Oil pastels are pigments that are mixed with oil and compressed into sticks. They are used like crayons. By pressing with gentle force and coloring over an area several times, students can create the effect of paint.

- Students can create lines by drawing with the tip. Textures can be created by making marks such as dots and lines. Textures can also be made by layering colors and scratching though with a paper clip that has been straightened.

- Colors can be mixed or blended by smearing them with a paper towel wrapped around a finger.

- Oil pastels break easily. Reassure the students that these pieces can still be used like new ones. If the oil pastels become dirty from use, instruct the students to mark on a paper towel until the colors are clean again.

Colored Chalk

- Colored chalks are used to make colorful, soft designs. The use of dustless chalk is recommended for elementary classrooms. The tip of the chalk is used much like an oil pastel to make lines. To fill a space or shape with solid color, use gentle force and color over an area more than once.

- Colors can be mixed or blended by smearing them together with a paper towel wrapped around a finger.

- Like oil pastels, colored chalks break easily. Reassure the students that these pieces can still be used like new ones. Colored chalks also become dirty from use. Instruct students to mark on a paper towel until the colors are clean.

Technique Tips

Oil Pastel

Lines

Color in large spaces.

Blend colors.

Colored Chalk

Lines

Color in large spaces.

Blend colors.

Painting

Taking Care of Your Paintbrush

Rinse and blot to change colors.

Technique Tips

Taking Care of Your Paintbrush

Clean your brush when you are done.

1. Rinse.

2. Wash with soap.

3. Rinse again.

4. Shape.

5. Store.

Painting

Taking Care of Your Paintbrush

- Taking proper care of a paintbrush will increase its time in use. By teaching students the rules for proper care, good habits will be established in the beginning.

- Students should always thoroughly rinse the brush tips after switching to a new color of paint. Next, they should gently blot the brush on a paper towel to test for missed paint. If paint appears on the towel, the brush should be rinsed and tested again. Sometimes paint gets deep inside the bristles and the brush needs more rinsing.

- To properly wash and store the brush when finished, students should:

  1. Rinse the brush under gently flowing water. Do not use hot water.

  2. Place a small amount of soap in the palm of one hand. Gently rub the bristles of the brush in their soapy palms. This will remove stubborn paint from deep inside the bristles.

  3. Rinse the brush under gently running water to remove all of the soap.

  4. Reshape the bristles into a point.

  5. Store the brushes in a container with the bristles up so the shape will be kept when the brush dries.

- When these habits are established early in the school year, the students will be more likely to respect the importance of proper care of the art media and tools.

Tempera

- For best results, it is recommended that quality liquid tempera paint is used. Powdered tempera paints seldom mix with water thoroughly. Tempera paint of a lesser quality is usually not opaque with one application. Also, the colors of cheaper temperas don't mix as well.

- Students should have the opportunity to experiment with a variety of brush sizes when using tempera.

- Demonstrate the following steps:

  1. In general, students should hold the brush as they would a pencil, but farther back on the handle.

  2. When getting ready to paint, dip the brush into water to moisten the bristles. To remove excess water from the brush, gently wipe the end of the brush on the inside edge of the container. This will allow the water to run back into the container. Discourage the students from tapping their brushes on the rim of the container. This will prevent paint splatters.

  3. Dip the brush into the paint and brush paint over the area that is to be covered, using only as much paint as needed. Remind students not to scrub the brush.

  4. To change colors, review the steps on page 217.

  5. When mixing paints on a palette, always mix the darker color into the lighter color a little at a time until the desired color is reached. This reduces wasted paint. Paper plates work well as palettes and reduce cleanup.

  6. To paint rough textures, use a dry brush with a small amount of paint.

  7. To create smooth textures, use a moist brush with a normal amount of paint.

Technique Tips

Tempera

Wipe the brush.

Mix the paint on a palette.

Use a wide brush for large spaces.

Use a thin, pointed brush for details.

Technique Tips

Watercolor

Put water on each color.

Dip the brush in the paint.

Mix on a palette.

Press firmly for thick lines.

Press lightly for thin lines.

Watercolor Resist

Crayons and oil pastels show through.

Watercolor

- School watercolors come in semimoist cakes. Moisten each cake that is going to be used by dripping a little water from the brush onto the cake and gently stirring the water on the surface of the paint.

- Create thick lines by gently pressing down on the brush.

- Create thin lines by lightly touching the surface of the paper with the tip of the brush.

Watercolor Resist

- By drawing on the paper first with crayons and/or oil pastels, students can achieve a resist effect. Because of their waxy or oily compositions, crayons and oil pastels show through watercolors. Best results are achieved when cool-colored drawings are painted over with warm colors, or vice versa.

Painting Texture with Watercolor

■ To create textures such as stipple (dots) or lines, demonstrate this technique for students.

1. Wet a round, soft-bristled watercolor brush.

2. Hold the brush over the container of water and gently squeeze the excess water from the bristles. Stress that this is a squeeze and not a pull or the bristles may pull out from the brush.

3. Gently divide the bristles into spikes.

4. Carefully touch the moistened paint cake with the bristle tips so that some paint is absorbed by the bristles. Gently touch the paper with the separated bristles.

5. When finished, rinse, clean, and reshape the brush.

■ This technique will take some practice. Gentle taps will create irregular dots for bushes, treetops, and other textures. Gentle, upward strokes will create irregular lines for grass, fur, and other textures.

Technique Tips

Painting Rough Texture with Watercolor

1. Dip the brush in water.

2. Hold the brush over a container. Squeeze water out.

3. Divide the bristles into spikes.

4. Dip the brush in paint. Lightly touch the brush to paper.

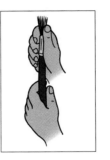

5. Rinse. Shape the bristles into a point.

Technique Tips

Collage

Using Scissors

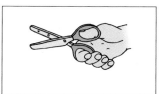

Hold scissors this way.

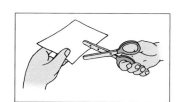

Hold the paper by its edge with your other hand.

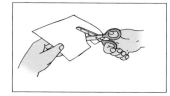

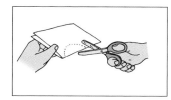

Always cut away from your body.

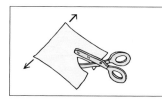

Have a friend stretch cloth as you cut.

Do the same with yarn.

Collage

Scissors

- It is important to teach students safety when they use scissors. They should always cut away from their bodies. Of course they should never point their scissors at others, spin them on the table, or walk around the room with them.

- There are scissors specially made to spring open for students with physical disabilities, or who are not yet developmentally ready to use standard school scissors. Many scissors on the market today can be used with the right or left hand. If these are not available, keep a supply of "lefty" scissors for students who need them.

- To cut thick yarn or fabric, encourage students to work in pairs. While one cuts, the other can stretch the yarn or fabric. This makes cutting easier and encourages cooperation.

Glue

Below are a few tips to share with the students to prevent waste, mess, and wrinkling of paper.

- To attach two pieces of fabric or paper, use only a few drops of glue and smooth them with the tip of the bottle.

- When finished, students should close the top first, then clean the bottle and store upright.

Technique Tips

Using Glue

Use only a few glue dots on one paper.

Smooth with the tip of the glue bottle.

Press the papers together.

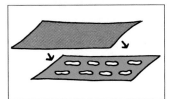

Close the bottle and clean the top.

Technique Tips
Arranging a Design

Tear shapes.

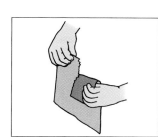

Tear strips.

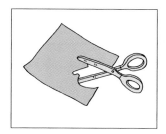

Cut shapes.

Use found objects.

Make a design.

Glue the pieces
into place.

Arranging a Design

- Provide a variety of textured and colored papers, yarns, fabrics, and found objects for students to use. Hard-to-cut materials should be precut for students.
- When using paper, students may choose to tear and/or cut their shapes.
- Encourage students to arrange the design first. They should pay as much attention to the negative spaces as the positive ones.
- Glue only after the final colors, shapes, and textures have been chosen and arranged. White glue will attach most porous items to the background surface.

Paper Sculpture

Making Strip Forms

Paper strips can be folded, curved, twisted, and then glued to create many different forms. A few basic forms are described here. Students will create many more.

1. Prepare by precutting enough paper strips for class use. This can be done on a paper cutter. The strips should be one to three inches wide in a variety of lengths.

2. Make a circle by curving the strip around to its beginning and gluing the ends together.

3. Make a box by folding a strip into four equal sections, leaving a small section for a tab. Bend the tab over its matching end and glue.

4. Make a triangle form by folding a strip into three sections plus a tab. Glue together.

5. Make a cone by cutting out a circle, cutting along its radius, overlapping the side of the cut, and gluing into a cone shape.

Building with Forms

- To join two cardboard forms, it is best to put the tape on one piece and then place it against the second piece before pressing the tape firmly in place.

- Tacky glue can also be used to join two forms. Apply a small amount of tacky glue to one surface, spread it thin with the bottle tip, and then gently press the two pieces together and hold them for a count of ten.

Paper Sculpture
Making Strip Forms

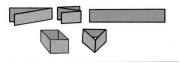

Use paper strips to make stairs, stars, tunnels, and other things.

Cones

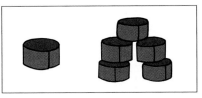

Building with Forms

Technique Tips

Weaving

Making a Paper Loom

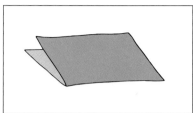

1. Fold paper in half.

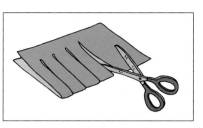

2. Cut wide strips from the folded edge. Don't cut to the other edge.

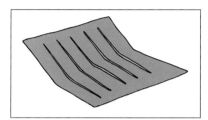

3. Open the paper.

Weaving on a Paper Loom

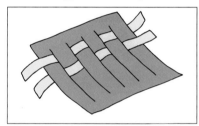

Over and under.

Weaving

Making a Paper Loom

- To make a paper loom, instruct the students to:
  1. Fold a rectangular piece of construction paper in half.
  2. Begin cutting lines from the folded edge, but don't cut all the way to the other end.

- The students can find the stopping point by locating a point three to four finger widths from the open end of the paper. Another method for finding the stopping point is to use a ruler to draw lines for the students to cut along. Draw a thicker line across the stopping point. If you have access to a copy machine that accepts heavy paper, pre-draw one loom and make copies to distribute to students.

Weaving on a Paper Loom

- Precut enough paper strips for each loom. These can be different widths, but the length should be at least the width of the loom.

- To ensure success, have students practice weaving a single strip over and under until they understand the concept.

- Next, students should practice alternating the beginning of each new strip over and under. When this concept has been grasped, they can continue weaving until completion.

- Use a dot of glue to fasten the ends of the strips to the loom.

Printmaking

- Oil-based modeling clay can be used to make a stamp. This is done by drawing or sculpting a design on a flat piece of modeling clay. There are a variety of tools manufactured for carving clay. Some classroom items that will work just as well include plastic eating utensils, craft sticks, and paper clips. The straightened end of a paper clip can be used to draw in the clay. The rounded end can be used as a gouge to carve clay away. To create a raised stamp, simply add pieces of clay to the bottom of the clay stamp.

Using a Brayer

- Below is the procedure for using a brayer, which is a soft roller, to make prints.

  1. Pour a small amount of water-based printing ink or paint onto a flat, solid surface. Roll the brayer in the ink or paint until there is an even coating on the surface and brayer.
  2. Roll the brayer over the top of the stamp. The ink should cover the stamp evenly without getting into the grooves of the design.
  3. Apply the stamp carefully to the paper, rubbing the back of the stamp with the side of the fist.
  4. Peel the paper and stamp apart.
  5. Reink the stamp as needed if you wish to make more than one print.
  6. When finished, wash the brayer, surface, and stamp.

- Another method for making prints calls for a paintbrush to apply the ink or paint. This method works better than the brayer with a raised stamp that the brayer would flatten out. Brush the ink or paint onto the stamping surface. Then follow the steps above, ending with thoroughly cleaning the brush.

Technique Tips

Printmaking

Making a Stamp Print

1. Paint the stamp.

Or, press the stamp into a paint-filled sponge.

2. Press the stamp onto paper and lift.

Using a Brayer

  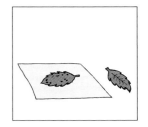

1. Roll the brayer through the ink.

2. Roll the brayer over a leaf.

3. Press the leaf onto paper and lift.

Technique Tips

Printmaking

Making a Sponge Print

Use a different sponge for each color. Dip a sponge in paint. Press it onto paper.

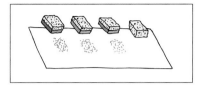

Making a Stencil

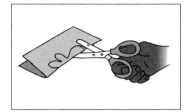

Cut a shape from folded paper.

Sponge Printing with a Stencil

Hold the stencil in place. Press paint into the stencil with a sponge.

Making a Sponge Print

- If students wish to cut a sponge into a specific shape, use thin sponges. Draw the shape on the sponge with a marker and use scissors to cut it out.

- Dispense colors onto individual palettes, or spread out on a surface large enough to avoid mixing. Lightly press the sponge into the paint, being careful not to get too much paint on it. Lift the sponge and lightly press it into place on the paper. The sponge should be thoroughly rinsed between colors.

Making a Stencil

Have students use the following procedure for making a stencil.

1. Fold a 6″ × 9″ piece of stiff paper in half.

2. Begin cutting on the folded edge, and cut out half the shape. Make sure to finish cutting the shape back on the folded edge. This will result in a solid shape to unfold and a matching negative shape.

3. If the shape cannot be cut from a fold, just cut the shape from the middle of the paper. Save both the positive and the negative shapes. Both can be used as stencils.

Sponge Printing with Stencils

Have students use the following procedure for sponge painting with stencils.

1. Have a sponge for each color.

2. Hold the stencil firmly in place. Don't let it slip. Tape it if necessary.

3. Dip the sponge into the paint.

4. Press the sponge *into* the negative stencil. Press the sponge *around* the positive stencil.

Technique Tips

Printmaking

Monoprint

1. Make a design in paint.

2. Lay paper on top. Rub the back.

3. Peel away the paper.

Technique Tips

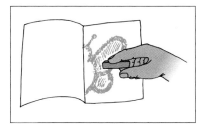

1. Fold paper in half. Unfold and draw on one half.

2. Refold the paper and rub.

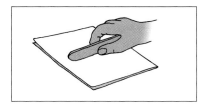

3. Open the paper.

Sculpting

Working with Clay

- Always protect the work area with a cloth or newspaper. Clay dust is messy. Always wash the tables after working with clay.

- To help prevent earth clay from drying and cracking, students should not overhandle the clay. Keep damp paper towels nearby for students to keep their hands moist.

- Clay is often sold in 25-pound bags. The bags are usually strong enough to keep the clay damp, but be sure to close the bag tightly with a twist tie or some other device to keep it sealed. It is a good idea to place the bag inside a second bag, like a heavy duty garbage bag, for long-time storage.

- The following steps are for modeling a person or animal from clay:

  1. Roll the piece of clay into an oval-shaped form. Describe this to the students as a "potato" shape.
  2. Pinch a head shape on one end.
  3. Pinch and pull out arms and legs.
  4. Leave some, but not too much, clay for the body.
  5. Squeeze the head, arms, legs, and body into the desired shapes.

- Because students at this level are not developmentally ready to grasp the idea of proportion, arms and legs may be skinny. The concept is to identify and sculpt the major body parts. Details can be added by pinching, pulling, squeezing, or by using carving techniques.

Carving Clay

There are a variety of tools manufactured for carving clay. Some classroom items that will work just as well are plastic eating utensils, craft sticks, and paper clips. The straightened end of a paper clip can be used to draw in the clay. The rounded end can be used as a gouge to carve clay away.

Sculpting

Working with Clay

Squeeze, pull, and shape the clay to make it soft. Form clay into an oval shape.

Squeeze and pinch.

Pinch and pull.

Adding Texture to Clay

Carve the clay. Use a pointed tool.

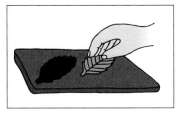

Press an object that has texture into the clay.

Technique Tips

Sculpting
Joining Clay

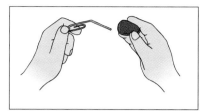

Score the edge.

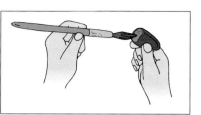

Apply slip.

Squeeze and smooth.

Stitchery
The Running Stitch

Thread a needle.

Use a running stitch.

Joining Clay

- Clay is joined by using **slip,** a creamy mixture of clay and water. Slip can be made by putting a few dry pieces of clay in a container and covering them with water. When the clay dissolves, stir to achieve a creamy consistency.

- Joining clay also requires a scoring tool such as a straightened paper clip. The steps below are called the four S's—score, slip, squeeze, and smooth. You have to put the surfaces together before you can smooth the seam.

  1. **Score** the two pieces to be joined.
  2. Apply **slip** to one of the surfaces.
  3. **Squeeze** the two surfaces together.
  4. **Smooth** the seam.

Stitchery

- Large tapestry needles purchased at fabric stores, craft shops, or from art supply catalogs are appropriate for embroidery. They have blunt points and large eyes for easier threading.

- When threading the needle, discourage students from moistening the end of the yarn or thread. It doesn't work and spreads germs. Below are two alternate methods. Either of them will require some patience to master.

  1. Demonstrate twisting the end of the yarn or thread to make a point. Then push it through the eye of the needle.
  2. Another method is to bend the end of the yarn or thread back against itself and then push the looped end through the eye of the needle. This method keeps the frayed end from blocking the opening of the eye of the needle.

- Pull about one fourth of the length of the yarn or thread through the needle. The students can grasp this in their stitching hand as they embroider to keep the yarn or thread from pulling out of the needle. Do not encourage them to tie knots.

- The **running stitch** is made by simply pulling the needle and yarn or thread up through the fabric and pushing it back through the front in a path. When finished, let the loose ends hang out the back. Trim them.

Activity Tips

Lines

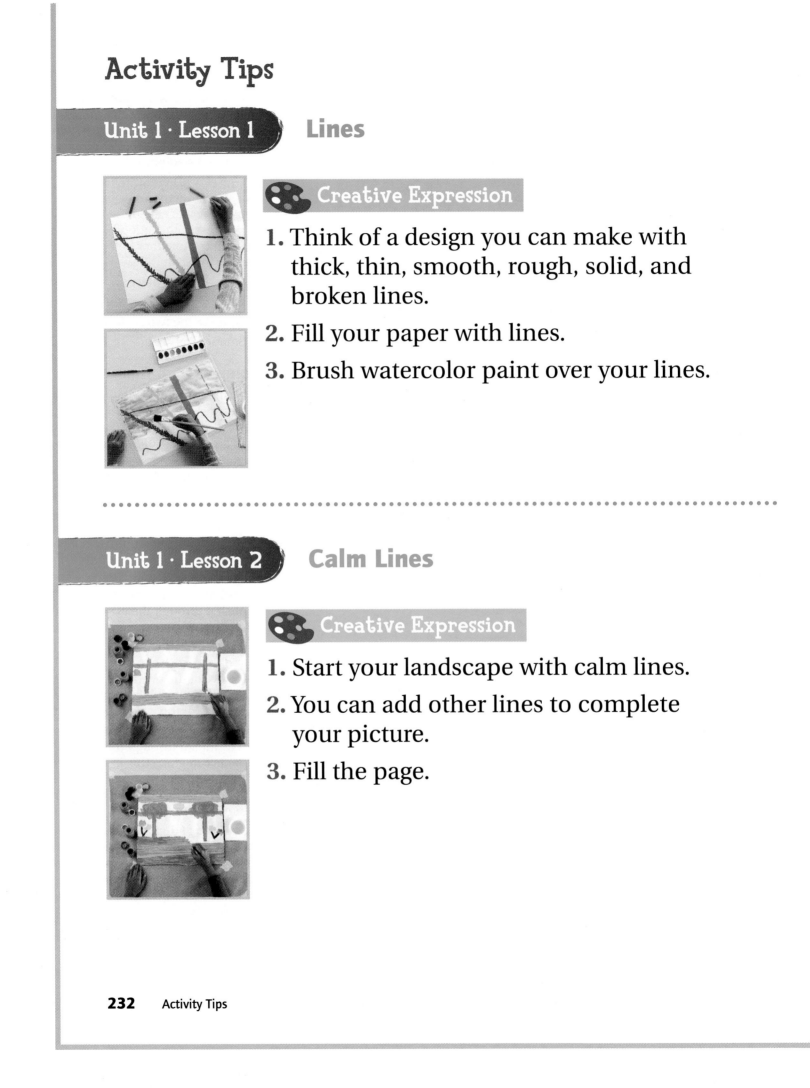

🎨 Creative Expression

1. Think of a design you can make with thick, thin, smooth, rough, solid, and broken lines.

2. Fill your paper with lines.

3. Brush watercolor paint over your lines.

· ·

Unit 1 · Lesson 2 **Calm Lines**

🎨 Creative Expression

1. Start your landscape with calm lines.

2. You can add other lines to complete your picture.

3. Fill the page.

232 Activity Tips

Activity Tips

Diagonal Lines

 Creative Expression

1. Think about how a tree changes as it grows.

2. Tear a sheet of paper to make a tree trunk. Tear thick branches and thin branches. Tear leaves.

3. Glue your tree onto another sheet of paper.

- -

Unit 1 · Lesson 4 **Curved Lines**

Creative Expression

1. Tape a square of plastic wrap to the table. Spread paint on it.

2. Pull a comb through the paint to make curved lines. Use gentle movement.

3. Lay paper on top of the paint to make a print.

Activity Tips

Buildings Have Lines

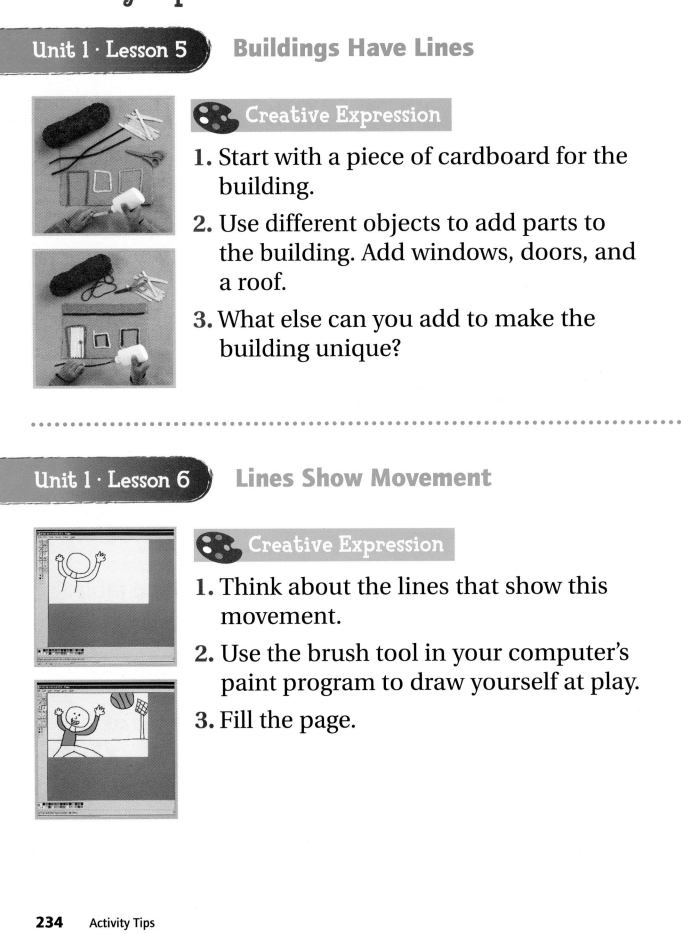

🎨 Creative Expression

1. Start with a piece of cardboard for the building.

2. Use different objects to add parts to the building. Add windows, doors, and a roof.

3. What else can you add to make the building unique?

Lines Show Movement

🎨 Creative Expression

1. Think about the lines that show this movement.

2. Use the brush tool in your computer's paint program to draw yourself at play.

3. Fill the page.

234 Activity Tips

Activity Tips

Unit 2 · Lesson 1 — Lines Outline Shapes

🎨 Creative Expression

1. Use crayons to draw outlines of fish shapes and plant shapes.
2. Use big shapes, medium-sized shapes, and small shapes.
3. Brush watercolor over your page.

Unit 2 · Lesson 2 — Geometric Shapes

🎨 Creative Expression

1. Make texture rubbings on paper.
2. Trace the outlines of geometric shapes on the paper.
3. Cut out the shapes. Arrange them to make a design. Glue the shapes to black paper.

Activity Tips

Unit 2 · Lesson 3   Free-Form Shapes

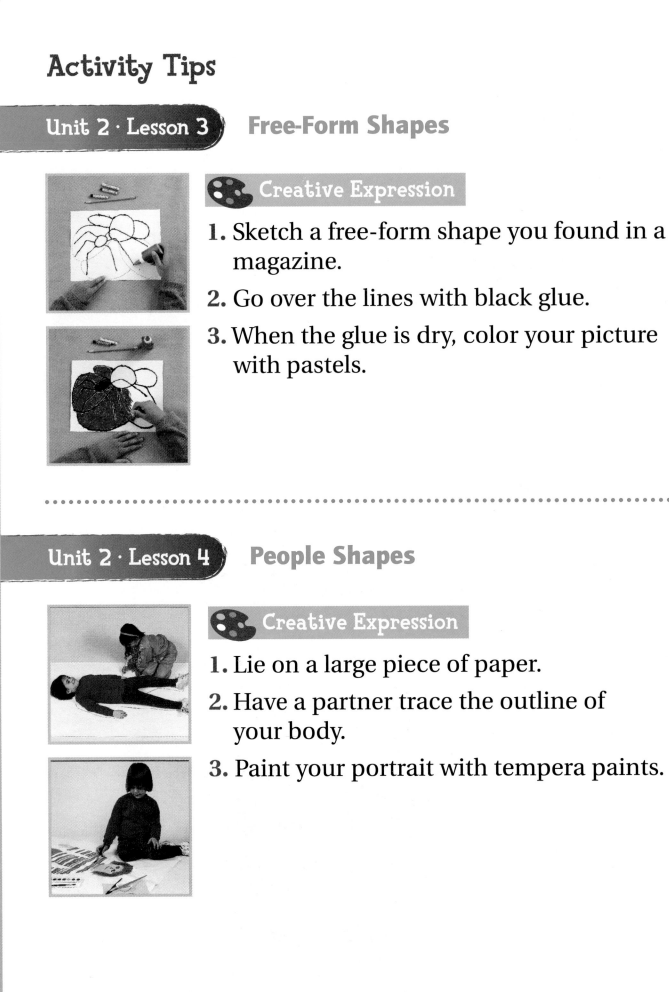

🎨 **Creative Expression**

1. Sketch a free-form shape you found in a magazine.

2. Go over the lines with black glue.

3. When the glue is dry, color your picture with pastels.

Unit 2 · Lesson 4   People Shapes

🎨 **Creative Expression**

1. Lie on a large piece of paper.

2. Have a partner trace the outline of your body.

3. Paint your portrait with tempera paints.

Activity Tips

Shapes of People in Action

Creative Expression

1. Think about what your body looks like when you play your favorite game.

2. Draw yourself at play. Use action shapes to show how you move.

Still-Life Shapes

Creative Expression

1. Choose your objects. Decide how you would arrange them.

2. Use the shape tools in your computer's paint program to draw objects with geometric shapes. Use the brush tool to draw objects with free-form shapes.

3. Use the fill tool to paint the objects. Use other tools to decorate your picture.

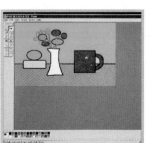

Activity Tips

A Rainbow of Colors

Creative Expression

1. Think of objects you would like to make colorful. Draw the outlines of the objects with a black marker.

2. Using crayons, color the objects with rainbow colors in order.

3. Paint the background with rainbow colors in order.

Unit 3 · Lesson 2   Primary Colors

Creative Expression

1. Use the computer's paint program. Choose a primary color to draw horizontal and vertical lines that represent streets.

2. Use the other primary colors to draw lines that represent cars and trucks on the streets.

3. Draw primary-colored shapes to represent buildings in the white space.

Activity Tips

Red and Yellow Make Orange

🎨 **Creative Expression**

1. Think of a shape for yellow and one for red. Paint your shapes.

2. Mix red and yellow paint to make orange. See how many oranges you can make.

3. Fill the rest of the paper with orange.

Blue and Yellow Make Green

🎨 **Creative Expression**

1. Imagine a summer day outdoors. Choose green things to put in your scene.

2. Make green things by mixing blue and yellow.

3. Use blue and yellow to fill the background.

Activity Tips **239**

Activity Tips

Unit 3 · Lesson 5   Red and Blue Make Violet

Creative Expression

1. Overlap torn pieces of red and blue tissue paper.

2. Glue the tissue paper to a sheet of white paper to make the shape of your creature.

3. Add details to your creature with black marker.

Unit 3 · Lesson 6   Primary and Secondary Colors

Creative Expression

1. Fold your paper in half. On one half, paint squares of each primary color. On the other half, paint squares of the primary color needed to make each secondary color.

2. Fold your paper and press to mix the paint.

3. Use craft sticks to draw your scene in the wet paint.

Activity Tips

Unit 4 · Lesson 1   Shapes and Forms

🎨 Creative Expression

1. Cut paper into shapes. Twist, fold, or bend some of the shapes into forms.
2. Glue the paper shapes and forms to cardboard.
3. Tie a string to the cardboard.

Unit 4 · Lesson 2   Forms Take Up Space

🎨 Creative Expression

1. Draw designs on posterboard with crayons and markers.
2. Fold your posterboard in half. Cut slits into it.
3. Bend the posterboard to make some sections stand out.

Activity Tips

Unit 4 · Lesson 3 — Free-Form Forms

Creative Expression

1. Think about the forms you would see in your sculpture.

2. Mold clay to make free-form forms.

3. Join the clay pieces together to make your sculpture. Paint the sculpture when you are finished.

Unit 4 · Lesson 4 — 3-D Me!

Creative Expression

1. Start with a chunk of clay for the torso. Form a neck and head.

2. Make arms and legs and attach them.

3. Add details to make your sculpture look like you.

Activity Tips

Buildings and Spaces

🎨 Creative Expression

1. Use boxes, tubes, bottles, and other objects.
2. Join the objects together with tape and glue.
3. Paint the house.

Space in Pictures

🎨 Creative Expression

1. Look at a still-life arrangement.
2. Draw the outlines of the objects. Show the space.
3. Paint your still life.

Activity Tips

Unit 5 · Lesson 1   Real Texture

Creative Expression

1. Choose materials with different textures.
2. Cut or tear them into geometric and free-form shapes.
3. Arrange the materials. Glue them to the paper.

Unit 5 · Lesson 2   Visual Texture

Creative Expression

1. Draw your self-portrait with crayon.
2. Use lines that show the textures of your body and clothing.
3. Paint over your drawing with watercolors.

Activity Tips

Unit 5 · Lesson 3   Raised Texture

🎨 Creative Expression

1. Flatten a ball of clay into a square or circle.

2. Carve and press different lines and shapes into the clay to make a design.

3. Carve your initials into the back of the clay.

Unit 5 · Lesson 4   Pattern

🎨 Creative Expression

1. Carve texture into clay to make a stamp.

2. Press the stamp in paint and then on your paper.

3. Make a design that has a pattern.

Activity Tips

Changing Pattern

🎨 **Creative Expression**

1. Make a paper loom. Your teacher will show you how.

2. Cut strips of paper.

3. Weave the strips over and under the strips of paper that make the loom.

Rhythm

🎨 **Creative Expression**

1. Choose a parade theme. Think about what to include. Make yourself an important part of the parade.

2. Draw your parade. Repeat a motif to create rhythm.

246 Activity Tips

Activity Tips

Balance

🎨 **Creative Expression**

1. Think about the symbols you would like to wear on a shirt.

2. Fold your paper in half and open it. Draw half of your shirt design on one half of the paper. Press hard with the oil pastels.

3. Refold your paper. Rub the back. Open the paper.

Balance in Masks

🎨 **Creative Expression**

1. Stuff a small paper bag with newspaper to make a head.

2. Use tape to attach a paper-towel tube to the head. Cover the tube with fabric to make a body.

3. Attach buttons, yarn, and other objects to the head to make a face with balance.

Activity Tips

Unit 6 · Lesson 3 — Emphasis in Paintings

Creative Expression

1. Look through a magazine. Find a picture of an object you would normally find outside.

2. Carefully cut out the object.

3. Glue the object to a sheet of paper. Draw and paint a landscape around the object.

Unit 6 · Lesson 4 — Emphasis in Forms

Creative Expression

1. Trace your foot on a sheet of construction paper. Cut out the foot shape.

2. Glue a strip of paper to make the top of the slipper.

3. Decorate the top of the slipper. Make it look like an animal.

Activity Tips

Unity with Words and Symbols

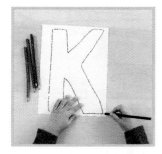

🎨 **Creative Expression**

1. Think of your favorite letter. You could choose one of your initials.

2. Draw the letter. Imagine how the shape of the letter could become an animal, person, or creature.

3. Add more lines and shapes to complete the picture.

Unity in Sculpture

🎨 **Creative Expression**

1. Select wood scraps to use in your sculpture.

2. Arrange the wood scraps on a board. Glue them together.

3. Paint your sculpture.

Visual Index

Artist Unknown
The Thinker
5500–4700 B.C.
(page 150)

Artist Unknown
Standing Youth
late 5th–early 4th
century B.C. (page 134)

Artist Unknown
Ritual Figure
c. 1962–1928 B.C.
(page 138)

Artist Unknown
Plaque
A.D. 700–1100. (page 164)

Artist Unknown
Seated Arhat
c. 1300–1450. (page 139)

Leonardo da Vinci
Mona Lisa
1503. (page 184)

Albrecht Dürer
Rhinoceros
1515. (page 34)

John Singleton Copley
Mrs. Ezekiel Goldthwait
1771. (page 160)

Artist Unknown
*Ngady Amwaash
(Mweel) Mask*
c. 19th–20th century.
(page 190)

Artist Unknown
Bridal Bed Cover
19th century.
(page 49)

Artist Unknown
Potawatomi Turban
c. 1880. (page 156)

Artist Unknown
Arapaho Man's Shirt
c. 1890. (page 187)

Artist Unknown
Corn Palace
c. 1892. (page 142)

Winslow Homer
The Lookout—"All's Well"
1896. (page 161)

Artist Unknown
*Man's Headband of
Toucan Feathers*
c. 20th century.
(page 104)

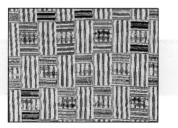

Artist Unknown
Kente Cloth
20th century. (page 172)

Artist Unknown
Mola
20th century.
(page 186)

Artist Unknown
Sioux Moccasins
c. 1900. (page 199)

Artist Unknown
Letter Holder or
Book Cover
c. 1900–1925.
(page 157)

Henri Matisse
A Glimpse of Notre Dame
in the Late Afternoon
1902. (page 113)

Mary Cassatt
In the Garden
1904. (page 94)

Paul Cézanne
Still Life with Apples and
Peaches
c. 1905. (page 86)

Albert Marquet
Le Pont Saint-Michel
in Paris
1908. (page 71)

Henri Rousseau
The Equatorial Jungle
1909. (page 74)

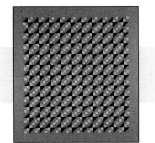

Barbara Zook Peachey
Four Patch in Triangles
Quilt
1910–1920. (page 169)

Gabriele Münter
Still Life with
Porcelain Dog
1911. (page 147)

Maurice Prendergast
Summer, New England
1912. (page 117)

Piet Mondrian
Composition V
1914. (page 41)

Seldon Conner Gile
Two Fishermen and a Boat
c. 1917. (page 101)

Lawren S. Harris
Shacks
1919. (page 52)

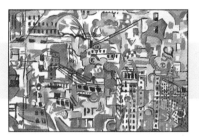

Joaquín Torres-García
New York City
Bird's Eye View
c. 1920. (page 36)

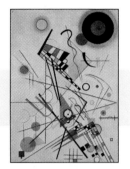

Wassily Kandinsky
Composition 8
1923. (page 37)

Pablo Picasso
The Red Foulard
1924. (page 87)

Jacques Lipchitz
Figure
1929–30.
(page 131)

Artist Unknown
Tortilla Molds
1930s. (page 165)

Pierre Bonnard
The Breakfast Room
1930–1931.
(page 90)

Agnes Tait
Skating in Central Park
1934. (page 48)

Blanche Lazzell
*The Monongahela
at Morgantown*
1935. (page 53)

Antonio Ruiz
School Children on Parade
1936. (page 177)

René Magritte
Time Transfixed
1938. (page 194)

Georgia O'Keeffe
Papaw Tree– 'Iao Valley
1939. (page 109)

Isabel Bishop
Ice Cream Cones
1942. (page 79)

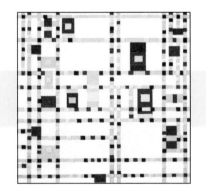

Piet Mondrian
Broadway Boogie Woogie
1942–1943. (page 100)

Thomas Hart Benton
July Hay
1943. (page 116)

Marc Chagall
Birthday
1945. (page 195)

Joe Seaweed
Mask of the Moon
c. 1946. (page 191)

Harrison Begay
Night Chant Ceremonial Hunt
1947. (page 57)

Jacob Lawrence
Children at Play
1947. (page 56)

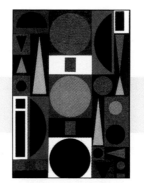

Auguste Herbin
Vie no. 1 (Life No. 1)
1950. (page 70)

Stuart Davis
Visa
1951. (page 202)

Barbara Hepworth
Figure: Churinga
1952. (page 135)

Henry Moore
Study for Time-Life Frieze
1952. (page 207)

Hans Hofmann
Au Printemps, Springtime
1955. (page 120)

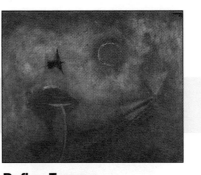

Rufino Tamayo
Toast to the Sun
1956. (page 105)

George Sugarman
Yellow Top
1959. (page 130)

Grace Hartigan
Dido
1960. (page 112)

Harrison Mc Intosh
Stoneware Vase #661
1966. (page 168)

Claes Oldenburg
*Shoestring Potatoes
Spilling from a Bag*
1966. (page 124)

Ellsworth Kelly
Spectrum III
1967. (page 96)

Loïs Mailou Jones
*Esquisse for Ode to
Kinshasa*
1972. (page 64)

256 Visual Index

Ivan Eyre
Touchwood Hills
1972–1973. (page 108)

Alexander Calder
Red Rudder in the Air
1975. (page 126)

Jacob Lawrence
*Builders—Red and
Green Ball*
1979. (page 82)

Jasper Johns
*Between the Clock
and the Bed*
1981. (page 44)

Ida Kohlmeyer
Symbols
1981. (page 203)

David Hockney
Hollywood Hills House
1982. (page 97)

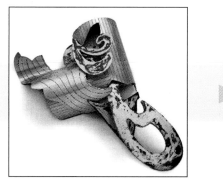

Frank Stella
Loomings 3X
1986. (page 127)

Artist Unknown
Hmong Story Cloth
c. 1988. (page 180)

Carmen Lomas Garza
Naranjas (Oranges)
1988. (page 78)

Jesús Moroles
Granite Weaving
1988. (page 154)

Gilda Snowden
Monument
1988. (page 206)

Artist Unknown
Chinese Children's Slippers
1991. (page 198)

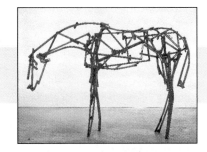

Deborah Butterfield
Rex
1991. (page 67)

Sylvia Plimack Mangold
The Elm Tree (Summer)
1991. (page 45)

Harry Fonseca
Coyote Koshare
1993. (page 176)

Joseph Norman
Spanish Garden #IV
1994–1995. (page 60)

Janet Fish
Jump
1995. (page 83)

Patricia Walker
Still Life
1995. (page 146)

**Francesca
Puruntatameri**
Muniti Red Snapper
c. 1998. (page 66)

Wolf Kahn
Lilac-colored Landscape
1998. (page 40)

Martha Berry
*Dance By Numbers
Bandolier Bag*
2000. (page 173)

Hung Liu
*Hong Shancha:
Red Camellia*
2002. (page 75)

Miriam Schapiro
Offering
2002. (page 210)

**Central Office of
Architecture**
The Dwell House
2003. (page 143)

Glossary

balance

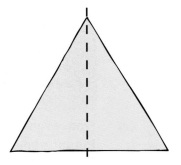

broken line

building
a structure where we live, work, meet, or play

carving

circle

collage
objects glued onto paper

color wheel

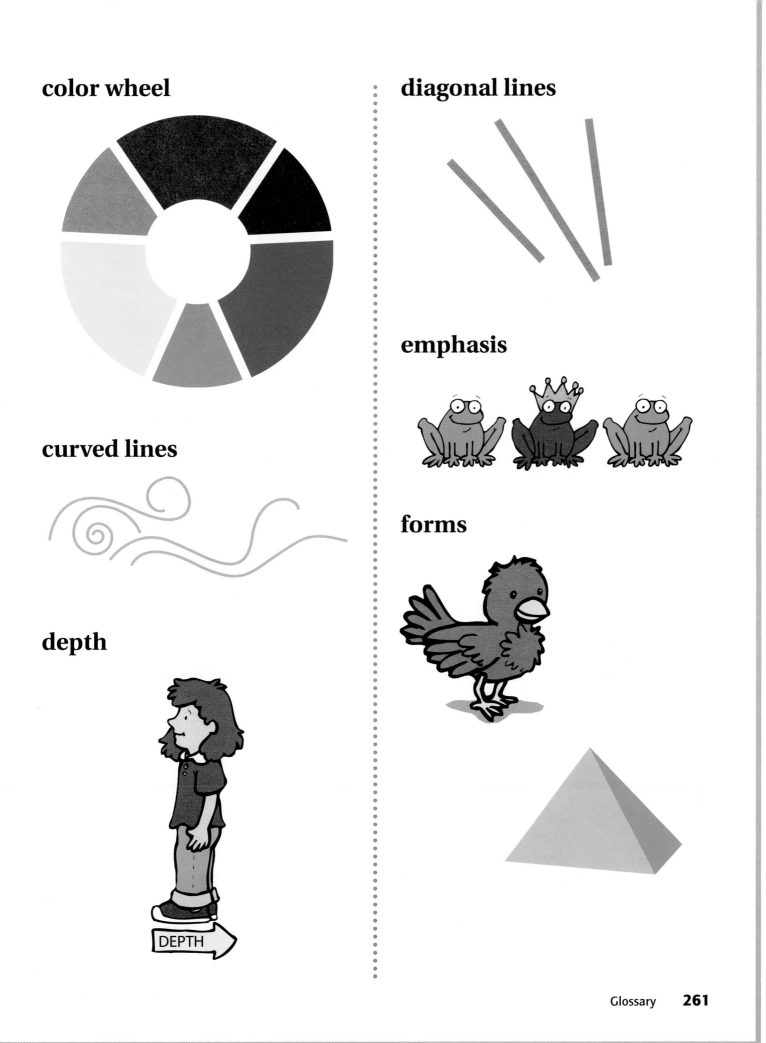

curved lines

depth

DEPTH

diagonal lines

emphasis

forms

free-form form

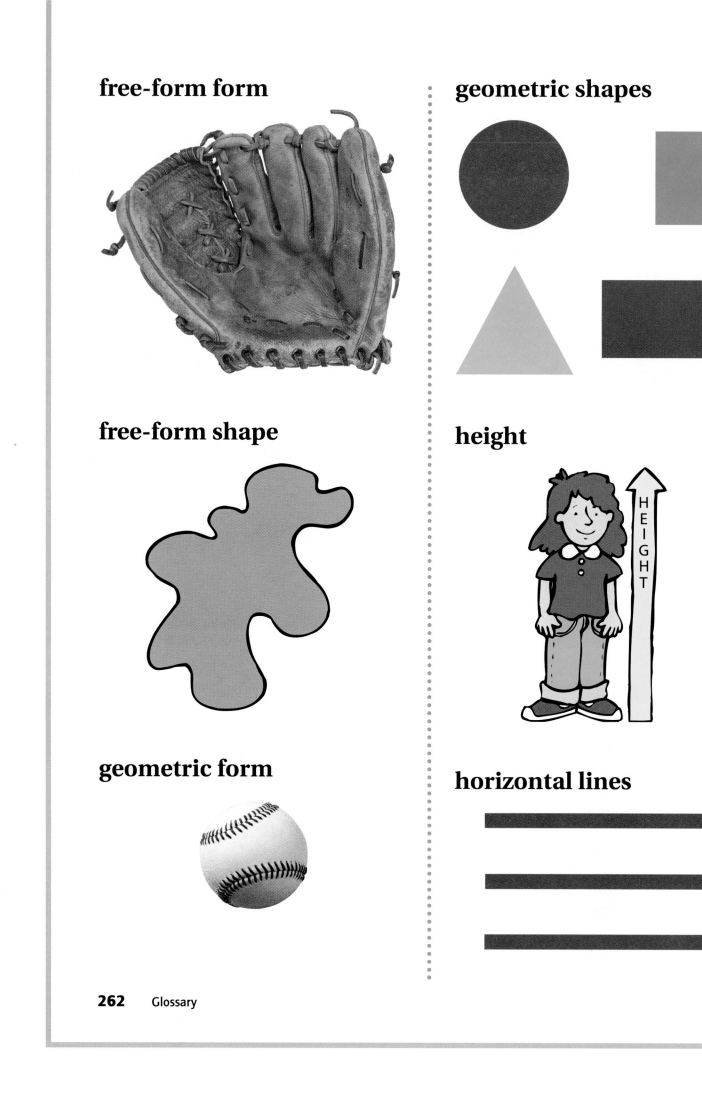

free-form shape

geometric form

geometric shapes

height

horizontal lines

landscape

a picture of the outdoors

line

_____

mask

three-dimensional art worn to cover the face

motif

what is repeated in a pattern

outline

pattern

position

how body parts are arranged

primary colors

rainbow

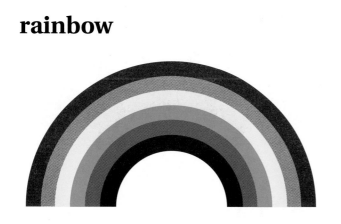

real texture

texture you can feel

rectangle

rhythm

rough line

sculpture

art that can be seen from all sides

secondary colors

shapes

smooth line

solid line

space
the emptiness between, around, and within objects

square

still life

texture
the way something feels when you touch it

thick line

thin line

triangle

Glossary **265**

unity

a feeling of belonging together

vertical lines

visual texture

texture you can see but cannot touch

weave

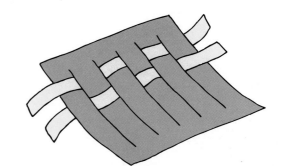

width

zigzag line

Index

title **267**

Acknowledgments

Grateful acknowledgement is given to the following publishers and copyright owners for permissions granted to reprint selections from their publications. All possible care has been taken to trace ownership and secure permission for each selection included. In case of any errors or omissions, the Publisher will be pleased to make suitable acknowledgements in future editions.

Reprinted with the permission of Simon & Schuster Books For Young Readers, an imprint of Simon & Schuster Children's Publishing Division, From THE CHICK AND THE DUCKLING by Mirra Ginsburg, pictures by Jose & Arianne Aruego. Cover illustration, Copyright © 1972 by Jose Aruego. All rights reserved.

Reprinted with the permission of Simon & Schuster Books For Young Readers, an imprint of Simon & Schuster Children's Publishing Division, from 1 IS ONE by Tasha Tudor. Copyright © 1956 by Oxford University Press. Copyright © renewed 1984 by Corgi Cottage Industries, L.L.C. All rights reserved.

THE STORY OF LIGHTNING AND THUNDER. Copyright © Ashley Bryan (1993). Used by permission of the author.

From TIMOTHY GOES TO SCHOOL by Rosemary Wells, copyright © 1981 by Rosemary Wells. Used by permission of Dial Books for Young Readers, A Division of Penguin Young Readers Group, A Member of Penguin Group (USA) Inc., 345 Hudson Street, New York, NY 10014. All rights reserved.

From OX-CART MAN by Donald Hall, copyright © 1979 by Donald Hall, text. Used by permission of Viking Penguin, A Division of Penguin Young Readers Group, A Member of Penguin Group (USA) Inc., 345 Hudson Street, New York, NY 10014. All rights reserved.

From THE VERY HUNGRY CATERPILLAR by Eric Carle, copyright © 1969 and 1987 by Eric Carle. Used by permission of Philomel Books, A Division of Penguin Young Readers Group, A Member of Penguin Group (USA) Inc., 345 Hudson Street, New York, NY 10014. All rights reserved.

Photo Credits

Table of Contents

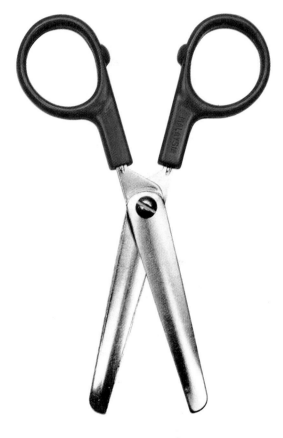

The Elementary Art Curriculum

Rosalind Ragans, Ph.D., Associate Professor Emerita, Georgia Southern University

Art education is for all students. It provides learning opportunities for the artistically talented few, as well as the many students who may never produce art outside the classroom.

A strong elementary visual arts curriculum teaches students that they can communicate a variety of ideas and emotions in many different ways. Students learn that some problems have many different solutions, and they will not be afraid to use divergent-thinking strategies. They will learn concepts and techniques that will give them control of the visual images they produce.

A strong elementary art curriculum also enables students to expand their perceptive, interpretive, and analytical abilities. They learn to find meaning in visual images, and they learn to identify aesthetic qualities in a variety of works of art and in the environment. They begin to develop the ability to make aesthetic judgments.

The visual arts have always been an integral component in the history of humanity, and through the study of art history, students will develop a better understanding of beliefs and ideas that are different from their own.

The four components of a quality art program are Aesthetic Perception, Art Criticism, Art History and Culture, and Art Production and Creative Expression.

Aesthetic Perception

Aesthetics is a branch of philosophy. In visual art, aesthetics becomes the study of the nature of beauty and art. Aesthetics is concerned with the question "What is art?" In the past, aesthetics was defined as the study of beauty because the creation of beauty was thought to be the purpose of art. Today, some aestheticians still believe that the purpose of art is to create beauty or beautifully organized arrangements of the elements of art. Some believe that art must imitate reality. Others think of art as a strong means to communicate ideas and emotions.

Aesthetic concepts are the core of the *Art Connections* curriculum. They are the framework upon which all aspects of art learning are constructed. The **About Aesthetic Perception** section in the *Student Edition* and *Teacher Edition* offers concrete methods for introducing students to aesthetics.

Art Criticism

Works of art are the focus of every lesson. Art criticism is the sequential process used in this textbook to guide students through the procedures needed to learn from these works of art. Art criticism enables students to learn from works of art that have been created by artists from many cultures and time periods. Art criticism also provides a procedure that students can use to objectively study their own art products.

The four-step process of art criticism will help students expand their perceptive, analytical, interpretive, and aesthetic valuing abilities. The sequential steps of art criticism are similar to those used in the scientific method. During the first two steps, **Describe** and **Analyze,** students are asked to collect data objectively. During the third step, **Interpret,** students speculate about the meaning of the work based on the data collected: they make a hypothesis abut the idea, emotion, or mood expressed by the artist. During the fourth step, **Decide,** or aesthetic judgment, the students offer their conclusions about the work of art.

Art criticism helps students study a work of art before making an aesthetic judgment. Too often, beginners look at a work of art briefly and immediately make a value judgment. The sequential procedures in art criticism force the students to postpone judgment while becoming immersed in the image.

In this program art criticism is used as a higher-level method of thinking about the concepts taught in each unit. One work of art has been selected that emphasizes the elements or principles that were the focus of the lesson. Art criticism is also used to help students make a personal assessment of the artwork produced during the Creative Expression activities. The questions offered are neutral and avoid judgments involving likes and dislikes. This avoids embarrassing moments when discussing works in front of peers.

Art History and Culture

Art Connections is not an art history text, but any study of art should begin with learning something about the history of world art and the people who created it. Information about art history related to the featured work of art in each lesson is provided for the students throughout the text. The **About Art History and Culture** section provides an overview of how to include art history information in classroom instruction. Additional information is provided for the teacher in each lesson and in ancillary materials such as the *Artist Profiles* books and on the backs of the *Large Prints.* The *Art Around the World* collection and *The National Museum of Women in the Arts Collection* contain works of art from many countries and provide additional historical and cultural information.

Art Production and Creative Expression

Each lesson includes an art production activity identified as **Practice** and **Creative Expression** in the *Student Edition.* This is the place for each student to creatively explore the lesson concept. Hands-on activities are often the most enjoyable aspect of art learning. The student integrates and internalizes the verbal and visual concepts of the lesson during the creative manipulation of art materials. While every component in the art program is equally important, every component does not need equal time. Art production requires the longest amount of time.

Do not skip the self-assessment section of the lesson. Most students would be embarrassed to offer subjective statements about their own work or the work of classmates. The four steps of art criticism offer an objective procedure for thinking about the concepts and technical procedures used during the creation of art.

Art Magazine Resources for Teachers

American Artist	*ARTnews*	*Crayola Kids*
Art Education	*Arts and Activities*	*Scholastic Art*
Art to Zoo	*Arts Education Policy Review*	*School Arts*

About Aesthetic Perception

Richard W. Burrows , Executive Director, Institute for Arts Education, San Diego, California

The Association of Institutes for Aesthetic Education promotes and fosters aesthetic education principles and practices through professional and institutional development. The Association provides policy and program leadership to the arts and education field at the national, state, and local levels.

Aesthetics has been defined as the branch of philosophy that focuses on the nature of beauty, the nature and value of art, and the inquiry processes and human responses associated with those topics.

Aesthetic perception can be most simply defined as an educational approach designed to enhance understanding of artistic expression. Aesthetic perception requires two primary elements to exist: a work of art and a viewer to perceive it. An aesthetic perception approach to viewing works of art is predicated on the belief that the arts can be studied in an active, experiential way. The focus is on developing skills of perception by using works of art as a "textbook" or a focus for study. The instruction delivered by teachers is in partnership with the work of art.

Aesthetic perception provides opportunities to heighten perception and understanding through direct encounters with a broad spectrum of works of art. Students and teachers become actively involved with the artwork—observing, listening to and discussing works of art, and exploring their perceptions of these works through participatory activities. The focus is on developing skills of perception through greater understanding of art forms, of how artists make aesthetic choices, and of how these understandings relate to other aspects of life.

Misconceptions About Aesthetic Perception

As aesthetic perception approaches have become more widely used, a number of misconceptions have developed about the purpose of aesthetic perception education in the understanding of works of art.

Multidisciplinary Versus Interdisciplinary

The purpose of aesthetic perception is not to explore the commonalities among works of art. Each work of art must be studied separately first; connections should be made after an in-depth understanding of that particular work. Every work of art has a separate intention and different meaning. If aesthetic perception is to develop a thinking- or meaning-based understanding of the work of art, then activities must reflect that point of view.

You Cannot Teach What You Do Not Like

A strong "personal" negative reaction to a work of art does not invalidate it as an object of study for students.

Arts Integration

While arts experiences must integrate with all other areas of the curriculum, it is important to understand the separate language that the arts have and acknowledge the connections with other cross-curricular areas as they arise.

The Therapeutic Value of Aesthetic Perception

Very often students and teachers will comment on the therapeutic value of aesthetic perception—it seems separate from the actual art-making processes. This is often a side effect of active engagement in artistic creation and perception. This is not the purpose of aesthetic perception, which should be seen as an alternative way of viewing the work of art and the world in which it is created.

Using Aesthetic Perception

Below are some guidelines for using an aesthetic-perception approach to education.

Deciding What to Teach

It would not be appropriate to teach the same elements over and over in connection with each work of art. Instead, knowledge of all of the elements within a given art discipline should provide the background knowledge for making a decision about what aesthetic perception experiences to design. These decisions should be based on the most predominant elements in the work of art—the responses and the backgrounds of the students.

Creating a Safe Space and Adopting a Critical Stance

It is important to create a working and learning environment with both students and teachers in which they feel comfortable taking risks and trying out new ideas. This does not mean, however, that everything that occurs in aesthetic perception has to be met with uncritical approval. Instead, experiences can be structured so that participants receive feedback on their aesthetic choices and are given an opportunity to revise and improve their solutions to problems.

Documenting the Experience

Various types of documentation serve as a way of recording the aesthetic perception events as they occur or are revisited. This documentation should include written observations, interviews, journals, and student projects. It is important in any case to record this work in order to be able to see the "habits of mind" that reveal themselves in this complex and rich way of thinking and knowing.

Aesthetic perception is a long-term undertaking and requires a patient conviction that the arts and aesthetic perception should be a part of the learning experience of young people. It requires flexibility, stamina, ingenuity, and perseverance. The rewards are astronomical in terms of student response, content understanding, and classroom relationships.

Introduction to Art History

Gene A. Mittler, Ph.D., Professor Emeritus, Texas Tech University

> "The art of the Greeks, of the Egyptians, of the great painters who lived in other times, is not an art of the past; perhaps it is more alive today than it ever was. Art does not evolve by itself; the ideas of people change and with them their mode of expression."   —Pablo Picasso

One of the primary goals of education in the visual arts is to prepare students to make and support intelligent and sensitive decisions about works of art. In order to make those kinds of decisions students can employ two ways of examining and responding knowledgeably to visual art forms. One of these ways, art criticism, involves them in learning *from* works of art. Another approach is art history, which enables students to learn *about* works of art and the artists who created them.

The Art History Approach to Learning about Art and Artists

Art historians contend that no work of art can be fully understood unless it is viewed in relation to the circumstances in which it was created. Every artwork is created in a particular place at a particular time in history and to some degree is bound to reflect the prevailing conditions of that time and place. For example, an art history approach to the study of a painting by Rembrandt would include an examination of seventeenth century Holland—the time and place in which that particular artist lived and worked. Adhering to this approach would require that students focus attention on the social, religious, and economic conditions that existed in the republic at that time in history before focusing attention on the painter and his work. All these conditions would have impacted Rembrandt's choice of subject matter, medium, his way of handling materials, and the visual language he chose to use in expressing his ideas and feelings.

Art history, then, involves a study of the visual arts in relation to the times and places from which they sprang. This study will provide students with a richer, broader, and deeper understanding of the specific art objects selected for study and the world as it existed when those art objects were created. However, to determine the significance of the place of a particular work, such as a picture by Rembrandt, involves more than just an examination of the world conditions at the time that artist lived. It also requires a study of what went on in the world *before* and *after* Rembrandt painted his picture. A study of this kind will show students that Rembrandt, like all artists, took into account the works of other artists, selecting some ideas and techniques to use in his own painting while rejecting other ideas and techniques. This is a valuable lesson that students can apply to their own efforts to create art.

Consequently, a historical examination of a painting by Rembrandt would include the identification of any artists who may have influenced his style of painting. The most important of these artists was the Italian painter Caravaggio, whose paintings Rembrandt never saw, but without which his own work would not have taken on certain stylistic innovations. However, to understand Caravaggio, students would have to become acquainted with the artists *he* admired as well as the ones he rejected while arriving at his own revolutionary painting style. Thus, students adhering to an art history approach will find themselves involved in a fascinating learning process not unlike a game of dominoes, in which an entire row of game pieces is seen to collapse by upsetting the first domino in that row. The very last "domino" to fall in this comparison of art history to dominoes would be the very first visual image ever created—perhaps an image scratched on the rough wall of a cave by the very first prehistoric artist.

The Use of Historical Periods

For convenience, art historians divide the history of art into more or less artificial periods such as Medieval, Renaissance, Baroque, and Rococo. Doing so does no harm as long as students are reminded that the changes in art history identified by these labels, like changes of the seasons, are gradual. Each historical period passes into the next as smoothly as spring passes into summer.

If it can be assumed that an understanding of the present can be illuminated by a study of the past, then a chronological ordering of art history periods can be most helpful. By beginning at the beginning and observing the changes in art created from one year, decade, or century to the next, students will find it easier to understand how the art produced today has its roots in the art produced in the past. If students are to gain an understanding of art history, they should be afforded opportunities to see and learn about art examples from every corner of the world representing every historical period, not just those created by Western artists.

In every art history period students will encounter artists whose works preserve the traditional values of earlier artists, artists who chose to build upon current art trends, and still other artists who opted to explore revolutionary ways of expressing themselves through their art. Art history is filled with the stories of artists who accepted or rejected, endorsed or protested, conformed or reformed, contrasted or destroyed, dreamed of the past or conjured up visions of the future—but every one of those artists did so from the springboard of his or her own time and place, be that tenth-century China or twentieth-century America.

Art History as a Means of Understanding Each Other

Through art history students learn that a painting, a statue, or a temple is a consequence of how imaginative, sensitive members of any given society viewed and responded to the world around them. Art history also encourages students to regard works of art as more than objects that are pleasing to the eye, more than splendid and original products of human skill and inventiveness. Works of art also represent springboards for learning, revealing how differently people thought and acted at different times and in different geographical locations throughout the long history of humankind. A work of art reveals not only the customs, social habits, architecture, and technical achievements of its time and place; it also reflects the prevailing fears, beliefs, superstitions, desires, and values of people living in different ages at different geographic locations. Art history, then, is a vital part of the history of the human race.

Art History and Changing Tastes

As they study art history, students will discover that, over time, works of art do not always look the same to the people viewing them. This happens because people from different times and places look at art from different points of view. Cultures vary and change and so do tastes. Take any great artist or any great work of art from a bygone era and note how there have been periods in which that artist or work has been highly regarded, treated with indifference, or even ridiculed. For example, few today would venture a negative judgment of a painting created by Rembrandt, who is universally regarded as one of the greatest artists of all time. Yet, over the years, this Dutch master has not always been understood or appreciated. Indeed, when Italian artists first viewed a painting by Rembrandt they were puzzled and disappointed. They failed to understand why this artist was so highly regarded. His style, they concluded, was most peculiar because it made use of large areas of dark values and made no use of outlines favored by Italian artists.

Students must learn that art is a two-way process involving *both* artist and viewer. If students are to grasp more than the superficial appearance of a work of art, they must be prepared to learn its purpose, its *contemporary* meaning within the society in which it was produced, and its place in the historical process. No work of art is created in a vacuum. If students are to share in the ideas and feelings that contributed to the creation of a work of art, they must recognize the concepts, desires, and expectations of the person expressing those ideas and feelings at a particular point in time. This will result in a richer, broader, deeper understanding of both the artwork and the culture that witnessed its creation.

The Art History Operations

The study of art history is made easier for students if a plan of action is offered. One such plan makes use of four steps, or operations, that bear the same labels used to describe the four steps used in art criticism. These operations are description, analysis, interpretation, and decision. However, while these operations enable students to gain information from works of art during art criticism, they also are used to help students gather information about those works during art history. Briefly, the four art history operations are:

Description During this first operation, students seek to discover when, where, and by whom the work was created. In other words, they determine the period in which the work was created, the place where the artist lived, and, assuming it is known, the name of the artist.

Analysis This operation requires students to identify the unique features in a work of art that determine its artistic style. In the visual arts, style has come to mean the personal and unique way in which the artist uses the elements and principles of art to express ideas and feelings. For example, one artist may choose to delineate shapes in his painting by surrounding them with a heavy dark outline. Another painter might ignore the use of an outline and suggest shapes by creating areas of bright hues that contrast with the dull hues surrounding them.

> "Art historians contend that no work of art can be fully understood unless it is viewed in relation to the circumstances in which it was created."

Interpretation When interpreting a work of art, students take into account the impact of time and place upon the artist. It is during this operation that they learn that pictures of the same subject painted at the same time but in different geographic locations typically differ in appearance because they reflect different traditions and values. A landscape painted in fifteenth-century Italy will differ dramatically from a landscape painted at the same time in Japan. Moreover, a work of art created in the same country but at different times may also bear few stylistic similarities. A landscape painted by a French artist living and working in the late nineteenth century would have little in common with a landscape done by a French artist living and working at the beginning of the same century.

In an effort to express themselves in visual terms, artists make use of the materials and processes placed in their hands by the circumstances of time and place. Thus, a

nineteenth-century African artist might have carved a figure from a piece of wood to serve as a dwelling place for a departed spirit, while a seventeenth-century artist applied his brush to canvas to paint a lifelike portrait of his king. In the spotlight of history, the efforts of both artists are magnified or diminished, honored or dismissed by forces that neither could predict or control but that had little to do with the values the artists sought to express in their work. It is the desire to discover those values that motivates students when interpreting artists' works.

Decision The final art history operation requires that students make a decision about the historical importance of a work of art. They will discover that some works are more important than others because they were the first examples of a new, revolutionary style. Others are found to be significant because they are the most accomplished and successful examples of a particular style. As their knowledge and understanding of art grows, students will find themselves liking a great many more works of art than they thought possible at the start. Gradually they will gain confidence in their historical judgments and exercise skill in defending those judgments.

Art history is a fascinating, provocative learning experience affording students the opportunity to travel through time and space. It provides them with access to the inner lives of many kinds of people and offers clues to where we come from and who we are. Finally, art history reveals that artists and their art have succeeded in helping people communicate with each other in a manner we cannot express in any other way.

Art Criticism

Rosalind Ragans, Ph.D., Associate Professor Emerita, Georgia Southern University

Art criticism is organized discussion about art. The art criticism procedures used in this program were developed by Edmund B. Feldman based on his analysis of the writings of professional art critics. He organized the elaborate procedures followed by critics and summarized them into four steps. The purpose of these four steps is to delay impulse judgments of visual images and to involve the viewer in a complex interaction with the image that can result in a truly aesthetic experience.

Art criticism involves the use of high-level thinking skills. The viewer translates the visual language of the image created by an artist into everyday words. To have a truly aesthetic experience the viewer must go beyond simple identification and recognition to the types of thinking required to analyze, interpret, and judge visual clues.

Anyone can do art criticism. All that is needed are eyes to see the image and a brain to think about what is seen. Art criticism gives a viewer of any age the confidence to discuss a work of art without worrying about what other people have said about it. One does not need to know anything about the artist, the style, or the time when the work was made to get involved with the work. After the steps of art criticism have been followed in a school setting, students are usually so interested in the art that they want to know more about the who, what, where, when, and how of the work. In other words, the students are ready to learn about art history and culture.

Description

The first step of art criticism is a clue-collecting step. The purpose of this step is to get to know the work as intimately and deeply as one can. All the information from the credit line should be noted. It is important for the viewer to know whether the artwork is 20 × 30 inches or 20 × 30 feet. The medium with which the work is made is also important. Whether a piece of sculpture is modeled with clay or carved from stone affects the viewer's impression. Then the observer names everything that is seen in the image. During description the observer must remain objective. All the descriptive terms must be neutral, value-free words.

Analysis

This is an advanced form of description. It is also an objective, clue-collecting step. During this stage the viewer studies the elements of art and the principles that have been used to organize those elements. It is during this step that the viewer begins to discover how the artist has organized the formal qualities of the work to create the content or meaning. In this program you will see how the art criticism lesson at the end of each unit is used to reinforce the concepts taught during each unit. Works of art have been selected that will help the student comprehend the artist's use of the specific elements or principles that were introduced in that unit.

Interpretation

This is the most important part of art criticism. It is during this step that the viewer pulls together all the descriptive and analytical observations to make sense of the work. The viewer makes inferences about the mood, meaning, or message being conveyed by the work. This step goes beyond narration to a generalization about life. The viewer makes guesses, but these ideas must be supported by the clues collected during the first two steps. This can be the most difficult step because it requires imagination and courage. Every interpretation can be different because each is based on the feelings and life experiences of the viewer. No one individual has done or seen exactly the same things as the next person. The viewer may see ideas in a work of art that were never dreamed of by the artist. That is not wrong. It simply means that the work is so powerful that it carries special meanings for everyone.

A good interpretation goes beyond answering "What is happening?" to answering "What does it mean?"

Decision (Judgment)

This is the step where a professional critic will decide the quality of a work. Is this as good as the rest of the works by this artist? How does it measure up to the works of other artists in the same group? The students who are using this program do not have enough experience to make that level of decision, so the works of art in *Art Connections* have been selected because they have already been judged to be outstanding examples of art.

The students are asked to make personal decisions. There are two levels of judgment to be made. The first is "Do you like the work?" This opinion may be embarrassing for students to share in front of classmates, and it is best left unspoken. No one can ever tell someone else what they should like or dislike.

The second level of judgment is also subjective. We ask the student to decide why the work is successful, and we use aesthetic theories to help each individual make decisions about the work. The three aesthetic theories that we employ are the most common theories: imitationalism/realism, formalism/composition, and emotionalism/expressionism. More than one theory can be used to judge a work of art.

- Some critics think the most important thing about a work of art is the realistic presentations of the subject matter. People with this point of view think that an artwork should imitate life. This theory, called **imitationalism** or **realism,** focuses on realistic representation.
- Other critics think that composition is the most important factor in a work of art. This aesthetic theory, called **formalism** or **composition,** places emphasis on the design qualities, the arrangement of the elements of art using the principles of art.
- **Emotionalism** or **expressionism** is the theory concerned with the content or meaning of the work. This theory requires that a work of art convey a message. It must arouse a response of feelings, moods, or emotions in the viewer.

In this program we provide leading questions to help the teacher and student delve into a work of art by using the steps of art criticism. These are not all the questions that can be addressed in viewing a work, and teachers are encouraged to go beyond what is presented on the pages of these books.

Meeting National and State Standards for Art Education

Nan Yoshida

Art Connections has been carefully designed to help educators meet the standards of state and national art curriculum guidelines.

The *National Standards for Arts Education* are part of Goals 2000, the overarching plan for improving American education. Approved by the United States Congress in 1994, the standards describe what every young American student should know and be able to do in the arts.

In addition to the national standards, individual states have curriculum documents that set forth guidelines and requirements in subject areas. For example, both the *Texas Essential Knowledge and Skills for Art* and the *Visual and Performing Arts Framework for California Public Schools, Kindergarten through Grade Twelve* discuss four components of visual arts education common to most other state guidelines.

Placing the national standards side by side with the Texas and California standards, one can readily see that the documents match in their expectations of what students should know and be able to do in the visual arts.

Art Connections has been developed with these national and state expectations in mind. Every lesson in the program was designed to address the components of art education in Aesthetic Perception, Art History and Culture, Creative Expression, and Art Criticism.

Aesthetic Perception

(Artistic Perception)

Each lesson begins with Activate Prior Knowledge, which asks students to recall and visualize an image from personal experience that will help them take a purposeful look at the artwork.

Introduce the Art focuses students' attention on specific attributes of the artwork, design elements and principles, underlying structures, and functions. As students answer the questions about the work of art, they develop critical *observation* skills.

Aesthetic Perception directs students to extend their artistic perception to their environment and objects in the environment. The transition is made to use keen visual and tactile perception of formal art objects in everyday life (lifelong learning).

> "In **Art Connections** students are exposed to a variety of types and styles of art from many cultures and historical periods."

Art History and Culture

(Cultural Context)

In *Art Connections* students are exposed to a variety of types and styles of art from many cultures and historical periods. Students study art from Africa; Asia; Australia; Europe; and North, Central, and South America. They learn about the role of the artist in societies. They develop appreciation for paintings, drawings, prints, photographs, sculptures, textiles, and architecture. They relate to folk, decorative, functional, and formal arts.

While information about the works of art and the artist is necessarily brief in the *Student Edition,* teachers are encouraged to use the Art History and Culture feature of the *Teacher Edition* and the *Artist Profiles* books to provide students with enriching information about the artists, the periods of art history, and cultural perspectives.

 Creative Expression

(Art Production)

Creative expression is fundamental to every art lesson. The Practice activity provides a structure for students to apply lesson concepts in meaningful practice. In the Creative Expression activity, students refine their new knowledge and skills by producing original artwork based on their personal visions. The lessons throughout the program introduce a variety of art media and techniques.

 Art Criticism

(Aesthetic Valuing)

Reflection and self-assessment are inherent in the art-making process. Upon completion of the Creative Expression activity, students

evaluate their own work using the four steps of art criticism: Describe, Analyze, Interpret, and Decide. These four steps of art criticism are a method for making an informed critique of others' artwork as well.

Arts Integration

In addition to the high priority placed on teaching the visual arts as a unique discipline, both national and state standards recommend the appropriate integration or interrelation of the visual arts with the other arts disciplines of music, dance, and theatre. Toward this goal, every unit in *Art Connections* culminates with a lesson integrating one of these performing arts. In addition, connections are made to music and movement/dance in every lesson of the *Teacher Edition.*

Curriculum Integration

The *Teacher Edition* has an Art Across the Curriculum section that ties art concepts to other curriculum areas. Every lesson has a connection to Reading/Language Arts, Math, Science, Social Studies, and Technology.

National Standards for Arts Education © 1994

1. Understand and apply media, techniques, and processes.
2. Use knowledge of structures and functions.
3. Choose and evaluate a range of subject matter, symbols, and ideas.
4. Understand the visual arts in relation to history and cultures.
5. Reflect upon and assess the characteristics and merits of their work and the work of others.
6. Make connections between the visual arts and other disciplines.

The Development of Children's Art

Rosalind Ragans, Ph.D.

A child's ability to make and understand art develops along with his or her cognitive, social, emotional, and physical development. In 1947 Victor Lowenfeld was the first to identify and label the sequential stages that students move through as they create images. Since then many others have continued to study the development of children's visual images.

Understanding these stages will help you recognize what your students are doing; however, you must also understand that these stages describe untutored progression through the making of images. There are many outside influences on students, and these will show in their work. A well-meaning adult might teach a child to make stick figures, and because they are so easy to make, the child adopts this symbol.

Just as reading levels vary widely within one class, so do art abilities. Just as you teach students to appreciate differences in ability in other subject areas, you must help them understand that not everyone will have the same art abilities at the same time.

There are many different versions of the developmental stages; here we present a three-step version of art development. The stages of artistic development are useful norms that can help you, but they are **not** rules that must be followed.

The Manipulative Stage
Ages 2–5 (Grade K)

This has been called the scribble stage, and it is usually seen in children from two to five years old. During the early part of this stage, the child makes random, disordered scribbles. Making art at this stage is such a sensory experience that the child may hold crayons in both hands. Children who have opportunities to scribble produce a wide variety of lines, marks, dots, and shapes. The child who develops a variety of graphic marks during the scribble years will use them to produce complex symbolic drawings as he or she matures. Children who rarely scribble will have a more limited range of expression, and they will need a great deal of encouragement to continue drawing.

As the random scribbles become more controlled, the child starts to pull the marks into circular patterns until a mandala, or rough circle, is created. Rhoda Kellogg, who studied thousands of children's drawings from all over the world, found that the mandala appears as the final stage between random scribbling and representation. This controlled scribble becomes a named scribble. Expressive concepts develop as children recognize the relationship between their marks and the visual outcome.

The Symbol-Making Stage
Ages 4–9 (Grades 1–4)

When a child makes the connection between images and an idea, a shape becomes a symbol. During this stage children develop a series of distinct images that stand for objects in their experiences. These symbols are eventually related to an environment within the drawing. The first representation of a person is a mandala. This can represent anyone the child wants it to be. Although this shape appears to be just a head, it represents the entire person. Soon the child adds a line and two marks, which represent a person with a mouth and two eyes. Then two lines are added to the shape to represent legs, two lines for arms, and a scribble for hair. The child is drawing what he or she knows, not what he or she sees. As children develop from the early symbolic stage into the symbol-making stage, they start to add more details and develop a symbol that includes all the body parts.

At first, space is not a consideration, and the size of symbols in a work is related to importance. Objects and people seem to float. Eventually the child wants to make people and objects stand up and will line things up on the bottom of the paper or on a baseline. Along with a baseline, the child starts to represent the sky with a strip of color across the top of the paper that includes a round symbol with radiating lines for the sun. As far as the child is concerned, the space between the sky and the baseline is air. The sky will not touch the earth until the child develops a more mature sense of perception, usually the result of sensitive art instruction.

Another spatial problem is overlap. Children realize that two objects cannot occupy the same space at the same time, and they avoid overlapping. As the environments they depict become more complex, children may use a bird's-eye view, a foldover view, or multiple views to represent space.

Children in this stage develop their own schema, or image, that resembles an actual object. Once a schema has been invented it will be used over and over. As the child continues to make art, the schema will become more detailed and sophisticated.

Giving a child this age coloring books may lead to self-doubt because of the conflict between the child's schema and the adult image. After coloring a seated dog in a coloring book, the child may become frustrated when his or her own drawing of a dog does not measure up to his or her memory of the adult image. Because children are exposed to so many adult images, many of which have low artistic quality, it is helpful for the teacher to expose children to the many high-quality works of art available in this program.

The Preadolescent Stage
Ages 8–13 (Grades 3–8)

Preadolescent children are still naturally inquisitive and creative, but they have learned to be more cautious. They have become very sensitive to peer opinion. They have reached a "crisis of confidence" regarding the images they make. If a work doesn't look exactly the way they think it should, or if it looks childlike, they reject the art product. This is the time when many children become frustrated and stop making art.

This is a critical time in students' visual development. They need to be taught to work slowly and with patience. They need to be taught drawing skills such as perspective and human proportions. They need to master the language of art and the use of design principles. They need the technical skills to master the various media such as painting, printmaking, ceramics, and sculpture.

Students need to see how different artists in the past have solved problems, and to observe what contemporary artists are doing today. Artists solve problems differently, and young people need to be exposed to many different ideas as they try to create their own solutions to visual problems.

The strong art teacher will lead students over this perilous bridge of doubt by gently stretching their minds to help them see more so that they can do more. At every stage in the child's visual development, a strong, understanding teacher can help the child move forward.

Brain-Based Learning

Jamye Ivey, K–12 Art Supervisor, Dougherty County School System, Georgia

At the end of the school day, teachers often face many unanswered questions concerning the young people whose education is their responsibility. Educators cannot help but wonder why students fail to respond to instructional strategies that were successful in their own experiences. Why is today's student so different?

Brain Research

Neuroscientists are now able to supply some of the answers that have plagued educators for years. The amazing, constantly changing world of technology has unlocked for researchers a new realm of understanding of the human brain. With the aid of advanced medical techniques and strategies using equipment such as MRI, FMRI, CAT, and PET scans, the working brain can be observed. Translating these new and often startling medical findings into the educational arena has provided the classroom teacher with practical methodologies and a better understanding of how, why, and when students learn best.

The brain is the most powerful organ in the body. Researchers have discovered that today's brains grow better in the real world than in artificial learning environments. Students must be able to connect their learning to previous experience in order for new learning to occur. For years teachers have designed and taught units with the activities culminating in field trips. When we consider these recent findings, we realize this procedure should be reversed. The field trip provides the student relevance that would facilitate learning. Without a related experience in the memory bank of past experiences, the learner finds no significance in the new material.

It is also important to note that synapses in the brain are formed, strengthened, and maintained by interaction with experience. The stronger the synapses, the faster the messaging travels and the greater the number of neural pathways that are created in the brain. This enables a person to be capable of creating more flexible thought processing and better memory.

Research confirms that environments shape brains. Teachers should create an environment that provides the best opportunities for this generation of young people to learn. Students of today need to move, talk, and touch more than previous learners did. Eric Jensen explains that the part of the brain that processes movement is the same part that processes learning. Thus, there needs to be movement in the classroom.

Today, we know that lecturing is the poorest way to present new learning. Only about fifty percent of the audience is actively listening in any given oral presentation. Students learn the most at the beginning of a presentation, the second-most at the end, and the least in the middle. Learners need breaks during teacher talk sessions. The attention span of a preadolescent is ten to twelve minutes.

This generation of children has more trouble organizing thoughts and learns on a more global scale. Expect students to want to understand the big picture before dealing with the details. One way to accomplish this is to let the class spend a few minutes looking through the whole chapter before focusing on the first page.

We know now that students cannot learn if they feel threatened or stressed. If a teacher shouts at a student, it takes fifteen minutes for the adrenaline levels to subside in all the students in the class. The glucose needed for cognitive functioning is redirected to combat stress, so all learning is governed to some extent by emotions. The constant threat of failure needs to be removed and recognition should be placed on individual performance, experience, and interest. Pressure, tension, and stress slow down or eliminate learning.

Brain-Based Learning and the Arts

Art teachers are known for using creative methods to capture the imaginations of their students. Need, novelty, meaning, and emotion are four ways to gain a student's attention, and using humor during instruction increases attention by fifty percent. A happy classroom is a more brain-compatible classroom.

The arts are an important part of effective teaching and an essential component of brain-compatible instruction. There is evidence that art-making has been around for over one million years. Brain research documents the arts as basic to the brain. Every culture in human history has one common thread: all had the arts. Stable art, music, and dance experiences not only enhance the aesthetic life of the learner, but they also provide important activity for the growing neurological system.

For both teacher and student, the most encouraging summation from recent research is that we continue to grow brain cells regardless of our age. Noted neuroscientist

Marion Diamond explains that it is best to keep the brain curious and active. In her opinion the most significant finding of her career has been that the brain can learn at any age. Be a lifelong learner and engage in physical activitities, which also helps build brain cells. Stay curious and stay active. How affirming this is for art educators because the successful teaching of art daily demands both creative curiosity and physical endurance.

References

Sousa, David A. (2002). *How the Brain Learns, Second Edition.* Corwin Press.

Sylwester, Robert (1995). *A Celebration of Neurons, an Educator's Guide to the Brain.* Alexandria, VA: Association for Supervision and Curriculum Development.

Eric Jensen (2001). *Arts With the Brain in Mind.* Alexandria, VA: Association for Supervision and Curriculum Development.

Sprenger, Marilee (1999). *Learning & Memory-The Brain in Action.* Alexandria, VA: Association for Supervision and Curriculum Development.

Armstrong, Thomas (1987). *In Their Own Way.* G.P. Putnam's Sons.

Armstrong, Thomas (1991). *Awakening Your Child's Natural Genius.* G.P. Putnam's Sons.

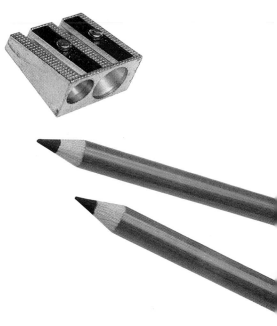

Classroom Management and Motivation Strategies for Teaching Elementary Art

Bunyan Morris, Art Teacher, Effingham County School System, Georgia

While motivating students to express themselves visually through creative means, the elementary art teacher is challenged with the task of maintaining proper classroom management. The purpose of this article is to provide some practical methods of motivating creative thought and action under the guidance of successful classroom management. Combine these methods with your own to give students the best learning experience possible.

Be Prepared. Begin the lesson excited and ready. Students will pick up on your mood the moment they walk into the room. If you set the tone at the beginning and grasp immediate control, it will be much easier to keep it throughout the lesson. It is important to have art prints and demonstration materials ready and in place for the initial focus. Practice an activity before demonstrating it if it is the first time that it has been taught. Something might happen that could not be foreseen; prepare for the best and the worst. Also, it might be a good idea to practice a concept or an activity that has not been taught in a long time. Even classroom veterans forget things.

Focus. For the initial focus of the lesson, gather the students into a group on the floor, in chairs, or on benches in an area of the room that is ready for discussion and demonstration. By gathering the students into a compact group, it is easier to make eye contact and to keep the attention of all learners. If there is no room for a separate demonstration and discussion spot, gather the tables or desks into a closer group so that no one is "out of reach."

Introduce the Art. Always introduce a lesson with a work of art that relates to what the students will be learning. Students get excited playing detective. Finding clues and ideas in a painting or sculpture allows them to make their own interpretations and assessments about art. They will in turn learn to apply this to their own work. The students don't have to know that this activity has a lofty term called *art criticism* to gain from its purpose. Encouraging them to ask questions and share ideas about a master work will give the students motivation and fresh ideas to take into the Creative Expression portion of the lesson.

Moving to Art Production. Always control the manner in which students move to the Creative Expression area from the Demonstration/Discussion center. Release students in a manner that will keep order but not quell their enthusiasm about the lesson. Use positive reinforcement by complimenting those who are sitting quietly, and send them first. It will not take long for the others to catch on. After time most of the students will become conditioned to this expectation. Even if they've been involved in a lively discussion, they will automatically become settled as this transitional period approaches.

Classroom Design. Not only should the students be orderly, but the classroom must also be organized and conducive to the movement of the teacher and students. The Creative Expression stations should have enough space between them for the teacher to reach every student. There should be enough space in traffic areas for student movement. Children need easy access to supply shelves and sinks, and should be able to move from one Creative Expression station to another unencumbered. The supplies should be organized on leveled shelves so that the students will return them to their proper places. If the teacher keeps the room and supplies organized, hopefully the students will too.

As well as keeping the room and supplies organized, the rest of the room should be visually pleasing. Display student art with master prints. This builds self-esteem. When possible, display every child's work. Make learning centers organized and interesting. Keep interesting objects around the room for visual reference. These objects might include plants, pottery, old bottles, discarded sports equipment, old toys, or anything that might capture the attention and interest of your students. Use these objects in still lifes and as objects of visual reference for lines, shapes, and other elements and principles of art.

When moving about the room assisting students, it is important to keep the senses alive and be aware of what is happening with the other students. See and hear what they think you can't.

Closing the Lesson. Normally one should try to close the class with a review of the lesson's objectives. This should be short and interesting. This is also the time to reward the students for good behavior. The art teacher must set the criteria for earning the award. Do not give the award if it is not earned. Of course, the students must be aware of the opportunity to earn an award ahead of time.

One method that works is to award the students with a "Super Behavior Card." This is simply a colorful card that can be given to the class to take back to their classroom teacher for having good behavior during art. This requires the cooperation of the classroom teacher to award the students in some manner for collecting a certain number of Super Behavior Cards. Awards might include a popcorn party or extra time at recess. If the classroom teacher is unwilling, you will have to provide the award in your class. Awarding of the Super Behavior Card can be coordinated with cleanup at the end of the period. Choose one student at the table who cleans up most thoroughly and quietly to carry the Super Behavior Card back to the classroom teacher. The students at each table will work together to earn the Super Behavior Card.

Hopefully these ideas and suggestions will reduce the challenge of maintaining classroom control and motivating students. The individual teacher must decide what works best for each situation. All of the motivation and management techniques suggested here have been tried and have been proven to work. Combined with each teacher's individual strategies, they will increase the probability of success in the art classroom.

A Sampling of Art Games for Home or School

Art Lotto: National Gallery of Art. Safari Limited, Miami, Florida.

ARTDECK. Aristoplay, Ann Arbor, Michigan.

The Fine Art Game. Piatnik, Wiener Spielkartenfabrik, Ferd. PIATNIK & Söhne.

Where Art Thou? WJ Fantasy, Inc., Bridgeport, Connecticut.

Art Instruction for Students with Disabilities

Mandy Yeager, Art Educator, Ph.D. Student, The University of North Texas, Denton, Texas

Art education empowers all students to look at, respond to, create, and enjoy works of art. Students who are disabled are no exception to this privilege. The arts have often been understood as an equalizing force in the education of students with disabilities; often these students experience discrimination from peers and adults because of their disability. This discrimination often manifests itself in avoidance of or lowered expectations for these students. Stereotypes of persons with disabilities cast them as helpless, unintelligent, dangerous, or contemptible. These stereotypes are maintained by a lack of knowledge or personal experiences with persons who are disabled.

The visual arts, because they use images to express ideas about the human experience, play a vital role in challenging and eliminating many of these stereotypes. The current emphasis of art education upon visual literacy allows students to examine and transform stereotypes that exist in the media regarding all types of differences (including age, race, class, gender, and ability). Artists throughout time have engaged in this process of recording and seeking to transform societal injustices through visual imagery.

The benefits of art for students with disabilities cannot be underestimated. The skills gained in visual arts often result in increased confidence and ability in other academic subjects. Arts-based learning is often effective because of the ways it engages the multiple senses and abilities of students.

The arts also give students opportunities to explore, express, and celebrate their identities. Teachers who include the work of artists with disabilities in their art curriculum help all students realize that disability is a part of the human experience and does not prevent anyone from being a creator of art.

Resources to Assist Art Educators

The first step to developing competence is to develop an understanding of the child's disability. There are a number of resources to assist the art teacher in this regard.

Resources at the School Level

Resources at the school level include special-education staff and related service providers who have contact with the child such as occupational and physical therapists. All of these staff members can provide the art teacher with insight into the child's learning strengths and needs and his or her physical and emotional development. They can also provide helpful suggestions for how a particular art medium or tool can be made accessible to a particular student.

Another valuable resource for the art teacher is the student's Individualized Education Plan (IEP). This plan exists for every student receiving special education services and provides information about learning styles, needs, and modifications. The *Individuals with Disabilities Education Act* (IDEA) requires that all regular education teachers of students with disabilities have access to the child's IEP and are provided support in implementing modifications to the general curriculum.

Art educators can design their art curricula to meet students' annual IEP goals. For instance, art criticism activities have the potential to enhance students' expressive language skills. Cooperative learning activities such as mural painting can foster social skills. Art production often produces self-efficacy in students with disabilities as they learn to trust their ability to achieve success. Art teachers who engage in this process of reviewing a child's IEP and delineating the ways that art curricula can address annual goals become more confident in their abilities to successfully instruct students with disabilities.

Art Education and Disability Organizations

VSA arts has been designated by the U.S. Congress as the National Coordinating Agency of Arts in Learning for Persons with Disabilities. The agency fulfills this role through a vast network of state affiliates. VSA arts produces art and disability awareness curricula and showcases the work of students with disabilities by regularly sponsoring national calls for art. It also provides access to the work of artists with disabilities.

The Special Needs Interest Group of the National Art Education Association (NAEA) meets annually at the NAEA convention to discuss best practices in art education and disability. This group publishes a column in the bimonthly publication *NAEA News*.

Adapting the Art Experience for Students with Disabilities

It is often necessary to adapt some aspect of the art experience for students with disabilities. Adaptations ensure that learning is accessible to every child; as such, adaptation is a principle of good instruction.

Adapting the art experience is essentially a creative activity, as many different combinations of students, media, and processes coalesce in one semester of art instruction. Accordingly, effective adaptations are individualized and begin with knowledge of a particular student's learning strengths and needs. Teachers may choose to adapt art media, instructional strategies, and/or physical space, depending upon the situation. This process of adaptation often begins by observation of students in an introductory art-making experience. If a student is having difficulty with an art task, try to determine the source of the difficulty. Consult with other school staff and use some of the resources listed below to determine what is most appropriate for the student and situation.

The adaptations accompanying every lesson in this text are provided as suggestions only, because learning needs and strengths vary with each child, medium, and project. It is hoped that art educators, upon reading this article, will feel equipped to utilize available resources to design and implement empowering learning experiences for all students.

Resources

Disability Education Organizations

National Dissemination Center for Children with Disabilities (NICHCY), www.nichy.org/index.html

The Council for Exceptional Children, www.cec.sped.org/

ERIC Clearinghouse on Disability and Gifted Education, http://ericec.org

Art and Disability Organizations and Resources

VSA arts, www.vsarts.org

Art, Disability and Expression Online Exhibit, www.vsarts.org/showcase/exhibits/disability/index.html

The National Art Education Association Special Needs Interest Group

EDGE: Education for Disability and Gender Equity, www.disabilityhistory.org/dwa/edge/curriculum/index-netscape.htm

National Arts and Disability Center (NADC), http://nadc.ucla.edu/

Safe Use of Art Materials

Mary Ann Boykin, Director, The Art School for Children and Young Adults
University of Houston—Clear Lake, Texas

Elementary art teachers need to be aware of safety issues that can affect the well-being of the children they teach, as well as themselves. Follow the guidelines established by the Center for Safety in the Arts to assure that neither students nor teachers are injured by the unsafe use of art materials.

Elementary teachers should do two things to prevent problems. The first is to keep all toxic and hazardous substances out of the classroom. The second is to know how to use the materials safely, because any materials can become hazardous when used inappropriately.

Toxic Substances

A toxic substance is defined by the Center for Occupational Hazards as "a poison which can damage your body's organ systems when you are overexposed to it." This harm can be immediate or can be the result of repeated exposure over time. Toxic substances can enter the body in three ways:

1. absorption through the skin
2. inhalation through the nose or mouth
3. ingestion through eating or drinking in the area where toxic materials are being used

It is up to the teacher to make sure toxic substances do not enter the classroom and that all materials are used safely to avoid problems.

Pregnant women and those who are nursing must be especially careful to prevent exposure to toxic substances. Fumes, sprays, dusts, and powders present a real hazard to the fetus, can be transferred to the infant through the mother's milk, and can be carried home to the infant or young child through dusts and residue picked up by clothing and hair. The safe path is to completely avoid exposure to any toxin by carefully reading labels and applying common sense to the situation. For example, if you plan to mix powdered tempera paint or work with chalks or clay, the safe method would include use of a respirator mask, which would prevent inhalation of these substances.

Children and Safe Art Materials

Preschool and elementary children are particularly vulnerable to unsafe art materials for a variety of reasons. Their lower body weight allows a toxic substance to become more concentrated in their bodies. Because children have a more rapid metabolism than adults, toxic substances are more quickly absorbed into their bodies. Children also tend to have more hand-to-mouth contact than adults, which allows ingestion of toxic materials. Furthermore, children are easily distracted from safety warnings regarding materials as they become involved in the art process. The tendency of children to have cuts and scratches also allows for ready entry of toxins into their bodies.

What the Labels Mean

Since 1990 our government has required the labeling of all hazardous materials. Any product labeled as hazardous is totally inappropriate for the elementary school. Safe art materials carry the statement that the material "Conforms to ASTMD-4236." A simple "nontoxic" statement on a product is not adequate.

The Arts and Crafts Materials institute developed a voluntary program to provide a safe standard for materials used by children. Products bearing the labels AP (Approved Product) or CP (Certified Product) have been tested by toxicologists in major universities and have been deemed safe for children to use. The HL (Health Label) on art products indicates that these products are appropriate to use with children 12 years old or older under the supervision of an art teacher. Products with HL labels are not safe for elementary children.

Safe Art Materials

The following are guidelines for choosing and using basic art materials in a safe manner.

Drawing Materials

- Use only water-soluble AP- or CP-designated markers. Permanent markers are extremely dangerous and can cause lung and liver damage if inhaled. Never use permanent markers in the elementary classroom.
- Do not use scented markers. This teaches children to sniff or smell materials.
- Use only dustless chalk. The amount of dust created in a classroom by twenty children wiping and blowing chalk can be irritating to those who suffer from allergies, asthma, and other respiratory problems.
- Use oil pastels; the colors are richer than crayons and the satisfaction is greater! Crayons should also bear the AP or CP label to ensure that no lead is present in these materials.

Painting Materials

- Use only liquid tempera and/or watercolor paints. If you must use powdered tempera paints, mix these outside and have the paints ready before children enter the classroom. Avoid inhaling the powders of tempera paints.
- Do not use any spray paints or fixatives. These are extremely dangerous.

Printmaking Materials

- Use only water-soluble printers' inks. Do not use any solvent-based inks.
- Use pencils to carve into unused foam trays for printing blocks. Do not use mat knives or other sharp instruments.

Collage Materials

- Sharp scissors should not be used by young children; blunt points are safe. Fourth- and fifth-graders may use rounded points with teacher supervision.
- Use only school paste or white glue for adhering papers. Do not use rubber cement unless it bears the AP or CP label. Do not use any solvent-based glues.

Sculpture and Three-Dimensional Materials

- Use premixed, moist clay for sculpture and pottery. Do not allow students to take home any unfired clay.
- Remind students to wash their hands thoroughly after using clay. The residual dust can be harmful and irritating if inhaled.
- Paint clay pieces with tempera or watercolor paints. Do not use glazes. Some have the approved labels, but they are not recommended for elementary use.
- Use pencils, craft sticks, or other blunt tools to carve clay. Soapstone should not be used for carving in a closed environment.
- Read labels carefully on pastes used for papier-mâché, because some pastes contain pesticides or preservatives that are extremely harmful.

Stitchery, Weaving, and Fiber Materials

- Use blunt plastic needles and loosely woven fabrics such as burlap for stitchery. Blunt metal tapestry needles are safe if their use is supervised.
- Young children will have trouble cutting fabric and yarn with their scissors. Precut lengths of fabric and yarn prior to introducing a task.

The Community as a Resource for Art Materials

Willis "Bing" Davis, Associate Professor Emeritus, Central State University, Ohio
President and Founder of SHANGO: The Center for the Study of African American Art & Culture

Ingenuity, resourcefulness, and creative survival have always been important to most successful art and classroom teachers when it comes to providing meaningful arts experiences for students. We are known as collectors who almost never throw anything away. Some art and classroom teachers will need to acquire the skill of always being on the lookout for resources, materials, and supplies that can supplement art materials in the classroom. It can be fun; plus, it stimulates the imagination and creative impulse. This is also a great way to build bridges and advocates for arts education.

Think of all the things you use in the art room. How many can be found locally? Safe, usable materials or supplies that can be found free or reduced in price leave more of the art budget to buy the things that have to be purchased. There are different forms of searching for inexpensive and free materials for art activities. The following are a few tried and proven ways to acquire materials, supplies, and resources that can be used for art and other educational activities.

Materials in the School Building

- Leftover wood or metal from a shop class
- Clean, empty food containers from the food-service area
- Cardboard tubes from the food-service area or copy machine
- Scrap paper from copy machines

Annual Open-House Night Resources

Open house is a great time to post a small list of hand tools needed for the art program. You would be surprised by how many extra hammers, pliers, screwdrivers, bent forks, and so on are in garages and basements. Many parents or caregivers also work at places that have by-products that could supplement the art materials in the art program.

Local Business Material Sources

- *Wood* Lumberyards are usually willing to let teachers collect boxes of scrap wood for art production. Some lumberyards will even let you leave a box with your school's name on it.
- *Wallpaper* Ask for discontinued wallpaper design sample books from paint stores.
- *Paper* Large quantities of damaged paper may be available from local paper or paper distribution companies.

> "Many local service organizations have an interest and commitment to youth and the arts."

Community Resources

- Many communities participate in the popular "Take a Child to Work" programs that allow children to see and experience where their parents or caregivers work. Almost every school also has a career day when many professional individuals visit schools to talk to students about potential careers. Both programs put schools, students, and teachers into direct contact with local businesses.
- Teachers may find that companies with national headquarters in their communities often have a strong commitment to those communities and their educational systems. Teachers can assist these companies in reaching their community commitment goals by suggesting ways to assist the school art program. Local businesses may want to sponsor the visit of a local artist or donate materials.
- Many local service organizations have an interest and commitment to youth and the arts. They often look for art and cultural events and activities to which they can

contribute. Find out how they want to contribute and help them reach their goal. These events could be funding an exhibit, hosting an art reception, donating materials and supplies, framing student artwork for display in the hallways, sponsoring a local or major art field trip, and so on.

Artist Resources

- Local and regional emerging artists live in every community and can make meaningful contributions to the school art program. Artists from the community or region offer a "realness" to the program from knowing and living in the area.
- Some artists do a good job at demonstrating, some do a good slide lecture, some are more effective in large or small groups, some do great critique sessions, and some may be better mentoring one-on-one. Each individual teacher or school district can develop an annotated artist directory listing the artists' strong points for reference.
- Most communities also have one or more local arts groups or arts organizations that can assist schools in identifying and securing the services of local artists. A local arts group may be willing to do a series of Member Art Demos over the course of the year in your school.
- Another great source of local and regional artists can be found in the colleges and universities in your area. The college or university art program can show your students some of the quality art teachers students might be working with in the future. This is a great source of judges for student competitions.

Art Agencies at Local and State Levels

While everyone is aware of the existence of the National Endowment for the Arts in Washington, D.C., many may not be aware that there are state arts agencies and many community-based arts councils that can be an important resource for your art program. Find ways to let everyone in the community help your art program to be the best it can be.

Displaying Students' Art

Jackie Ellett

"My picture is hanging in the hall!" exclaims an excited second-grader. Yes, having one's work displayed is exciting. When you display a child's artwork, you are communicating two things to that child: you value what he or she has created *and* you value the child.

Why Display Students' Art?

Students are intrigued by the work their peers produce and are eager to join in any discussion that arises from the shared experiences of the work. They often compare what they have created to the work made by their peers. A natural aesthetic experience occurs, and questions and comparisons arise. These are either verbalized or internalized, depending on the circumstance of the viewing. "Why did Erin paint that flower large and the others small?" "I like the details of the seeds that Galvin added to his painting; I'll do more details next time." These are examples of questions, comments, or thoughts that may arise when students are viewing a display. Not only do displays allow students to appreciate their completed projects, but they also allow students to aspire to better art endeavors.

A class display allows students the opportunity to stand back and critique their work. A teacher-led critique is best. Students are able to evaluate their work, gain insight into things they may not have thought about, and may learn a new solution to a problem they have encountered. Discussing their works as you would a fine-art print validates the importance of what they have created. Art is so personal that a discussion can become quite insightful.

Preschool and early elementary-aged students are eager to take their works of art home to show their parents what they have created. You should ask permission of all students to display their work. By asking permission you are showing respect for their work, and for those students as individuals.

Displays are also a good way to show administrators, parents, and the community what students are learning.

Where to Display Students' Art

Many art educators believe that the farther away from the classroom the display, the more selective the images need to be. In the classroom, every student's art may be displayed.

This area can be controlled by the teacher, students, or both. Students can be allowed to change their own work when they decide to.

Outside of the classroom there is usually an assigned area for each class to display its work. Bulletin boards made of composition board are the most desirable of all surfaces for two-dimensional art. Artwork is easily attached using staples, and the walls are protected from any damage.

Setting up a school gallery of permanent or rotating student art is wonderful for promoting the art program within a school. This should be housed in a high-traffic area where parents, administrators, and visitors can view students' art. In "Leadership and the Elementary Art Specialist: Twenty Ways to Improve Your Program's Position in the Educational System," Phillip Dunn recommends establishing a "Principal's Permanent Art Collection." Having a gallery within the school with professionally matted and framed student art communicates that students' works and the art program are valued. In an era where budget cuts are customary, promoting the work of students is very important to the survival of art programs.

Displays in local businesses, civic centers, or art centers help educate the public about the work being done within their schools. These exhibits contain a mix of student art that has gone through a selection process. Depending on the guidelines and formality of the display, the works can be mounted, matted, or framed, with three-dimensional works displayed in sculpture cases or on sculpture stands.

How to Display Students' Art

Student art can be displayed in a variety of ways. Some teachers take digital photos of their students in the process of creating a work of art and critiquing their work, and then take a photo of the finished art itself. These images can be posted on a school Web site with descriptions of the activity. Digital images are sometimes used as screen savers on the school's computer system and highlighted on closed-circuit TVs in the classrooms. The most common method of display, however, is the bulletin board. These have evolved from simple displays to elaborate descriptions of the process and documentation of student learning. Teacher-focused bulletin boards have given way to student-focused displays that often include student reflections

and interpretations. Including descriptions of the process and background information adds to better understanding of the learning that has taken place.

Two-dimensional works of art should be mounted on larger contrasting or neutral-toned paper. The top and sides are usually of equal width with the bottom larger, unless the work is square, in which case all four sides are equal in width. When matting art, a two- to three-inch mat is standard, with the bottom being an inch wider than the top and sides. The mat acts as a resting place, so when arranging mounted or matted art, the works should not overlap.

A sheet of butcher paper or bulletin-board paper can be attached to a wall to define a display area and unify the works of art. Poster board or construction paper cut wider on all sides than the largest paper used by a class can be attached to the wall as an area for mounting individual students' work. Glue a clothespin to the top of the mounted paper so students can easily change their artwork. The background papers are usually in neutral colors, although primary colors may be used in classrooms for younger children. Each background paper is individually identified by placing the child's name in large print on a label.

Three-dimensional works look best in sculpture cases or on sculpture stands. Not every school can afford these. Arranging sturdy boxes of varying heights and covering them with complementary cloths allow sculptures to be equally viewed. If sculptures are of varying sizes, the largest should always be placed toward the back and the small works in front. Arranging works in odd numbers creates interest as well.

Mobiles and kites are best displayed from the ceiling. Make certain that all materials are well attached and that the items hung from the ceiling are secure so they do not fall or set off sensor alarms. As with all displays, it is important to know your school's policies about the types of adhesives allowed. Hot glue has a tendency to peel paint, low-temperature glue guns may not work on some surfaces, and double-sided tape can leave a residue. Humidity and the wall's surface both affect what will and will not work. Reusable tacky putty sticks to most surfaces and leaves few marks.

Displays do much to enhance and rejuvenate students' spirits and allow students to communicate in a way that is neither mathematical nor verbal. The art that students make is very personal and deserves careful attention when being displayed.

Art Assessments

Assessment in art can be problematic for a variety of reasons. Many educators are reluctant to evaluate a student's creative expression as good or bad. Because there are often no right or wrong answers, students and their parents could challenge a teacher's subjective opinion of a work if it is reflected in a letter grade. Furthermore, many teachers without a strong art background do not feel qualified to grade student artwork. In addition, teachers do not want to discourage creative expression by giving a low grade or an undeserved grade. Many people also often feel that talented students have the advantage in art class and that students should not be evaluated on how talented they are, but rather on how much effort they put into their work and how much progress they make.

All of these assessment difficulties stem from the focus on art production in the art classroom, rather than a reflection of art history and culture, aesthetics, or art criticism. A broader focus in the art classroom and a variety of assessment options may help in more effective art assessment.

Assessment of Lesson Objectives

Instead of subjective opinions of whether or not one likes a student's artwork, students can be evaluated on whether or not they meet the art lesson objectives or demonstrate the knowledge and skills introduced in the lesson. In a quality art program, there are objectives for aesthetic perception, art history, and art criticism, as well as for demonstrating understanding of the elements and principles of art in art production.

In *Art Connections,* every lesson has four clear, measurable objectives. At the end of each lesson, a rubric provides evaluation criteria for each objective.

Art Production: Evaluating Student Artwork

Art teachers frequently evaluate student artwork on the basis of how well it reflects the elements and principles of art that are being stressed in the lesson and how well the student meets the criteria for the artwork. Some teachers can construct rubrics or standards for the artwork beforehand and tell students how their work will be evaluated at the time it is assigned. Other teachers use written or mental checklists of their standards as they look at student artwork. Teachers may use this form of evaluation as an opportunity to discuss the work with a student and find out whether the student thought he or she met the objectives for the artwork.

In *Art Connections,* teachers can also use the Assessment Masters in the *Assessment* book to get an idea of whether a student understands the elements or principle of art for a lesson.

Art Criticism and Aesthetic Perception: Self- and Peer-Assessment

The four-step process of art criticism (Describe, Analyze, Interpret, Decide) provides a procedure that students can use to objectively study their own art products, as well as the works of others. The sequential steps of art criticism are similar to those used in the scientific method. During the first two steps, Describe and Analyze, students are asked to collect data objectively. During the third step, Interpret, students speculate about the meaning of the work based on the data collected: they make a hypothesis about the idea, emotion, or mood expressed by the artist. During the fourth step, Decide, students offer their aesthetic judgment about the work of art. The sequential procedures in art criticism force students to postpone judgment while becoming immersed in the image. It forces them to have a fully funded visual experience before drawing conclusions about a work.

Art Connections includes art criticism questions for every Creative Expression activity. Additionally, the Aesthetic Perception feature in every lesson of the *Student Edition* provides students with an opportunity to evaluate their developing aesthetic perception.

Art History and Culture

Art is a visual record of history and diverse cultures. The goals for elementary art education are that students understand and appreciate different historical periods, cultures, and artistic styles and develop respect for the traditions and contributions of diverse societies.

In *Art Connections* every lesson introduces a work of art from a particular culture, time, and style. In the Introduce the Art strategies, teachers are encouraged to compare, contrast, and share the Art History and Culture information as well as the information provided in *Artist Profiles* to help students develop an understanding of the visual arts in relation to history and cultures. Through discussion and elements in students' own artwork, teachers can evaluate students' awareness in this area.

Portfolio Assessment

Art educators could claim to have inspired the growing use of portfolio assessment in other subject areas. Many art teachers collect the best examples of a student's work and look at the progress over time. They display it and discuss it with students and parents. Student art journals with ideas, drawings, and sketches also provide an opportunity for portfolio assessment.

In *Art Connections* students are encouraged to keep their best work in a Student Portfolio and to maintain an Art Journal. Reminders of these types of portfolio assessments appear in the *Teacher Edition.*

Performance Assessment

Unlike other subject areas, art education has a long tradition of performance assessment. In art class students make things to demonstrate what they can do. In quality art programs, teachers use performance descriptions not only for art production, but also for art criticism, art history and culture, and aesthetic perception to aid them in evaluating student demonstrations of their knowledge and skills in art.

In *Art Connections,* every work of art a student produces can be considered for performance assessment of the lesson concept. Performance assessments can also involve discussions about the works of art to introduce the lesson concept and art criticism questions.

Art not only enables teachers to evaluate student knowledge and skills in art each year, but it also provides a wonderful opportunity to assess students' growth and development over time. Students and parents are often reluctant to discard artwork and fondly review it from time to time to see how children's ideas and skills have changed. Schools often keep examples of student artwork in student portfolios from year to year.

A thoughtful and fair art assessment program enables teachers to really see how much their students are capable of accomplishing.

Art and Cross-Curricular Connections

Tina Farrell

The study and production of artwork enhances learning in all areas of the curriculum. When teachers and students connect art to other subjects, learning occurs in the natural and interrelated way that it exists in the real world. We know from experience that learning is most meaningful when it is interconnected, not isolated. Therefore, making the natural connections that exist within each discipline of study, art including, enhances total understanding and brings meaning to fragmented information.

Below are a few of the ways that art education can impact the study of other subjects.

Reading/Language Arts In the viewing and analysis of a work of art, students develop oral and written communication skills. Teachers can enhance the language process by writing art terms and concepts on the board, having students generate lists of adjectives and adverbs to describe works of art, encouraging reflective inquiry into art, having students read about art and artists, and having students use works of art as stimuli for all forms of writing.

Mathematics Mathematics concepts are enhanced through art. When math concepts are presented or expressed in a visual or manipulative manner, students can more easily grasp them. The comparison and development of shapes and forms, visual-spatial relationships, measurement, proportion, estimation, and grids and graphs, for example, all are best explained through art.

> "We know from experience that learning is most meaningful when it is interconnected—not isolated."

Science In the art-making process, children learn that multiple ways to solve problems exist. They learn to discover, imagine, try new materials and techniques, experiment, develop and test hypotheses, and observe and record visual data. These are many of the skills, objectives, and habits of mind taught in science.

Social Studies The history of the world is reflected in the functional and aesthetic works of art produced by the peoples of the world. Children can gain great insights about near and distant cultures through the study of art, artifacts, and architecture.

The Arts The arts all complement each other in the skills, elements, principles, and beliefs that are emphasized in each one. Each discipline presents a unique way to express ideas and transform emotions into song, dance, interactions, words, or images. Visual artists research, develop rough drafts (sketches), plan, develop ideas, produce completed visual ideas, and sign and title their works. These are the processes that authors, writers, dancers, composers, actors, and poets also employ.

Life Skills In art, children develop craftsmanship, self-discipline, dedication to a task, skills for working both individually and cooperatively, and pride in one's work. These skills are necessary for success in all areas of their lives.

Critical-Thinking Skills Studying the visual arts develops higher-level thinking skills as studenst analyze, compare, interpret, synthesize, and make inferences and judgments about works of art.

Art is a great integrating subject because art, first and foremost, is a form of human communication. Art is one of the first forms of communication for children. Children often express complex ideas through visual symbols that represent their beginning language systems. Art is a vehicle for children to learn about the world around them and to organize the information in a comprehensive format. As young children draw, they take textures, shapes, and colors from a complex world and form them into coherent visual images. This visual cognition, a powerful way for children to process information, is the basis for learning in and through art.

A Sampling of Art Program Resources for Schools

The California Arts Project
  (http://www.ucop.edu/tcap/aeol.html)
Getty Education Institute for the Arts
  (http://www.artsednet.getty.edu)
The Kennedy Center ArtsEdge
  (http://artsedge.kennedy-center.org)
The Metropolitan Museum of Art
  (http://www.metmuseum.org/explore/index.asp)
The Educator's Reference Desk
  (http://www.eduref.org/cgi-bin/res.cgi/Subjects/Arts)

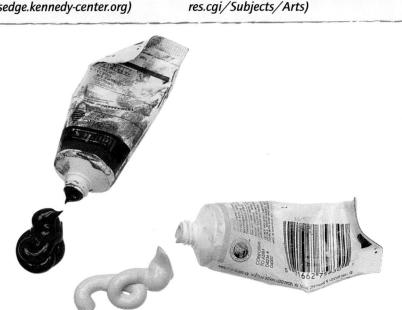

Integrating the Four Art Forms

Susan Cambigue-Tracey, Education Division, The Music Center of Los Angeles County

Albert Einstein said, "Imagination is more important than knowledge." Without exercising the imagination, knowledge is stored in the individual containers of the mind, but connections are not made. When students are taught to use the elements, skills, and content of the visual and performing arts the possibilities for synthesizing and applying what they know are multiplied. Teachers need to ensure that imagination and creativity are always nourishing the roots of learning.

The importance of artistic activity for all students goes beyond the intrinsic value of each art form in itself. Real arts investigation requires the rigor of being able to focus, make decisions, develop discipline, promote originality, and undertake research, study, and practice. Helping students to experience new ways of thinking and seeing allows them to construct personal meaning from what they experience and to build confidence and motivation.

Each art form is a discrete discipline with its own elements, vocabulary, and strategies. However, it is interesting to see connections among them where there are fundamental concepts shared across the arts and other subjects. For example, lines in art are the marks used to create images. Line in dance is the path of gestures and traveling movements, as well as body design. Line in music is a melody and also the lyrics of a song, while lines in theatre are the words that the actors speak.

A common core of knowledge is built through the arts. The principles of visual art, such as emphasis, variety, harmony, unity, and contrast, are the underlying principles used to creating anything—an architectural structure, a musical composition, a piece of literature, a dance, or a play.

It is easy to find ways to integrate one or more of the art forms and still make connections that are viable and authentic. For example, when viewing and discussing a work of art from a particular time period or culture, select music from that same time period or culture. Aztec art will have more relevance when Aztec-inspired music is played or students can view an Aztec dance and see the colors and design of the costumes. A style of music might also inspire art. Matisse did a jazz series that begs for jazz music and dance. Students can then see and hear the structural and improvisational aspects of this style in three different art forms.

When viewing or painting family scenes in art, challenge students to think of family activities that can be portrayed in a tableau, or live,

frozen picture. When viewing or creating sculpture, pair students and have one person become the "clay" and the other the "sculptor" who shapes the clay with respect and cooperation. This can extend into dance by directing the sculpted person (clay) to develop a movement idea lasting eight counts that starts and ends with the sculpted pose or form. Two people in contrasting sculptural poses can have eight counts to slowly transform from one into the other.

Three-dimensional forms in art can inspire counterbalanced (push, pull, leaning) designs made by small groups. A story, such as "The Two Skyscrapers Who Wanted to Have a Child" by Carl Sandburg, could be retold using story theatre or be portrayed in tableaux or as dramatized scenes. Students could also research musical selections to accompany their work.

> "Imagination is more important than knowledge."
> –Albert Einstein

Students will be better able to express emotions in their visual artwork if they first work with them through drama, music, and dance. Students can begin by showing a variety of emotions in the face, hands, and feet and then move toward portraying these emotions in postures such as sitting, standing, and walking. Everyday activities such as cooking or brushing teeth can be done with different emotional motivations. Students can also create short musical pieces depicting an emotion or mood or find music that expresses specific feelings or moods.

All four performing arts can become a powerful component of integrated learning. For example, during a fifth-grade project focused on the Lewis and Clark expedition, students did research in books and on the Internet to collect historical, scientific, geographical, and cultural content. This information served as the basis for group projects in music, dance, theatre, visual arts, technology, and language.

Challenged by well-designed tasks, students discussed what they knew and selected different aspects to explore through dance, music, theatre, and visual art. They learned songs of the times, listened to traditional fiddle music, and learned a rhythmic chant that was used to measure the depth of rivers. In dances, they captured the sense of traveling through "boundless space"; portrayed animals encountered during the expedition; created weather conditions such as storms; and showed the struggles in navigating rivers, waterfalls, and mountains. In theatre, students drew upon the historical characters, interpreted various scenarios, and read journal entries of Lewis and Clark. Visual art classes focused on observation drawings of plants and wild animals.

Students also created journals in which they recorded their feelings, observations, sketches, and discoveries. They were able to make connections between their own journeys and that of the Corps of Discovery. Finally, the students shared what they had learned about this epic journey in a multi-arts culmination.

The arts bring accessibility and vitality to learning, empowering students to construct meaning that has relevance for their lives. When children learn to draw, they learn to see. When children learn to act, they learn how it feels to be in different roles, cultures, and circumstances. When children learn to dance, they learn to feel comfortable in their bodies and to use movement expressively. When children learn to play an instrument, they learn perseverance and the rewards of expression through music. When children learn to sing, they release their voices and are empowered to harmonize. When children learn to write a play, they learn to observe life by thinking, reflecting, and writing. When creativity and imagination are nurtured, children learn how to use all of their resources to solve problems, to dream, and build on the ideas of others.

The Creative Process and Problem Solving

Bunyan Morris, Art Teacher, Effingham County School System, Georgia

There is great reward in watching the artistic growth of a child. Simply providing the media and the time for creating is not enough. The student's natural curiosity and desire to create must be nurtured, encouraged, and challenged. Even the brightest and most talented students need a teacher's guidance in developing the critical-thinking skills necessary for creative problem solving. The intention of this article is to provide ideas and methods for fostering creativity by developing and encouraging divergent problem solving and critical-thinking skills in elementary school art students.

Classroom Management

Fostering creativity in the art classroom is possibly an art teacher's most important skill. In order to encourage creativity, a teacher must be able to relate to students at their thinking level and then guide them to a higher level of cognitive reasoning. Classroom and behavior management are essential. There cannot be an atmosphere of creativity in a room with chaos. That is not to say that one must be a firm authoritarian. A good art teacher will learn how to walk the fine line between maintaining order and maximizing creative energy among students. Although some may not admit it, all students prefer an educational environment that is free from annoying distractions created by other students. Therefore, good behavior management is a must for maintaining a creative environment.

Visual References

Introducing a lesson with a work of art and going through the art criticism process is a tried and true method of encouraging creativity. It is important to discuss works of art that are related to the objectives of the lesson. Working strictly from imagination and memory is usually not effective. Students must have visual references from which to gather ideas.

Picture files, reference books, and the Internet are just a few sources for visual images. Photographs of people and various natural and humanmade objects provide ideas and references for drawing. Images can be collected from magazines and calendars or unwanted photographs. The image file should be organized according to subject matter or theme.

Reference books filled with images related to the lesson should be available to students. They may be checked out of the media center and kept in the room, or they may belong to the classroom. Some media specialists are willing to search for and reserve books that a teacher may need for an upcoming lesson.

An image search on the Internet is one method to help students access a visual reference that may not be available in the classroom's image file, reference books, or the school's media center.

Art Journals

Students who keep art journals maintain handy reference tools. An art journal is the best way to record ideas through sketching and writing. If art journals and writing tools are kept handy, students can jot down ideas or make sketches to save for future use. Ideas can come to mind any place or any time such as in the cafeteria, on the playground, or at the bus stop. The method or tool doesn't really matter that much. It is just important that students have a way of practicing and recording creative ideas.

Exercising the Brain

Reading should be encouraged. Students who like to read perform better in all subjects. Descriptive language stimulates the imagination. Reading a passage about the beauty of a tree or the sound of a waterfall creates a visual image in the brain. This visual image can be stored in the sketchbook and later rendered as a sculpture, painting, or drawing. Encouraging reading encourages creativity. Teachers and schools should encourage parents to limit their children's time watching television because this takes away from reading and creative play time.

Resting the Brain

Teachers should be tolerant of students taking small breaks. Sometimes students need down time to regenerate their mental energy. This down time can take the form of daydreaming or play. Both are important to the creative process. Common sense and good judgment is used to determine when a student is using time for thinking as opposed to just wasting time. Students should be reminded to get a

"Fostering creativity in the art classroom is possibly an art teacher's most important skill."

good night's sleep every night. This is not something teachers can control, but it should be encouraged. We all know that brains function better after a good night's rest.

Enriching Observation Skills

Enriched observation skills lead to more focused experimentation in art. Artists are naturally observant, but teachers know that most students are not born with natural talent. Through practice, all students can enrich their observation and critical-thinking skills. It is important to get students to slow down and see what they might not otherwise observe. One way to do this is to play an observation game. With the students' help, the teacher can set up a still life in the room. A fun game similar to "I Spy" can be played once the still life is ready. The students describe textures, lines, shapes, colors, and other elements and principles of art found within the real-life objects. The teacher writes the observations and descriptions on the board. Once the game is over and students move to the project portion of the lesson, they will be better equipped with enriched observation skills and more focused critical-thinking skills as they create.

In order to gain more focused and creative experimentation from students, an important goal of every art teacher should be to encourage creativity and divergent problem solving and critical thinking. Hopefully, teachers will find value in the ideas shared in this article and combine them with their own ideas to encourage creativity in their students.

Using Writing to Enhance Your Art Curriculum

Mary Lazzari, Ed.S., Elementary Art Teacher, Clarke County School District, Athens, Georgia

In recent decades, art teachers have expanded their area of expertise from art production to lessons that include art criticism, art history, and aesthetics. Art is being used as a vehicle not only for increasing creativity but also for developing thinking skills. One way to broaden the art experience and enhance these skills is through guided, interactive writing techniques. Writing about art is an essential component of a well-rounded art curriculum because it provides students with the opportunity to transform thoughts and feelings into words and images. It can also provide the art teacher a more personalized format for communicating with a large student population and assist art teachers in meeting the increased demand to qualify and quantify their students' learning.

> "Art is being used as a vehicle not only for increasing creativity but also for developing thinking skills."

A visual arts curriculum rich in written language activities can facilitate the development of higher-order thinking skills, such as the ability to analyze, defend, and interpret. The use of written statements can help students slow down and refine their thoughts about their own art and the art of others. Words can become the voice for a shy or inarticulate student. With writing as a means of self-expression, art educators can be more in tune with their students' inner thoughts. Some art teachers may be reluctant to incorporate writing into their curriculum because they fear a less than enthusiastic response from their students. Here are a variety of suggestions that can help motivate elementary students to write about art.

Journals

Whether it is a few sheets of paper stapled together or a spiral notebook, students enjoy having a place to write their private thoughts and feelings. Journals can be used to record the thought process from the beginning to the end of a project. It can also be a place to brainstorm ideas or vent frustrations. Art teachers can give written feedback and encouragement to each student in his or her journal.

Titles

Materials: Selected works of art, pencil and paper

At the completion of a project, students can write descriptive titles for their works of art. A title can inform, challenge, or even surprise a viewer. Younger children or students with a language deficit can dictate the title as the teacher writes. Include the student's title when displaying the artwork. Students can also think of a new title for a famous work of art. Compare it to the artist's original title and discuss the similarities and differences.

Acrostic Poems

Materials: Selected works of art, pencil and paper (for individual writings), or dry/wipe board (for group writing)

Select an artist's name or art topic and write the letters vertically. Instruct students to think of words that describe the artist or topic. Students should think of a decriptive word for each letter in the artist's name or art topic. Descriptive words can start, end, or have the letter anywhere in the selected word. Display acrostic poems with the art work that inspired them.

Venn Diagrams

Materials: Individual sheets of Venn diagrams (or draw a large diagram on the board for a whole group discussion); a set of art postcards

Place an image in each of the two outer circles of the Venn diagram. Students describe qualities they see in each of the two works of art. Qualities that are unique to each image are written in the circle that contains the image. Qualities that they have in common are written in the center of the diagram where the two circles overlap. Invite individuals or groups to share their observations. Mount and display Venn diagrams with student artwork.

Artist Statements

Materials: Pencil and paper

Direct students to write three to five sentences about their artwork. Have the students consider these questions: What did I study? What did I create? What did I learn? Display the artist statements with the completed artwork.

Writing Buddies

If you have students who are reluctant or unmotivated to write during art class, have them work in groups. Ask for a student volunteer to be the group secretary. This student is responsible for writing down the group's thoughts and ideas. Students who are not strong in written expression will still feel success in sharing their ideas and opinions.

Brainstorming Ideas

Incorporate writing at the beginning of a lesson by having students use writing devices such as webs. The main topic is placed on the center of the page and ideas that support or expand it are written on the sides.

Vocabulary

Incorporate vocabulary into the art room. Post the "Word of the Day" on a chart or bulletin board display. Build a "Word Wall" with art vocabulary that is added throughout the year. Use word labels on art materials and equipment around the room. Create art flash cards with art words or concepts printed on them. Use the flash cards to find elements such as line, shape, and color in works of art or to review these concepts at the beginning or end of a lesson.

Try writing yourself!

Post statements about projects when displaying your students' works of art. Describe the learning objects and concepts in your statement. Use the display to inform parents, teachers and administrators about the rich and interesting learning that is taking place in your art class. Include articles about lessons, projects, and student achievements in your school or district newsletter.

Writing is an important means of creative expression. It is as valid and essential to the art curriculum as drawing or painting. Using writing to augment the art curriculum not only improves the students' ability to express ideas, it helps the art teacher communicate more effectively with every student. When art teachers integrate art instruction and writing about art, the entire curriculum is enhanced. By pairing art production, a realization of students' thoughts and ideas, with writing, a reflective way to understand and validate their opinions and feelings, art teachers can broaden the scope of the art experience. At the same time, the art teacher will develop a critical means to record and assess student learning.

The Importance of Cultural Diversity Through Art in the Elementary Classroom

Jane Rhoades Hudak, Ph.D., Professor of Art, Georgia Southern University

Culture is learned. People acquire information about the world and how to deal with it as members of a society. Individuals do not learn about their culture by themselves. Children learn about the art of their own culture and other cultures through family and friends, through the mass media, and through the Internet. The information learned this way is often valuable, but it cannot be relied upon to always give adequate and correct information. Schools are often the most effective place for giving students the opportunity to learn about the art of their culture and other cultures.

Our view of the nature of the world and our place in it is expressed and communicated culturally. Every society has institutions that teach culture—family and school are two of the best examples in our society. All societies have religions, which are bodies of cultural knowledge and practices. We also have rituals for birth and death. All cultures have objects that are used for everyday living. We express our world and views through dance, drama, music, and art. We decorate our world and our bodies. We paint our faces and the walls of our houses. We make music with instruments and our voices. All this activity is shaped by our participation in a cultural tradition.

A quality elementary art program provides a wonderful opportunity for teachers to expose students to a variety of cultures as well as their own and to help them to become culturally aware. Following are several of the areas such a program can enhance.

Art Promotes Intracultural Understanding

Through a culturally diverse art program, students begin to understand the role and function that art and artists play in society. Through learning about the art of other cultures, they have the opportunity to identify similarities and differences among their culture and others. They learn that art reflects the religion, politics, economics, and other aspects of a culture.

Through a quality art program, students can address issues of ethnocentrism, bias, stereotyping, prejudice, discrimination, and racism. Students can learn that no one racial, cultural, or national group is superior to another and that no one group's art is better than another.

Art Teaches Self-Esteem Through Diversity

Through a quality art program, students learn to recognize, acknowledge, and celebrate racial and cultural diversity through art within their own society. A good program helps promote the enhancement and affirmation of their self-esteem and encourages pride in their heritage. Personal expression is encouraged, and the result is often a statement in visual form that is both inventive and filled with personal meaning.

Art Teaches Effective Communication

When a quality art program is implemented, students are encouraged to increase their visual literacy skills. Students begin to understand that artists transmit information that cannot be disclosed through other modes of communication. Students learn visual literacy by looking, understanding, talking, writing, and making images. They learn that each society has its own way of communicating through image. Through a culturally sensitive art program, students will be able to discuss and compare art from other societies.

Art Teaches about the Past

Through a quality art program, students develop sensitivity and understanding for the history of humankind. For many periods in history, it is only through visual remains or material culture that societies' cultures can be pieced together. Experiences that students have with these art objects from the past teach them respect for others, challenge their minds, and stimulate not only their intellect but also their imagination.

Art Teaches Critical Thinking

A culturally sensitive art program encourages a variety of critical thinking skills. When students look at art from other cultures, they make critical judgments and develop their own opinions. Students are asked to identify and recall information; to organize selected facts and ideas; to use particular facts, rules, and principles; to figure out component parts or to classify; and to combine ideas and form a new whole.

Art Teaches Perceptual Sensitivity and Aesthetic Awareness

As a result of a quality art program, students develop a keen sense of awareness and an appreciation for beauty. They learn that each culture has its own criteria for beauty. Art experiences help cultivate an aesthetic sensitivity and respect for the natural and humanmade environment. Art classes are the only place in the school curriculum where students learn about what constitutes quality visual design—about harmony, order, organization, and specific design qualities such as balance, movement, and unity.

Art Teaches Creativity

When a culturally sensitive art program is implemented, creativity in all students is stimulated and nurtured. Students learn to solve problems creatively. They learn that every society has some form of creative expression. In some societies, no one special person is called an artist—everyone in the culture makes "art" objects.

Teachers can help prevent students from having a simplistic view of other cultures and help them understand the cultural context of how and why works of art are created. *Art Connections* has been carefully constructed so that students will be exposed to works of art that represent a wide variety of cultures. Questions and strategies are designed to help teachers put art in a cultural context for students. The Art History and Culture feature in the *Teacher Edition* and the *Artist Profiles* book provide additional information about the works of art and the artists.

As a teacher, you are a cultural transmitter. A quality art program taught by a culturally sensitive teacher benefits every student. When educators teach in a systematic, meaningful way, students acquire knowledge about art and cultures that will benefit them throughout their lives.

Museum Education

Marilyn J.S. Goodman, Director of Education, Solomon R. Guggenheim Museum

Museums are truly magnificent places. In recent years, these bastions of culture have taken tremendous strides toward making their collections accessible to a broader audience. Museum educators are usually eager to share new information and ideas and are delighted to assist school educators with programs and materials that can easily be incorporated into the classroom. Museums contain a wealth of treasures that offer extraordinary resources for teachers and students, and which will undoubtedly enrich the overall classroom experience.

Getting acquainted with museums in your region can be a real eye-opener. Museums collect objects that document human achievement, both in our own and in other cultures. A local historical society or farm museum might contain a variety of clothing and tools that can bring history to life. A science museum may offer interactive exhibits about phenomena in the natural or physical sciences, sensory perception, new technologies, or space exploration. A children's museum will offer hands-on displays specially designed to motivate young children to learn by doing. Art museums contain visually stunning works that reflect the diversity of human thought and experience.

Museums do not supplant classroom instruction. They enhance and reinforce what is taught by providing raw materials in the forms of objects, artifacts, and exhibits. Museums give students the chance to see and sometimes handle the real thing. It is one thing to talk about Egypt's role in the history of civilization; it is another thing entirely to see the wrappings on a cat mummy, discover hieroglyphs on a sarcophagus, or be overwhelmed by the power and grandeur of large stone sculptures of kings and queens.

When students have the chance to look at portraits, still lifes, landscapes, genre scenes, furniture, clothing, and artifacts, they learn more than by just seeing a picture of a person, place, or thing. They learn how to "read" a culture. Perhaps more importantly, they learn to develop their own process of investigation and critical inquiry. What was this person's life really like? What can one learn about the class structure of this society? What can we tell about craftspeople, available materials, or the objects this society valued? What does the clothing tell us about the climate of the region? What can we learn about the geography, topography, and vegetation? What did people eat? How did they spend leisure time? What were their religious beliefs? Is there any evidence of trade and communication with other regions? What scientific inventions were present at the time? Can one tell if they communicated through language or by writing? Because children are naturally curious, objects will motivate them to think, research, and learn.

> "A visit to a museum will make the curriculum come alive as students begin to explore objects and learn about their meanings."

A visit to a museum will make the curriculum come alive as students begin to explore objects and learn about their meanings. Museum objects give us information in a way that is very different from reading about the objects. Students must think critically to determine both the questions and answers for themselves. A first-hand, visual investigation of an object's style, material, subject matter, and physical characteristics offers preliminary clues to deciphering its meaning. When the exploration is combined with other knowledge, such as the geography and natural resources of a region; the historical context; the social, political, and economic structure of a culture; or even advances in science and technology, students can be engaged in a type of learning that is truly multidisciplinary and may lead them into other areas of study. Moreover, methods for gathering information go far beyond what people see. Exploring objects and works of art allows students to use all of their senses, combining intellect with intuition. The opportunity for experiential, emotional, and intellectual learning is always present.

Museum objects present different historical and cultural perspectives. Students can gather information about people, culture, belief systems, values, and the ways people lived in the past. Museum visits encourage students to see things from broader global and intellectual points of view, developing respect for the work, lives, and points of view of others. Students are encouraged to respond in a variety of ways and on different levels. Most importantly, students are invited to formulate and express their ideas and then discuss them with others.

To learn about museum resources, teachers can contact the education departments of museums in their region. If teachers explain the level of their students, the subjects they are studying, and the specific aspects of the curriculum they would like to supplement, the museum's education department can help to tailor the resources to the class. In addition to guided tours and workshops, the museum education department may offer materials for loan, including slides, pamphlets, posters, postcards, kits, and other printed materials. Some museums have teacher resource rooms filled with books, films, videos, CD-ROMs, and computer databases geared toward educators. Trained staff is available to answer questions or to help teachers develop a complete learning unit that can integrate museum objects with classroom studies.

Using museums is an excellent way to enrich and enliven the classroom experience. Educators can take the first step by learning all they can about the rich and diverse resources available to them and their students.

U.S. Museum Resources

Alabama

1 Birmingham Museum of Art
2000 8th Avenue North, Birmingham
http://www.ARTSbma.org

2 Mobile Museum of Art
4850 Museum Drive, Mobile
http://www.mobilemuseum ofart.com

3 Montgomery Museum of Fine Arts
1 Museum Drive, Montgomery
http://www.mmfa.org

Alaska

4 Alaska State Museum
395 Whittier Street, Juneau
http://www.museums. state.ak.us/asmhome.html

5 Anchorage Heritage Library Museum
301 West Northern Lights Boulevard, Anchorage
http://www.wellsfargohistory. com/museums/alaska.ht

6 Anchorage Museum of History and Art
121 West 7th Avenue, Anchorage
http://www.anchorage museum.org

Arizona

7 Heard Museum
2301 N Central Avenue, Phoenix
http://www.heard.org/

8 Phoenix Art Museum
1625 North Central Avenue, Phoenix
http://www.phxart.org

9 Scottsdale Museum of Contemporary Art - (SMOCA)
7380 E 2nd St, Scottsdale
http://www.scottsdalearts.org

Arkansas

10 Arkansas State University Museum
Jonesboro, AR 72467
http://museumastate.edu

11 Historic Arkansas Museum
200 East 3rd Street, Little Rock
http://www.arkansashistory. com/

12 Old State House Museum
300 West Markham Street, Little Rock
http://www.oldstatehouse.com

California

13 Asian Art Museum of San Francisco
Golden Gate Park, San Francisco
http://www.asianart.org

14 Berkeley Art Museum and Pacific Film Archive
2625 Durant Avenue, Berkeley
http://www.bampfa.berkeley. edu

15 El Museo Mexicano - Mexican Museum
Fort Mason Center, Building D, San Francisco
http://www.mexican museum.org

16 J Paul Getty Center Museum
1200 Getty Center Drive, Los Angeles, CA
http://www.getty.edu

17 Japanese American National Museum
369 East 1st Street, Los Angeles
http://www.janm.org

18 Korean American Museum
3780 Wilshire Boulevard # 220, Los Angeles
http://www.kamuseum.org

19 L A County Museum of Art
5905 Wilshire Boulevard, Los Angeles
http://www.lacma.org

20 San Francisco Museum of Modern Art
151 3rd Street Building A, San Francisco
http://www.sfmoma.org/

21 Santa Barbara Museum of Art
1130 State Street, Santa Barbara
http://www.sbmuseart.org

22 Southwest Museum
234 Museum Drive, Los Angeles
http://www.southwest museum.org/

Colorado

23 Aspen Art Museum
590 North Mill Street, Aspen
http://www.aspenart museum.org

24 Boulder Museum of Contemporary Art
1750 Thirteenth Street, Boulder
http://www.bmoca.org/

25 Denver Art Museum
100 West 14th Avenue, Denver
http://www.denverart museum.org

Connecticut

26 New Britain Museum of American Art
56 Lexington Street, New Britain
http://www.nbmaa.org

27 Norwalk Museum
41 North Main Street, Norwalk
http://www.norwalkct.org/ norwalkmuseum/index.htm

28 Wadsworth Atheneum Museum of Art
600 Main Street, Hartford
http://www.wadsworth atheneum.org/

Delaware

29 Delaware Art Museum
800 S Madison Street Suite B, Wilmington
http://www.delart.org

30 Sewell C Biggs Museum of American Art
406 Federal Street, Dover
http://www.biggsmuseum. org

31 Winterthur Museum
Route 52, Winterthur
http://www.winterthur.org/

Florida

32 Bass Museum of Art
2121 Park Ave, Miami
http://www.bassmuseum.org/

33 Key West Art and Historical Society
281 Front Street, Key West
http://www.kwahs.com

34 Lowe Art Museum
1301 Stanford Drive, Miami
http://www.lowemuseum. com/

35 Miami Art Museum
101 West Flagler Street, Miami
http://www.miamiart museum.org/

36 Museum of Fine Arts, St Petersburg
255 Beach Drive Northeast, St Petersburg
http://www.fine-arts.org

37 Salvador Dali Museum
1000 3rd Street South, St Petersburg
http://www.salvadordali museum.org

Georgia

38 Albany Museum of Art
311 Meadowlark Drive, Albany
http://www.albany museum.com/

39 High Museum of Art
1280 Peachtree Street Northeast, Atlanta, GA
http://www.high.org

40 Morris Museum of Art
1 10th Street, Augusta
http://www.themorris.org

Hawaii

41 Contemporary Museum, Honolulu
2411 Makiki Heights Drive, Honolulu
http://www.tcmhi.org

42 Kauai Museum
4428 Rice Street, Lihue
http://www.kauaimuseum.org

43 University of Hawaii at Manoa Art Gallery
University of Hawaii at Manoa, Honolulu
http://www.hawaii.edu/ artgallery

Idaho

44 Boise Art Museum
670 Julia Davis Drive, Boise
http://www.boiseart museum.org

45 Eagle Rock Art Museum and Education Center, Inc.
300 S Capital Avenue, Idaho Falls
http://www.eaglerockart museum.org

Illinois

46 Art Institute of Chicago
111 South Michigan Avenue, Chicago
http://www.artic.edu/aic/

47 Krannert Art Museum
500 East Peabody Drive, Champaign
http://www.kam.uiuc.edu

48 Martin D'Arcy Museum of Art
6525 N Sheridan Road, Chicago
http://darcy.luc.edu

49 Mitchell Museum of the American Indian
2600 Central Park Ave, Evanston
http://www.mitchell museum.org/

50 Museum of Contemporary Art
220 East Chicago Avenue, Chicago
http://www.mcachicago.org

51 Smart Museum of Art
5550 South Greenwood Avenue, Chicago
http://smartmuseum. uchicago.edu/

Indiana

52 Brauer Museum of Art
Valparaiso University Center for the Arts, Valparaiso
http://wwwstage.valpo.edu/ artmuseum/index.html

53 Eiteljorg Museum of American Indian and Western Art
500 West Washington Street, Indianapolis
http://www.eiteljorg.org

54 Indianapolis Museum of Art
1200 West 38th Street, Indianapolis
http://www.ima-art.org

U.S. Museum Resources (continued)

Iowa

55 Cedar Rapids
Museum of Art
*410 3rd Avenue Southeast,
Cedar Rapids*
http://www.crma.org

56 Davenport Museum of Art
*1737 West 12th Street,
Davenport*
http://www.art-dma.org

57 Dubuque Museum of Art
36 East 8th Street, Dubuque
http://www.dbqart.com

Kansas

58 Coutts Memorial Museum
*110 North Main Street,
El Dorado*
http://skyways.lib.ks.us/
kansas/museums/coutts/ind

59 Spencer Museum of Art
*1301 Mississippi Street,
Lawrence*
http://www.ukans.edu/~sma/

60 Wichita Art Museum
*West Museum Boulevard,
Wichita*
http://www.wichitaart
museum.org

Kentucky

61 Kentucky Museum
of Arts + Design
609 West Main Street, Louisville
http://www.kentuckycrafts.org

62 Speed Art Museum, the
2035 South Third St., Louisville
http://www.speedmuseum.org

63 University of Kentucky
Art Museum
*Rose and Euclid Avenue,
Lexington*
http://www.uky.edu/Art
Museum/

Louisiana

64 African-American Museum
*125 New Market Street,
St Martinville*
http://stmartinparish-
la.org/tourism_africanmuseum

65 Louisiana State Museum
751 Chartres Street, New Orleans
http://lsm.crt.state.la.us/

66 New Orleans
Museum of Art
*City Park 1 Collins Diboll Circle,
New Orleans*
http://www.noma.org

Maine

67 Farnsworth Art Museum
*352 Main Street, Box 466,
Rockland*
http://farnsworthmuseum.org/

68 Ogunquit Museum
of American Art
Shore Road, Ogunquit
http://www.ogunquit
museum.org

69 Portland
Museum of Art
7 Congress Square, Portland
http://www.portlandmuseum.
org

Maryland

70 African Art
Museum of Maryland
*5430 Vantage Point Road,
Columbia*
http://www.Africanart
museum.org

71 Baltimore
Museum of Art
10 Art Museum Drive, Baltimore
http://www.artbma.org/

72 Walters Art Museum
*600 North Charles Street,
Baltimore*
http://www.thewalters.org

Massachusetts

73 Harvard University
Art Museums
32 Quincy Street, Cambridge
http://www.artmuseums.
harvard.edu/

74 Institute of Contemporary
Art
955 Boylston Street, Boston
http://www.icaboston.org

75 MASS MoCA -
Massachusetts Museum
of Contemporary Art
87 Marshall Street, North Adams
http://www.massmoca.org

76 Mead Art Museum
*Amherst College, PO Box 5000,
Amherst*
http://www.amherst.edu/
~mead/

77 Museum of Fine Arts
Boston
465 Huntington Avenue, Boston
http://www.mfa.org/

78 Worcester Art Museum
55 Salisbury Street, Worcester
http://www.worcesterart.org

Michigan

79 Cranbrook Art Museum
*39221 Woodward Avenue,
PO Box 801, Bloomfield Hills*
http://www.cranbrook.
edu/art/museum/

80 Detroit Institute of Arts
*5200 Woodward Avenue,
Detroit*
http://www.dia.org

81 Grand Rapids
Art Museum
55 Division Ave N, Grand Rapids
http://www.gramonline.org

Minnesota

82 Frederick R Weisman
Art Museum
*333 East River Road # 200,
Minneapolis*
http://hudson.acad.umn.edu/

83 Minnesota Museum
of American Art
*Landmark Center 75 West 5th
Street West, St Paul*
http://www.mmaa.org

84 Walker Art Center
*725 Vineland Place,
Minneapolis*
http://www.walkerart.org

Mississippi

85 Lauren Rogers
Museum of Art
*5th Avenue and 7th Street,
Laurel*
http://www.lrma.org/

86 Mississippi Museum
of Art
*201 E Pascagoula St
Ste 103, Jackson*
http://www.msmuseumart.
org/

87 Walter Anderson
Museum of Art
*510 Washington Avenue,
Ocean Springs*
http://www.walteranderson
museum.org/

Missouri

88 Albrecht-Kemper Art Museum
2818 Frederick Avenue, St Joseph
http://www.albrecht-
kemper.org/

89 Nelson-Atkins
Museum of Art
4525 Oak Street, Kansas City
http://www.nelson-
atkins.org/

90 St Louis Art Museum
1 Fine Arts Drive, St Louis
http://www.slam.org

Montana

91 Art Museum of Missoula
*335 North Pattee Street,
Missoula*
http://www.artmissoula.org/

92 Hockaday Museum
of Art
*2nd Avenue East at
Third Street, Kalispell*
http://www.hockadayart
museum.org/

93 Montana Museum
of Art and Culture
University of Montana, Missoula
http://www.umt.edu/partv/
famus/

Nebraska

94 Joslyn Art Museum
2200 Dodge St., Omaha
http://www.joslyn.org

95 Museum of Nebraska Art
(MONA)
2401 Central Avenue, Kearney
http://monet.unk.edu/mona/

96 Sheldon Memorial
Art Gallery and
Sculpture Garden
*University of Nebraska-Lincoln,
12th and R Streets, Lincoln*
http://sheldon.unl.edu/

Nevada

97 Las Vegas Art Museum
*9600 West Sahara Avenue,
Las Vegas*
http://www.lvam.com

98 Nevada Museum of Art
160 West Liberty Street, Reno
http://www.nevadaart.org

99 Walker African-American
Museum and Research Center
*705 W Van Buren Ave,
Las Vegas*
http://members.aol.com/
Bigbrwnsis/

New Hampshire

100 Currier Museum of Art
201 Myrtle Way, Manchester
http://www.currier.org

101 Hood Museum of Art
Wheelock Street, Hanover
http://web.dartmouth.
edu/~hood/

102 Mariposa Museum
26 Main Street, Peterborough
http://www.mariposa
museum.org

New Jersey

103 Jane Voorhees
Zimmerli Art Museum
*71 Hamilton St, Rutgers
University, New Brunswick*
http://www.zimmerlimuseum.
rutgers.edu

104 Jersey City Museum
*350 Montgomery Street,
Jersey City*
http://www.jerseycity
museum.org/

105 Princeton University
Art Museum
Princeton University, Princeton
http://www.princetonart
museum.org/

New Mexico

106 Georgia O'Keeffe Museum
217 Johnson Street, Santa Fe
http://www.okeeffe
museum.org

107 Harwood Museum of Art
*238 Ledoux Street, 4080
NDCBU, Taos*
http://www.harwood
museum.org

108 Institute of American
Indian Arts Museum
Cathedral Place, Santa Fe
http://www.iaiancad.org

New York

109 Albright-Knox
Art Gallery
1285 Elmwood Avenue, Buffalo
http://www.albrightknox.org

110 Metropolitan Museum
of Art
*6626 Metropolitan Avenue
FL 2, Flushing*
http://www.Metmuseum.org/

111 Museum of Modern Art
MoMA
11 West 53 Street , New York
http://www.moma.org/

112 New Museum
of Contemporary Art
583 Broadway, New York
http://www.newmuseum.org/

113 Solomon R Guggenheim
Museum, New York
1071 5th Ave at 89th, New York
http://www.guggenheim.org
/new_york_index.html

114 Whitney Museum
of American Art
*945 Madison Avenue FL 5,
New York*
http://www.whitney.org

North Carolina

115 Ackland Art Museum
*Columbia and Franklin Street,
Chapel Hill*
http://www.ackland.org

116 Duke University
Museum of Art
*Buchanan Blvd-Trinity Avenue,
Durham*
http://www.duke.edu/web/
duma/

117 North Carolina Museum
of Art
2110 Blue Ridge Road, Raleigh
http://www.ncartmuseum.org/

North Dakota

118 *North Heritage Center of
the State Historical Society of
North Dakota, Bismarck*
http://www.state.nd.us/hist/
index.html

119 North Dakota
Museum of Art
Centennial Drive, Grand Forks
http://www.ndmoa.com

120 Plains Art Museum
219 7th Street South, Fargo
http://www.plainsart.org/

Ohio

121 Cincinnati Art Museum
953 Eden Park Drive, Cincinnati
http://www.cincinnatiart
museum.com/

122 Cleveland Museum of Art
11150 East Boulevard, Cleveland
http://www.clemusart.com/

123 Columbus Museum of Art
480 East Broad Street, Columbus
http://www.columbusmuseum.
org

Oklahoma

124 Fred Jones Jr
Museum of Art
*410 West Boyd Street,
University of Oklahoma, Norman*
http://www.ou.edu/fjjma/

125 Oklahoma City
Art Museum
*3113 Pershing Boulevard,
Oklahoma City*
http://www.okcartmuseum.
com/

126 Philbrook Museum of Art
*2727 South Rockford Road,
Tulsa, OK*
http://www.philbrook.org/

Oregon

127 Coos Art Museum
235 Anderson Avenue, Coos Bay
http://www.coosart.org

128 Portland Art Museum
1219 SW Park Ave., Portland
http://www.pam.org

129 University of Oregon
Museum of Art
*1223 University of Oregon,
Eugene*
http://uoma.uoregon.edu/

Pennsylvania

130 The Andy Warhol
Museum
117 Sandusky Street, Pittsburgh
http://www.clpgh.org/warhol/

131 The Palmer
Museum of Art
*Curtin Rd, The Pennsylvania
State University, University Park*
http://www.psu.edu/dept/
palmermuseum/

132 Philadelphia
Museum of Art
*26th Street and the Benjamin
Franklin Parkway, Philadelphia*
http://pma.libertynet.org/

Rhode Island

133 Museum of Art,
Rhode Island School of Design
224 Benefit Street, Providence
http://www.risd.edu/

134 Museum Of Primitive
Art & Culture
*1058 Kingstown Road,
South Kingstown*

135 National Museum
of American Illustration
*Vernon Court 492 Bellevue
Avenue , Newport*
http://www.american
illustration.org

South Carolina

136 Gibbes Museum of Art
135 Meeting Street, Charleston
http://www.gibbes.com/

137 Columbia Museum of Art
*Main and Hampton Streets,
Columbia*
http://www.colmusart.org/

138 The Spartanburg County
Museum of Art
385 S Spring St., Spartanburg
http://www.sparklenet.com/
museumofart

South Dakota

139 Journey Museum
222 New York Street, Rapid City
http://www.journeymuseum.org

140 Oscar Howe Art Center
and Middle Border Museum
*1300 E University Street P.O
Box 1071 Mitchell*
http://www.oscarhowe.com/
index.htm

141 South Dakota Art Museum
P.O Box 2250, Brookings
http://web.sdstate.edu/sites/
artmuseum/

Tennessee

142 Hunter Museum of Art
10 Bluff View, Chattanooga
http://www.huntermuseum.
org/

143 Institute of Egyptian
Art and Archaeology
*The University of Memphis,
Memphis*
http://www.memst.edu/
egypt/about.html

144 Knoxville Museum of Art
*1050 Worlds Fair Park Drive,
Knoxville*
http://www.knoxart.org

Texas

145 Dallas Museum of Art
1717 North Harwood, Dallas
http://dm-art.org/

146 Kimbell Art Museum
*3333 Camp Bowie Blvd.,
Fort Worth*
http://kimbellart.org/

147 Mexic-Arte Museum
419 Congress Avenue, Austin
http://www.mexic-arte
museum.org

148 The Museum of Fine Arts
1001 Bissonnet, Houston
http://mfah.org/

149 Panhandle-Plains
Historical Museum,
West Texas A&M University
2401 4th Ave., Canyon
http://www.wtamu.edu/
museum/

150 San Antonio Museum
of Art
*200 West Jones Avenue,
San Antonio*
http://www.sa-museum.org

Utah

151 BYU Museum of Art
*Brigham Young University,
Provo*
http://www.byu.edu/moa/

152 St George Art Museum
175 East 200 North, St George
http://www.ci.st-george.ut.us/
arts/artmuseum.php

153 Utah Museum of Fine
Arts, University of Utah
*370 South 1530 East
University of Utah , Salt Lake City*
http://www.utah.edu/umfa/

Vermont

154 The Bennington Museum
West Main St., Bennington
http://www.bennington
museum.com

155 Robert Hull
Fleming Museum
Colchester Avenue, Burlington
http://www.uvm.edu/
~fleming/home/

156 Shelburne Museum
*US Route 7, PO Box 10,
Shelburne*
http://www.shelburne
museum.org

Virginia

157 Chrysler Museum of Art
245 West Olney Rd., Norfolk
http://www.chrysler.org/

158 Maier Museum of Art
*2500 Rivermont Avenue,
Lynchburg*
http://www.rmwc.edu/
Maier/

159 Virginia Museum
of Fine Arts
2800 Grove Ave., Richmond
http://www.vmfa.state.va.us/

Washington

160 Frye Art Museum
704 Terry Ave., Seattle
http://fryeart.org/

161 Jundt Art Museum
*502 East Boone Avenue,
Spokane*
http://www.gonzaga.edu/
Campus+Resources/Museums
+an

162 Seattle Art Museum
100 University St., Seattle
http://seattleartmuseum.
org/

Washington, D.C.

163 Arthur M Sackler Gallery
and the Freer Gallery of Art
1050 Independence Avenue, SW
http://www.asia.si.edu/
default.htm

Oklahoma (continued)

164 Corcoran Gallery of Art
500 17th Street Northwest
http://www.corcoran.org/

165 Hirshhorn Museum
and Sculpture Garden
*Independence Avenue
and 7th Street Southwest*
http://hirshhorn.si.edu/

166 National Gallery of Art
http://www.nga.gov/

167 The National Museum
of Women in the Arts
1250 New York Ave., NW
http://www.nmwa.org/

168 Smithsonian Museums
Smithsonian Institution
http://www.si.edu/

West Virginia

169 Huntington Museum
of Art
2033 McCoy Rd., Huntington
http://www.hmoa.org/

170 Oglebay Institute:
Mansion Museum and
Glass Museum
Burton Center, Wheeling
http://www.oionline.com/

Wisconsin

171 Elvehjem Museum of Art
*800 University Avenue,
Madison*
http://www.lvm.wisc.edu

172 Leigh Yawkey Woodson
Art Museum
700 North Twelfth St, Wausau
http://www.lywam.org/

173 Milwaukee Art Museum
*750 North Lincoln Memorial
Dr., Milwaukee*
http://www.mam.org/

Wyoming

174 National Museum
of Wildlife Art
2820 Rungius Road, Jackson
http://www.wildlifeart.org

175 University of Wyoming
Art Museum
2111 Willett Dr., Laramie
http://uwadmnweb.uwyo.
edu/artmuseum/

World Museum Resources

Argentina

1 Fundacion Federico Klemm
Buenos Aires, Argentina
www.fundacionfjklemm.org

Australia

2 Art Gallery of New South Wales
Sydney, Australia
www.artgallery.nsw.gov.au/

3 Australian National Art Gallery
Canberra, Australia
www.nga.gov.au/Home/index.cfm

4 Museum of Contemporary Art
Sydney, Australia
www.mca.com.au/

Austria

5 Kunsthistorisches Museum Wien
Vienna, Austria
www.khm.at/

Bahrain

6 Al Hayat Museum
Manama, Bahrain
www.beitalquran.com/

Brazil

7 Museu Historico Nacional
Rio de Janeiro, Brazil
www.museuhistoriconacional.com.br/ingles/index.htm

Canada

8 Art Gallery of Calgary
Calgary, Canada
www.artgallerycalgary.com/

9 Morris and Helen Belkin Art Gallery, University of British Columbia
Vancouver, Canada
www.belkin-gallery.ubc.ca/

10 Art Gallery of Newfoundland and Labrador
St. Johns, Canada
www.mun.ca/agnl/main.html

11 Art Gallery of Nova Scotia
Halifax, Canada
www.agns.gov.ns.ca/

12 Art Gallery of Ontario
Toronto, Canada
www.ago.net/navigation/flash/index.cfm

13 National Gallery of Canada
Ottawa, Canada
www.national.gallery.ca/

14 The Montreal Museum of Fine Arts
Quebec, Canada
www.mmfa.qc.ca/en/index.html

15 McMichael Canadian Art Collection
Toronto, Canada
www.mcmichael.com/

16 Winnipeg Art Gallery
Winnipeg, Canada
www.wag.mb.ca/

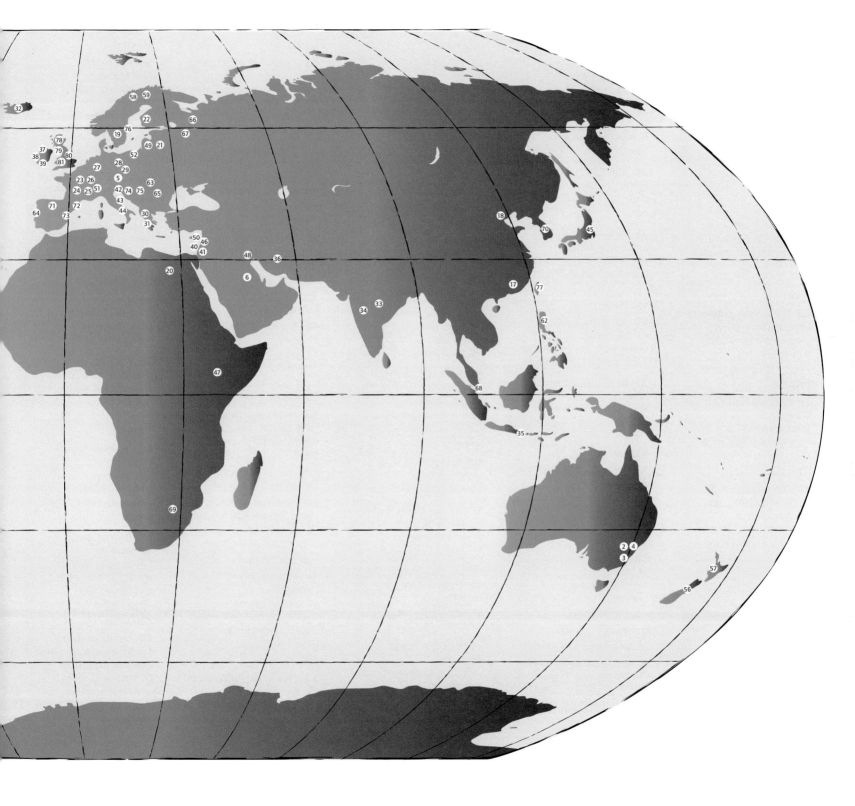

World Museum Resources

China

17 Hong Kong
Museum of Art
Hong Kong, China
www.lcsd.gov.hk/CE/Mus
eum/Arts/english/intro/
eintro.html

18 Palace Museum
Beijing, China
www.dpm.org.cn/

Denmark

19 National Museum
Copenhagen, Denmark
www.natmus.dk/sw1413.
asp

Egypt

20 The Egyptian Museum
Cairo, Egypt
www.egyptianmuseum.
gov.eg/

Estonia

21 Estonian National
Museum
Tartu, Estonia
www.erm.ee/?lang=ENG

Finland

22 The Finnish
National Gallery
Helsinki, Finland
www.fng.fi/fng/rootnew/
en/vtm/etusivu.htm

France

23 The Louvre
Paris, France
www.louvre.fr/louvrea.htm

24 Musee d'Orsay,
Paris, France
www.musee-orsay.fr/

25 Centre Georges
Pompidou
Paris, France
www.cnac-gp.fr/Pompidou/
Accueil.nsf/tunnel?
OpenForm

Germany

26 Neues Museum
Nuremberg, Germany
www.nmn.de/

27 Hamburg Kunsthalle
Hamburg, Germany
www.hamburger-
kunsthalle.de/

28 Alte National Galerie
Berlin, Germany
www.alte-nationalgalerie.
de/

29 Bauhaus Archiv
Museum of Design
Berlin, Germany
www.bauhaus.de/english/

Greece

30 Acropolis Museum
Athens, Greece
www.culture.gr/2/21/211/
21101m/e211am01.html

31 Benaki Museum
Athens, Greece
www.benaki.gr/index-
en.htm

Iceland

32 Living Art Museum
Reykjavik, Iceland
www.nylo.is/English/
index.html

India

33 National Museum
of India
New Delhi, India
www.nationalmuseumindia
.org/index.html

34 Chhatrapati Shivaji
Maharaj Vastu Sangrahalaya
(Formerly the Prince of Wales
Museum of
Western India)
Mumbai (Bombay), India
www.bombaymuseum.org/

Indonesia

35 Agung Rai
Museum of Art
Ubud, Bali, Indonesia
www.nusantara.com/
arma/

Iran

36 National
Museum of Iran
Tehran, Iran
www.nationalmuseumofira
n.com/

Ireland

37 Hunt Museum
Limerick, Ireland
www.huntmuseum.com/

38 Irish Museum
of Modern Art
Dublin, Ireland
www.modernart.ie/

39 National Gallery
of Ireland
Dublin, Ireland
www.nationalgallery.ie/

Israel

40 The Israel Museum
Jerusalem, Israel
www.imj.org.il/

41 Tel Aviv Museum of Art
Tel Aviv, Israel
www.tamuseum.com/

Italy

42 Uffizi Gallery
Florence, Italy
www.uffizi.firenze.it/
welcomeE.html

43 Museo di Roma
Rome, Italy
www.museodiroma.comune
.roma.it/PalazzoBraschi/
inizio.mostra

44 Vatican Museum
Vatican City
http://mv.vatican.va/
3_EN/pages/MV_Home.
html

Japan

45 Kyoto National Museum
Tokyo, Japan
www.kyohaku.go.jp/index
e.htm

Jordan

46 Darat al Funun
Home for the Arts
Amman, Jordan
www.daratalfunun.org/

Kenya

47 National Museum
of Kenya
Nairobi, Kenya
www.museums.or.ke/

Kuwait

48 Kuwait National
Museum
Kuwait City, Kuwait
www.kmia.org.kw

Latvia

49 State Museum of Art
Riga, Latvia
www.vmm.lv/en/muzejs.
html

Lebanon

50 American University of
Beirut Archaeology Museum
Beirut, Lebanon

Liechtenstein

51 Kunstmuseum
Liechtenstein
Vaduz, Liechtenstein
www.kunstmuseum.li/web
2306e/index.html

Lithuania

52 Lithuanian Art Museum
Vilnius, Lithuania
www.ldm.lt/ldm_en.htm

Mexico

53 Museo de
Arte Moderno
Mexico City, Mexico
www.arts-history.mx/
museos/mam/home2.html

54 National Museum
of Anthropology
Mexico City, Mexico
www.mna.inah.gob.mx/

55 Museo de Arte
Contemporaneo de Oaxaca
Oaxaca, Mexico
www.arts-history.mx/
museos/maco/home.html

New Zealand

56 Centre of
Contemporary Art
Christchurch, New Zealand
www.coca.org.nz/

57 Auckland Art Gallery
Auckland, New Zealand
www.aucklandartgallery.
govt.nz/

Norway

58 National Gallery
of Norway
Oslo, Norway
www.museumsnett.no/
nasjonalgalleriet/flash_
versjon_engelsk/

59 Lillehammer
Art Museum
Lillehammer, Norway
www.lillehammerart
museum.com/

Panama

60 Museo de Arte
Contemporaneo de Panama
*Panama, Republic
of Panama*
www.macpanama.org/

Peru

61 Museo Arqueologico
Rafael Larco Herrera
Lima, Peru
museolarco.perucultural.
org.pe/

Philippines

62 Philippine National
Museum
Manila, Philippines
http://nmuseum.tripod.
com/

Poland

63 Polish National Museum
Warsaw, Poland
www.mnw.art.pl/

Portugal

64 Museu Calouste
Gulbenkian
Lisbon, Portugal
www.gulbenkian.pt/

Romania

65 The National Museum
of Art of Romania
Bucharest, Romania
http://art.museum.ro/
museum.html

Russia

66 The State Hermitage
Museum
St. Petersburg, Russia
www.hermitagemuseum.
org/

67 Pushkin Museum
of Fine Arts
Moscow, Russia
www.museum.ru/gmii/

Singapore

68 Singapore Art Museum
*Singapore, Republic of
Singapore*
www.nhb.gov.sg/SAM/
sam.shtml

South Africa

69 Pretoria Art Museum
Pretoria, South Africa
www.pretoriaartmuseum.
co.za/

South Korea

70 Seoul Metropolitan
Museum of Art
Seoul, South Korea
www.metro.seoul.kr/
muse/eng/

Spain

71 Guggenheim
Bilbao Museum
Bilbao, Spain
www.guggenheim-
bilbao.es/idioma.htm

72 Museu d'Art
Contemporani
Barcelona, Spain
www.macba.es/home.php

73 Valencian Institute
of Modern Art
Valencia, Spain
www.ivam.es/

Switzerland

74 Kunstmuseum Basel
Basel, Switzerland
www.kunstmuseumbasel.
ch/de/

75 Kunsthaus
Zurich, Switzerland
www.kunsthaus.ch/

Sweden

76 National Museum
Stockholm, Sweden
www.nationalmuseum.se/

Taiwan

77 National Palace Museum
T'aipei, Taiwan
www.npm.gov.tw/english/
index-e.htm

United Kingdom

78 National Gallery
of London
London, England
www.nationalgallery.
org.uk/

79 British Museum
London, England
www.thebritishmuseum.
ac.uk/

80 Tate Gallery
London, England
www.tate.org.uk/home/
default.htm

81 Victoria and
Albert Museum
London, England
www.vam.ac.uk/

Uruguay

82 Museo Nacianal
de Artes Visuales
Montevideo, Uruguay
www.mnav.gub.uy/

Elements and Principles of Art

Scope and Sequence

Elements of Art	Level K U1	U2	U3	U4	U5	U6	Level 1 U1	U2	U3	U4	U5	U6	Level 2 U1	U2	U3	U4	U5	U6	Level 3 U1	U2	U3	U4	U5	U6
Line	1–6						1–6	1					1–4						1–2					
Shape		1–6			6			1–6	1				5–6					2, 4	3–6					
Color			1–6						1–6						1–3			1, 3			1–6			
Value																4–6					1			
Space				1, 3						2, 5, 6				5–6						1–3				
Form				2–6	5					1–4		4	1–4					2, 4	4–6					
Texture					1–6						1–3						5–6						5–6	

Principles of Art	Level K U1	U2	U3	U4	U5	U6	Level 1 U1	U2	U3	U4	U5	U6	Level 2 U1	U2	U3	U4	U5	U6	Level 3 U1	U2	U3	U4	U5	U6
Pattern						1					4–5					1–2							1–3	
Rhythm						2					6					3–6							4–6	
Balance					3–4							1–2					1–2					1–4		
Proportion																								
Emphasis											3–4						3–4							3–4
Variety																		3–4						2
Harmony																		1–2						1
Unity						5–6						5–6						5–6						5–6

*Numbers indicate lesson numbers within a given unit.

Level 4						Level 5						Level 6						Level 7	Level 8
U1	U2	U3	U4	U5	U6	U1	U2	U3	U4	U5	U6	U1	U2	U3	U4	U5	U6	Exploring Art	Understanding Art
1-6						1-2						1						Chapter 2, 6, 7, 8, 9, 10, 11	Chapter 2, 6, 8, 9, 12, 15, 16
	1-2					3	1					2						Chapter 2, 6, 8, 9, 10, 11	Chapter 2, 3, 5, 8, 9, 13, 14, 16, 17
		1-4						1-4						1-4				Chapter 2, 4, 8, 9, 11, 13	Chapter 2, 3, 4, 8, 11, 12, 14-17
		5-6				4-6								2-3				Chapter 14	Chapter 13, 14, 15
			1-3				1-3							5-6				Chapter 2, 4, 10, 12	Chapter 6, 7, 13, 15
		1-3					4-6							3-4				Chapter 2, 6, 11, 12, 13	Chapter 6, 14, 15
		4-5								1				5-6				Chapter 2, 14	Chapter 3, 5, 6, 11-16

Level 4						Level 5						Level 6						Level 7	Level 8
U1	U2	U3	U4	U5	U6	U1	U2	U3	U4	U5	U6	U1	U2	U3	U4	U5	U6	Exploring Art	Understanding Art
	3							5-6					1-3					Chapter 3, 6	Chapter 7, 8, 10, 15, 17
	4-6								2-3				4-6					Chapter 3, 4, 7	
			1-3						4-6						1-4			Chapter 3, 11, 12	Chapter 5, 7, 9, 10, 11, 13
			4-6					1-6								1-6		Chapter 3, 11, 14	Chapter 5, 11, 12
		6		5										3-4		5-6		Chapter 3, 11	Chapter 5, 10, 11, 12, 16
				5											2		1-2	Chapter 3, 6, 13	Chapter 3, 4, 5, 10, 15
				4											1		3-4	Chapter 3, 6, 7	Chapter 4, 5, 7, 12, 16
				6										5-6			5-6	Chapter 3	Chapter 7

Media

Scope and Sequence

Media	Level K						Level 1						Level 2						Level 3					
	U1	U2	U3	U4	U5	U6	U1	U2	U3	U4	U5	U6	U1	U2	U3	U4	U5	U6	U1	U2	U3	U4	U5	U6
Collage	6	2	2, 3		1	3	3		5			3, 4	5	5						4				
Drawing	2, 4, 5	4, 5	1, 4, 5	1	2	1, 2	1	1–3, 5	1, 4		2, 6	1, 5				2, 3	2–4, 6	4	1, 2, 5, 6	3	1	1	3, 5	6
Fiber Arts				4, 6							5						5						6	2
Mixed Media		6		3, 4	3		5			5	1	2	2, 6	2	2, 3	6				6	4, 6			4
Painting	1		6				1, 2, 4	4	3, 6	6			3, 4	6	1, 4–6		1, 3		3	2	2, 3, 5	4		
Photography																								
Printmaking		3								4						1				1			1	
Three-Dimensional Forms				2, 5, 6	5	4, 6			1–4	3	6		1	1, 3, 4		4	1	5		4, 5		2, 3	4, 6	1, 5
Technology	3	1			5		6	6	2							5		2, 6				5	2	3

*Numbers indicate lesson numbers within a given unit.

Level 4 · U1	U2	U3	U4	U5	U6	Level 5 · U1	U2	U3	U4	U5	U6	Level 6 · U1	U2	U3	U4	U5	U6	Level 7 (Exploring Art)	Level 8 (Understanding Art)
	6	3				1		4	2		5	6					1	Chapter 1, 6, 10	Chapter 10
1–6	3, 4	2		1, 2, 4, 5		2, 4, 5	1, 4	1, 5	1, 4	3	2	1	3	1, 2, 4	3–5	1, 2, 5		Chapter 2, 7, 11, 14	Chapter 3, 15, 16
					3, 6					2	4		2				3, 5	Chapter 1, 2, 3, 13	Chapter 7, 8, 10, 12
	1, 5		4, 5			1, 4				1			6			6	4	Chapter 5, 13	Chapter 2, 3
		4–6				2, 5		2, 3	3	3	4, 5	1	5	1, 2, 4	5	1		Chapter 2, 3, 4, 5, 6, 9, 11, 14	Chapter 1–8, 10, 11, 13–17
			3			6											2	Chapter 10	Chapter 1, 17
											3							Chapter 3, 4, 8	Chapter 1, 3, 6, 8, 14–17
		1–3						5, 6	6	5, 6		6	3, 4	3, 6	6	3	6	Chapter 2, 3, 4, 5, 7, 12, 13	Chapter 1, 2, 3, 5–13, 15–17
	2	1	6		6	3		2		6			5			2	4	Chapter 4, 11, 15	Chapter 3, 17

Program Glossary

A

active lines *noun* Lines that show action and add energy and movement to a work of art. Diagonal, zigzag, and curved lines are examples of active lines.

additive sculpture *noun* When something is added to either relief or freestanding sculpture

alternating pattern *noun* Can repeat a motif, but change position; alter spacing between motifs or add a second motif

analogous color scheme *noun* Uses colors that are side by side on the color wheel and have a common color

analogous colors *noun* Colors that sit side by side on the color wheel and have a common hue. Violet, blue-violet, blue, blue-green are examples of analogous colors.

angle *noun* A shape formed when two lines extend in different directions from the same point

animal forms *noun* A three-dimensional representation of an animal

ant's view *noun* Viewers feel they are looking up, toward an object or figure.

appliqué *noun* An art form in which cutout fabrics are attached to a larger surface

approximate symmetry *noun* A special kind of formal balance where both sides of a design are almost exactly the same. One example is the human face: each side is almost the same as the other.

arc *noun* Any portion of a curved line from a circle

architects *noun* Artists who design buildings, cities, and bridges using three-dimensional forms

architecture *noun* The art of designing and planning buildings, cities, and bridges

armature *noun* A framework for supporting material used in sculpting

art form *noun* A type of art

assemblage *noun* A sculpture technique in which a variety of objects is assembled to create one complete piece

B

asymmetrical balance *noun* Another name for informal balance

asymmetry *noun* Another name for informal balance. Something asymmetrical looks balanced even if it is not the same on both sides.

atmospheric perspective *noun* The effects air and light have on how we perceive an object

axis *noun* A real or imaginary line across the center of a work of art

background *noun* The area of the picture plane farthest from the viewer

balance *noun* The principle of design that deals with visual weight in an artwork

bird's-eye view *noun* Or aerial view; viewers feel they are looking down on a scene.

black ▮▮▮

blending *noun* A shading technique that creates a gradual change from light to dark or dark to light

blind contour drawing *noun* A drawing that is made by looking at the object being drawn, not at the paper.

blob *noun* A type of free-form shape

body forms *noun* Three-dimensional representations of a person

body proportions *noun* The size relationship of one part of the body to another

brass *noun* A metal made by combining copper and zinc

bright colors *noun* colors that appear to reflect light

broken (line) *noun* A line that is made of a series of dashes, not solid

building *noun* a structure where we live, work, meet, or play

C

calm lines *noun* Lines that give a work of art a quiet and peaceful mood. Horizontal and vertical lines are calm lines.

carving *noun* Art made by cutting into the surface of the medium.

central axis *noun* A real or imaginary dividing line that can run in two directions, vertically and horizontally

circle *noun* A round, geometric shape made when all points are placed the same distance from a center point.

close-up view *noun* Viewers feel they are right next to an object, or are a part of the action in a picture.

coil *noun* A long roll of clay joined into a circle or spiral. Clay coils are used to make pottery.

collage *noun* A two-dimensional work of art made up of pieces of paper and/or fabric to create the image.

collograph *noun* A printmaking technique where cut papers or thin boards are arranged to create an image on a stiff printing plate.

color *noun* 1. The art element that is created from reflected light; 2. In balance: a brighter color has more visual weight than a dull color; 3. In perspective: bright-colored objects seem closer, while dull or pale objects appear farther away.

color intensity *noun* The brightness or dullness of a color

color scheme *noun* A plan for organizing the colors used in an artwork

color spectrum *noun* The effect that occurs when light passes through a prism and separates into a band of colors in the order of red, orange, yellow, green, blue, and violet.

color wheel *noun* Shows the color spectrum bent into a circle

column *noun* A supporting pillar on a building

complementary color scheme *noun* Uses one set of complementary colors; for example, red and green, blue and orange, and yellow and violet

complementary colors *noun* Colors that are opposite each other on the color wheel

complex geometric shapes *noun* Shapes made by combining simple geometric shapes such as triangles, squares, and rectangles. Some examples of complex geometric shapes are diamonds, pentagons, trapezoids, hexagons, parallelograms, and octagons.

contour *noun* The edges and surface ridges of an object

contour hatching *noun* A shading technique that follows the form of an object

contour lines *noun* Continuous, unbroken lines that show the edges and surface ridges of an object or figure

contrast *noun* 1. A technique for creating a focal point or area of interest in a work of art using differences in elements; 2. In emphasis: contrast occurs when one element stands out from the rest of the work; 3. showing differences between things

converging *adj.* (*verb*) Coming together at one point or place

converging lines *noun* One of the six perspective techniques. Parallel lines seem to converge or move toward the same point as they move away from you.

cool colors *noun* Green, violet, and blue. They suggest coolness and move away from the viewer.

cool hues *noun* Blue, green, and violet. Cool hues are associated with cool things like snow, water, and grass.

cross-hatching *noun* A shading technique created when sets of parallel lines cross or intersect

culture *noun* Another word for custom

curling *verb* Hold one end of a long strip of paper. Grip the middle of the paper strip next to the side of a pencil. With a quick motion, pull the strip firmly across the pencil.

curved *adj.* Lines that bend and change gradually or turn inward to form spirals

curved (line) *noun* A line that changes directions slowly and bends in arcs

curving movement *verb* Using curved lines to move the viewer's eyes through a work of art and make the viewer feel that objects in the work of art are moving along curves

D

dark lines *noun* Created by using less water for watercolor paints

dark value *noun* A value that has more black added to it

decorative *adj.* Serving to make more beautiful; to adorn with ornaments

depth *noun* 1. The appearance of distance; 2. How far something extends toward or away from the viewer.

detail *noun* One of the six perspective techniques. Objects with fuzzy, blurred edges appear farther away than those with clear sharp edges.

diagonal *noun* (*adj.*) Lines that are slanted. They look as if they are falling or rising. They make things look active.

diagonal movement *verb* Using diagonal lines to move the viewer's eyes through a work of art and make the viewer feel that objects in the work of art are moving along diagonals

dimension *noun* A measurement of the amount of space an object takes up in one direction

diorama *noun* A display of a scene using sculpted, miniature figurines

directional lines *noun* How a line moves: diagonally, vertically, or horizontally

distortion *noun* A deviation from normal or expected proportions

dominant *noun* (*adj.*) The part of the work of art that seems more important to the viewer. Dominant elements have been emphasized.

dominant element *noun* The element in a work of art that is noticed first.

dull colors Colors that are not bright

E

earthenware *noun* Ceramics made out of clay and fired at a low heat

elongate *verb* To stretch out or make long

embroidery *noun* The art of decorating designs with needle and thread

emphasis *noun* The principle of design that stresses one area in an art work over another area

even balance *adj.* Both halves are equal. Left side and right side are the same.

exaggerate *verb* To make much larger than actual size

exaggeration *noun* To increase or enlarge beyond what is expected or normal

F

facial proportions *noun* The relationship of one feature of a face to another feature

faraway view *noun* Or eye-level view; viewers feel they are standing far away from the scene.

fiber *noun* A material used to make baskets and cloth. Grass, yarn, and straw are kinds of fibers.

flowing lines *noun* Create a feeling of calm and gracefulness. Flowing lines are fluid; they change direction and size.

flowing rhythm *noun* Created when curved lines or shapes are repeated

focal point *noun* The point where the receding lines meet. It is the first part of a composition to attract the viewer's attention.

foreground *noun* The area of the picture plane that is closest to the viewer

form *noun* A three-dimensional object that is measured by height, width, and depth

formal balance *noun* Occurs when equal or similar elements are placed on opposite sides of a central axis

Program Glossary (continued)

free-form forms *noun* Three-dimensional forms with irregular edges often found in nature

free-form shapes *noun* Two-dimensional images made of straight or curved lines or a combination of both

freestanding *noun* Forms that can be seen from all around

freestanding sculpture *noun* A three-dimensional work of art that can be viewed on all sides because it is surrounded by space

fringing *verb* Make parallel straight cuts along the edge of a piece of paper to create a ruffled look.

frontal proportions *noun* A front view of the head that is divided by three horizontal lines across the central axis

futurists *noun* A group of Italian artists during the early twentieth-century who repeated and overlapped shapes and lines to create the illusion of movement

G

geometric forms *noun* Mathematically precise forms based on geometric shapes

geometric shapes *noun* Mathematically precise shapes: circle, square, and triangle

gesture *noun* An expressive movement

gesture drawings *noun* Quick drawings used to capture the position or pose of the body

gesture lines *noun* Lines drawn to capture the movement of a person, an animal, or an object in a painting or drawing

gesture sketch *noun* Quick drawings used to capture the position or movement of the body

guide lines *noun* Lines used by artists to create both full-face and profile portraits more accurately

H

hand tools *noun* Simple instruments for carving or sculpting

harmony *noun* The principle of art that creates unity by stressing similarities of separate but related parts

hatching *noun* A shading technique that looks like a series of parallel lines

height *noun* A vertical measurement, or how tall something is

high-intensity color *noun* A pure hue such as red

highlights *noun* Small areas of white or light value to show the brightest spots

horizon line *noun* The point at which the earth and sky meet. The horizon line is always at the viewer's eye level.

horizontal *noun* (*adj.*) A line that moves from side to side

hues *noun* The spectral colors, or colors of the rainbow. Hues do not include black or white. Hues are red, orange, yellow, green, blue, and violet.

I

informal balance *noun* A way of organizing parts of a design so that unlike objects have equal visual weight

installation *noun* An artwork that was created for a specific place, such as a gallery or outdoor location

intensity *noun* The brightness or dullness of a color

interior designers *noun* Artists who decorate the inside of a building

intermediate colors *noun* Colors made by mixing a primary color and a secondary color. There are six intermediate colors—red-orange, yellow-orange, yellow-green, blue-green, blue-violet, and red-violet.

intermediate hues *noun* Yellow-green, red-orange, blue-green, made by combining a primary hue with either of the secondary hues that are adjacent on the color wheel

invented texture *noun* Created when an artist uses lines or other elements to make a textural look without any specific texture in mind

irregular *adj.* Does not follow a rule or pattern

isolation *noun* An object is emphasized by its placement apart from other objects.

J

jeweler *noun* An artist who designs and makes jewelry

jewelry *noun* Three-dimensional artwork that is made for people to wear

K

kinetic movement *noun* Actual or real movement

kinetic sculpture *noun* A three-dimensional form that actually moves in space

L

landscape *noun* a picture of the outdoors

light lines *noun* Created by adding more water to watercolor paints

light value *noun* A value that has more white added to it

line *noun* A mark drawn by a tool such as a pencil, pen, or paintbrush as it moves across a surface

line variety *noun* The different possibilities in the character of lines. For example, lines can be long or short, thick or thin, rough or smooth, and broken or solid.

linear perspective *noun* A system used to create the illusion of depth on a flat surface

lines *noun* One of the six perspective techniques. Parallel lines seem to converge or move toward the same point as they move away from the viewer.

location *noun* Artists can emphasize an object by placing it closer to the center of the piece.

low-intensity color *noun* A dull hue made by mixing a color with its complement

M

mandala *noun* A radial design divided into sections or wedges, each of which contains a different image

maquette *noun* A small model for a larger sculpture

mask *noun* A three-dimensional art form of sculpted faces

matte *noun* A dull, sometimes rough finish

medium *noun* The supply an artist uses to create art. Some media are clay, paint, or wood.

middle ground *noun* The area of the picture plane that is usually toward the center

minimal details *noun* Used in gesture sketches to complete the drawing

mix a neutral color *verb* Mix a neutral color with another color to change its value

mixed-media *noun* An art object that has been created from an assortment of media or materials

mobile *noun* A moving sculpture in which shapes are balanced and arranged on wire arms and suspended from the ceiling to move freely in the air currents

monochromatic *adj.* A color scheme that is made up of one color and the tints and shade of that color

monochromatic color scheme *noun* Uses only one color and the values of that color

monotonous *adj.* Lack of variety; boring

monumental sculptures *noun* Sculptures that are larger than human forms

motif *noun* A unit that is made up of objects or art elements that can be repeated

movement *noun* The principle of art that leads a viewer's eyes throughout a work of art

mural *noun* A painting done on a wall

N

negative space *noun* The empty space that surrounds objects, shapes, and forms

neon *noun* A special kind of light that can be made to be many bright colors

neutral color scheme *noun* Uses black, white, and a variety of grays

neutral colors *noun* Black, white, and gray; give hues a range of values

nonobjective *adj.* Art that has no recognizable subject matter

O

one-point linear perspective *noun* A system used to create the illusion of depth on a flat surface where all receding lines meet at one point

opaque *adj.* Does not let light through

outline *noun* a line drawn around the edge of an object

overlap *verb* To place one object on top of another object and partially cover the first object up

overlapping *noun* 1. One object covers a portion of another object. 2. In perspective: one of the six perspective techniques; the object covering another will appear closer to the viewer, creating a feeling of depth.

P

painting *noun* An art form using paint on a flat surface

paper sculpting techniques *noun* Six different techniques used to create paper sculptures: scoring a straight line, scoring a curve, pleating, curling, fringing, tab and slot.

parallel lines *noun* Lines that move in the same direction and always stay the same distance apart

pattern *noun* A repeated surface decoration

perception drawing *verb* Looking at something carefully and thinking deeply about what you see as you draw

perspective *noun* The method used to create the illusion of depth in two-dimensional art: overlapping, size, placement, detail, color, converging lines

perspective techniques *noun* The six techniques an artist uses to create the illusion of depth in two-dimensional art: overlapping, size, placement, detail, color, converging lines

photograph *noun* A picture taken using light-sensitive film and a camera

picture plane *noun* The surface of a drawing or painting

placement *noun* One of the six perspective techniques. Objects placed lower in the picture appear to be closer than those placed near eye level. There are three areas on a picture plane: foreground, middle ground, and background.

pleating *verb* Fold piece of paper from edge to edge. Then fold the same amount of paper in the other direction. Continue folding the paper back and forth in this manner.

point of view *noun* The angle at which the viewer sees an object

portrait *noun* A two- or three-dimensional artwork created in the image of a person or animal

posed *verb* Arranged in a special way

position *noun* In balance: a larger, positive shape and a small, negative space can be balanced by a small, positive shape and a large, negative space.

positive space *noun* Refers to any object, shape, or form in two- and three-dimensional art

primary colors *noun* Red, yellow, and blue. They cannot be made by mixing colors.

primary hues *noun* Red, yellow, and blue, used to mix the other hues on the color wheel

print *noun* An image created by using a stamp or printing plate. When artists make prints, they can make many identical images.

printing *verb* Pressing a shape from one thing to another many times

printing plate *noun* A plate that holds the image that will be used to create a print

prism *noun* A wedge-shaped piece of glass that bends light as it passes through

profile *noun* A side view of a person or animal

profile proportions *noun* A side view of the head that is divided by three horizontal lines

proportion *noun* The principle of art that is concerned with the size relationship of one part to another

Program Glossary (continued)

R

radial balance *noun* A type of balance that occurs when the art elements come out, or radiate, from a central point

rainbow *noun* An arc of spectral colors, usually identified as red, orange, yellow, green, blue, indigo, and violet, that appears in the sky opposite the sun

random pattern *noun* Occurs when the motif is repeated in no apparent order

ratio *noun* A comparison of size between two things

real texture *noun* Texture you can feel

realistic scale *noun* When an artist creates a work of art where everything fits together and makes sense in size relation

rectangle *noun* A four-sided geometric shape made of all right angles and whose opposite sides are equal in length.

regular pattern *noun* Occurs when identical motifs are repeated with an equal amount of space between them

relief *noun* A type of sculpture where forms project from a flat background

relief sculpture *noun* A sculpture in which objects stick out from a flat surface

repeated lines *noun* Used to give the feeling of movement or motion in a gesture drawing

repetition *noun* Lines, shapes, colors, or textures that are repeated throughout an artwork

rest *noun* The negative space between repetitions of the motif

rhythm *noun* The principle of design that organizes the elements in a work of art by repeating elements and/or objects

rough *noun* (*adj.*) A surface that has ridges; not smooth

rough (line) *noun* A line that has jagged, uneven edges

S

sail *noun* A type of free-form shape

scale *noun* Size as measured against a standard reference

score *verb* The repeated scratching of the clay surface at the area that another scored piece will be attached

scoring a curve *verb* Gradually cut bending curves in the paper with the point of the scissors

scoring a straight line *verb* Hold a ruler in the center of a piece of paper. Run the point of the scissors along the edge of the ruler to cut the paper in a straight line.

sculpture *noun* Three-dimensional art

sculpture model *noun* The study or detailed example of what the sculpture will look like when completed

secondary colors *noun* Orange, green, and violet. These colors are made by mixing two primary colors.

secondary hues *noun* Orange, green, and violet; the result of mixing two primary hues

self-portrait *noun* A two- or three-dimensional artwork that an artist makes of him or herself

sets of complementary colors *noun* There are three sets on the color wheel: red and green, blue and orange, and yellow and violet.

shade *noun* Any hue blended with black

shading *noun* A technique for creating dark values or darkening an area by repeating marks such as lines or dots

shadows *noun* Shaded areas in a painting or drawing

shape *noun* A two-dimensional area that is measured by height and width

shape reversal *noun* Occurs when an object, shape, or form is positive space in one image and then in another image becomes negative space

shiny *noun* Bright from reflected light

silhouette *noun* The shape of a shadow

simulated texture *noun* Imitates real texture, see also visual texture

size *noun* 1. in perspective: objects that are closer look larger than objects that are farther away; 2. In balance: a large shape or form will appear to be heavier than a small shape, and several small shapes can balance one large shape.

slip *noun* A mixture of clay and water that is creamy to the touch and is used to attach two scored pieces of clay together

smooth *noun* A surface free from roughness; even

smooth (line) *noun* A line that has even edges

solid (line) *noun* A line that has no breaks, gaps, or holes

space *noun* The art element that refers to the areas above, below, between, within, and around an object

spectral color scheme *noun* Uses all the colors of the rainbow: red, orange, yellow, green, blue, and violet

spectral colors *noun* The colors of the light spectrum: red, orange, yellow, green, blue, and violet

spectrum *noun* The range of colors that it is possible to see; the rainbow

splash *noun* A type of free-form shape

square *noun* A four-sided geometric shape where all sides are the same length and all angles are right angles

statue *noun* Three-dimensional art that is a body form

still life *noun* The arrangement of common inanimate objects from which artists draw or paint

stippling *noun* A shading technique using dots to show value

stitchery *noun* Art made with yarn on cloth

storyteller doll *noun* A Native American sculpture that shows one person relating the history of the culture to many children

style *noun* A unique quality of an object

subordinate *noun* The parts of the artwork that seem less important. Subordinate objects are not emphasized.

subtractive sculpture *noun* When an artist carves pieces away from a form

surrealism *noun* An art movement that emphasized art in which dreams, fantasy, and the subconscious served as inspiration for artists

symmetrical When two sides of a work of art are mirror images of each other

symmetry *noun* A type of formal balance in which two halves of a balanced artwork are identical, mirror images of each other

T

tactile texture *noun* The texture that can be felt

texture *noun* 1. The art element that refers to the way something feels; 2. In balance: a rough texture has an uneven pattern of highlights and shadows. For this reason, a rough surface attracts the viewer's eyes more easily than a smooth, even surface.

thick (line) *adj.* Wide

thick line *noun* Created by beginning with a thin line and gradually pressing the brush down

thin (line) *adj.* Narrow

thin line *noun* Created when a brush is held vertically to paper and touched lightly with the tip of the brush

three-dimensional *adj.* Has measurements in three directions: height, width, and depth

three-dimensional patterns *noun* Patterns that have depth and are formed on the surface of a sculptural form

three-dimensional rhythm *noun* A principle of design that indicates movement by the repetition of elements in a form

tint *noun* Any hue blended with white

transparent *adj.* Allows light to pass through so objects on the other side can be seen

triangle *noun* A three-sided geometric shape

two-dimensional *adj.* Shapes that are flat and can be measured by length and width

two-dimensional decoration *noun* Flat decoration produced on the surface of a work of art

U

unity *noun* The feeling of wholeness in a work of art. Artists use repetition and grouping to show that different parts of a work belong together.

unrealistic scale *noun* When an artist makes size relationships that do not make sense

V

value *noun* The lightness or darkness of a hue

value contrast *noun* The lightness or darkness stands out from the value that surrounds it

vanishing point *noun* The point on the horizon line where all parallel receding lines meet

variety *noun* The principle of art which is concerned with difference or contrast

vertical *noun* (*adj.*) Lines that move straight up and down. They make things look tall, steady, and calm.

visual movement *noun* Occurs when the eye is pulled through a work of art by a rhythm of beats and rests

visual rhythm *noun* The feeling of movement created when artists repeat colors, shapes, lines, and textures to lead the viewer's eyes through a work of art

visual texture *noun* Or simulated texture, imitates real texture. It is the illusion of a three-dimensional surface.

visual weight *noun* cannot be measured on a scale; it is measured by which objects the viewer's eyes see first.

W

warm colors *noun* Red, yellow, and orange. They suggest warmth and come toward the viewer.

warm hues *noun* Red, orange, and yellow. Warm hues are associated with warm things such as fire or sunshine.

weave *verb* To interlace or interweave strips or strands of material

width *noun* A horizontal measurement, or how long across something is

Z

zigzag *noun* (*adj.*) A line that is made by joining diagonal lines

Program Index

Program Index (continued)

Program Index (continued)

Program Index (continued)

Program Index (continued)